BARRON'S

HOW TO PREPARE FOR THE

LSAT

LAW SCHOOL ADMISSION TEST

THIRD EDITION

BY

Jerry Bobrow, Ph.D.

Executive Director
Bobrow Test Preparation Services
Programs at major universities, colleges, and
law schools throughout California, Arizona, and Colorado
Lecturer, consultant, author of over eighteen nationally known test preparation books

IN COLLABORATION WITH

William Covino, Ph.D.
Department of English and Comparative Literature
San Diego State University
Assistant Director
Bobrow Test Preparation Services

Brian N. Siegel, J.D.
Attorney at Law
Practicing Attorney in West Los Angeles
Member Adjunct Faculty
Southwestern University School of Law

David A. Kay, M.S.
Former President
Los Angeles City Teachers, Mathematics Association

Daniel C. Spencer, M.S.
Administrative Analyst
California State University, Northridge

Merritt L. Weisinger, J.D.
Attorney at Law
Weisinger and Associates (Los Angeles)

BARRON'S EDUCATIONAL SERIES, INC.

Woodbury, New York • London • Toronto • Sydney

All inquiries should be addressed to:
Barron's Educational Series, Inc.
113 Crossways Park Drive
Woodbury, New York 11797

Library of Congress Catalog Card No. 84-24286

Paper Edition
International Standard Book No. 0-8120-2790-6
Cloth Edition
International Standard Book No. 0-8120-5555-1

Library of Congress Cataloging in Publication Data

Bobrow, Jerry.
  Barron's guide to the Law school admission
test, LSAT.

  1 Law schools—United States—Entrance examinations.
2. Law schools—United States—Directories. I. Title.
II. Title: Guide to the "new" Law school admission
test, LSAT.
KF285.Z9B6 1985   340'.076   84-24286
ISBN 0-8120-5555-1
ISBN 0-8120-2790-6 (pbk.)

PRINTED IN THE UNITED STATES OF AMERICA

678 100 9876

Contents

Chapter 6   Writing Sample   98

PART THREE PRACTICE—Mastering Problem Types and Time Pressure   123

Chapter 7   Model Test One   124

Chapter 8   Model Test Two   183

Chapter 9   Model Test Three   244

Chapter 10   Model Test Four   297

PART FOUR FINAL TOUCHES—Reviewing the Important Techniques   355

Chapter 11   A Summary of Strategies   356

PART FIVE ABOUT THE LAW SCHOOLS   361

Chapter 12   An Overall View of ABA-Approved Law Schools   362

Preface

YOU CAN PREPARE YOURSELF TO TAKE THE LSAT!

Regardless of your background and your fears about test taking, there are strategies, techniques, and practice exercises that can strengthen your test taking in general, and your LSAT score in particular.

In this book we have gathered the expertise and materials developed over 12 years of successful LSAT, GMAT, GRE, NTE, CBEST, and SAT preparation courses which are currently offered at 30 state universities, colleges, and law schools. By thoroughly surveying each of the sections on the LSAT and reviewing the skills necessary for top performance, this text aims at complete preparation. It is up to date with the most recent forms of the new test. The staff of writers and consultants includes specialists in problem solving, reading, writing, law, logic, and test psychology.

The most successful overall systems of objective test taking—the "One-Check, Two-Check System" and "Elimination Strategy"—are described in detail   (see page 8). They provide you with strategies for assessing every question on the LSAT, eliminating wrong answers, and answering correctly all the questions that you should get right. To supplement this overall strategy, we show you a variety of specific techniques for each section of the test. For instance, we describe how to analyze and chart many of the difficult types of analytical reasoning problems. And we show you how to be an active reader, giving you an efficient and effective method for handling those unexciting reading passages.

An introductory mini-exam will both acquaint you with the format of the LSAT, and help you to spot any of your test-taking weaknesses. Then a series of chapters on the most recent sections of the test will pinpoint specific test-taking strategies and include additional practice. Four full-length practice tests will allow you to get the feel of the real thing while you begin applying new skills and techniques. Your answer sheet will resemble the machine-graded LSAT answer sheet, and an analysis chart will enable you to assess your strengths and weaknesses. The answers to each practice test are fully explained.

Altogether, this book combines complete analysis, thorough instruction, extensive practice, and up-to-date examples. The test-taking strategies and approaches we've included have proved effective for over 500,000 graduate and undergraduate students and teachers whom we've assisted in preparing for these important exams.

REMEMBER: Success is finally up to you. To assure yourself the best preparation possible, work through the book using the Five-Week Study Program, which begins on page 6 . You'll be glad you did!

Jerry Bobrow, PH.D.

January 1985

ACKNOWLEDGMENTS

I gratefully acknowledge the following sources for granting permission to use materials from their publications:

American Bar Association, for a complete listing of approved law schools from its publication *A Review of Legal Education in the United States*—1981-82.

Wesley Barnes, *Existentialism,* © 1968 by Barron's Educational Series, Inc. Woodbury, N.Y.

Arthur Doerr and J. L. Guernsey, *Principles of Geography,* © 1975 by Barron's Educational Series, Inc. Woodbury, N.Y.

Farrar, Straus, and Giroux, Inc. for an excerpt from "Man in a Drawer" by Bernard Malamud from *Rembrandt's Hat* © 1968, 1972, 1973 by Bernard Malamud. Reprinted by permission of Farrar, Straus, and Giroux, Inc.

Ann Fagan Ginger, *The Law, the Supreme Court and the People's Rights,* © 1977 by Barron's Educational Series, Inc. Woodbury, N.Y.

John Hollister Hedley, *Harry S. Truman—The Little Man from Missouri,* © 1979 by Barron's Educational Series, Inc. Woodbury, N.Y.

Donald Heiney and Lenthiel H. Downs, *Recent American Literature After 1930,* Vol. 4, © 1974 by Barron's Educational Series, Inc. Woodbury, N.Y.

Donald Heiney and Lenthiel H. Downs, *Contemporary British Literature,* Vol. 1, © 1974 by Barron's Educational Series, Inc. Woodbury, N.Y.

Donald Heiney and Lenthiel H. Downs, *Contemporary British Literature,* Vol. 2, © 1974 by Barron's Educational Series, Inc. Woodbury, N.Y.

Nicholas Horvath, *Essentials of Philosophy,* © 1974 by Barron's Educational Series, Inc. Woodbury, N.Y.

George E. Riggs, publisher; news articles and editorials from *The Herald News,* Fontana, Calif.

C. Leland Rodgers, *Essentials of Biology,* © 1974 by Barron's Educational Series, Inc. Woodbury, N.Y.

Erwin Rosenfeld and Harriet Geller, *Afro-Asian Culture Studies,* © 1979 by Barron's Educational Series, Inc. Woodbury, N.Y.

Ernst B. Schulz, *Democracy,* 2nd ed., © 1977 by Barron's Educational Series, Inc. Woodbury, N.Y.

Roger-Gérard Schwartzenberg, *The Superstar Show of Government,* © 1980 by Barron's Educational Series, Inc. Woodbury, N.Y. © Flammarion, 1977, solely with respect to the French language edition.

Dr. Albert Upton, *Design for Thinking,* Stanford University Press, Stanford, Calif.

My thanks also to James Zinger, President, Hypmovation, for the use of excerpts from his writings; to Stacey Baum and Joy Mondragon, for their diligent assistance in assembling the manuscript; to Lynn Turner and Sally Reilly, for typing the manuscript; and to Ruth Pecan, Dora Rizzuto, Ruth Flohn and Max Reed, for manuscript editing and final preparation.

And finally, thanks to my wife, Susan Bobrow, for critical analysis and moral support; and to my two children, Jennifer Lynn, 6, and Adam Michael, 3, for comic relief.

Jerry Bobrow

PART ONE

GETTING ACQUAINTED
WITH THE TEST

Introduction to the LSAT

ANSWERS TO SOME COMMONLY ASKED QUESTIONS

What does the LSAT measure?

The LSAT is designed to measure a range of mental abilities related to the study of law; therefore it is used by most law schools to evaluate their applicants.

Will any special knowledge of the law raise my score on the LSAT?

No. The LSAT is designed so that candidates from a particular academic background are given no advantage. The questions measure reading comprehension, logical reasoning, and analytical reasoning, drawing from a variety of verbal and analytical material.

Does a high score on the LSAT predict success in law school or in the practice of law?

Success on the LSAT demonstrates your ability to read with understanding and to reason clearly under pressure; surely these strengths are important to both the study and the practice of law, as is the ability to write well, measured by the LSAT Writing Sample. To say that success on the LSAT *predicts* success in law school may overstate the case, however, because success in law school also involves skills that are not measured by the LSAT.

When is the LSAT administered?

The test is given nationwide four times each year, around the beginning of the fall, winter, spring, and summer seasons. Except for the summer month, the test is usually administered on a Saturday morning from 8:30 a.m. to about 1:00 p.m.. For the past few years, the *summer exam* has been given on a Monday afternoon. Dates are announced annually by the Law School Admission Council in Newtown, PA.

What if I cannot take the test on a Saturday?

Some special arrangements are possible: check the LSAS General Information Booklet in your registration packet. Those who must take the exam at a time when the regular administration occurs on Saturday, but who cannot participate on Saturday for religious reasons, may arrange for a special Monday administration.

How early should I register?

Regular registration closes about one month prior to the exam date. Late registration is available up to three weeks prior to the exam date. There is an additional fee for late registration.

Is walk-in registration available?

Walk-in registration will *only* be permitted for students who telephone the Law School Admission Services (LSAS) in advance. Telephone registration begins three days after the close of the late registration period and runs until the Wednesday prior to the test date. *Students who do not telephone the LSAS will not be permitted to be walk-ins the day of the test.* If you must be a walk-in, be sure to very carefully read the General Information Booklet section on walk-in registration at test centers.

What is the LSDAS?

The LSDAS (Law School Data Assembly Service) compiles a report about each subscribing applicant. The report contains LSAT results, a summary of the applicant's academic work, and copies of college transcripts. A report is sent to each law school that the applicant designates. Thus, if you register for the LSDAS, you will not need to mail a separate transcript to each of your prospective law schools. REMINDER: You can *only* register for the Candidate Referral Service at the same time you register for the LSDAS.

How is the LSAT used?

Your LSAT score is one common denominator by which a law school compares you to other applicants. Other factors also determine your acceptance to law school: a law school may consider your personal qualities, grade-point average, extracurricular achievements, and letters of recommendation. Requirements for admission vary widely from school to school, so you are wise to contact the law school of your choice for specific information.

How do I obtain registration forms?

The registration form covering both the LSAT and the LSDAS is available in the LSAT/LSDAS REGISTRATION PACKET. Copies of the packet are probably available at the Graduate Studies Office, Counseling Center, or Testing Office at your undergraduate institution, and at law schools. You may also obtain the packet by writing to LAW SCHOOL ADMISSION SERVICES, Box 2000, Newtown, Pennsylvania 18940.

What is the structure of the LSAT?

The present LSAT is a 210-minute test, consisting of six 35-minute sections; in addition there is a 30-minute Writing Sample. The four common sections of the test are Logical Reasoning, Reading Comprehension, Analytical Reasoning, and Evaluation of Facts. In addition to these four sections (which determine your score), two experimental sections appear; each experimental section will probably be a repeat of one of the four common sections, but will not count in your score.

How is the LSAT scored?

The score for the objective portion of the test ranges from 10 to 48, and there is no penalty for wrong answers. The Writing Sample is unscored, but copies are sent to the law schools of your choice for evaluation.

What about question structure and value?

All LSAT questions, apart from the Writing Sample, are multiple-choice with either four or five choices. All questions within a section are of equal value, regardless of difficulty.

Should I guess?

There is no penalty for guessing on the LSAT. Therefore, before you move on to the next question, at least take a guess. You should fill in guess answers for those you have left blank or did not get to, before time is called for that section. If you can eliminate one or more choices as incorrect, your chances for a correct guess increase.

How often can I take the LSAT?

You may take the LSAT more than once if you wish. But keep in mind that any report sent to you or to law schools will contain up to your two most recent scores for any exams taken after June 1981, along with an average score for those exams. The law school receiving your scores will decide which score is the best estimate of your ability; many law schools rely on the average score as a reliable figure.

LSAC/LSAS have also initiated a new 12-month subscription service. Check carefully to make sure that you select the program that best fits your needs. THERE ARE NO REFUNDS OF THE FEES FOR THESE SERVICES.

Is it at all possible to cancel my LSAT score?

You may cancel your score only within 5 days after taking the test.

How early should I arrive at the test center, and what should I bring?

Arrive at the test center 15 to 30 minutes before the time designated on your admission ticket. Bring three or four sharpened No. 2 pencils, an eraser, and a watch. New identification requirements state that you must bring a 2½″ by 2½″ close-up color photograph that makes you clearly identifiable. This photograph should be inserted in the designated place in your Admission Ticket/Identification Card. You must also have two alternative forms of identification, such as a driver's license, employee ID, student ID, or passport. Your signature and appropriate descriptive information should be on the alternative ID.

No calculators, scratch paper, or other aids are allowed; all figuring is done in the margins of your test booklet. (Scratch paper is provided for organizing your essay.)

Can I prepare for the LSAT?

Yes. Reading skills and test-taking strategies should be the focus of your preparation for the test as a whole. Success on the more specialized analytical sections of the test depends on your thorough familiarity with the types of problems you are likely to encounter and the reasoning process involved. For maximum preparation, work through this book and practice the strategies and techniques outlined in each section.

NOTE: For your convenience, this Barron's text labels each section of the practice tests (e.g., Reading Comprehension, Logical Reasoning, etc.) In contrast, sections of the actual LSAT exam are not usually labeled, and some lists are presented without numbering or lettering.

BASIC FORMAT OF THE LSAT AND SCORING

THE *ORDER* OF THE FOLLOWING SECTIONS *WILL VARY*.

Section	Number of Questions	Minutes
Writing Sample	1 essay	30
I. Reading Comprehension	25–30 (4–5 passages)	35
II. Analytical Reasoning	21–27 (4–5 situations)	35
III. Evaluation of Facts	32–38 (6–9 sets)	35
IV. Logical Reasoning	24–29	35
V. Experimental Section	(varies)	35
VI. Experimental Section	(varies)	35

Important Notes

The two experimental or pretest sections will usually be repeats of other sections and can appear in different places on the exam. At the time of the exam, you will not know which sections are experimental.

Scoring will be from 10 to 48, with all questions having equal value.

There is NO PENALTY for guessing.

The 30-minute Writing Sample will not be scored, but copies will be forwarded to the law schools to which you apply. Scratch paper will be provided for the Writing Sample only. The 10-minute break will probably be given between sections III and IV.

A Sampling of Formats

Writing Sample	Writing Sample	Writing Sample
Reading Comprehension	Reading Comprehension	Logical Reasoning
Reading Comprehension	Analytical Reasoning	Evaluation of Facts
Analytical Reasoning	Evaluation of Facts	Reading Comprehension
Evaluation of Facts	Logical Reasoning	Logical Reasoning
Analytical Reasoning	Evaluation of Facts	Analytical Reasoning
Logical Reasoning	Logical Reasoning	Reading Comprehension

IT IS EVIDENT THAT MANY ADDITIONAL COMBINATIONS ARE POSSIBLE.

An Effective Study Program— Some Words to the Wise

A Five-Week Study Plan

Many students don't even bother to read the LSAT bulletin, let alone do any thorough preparation for the test. You, however, should begin your LSAT preparation by reading the LSAT bulletin carefully; information about how to obtain one is on page 4. The bulletin is filled with information about registration and score reporting. Also provided in the registration packet is an "official" practice test. You should also send for copies of old exams (good practice).

Check with the law schools to which you are applying to find out what score each requires for admission. Requirements vary widely and are often influenced by your grade-point average and other achievements.

With these preliminaries out of the way, begin working through this book. If you have the time, the following study plan is ideal and is used in many LSAT preparation programs at major universities and colleges. However, if you have a shorter time to prepare, simply adjust the following five-week plan to meet your needs (remember, lots of practice and analysis). You will find the techniques, strategies, practice, and analyses in this book invaluable to your preparation, either with the ideal five-week plan or with the shorter study plan.

Most people can keep up with the following study sequence by devoting about 6 to 8 hours a week. It is most important that you review and practice *daily,* for about an hour each day. Don't "save up" your practice for one long session each week. Shorter, regular practice sessions will allow you to assimilate skills and strategies more effectively and efficiently.

Week 1

- Read the section "Answers to Some Commonly Asked Questions" (p. 1).
- Complete, correct, and analyze the Diagnostic Mini-Exam (p. 11).
- Read carefully "Before You Begin...Some Words to the Wise" (p. 6), paying special attention to the "One-Check, Two-Check System" and the "Elimination Strategy." Applying these techniques confidently should make quite a difference in your test taking.
- Read carefully the chapters on Reading Comprehension, Logical Reasoning, Analytical Reasoning, Evaluation of Facts, and the Writing Sample.

Week 2

- Review the chapter on Reading Comprehension. Do the Reading Comprehension problems in the chapter, the ones in the LSAT bulletin, and those in Model Test One (pp. 130 and 154). Correct and analyze your performance.

  Note: Do not time yourself on these practice tests. Your task at present is to familiarize yourself with strategies and techniques, a task that is best done slowly, working back and forth between the introductory chapter and the practice problems. You may get an uncomfortable number of problems wrong at this stage, but, instead of being discouraged, you should attempt to understand clearly the reasons for your errors. Such understanding will become a plus in the future.
- Review the chapter on the Writing Sample, and write an essay about one of the given topics. Ask a friend with good writing skills to read your essay and offer constructive criticism.
- Review the chapter on Logical Reasoning. Do the Logical Reasoning problems in the chapter, those in the LSAT bulletin, and the ones in Model Test One (p. 147). Correct and analyze your performance.

Week 3

- Review the chapter on Analytical Reasoning. Do the Analytical Reasoning problems in the chapter, those in the LSAT bulletin, and those in Model Test One (pp. 137 and 161). Correct and analyze your performance.
- Do the Reading Comprehension problems in Model Test Two (pp. 195 and 219), and the Logical Reasoning problems in Model Test Two (pp. 190 and 208). Correct and analyze your performance.
- Do the Analytical Reasoning problems in Model Test Two. Correct and analyze your performance.
- Write another essay about one of the given topics in the Writing Sample chapter, and have a friend read and respond to your effort.

Week 4

- Review the chapter on Evaluation of Facts. Do the Evaluation of Facts problems in the chapter, those in the LSAT bulletin, and those in Model Test One (p. 141) and in Model Test Two (p. 214). Correct and analyze your performance.

  Note: At this point you have introduced yourself to the whole test, and have tried some effective strategies. Now you should begin timing each of your practice tests.
- Do all of Model Test Three; practice and review only one or two sections each day. For each section, time yourself (always short yourself on time during practice by about 10–15%), then correct and analyze your performance.
- Write another essay about one of the given topics in the Writing Sample chapter (or in Model Test Three), observing the time limit, and have a friend read and respond to your effort.

Week 5

- Do all of Model Test Four; practice and review only one or two sections each day. For each section, time yourself, then correct and analyze your performance.

- Write another essay about one of the given topics in the Writing Sample chapter (or in Model Test Four) (observing the time limit), and have a friend read and respond to your efforts.
- Finally, carefully read the review of test-taking strategies at the end of the book (p. 356). It will recap the highlights of the book, and also supply a variety of tips for putting yourself into an effective state of mind and body before you take the LSAT.

BEFORE YOU BEGIN

THE ONE-CHECK, TWO-CHECK SYSTEM

Many people score lower than they should on the LSAT simply because they do not get to many of the easier problems. They puzzle over difficult questions and use up the time that could be spent answering easy ones. In fact, the difficult questions are worth exactly the same as the easy ones, so it makes sense not to do the hard problems until you have answered all the easy ones.

To maximize your correct answers by focusing on the easier problems, use the following system:

The One-Check, Two-Check System

1. Attempt the first question. If it is answerable quickly and easily, work the problem, circle the answer in the quesion booklet, and then mark that answer on the answer sheet. The mark on the answer sheet should be a complete mark, not merely a dot, because test takers may not be given time at the end of the test to darken marks.

2. If a question seems impossible, place two checks (✔ ✔) on or next to the question number in the question booklet and mark the answer you guess on the answer sheet. The mark on the answer sheet should be a complete mark, not merely a dot, because test takers may not be given time at the end of the test to darken marks.

3. If you're in the midst of a question that seems to be taking too much time, or if you immediately spot that a question is answerable but time-consuming (that is, it will require more than two minutes to answer), place one check (√) next to the question number, mark an answer you guess on the answer sheet, and continue with the next question.

   NOTE THAT NO QUESTIONS ARE LEFT BLANK. AN ANSWER CHOICE IS *ALWAYS* FILLED IN BEFORE LEAVING THAT QUESTION.

4. When all the problems in a section have been attempted in this manner, there may still be time left. If so, return to the single-check (√) questions, working as many as possible, changing each guessed answer to a worked-out answer, if necessary.

5. If time remains after all the single-check (√) questions are completed, the test taker can choose between

   a. attempting those "impossible" double-check (√√) questions (sometimes a question later on in the test may trigger one's memory to allow once-impossible questions to be solved);

   or

   b. spending time checking and re-working the easier questions to eliminate any careless errors.

6. Test takers should be reminded to use *all* the allotted time as effectively as possible.

You should use this system as you work through the practice tests in this book; such practice will allow you to make "one-check, two-check" judgments quickly when you actually take the LSAT. As our extensive research has shown, use of this system results in less wasted time on the LSAT.

THE ELIMINATION STRATEGY

Faced with four or five answer choices, you will work more efficiently and effectively if you *eliminate unreasonable or irrelevant answers immediately*. In most cases, two or three choices in every set will stand out as obviously incorrect. Many test takers don't perceive this because they painstakingly analyze every choice, even the obviously ridiculous ones.

Consider the following Logical Reasoning problem:

According to the theory of aerodynamics, the bumblebee is unable to fly. This is because the size, weight, and shape of his body in relationship to the total wingspan make flying impossible. The bumblebee, being ignorant of this "scientific truth," flies anyway.

The author's statement would be strengthened by pointing out that   Ⓐ Ⓑ Ⓒ Ⓓ Ⓔ
- (A) the theory of aerodynamics may be readily tested
- (B) the bumblebee does not actually fly but glides instead
- (C) bumblebees cannot fly in strong winds
- (D) bumblebees are ignorant of other things but can't do all of them
- (E) nothing is impossible

A student who does not immediately eliminate the unreasonable choices here, and instead tries to analyze every choice, will find herself becoming confused and anxious as she tries to decide how even silly choices might be correct. Her thinking goes something like this: "I wonder if bumblebees do glide; I've never looked that closely—maybe the test has me on this one . . . come to think of it, I've never seen a bumblebee in a strong wind; (C) is tricky, but it just might be right . . . I can't understand (D); it seems irrelevant but that just might be a trick . . . ."
On and on she goes, becoming more and more uncertain.

Using the elimination strategy, a confident test taker proceeds as follows:

"(A)?   Possible choice.
(B)?   Ridiculous. Both false and irrelevant. Cross it out.
(C)?   Another ridiculous, irrelevant one. Cross it out.
(D)?   Incomprehensible! Eliminate it.
(E)?   Too *general* to be the best choice."

This test taker, aware that most answer choices can be easily eliminated, does so without complicating the process by considering unreasonable possibilities.
To summarize the elimination strategy:

- Look for unreasonable or incorrect answer choices first. Expect to find at least two or three of these with every problem.
- When a choice seems wrong, cross it out in your test booklet *immediately*, so that you will not be tempted to reconsider it.

Eliminating choices in this fashion will lead you to correct answers more quickly, and will increase your overall confidence.

MARKING IN THE TEST BOOKLET

Many test takers don't take full advantage of opportunities to mark key words and draw diagrams in the test booklet. Remember that, in the Reading Comprehension, Logical Reasoning, and Evaluation of Facts sections, *marking key words and phrases will significantly increase your comprehension and lead you to a correct answer*. Marking also helps to keep you focused and alert. In the Analytical Reasoning section, *drawing diagrams is absolutely essential*.

Further, more specific hints about marking are given in the introductory chapters that follow. The important general point to stress here is that active, successful test taking entails marking and drawing, and that passive, weak test takers make little use of this technique.

THE "MULTIPLE-MULTIPLE-CHOICE" ITEM

You are sure to encounter a number of test problems that contain two sets of multiple choices. Here is an example:

According to the theory of aerodynamics, the bumblebee should be unable to fly. But it flies anyway.

Which of the following can be logically inferred from the above statement? Ⓐ Ⓑ Ⓒ Ⓓ Ⓔ

  I.   The bumblebee's behavior contradicts scientific theory.
  II. The bumblebee is not really able to fly.
  III. Some theories don't hold true in all cases.
  (A) I only   (B) II only   (C) I and II   (D) I, II, and III   (E) I and III

When faced with a problem of this structure, first try to quickly answer each of the roman numerals and label them accordingly. They would therefore be labeled as follows:

T I.   The bumblebee's behavior contradicts scientific theory.
F II. The bumblebee is not really able to fly.
T III. Some theories don't hold true in all cases.
  (A) I only   (B) II only   (C) I and II   (D) I, II, and III   ((E)) I and III

Therefore since I and III are true, the answer is (E).

Quite frequently, however, determining each of the roman numerals as true or false is not always a quick or easy proposition. In such a case it may be effective (and possibly less time consuming) to skip the difficult roman numerals, solve the easy ones, and then eliminate the final choices, as follows:

? I.   The bumblebee's behavior contradicts scientific theory.
F II. The bumblebee is not really able to fly.
T III. Some theories don't hold true in all cases.
  (A̶) I only   (B̶) II only   (C̶) I and II   (D̶) I, II, and III   (E) I and III

Notice that since II is false, any choice containing a false II may be eliminated. Thus (B), (C), and (D) should be crossed out. Continuing, since III is true, any remaining choice must contain a true III for it to be correct. Thus choice (A) may be eliminated as it does not contain a true III. This leaves only choice (E) as the correct answer.

In some cases you will be able to eliminate all but the correct answer, as above. In other cases you may find several possible choices remaining, and thus have a more educated guess.

Becoming familiar with this technique will often save you time and allow you to take better educated guesses in those cases when you have partial information, when parts of the problem appear too difficult, or when the question itself does not appear to give enough direction.

Chapter

1

A Diagnostic Mini-Exam

The purpose of this mini-exam is to familiarize you with the common areas on the LSAT by giving you a sampling of typical problems. It is designed to introduce the testing areas. The chapters to follow on each exam area will give you a much more complete range of the problem types and difficulties.

This mini-exam should be taken under strict test conditions with each section timed as follows:

Section	Description	Number of Questions	Time Allowed
	Writing Sample		30 minutes
I	Reading Comprehension	8	10 minutes
II	Analytical Reasoning	7	10 minutes
III	Evaluation of Facts	10	10 minutes
IV	Logical Reasoning	9	10 minutes
TOTALS:		34	70 minutes

The actual LSAT contains six 35-minute sections plus a 30-minute Writing Sample for a total of 4 hours of testing. Note that two sections will be experimental and will probably be duplications of the above sections. Also note that they may appear anywhere in the test. Thus only four sections will count toward your score.

After correcting the mini-exam and assessing your strengths and weaknesses, you should start your area analysis with Chapters 2 through 6.

Now tear out your answer sheet from this book, turn to the next page, and begin the mini-exam.

ANSWER SHEET—PRACTICE MINI EXAM
LAW SCHOOL ADMISSION TEST (LSAT)
Note: The actual LSAT has six sections, plus a Writing Sample.

Section I:
Reading Comprehension

1. Ⓐ Ⓑ Ⓒ Ⓓ Ⓔ
2. Ⓐ Ⓑ Ⓒ Ⓓ Ⓔ
3. Ⓐ Ⓑ Ⓒ Ⓓ Ⓔ
4. Ⓐ Ⓑ Ⓒ Ⓓ Ⓔ
5. Ⓐ Ⓑ Ⓒ Ⓓ Ⓔ
6. Ⓐ Ⓑ Ⓒ Ⓓ Ⓔ
7. Ⓐ Ⓑ Ⓒ Ⓓ Ⓔ
8. Ⓐ Ⓑ Ⓒ Ⓓ Ⓔ

Section II:
Analytical Reasoning

1. Ⓐ Ⓑ Ⓒ Ⓓ Ⓔ
2. Ⓐ Ⓑ Ⓒ Ⓓ Ⓔ
3. Ⓐ Ⓑ Ⓒ Ⓓ Ⓔ
4. Ⓐ Ⓑ Ⓒ Ⓓ Ⓔ
5. Ⓐ Ⓑ Ⓒ Ⓓ Ⓔ
6. Ⓐ Ⓑ Ⓒ Ⓓ Ⓔ
7. Ⓐ Ⓑ Ⓒ Ⓓ Ⓔ

Section III:
Evaluation of Facts

1. Ⓐ Ⓑ Ⓒ Ⓓ
2. Ⓐ Ⓑ Ⓒ Ⓓ
3. Ⓐ Ⓑ Ⓒ Ⓓ
4. Ⓐ Ⓑ Ⓒ Ⓓ
5. Ⓐ Ⓑ Ⓒ Ⓓ
6. Ⓐ Ⓑ Ⓒ Ⓓ
7. Ⓐ Ⓑ Ⓒ Ⓓ
8. Ⓐ Ⓑ Ⓒ Ⓓ
9. Ⓐ Ⓑ Ⓒ Ⓓ
10. Ⓐ Ⓑ Ⓒ Ⓓ

Section IV:
Logical Reasoning

1. Ⓐ Ⓑ Ⓒ Ⓓ Ⓔ
2. Ⓐ Ⓑ Ⓒ Ⓓ Ⓔ
3. Ⓐ Ⓑ Ⓒ Ⓓ Ⓔ
4. Ⓐ Ⓑ Ⓒ Ⓓ Ⓔ
5. Ⓐ Ⓑ Ⓒ Ⓓ Ⓔ
6. Ⓐ Ⓑ Ⓒ Ⓓ Ⓔ
7. Ⓐ Ⓑ Ⓒ Ⓓ Ⓔ
8. Ⓐ Ⓑ Ⓒ Ⓓ Ⓔ
9. Ⓐ Ⓑ Ⓒ Ⓓ Ⓔ

EXAMINATION

WRITING SAMPLE

Time—30 Minutes

Directions:

You have 30 minutes to write an essay in response to a given topic. Take a few minutes to plan your work before you begin writing. DO NOT WRITE ON A TOPIC OF YOUR OWN CHOICE. ESSAYS THAT DO NOT ADDRESS THE GIVEN TOPIC ARE UNACCEPTABLE.

The quality of your writing is more important than the length of your response and content. There is no "right" or "wrong" answer to the question. Pay attention to organization, appropriate diction, and correct usage. You will not be expected to display any specialized knowledge in your response, nor will you be expected to write a "perfect" essay; law schools understand that you are writing under a time constraint and pressured circumstances.

Only the lined area in your booklet will be reproduced for the law schools, so do not write outside this space. *Do not* skip lines or use wide margins. These precautions, along with careful planning and legible handwriting that is not unduly large, will keep you within the allowed space.

Special Note: Two complete "model" essays on the following topic are given in Chapter 6.

SAMPLE TOPIC:

Read the following descriptions of Bergquist and Kretchmer, applicants for the job of Assistant Director on a major motion picture. *Then, in the space provided, write an argument for hiring either Bergquist or Kretchmer.* The following criteria are relevant to your decision:

1. In addition to working closely with and advising the Director on creative decisions, the Assistant Director must work with all types of individuals—from stars to Teamster truck drivers—and elicit the best from every cast and crew member for the good of the motion picture.

2. The Assistant Director is responsible for all the planning and organization—including paperwork, travel itinerary, meals, etc.—of the entire film project. He/she lays the groundwork for a successful "shoot."

BERGQUIST began her career in films as an Administrative Assistant to the president of a major film studio. As such, she often accompanied her employer in his wining and dining of stars, or to the set when problems arose. She doublechecked contracts, shooting schedules, cast and crew checks, and kept a close eye on the budget of several multimillion-dollar films. When her boss was subsequently fired due to a poor season of films, Bergquist was able to secure a position as Assistant Editor at the studio, helping several highly respected film editors "cut" feature films. It was here that she learned about the creative end of the business, and soon after became the chief editor of an hour-long studio documentary, which won several awards. After two years, Bergquist was accepted into the Assistant Directors Training Program, and is presently a candidate for Assistant Director of this new $15,000,000 motion picture.

KRETCHMER was a principal/teacher for 12 years before embarking on a film career. Not only did she teach math at the New York School for the Creative Arts, but she worked with parents in the community, the board of education, and local government representatives in securing financing for the $20,000,000 school building. As Chairperson of the New Building Committee, she worked closely with architects, townspeople, contractors, and even children to understand their needs for the building. Today the building stands as a model for such schools everywhere. Eight years ago Kretchmer came to Hollywood and, through persistence and charm, secured a studio position and worked her way up to Chief Auditor, where she oversaw budgets on several multimillion-dollar films. She enrolled in the Assistant Directors Training Program, which she recently completed, and is now the other candidate being considered for the postion of Assistant Director of this new film.

SECTION I
READING COMPREHENSION

Time—10 Minutes
8 Questions

Directions:
Read the passages and answer the questions following each passage by blackening the appropriate space on the answer sheet. You may refer back to the passages when answering the questions. Answer all questions on the basis of what is stated or implied.

Passage 1

My course of study had led me to believe that all mental and moral feelings and qualities, whether of a good or of a bad kind, were the results of association; that we love one thing, and hate another, take pleasure in one sort of action or contemplation, and pain in another sort, through the clinging of pleasurable or painful ideas to those things, from the effect of education or of experience. As a corollary from this, I had always heard it maintained by my father, and was myself convinced, that the object of education should be to form the strongest possible associations of the salutary class; associations of pleasure with all things beneficial to the great whole, and of pain with all things hurtful to it. This doctrine appeared inexpugnable; but it now seemed to me, on retrospect, that my teachers had occupied themselves but superficially with the means of forming and keeping up these salutary associations. They seemed to have trusted altogether to the old familiar instruments, praise and blame, reward and punishment. Now, I did not doubt that by these means, begun early, and applied unremittingly, intense associations of pain and pleasure, especially of pain, might be created, and might produce desires and aversions capable of lasting undiminished to the end of life. But there must always be something artificial and casual in associations thus produced.

1. The main point of this passage is that
   (A) pain is easier to feel than pleasure
   (B) all that we know and feel is the product of association
   (C) education causes more pain than pleasure
   (D) pleasure is preferable to pain
   (E) teachers believe that pain is inexpugnable

2. By "salutary" the author means
   (A) "the strongest possible associations"
   (B) ideas that "salute" one's mind
   (C) capable of giving pleasure
   (D) promoting some good purpose
   (E) those earning a middle-class income or better

3. We may infer that the pain and pleasure caused by the author's teachers were
   (A) the cause of his theory of association
   (B) not always coincident with respect for the natural order of things
   (C) aspects of the "great whole"
   (D) casual
   (E) artificial

4. Which of the following questions is (are) answered in the passage?

   I.   Is there any sort of thinking that is not associational?
   II. Is schooling the only cause of our lifelong "desires and aversions"?
   III. What do teachers praise and what do they blame?

(A) I only   (B) I and III   (C) II only   (D) I, II, and III   (E) I and II

Passage 2

It is interesting to contemplate an entangled bank, clothed with many plants of many kinds, with birds singing on the bushes, with various insects flitting about, and with worms crawling through the damp earth, and to reflect that these elaborately constructed forms, so different from each other, and dependent upon each other in so complex a manner, have all been produced by laws acting around us. These laws, taken in the largest sense, being Growth with Reproduction; Inheritance, which is almost implied by reproduction; Variability from the indirect and direct action of the external conditions of life, and from use and disuse; a Ratio of Increase so high as to lead to a Struggle for Life, and as a consequence to Natural Selection, entailing Divergence of Character and the Extinction of less-improved forms. Thus, from the war of nature, from famine and death, the most exalted object which we are capable of conceiving, namely, the production of the higher animals, directly follows. There is grandeur in this view of life, with its several powers, having been originally breathed into a few forms or into one; and that, whilst this planet has gone cycling on according to the fixed law of gravity, from so simple a beginning endless forms most beautiful and most wonderful have been, and are being, evolved.

5. The primary purpose of the passage is to
   (A) distinguish forms such as birds from forms such as worms
   (B) use the capitalization of common nouns as a rhetorical strategy
   (C) explain that the complexity of life around us is a product of certain laws
   (D) instruct the reader in the art of contemplation
   (E) instruct the reader in the production of higher animals

6. The author would agree that "higher" species are a product of
   (A) competition   (B) contemplation   (C) chaos   (D) character   (E) conception

7. Which of the following maxims might prevail if the author's theory of natural selection were applied to human society?
   (A) Might makes right.
   (B) We shall overcome.
   (C) War is hell.
   (D) As ye sow, so shall ye reap.
   (E) The rich get richer, the poor get poorer.

8. Which of the following terms best summarizes the process of natural selection that the passage describes?
   (A) creationism   (B) evolution   (C) the "big bang"   (D) social Darwinism
   (E) naturalism

STOP

IF YOU FINISH BEFORE TIME HAS ELAPSED, CHECK YOUR WORK ON THIS SECTION OF THE TEST ONLY. DO NOT GO ON TO THE NEXT SECTION OF THE TEST UNTIL TIME IS UP FOR THIS SECTION.

SECTION II
ANALYTICAL REASONING

Time—10 Minutes
7 Questions

Directions:
In this section you will be given a group of questions based on a specific set of conditions. Drawing a simple diagram may be helpful in answering some of the questions. You are to choose the best answer and mark the corresponding space on your answer sheet.

Eight students, A, B, C, D, E, F, G, and H, are standing in a straight line, not necessarily in order.

The first and last people in line are the two tallest.
The 4th, 5th, and 6th students in line are the only girls.
C is always third in line.
E is always next to F, and they are not girls.
H is a boy.
A and D are sisters, but will not stand next to each other.

1. If G is a girl, then which of the following MUST be true?
   (A) D is in the 4th place.
   (B) A is next to C.
   (C) D is in the 5th place.
   (D) G is in the 5th place.
   (E) G is next to C.

2. If H is one of the two tallest, then H may be next to
   (A) F   (B) B   (C) C   (D) D   (E) E

3. If G is a girl and H is last in line, then
   (A) E must be the other tallest student
   (B) E may be next to a girl
   (C) D must be next to C
   (D) G may be next to C
   (E) B must be next to H

4. If F is 2nd in line, which of the following MUST be true?

   I.   E is one of the tallest.
   II. B is either 7th or 8th in line.
   III. H is either 7th or 8th in line.
   (A) I   (B) II   (C) III   (D) I and II   (E) I and III

5. If E and B are the two tallest students, then the correct order in line may be:
   (A) E F C D H A G B
   (B) E H C A G D F B
   (C) B H C A G D F E
   (D) B G C D H A F E
   (E) E F C G A D H B

6. If H is last in line, which of the following may be true?

    I.   B is one of the tallest.
    II. G is next to C.
    III. E is one of the tallest.
    (A) I   (B) II   (C) III   (D) I and III   (E) II and III

7. If E and G are the two tallest, then the order in line may be:
    (A) G F C A B D H E
    (B) G B C A H D F E
    (C) E H C D B A F G
    (D) E F C D B A H G
    (E) E F C D H A B G

STOP

IF YOU FINISH BEFORE TIME HAS ELAPSED, CHECK YOUR WORK ON THIS SECTION OF THE TEST ONLY. DO NOT GO ON TO THE NEXT SECTION OF THE TEST UNTIL TIME IS UP FOR THIS SECTION.

SECTION III
EVALUATION OF FACTS

Time—10 Minutes
10 Questions

Directions:
This section consists of several sets; each set presents a factual statement, the description of a dispute, and two rules. In some sets, the rules will be conflicting. Be sure that you consider each rule independently and not as an exception to the other. Following each set are questions; select from four choices (given below) the one that best categorizes each question, based upon the relationship of one or both of the rules to the dispute. Darken the appropriate space on your answer sheet.

(A) A relevant question which you can only answer by choosing between the rules.

(B) A relevant question which you cannot answer because you need more information or additional rules, but which does not require a choice between the rules.

(C) A relevant question which you can answer by referring to the facts or rules, or both.

(D) An irrelevant question or one which is only remotely relevant to the outcome of the dispute.

Set 1

FACTS

Wearing a navy suit and carrying a new blue handbag, Mrs. Jones was going shopping. As she was leaving her car in the parking lot of the department store, she realized that a second new handbag—one that she had used yesterday—was on the back seat. Fearing its loss, she took the second bag into the store as well. She bought a small bottle of perfume, which she put into her handbag. As she was leaving the store, Mrs. Jones was observed by Ralston, the store detective to whom the theft of a red handbag had just been reported. Looking for the stolen red bag, Ralston followed Mrs. Jones to her car, and when she put her keys in the ignition, he reached in and took the keys. He asked her if she had a receipt for either bag. "I bought them at another store," she replied. "Give me back my keys." The detective said she would have to wait for the store manager, and left the parking lot with her keys. When the detective and the manager returned, Mrs. Jones emptied the contents of both bags on the front seat. They contained only her personal effects, including a second set of car keys. The detective apologized and returned her keys. Mrs. Jones was so upset by this incident that she had to remain in bed for a week under the care of a doctor.

DISPUTE

Mrs. Jones sued Ralston for compensation for her illness. Ralston contested.

RULE I

A shopkeeper or an employee may detain a person who appears to have taken merchandise from a store without paying for it if the shopkeeper or employee detains the person immediately after the suspected wrongful taking and only for such a period of time and in such a manner as is reasonable.

RULE II

A person who restricts the freedom of movement of another person is guilty of illegal restriction, and is liable for any loss resulting to that person because of the act of restriction.

Questions

1. If Ralston and the store manager returned to the car promptly, and if Mrs. Jones did not realize that her second handbag contained another set of car keys, has Ralston illegally restricted Mrs. Jones?

2. Was the perfume put in the paper bag normally used by the store to identify completed purchases?

3. What was the color of Mrs. Jones's second handbag?

4. Was Mrs. Jones's blue handbag similar in style to those on sale in the store?

5. If Mrs. Jones had locked the second handbag in the trunk of her car before entering the store, and if Ralston returned her keys to her soon after he came back with the manager, would Ralston be liable for the costs of Mrs. Jones's illness?

Set 2

FACTS

Rostow Street intersects Fremont Avenue. There is a stop sign on Rostow, approaching Fremont, but there is no stop sign on Fremont. Jackson was listening attentively to a baseball game as he drove along Rostow, and he failed to notice the stop sign, which was clearly visible. Consequently, his speed was undiminished when he entered the intersection. Fodor approached the same intersection on Fremont, driving 10 miles faster than the speed limit. Although he saw Jackson's car about to enter the intersection without slowing down or halting, Fodor did not stop in time to avoid a collision. Both cars were badly damaged, and Jackson suffered a broken wrist.

DISPUTE

Jackson sues Fodor for damages. Fodor contests.

RULE I

A person cannot recover from another for damages from an accident if the person was responsible in substantial part for the accident.

RULE II

One who is negligent may nevertheless recover from another party for damages if the other party had the ability to avoid an accident but made no attempt to do so.

Questions

6. Did Jackson know Fodor?

7. Did Fodor see Jackson's car approaching the intersection?

8. If both Fodor and Jackson had attempted unsuccessfully to stop their cars before the collision, will Jackson win his suit?

9. Did Fodor try to avoid the collision?

10. Were the brakes on Fodor's car in good working order?

STOP

IF YOU FINISH BEFORE TIME HAS ELAPSED, CHECK YOUR WORK ON THIS SECTION OF THE TEST ONLY. DO NOT GO ON TO THE NEXT SECTION OF THE TEST UNTIL TIME IS UP FOR THIS SECTION.

SECTION IV
LOGICAL REASONING

Time—10 Minutes
9 Questions

Directions:
In this section you will be given brief statements or passages and will be required to evaluate the reasoning involved. In some instances, more than one choice will appear to be a possible answer. You are to choose the *best* answer. Use common sense and reasonableness in making your selection; then mark the proper space on the answer sheet.

1. The theory that the subconscious is simply the unsymbolized suggests the desirability of adequate verbalization at the earliest possible stage of emotional development. It is the nameless fears and frustrations that defy analysis.

   The author of this passage would most likely agree that
   (A) there is nothing to fear but fear itself
   (B) emotional development starts at birth
   (C) verbalization is the key to complete emotional development
   (D) unsymbolized thoughts and emotions cannot be analyzed
   (E) the subconscious initiates only nameless fears and frustrations

2. Anyone who thinks that ignorance is no excuse isn't paying attention. Therefore
   (A) ignorance is an excuse
   (B) not paying attention is no excuse
   (C) ignorance comes from not paying attention
   (D) no one is ignorant
   (E) ignorance is no excuse

3. The most serious threat to modern man, it would seem, is not physical annihilation but the alleged meaninglessness of life. This latent vacuum becomes manifest in a state of boredom. Automation will lead to more and more free time and many will not know how to use their leisure hours. This is evidenced today by what Dr. Frankl refers to as Sunday Neurosis, the depression which afflicts people who become conscious of the lack of content in their lives when the rush of the busy week stops. Nothing in the world helps man to keep healthy so much as the knowledge of a life task. Nietzsche wisely said, "He who knows a Why of living surmounts every How."

   Which of the following is the best refutation of the above argument?
   (A) The availability of free time does not afford people more opportunity to enjoy their blessings.
   (B) Nuclear annihilation would vastly transcend the issue of personal meaningfulness.
   (C) Automation may actually result in more people working in such fields as computer science and technology.
   (D) The problem of personal meaning has existed since the beginning of modern times.
   (E) Most people actually enjoy their weekends when their work week ends on Friday.

4. Reading is an activity involving the use of the visual apparatus by means of which printed words are recognized.

   The above definition would be weakened most by pointing out that
   (A) skimming is a form of reading
   (B) a "nonreader" can recognize words
   (C) some printed words can be difficult to interpret
   (D) seeing is necessary for reading
   (E) lengthy printed words are not easily recognized

Questions 5–6 refer to the following passage.

Juan said, "It takes a good swing to be a good golfer. It takes practice to develop a good swing. Thus, it takes practice to be a good golfer."

5. Which of the following most closely parallels the logic of this statement?
   (A)   Betsy can bake a good cake if she wants to. Betsy baked a good cake. Thus she must have wanted to bake a good cake.
   (B)   A vote for Senator Cobb is a vote for peace. I voted for Senator Cobb. Thus, I want peace.
   (C)   You must work to earn money. You need money to pay the rent. Thus, you must work to pay the rent.
   (D)   It costs $200 to buy the TV. It costs $50 to buy the radio. Thus, the TV costs more than the radio.
   (E)   It is important to be alert when you take an exam. If you take a cold shower, you will be alert. Thus, you should take a cold shower before you take your exam.

6. Which of the following would weaken Juan's argument the most?
   (A)   It takes more than a good swing to be a good golfer.
   (B)   Some good golfers have average swings.
   (C)   Some people are born with a good golf swing.
   (D)   It takes strong forearms to have a good golf swing.
   (E)   Many good golfers lift weights.

Questions 7–8 require you to complete missing portions of the following passage by selecting from the five alternatives the one that best fits the context of the passage.

We suggest making a distinction between a highly developed or complex culture and a civilization. Culture may be defined in passing as the relatively rigid and unreasoned type of social behavior found in hives, lodges, and sometimes even in pentagons. It may be impressive and its achievements marvelous. We suggest a meaning for "(7) —————————————" that would make it rather a special sort of complex culture in which the constituent parts have developed linguistic, that is to say, parliamentary, techniques for resolving the "(8) ————————————" that arise from the conflicts of interest, real or apparent.

7. (A) culture   (B) behavior   (C) civilization   (D) parliamentary   (E) life

8. (A) inevitable disputes   (B) unfortunate circumstances   (C) complex situations
      (D) meaningless subsidies   (E) total carelessness

9. Many people believe that capital punishment acts as a deterrent to crime. This belief would be most weakened by
   (A)   examination of the number of murders before and after the abolition of the death penalty in a number of areas
   (B)   supplying statistics explaining the number of occurrences of crimes that are punishable by death
   (C)   a study of which crimes occur most and when they occur
   (D)   the fact that most crimes are not punishable by death
   (E)   the fact that the death penalty has not been enforced in 10 years

STOP

END OF EXAMINATION. IF YOU FINISH BEFORE TIME HAS ELAPSED, CHECK YOUR WORK ON THIS SECTION ONLY. DO NOT GO BACK TO ANY OTHER SECTION OF THE EXAMINATION.

ANSWER KEY

Section I:
Reading Comprehension

1. B	4. E	7. E
2. C	5. C	8. B
3. B	6. A	

Section II:
Analytical Reasoning

1. D	4. E	7. D
2. B	5. C	
3. E	6. C	

Section III:
Evaluation of Facts

1. A	5. C	9. B
2. D	6. D	10. D
3. C	7. C	
4. D	8. C	

Section IV:
Logical Reasoning

1. D	4. B	7. C
2. A	5. C	8. A
3. B	6. B	9. D

MINI-TEST ANALYSIS

Section	Total Number of Questions	Number Correct	Number Incorrect	Number Unanswered*
I: Reading Comprehension	8			
II: Analytical Reasoning	7			
III: Evaluation of Facts	10			
IV: Logical Reasoning	9			
TOTAL:	34			

*Since there is no penalty for incorrect answers on the LSAT, you should leave no question unanswered. Even if you don't have time to answer a question, at least fill in the answer space with a guess.

EXPLANATIONS OF ANSWERS

Section I

1. **B** This point is stated in the first sentence. Each of the other choices is either a subsidiary point or an irrelevant one.

2. **C** The context suggests that salutary associations are positive ones, and the phrase *associations of pleasure* immediately following the first mention of *salutary* certifies (C) as the best choice. (D) is also possible, but not as explicitly indicated in the passage.

3. **B** The author stresses that his teachers gave only *superficial* attention to salutary associations, associations which he calls *beneficial to the great whole*, that is, in a positive relationship to the natural order of things.

4. **E** Question I is answered in the first sentence, as is question II. In the first sentence we are told that *all* thinking is associational, and in the second that both *education and experience* promote associations. Nowhere, however, does the author mention just what teachers blame and praise.

5. **C** This choice summarizes the message of the paragraph: the author first describes the complexity of life by contemplating an entangled bank, and then enumerates the laws that account for this complexity, such as Growth with Reproduction, and Variability. (A) may be true, but it is not a *primary* purpose.

6. **A** The author asserts that higher animals follow directly from the *war of nature*, a phrase that clearly denotes competition.

7. **E** In the author's conception, the *less-improved* life forms become extinct, and those naturally selected prevail. He thus suggests a "rich" and a "poor" class of life in nature. (A) is not the best choice because the author does not specify that *might* is the primary attribute of the "right" (prevailing) life form.

8. **B** Without recognizing this passage as one of Charles Darwin's statements about evolution, you still might choose (B) by realizing that, according to the passage, life forms evolve through the interplay of natural laws. Creationism (A) implies divine guidance, which the author does not mention; the big bang (C) suggests some explosion, an occurrence not in the passage; social Darwinism (D) suggests a phenomenon of society rather than of nature; and naturalism (E) is a much more vague term in this context than is evolution.

Section II

From the information given, a "position" diagram may be drawn as follows:

$\underline{\qquad}$	$\underline{\qquad}$	$\underline{C}$	$\underline{A/D}$	$\underline{\qquad}$	$\underline{D/A}$	$\underline{\qquad}$	$\underline{\qquad}$
1	2	3	4	5	6	7	8
tallest			girl	girl	girl		tallest

Now notice that, since E and F are always adjacent, they may be in positions 1 and 2, or in positions 7 and 8. And, for instance, if they are in 7 and 8, then H (a boy) must be in 1 or 2 (and vice versa).

1. **D** If G is a girl, then she must be in 5th place, since the sisters (A and D) will not stand next to each other.

2. **B** If H is one of the two tallest, then H will be on one end. Thus at the other end must be E and F. Therefore, H may be next to either B or G, depending upon who is the boy.

3. **E** If G is a girl, and H is last in line, your diagram must look like this:

$\underline{E/F}$	$\underline{F/E}$	$\underline{C}$	$\underline{A/D}$	$\underline{G}$	$\underline{D/A}$	$\underline{B}$	$\underline{H}$

Thus, the only true statement is (E), B must be next to H.

4. **E** If F is second in line, then your diagram should look like this:

$\underline{E}$	$\underline{F}$	$\underline{C}$	$\underline{A/D}$	$\underline{\qquad}$	$\underline{D/A}$	$\underline{H?}$	$\underline{H?}$

Notice that statements I and III are true and statement II isn't true, because B could possibly be 5th in line.

5. **C** If E and B are the two tallest, then two diagrams are possible:

$\underline{E}$	$\underline{F}$	$\underline{C}$	$\underline{A/D}$	$\underline{G}$	$\underline{D/A}$	$\underline{H}$	$\underline{B}$

and

$\underline{B}$	$\underline{H}$	$\underline{C}$	$\underline{A/D}$	$\underline{G}$	$\underline{D/A}$	$\underline{F}$	$\underline{E}$

Notice that (A) and (D) are incorrect because H, a boy, cannot be in the 5th place. (B) is incorrect because E and F must be adjacent. Finally, (E) is incorrect because A and D will not stand next to each other in line.

6. **C** If H is last in line, then your diagram should look like this:

E/F	F/E	C	A/D	___	D/A	___	H

Notice that B and G must go in the 5th and 7th spots, but we cannot tell which one goes where. Therefore, the only statement that may possibly be true is statement III, E is one of the tallest.

7. **D** If E and G are the two tallest, your diagram is either

E	F	C	A/D	B	D/A	H	G

or

G	H	C	A/D	B	D/A	F	E

Notice that, since H is a boy, he must be next to G. Therefore, (D) is the only possible correct order of the students.

Section III

Set 1

1. **A** To answer this relevant question, you must choose between the two rules. Each rule gives a different outcome. Since Mrs. Jones was carrying two bags, a bag had been reported stolen, and Ralston detained Mrs. Jones for a reasonable period of time, Rule I applies. But Rule II also applies since Ralston did restrict Mrs. Jones's freedom of movement.

2. **D** The perfume is irrelevant. It is the handbag, not the perfume, which may have been stolen.

3. **C** This relevant question can be answered by logical deduction from the facts. Since a red handbag was reported missing, and Ralston followed Mrs. Jones looking for the red handbag, it can be deduced that the second handbag was red.

4. **D** This question is irrelevant. Since the stolen handbag was red, the likeness or unlikeness of Mrs. Jones's blue handbag to those in the store is irrelevant.

5. **C** This relevant question can be answered by applying the rules. If Mrs. Jones had carried only her blue handbag into the store, there would be no reason to think she had taken a red handbag and only Rule II would apply.

Set 2

6. **D** The question is irrelevant. Both drivers were negligent.

7. **C** This relevant question can be answered by applying the rules to the facts in the case: "he [Fodor] saw Jackson's car about to enter the intersection."

8. **C** This relevant question can be answered by applying the rules. If Fodor attempted to avoid the accident, Jackson cannot win under Rule II. Under Rule I Jackson cannot win, so Jackson will not win his suit.

9. **B** To answer this relevant question, you need additional information. If Fodor did try to avoid the collision, Jackson will lose under Rule II. The facts do not answer this relevant question.

10. **D** The question is irrelevant. The issue is whether or not Fodor *tried* to avoid the collision.

Section IV

1. **D** The passage states that nameless fears and frustrations defy analysis and implies that unsymbolized thoughts and emotions constitute nameless fears and frustrations. (C) and (E) are close, but note the absolute words "complete" and "only" in each.

2. **A** If anyone who thinks that ignorance is no excuse isn't paying attention, then those who are paying attention will know that ignorance is an excuse.

3. **B** The consequences of nuclear annihilation—namely the end of human life—would include the disappearance of all other human questions. Thus, the author's contention that the most serious threat to modern man may be the alleged meaninglessness of life is seriously challenged by the magnitude of nuclear annihilation.

4. **B** If a "nonreader" (one who cannot read) can recognize words, then reading cannot be defined as the act of recognizing words.

5. **C** Good swing implies good golfer and practice implies good swing; therefore practice implies good golfer. (X implies Y and Y implies Z; therefore X implies Z.) This is most closely paralleled by (C), even though the terms are in slightly different order, or not exactly parallel. (B) is wrong since voting for peace and wanting peace are two different things. Betsy may have baked a good cake (A) even if she did not want to. (E), although in proper form, brings in excess subjectivity.

6. **B** This is the only answer that refutes the premise that you need a good swing. (A) talks about what else you need, and (C) says nothing about the need for a good swing.

7. **C** None of the other choices is a "special sort of culture."

8. **A** "Disputes" are the most specific and logical results of "conflicts."

9. **D** If most crimes are not punishable by death, then, even if capital punishment were reinstated, most criminals would not be deterred by it. (A) would be a good answer, except that it might strengthen the belief, depending on the outcome of the statistics.

PART TWO

ANALYSIS
Understanding the Sections and the Key Strategies

Chapter

2

Reading Comprehension

INTRODUCTION TO QUESTION TYPE

The entire LSAT is, generally speaking, a test of reading comprehension. However, the Reading Comprehension section itself is a test of general reading skills rather than the more particular analytical skills stressed in other sections. Each Reading Comprehension section usually consists of four passages, each of approximately 450 words, and 28 questions to be answered in 35 minutes.

The passages are drawn from three basic areas: the humanities, the social sciences, and the sciences—for instance, you may read one passage about Beethoven's life, one about the discovery of Neanderthal man, one about behavioral psychology, and one about the virtues of organic gardening. Each passage assumes a general college background but does not give an advantage to expertise in any one area; thus, for example, a psychology major has no edge on a music major. Often the passages are excerpts from published material.

ACTIVE READING

The Reading Comprehension section presents long passages demanding your steady concentration. Because such passages are complex and often dull, you must approach them *actively*, focusing in with a specific plan of attack.

Suppose that midway through the first paragraph of a passage you encounter a sentence like this:

Ordinarily, of course, we are invited only to criticize the current neglect of government programs; politicians cling to their own fringe benefits while the strife in our inner cities is only nominally contained with a plethora of half-baked local projects whose actual effect is the gradual erosion of trust in the beneficence of the republic.

Different students may respond in different ways:

> "What? Let me read that again" (and again and again).
> "I used to know what *beneficence* meant; uh. . . ."
> "Boy, am I tired."
> "I should have eaten a better breakfast; my head aches."
> "I wonder what I'll wear tonight. . . ."
> "This writer is screwy; I was a Senator's aide and I know he's wrong."
> "How can I read this!? It's written so poorly; that word *plethora* is a terrible choice."

These typical responses—getting stuck, getting distracted, getting angry—all work against your purpose: using the passage to increase your LSAT score. The techniques described below should help you avoid some common reading test pitfalls.

Essentially, active reading consists of marking as you read. But the marking you do must be strategic and efficient. To present some effective active reading techniques, we will consider a sample reading passage and seven typical LSAT questions.

SAMPLE PASSAGE AND QUESTIONS

With the possible exception of equal rights, perhaps the most controversial issue across the United States today is the death penalty. Many argue that it is an effective deterrent to murder, while others maintain there is no conclusive evidence that the death penalty reduces the number of murders.

The principal argument advanced by those opposed to the death penalty, basically, is that it is cruel and inhuman punishment, that it is the mark of a brutal society, and finally that it is of questionable effectiveness as a deterrent to crime anyway.

In our opinion, the death penalty is a necessary evil. Throughout recorded history there have always been those extreme individuals in every society who were capable of terribly violent crimes such as murder. But some are more extreme, more diabolical than others.

For example, it is one thing to take the life of another in a momentary fit of blind rage, but quite another to coldly plot and carry out the murder of one or more people in the style of an executioner. Thus, murder, like all other crimes, is a matter of relative degree. While it could be argued with some conviction that the criminal in the first instance should be merely isolated from society, such should not be the fate of the latter type murderer. To quote Moshe Dayan, "Unfortunately, we must kill them."

The value of the death penalty as a deterrent to crime may be open to debate, but there remains one irrefutable fact: Gary Gilmore will never commit another murder. Charles Manson and his followers, were they to escape, or—God forbid—be paroled, very well might.

The overwhelming majority of citizens believe that the death penalty protects them. Their belief is reinforced by evidence which shows that the death penalty deters murder. For example, the Attorney General points out that from 1954 to 1963, when the death penalty was consistently imposed in California, the murder rate remained between three and four murders for each 100,000 population. Since 1964 the death penalty has been imposed only once (in 1967), and the murder rate has skyrocketed to 10.4 murders for each 100,000 population. The sharp climb in the state's murder rate, which commenced when executions stopped, is no coincidence. It is convincing evidence that the death penalty does deter many murderers.

If the Governor's veto of the bill reestablishing the death penalty is upheld, an initiative will surely follow. However, an initiative cannot restore the death penalty for six months. In the interim, innocent people will be murdered—some whose lives may have been saved if the death penalty were in effect.

This is literally a life or death matter. The lives of hundreds of innocent people must be protected. The Governor's veto must be overridden.

1. The primary purpose of the passage is to   Ⓐ Ⓑ Ⓒ Ⓓ Ⓔ
   (A) criticize the governor
   (B) argue for the value of the death penalty
   (C) initiate a veto
   (D) speak for the majority
   (E) impose a six-month moratorium on the death penalty

2. The passage attempts to establish a relationship between   Ⓐ Ⓑ Ⓒ Ⓓ Ⓔ
   (A) Gary Gilmore and Charles Manson
   (B) the importance of both equal rights and the death penalty
   (C) the murder rate and the imposition of the death penalty
   (D) executions and murders
   (E) the effects of parole and the effects of isolation

3. It can be inferred that the author assumes which of the following about the
   Governor's veto of the death penalty legislation?   Ⓐ Ⓑ Ⓒ Ⓓ Ⓔ
   (A) It might be upheld.
   (B) It will certainly be overridden.
   (C) It represents consultation with a majority of citizens.
   (D) The veto is important, but not crucial.
   (E) It is based on the principle of equal protection for accused murder-
   ers.

4. The author's response to those who urge the death penalty for all degrees of
   murder would most likely be   Ⓐ Ⓑ Ⓒ Ⓓ Ⓔ
   (A) supportive   (B) noncommittal   (C) negative   (D) friendly
   (E) ambivalent

5. In the passage the author is primarily concerned with   Ⓐ Ⓑ Ⓒ Ⓓ Ⓔ
   (A) supporting a position
   (B) describing an occurrence
   (C) citing authorities
   (D) analyzing a problem objectively
   (E) settling a dispute

6. In paragraph 7, "initiative" refers to   Ⓐ Ⓑ Ⓒ Ⓓ Ⓔ
   (A) a demonstration against the Governor's action
   (B) a rise in the murder rate
   (C) a more vocal response by the majority of citizens
   (D) the introduction of legislation to reinstate the death penalty
   (E) overriding the Governor's veto

7. The passage provides answers to which of the following questions?   Ⓐ Ⓑ Ⓒ Ⓓ Ⓔ
   I. Are all murders equally diabolical?
   II. Should the death penalty be a controversial issue?
   III. Are there factors other than the death penalty that may account for an
   increased murder rate?
   (A) I only   (B) II only   (C) III only   (D) I and II only
   (E) II and III only

FOUR-STEP APPROACH

STEP ONE: SKIM THE QUESTIONS.

Before reading the passage, spend a short time familiarizing yourself with the questions. You should preread or "skim" the questions for two reasons: (1) to learn what *types* of questions are being asked; and (2) to learn what specific *information* to look for when you do read the passage. In order to skim efficiently and effectively, you should read over only the portion of each question that *precedes* the multiple choices, and you should mark *key words* as you do so.

A *key word* or phrase is any segment that suggests what you should look for when you read the passage. Marking these key words will help you remember them as you read (luckily, the questions will be printed directly below and alongside the passage, so that as you read the passage you will be able to glance at the questions and remind yourself about what you've marked). In order to further explain and clarify these tips on skimming, let's examine the questions that follow the passage above.

The key words for each of them are circled.

1. The primary purpose of the passage is to . . . .
This is a "main idea" or "primary purpose" question; most LSAT reading passages are followed by at least one of these. You are asked what the passage is trying to *do* or *express*, as a whole. Here is a list of possible purposes that may be embodied in a reading passage:

to inform	to criticize	to show
to persuade	to argue for or against	to question
to analyze	to illustrate	to explain
to change	to represent	to prove
to restore	to parody	to describe

This list is by no means exhaustive; the possible purposes are almost endless, and you might try thinking of some yourself.

The main idea or primary purpose of a passage is usually stated or implied in the *thesis sentence* of one or more of the paragraphs. A thesis sentence tells what the paragraph as a whole is about; it states a main idea or primary purpose. For example, the second sentence of paragraph 6 in the passage is the thesis sentence; it sums up the evidence of that paragraph into a single statement.

A primary purpose or main idea question should direct your attention to the thesis sentences in the passage, that is, the *general statements* that sum up the specific details.

2. The passage attempts to establish a relationship between . . . .
This question requires that you locate *explicit* (established) *information* in the passage, information that defines a relationship. The question allows you to anticipate the mention of at least one relationship in the passage, and warns you through its wording that the relationship is not "hidden," but is instead one that the author deliberately attempts to establish.

3. It can be inferred that the author assumes which of the following about the veto of the Governor's death penalty legislation?
This question requires that you locate *implicit*, rather than explicit information; you are asked to draw an *inference* (a conclusion based on reasoning), not just to locate obvious material. It is more difficult than question 3. When you read about the Governor's veto in the passage, you should take mental note of any unstated assumptions that seem to lie behind the author's commentary.

4. The author's response to those who urge the death penalty for all degrees of murder would most likely be . . . .
This question type, usually more difficult than the types previously discussed, requires you to *apply* the information in the passage itself. As you read the passage, you should pay special attention to the author's attitude toward types, or degrees, of murder; applying this attitude to the situation described in the question should lead toward the answer.

5. In the passage the author is (primarily concerned) with . . . .
This is another variety of the "primary purpose" or "main idea" question.

6. In paragraph 7, "initiative" refers to . . . .
The question requires you to focus on specific language in the passage, and define it in context. Such a question is relatively easy insofar as it specifies just where to look for an answer; its difficulty varies according to the difficulty of the word or phrase you are asked to consider.

7. The passage (provides answers to) which of the following questions?
This question is significant because of its "multiple-multiple-choice" form, which was discussed more fully on page 10 . As a guide to reading the passage, it is not very helpful. Although most questions that you skim will lead you to useful information in the passage, some, like this one, do not.

In general, spend only a few seconds skimming the questions. Read each question, mark key words, and move on.
DO NOT:
- dwell on a question and analyze it extensively.
- be concerned with whether you are marking the "right" words (trust your intuition).
- read the multiple choices (this wastes time).

STEP TWO (OPTIONAL): SKIM THE PASSAGE.

Some students find skimming the passage helpful. Skimming the passage consists of quickly reading the first sentence of each paragraph, and marking key words and phrases. This will give you an idea of what the paragraph as a whole is about. The first sentence is often a general statement or thesis sentence that gives the gist of the paragraph.
paragraph.
Consider the passage given above. Reading the first sentence of each paragraph, we mark the key words and phrases, and may draw the following conclusions:

Paragraph 1: "With the possible exception of equal rights, perhaps the most controversial issue across the United States today is the death penalty." This sentence suggests that the passage will be about the death penalty, and the word "controversial" suggests that the author is about to take a stand on the controversy.

Paragraph 2: "The principal argument advanced by those opposed to the death penalty, basically, is that it is cruel and inhuman punishment, that it is the mark of a brutal society, and finally that it is of questionable effectiveness as a deterrent to crime anyway." This sentence (which is also the whole paragraph) presents opposition arguments, and because those arguments are presented as the views of others, not the views of the author, we begin to suspect that he does not align himself with the opposition.

Paragraph 3: "In our opinion, the death penalty is a necessary evil." This confirms our suspicion; the author is beginning an argument *in favor of* the death penalty.

Paragraph 4: "For example, it is one thing to take the life of another in a momentary fit of blind rage, but quite another to coldly plot and carry out the murder of one or more people in the style of an executioner." Here the author is distinguishing between *degrees* of murder, and you may at this point recall question 4; this information seems relevant to that question.

Paragraph 5: "The value of the death penalty as a deterrent to crime may be open to debate, but there remains one irrefutable fact: Gary Gilmore will never commit another murder." The most significant feature of this sentence is that the author's tone is so absolute, indicating his strong belief in his own position.

Paragraph 6: "The overwhelming majority of citizens believe that the death penalty protects them." This sentence points toward statistical evidence in favor of the author's view.

Paragraph 7: "If the Governor's veto of the bill reestablishing the death penalty is upheld, an initiative will surely follow." Coincidently with the author's faith in the will of the majority, here he suggests that the death penalty will be upheld one way or another, by overriding a veto or through initiative.

Paragraph 8: "This is literally a life or death matter." The author here reemphasizes the seriousness and importance of his position.

Do not expect your own skimming of the passage to necessarily yield a series of conclusions such as those expressed above. Most of the knowledge you gather as you skim will "happen" without a deliberate effort on your part to translate your intuitions into sentences. Just read and mark the sentences, without slowing yourself down by analyzing each sentence. The preceding analysis suggests some possible conclusions that may occur to a reader, but drawing such full conclusions from sentence clues will take both practice and a relaxed attitude; don't push yourself to make sense out of everything, and don't reread sentences (skimming the passage should take only a few seconds). Some sentences you read may be too difficult to make sense of immediately; just leave these alone and move along. Remember that getting stuck wastes time and raises anxiety.

STEP THREE: READ AND MARK THE PASSAGE.

Now you are ready to read the entire passage. To read quickly, carefully, and efficiently, you must be *marking* important words and phrases while you read. At least such marking will keep you alert and focused. At most it will locate the answers to many questions.

Skimming the questions will have helped you decide what to mark. If a question refers to a specific line, sentence, or quotation from the passage, you will want to mark this reference and pay special attention to it. Whenever a key word from a question corresponds with a spot in the passage, mark the spot. In the scheme for marking a passage, these spots are called, simply, ANSWER SPOTS. There are two other kinds of "spots" that you should mark as you read: REPEAT SPOTS and INTUITION SPOTS. Repeat spots are sections of the passage in which the same type of information is repeated. Consider the following excerpt from a passage:

Proposed cutbacks in the Human Resources Agency are scheduled for hearing 9 A.M. on the 17th. Included in possible program reductions are cutbacks in the veterans' affairs program, including closure of the local office; in potential support for the county's Commission on the Status of Women; and in payments provided by the county for foster home care, which are not being adjusted for cost-of-living increases this year.

Programs in the Environmental Improvement Agency will be examined by the board beginning 9 A.M. Friday, August 18. The milk and dairy inspection program has been recommended by County Administrative Officer Fred Higgins for transfer to state administration. In addition, budget recommendations do not include funds for numerous community general plans which have been discussed previously by the board of supervisors. Such areas as Joshua Tree, Crestline, Lytle Creek, and Yucaipa are not included in the Planning Department's program for the upcoming year.

A special session to discuss proposed budget cuts in the county's General Services Agency will be conducted at 9 A.M. Saturday, August 19. A number of county branch libraries have been proposed for closure next year, including the Adelanto, Bloomington, Crestline, Joshua Tree, Mentone, Morongo, Muscoy, and Running Springs locations. A rollback in hours of operation will also be considered. Branches now open 60 hours a week will be cut to 52 hours. Other 50-hour-a-week branches will be reduced to 32 hours a week. Testimony will be heard on cutbacks in various agricultural service programs, including the county trapper program in the Yucaipa region and support for 4-H activities.

Generally, this excerpt stresses information about times, dates, and locations; we are conscious of repeated numbers and repeated place names. Marking the spots in which such information is found will help you to sort out the information, and also to answer more efficiently a question that addresses such information, a question such as, "Which of the following cities are (is) *not* included in the Planning Department's program and *are* (is) liable to lose a branch library?" Having marked the repeat spots that contain location names, you may be better able to focus on the appropriate information quickly.

INTUITION SPOTS are any spots that strike you as significant, for whatever reason. As we read, we tend to pay special attention to certain information; marking those spots that your intuition perceives as important will help increase your comprehension and will therefore contribute to correct answers.

You may notice that ANSWER SPOTS, REPEAT SPOTS, and INTUITION SPOTS are not necessarily different spots. An answer spot may also be a spot that contains repeat information AND appeals to your intuition.

Don't overmark. Some students, fearing that they will miss an important point, underline everything. Such misplaced thoroughness makes it impossible to find any specific word or phrase. Just mark the main idea of each paragraph and several important words or phrases. And vary your marks. You may want to underline main ideas, use circles or brackets or stars to indicate other important spots, and jot some notes to yourself in the margin. Here is how you might mark the death penalty passage:

With the possible exception of equal rights, perhaps the most (controversial issue) across the United States today is the (death penalty.) Many argue that it is an effective deterrent to murder, while others maintain there is no conclusive evidence that the death penalty reduces the number of murders. *contrast*

The (principal argument) advanced by those opposed to the death penalty, basically, is that it is cruel and inhuman punishment, that it is the mark of a brutal society, and finally that it is of questionable effectiveness as a deterrent to crime anyway. *opposition points*

* (In our opinion, the death penalty is a necessary evil.) Throughout recorded history there have always been those extreme individuals in every society who were capable of terribly violent crimes such as murder. But some are more extreme, more diabolical than others.

For example, it is one thing to take the life of another in a momentary fit of blind rage, but quite another to coldly plot and carry out the murder of one or more people in the style of an executioner. Thus, murder, like all other crimes, is a matter of (relative degree.) While it could be argued with some conviction that the criminal in the first instance should be merely isolated from society, such should not be the fate of the latter type murderer. To quote Moshe Dayan, "Unfortunately, we must kill them." *degrees of murder penalty*

The value of the death penalty as a deterrent to crime may be open to debate, but there remains one irrefutable fact: Gary Gilmore will never commit another murder. Charles Manson and his followers, were they to escape, or—God forbid—be paroled, very well might. ←

[The overwhelming majority of citizens believe that the death penalty protects them.] Their belief is reinforced by evidence which shows that the death penalty deters murder. For example, the Attorney General points out that from 1954 to 1963, when the death penalty was consistently imposed in California, the murder rate remained between three and four murders for each 100,000 population. Since 1964 the death penalty has been imposed only once (in 1967), and the murder rate has skyrocketed to 10.4 murders for each 100,000 population. The sharp climb in the state's murder rate, which commenced when executions stopped, is no coincidence. It is convincing evidence that the death penalty does deter many murderers. *STATS*

If the (Governor's veto) of the bill reestablishing the death penalty is upheld, an initiative will surely follow. However, an initiative cannot restore the death penalty for six months. In the interim, innocent people will be murdered—some whose lives may have been saved if the death penalty was in effect. *veto effects*

This is literally a life or death matter. The lives of hundreds of innocent people must be protected. The Governor's veto must be overridden.

Your marking method should be active, playful, and personal. While you are marking, don't worry about whether you are doing it correctly. You may notice that, in the discussion of skimming the passage, some sentences are marked differently than they are here, in order to stress that there is no single, "correct" method.

Remember not to react subjectively to the passage, or add to it. Your own background may have you disagreeing with the passage, or you may be tempted to supply information from your own experience in order to answer the question. You must use only the information you are given, and you must accept it as true.

Avoid wasting time with very difficult or technical sentences. Concentrating on the sentences and ideas you do understand will often supply you with enough material to answer the questions. Rereading difficult sentences takes time, and usually does not bring greater clarity.

STEP FOUR: ANSWER THE QUESTIONS.

As you attempt to answer each question, follow these steps: (1) assess the level of difficulty, and skip the question if necessary; (2) eliminate unreasonable and incorrect answer choices; (3) make certain that information in the passage supports your answer. We will follow this procedure, using the questions on the "death penalty" passage above as examples.

ANSWERS AND EXPLANATIONS

1. **B**   Remember that this sort of question asks for the *primary* purpose, not a subsidiary purpose. Often the incorrect answer choices will express minor or subsidiary purposes; this is true of (A) and (D). Another type of incorrect answer choice *contradicts* the information in the passage. So it is with (C) and (E). Both contradict the author's expressed support of the death penalty. Having marked thesis sentences in the passage, you should be aware of the author's repeated arguments for the value of the death penalty, and choose (B).

2. **C**   "Equal rights" is mentioned only in passing, and a relationship between parole and isolation is scarcely even implied; therefore (B) and (E) should be eliminated. (A) is not a good answer because, strictly speaking, Gary Gilmore and Charles Manson are not compared; their *sentences* are. (D) is a true answer, but not the best one because it is more vague and general than the best choice, (C); paragraph 6 makes this specific comparison.

3. **A**   We are looking for information that is (1) assumed but not explicit, and (2) relevant to the Governor's veto. Having marked the appropriate section of the passage, you are able to return immediately to the final two paragraphs, which discuss the veto. (B), (C), and (D) contradict passage information: (C) contradicts the author's earlier explanations that most citizens approve of the death penalty, and (D) contradicts the author's emphatic final statement. (B) contradicts the author's acknowledgment that the veto might be upheld (first sentence of paragraph 7). (E) is irrelevant to the veto issue. (A) is correct because the assumption that the veto might be upheld would certainly underlie an argument against it.

4. **C**   Having marked the section that refers to different degrees of murder, you are once again able to focus on the appropriate section. In paragraph 4, the author argues that unpremeditated murder may not warrant the death penalty. This argument suggests his negative attitude toward someone who urges the death penalty for all murderers. You should have immediately eliminated (B) and (E), concluding that this is a passage in which the author is *never* noncommittal or ambivalent.

5. **A**   With your general knowledge of the passage, you should immediately eliminate (B) and (D), because the author is *argumentative* throughout, never merely descriptive or objective. Citing authorities (C) is a *subsidiary* rather than a primary concern; the author does so in paragraph 5. (E) is incorrect because it is the author himself who is *creating* a dispute over the death penalty. A review of the thesis sentences alone shows that the author is consistently supporting a position; (A) is certainly the best answer.

6. **D** Skimming this question has allowed you to pay special attention to "initiative" as you read the passage. The sentence suggests that the initiative is a response to the Governor's veto of the death penalty; and it is a *certain* response, as indicated by "surely." It is also an action that can eventually restore the death penalty; this fact especially signals (D) as the answer. (B) states information mentioned apart from the initiative; the murder rate will rise "in the interim." Demonstrations (A) or vocal responses (C) are not suggested as possibilities anywhere. (E) is eliminated because the last sentence of the passage urges an override, thus distinguishing this action from an initiative.

7. **D** To approach this "multiple-multiple-choice" question, work from the roman numerals first, asking yourself whether each is true or false. (I) is true; the author answers this question in paragraph 4. At this point, eliminate (B) and (C) because they do not include (I). (II) is true; the author answers this question by attempting to eliminate the controversy and establish his side. The only answer choice including (I) and (II) is (D). You do not need to consider (III). Remember: When you encounter this type of question, work from the roman numerals first, and eliminate letter choices accordingly.

ACTIVE READING, A SUMMARY CHART

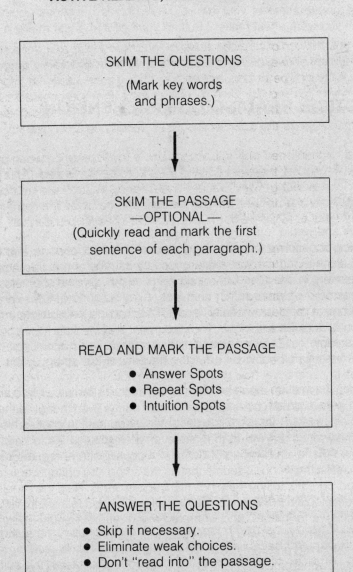

SKIM THE QUESTIONS

(Mark key words
and phrases.)

↓

SKIM THE PASSAGE
—OPTIONAL—
(Quickly read and mark the first
sentence of each paragraph.)

↓

READ AND MARK THE PASSAGE

● Answer Spots
● Repeat Spots
● Intuition Spots

↓

ANSWER THE QUESTIONS

● Skip if necessary.
● Eliminate weak choices.
● Don't "read into" the passage.

BASIC TRAINING: EXTRA, EFFECTIVE PRACTICE

The following procedure, *practiced daily*, should strengthen precisely the kinds of skills that you will need for the Reading Comprehension section of the LSAT:

1. Locate the editorial page in your daily newspaper. There you will probably find three or four editorials on different subjects.

2. Read several editorials, at your normal reading speed, marking them if possible.

3. Set the editorials aside, and try to write a summary sentence describing each editorial. Make your summary as precise as possible. Do not write, "This editorial was about the economy." Instead, try to write something like this: "The editorial argued against the value of supply-side economics by referring to rising unemployment and interest rates."

    You may not be able to write so precise a summary right away, but after a few days of practicing this technique, you will find yourself better able to spot and remember main ideas and specific details, and better able to anticipate and understand the author's point of view.

    It is most important that you *write down* your summary statements. This takes more time and effort than silently "telling" yourself what the editorial means, but the time and effort pay off.

4. Every few days, create some of your own multiple-choice questions about an editorial. What would you ask if you were a test maker? Putting yourself in the test maker's shoes can be very instructive. You will realize, for instance, how to construct weak or incorrect answer choices, and that realization will help you to eliminate choices when you take the LSAT.

EXTRA PRACTICE: READING COMPREHENSION

Passage 1

A recent Harris Survey revealed that a majority of Americans say the price of gasoline would have to go to $1.50 a gallon before they would cut back on the use of their automobiles for pleasure driving. The survey, conducted among 1517 adults nationwide, also found that gasoline prices would have to go to $1.85 per gallon before adults would cease to use their own cars to go to work and would turn to public transportation and car pooling.

In fact, the price of gasoline is presently going *down* rather than up. Major oil companies have announced plans to reduce wholesale prices by as much as eight cents a gallon. As a result, those drivers who insisted that only rising gasoline costs would cut their consumption will now probably begin to drive more rather than less. Already, according to the Highway Patrol, highways are becoming more crowded with cars carrying only one passenger, and with gas-guzzling recreational vehicles.

These results are interesting when one considers that we are presently at the height of the smog season. As most of us know by now, the majority of our smog problem is caused by exhaust emissions from cars. Yet how many of us have actually made an effort to drive less? In fact, how many of us have even made an effort to drive more slowly to help conserve gasoline? Unfortunately, the answer to both questions is: not very many. Even though we all are aware—or certainly should be by now—that there is a desperate need both to conserve fuel and to clean up our air, far too few of us are willing to make even a small sacrifice to help.

Recently we read that a small group of botanists is busily attempting to develop a strain of pine tree that can resist the smog. It seems that as the smog has gotten worse each year it has taken an increasingly greater toll on the pines in mountain areas. Now the situation is becoming critical; either we develop a hardier tree or they will all die. It's sad to think that in a country which professes so much love for nature, and where so much natural beauty abounds, we have to develop a breed of "supertrees" which can cope with the polluted air we create.

The solution to our smog problem lies not in eliminating the steel industry's coke oven emissions, or any other industrial emissions, but in convincing the millions of people who traverse our freeways daily to try at least to drive less. Obviously it's necessary to drive in order to get to and from work, but if each of us could at least reduce the pleasure driving a little, drive the speed limit, and have our automobile engines tuned regularly, the improvement would be immediately noticeable. If we make these small sacrifices we won't have to worry about eventually paying $1.85 per gallon for gasoline. The reduced consumption will keep prices low because there will be enough for everyone without having to increase prices to "force" us to use less.

1. The primary purpose of this passage is to   Ⓐ Ⓑ Ⓒ Ⓓ Ⓔ
   (A) convince smog producers to reduce emissions
   (B) convince drivers to reduce smog
   (C) convince drivers to drive less
   (D) describe an instance of the supply/demand phenomenon
   (E) argue against higher gasoline prices

2. The author puts the blame for air pollution on   Ⓐ Ⓑ Ⓒ Ⓓ Ⓔ
   (A) individuals   (B) institutions   (C) corporations   (D) botanists
   (E) pollsters

3. With which of the following statements about the effects of smog would the
   author be most likely to agree?   Ⓐ Ⓑ Ⓒ Ⓓ Ⓔ
   (A) A greater number of vans and campers at our national parks threatens
        the parks' beauty.
   (B) Smog encourages the survival of hardy vegetation.
   (C) The price of gasoline may rise in the future.
   (D) People who drive alone have no respect for nature.
   (E) Smog will gradually become something we can live with.

4. Who of the following would be most likely to object to the author's argu-
   ment?   Ⓐ Ⓑ Ⓒ Ⓓ Ⓔ
   (A) an industrialist
   (B) an auto mechanic
   (C) a botanist
   (D) a Highway Patrol officer
   (E) a manufacturer of recreational vehicles

5. The author implies which of the following in his argument?   Ⓐ Ⓑ Ⓒ Ⓓ Ⓔ
   (A) Industrial emissions are uncontrollable.
   (B) Reduced driving will occur even if drivers do not follow his advice.
   (C) Reduced driving will not inconvenience drivers.
   (D) The diminishing supply of fuel is not a problem.
   (E) Gasoline prices should not go down.

6. The author's tone in this passage is   Ⓐ Ⓑ Ⓒ Ⓓ Ⓔ
   (A) cynical   (B) analytical   (C) satirical   (D) urgent
   (E) objective

7. To accept the author's argument, we MUST assume which of the following
   about the Harris Survey?   Ⓐ Ⓑ Ⓒ Ⓓ Ⓔ
   (A) That the people conducting the survey were opposed to pleasure driv-
        ing.
   (B) That the people conducting the survey were not drivers.
   (C) That the survey was conducted recently.
   (D) That the 1517 adults actually represent a majority of Americans.
   (E) That the people conducting the survey were not employed by the steel
        industry.

Passage 2

Just as the members of the Inter-American Tropical Tuna Commission have subscribed to annual quotas on the tuna harvest, they are agreed that cooperation is essential in limiting the porpoise kill. The common interest is preservation of the tuna industry. And since modern fishing methods exploit the cozy relationship between the yellowfin tuna and the porpoise, according to a report presented at recent commission meetings in San Diego, California, "the fishery for tuna would . . . become less profitable" as the number of porpoises decreased. Tuna and porpoise are often found together at sea, and the fishermen have learned to cast their nets where they see the porpoises, using them to locate the tuna. The problem is that many porpoises die in the nets.

The commission deliberations acknowledged the environmental pressures that have led to strict regulation of U.S. tuna crews under federal law. Delegates also recognized that porpoise protection goals are relatively meaningless unless conservation procedures are adopted and followed on an international basis. Commission supervision of survey, observer, and research programs won general agreement at the eight-nation conference. The method and timetable for implementing the program, however, remain uncertain.

Thus the federal regulation that leaves U.S. crews at a disadvantage in the tuna-harvest competition remains a threat to the survival of the tuna fleet. Still, the commission meetings have focused on the workable solution. All vessels should be equipped with the best porpoise-saving gear devised; crews should be trained and motivated to save the porpoise; a system must be instituted to assure that rules are enforced.

Above all, the response must be international. Porpoise conservation could well be another element in an envisioned treaty that remains unhappily elusive at the continuing Law-of-the-Sea Conference in New York City.

The tuna industry interest in saving porpoises is bothersome to many who also want to "save the porpoise," but object to the industry motivation for doing so. For fishermen, saving the porpoise is valuable only because the porpoise leads them to tuna. For more compassionate souls, however, the porpoise is not just a tuna finder, but, more important, the sea creature that seems most "human." Fredson Delacourte, national chairman of the "People for Animals" drive, says this: "It is especially sad that these sea creatures, in spite of their keen intelligence, cannot outwit the tuna fishermen who, anxious to meet their annual quota, ensnare and destroy porpoises as well. But it is even sadder that the tuna industry is so intent upon using the porpoise so greedily." Mr. Delacourte praises the fishing industry for its plans to save the porpoises, at the same time that he wishes their motives were more altruistic. He insists that any "law of the sea" should be essentially a moral law rather than an economic one.

8. The primary purpose of this passage is to   Ⓐ Ⓑ Ⓒ Ⓓ Ⓔ
   (A) resolve a controversy
   (B) discuss the protection of porpoises
   (C) praise the Law-of-the-Sea Conference
   (D) implement a program for new fishing techniques
   (E) create international cooperation

9. Fredson Delacourte and the tuna industry do not share which of the following?   Ⓐ Ⓑ Ⓒ Ⓓ Ⓔ
   (A) a wish that international fishing crews cooperate
   (B) information about the tuna/porpoise relationship
   (C) a common interest in the porpoise/tuna relationship
   (D) a common desire to protect porpoises
   (E) a common motive for the preservation of porpoises

10. The author presents the information in this passage   Ⓐ Ⓑ Ⓒ Ⓓ Ⓔ
   (A) cynically   (B) angrily   (C) objectively   (D) humorously
   (E) indifferently

11. The author implies that the government and industry representatives concerned with porpoise conservation may lack which of the following?
(A) knowledge   (B) influence   (C) greed   (D) compassion
(E) purpose

Ⓐ Ⓑ Ⓒ Ⓓ Ⓔ

12. Fredson Delacourte would probably object to which of the following?
(A) a reduced tuna quota
(B) the use of animal fur for coats
(C) an international treaty that requires porpoise conservation
(D) the enforcement of rules for porpoise conservation
(E) the regulation of the tuna industry

Ⓐ Ⓑ Ⓒ Ⓓ Ⓔ

13. Which of the following is (are) not described explicitly in the passage?
(A) Fredson Delacourte's sentiments
(B) the federal regulations that U.S. fishermen must obey
(C) the items that won general agreement at the conference
(D) the relationship between porpoise and yellowfin
(E) the elements of a solution to the porpoise conservation problem

Ⓐ Ⓑ Ⓒ Ⓓ Ⓔ

14. The passage provides answers to which of the following questions?

I.   Has the tuna industry finalized a law of the sea?
II. Are fishing regulations moral as well as economic issues?
III. Has the general public expressed interest in a moral law of the sea?
(A) I only   (B) II only   (C) I and II only   (D) II and III only
(E) I, II, and III

Ⓐ Ⓑ Ⓒ Ⓓ Ⓔ

Passage 3

There are many dictionary definitions of "existentialism"; each carries some degree of truth. These will not be discussed, nor will they be analyzed since that process would involve several volumes. However, central to each definition is the assertion that existentialism is a theory or statement about the nature of man's existence. There is entire agreement about that point. Errors come from accompanying statements that scientific or idealistic approaches are not adequate in defining or understanding existentialism.

Let us understand clearly that no theory of any kind of human existence can be defined in terms solely those of a scientific or idealistic process. Definition, as must be true of any other process, must be a matter of total personality. As such, existentialism must involve the viewpoints of thinking, feeling, and sensing. Second, existentialism, overall, and existentialism, as reflected specifically in any behavioral account of its operation—is subject to the scientific detection of its operation through any one of several modern psychological approaches. Different emotive states carry their principles into operation through certain unique linguistic structures, both macroscopic and microscopic. Those operating in an "existential way" can be identified as uniquely different from the other theories of human existence.

Existentialism is one of a limited number of views of man's nature, central to which is his existence. The other views are that man's nature is one that falls into one of the following categories: an operational balance among the elements of thought, feeling, and sensation—classicism, an imbalance weighted in favor of the world of volitions (feeling, emotions, and will) over the world of mind and senses—romanticism, an imbalance among the categories of head, heart, and hand in favor of thought—rationalism, an imbalance resulting from choosing the world of materiality—the world of the senses and things, over the claims of spirit and thought—naturalism.

Then existentialism is a view of human existence, and, as such, finds itself in the class with classicism, romanticism, rationalism, and naturalism. Obviously, for each individual, the meanings of each view must be carried by words which have ranges of meaning. If we can find one of the views which differs from all other views in accepting a range of meaning, then the view can be defined at least from a semantic point of view. Whether one is a romanticist, a rationalist, a classicist, or one in the grim hold of naturalism, he accepts words describing each as holding the same range of meanings for all views, even including that of existentialism. He accepts the range of meanings describing each one, although he selects from the range according to his unique viewpoint. However, since the existentialist denies that he can be bound to the external control of any range of meanings, including those of words, he can be defined as uniquely different from his *philosophers*. Here, the definition, and an effective one, is on semantical grounds. He creates his own range of meanings of words; if they approach those used in the other philosophies of man's existence, they do so only accidentally. The existentialist deliberately—and unconsciously sometimes—rejects traditional ranges of meaning in his own language environment. Quite often he does so through using the words in an opposite sense. We could rest on this linguistic view, and do so safely, did we so desire. However, we can also define existentialism in the light of a historical uniqueness.

15. The author does not imply that a full definition of existentialism should be Ⓐ Ⓑ Ⓒ Ⓓ Ⓔ
(A) pithy (B) prolix (C) many-faceted (D) difficult
(E) complex

16. Despite all the different definitions of existentialism, one central point around which they all cohere says that Ⓐ Ⓑ Ⓒ Ⓓ Ⓔ
(A) there is no central point
(B) existentialism is the essence of existence
(C) existentialism tries to explain the nature of human existence
(D) existentialism tries to define the nature of human nature
(E) existential theorists are tending toward universal agreement

17. The existentialist is different from other philosophers because he Ⓐ Ⓑ Ⓒ Ⓓ Ⓔ
(A) rejects definitions
(B) embraces all theories
(C) makes a pact with his existence
(D) is uniquely grim
(E) is more astute than the others

18. According to the passage, several existentialists would be likely to define "reality" in Ⓐ Ⓑ Ⓒ Ⓓ Ⓔ
(A) two ways (B) strange ways (C) similar ways
(D) unseemly ways (E) several ways

19. Each dictionary definition of existentialism is, at best, Ⓐ Ⓑ Ⓒ Ⓓ Ⓔ
(A) partial (B) equivocal (C) abstract (D) redundant
(E) in error

20. The best title for this passage would be: Ⓐ Ⓑ Ⓒ Ⓓ Ⓔ
(A) "Modern Philosophy and Its Complexities"
(B) "Existence vs. Essence"
(C) "Where the Dictionary Goes Wrong"
(D) "Is Existentialism Definable?"
(E) "Words Do Not Have Meanings"

21. According to the passage, which of the following is not an alternative view to existentialism? Ⓐ Ⓑ Ⓒ Ⓓ Ⓔ
(A) classicism (B) romanticism (C) rationalism (D) naturalism
(E) dogmatism

22. The existentialist's use of words may often be   Ⓐ Ⓑ Ⓒ Ⓓ Ⓔ
(A) lucid   (B) partial   (C) contradictory   (D) precise
(E) obscure

Answers and Explanations

Passage 1

1. **C**   This purpose is stated most explicitly in paragraph 5, although there are several other points in the passage where the author urges drivers to drive less. (A) is weak because it is too general and inclusive; (B) is vague about the means of reducing smog; (D) and (E) are very minor points.

2. **A**   This is stated explicitly in paragraph 5, where the author blames individual drivers rather than industry.

3. **A**   The second paragraph implies that recreational vehicles create more smog, and the fourth paragraph describes smog's effects on nature; therefore, we may conclude that gas-guzzling vacation vehicles help to damage the natural beauty of vacation spots. The author *might* also agree with (D), but the evidence in the passage itself points more substantially to (A).

4. **E**   The author criticizes the increased use of recreational vehicles (see explanation for question 3).

5. **B**   The final sentence in the passage implies that we will be "forced" to conserve if we do not do so voluntarily. (A) is neither stated nor implied; the author does imply that industrial emissions *should not be controlled*, but this is not the same as suggesting that they are *uncontrollable*.

6. **D**   The author is almost pleading that drivers make immediate changes in their habits; the urgency of his purpose coincides with the urgency of his tone.

7. **D**   The author begins the passage by claiming that the Harris Survey represents a "majority of Americans"; we must share that assumption in order to accept the importance of his argument. All other choices are irrelevant.

Passage 2

8. **B**   The passage is essentially neutral; the author does not take sides or suggest his own program or solution. "Discuss," the most neutral term of the five choices, signals (B) as the appropriate answer.

9. **E**   Delacourte's motive is *moral*, and the industry's motive is *economic*; this difference is stressed in the final sentence of the passage.

10. **C**   The author is *reporting* information without attempting to slant it subjectively. His impersonal tone should lead you to eliminate (A), (B), and (D), all of them suggesting personal involvement. However, the author is not indifferent (E) to the issue he describes; otherwise, he would not choose to discuss it so extensively.

11. **D**   Without explicitly criticizing the tuna industry, the author does contrast fishermen with "compassionate souls" such as Delacourte (final paragraph).

12. **B** .The chairman of a "People for Animals" drive would be certain to object to clothing produced through the destruction of animals. Delacourte would probably be in favor of the other choices.

13. **B** Although we are told that U.S. fishermen must conform to federal regulations, those regulations are not mentioned explicitly; we may *infer* that the regulations entail porpoise conservation.

14. **C** I is true; the answer to that question is No. II is true; the answer to that question, Yes, emerges from the contrast between Delacourte's motives and those of the industry. III is false; the opinion of the general public is neither expressed nor implied in the passage.

Passage 3

15. **A** A definition of existentialism cannot be pithy (short, brief) because the process of full definition "would involve several volumes" (paragraph 1).

16. **C** Paragraph 1 states, "Central to each definition is the assertion that existentialism is a theory or statement about the nature of man's existence."

17. **A** According to paragraph 4, "The existentialist deliberately . . . rejects traditional ranges of meaning."

18. **E** In paragraph 4, the writer claims that each existentialist creates his own range of meanings of words.

19. **A** Paragraph 1 states that each dictionary definition of existentialism "carries some degree of truth."

20. **D** The passage as a whole deals with problems and approaches to defining existentialism. (A) is too general; (B), (C), and (E) are too specific.

21. **E** Paragraph 3 lists all the terms except (E) as alternatives.

22. **C** According to paragraph 4, the existentialist rejects traditional meanings of words and often "uses words in an opposite sense."

Chapter

3

Analytical Reasoning

INTRODUCTION TO QUESTION TYPE

The Analytical Reasoning section is designed to measure your ability to analyze, understand, and draw conclusions from a group of conditions and relationships. This section contains 21–27 problems (four or five sets of conditions). Three to eight conditions or statements comprise a set, and each set is followed by three to seven questions.

A form of Analytical Reasoning has been used on the Graduate Record Exam for many years.

Analytical reasoning situations can take many forms, but there are some general things you should be aware of before reviewing the variety of problem types:

1. REMEMBER: No formal logic is required.

2. Making simple charts or diagrams can be very helpful.

3. If you decide to make a diagram, fill in as much of the diagram or chart as possible, but do not spend a great deal of time trying to complete it. (This may not be possible or necessary in order to answer the questions.)

4. You may need to redraw all or part of your diagram several times (typically, once for each question) as different conditional information is given for specific questions.

5. When drawing a chart or diagram, keep the following techniques in mind:
  (a) Look for the framework of the diagram. Sometimes this is given in the first statement, but in other cases you may need to read a number of the conditions before constructing the type of drawing that will be most effective.
  (b) If a framework is not given, see if the information can be grouped by similarities or differences.
  (c) Place a small check next to each statement or condition as you read it, in order to avoid skipping a statement.
  (d) As you read each statement, try to enter that information into your chart. Some statements, however, will be very important but may not fit neatly into your chart. These may be large, general rules, and you should note these with a star or an asterisk, etc.
  (e) If some statements are not immediately placeable in your chart, you may have to return to these after placing others. Mark such statements with a special symbol (an arrow or an exclamation mark, etc.) so you don't forget to return to them.
  (f) Apply evidence in "both directions." For instance, if a statement tells you that a condition must be true, consider whether this means that certain other conditions must *not* be true. Example: "All blue cars are fast" tells you that a slow car is *not blue*.
  (g) Look for the first piece of concrete information that you can put into the diagram.
  (h) Use question marks (?) to mark information that is variable or could be placed in a number of different places in the diagram.
  (i) Understand the distinction between *must be* and *could be*:

MUST BE	COULD BE
No exceptions All the time Always	May be, but doesn't necessarily have to be

(j) Keep the drawing simple; don't complicate your thinking.

(k) Sometimes looking at the questions can indicate the type of drawing that will be most useful.

(l) Sometimes no standard type of chart will apply to the problem, and you may wish to merely pull out information in a simple type of graphic sketch or through simple notes.

The following sections provide some detailed examples of typical problem types and charts. These samples are intended to give you insight into the methods of charting that are possible. REMEMBER: Different students may prefer different types of charts. Use what is effective and efficient for you, but *keep the drawing simple!*

SOME TYPES OF CHARTING

THE CONNECTION CHART

One of the many types of charts is the *connection chart.* In constructing such a chart, your first step is usually to group or align items into *general* categories. Then the second step is to draw connections according to relationships between *specific* items.

Example

Sales manager Tom Forrester is trying to put together a sales team to cover the Los Angeles area. His team will consist of four members—two experienced and two new salesmen.
1. Sam, Fred, Harry, and Jim are the experienced salesmen.
2. John, Tim, and Tom are new.
3. Sam and Fred do not work together.
4. Tim and Sam refuse to work together.
5. Harry and Tom cannot work together.

1. If Sam is made part of the team, the following MUST be the other members:
(A) John, Tim, Tom
(B) John, Tom, Jim
(C) Tim, Harry, Jim
(D) Tom, John, Fred
(E) John, Tom, Harry

Ⓐ Ⓑ Ⓒ Ⓓ Ⓔ

2. If Sam is not chosen as part of the sales team and Tim is, then which of the following MUST be true?
(A) Tom and Harry are on the team.
(B) Jim and John are on the team.
(C) Harry and Fred are on the team.
(D) John or Tom is not on the team.
(E) Fred or Jim is not on the team.

Ⓐ Ⓑ Ⓒ Ⓓ Ⓔ

3. Which of the following MUST be true?

I. Fred and Sam never work together.
II. Jim and Tom never work together.
III. Jim and Fred always work together.
(A) I only   (B) II only   (C) I and II only   (D) II and III only
(E) III only

Ⓐ Ⓑ Ⓒ Ⓓ Ⓔ

4. If Tom is chosen as part of the sales team, but John is not, then the other three
members MUST be   Ⓐ Ⓑ Ⓒ Ⓓ Ⓔ
   (A)   Fred, Tim, and Harry
   (B)   Fred, Tim, and Jim
   (C)   Harry, John, and Tim
   (D)   Tim, Tom, and Jim
   (E)   Sam, Fred, and Harry

5. Which of the following MUST be true?   Ⓐ Ⓑ Ⓒ Ⓓ Ⓔ
   I.   If Harry works, then John works.
   II.   If Jim works, then John works.
   III.   If John works, then Tom works.
   (A) I   (B) II   (C) III   (D) I and II   (E) I and III

ANSWERS AND EXPLANATIONS

When drawing a connection chart, always prefer fewer connections to many connections. In this case, drawing connections between the workers who can work together will result in a complicated system of intersecting lines. Connecting those who *do not* or *cannot* work together results in a simple, clear chart:

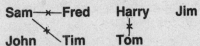

This chart encourages you to use information in both directions, recognizing that, because connected workers *cannot* work together, unconnected workers *can* work together.

Notice that the conditions gave initial information about those who cannot work together, helping you to formulate the most efficient method of connecting the diagram. If the conditions had stated that some salesmen always work together and some never work together, you would have used a different type of marking to denote each type of connection.

1. **B**   The team must consist of two experienced and two new salesmen. Sam is experienced, so the rest of the team must include one experienced and two new salesmen. (C) should be eliminated both because it contains two experienced salesmen and because Sam does not work with Tim; also eliminate (A) because it includes Tim. Eliminate (D) because Sam does not work with Fred, and eliminate (E) because Tom does not work with Harry.

2. **D**   With Tim on the team, there is room for one other new salesman. Therefore, *either* John *or* Tom is on the team, but not both.

3. **A**   The key word in this question is "must," which excludes *possible* but not *necessary* combinations. I is true, as inspection of the chart reveals. II *may* be true, depending upon whether Jim always works with Harry. III cannot be true. Consider the following counterexample: Jim, Sam, John, and Tom. Thus Jim and Fred do not have to work together.

4. **B**   If Tom is chosen as part of the team, and John is not, then Tim must be the other inexperienced member. So, if Tom and Tim both are chosen, then Sam and Harry are not chosen. The team now consists of Tom, Tim, Fred, and Jim.

5. **A**   Since Harry will not work with Tom, then John must be one of the other inexperienced members in the group when Harry works. The other combinations (Jim and John, John and Tom) do not always work together.

THE POSITION CHARTS

Another type of diagram is the position chart. This type is very common on the LSAT and appears in a variety of forms. Often a framework will be given in the first condition or in a statement preceding the conditions.

Example 1

John, Paul, George, and Herman sit around a square table with eight chairs, which are equally distributed.
Bob, Carol, Ted, and Alice join them at the table.
The two women (Carol and Alice) cannot sit next to each other.
John and Herman are seated on either side of George and are next to him.
Ted is seated next to Herman.
Carol is seated next to John, but not directly across from George.
John is directly across from Alice.

1. Which men could switch positions without contradicting the seating arrangement?
   (A) George and Herman
   (B) John and George
   (C) Paul and Ted
   (D) Bob and Paul
   (E) Bob and George

   (A) (B) (C) (D) (E)

2. Which of the following MUST be false?
   (A) George is not next to Ted.
   (B) Alice is not next to Carol.
   (C) Herman is next to Carol.
   (D) George is across from Paul.
   (E) Bob is not next to Paul.

   (A) (B) (C) (D) (E)

3. Which of the following could be true?
   (A) Herman sits next to Carol.
   (B) Herman sits next to John.
   (C) Ted sits next to Paul.
   (D) John sits next to Paul.
   (E) George sits next to Alice.

   (A) (B) (C) (D) (E)

4. Which of the following MUST be true?
   (A) Ted sits next to Paul.
   (B) Alice sits next to Paul.
   (C) George sits next to Carol.
   (D) Ted sits next to Bob.
   (E) Bob sits next to John.

   (A) (B) (C) (D) (E)

5. If Arnold were now to take Ted's seat, then Arnold
   (A) must now be next to Bob
   (B) must be next to Alice
   (C) must be across from Bob
   (D) is either next to or across from Paul
   (E) is either next to or across from George

   (A) (B) (C) (D) (E)

ANSWERS AND EXPLANATIONS

Note that the statement preceding the six conditions immediately suggests that you draw a square table with two spaces on each side. The first piece of concrete information is condition 3, which tells you to seat John, George, and Herman in that order. Next, seat Ted next to Herman (#4), seat Carol next to John (#5), and seat Alice across from John (#6). Note that Carol and Alice are not sitting next to each other (#2), and that Paul and Bob are in *variable* positions on either side of Alice. The resulting chart is as follows:

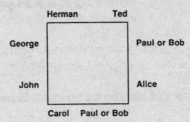

1. **D** As the chart points out, only Bob and Paul are in variable positions and, thus, interchangeable.

2. **C** Working from the answer choices and inspecting the chart, you see that (C) *must* be false in any case, and that (D) *may* be false, depending upon where Paul is seated.

3. **C** From the diagram you can see that Paul could be in the seat next to Ted. None of the other choices are possible.

4. **B** Since the two seats next to Alice are taken by Paul and Bob, then Alice must sit next to Paul.

5. **D** If Arnold takes Ted's seat, then either he is seated next to Paul, or else Paul is seated across from him.

Example 2

A is taller than B but shorter than C.
B is shorter than D but taller than E.
F is shorter than A but taller than B.
G is taller than D but shorter than F.
H is shorter than B.

1. Which of the following may be false, but is not necessarily false?   Ⓐ Ⓑ Ⓒ Ⓓ Ⓔ
   (A) E is shorter than D.   (D) H is taller than E.
   (B) C is taller than E.   (E) E is shorter than A.
   (C) D is taller than F.

2. Which of the following may be true?   Ⓐ Ⓑ Ⓒ Ⓓ Ⓔ
   (A) D is taller than most of the others.   (D) D is not shorter than G.
   (B) A is the tallest.   (E) H is taller than F.
   (C) H is the shortest.

3. Which of the following MUST be true?   Ⓐ Ⓑ Ⓒ Ⓓ Ⓔ
   I.   F is taller than D.
   II. H is the shortest of all.
   III. H is shorter than D.
   (A) I only   (B) I and II   (C) I and III   (D) I, II, and III   (E) III

4. If Q is added to the group and Q is taller than B but shorter than G, then   Ⓐ Ⓑ Ⓒ Ⓓ Ⓔ
(A)   Q must be taller than F.
(B)   Q must be shorter than D
(C)   Q must be between D and F
(D)   Q must be taller than only three of the others
(E)   Q must be shorter than at least three of the others

5. If Q and Z are both added to the group, and both are taller than H, then   Ⓐ Ⓑ Ⓒ Ⓓ Ⓔ
(A)   H is the shortest of all   (D)   either Q or Z is the tallest of all
(B)   E is the shortest of all   (E)   either H or E is the shortest of all
(C)   C is the tallest of all

ANSWERS AND EXPLANATIONS

From the information given, a simple chart may be constructed. It will look like this:

```
        C
        A
        F
        G
        D
        B
       ←H
        E⌐
         ⌎
```

Note that H is in a variable position.

1.   **D**   H may be taller than E, or it may be shorter than E. This is the only part of the chart that isn't definitely resolved.

2.   **C**   H may be the shortest, because it could possibly be shorter than E.

3.   **C**   Inspection of the chart reveals that F is taller than D, and that H is shorter than D, but because H is in a relatively variable position, we cannot be certain that H is the shortest of all.

4.   **E**   If Q is added to the group, it may be either taller or shorter than D. Therefore, only (E) is true.

5.   **E**   If Q and Z are added, and both are taller than H, we know little more except that H or E must still be the smallest. Q or Z could possibly be the tallest, but not necessarily so. Only (E) *must* be true.

Example 3

In a parking lot, seven company automobiles are lined up in a row in seven parking spots.
(1) There are two vans, which are both adjacent to the same sports car.
(2) There is one station wagon.
(3) There are two limousines, which are never parked adjacent to each other.
(4) One of the sports cars is always on one end.

1. If the station wagon is on one end, one of the sports cars MUST be in the   Ⓐ Ⓑ Ⓒ Ⓓ Ⓔ

   I.   2nd spot
  II.   3rd spot
  III.   4th spot
(A) I only   (B) II only   (C) III only   (D) Either I or II
(E) Either I, II, or III

2. If one of the vans is on one end, then the station wagon MUST be   Ⓐ Ⓑ Ⓒ Ⓓ Ⓔ
   (A) only in the 4th spot
   (B) either in the 2nd or the 6th spot
   (C) only in the 3rd spot
   (D) either in the 3rd or the 5th spot
   (E) only in the 6th spot

3. If a limousine is in the 7th spot, then the station wagon could be in the   Ⓐ Ⓑ Ⓒ Ⓓ Ⓔ

   I. 2nd spot
   II. 3rd spot
   III. 6th spot
   (A) I only   (B) II only   (C) III only   (D) Either I or III
   (E) Either I, II, or III

4. If one of the sports cars is in the 2nd spot, then the station wagon   Ⓐ Ⓑ Ⓒ Ⓓ Ⓔ
   (A) could be in the 5th spot
   (B) could be in the 6th spot
   (C) must be in the 5th spot
   (D) must be in the 6th spot
   (E) not enough information to tell

5. If both sports cars are adjacent to a van, the station wagon MUST be in
   the   Ⓐ Ⓑ Ⓒ Ⓓ Ⓔ

   I. 2nd spot
   II. 4th spot
   III. 6th spot
   (A) I only   (B) II only   (C) III only   (D) Either I or II
   (E) Either I or III

6. If an eighth car (a limousine) is added, and another parking spot is also
   added, then in order not to violate any of the original statements except
   the number of limousines in statement 3   Ⓐ Ⓑ Ⓒ Ⓓ Ⓔ
   (A) a limousine must be parked in the 2nd spot
   (B) the station wagon must be parked in the 2nd spot
   (C) the station wagon must be parked in the 6th spot
   (D) a limousine must be parked on one end
   (E) at least one of the original statements must be violated

Answers and Explanations

1. C In this question, two charts are possible:

| S | ___ | ___ | ___ | ___ | ___ | SW |

and

| SW | ___ | ___ | ___ | ___ | ___ | S |

Now notice that for *both* of the vans to be adjacent to the same sports car, there must be another sports car, and they must always be in the order V S V. Thus, the only way to place V S V in either of the above diagrams so that two limousines are never adjacent is to place V, S, and V in spots 3, 4, and 5, as follows:

| S | ___ | V | S | V | ___ | SW |

or

| SW | ___ | V | S | V | ___ | S |

Thus, the limousines will not be adjacent if one of the sports cars is in the 4th spot.

2. D Again there are two possible diagrams for this question:

| V | S | V | ___ | ___ | ___ | S |

and

| S | ___ | ___ | ___ | V | S | V |

Now notice that, in order that the limousines not be adjacent, the station wagon must be in either the 5th spot or the 3rd spot.

3. E If a limousine is in the 7th spot, then a sports car, to be on an end, must be in the 1st spot:

| S | ___ | ___ | ___ | ___ | ___ | L |

Notice that the station wagon could now be in the 6th spot:

| | | V | S | V | L | |
| S | L | V | S | V | SW | L |

or else in either the 2nd or the 3rd spot:

| | L | SW | | | | |
| S | SW | L | V | S | V | L |

So the station wagon could be in either the 2nd, the 3rd, or the 6th spot.

4. C If one of the sports cars is in the 2nd spot, the other sports car must be in the 7th spot:

| V | S | V | ___ | ___ | ___ | S |

Thus, in order for the limousines not to be adjacent, the station wagon must be in the 5th spot.

5. E Two diagrams are necessary for this problem. If both sports cars are adjacent to a van, your diagrams will be:

| S | V | S | V | ___ | ___ | ___ |

and

			V	S	V	S
___	___	___	___	___	___	___

Thus, in order for the limousines not to be adjacent, the station wagon must be in either the 2nd spot or the 6th spot.

6. **D** If another limousine is added along with an eighth parking spot, all the original statements can be obeyed ONLY if a limousine is parked on one end. For example:

S	L	V	S	V	L	SW	L
___	___	___	___	___	___	___	___

THE INFORMATION CHART

The *information* chart is helpful for spotting specific information and making deductions quickly.

Example

Unless otherwise stated, each workman must work alone in the store.
Unless otherwise stated, each workman is able to complete his own job in half a day.
(1) In order to open a new furniture store the following week, Mr. Worble hired a painter, a carpet layer, an electrician, and a carpenter.
(2) The painter is available only on Tuesday morning, Wednesday afternoon, and all day Friday.
(3) The carpet layer is available only on Monday, Wednesday, and Friday mornings.
(4) The electrician is available only on Tuesday morning and Friday afternoon.
(5) The carpenter is available only on Monday morning, Tuesday all day, and Wednesday afternoon.

1. If the carpenter and the electrician must work on the same day to coordinate their efforts, but cannot work at the same time, who of the following will not be able to start work until Wednesday, at the earliest?   Ⓐ Ⓑ Ⓒ Ⓓ Ⓔ

    I. Painter
    II. Carpet layer
    (A) I only   (B) II only   (C) I or II   (D) I and II   (E) None of these

2. If the painter needs the whole day on Friday to complete his job, the   Ⓐ Ⓑ Ⓒ Ⓓ Ⓔ
    (A) carpenter must work on Thursday
    (B) electrician and carpet layer must work on the same day
    (C) total job cannot be completed in one week
    (D) electrician must work on Tuesday
    (E) carpet layer and carpenter must work on the same day

3. Mr. Worble is expecting a supply of furniture on Thursday morning. Which of the following MUST be true?   Ⓐ Ⓑ Ⓒ Ⓓ Ⓔ
    Before the merchandise arrives
    (A) the carpenter will be the only one finished
    (B) the painter will be finished, but the electrician will have to work Wednesday night
    (C) the carpet layer, the carpenter, and the electrician will be the only ones finished
    (D) the carpet layer will have to work on Tuesday
    (E) all of the jobs could be finished with simple planning

4. If the store must be closed Monday and Tuesday and no worker may enter on those days, then, for all the work to be completed by the end of the week,　　Ⓐ Ⓑ Ⓒ Ⓓ Ⓔ
   (A)   the carpet layer must work Friday morning
   (B)   the painter must work Friday morning
   (C)   the painter must work Wednesday afternoon
   (D)   the painter must work Friday afternoon
   (E)   it won't be possible to complete the work

5. If the store must be painted before any of the other work may begin, then, for all the work to be completed, all the following are true *except*　　Ⓐ Ⓑ Ⓒ Ⓓ Ⓔ
   (A)   the carpenter may work Tuesday or Wednesday afternoon
   (B)   the electrician must work Friday afternoon
   (C)   the carpet layer must work Wednesday or Friday morning
   (D)   the electrician and the carpet layer may work the same day
   (E)   the painter and the electrician may work the same day

ANSWERS AND EXPLANATIONS

An information chart is suggested whenever you are trying to determine the points at which two sets of facts coincide. In this case, we chart the daily schedule of each worker, simply following the explicit information given in conditions 2–5:

	M	T	W	T	F
Painter		Morning	Afternoon		All day
Carpet layer	Morning		Morning		Morning
Electrician		Morning			Afternoon
Carpenter	Morning	All day	Afternoon		

Although we have written out "morning," "afternoon," and "all day," you may wish to abbreviate such terms.
   The chart reveals that:

1. **A**   The carpet layer may work on Monday, and the carpenter and the electrician *must* work Tuesday (the only day they are available together). In this case, the painter may not begin until Wednesday.

2. **D**   The electrician *must* work Tuesday, because his only other working day, Friday, interferes with the painter's work.

3. **E**   One possible plan is this: The carpet layer works Monday morning, the electrician works Tuesday morning, the carpenter works Tuesday afternoon, and the painter works Wednesday afternoon.

4. **B**   If the store must be closed on Monday and Tuesday, then the carpenter must work Wednesday afternoon, and the electrician must work Friday afternoon, as these workers have no other available days to work. Since the painter cannot work Wednesday afternoon (the carpenter is already working then), he must work Friday morning. This leaves the carpet layer Wednesday morning to complete his work.

5. **E**   If the store must be painted first, then the painter could do his work Tuesday morning. All of the choices then are true, except (E). The painter and electrician may not work the same day, because if it's Tuesday, then they both would work in the morning, which is not allowed. The only other day they could both work is Friday, but that wouldn't allow all the work to be completed if the painter first works Friday morning.

THE ELIMINATION GRID

This type of chart will assist you in eliminating many possibilities, thus narrowing your answer choices and simplifying the reasoning process.

Example

Two boys (Tom and Sal) and two girls (Lisa and Molly) each receive a different grade of four different passing grades (A,B,C,D) on an exam.
(1) Both boys receive lower grades than Lisa.
(2) Sal did not get a B.
(3) Tom got a B.
(4) Molly did not get an A.

1. Which statement may be deduced from only one of the other statements?   Ⓐ Ⓑ Ⓒ Ⓓ Ⓔ
   (A) Statement 1   (B) Statement 2   (C) Statement 3
   (D) Statement 4   (E) None of these

2. If Molly received the lowest grade, then Sal MUST have received the   Ⓐ Ⓑ Ⓒ Ⓓ Ⓔ
   (A) A   (B) B   (C) C   (D) D   (E) not enough information to tell

3. Sal could have received   Ⓐ Ⓑ Ⓒ Ⓓ Ⓔ

   I.   the A
   II. the C
   III. the D
   (A) I   (B) II   (C) III   (D) II or III   (E) I, II, or III

4. Molly could NOT have received   Ⓐ Ⓑ Ⓒ Ⓓ Ⓔ

   I.   the A
   II.   the B
   III. the C
   IV. the D
   (A) I   (B) II   (C) III   (D) IV   (E) Two of these

5. If Sal received the D, then Molly received the   Ⓐ Ⓑ Ⓒ Ⓓ Ⓔ
   (A) A   (B) B   (C) C   (D) D   (E) not enough information to tell

6. If the grades that Sal and Lisa received were reversed, then which of the original statements would no longer be true?   Ⓐ Ⓑ Ⓒ Ⓓ Ⓔ
   (A) Statement 1   (B) Statement 2   (C) Statement 3
   (D) Statement 4   (E) Statements 2 and 3

ANSWERS AND EXPLANATIONS

1. **B** Statement 2 may be deduced from statement 3. If Tom got the B, it then must be true that Sal did not get the B.

2. **C** This question requires you to complete a chart, using the information from the statements. First, since both boys received lower grades than Lisa, we know that Lisa could not have gotten the C or D, and that neither of the boys could have gotten the A. Thus, your chart will look like this:

	A	B	C	D
Tom	X			
Sal	X			
Lisa			X	X
Molly				

From statements 2 and 3, we can fill in that Tom received the B (and thus the others didn't):

	A	B	C	D
Tom	X	✓	X	X
Sal	X	X		
Lisa		X	X	X
Molly		X		

Statement 4 allows us to indicate on our chart that Molly didn't get an A. Thus, we can see from our chart that Lisa *must* have gotten the A:

	A	B	C	D
Tom	X	✓	X	X
Sal	X	X		
Lisa		X	X	X
Molly	X	X		

Notice that we could have deduced that even without statement 4, as there was no other grade Lisa could possibly receive.

Now we know that Lisa received the A, and Tom received the B. But we cannot deduce Sal's or Molly's grade. Be aware that, on many problems like this, you will have to proceed to the questions with an incomplete chart. We can, however, now answer the rest of the questions: If Molly received the lowest grade (D), then Sal must have gotten the C.

3. **D** From our chart we can easily see that Sal could have received either the C or the D.

4. **E** From our chart we can easily see that Molly could not have received either the A or the B. We could also have determined this from statements 3 and 4.

5. **C** From our chart we can easily see that, if Sal received the D, then Molly must have received the C.

6. **A** If Sal and Lisa reversed their grades, then

> Sal would get the A.
> Tom would get the B.
> Lisa received either the C or the D.
> Molly received either the C or the D.

Therefore, only statement 1 ("Both boys receive lower grades than Lisa") would no longer be true.

THE DEPENDENT CONNECTION CHART

This type of chart is usually more complex than the linear position chart, because the conditions create a dynamic rather than a static relationship between interdependent factors in a sequence.

Example

(1) To enter the bar, you need a blue ticket and a yellow card.
(2) To get a blue ticket, you need an orange hat or a green bicycle.
(3) To get a yellow card, you need a blue card and a yellow hat.
(4) If you have a red ticket, you can get a green bicycle and a yellow hat.
(5) A blue hat will get you a red ticket.

1. Which of the following will allow you to enter the bar?
  (A) an orange hat and a blue card
  (B) a red ticket and a green bicycle
  (C) a green bicycle and a yellow hat
  (D) a yellow hat and a blue card
  (E) a blue card and a red ticket

2. What will get you a blue ticket?
  (A) a yellow card
  (B) a blue card
  (C) a blue hat
  (D) a yellow hat
  (E) an orange bicycle

3. If a purple card will get you a yellow hat, what is also needed to get a yellow card?
  (A) a purple hat
  (B) a blue card
  (C) a green bicycle
  (D) an orange hat
  (E) a blue ticket

4. If you have a blue ticket and a blue card, which of the following will get you into the bar?

  I. A yellow hat
  II. A red ticket
  III. A blue hat
  (A) I   (B) II   (C) III   (D) I and II   (E) I, II, and III

ANSWERS AND EXPLANATIONS

The following diagram results from the given conditions:

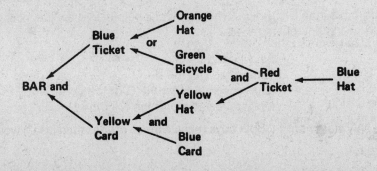

You can begin constructing this diagram by working backwards from the endpoint or goal (BAR); note that when you get to condition 4 you may want to switch from thinking backwards through the sequence to thinking forwards.

1. **E** A red ticket will get you a green bicycle and a yellow hat. A green bicycle, a yellow hat, and a blue card will get you a yellow card and a blue ticket, and you may then enter the bar.

2. **C** Since a blue hat gets a red ticket, and a red ticket gets a green bicycle, and a green bicycle gets a blue ticket, then a blue hat ultimately gets a blue ticket.

3. **B** To get a yellow card you need *both* a yellow hat and a blue card.

4. **E** If you have a blue ticket and a blue card, then a yellow hat (with the blue card) will get you a yellow card, and that yellow card (with the blue ticket) will get you into the bar (item I).
A red ticket will also get you that yellow hat, which will start the whole process rolling until you get into the bar (item II).
And a blue hat will also get you a red ticket, which will again begin the process that gets you into the bar (item III).
So all of the listed items will get you into the bar.

VENN DIAGRAMS/GROUPING ARROWS

Another type of charting (also mentioned in Chapter 5: Logical Reasoning) is the Venn Diagram/Grouping Arrow. This type of diagram can be useful when information is given that shows relationships between sets or groups of sets. Venn diagrams should only be used in *very simple situations* involving a small number of items. Grouping arrows seem to be more effective and simpler to work with, especially in complex situations.

Some very basic Venn diagrams and grouping arrows look like this:

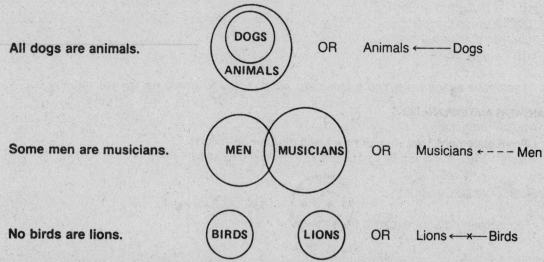

All dogs are animals.   OR   Animals ←——— Dogs

Some men are musicians.   OR   Musicians ← – – – Men

No birds are lions.   OR   Lions ←—×— Birds

In diagramming more than two groups, you may find it helpful to draw the most general or largest category before drawing any of the others.

Example

(1) All A's are B's.
(2) All B's are C's.
(3) Some, but not all, D's are A's.
(4) All D's are B's.
(5) No E's are C's.

1. Which of the following MUST be true?   Ⓐ Ⓑ Ⓒ Ⓓ Ⓔ

    I.   All A's are C's.
    II. Some E's are B's.
    III. No B's are E's.
    (A) I   (B) II   (C) III   (D) I and III   (E) I, II, and III

2. Which of the following MUST be false?   Ⓐ Ⓑ Ⓒ Ⓓ Ⓔ

    I.   All D's are A's.
    II. No A's are E's.
    (A) I   (B) II   (C) Both I and II   (D) Either I or II, but not both
    (E) Neither I nor II

3. If all E's are F's, then which of the following MUST be true?   Ⓐ Ⓑ Ⓒ Ⓓ Ⓔ
    (A) All F's are E's.
    (B) Some F's are E's.
    (C) All A's are F's.
    (D) Some B's are F's.
    (E) No F's are C's.

4. If some G's are A's, then   Ⓐ Ⓑ Ⓒ Ⓓ Ⓔ

    I.   Some G's are B's
    II. Some G's are C's
    III. Some G's could be E's
    (A) I   (B) II   (C) III   (D) I and II   (E) I, II, and III

ANSWERS AND EXPLANATIONS

From statement 1 we may draw a Venn diagram as follows:

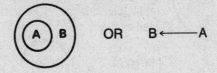

From statement 2 our Venn diagram grows to look like this:

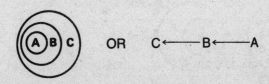

Now statements 3 and 4 add another circle (note that we needed the fourth statement in order to "contain" the D circle within the B circle) as follows:

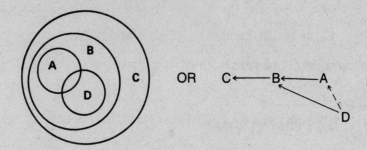

And, finally, from statement 5 we get:

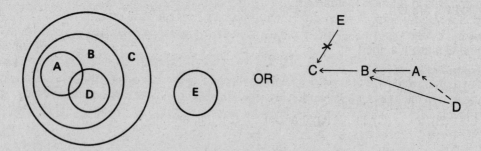

Now it will be relatively simple to answer the questions simply by referring to our final Venn diagram.

1. **D**
2. **A**
3. **B**   Note that this problem requires us to add another circle to our Venn diagram, as follows:

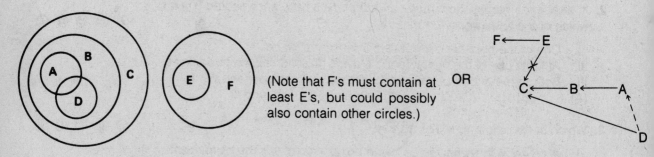

(Note that F's must contain at least E's, but could possibly also contain other circles.)

4. **E**   This problem, too, requires us to add to our original Venn diagram. If some G's are A's, our Venn diagram must *at least* contain some G's in the A circle (x notes location of some G's):

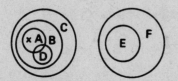

(thus I and II are true)

OR

but it *could* also look like this:

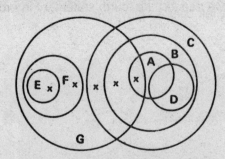 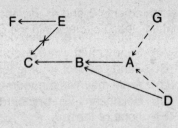

(thus III is also true)

PULLING OUT INFORMATION

In some instances, no chart appears to fit the situation. If this is the case, then simply pull out whatever information seems important to you.

Example

One left-handed tongo player (Sandy) and two right-handed tongo players (Arnie and Betsy) are the only entrants in a tongo tournament.
Tongo is a sport where, in each game, three players oppose each other.
The winner of each game receives 5 points; the second place finisher gets 3 points; and the third place finisher gets 1 point.
There are no tie games.
The one player with the most game points at the end of the tournament is the grand winner.
If, at the end of the tournament, two or more players have the same total number of points, there will be a playoff.

1. Which of the following MUST be true?   Ⓐ Ⓑ Ⓒ Ⓓ Ⓔ
  (A) Betsy plays only right-handed opponents.
  (B) Arnie never plays a right-handed opponent.
  (C) Arnie just plays right-handed opponents.
  (D) Sandy never plays right-handed opponents.
  (E) Sandy always plays right-handed opponents.

2. If, after three games, both right-handed players have each scored 9 points,
    which of the following could be true?   Ⓐ Ⓑ Ⓒ Ⓓ Ⓔ

  I.   One of the right-handed players finished first twice.
  II. At least one of the right-handed players finished second three times.
  III. Both right-handed players each finished first, second, and third.
  (A) I   (B) II   (C) III   (D) II and III   (E) I, II, and III

3. Which of the following MUST be true?   Ⓐ Ⓑ Ⓒ Ⓓ Ⓔ

  I.   A player with no first-place game points cannot win the tournament.
  II. A player with only second-place game points can win the tournament.
  III. A player with no first-place game points can win the tournament.
  (A) I   (B) II   (C) III   (D) II and III   (E) None of these

4. If, after three games, Arnie has 11 points, Betsy has 9 points, and Sandy has 7
    points, which of the following could be true?   Ⓐ Ⓑ Ⓒ Ⓓ Ⓔ

  I.   After four games, there is a three-way tie.
  II. After four games, Sandy is alone in first place.
  III. After four games, Betsy is alone in first place.
  (A) I   (B) II   (C) III   (D) I and III   (E) I, II, and III

5. If, just before the last game, it is discovered that the left-handed player has finished first in every even-numbered game, then

Ⓐ Ⓑ Ⓒ Ⓓ Ⓔ

(A) Sandy must win the tournament

(B) Sandy cannot win the tournament

(C) Arnie may win the tournament

(D) Betsy can't win the tournament

(E) none of these

ANSWERS AND EXPLANATIONS

You probably found that this set of conditions was not conducive to constructing any standard chart. As soon as this was evident, you should have simply pulled out information as follows:

L—Sandy	1st—5 pts.
R—Arnie	2nd—3 pts.
R—Betsy	3rd—1 pt.

Sometimes just pulling out information can be very helpful. Now let's look at the answers.

1. **E** Since Sandy is the only left-handed player, then she must play only right-handed opponents.

2. **C** Only statement III may be true. Statement I is blatantly false, since two first-place wins would result in 10 points. Statement II is incorrect because, if one player finishes second all three games, then there is no way a second player could score exactly 9 points in three games.

3. **A** Only statement I is true. With no first-place game points, the most a player could score per game is 3 points. The best that that player could hope for would be that the other two players would split first place and third place on all the games. But even then, the other two players would average 3 points per game. At best a playoff would be necessary, and the player without a first-place finish would thus lose the tournament.

4. **D** The only statement that could not be true is statement II. Since the most Sandy could score after four games would be 12 points, Betsy and/or Arnie will at least tie her for first place.

5. **C** Even though Sandy may have scored 5 points in every even-numbered game, she may not necessarily win the tournament. For instance, if, say, Arnie scores 5 points in every odd-numbered game, and if the tournament consists of an odd number of games, then Arnie will win the tournament. Sandy *can* win the tournament, but not necessarily *must* win the tournament. Betsy, also, could possibly win the tournament, if she scores first-place wins in every odd-numbered game.

IN CONCLUSION

You have just worked through some of the basic types of charts that you may encounter on the LSAT. Be aware that there are *many other possible charts and modifications of the charts presented.* In the following practice tests, as you work through some of the other possible charts, carefully review the explanations of each to assist you in understanding these other types.

Remember that the exact type of chart you make is not of critical importance. What is important is that you can get the necessary information from your chart, and that it is simple to understand. Do not spend a great deal of time trying to make an elaborate chart: a simple one will usually serve the purpose.

EXTRA PRACTICE: ANALYTICAL REASONING

Questions 1–4

(1) Four books are standing next to each other on a shelf in order from left to right. One of the books is red, one is yellow, one is blue, and one is orange.
(2) The red book is between the yellow and blue books.
(3) The blue book is between the orange and red books.
(4) The orange book is not fourth.

1. Which of the following can be deduced from statements 1, 2, and 3?   Ⓐ Ⓑ Ⓒ Ⓓ Ⓔ

  I.   The red book is not fourth.
  II. The blue book is not first.
  III. The yellow book is not second.
(A) I and II   (B) I and III   (C) II and III   (D) One of these
(E) All of these

2. Statement 4 eliminates which of the following orders (from left to right)?   Ⓐ Ⓑ Ⓒ Ⓓ Ⓔ
(A) O B R Y   (B) Y R B O   (C) Y B O R   (D) Y O R B
(E) O R B Y

3. Which of the following pairs are next to each other on the shelf?   Ⓐ Ⓑ Ⓒ Ⓓ Ⓔ

  I.   Orange and blue
  II. Blue and yellow
  III. Red and yellow
(A) I and II   (B) I and III   (C) II and III   (D) One of these
(E) All of these

4. If a green book were placed just to the left of the blue book, what position would it be in (counting from the left)?   Ⓐ Ⓑ Ⓒ Ⓓ Ⓔ
(A) first   (B) second   (C) third   (D) fourth   (E) fifth

Questions 5–8

Disease J is always communicable; its symptoms are red splotches, which appear the day after infection.

Disease K is only communicable the day after infection; its symptoms are blue lips or red splotches, which appear the day of infection.

Disease L only infects concurrently with Disease J; its symptoms—swollen ears, which appear the day after infection—are negated by Disease K.

These are the only diseases possible.
Peter had lunch with Paul on Tuesday.
Paul had dinner with Mary on Wednesday.
Symptoms appear for only one day.

5. If Peter broke out in red splotches on Tuesday, which of the following MUST be true?   Ⓐ Ⓑ Ⓒ Ⓓ Ⓔ
(A) Peter was infected with Disease K.
(B) Peter was infected with Disease J.
(C) Peter was infected with Disease L.
(D) Peter could have given Disease K to Paul on Tuesday.
(E) Peter didn't give Paul Disease K on Tuesday.

6. Which of the following pairs of symptoms are possible? Ⓐ Ⓑ Ⓒ Ⓓ Ⓔ

   I.   Blue lips and swollen ears
   II. Swollen ears and red splotches
   III. Blue lips and red splotches
   (A) I   (B) II   (C) III   (D) II and III   (E) I and III

7. If Paul had red splotches on Tuesday, then he could have Ⓐ Ⓑ Ⓒ Ⓓ Ⓔ

   I.   given Peter Disease J
   II. given Peter Disease K
   III. given Mary Disease J
   IV. given Mary Disease K
   (A) I and III   (B) I and IV   (C) II and III   (D) I, III, and IV
   (E) I, II, and IV

8. If on Monday Peter was only infected with Disease K, then which of the following could be true on Wednesday only because of Peter's passing Disease K on? Ⓐ Ⓑ Ⓒ Ⓓ Ⓔ

   I.   Mary's lips were blue.
   II. Mary's ears were swollen.
   III. Mary had red splotches.
   (A) I   (B) II   (C) III   (D) I and II   (E) I and III

Questions 9–17

A head counselor is choosing people to go on a hiking trip. The head counselor must choose from among 3 adult counselors (A, B, C) and 9 campers (boys, D, E, F, G, H, and girls J, K, L, M).
At least two adult counselors must go on the hike.
Camper D will not go without friends E and F.
Campers J and L will not hike together.
Camper M will not hike with counselor C.
There can never be more boy campers than girl campers.

9. If camper D is chosen for the hike Ⓐ Ⓑ Ⓒ Ⓓ Ⓔ
   (A) camper L must be chosen
   (B) camper J cannot be chosen
   (C) camper L cannot be chosen
   (D) camper G cannot be chosen
   (E) camper H must be chosen

10. If camper K is not chosen for the hike Ⓐ Ⓑ Ⓒ Ⓓ Ⓔ
   (A) camper G cannot be chosen
   (B) camper H cannot be chosen
   (C) camper E cannot be chosen
   (D) camper D cannot be chosen
   (E) camper L cannot be chosen

11. If camper D is chosen for the hike, which of the following cannot be true? Ⓐ Ⓑ Ⓒ Ⓓ Ⓔ
   (A) Camper H goes on the hike.
   (B) Camper K goes on the hike.
   (C) Counselor A goes on the hike.
   (D) Counselor B goes on the hike.
   (E) Camper M goes on the hike.

12. An acceptable combination of campers and counselors is   Ⓐ Ⓑ Ⓒ Ⓓ Ⓔ
- (A) ABCDEFJKM
- (B) ABDEFJLM
- (C) ABGHJKM
- (D) ACDEFJK
- (E) ACEFGKLM

13. If counselor A is not chosen for the hike then   Ⓐ Ⓑ Ⓒ Ⓓ Ⓔ
- (A) camper D must be chosen
- (B) camper D cannot be chosen
- (C) camper J must be chosen
- (D) camper L cannot be chosen
- (E) camper F cannot be chosen

14. If counselor A is not chosen for the hike, then which of the following must be true?
- (A) If camper E is chosen, camper K must be chosen.   Ⓐ Ⓑ Ⓒ Ⓓ Ⓔ
- (B) If camper F is chosen, camper K must be chosen.
- (C) Camper J cannot be chosen.
- (D) Camper D cannot be chosen.
- (E) If camper L is chosen, camper F must be chosen.

15. If camper D is chosen for the hike, which of the following could represent the other hikers?
- (A) ACEFJKM   Ⓐ Ⓑ Ⓒ Ⓓ Ⓔ
- (B) ABGHKML
- (C) ABEFJKM
- (D) ABFGJKL
- (E) ACEFGKLM

16. What is the largest number of hikers that can go on the hike?   Ⓐ Ⓑ Ⓒ Ⓓ Ⓔ
- (A) 5   (B) 6   (C) 7   (D) 8   (E) 9

17. Which of the following must be true?   Ⓐ Ⓑ Ⓒ Ⓓ Ⓔ
- (A) Campers K and M never hike together.
- (B) Campers E and G never hike together.
- (C) Campers D and G never hike together.
- (D) Campers J and M never hike together.
- (E) Campers D and M never hike together.

Questions 18–23

Four people, Q, R, S, and T, compete in a round robin tournament, playing one game against each of the other three.

Each player scores only when a player that he defeats, beats another player. (For example, A beats B, and B beats C and D. A receives 2 points because B won two games. Note that A does not get a point for beating B.)

- (1) No one won all three of his games.
- (2) No one lost all three of his games.
- (3) Q won the tournament by scoring the most points.
- (4) S came in last by scoring 1 point and winning the smallest number of games.
- (5) T beat Q.
- (6) The most points scored was 3.

18. How many points did Q score?   Ⓐ Ⓑ Ⓒ Ⓓ Ⓔ
- (A) 1   (B) 2   (C) 3   (D) 4   (E) 5

19. Who beat T?　　　　　　　　　　　　Ⓐ Ⓑ Ⓒ Ⓓ Ⓔ
(A) Q and R　　(B) R and S　　(C) Q and S　　(D) R only　　(E) S only

20. Who won two games?　　　　　　　　　Ⓐ Ⓑ Ⓒ Ⓓ Ⓔ
(A) Q and R　　(B) R and S　　(C) Q and T　　(D) Q only　　(E) R only

21. How many points did T score?　　　　Ⓐ Ⓑ Ⓒ Ⓓ Ⓔ
(A) 1　　(B) 2　　(C) 3　　(D) 4　　(E) 5

22. A tie in total points scored occurred between which players?　Ⓐ Ⓑ Ⓒ Ⓓ Ⓔ
(A) R and S　　(B) S and T　　(C) R and T　　(D) R, S, and T　　(E) No tie

23. If one player had won all three of his games, how many points would he
have scored?　　　　　　　　　　　　Ⓐ Ⓑ Ⓒ Ⓓ Ⓔ
(A) 3　　(B) 4　　(C) 5　　(D) 6　　(E) Cannot be determined

Answers and Explanations

Answers 1–4

By following statements 1–3, you could have made these two possible orders:

YRBO　or　OBRY

but statement 4 eliminates the first order, Y R B O.

1.　**E**　From statements 2 and 3, the red and blue books are between other books; thus, they cannot be first or fourth. Therefore, they are second and third. This leaves first and fourth positions for the orange and yellow books.

2.　**B**　Statement 4 eliminates the order with orange in fourth position.

3.　**B**　This follows directly after filling the grid.

4.　**B**　Since the blue book was in the second position, it will move to the third position, and the green book will take the second.

Answers 5–8

The following simple chart may be helpful in answering the questions:

Disease	When Communicable	Symptom
J	Always	Red splotches appear DAY AFTER INF.
K	Day after infection	Blue lips OR red splotches appear DAY OF INF.
L	Only with J	Swollen ears appear DAY AFTER INF. NEGATED BY DISEASE K

Tuesday	Wednesday
Peter and Paul	Paul and Mary

5. **E** Either (A) or (B) may be true, but neither necessarily *must* be true. (C) could be true if Disease L is concurrent with Disease J, but it doesn't necessarily have to be true. Choice (D) is false, since Disease K wouldn't be communicable until the day after, Wednesday. Thus (E) *is* true: Peter did not give Paul Disease K, because Disease K isn't communicable until a day later, on Wednesday.

6. **D**
   I. Blue lips and swollen ears are not possible together: Disease L's symptoms are negated by Disease K. FALSE
   II. Swollen ears and red splotches will both appear the day after infection with Diseases J and L. TRUE
   III. Blue lips and red splotches will appear together if a person is infected with Disease K a day after infection by Disease J. TRUE

7. **D** If Paul had red splotches on Tuesday, then he either was infected with Disease J on Monday or was infected with Disease K on Tuesday. Therefore:
   I. he could have given Peter Disease J because J is always communicable. TRUE
   II. Paul could *not* have given Peter Disease K on Tuesday, because Disease K isn't communicable until the day after (Wednesday). FALSE
   III. Paul could have given Mary Disease J because Disease J is always communicable. TRUE
   IV. Paul could have given Mary Disease K because Disease K is communicable a day after infection (Wednesday). TRUE

8. **E** If Peter was infected with Disease K on Monday, then:
   I. he could have infected Paul with Disease K on Tuesday (one day later); Paul in turn could have infected Mary on Wednesday. Thus, Mary could have blue lips. TRUE
   II. Mary's ears could not have been swollen because simply passing on Disease K would not manifest such a symptom. FALSE
   III. Peter could have given Paul Disease K on Tuesday; Paul in turn could have given it to Mary on Wednesday. Red splotches is also a symptom of Disease K, which Mary could have shown on Wednesday. TRUE

Answers 9–17

Drawing the simple diagram, below, will help answer the questions.

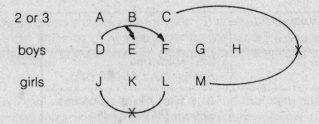

9. **D** If camper D is chosen, then campers E and F are also chosen. Thus three boys have been picked to go on the hike. Note that three girls, at most, can go on the hike. Since boys cannot outnumber girls, no other boys can be chosen.

10. **D** If camper K is not chosen, the maximum number of girls chosen can be two. Therefore, since boys cannot outnumber girls, D cannot be chosen, since selecting D means also selecting two more boys, E and F.

11. **A** If camper D is chosen, then boys E and F are also chosen. Since the maximum number of girls chosen can be three, no other boys may be chosen, since boys may not outnumber girls.

12. **C** Choices (A) and (E) include both C and M, which is not permitted. Choice (B) includes J and L, who will not hike together. In choice (D), boys outnumber girls, which is not permitted. Only choice (C) is an acceptable combination of campers and counselors.

13. **B** If counselor A is not chosen for the hike, then counselors B and C are chosen as there must be at least two counselors on the hike. Since counselor C is chosen, camper M (a girl) cannot be chosen. Therefore, the maximum number of girls on the hike can be two. Since boys cannot outnumber girls, D cannot be chosen, since selecting D would mean also selecting E and F, a total of three boys.

14. **D** If counselor A is not chosen, then counselors B and C will be chosen as there must be at least two counselors on the hike. If counselor C is chosen, camper M cannot be chosen, leaving the maximum number of girls possible on the hike at two. Therefore, since boys may not outnumber girls, D cannot be chosen as choosing D would mean also selecting E and F, thus outnumbering the girls.

15. **C** Choices (A) and (E) included both C and M, which is not permitted. Choices (B) and (D) do not include camper E, who must accompany camper D. Only choice (C) includes acceptable companions for a hike with camper D.

16. **D** The largest number of hikers that can go on the hike is eight, as follows: three boys, three girls, and counselors A and B. (Example: A, B, D, E, F, J, K, M)

17. **C** The maximum number of girls possible for the hike is three. Therefore, since choosing camper D means also choosing campers E and F, no other boys (for instance, G) can be chosen, as boys would then outnumber girls.

Answers 18–23

18. **C** Since no player won all three games and no player lost all three games, it is apparent that two players won two games each and two players won one game each. (Six games were played in all: Q vs. R, Q vs. S, Q vs. T, R vs. S, R vs. T, and S vs. T.) Since Q won the tournament, he must have been one of the two players who won two games. Therefore, Q must beat one player who won two games and one player who won one game, thus scoring a total of 3 points.

19. **B** We know that T beat Q. This eliminates (A) and (E). Player T has already earned 2 points by beating Q (who won two games). If T beat anyone else, then T would score more than 2 points. Since Q won the tournament with only 3 points, T must have lost to both R and S.

20. **A** Since Q won two games, the answer must be (A), (C), or (D). We also know that T won only one game. That eliminates (C). We know that R or S must have won two games, since Q won two games, T won one game, and two players won two games each. This eliminates (D). Thus the answer is (A).

21. **B** Since T beat only player Q, and since Q won two games, T must score 2 points.

22. **C** Since Q scored 3 points and won the tournament, and since S lost the tournament by winning only one game, S must have scored 1 point. Thus R and T must have scored 2 points each.

23. **A** Since six games are played, and if one player wins three of them, the other players must have won a total of three games. Thus 3 points is the maximum. The final chart is as follows:

		Opponent					
		Q	**R**	**S**	**T**		
	Q		W	W	L	=	3 points (R won 2; S won 1)
Player	**R**	L		W	W	=	2 points
	S	L	L		W	=	1 point
	T	W	L	L		=	2 points

KEY
W = won; L = lost.

Chapter

4

Evaluation of Facts

INTRODUCTION TO QUESTION TYPE

The Evaluation of Facts section has appeared previously as an experimental section on the LSAT; it is similar in some ways to the Cases and Principles section that was recently removed from the LSAT. You should expect at least one section of Evaluation of Facts questions, containing 32–38 questions distributed among six to nine sets (four to seven questions per set).

This section is designed to measure your reading and reasoning abilities. You will be given a set of facts and a dispute that must be resolved, followed by two rules that could govern the outcome of the dispute. The questions are issues that must be classified in relation to the rules in solving the dispute.

Here are some general tips that you should be familiar with before attempting the sample problems:

1. The facts and rules do not presuppose any specific legal knowledge.
2. The rules may be conflicting; do not assume automatically that one rule takes precedence over the other rule.
3. Technical or legal terms will be defined for you.
4. Work from the information on the page; do not bring in specific legal knowledge.
5. Some of the facts and conflicts may deal with games, quiz shows, and so on (not only legal issues); do not bring in specialized knowledge in these situations.
6. Each question must be evaluated independently of the other questions (new information brought in with a question refers only to that question).
7. Read actively, marking the facts that you feel are important.
8. Pay special attention to such words as *if, only, all, and, or, provided that, otherwise, only when, unless,* and so on. These types of words will help give direction to the rules and the relationships between them.

9. Note the differences between the two rules: what requirements and responsibilities are established.

10. Remember that you are being asked to classify the questions, not to answer them.

Make sure that you are familiar with the definitions of the choices before you enter the exam, but always read the directions carefully.

SAMPLE SET

Following are the directions for this section and a sample set, which will provide our basis for discussing strategies and techniques that will help you master this question type.

Directions:

This section consists of several sets; each set presents a factual statement, the description of a dispute, and two rules. In some sets, the rules will be conflicting. Be sure that you consider each rule independently and not as an exception to the other. Following each set are questions; select from four choices (given below) the one that best categorizes each question, based upon the relationship of one or both of the rules to the dispute. Darken the appropriate space on your answer sheet.

(A) **A relevant question that you can only answer by choosing between the rules.**
(B) **A relevant question that you cannot answer because you need more information or additional rules, but that does not require a choice between the rules.**
(C) **A relevant question that you can answer by referring to the facts or rules, or both.**
(D) **An irrelevant question or one that is only remotely relevant to the outcome of the dispute.**

A few words about the directions will be helpful before you start the sample set:

To choose (A) the question must fit both rules, the use of each rule gives a different outcome, and there is no basis for selecting one rule over the other.

To choose (B) the question cannot require a choice between the rules and must require clarification of important terms in one or both rules, information needed to establish important facts, or additional rules.

To choose (C) the question either leads to one of the rules, will give you the same answer from both rules, or can be answered from the facts.

To choose (D) the question should have no bearing on the outcome of the dispute as governed by the rules.

Questions that inquire about the outcome of the dispute cannot be (D).

Now try the sample set:

FACTS

Sid Warner, owner of S & W Bowling Ball Manufacturers, has been manufacturing top-quality bowling balls for the past 16 years. One day Sid is approached by Karl Lumb of K & L Bowling Equipment, whose company wishes to special-order 700 personalized bowling balls, with the K & L name engraved in gold lettering. Karl's company needs the bowling balls by November 15, to beat the Christmas rush.

Sid meets with his advisors the next day to discuss this $7000 transaction. Sid's advisors agree that he should take a chance, because business has been very slow for the past few months and the income is desperately needed.

After a lengthy meeting with Karl, Sid agrees to start production immediately, having been assured by Karl that the contract will be in the mail the next day. S & W then makes the machinery adjustment and starts manufacturing as quickly as possible to meet the deadline. After 4 days, Sid, who has not received the contract, phones Karl. Karl assures him that it was mailed 3 days ago but he will have another one sent out immediately.

After 3 more days, Sid becomes very anxious and has his company stop production. Upon being informed that production will remain at a standstill until the contract is received, Karl responds by telling Sid that he has changed his mind and decided to go with another company. Sid is enraged and immediately phones his attorney, whose later investigation proves that Karl never intended to complete the deal and was actually trying to put S & W out of business.

DISPUTE

Sid wanted the contract upheld in court, claiming that Karl had intentionally caused Sid financial loss. Karl contested.

RULE I

A contract for the sale of any goods for the price of $500 or more must be in writing.

RULE II

An oral contract for the sale of goods valued at over $500 will be enforced where the contract is to manufacture special goods and the seller has already started manufacturing the goods.

Questions

1. Will Sid win the suit against Karl? Ⓐ Ⓑ Ⓒ Ⓓ

2. Did Karl intentionally cause Sid financial loss? Ⓐ Ⓑ Ⓒ Ⓓ

3. Was there ever a written contract? Ⓐ Ⓑ Ⓒ Ⓓ

4. Did Sid's advisors give him poor advice? Ⓐ Ⓑ Ⓒ Ⓓ

5. If Sid had received the contract in the mail, but Karl decided he did not want the goods, will the contract be upheld? Ⓐ Ⓑ Ⓒ Ⓓ

6. If the total transaction came to $450, will the contract be upheld? Ⓐ Ⓑ Ⓒ Ⓓ

SUCCESSFUL TECHNIQUES AND STRATEGIES

READ THE STATEMENT OF FACTS, DISPUTE, AND RULES ACTIVELY, MARKING KEY WORDS AND PHRASES AS YOU READ.

In general, you should mark those places that seem most significant to you. Circle names, so that you can distinguish between the parties involved, and their relationship and/or dealings with one another. Mark the key words that delineate the conflict. THEN read the dispute slowly, carefully, and actively.

In the preceding set, note in particular the third paragraph, which establishes an oral agreement between Karl and Sid but leaves undetermined the existence of a written contract. Also note that in paragraph 4 Karl's intention to cause Sid financial loss is established.

In reading the rules, look for two important characteristics:

1. The relationship between the rules. Ask yourself whether the rules overlap or conflict in any way.
2. Terms that restrict or extend the applicability of the rules, usually words of degree (*all*, *some*, etc.), words that make the rule conditional (*if*, *only*, etc.), or conjunctions indicating whether items in a rule are necessarily linked ("this *and* that") or are alternatives to one another ("this *or* that").

Looking back at the rules presented in the case above, we notice several significant characteristics. First of all, note the general conflict between the rules: Rule I mandates a *written* contract, and Rule II allows an *oral* contract. Being aware of any conflict between the rules will help you to spot places in the facts that are relevant to that conflict, and to recall that conflict whenever you consider whether (A) is an appropriate answer.

Also notice terms that restrict or extend the applicability of the rules. We have repeated the rules below, with such key terms marked:

RULE I

A contract for the sale of⟨any⟩goods for the price of $500 or more⟨must⟩be in <u>*writing*</u>.

RULE II

An ⟨*oral contract*⟩ *for the sale of goods valued at* ⟨*over $500*⟩ *will be enforced* <u>*where*</u> *the contract is to* <u>*manufacture*</u> *special goods* ⟨*and*⟩*the seller has already* <u>*started manufacturing*</u> *the goods*.

Note that the key terms marked not only clarify the applicability of the rules, but also highlight the point of conflict between them.

After reading the rules carefully, reread and mark the dispute. Having read the rules, you may be better able to focus on the significant features of the dispute. This will aid in finding irrelevant questions. For instance, the dispute above centers on (1) the upholding of a contract; and (2) the claim of intentionally caused financial loss. Since a basic conflict between the rules concerns written versus oral contracts, you will want to pay particular attention to the nature of the contract in dispute as you check the facts, and will also want to pay attention to whether Karl's action was intentional.

As you consider each question, the classification will sometimes be immediately apparent. If this is the case, then quickly mark your answer choice and proceed to the next question. But in other cases involving more difficult questions, you should proceed systematically through your possible choices in order to arrive at your answer. One efficient method of systematic analysis is represented by the flow chart below:

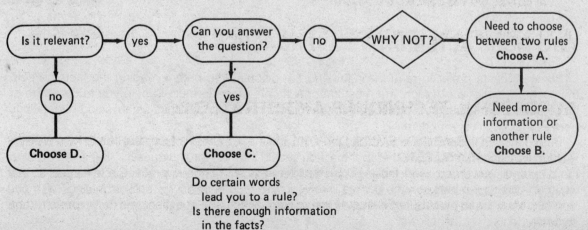

Do certain words
lead you to a rule?
Is there enough information
in the facts?

We will apply this method to answering the questions about the dispute between Sid and Karl.

1. Will Sid win the suit against Karl?
Is this question relevant? Yes—eliminate (D).
Can you answer the question? No—eliminate (C).
Why not? An answer requires a choice between the two rules; it must be decided whether an oral or a written contract is required in this case. Because the answer requires a choice, you pick (A).

2. Did Karl intentionally cause Sid financial loss?
Is this question relevant? Yes—eliminate (D).
Can you answer the question? Yes—the necessary information is given in paragraph 4. Pick (C).

3. Was there ever a written contract?
Is this question relevant? Yes, since the outcome might hinge on the nature of the contract—eliminate (D).
Can you answer this question? No; Karl didn't send the contract, but *may* have written one—eliminate (C).
Why can't you answer? You need more information. Pick (B).

4. Did Sid's advisors give him poor advice?
Is this question relevant to the dispute? No—choose (D).

5. If Sid had received the contract in the mail, but Karl decided he did not want the goods, will the contract be upheld?
Is this question relevant? Yes—eliminate (D).
Can you answer this question? Yes; in this case a written contract exists in addition to the oral agreement, so that both rules defining and verifying a valid "contract" apply, and suggest that the contract will be upheld. Pick (C).

6. If the total transaction came to $450, will the contract be upheld?
Is this question relevant to the dispute? Yes—eliminate (D).
Can you answer this question? No, because the rules apply only to more expensive goods. You need *additional* rules to cover goods valued at less than $500. Pick (B).

One additional point: Note that overtly factual questions, questions that ask simply *who, what, when, where,* or *how,* often *do not require a choice between the rules;* they do often require a consideration of *whether sufficient information exists.* In other words, when the question asks for a simple fact and no deductions are necessary, (A) is often *not* the correct choice.

TWO MORE ALTERNATIVE APPROACHES

Some students prefer to read the rules and the dispute first, before reading the facts, to help themselves predict which facts are most important. This procedure could help you to be aware of those places that seem most applicable to the rules and the dispute, thus establishing correlations between facts, rules, and dispute.

Before moving to the questions, reread the rules and the dispute efficiently but carefully, in order to reaffirm your understanding. Remember that you should pick (D) for any question that is irrelevant to the dispute as governed by the rules. You should try this technique in practice a few times to see whether it fits your needs.

A slightly different procedure for analyzing and classifying each question type that is preferred by some students goes as follows:

First ask, "Is the question relevant?" If no, answer (D); if yes, then ask, "Does an answer require a choice between the rules?" If yes, answer (A); if no, then ask, "Does an answer require more information or additional rules?" If yes, answer (B), if no, the question must be relevant and answerable, so choose (C).

Remember to practice and use whichever method is most efficient and effective for you.

Most important is to make sure that you have a good understanding of the directions and how to apply them as you proceed in classifying the questions. The following set will provide extra practice.

FACTS

Sally and Edna had been good friends and neighbors for many years. Sally, who enjoyed gardening, used one section of her property for a flower garden and another for a vegetable garden. In the spring of 1959, Sally asked Edna if she could use a small corner of Edna's property to extend her vegetable garden. Edna verbally agreed to let Sally use the property, and Sally began to cultivate the land immediately. As time passed, Sally used more and more of Edna's property and by 1964 was using over half of Edna's land for what was now her vegetable farming company. Sally had even erected a chain-link fence to protect her crops and put in sprinkler systems for easy watering. Edna, who had just returned from a 6-month trip to Europe, was appalled when she saw large produce trucks parked in front of her house and a chain-link fence surrounding half of her property. Edna approached Sally about the original agreement and requested that Sally not use the land anymore.

DISPUTE

Sally refused to remove the fence and continued to utilize the property, arguing that she had invested a great sum of money in the land's development. Edna contested, asking the court to order Sally to leave.

RULE I

One may use another's property only with the owner's oral or written consent. Owner may not withdraw consent without a written notice given 30 days prior to such action.

RULE II

Owner may withdraw consent to unpaid-for property use by another at any time, without notice, unless specified differently in a written contract.

Questions

1. Will the court force Sally to leave immediately?   Ⓐ Ⓑ Ⓒ Ⓓ

2. Should Edna sue Sally for damages?   Ⓐ Ⓑ Ⓒ Ⓓ

3. If Sally had been given written notice 30 days prior to the intended action, will Sally be forced to leave?   Ⓐ Ⓑ Ⓒ Ⓓ

4. If Edna had signed a written contract allowing Sally to use the property, will Sally be forced to leave?   Ⓐ Ⓑ Ⓒ Ⓓ

5. If Sally agrees to stop growing vegetables on Edna's land and removes the fence, should Edna withdraw her complaint?   Ⓐ Ⓑ Ⓒ Ⓓ

ANSWERS AND EXPLANATIONS

Note how the rules conflict in this set. Rule I does not allow the owner to withdraw consent without written notice, but Rule II does allow the owner to withdraw consent "unless specified differently in a written contract." Note also that the dispute involves the use of another's property.

1. Will the court force Sally to leave immediately?
   Is this question relevant? Yes—eliminate (D).
   Can you answer this question? No—eliminate (C).
   Why not? An answer requires a choice between the two rules; it must be decided whether the owner may withdraw consent immediately or not; Rule I says no, and Rule II says yes. Because the answer requires a choice, pick (A).

2. Should Edna sue Sally for damages?
   Is this question relevant to the dispute? No, the dispute is over utilization of the property, not damages. Pick (D).

3. If Sally had been given written notice 30 days prior to the intended action, will Sally be forced to leave?
   Is this question relevant to the dispute? Yes—eliminate (D).
   Can you answer this question? Yes; in this case the conditions specified in Rule I for withdrawing consent are in effect, and Rule II allows for the immediate withdrawal of consent in any case. Because both rules lead you to an answer, pick (C).

4. If Edna had signed a written contract allowing Sally to use the property, will Sally be forced to leave?
   Is this question relevant to the dispute? Yes—eliminate (D).
   Can you answer this question? No, because you are not told whether the written contract allows the withdrawal of consent; the answer to this question hinges primarily on whether such information is "specified . . . in a written contract" (see Rule II). Because you require more information to answer this question, pick (B).

5. If Sally agrees to stop growing vegetables on Edna's property, should Edna withdraw her complaint?
   Is this question relevant? Yes—eliminate (D).
   Can you answer this question? No, because you are not told whether or not Sally will continue to utilize the property in some manner. Since the dispute involves Sally's utilization of the property, and not her particular decision to grow vegetables, you need further information about Edna's consequent use of the property. Because you require more information, choose (B).

CAUTION: Although each set involves the analysis of rules of law and related facts, you must not apply any outside knowledge of the law when considering your answers. The rules presented may be real or imaginary, and may at times seem at odds with actual legal principles with which you may be familiar. Base your analysis and answer choices ONLY on the information given. This is a test of your reading comprehension and analytical ability, not your legal background.

EXTRA PRACTICE: EVALUATION OF FACTS

Set 1

FACTS

After examining the contents of his safe deposit box in a cubicle at Belmont National Bank, David Norris unwittingly carried an envelope along with other banking materials to the teller's window where he changed a $50 bill to smaller bills. He was unaware that the envelope contained three rare postage stamps. He accidently left the envelope on the counter beneath the window, where Martha Rudel found it 10 minutes later. Thinking the envelope was empty, she used the back to calculate the balance in her savings account, and put the envelope in her purse. Two weeks later she discovered the stamps. Realizing that she had found the envelope at the bank, she asked Belmont National to help her find the owner. Unable to locate the owner of the stamps, Belmont National Bank asked Mrs. Rudel to return the stamps.

DISPUTE

Belmont National Bank asks a court to require Mrs. Rudel to return the stamps to the bank. Mrs. Rudel contests.

RULE I

The finder of lost property has valid title to the property as against everyone else except the person who lost the property.

RULE II

Property lost on premises intended for the safekeeping of such property belongs to the custodians of said premises as against the finder of the property.

Questions

1. What was the value of the stamps?   Ⓐ Ⓑ Ⓒ Ⓓ

2. Had the stamps been in Norris's safety deposit box?   Ⓐ Ⓑ Ⓒ Ⓓ

3. Did the bank make a conscientious effort to find the original owner of the stamps?   Ⓐ Ⓑ Ⓒ Ⓓ

4. If the envelope containing the stamps had fallen from the box of the depositor who used the cubicle before Norris, to whom will the stamps belong?   Ⓐ Ⓑ Ⓒ Ⓓ

5. Would Norris get his stamps back if he realized they were missing from his safety deposit box and notified the bank?   Ⓐ Ⓑ Ⓒ Ⓓ

Set 2

FACTS

In 1946, Cabot took a lease on 200 acres of Vermont farmland owned by Forbes, and established a herd of 300 dairy cows. Cabot paid his rent to Forbes for 3 years, and then, when Forbes moved to Nevada, Cabot paid rent into a bank account Forbes had established in the town. In the fall of 1953, price supports for dairy products were removed and the farm ceased to be profitable; Cabot stopped paying the rent. Since the amount of the rent was small, and Forbes was wealthy, Forbes was not concerned about the unpaid rent, and Cabot remained in Vermont. In 1973, Forbes returned to Vermont to open a ski lodge on his property. When Forbes sought to have him evicted, Cabot claimed title to the property.

DISPUTE

Forbes and Cabot went to court to determine the ownership of the property.

RULE I

The ownership of or right to use private property cannot be transferred or nullified without the written consent of the owner or the owner's approved representative.

RULE II

An individual may acquire legal title to real property rightfully owned by another if that individual exercises dominion over the property for a period of at least 20 years. This dominion must be public, include continuous occupancy, and be without the express permission of or pursuant to the terms of a lease with the true owner of the property.

Questions

6. If Forbes filed his case in March 1964 and Cabot's occupancy of the property had been open and uninterrupted, who would be the legal owner of the property? Ⓐ Ⓑ Ⓒ Ⓓ

7. Did Forbes agree in writing to Cabot's nonpayment of rent? Ⓐ Ⓑ Ⓒ Ⓓ

8. Did Cabot ever pay any additional rent into Forbes's bank account after he stopped his rent payments in 1953? Ⓐ Ⓑ Ⓒ Ⓓ

9. If Forbes returned to Vermont in December 1973, and if Cabot had stayed on the Vermont farmland since 1951 without a lease, who will be the legal owner of the property? Ⓐ Ⓑ Ⓒ Ⓓ

10. Where did Cabot live between 1960 and 1970? Ⓐ Ⓑ Ⓒ Ⓓ

11. How much income did Forbes lose by not collecting rent between 1953 and 1963? Ⓐ Ⓑ Ⓒ Ⓓ

Set 3

FACTS

Edmond Boyle, publisher and editor of the *Bearwood Times*, was running for reelection as mayor of Bearwood. His opponent in a heated campaign was Arthur Hamilton, the owner of the town's general store. After obtaining information from a private investigator that during the Korean War Hamilton had spent some time in a Communist prison camp, Boyle presented the following statement in the election-eve edition of the *Bearwood Times*: "Arthur Hamilton has spent years in the company of our Communist enemies. He has been under their control and undoubtedly has carried out many of their orders." Notwithstanding the publication of this statement, Hamilton was elected mayor. In the next few months however, the number of customers at Hamilton's general store declined significantly. Hamilton attributed the decline to the statement in the newspaper.

DISPUTE

Hamilton sued Boyle for damages resulting from the defamatory paragraph in the *Bearwood Times*. Boyle contested.

RULE I

One is liable for defamation only if one has knowingly made a false statement injurious to the reputation of another.

RULE II

One is liable for damages caused by defamation even though the injurious statement is technically true if the meaning of the statement inferred by the ordinary persons who hear or read the statement is false and defamatory.

Questions

12. How long did Hamilton spend in a Communist prison camp? Ⓐ Ⓑ Ⓒ Ⓓ

13. Why did the number of customers at Hamilton's general store decline? Ⓐ Ⓑ Ⓒ Ⓓ

14. If Hamilton had made broadcasts sympathetic to the Communists during his imprisonment, how will his case be decided? Ⓐ Ⓑ Ⓒ Ⓓ

15. If Boyle believed the newspaper statement to be true and the decline in Hamilton's business is the consequence of that statement, will Boyle be liable for damages? Ⓐ Ⓑ Ⓒ Ⓓ

16. Had Boyle been a popular mayor? Ⓐ Ⓑ Ⓒ Ⓓ

Answers and Explanations

Set 1

1. **D** This question is irrelevant. The value of the stamps has no bearing on the case.

2. **B** To answer this relevant question, you need additional information. The facts do not make clear whether the stamps had been in Norris's safe deposit box. If they were, Rule II will be relevant.

3. **D** The question is irrelevant to the rules of this case.

4. **A** To answer this relevant question, you must choose between the two rules. Each rule gives a different outcome. Under Rule I the stamps will belong to the finder, but under Rule II the stamps will belong to the bank.

5. **C** This relevant question can be answered by applying the rules. Under these circumstances, Rule I will award the stamps to Norris and Rule II will no longer be relevant.

Set 2

6. **C** This relevant question can be answered by applying the rules. If Forbes filed his case in March 1964, Cabot has not exercised dominion over the property for 20 years in defiance of the terms of a lease.

7. **B** To answer this relevant question, you need additional information. If Forbes has agreed in writing, then Cabot does not occupy the land *without* the express permission of the owner.

8. **B** To answer this relevant question, you need additional information. Since 20 years without any observed rental contract must pass for Cabot's case, the question is relevant.

9. **A** To answer this relevant question, you must choose between the two rules. Each rule gives a different outcome. If Forbes did not return until December, 20 years have passed with Cabot in continuous possession, so Cabot will win according to Rule II. By Rule I, Forbes will win.

10. **B** To answer this relevant question, you need additional information, since under Rule II Cabot's dominion must be continuous.

11. **D** The amount of lost income is irrelevant.

Set 3

12. **B** To answer this relevant question, you need additional information. If Hamilton did not spend "years" in the prison camp and Boyle knows this, the article is false and Rule I will apply.

13. **B** To answer this relevant question, you need additional information. If the decline has been caused by the newspaper statement, Rule II will apply even if Rule I does not.

14. **C** This relevant question can be answered by applying the rules. If Hamilton had made such broadcasts, he would lose under either rule since there is no falsehood under either Rule I or Rule II.

15. **A** To answer this relevant question, you must choose between the two rules. Each rule gives a different outcome. If Boyle believed the statement to be true, he will win according to Rule I; but if Hamilton's customers have accepted the defamatory implication of the statement, Boyle will lose according to Rule II.

16. **D** This question is irrelevant and has no clear bearing on this case.

Chapter

5

Logical Reasoning

INTRODUCTION TO QUESTION TYPE

The Logical Reasoning section contains 24–28 questions and measures your aptitude for understanding, analyzing, utilizing, and criticizing various types of arguments. Your ability to reason logically and critically is tested by questions that require you to do the following:

1. Recognize a point.
2. Follow a chain of reasoning.
3. Draw conclusions.
4. Infer missing material.
5. Apply principles from an argument.
6. Identify methods.
7. Evaluate arguments.
8. Differentiate between fact and opinion.
9. Analyze evidence.
10. Assess claims critically.

Logical reasoning questions may take many forms. In analyzing these forms consider their basic component parts:

1. A *passage, argument,* or *discussion*
           followed by
2. A *question* based upon the preceding text
           followed by
3. The five *answer choices* (A, B, C, D, and E)

The following discussion offers some tips for each of these parts.

1. The Passage, Argument, or Discussion

For the passage, read *actively;* that is, as you read you should mark the important parts with circles, exclamation points, etc., directly on the page of your question booklet. Reading actively helps you stay involved in the passage, it keeps you an active participant in the testing process, and it helps you note and highlight the important points mentioned, should you need to refer back to the passage.

As you read you should also note the major issue being discussed, along with the few supporting points, if any.

2. The Question

For the question, it may be helpful to *pre-read actively.* That is, read the question first, *before* reading the passage. That way you have an idea of what to look for as you read the passage. This is an effective technique only if the question is short. If the question is as long as (or longer than) the passage, this technique may not be helpful. Use your judgment.

As you read the question, note the key words and *circle* them, in the same manner as you mark the passage. Also note the *reference* of the question. Is it positive or negative? Is it asking what would strengthen the author's argument or what would weaken the author's argument? Is it asking what the author would agree or disagree with? Is it asking what the author believes, or what his critics would believe? Finally, be aware that questions often refer to *unstated* ideas: assumptions (a supposition or a truth taken for granted); implications/inferences (what would logically follow from a previous statement); and conclusions (the necessary consequence or result of the ideas in the passage). Assumptions and implications/inferences are usually not directly mentioned in the passage. Conclusions may or may not be mentioned. You must arrive at all three through logical thinking.

3. The Choices

For the choices, note that you must select the *best* of the five choices. Therefore, there may not be a perfect choice. There may also be two good choices. You are to pick the best of the five. Therefore the elimination strategy (pp. 000 and 000) is an effective way to approach the answer choices. Eliminate choices that are irrelevant (having nothing to do with the particular topic or issue), off-topic, or not addressed by the passage. Note that often a choice will be incorrect simply because one word in that choice is off-topic. Learn to look for and mark these off-topic key words.

Finally, be very careful as you read the passage, question, and choices, to watch for words that have very special meanings. The following words, for instance, are frequently used.

except some all none only one
few no could must each

These types of words will often be the key to finding the best answer. Therefore, make sure to underline or circle them in your reading.

DISCUSSION OF QUESTION CATEGORIES

The following sections give detailed examples of the most common types of Logical Reasoning questions, complete with important techniques and strategies. You should not try to memorize the different categories presented here, but rather use them as an aid in identifying strategies needed and in practicing techniques.

1. Author Information

One of the most common Logical Reasoning questions refers to a reading passage or paragraph and asks you to understand some things about the author. You may be asked to *interpret* what the author means or is trying to accomplish by this statement, or to *predict* the action and feeling of the author on similar or unrelated subject matter (tell whether the author would agree or disagree with some other idea).

To answer this type of question, first look for the values and attitudes of the author. (Ask yourself, "Where is the author coming from?") Second, watch for word connotation: the author's choice of words can be very important. Third, decide the author's purpose and point of view, but don't OVER-READ. Keep within the context of the passage. Some times it will be advantageous to skim some of the questions (not the answer choices) before reading the short passage, so that you will know what to expect.

Remember while reading to mark the passage and look for *who, what, when, where, why*, and *how*. (See the section on "Active Reading" that begins on page 33).

Example

Recent studies show that the general public is unaware of most new legislation and doesn't understand 99% of the remaining legislation. This is mainly because of the public's inattention and lack of interest.

The author of this argument would most likely be   Ⓐ Ⓑ Ⓒ Ⓓ Ⓔ

   I.   in favor of new legislation
  II.   against new legislation
 III.   advocating public participation in legislation
 IV.   advocating the simplifying of the language of new legislation
(A) I   (B) II   (C) III   (D) II and IV   (E) III and IV

ANSWER AND EXPLANATION

The correct answer is (C). The statement does not imply that an increase or decrease in legislation would change the public awareness; therefore I and II are incorrect. III follows in the tenor of the argument because the author's purpose appears to be centered around involvement. He points out that the general public is unaware because of inattention and lack of interest. IV would be possible, making (E) a possible choice, *but* the author is not focusing his criticism on the complex wording of legislation and does not mention it as a reason for unawareness. Remember (1) *whom* the author is talking about—the general public, (2) *what* he mentions—their unawareness of most new legislation, and (3) *why* they are unaware—because of inattention and lack of interest.

2. Form of Argumentation or Author Identification

In this type of question, you are asked to decide what type of argument, logic, or reasoning the author is using (example, exaggeration, deduction, induction, etc.) or what field or profession the author is involved in (doctor, lawyer, engineer, etc.).

To answer this type of question, carefully follow the author's line of reasoning while focusing on his intent or purpose. Notice how he starts and finishes his argument. Consider what he has concluded or proved, or what point he has made.

Example

Once again, refer to the argument just used, concerning legislation.

This argument was probably written by a   Ⓐ Ⓑ Ⓒ Ⓓ Ⓔ
(A)   candidate for office
(B)   social psychologist
(C)   disgruntled politician
(D)   statistician
(E)   consumer advocate

The correct answer is (C). The author is making a statement specifically relevant to politics, but (A) may be eliminated because a candidate for office would not tend to criticize the general public. The "disgruntled" politician can be identified by his purpose and method of criticism.

3. Strengthening or Weakening the Author's Statement or Conclusion

This question type is very common on the LSAT. Here you are given a short reading passage or paragraph followed by the question "Which of the following would strengthen the author's statement the most?" or "Which of the following would most weaken the author's statement?" (Both of these questions may be asked. There are many possible varieties of this question type: "least likely to weaken," "strongest criticism of," etc.).

You may find it helpful to preread, or read the question before reading the short paragraph. Focus on the major point of the statement and "how" or "if" it is supported. Be aware of the *strength* of the statement or argument. Is it a harsh criticism of a certain system? Is it a mildly persuasive paragraph? What point is the author trying to make in supporting this cause?

Remember to always read actively, marking key words or phrases.

Example

Psychiatrists and laymen agree that the best sort of adjustment is founded upon an acceptance of reality, rather than an escape from it.

Which of the following would probably most weaken the author's point?   Ⓐ Ⓑ Ⓒ Ⓓ Ⓔ
(A) Psychiatrists and laymen do not often agree.
(B) Reality is difficult to define.
(C) Escaping reality has worked for many.
(D) Accepting reality is often traumatic.
(E) Psychiatrists' definition of reality and laymen's definition of reality are
     different.

The correct answer is (C). If escaping reality has worked for many, then it becomes more difficult to defend the acceptance of reality theory. (A) would probably strengthen the point being made. (B) could strengthen or weaken the point. (D) and (E) are irrelevant.

4. Author Assumptions, Implications, Deductions

This is another very common question type in the Logical Reasoning section. Here you are again given a short reading passage or paragraph followed by questions asking about the author's possible assumptions, implications, or deductions.

To answer this question type, you may wish to read the question first actively. Make a careful note of what part of the paragraph the question refers to. Is the question asking about the conclusion of the paragraph? Or the opening statement? Or about the complete paragraph? (The complete passage may be only one or two sentences.) Keep in mind that assumptions are things taken for granted, or supposed as facts. An implication is not expressed in words, but is something that may be fairly understood. Deductions are arrived at or attained from general premises . . . drawing or inferring information. Deductions are necessarily true.

Example

Use the statement in the example for Category 3:

Psychiatrists and laymen agree that the best sort of adjustment is founded upon an acceptance of reality, rather than an escape from it.

The author of this passage assumes that ⓐ ⓑ ⓒ ⓓ ⓔ

   I.   there are many sorts of adjustment
   II. escaping reality is possible
   III. psychiatrists and laymen disagree on most things
(A) I only   (B) I and II   (C) II only   (D) III only   (E) I and III

ANSWER AND EXPLANATION

The correct answer is (B). The author states that "the best sort of adjustment is," which implies the assumption that there are many sorts of adjustment. In stating "rather than an escape from it [reality]," he is assuming that escaping reality is possible.

5. Passage Completion or Fill-In

This question type requires you to fill in a word or words in a passage or to choose a phrase or sentence that best completes the passage.

It is initially important that you preserve the meaning of the passage, completing or maintaining the same thought. Unity (same subject) and coherence (order of thoughts) should be carefully noted. Second, it is important that the words you choose fit stylistically, use the same vocabulary, and are from the same context. Many times you will be able to eliminate some choices that "just don't sound good."

6. Word Reference

Here a word, or group of words, is taken out of context, and you are asked either what the word or words mean or what they refer to. In this type of question, first consider the passage as a whole; then carefully examine the key word or words surrounding the selected ones.

Examples of types 5 and 6

English, with its insatiable and omnivorous appetite for imported food, has eaten until it has become linguistically unbuttoned. And the glutton has cloaked his paunch with the pride of the gourmet. We would not imply that a large vocabulary is bad, but rather that it is self-destructive if uncontrolled by ————————.

Choose the completion that is best according to the context of this passage.   ⓐ ⓑ ⓒ ⓓ ⓔ
(A)   a smattering of slang
(B)   a fine sense of distinction
(C)   the removal of all but Anglo-Saxon derivatives
(D)   a professor who knows the limits of good usage
(E)   an unbuttoned tongue

ANSWER AND EXPLANATION

The correct answer is (B). The passage describes the English language itself; therefore, references to individuals, (D) and (E), are inappropriate. They do not maintain the same general level of thought.

Since the author does not condemn a large and distinguished vocabulary, (A) and (C), which do, are both poor choices. (B) preserves the meaning of the passage and fits stylistically.

Here is an example of word reference using the same passage:

The word "glutton" refers to

Ⓐ Ⓑ Ⓒ Ⓓ Ⓔ

(A) an English language with a lack of Anglo-Saxon derivation
(B) one who never stops talking about foreign food
(C) an English language bursting with pride
(D) one who is bilingual
(E) an English language bursting with derivatives from foreign languages

ANSWER AND EXPLANATION

The correct answer is (E). The passage, as a whole, is commenting on the English language, and (E) is the only choice that equates "glutton" with the subject of the passage.

7. Parallel Reasoning or Similarity of Logic

In this type you will be given a statement or statements and asked to select the statements that most nearly parallel the originals or use similar logic. First, you should decide whether the original statement is valid. (But don't take too much time on this first step because some of the others may tip you off to the correct choice.) If the statement is valid, your choice must be a valid statement. If the statement is invalid, your choice must be an invalid one. Your choice must preserve the same relationship or comparison.

Second, the direction of connections is important—general to specific (deduction), specific to general (induction), quality to thing, thing to quality, and so on.

Third, the tone of the argument should be the same. If the original has a negative slant, has a positive slant, or changes from negative to positive, then so must your choice.

Fourth, the order of each element is important. Remember: Corresponding elements must be in the same order as the original.

It may be helpful to substitute letters for complex terms or phrases, to simplify confusing situations and help you avoid getting lost in the wording. Direction and order are usually more easily followed by letter substitution.

Remember: Don't correct or alter the original; just reproduce the reasoning.

Example

Alex said, "All lemons I have tasted are sour. Therefore, all lemons are sour."

Which of the following most closely parallels the logic of the above statement?

Ⓐ Ⓑ Ⓒ Ⓓ Ⓔ

(A) I have eaten pickles four times and I got sick each time. Therefore, if I eat another pickle, I will get sick.
(B) My income has increased each year for the past four years. Therefore, it will increase again next year.
(C) I sped to work every day last week and I did not get a ticket. Therefore, they do not give tickets for speeding around here any more.
(D) All flormids are green. This moncle is red. Therefore, it is not a flormid.
(E) Every teacher I had in school was mean. Therefore, all teachers are mean.

ANSWER AND EXPLANATION

The correct answer is (E). First, the logic of the original is faulty; therefore, the correct choice must also be faulty, eliminating (D). Next, notice the direction of connections: generalization from a *few* experiences ⟶ generalization about *all* similar experiences. (A) and (B) each project the result of a few past experiences to only ONE similar experience. (C) starts from a few experiences, but finishes with a result that implies a change in a specific area. You could assume that "they" used to give tickets here.

Another example (with a slight twist)

Why do you want to stop smoking?

Which of the following most closely parallels the structure and reasoning of
this question?   Ⓐ Ⓑ Ⓒ Ⓓ Ⓔ
(A)   Why do you want to go to Italy?
(B)   When will you decide on the offer?
(C)   Will you ever play cards again?
(D)   When do you want to learn to play tennis?
(E)   Which desk do you like better?

ANSWER AND EXPLANATION

The correct answer is (C). This response is the only one that implies that the *action has already taken place*, as in the original question. (A) appears to be the closest, but this is only true regarding sentence structure, not reasoning. (B) and (D) are asking about future plans without implying anything about past actions. (D) does imply past lack of action. (E) merely asks for a comparison.

8. Argument Exchange

In this question type, two or more speakers are exchanging arguments or merely discussing a situation. You will then be asked to choose the statement that most strengthens or weakens either argument. Or you may be asked to find the inconsistency or flaw in an argument, or to identify the form of argument. In some instances you will be asked to interpret what one speaker might have thought the other meant by his response.

To answer these questions, you should first evaluate the strength and completeness of the statements. Are they general or specific? Do they use absolutes? Are they consistent?

Second, evaluate the relationship between responses. What kind of response did the first statement procure from the second speaker?

Third, evaluate the intentions of the author in making his remarks. What was his purpose?

Example

Tom: It is impossible to get a hit off the Yankee pitcher Turley.
Jim: You're just saying that because he struck you out three times yesterday.
Which of the following would strengthen Tom's argument most?   Ⓐ Ⓑ Ⓒ Ⓓ Ⓔ
(A)   Tom is a good hitter.
(B)   Turley pitched a no-hitter yesterday.
(C)   Tom has not struck out three times in a game all season.
(D)   Tom has not struck out all season.
(E)   Turley has not given up a hit to Jim or Tom all season.

ANSWER AND EXPLANATION

The correct answer is (B). Tom's is a general statement about Turley's relationship to *all* hitters. All choices except (B) mention only Tom or Jim, not hitters in general.

9. Group Questions

In some instances, you may be presented with five choices first, and then two or three questions that refer to these five choices.

Reading the questions first will clue you as to what to look for when reading the choices, and may save you time.

Example

(A)   Man cannot fly; therefore man was not meant to fly.
(B)   Jogging is good for you unless you have flat feet.
(C)   The homeowner doesn't need to pay the tax because he doesn't own a home.
(D)   The witness's testimony was truthful because he said he was telling the truth.
(E)   The car stalled because of lack of fuel.

1. Which of the statements uses circular reasoning?   Ⓐ Ⓑ Ⓒ Ⓓ Ⓔ
2. Which of the statements is internally inconsistent?   Ⓐ Ⓑ Ⓒ Ⓓ Ⓔ
3. Which of the statements uses an example to make a point?   Ⓐ Ⓑ Ⓒ Ⓓ Ⓔ

ANSWERS AND EXPLANATIONS

1.   **D**   Circular reasoning is the use of a statement to support itself. Thus, (D) is circular.

2.   **C**   Statement (C) is internally inconsistent because a homeowner, by definition, is someone who owns a home. Thus, stating that the homeowner doesn't own a home is inconsistent.

3.   **A**   Statement (A) posits an argument or statement that man is not meant to fly. To support this point, it uses an example: man cannot fly.

Notice that reading the questions first pinpointed what to look for in the preceding answer choices. Because this method may make you observe answers out of order, be careful that you are answering the right question number.

10. Syllogistic Reasoning

This type of question gives you some short propositions and asks you to draw conclusions, valid or invalid. You may be expected to evaluate assumptions: information that is or is not assumed.

First, if possible, simplify the propositions to assist your understanding.
Second, draw diagrams (Venn diagrams; see p. 50 in Chapter 3—or Euler circles) if possible.
Third, replace phrases or words with letters to help yourself follow the logic.

Example 1

All couples who have children are happy.
All couples either have children or are happy.

Assuming the above to be true, which of the following cannot be true?   Ⓐ Ⓑ Ⓒ Ⓓ Ⓔ

   I.   Some couples are not happy.
   II.   Some couples who are happy have children.
   III.   Some couples who have children are not happy.
(A) I only   (B) II only   (C) III only   (D) I and III only
(E) II and III only

ANSWER AND EXPLANATION

The correct answer is (D). If all couples who have children are happy, and if all couples who don't have children are happy, then all couples are happy. Simplifying the two statements to "all couples are happy" makes this question much more direct and easier to handle. Thus, I is false. III is also false, since it contradicts the first statement. Therefore, I and III are not true.

Example 2

All A's are B's.
Some C's are A's.

Which of the following is (are) warranted based upon the above?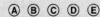

I.   All B's are A's.
II. Some C's are B's.
III. All B's are C's.
IV. Some B's are A's.
V.   All C's are B's.
(A) I only   (B) I and II only   (C) III only   (D) II and IV only
(E) III and V only

ANSWER AND EXPLANATION

The correct choice is (D)—II and IV only. Diagramming the original information gives:

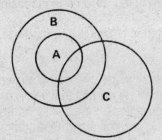

With this diagram, the following is evident:
I.   "All B's are A's" is false.
II. "Some C's are B's" is true.
III. "All B's are C's" is false.
IV. "Some B's are A's" is true.
V.   "All C's are B's" is false.

11. Chain Reasoning or Conclusion Validity

Here you will be given a list of conditionals, or statements, and asked to follow the logic or reach a valid conclusion.

In this type, you will first want to underline key terms to eliminate looking at excess wording.

Second, mark the direction of each statement. Where does it start and end? What connection is it making?

Third, look for the "kicker" statement. That's the one that starts the chain reaction; it gives you the information to work with other statements.

Example

Senator Jones will vote for the Pork bill if he is reelected. If the Pork bill passes, then Senator Jones was not reelected. Senator Jones was reelected.

Which of the following can be concluded from these statements?
(A)   Senator Jones assisted in the passage of the Pork bill.
(B)   The passage of the Pork bill carried Senator Jones to victory.
(C)   Senator Jones voted against the Pork bill, but it passed anyway.
(D)   The Pork bill didn't pass, even though Senator Jones voted for it.
(E)   The Pork bill was defeated by a large majority.

ANSWER AND EXPLANATION

The correct answer is (D). Notice that the "kicker" statement that started the chain reaction is "Senator Jones was reelected." From this, we know that he voted for the Pork bill. But the Pork bill could not have passed; otherwise he could not have been reelected.

12. Statement Evaluation or Ambiguity of Statements

This question type gives you a statement, argument, proverb, or cliché and asks you to deal with the possible meanings, either identifying them or applying them.

First, you should make sure that you understand the statement; simplify it to make sense if necessary. Take the simplest, most straightforward meaning first. Consider all other possible meanings from all angles only after you have read the choices.

Second, evaluate the strength and completeness of the statement. (Is it general? Specific? Absolute?)

Example

"One may go wrong in many directions, but right in only one," stated Aristotle.

This statement has many meanings. Which of the following could not be one
of the meanings?   Ⓐ Ⓑ Ⓒ Ⓓ Ⓔ

  I.   Right has an absolute direction.
  II. Going wrong is more possible than going right.
  III. One may go right more than once.
  IV. The right directions are more accessible.
  (A) I   (B) I and III   (C) II   (D) II and IV   (E) IV

ANSWER AND EXPLANATION

The correct choice is (E). Since statement IV says the right "directions," it actually contradicts the statement by mentioning more than one right direction. Also the original statement could not mean that the right directions are more accessible because it implies they are less accessible. I, II, and III are all either stated or can be easily inferred as one of the meanings.

As you have seen, Logical Reasoning includes a potpourri of problem types all requiring common sense and reasonableness in the answers. You should take care in underlining what is being asked so that you do not (for example) accidentally look for the valid conclusion when the invalid one is asked for. Because of the nature of the Logical Reasoning problems, it is very easy to get tangled in a problem and lose your original thought, spending too much time on the question. If you feel that you have become trapped or stuck, *skip the problem* and come back later if you have time. Remember that you must work within the context of the question, so do not bring in outside experiences or otherwise complicate a problem. The Logical Reasoning question is looking *not* for training in formal logic, just for common sense and reasonableness.

REVIEW OF SOME GENERAL STRATEGIES FOR LOGICAL REASONING

THE PASSAGE
Read *actively*, circling key words.
Note major issue and supporting points.

THE QUESTION
Pre-read (before reading the passage) *actively*.
Note its reference.
Watch out for *unstated* ideas:
assumptions, implications/inferences, and sometimes conclusions.

ANSWER CHOICES
Sometimes there may not be a *perfect* answer; thus choose the *best* of the five choices.
Use the elimination strategy.
Note that "wrong" words in choice make choice incorrect.
Watch for those off-topic key words.

EXTRA PRACTICE: LOGICAL REASONING

In this section you will be given brief statements or passages and be required to evaluate the reasoning involved. In some instances, more than one choice will appear to be a possible answer. You are to choose the *best* answer. Use common sense and reasonableness in making your selection; then mark the correct answer.

Questions 1–3 refer to the following passage.

Robots have the ability to exhibit programmed behavior. Their performance can range from the simplest activity to the most complex group of activities. They not only can build other robots, but also can rebuild themselves. Physically they can resemble humans, yet mentally they cannot. Even the most highly advanced robot does not have the capacity to be creative, have emotions, or think independently.

1. From the passage above, which of the following MUST be true?　Ⓐ Ⓑ Ⓒ Ⓓ Ⓔ
   (A) Robots could eventually take over the world.
   (B) The most complex group of activities involve being creative.
   (C) A robot can last forever.
   (D) Emotions, creativity, and independent thought cannot be programmed into a robot.
   (E) Building other robots involves independent thinking.

2. The author of this passage would agree that　Ⓐ Ⓑ Ⓒ Ⓓ Ⓔ

   I. robots would eventually be impossible to control
   II. in the near future, robots will be able to think independently
   III. robots have reached their peak of development
   (A) I   (B) II   (C) III   (D) All of the above   (E) None of the above

3. The author's assertions would be weakened by pointing out that　Ⓐ Ⓑ Ⓒ Ⓓ Ⓔ
   (A) humans exhibit programmed behavior for the first few years of life
   (B) robots' behavior is not always predictable
   (C) building other robots requires independent training
   (D) internal feeling is not always exhibited
   (E) the most complex group of activities necessitate independent thinking

4. Life is like a parachute jump—you had better get it right the first time.

The author of this statement assumes that   Ⓐ Ⓑ Ⓒ Ⓓ Ⓔ

   I.   you only live once
  II. starting over is possible but difficult
  III. there is no life after death
(A) I only   (B) II only   (C) I and III   (D) III only   (E) II and III

5. Man is free because he is rational.

This statement has many possible meanings. Which of the following could
be possible meanings?   Ⓐ Ⓑ Ⓒ Ⓓ Ⓔ

   I.   Man's being rational makes him free.
  II. Man is rational.
  III. Man is free.
(A) I only   (B) II only   (C) III only   (D) I and III only
(E) I, II, and III

6. The simplest conceivable situation in which one human being may communicate with another is one in which structurally complementary communi-
cants have been conditioned to associate the same words with the same
things.

The sentence that would best complete this thought is: Ⓐ Ⓑ Ⓒ Ⓓ Ⓔ
(A) Therefore, dictionaries are of little value to foreigners.
(B) Therefore, man cannot communicate effectively with animals.
(C) Therefore, communication is a matter of relation.
(D) Therefore, communication is simplest following a common experi-
     ence.
(E) Therefore, communication is dependent on complementary struc-
     tures.

7. In a nationwide survey, four out of five dentists questioned recommended
sugarless gum for their patients who chew gum.

Which of the following would most weaken the above endorsement for
sugarless gum?   Ⓐ Ⓑ Ⓒ Ⓓ Ⓔ
(A) Only five dentists were questioned.
(B) The dentists were not paid for their endorsements.
(C) Only one of the dentists questioned chewed sugarless gum.
(D) Patients do not do what their dentists tell them to do.
(E) Sugarless gum costs much more than regular gum.

8. In Tom and Angie's class, everyone likes drawing or painting or both, but
Angie does not like painting.

Which of the following statements MUST be true?   Ⓐ Ⓑ Ⓒ Ⓓ Ⓔ

   I.   Angie likes drawing.
  II. Tom likes drawing and painting.
  III. Everyone in the class who does not like drawing likes painting.
  IV. No one in the class likes painting.
(A) I and IV   (B) I and II   (C) II and III   (D) III and IV
(E) I and III

9. *Mark*: The big test is tomorrow and I didn't study. I suppose I'll just have to
cheat. I know it is wrong, but I have to get a good grade on the test.

Amy: I don't think that's a good idea. Just go to the teacher, tell the truth, and maybe you can get a postponement.

Amy attacks Mark's argument by   Ⓐ Ⓑ Ⓒ Ⓓ Ⓔ
(A) attacking his reasoning
(B) applying personal pressure
(C) implying that good triumphs over evil
(D) presenting another alternative
(E) suggesting a positive approach

Answers and Explanations

1. **C** The passage states that robots not only can build other robots, but also can rebuild themselves; therefore, they can last forever. (B) and (D) are probably true, but (C) *must* be true according to the passage. (A) and (E) are not implied anywhere in the passage.

2. **E** The author mentions nothing that shows he would agree with any of the statements. He mentions nothing of control, problems, or potential for independent thinking. He would probably disagree that robots have reached their peak of development.

3. **E** The author states that the robot can do the most complex group of activities, but "does not have the capacity to . . . think independently." If the most complex group of activities necessitate independent thinking, then the author's assertions are in *direct* contradiction. (C) would be a good choice if it mentioned independent thinking, not training, as training is not mentioned in the passage.

4. **C** The author must assume that you live only once and that there is no life after death, as he implies that you only get one chance in life, by stating ". . . you had better get it right the first time." II contradicts the implication of having to get it right the first time.

5. **E** I, II, and III are all implied meanings. Man as rational is free, could imply I. Man as rational, implies II. Man as free, is III.

6. **D** (A) and (B) are irrelevant, and (C) and (E) are not as effective as (D) because they are just restatements of the thought, rather than a clarification.

7. **A** The phrase "four out of five" implies 80% of a large sample (nationwide). If only five dentists were in the sample, the reliability would certainly be in question. (B) would strengthen the endorsement, while (D) and (E) are irrelevant. (C) could weaken it, but not nearly as much.

8. **E** I must be true by the first statement because everybody in the class likes drawing and painting or both, so if Angie does not like painting, she must like drawing. This same logic holds for III. Everyone in the class who does not like drawing, must like painting. II and IV could only possibly be true, as Tom could like both drawing and painting or either one, and it is possible that no one in the class likes painting.

9. **D** (A) is incorrect since there is no attack on Mark's reasoning. (B) is incorrect because personal pressure is not implied. (C) is incorrect since it is hearsay. (E) is incorrect, since who is to say what a "positive" approach is? (E) could have been the correct choice if (D) were not a possibility.

Chapter

6

Writing Sample

INTRODUCTION

The LSAT will include a 30-minute writing sample. You will be asked to respond to a general essay topic that requires no specialized knowledge, but does require you to write an argument for selecting one of two candidates or items based on given criteria. You should express yourself clearly and effectively.

The essay will *not* be scored, but will be forwarded to the law schools to which you apply. Different law schools have adopted different approaches to evaluating and weighing the quality of the essay.

You will write the essay in a "Writing Sample booklet," a paper folder with general directions on the outside, and the essay topic plus space for your response on the inside. A sheet of scratch paper is provided for organizing and/or outlining your ideas. A pen is also provided for the essay. The essay booklet restricts the length of your response to about *55 lines, each line 6 inches long.* Anything you write outside this restricted space will not be evaluated. Therefore, for practice purposes, restrict yourself to the same space that you will be given on the LSAT to become more comfortable with writing under these restricted conditions.

Following are general directions for the writing sample, a careful analysis of this new writing sample, and a series of steps you may want to follow as you compose your essay. You will examine two completed essays; each written from a different perspective.

GENERAL DIRECTIONS

You have 30 minutes to write an essay in response to a given topic. Take a few minutes to plan your work before you begin writing. DO NOT WRITE ON A TOPIC OF YOUR OWN CHOICE. ESSAYS THAT DO NOT ADDRESS THE GIVEN TOPIC ARE UNACCEPTABLE.

The quality of your writing is more important than the length of your response and content. There is no "right" or "wrong" answer to the question. Pay attention to organization, appropriate diction, and correct usage. You will not be expected to display any specialized knowledge in your response, nor will you be expected to write a "perfect" essay; law schools understand that you are writing under a time constraint and pressured circumstances.

Only the lined area in your booklet will be reproduced for the law schools, so do not write outside this space. *Do not* skip lines or use wide margins. These precautions, along with careful planning and legible handwriting that is not unduly large, will keep you within the allowed space.

ANALYSIS

Since the June, 1985 exam, the topic for the LSAT writing sample has had a new form. You are asked to write an argument for hiring, promoting, selecting, etc., one of two candidates or items based on two or more criteria and two brief sketches of the candidates or items. For example, the June, 1985, topic gave us its two criteria for hiring a mathematics teacher: (1) the high school's increased concern with computers and (2) its wish to develop the mathematics program at the school to incorporate work-study projects in the business community. The first candidate had a solid educational background, high-school teaching and minor administrative experience, good references, and recent training in computers. The second candidate had a slightly different but equally good educational background and no high-school teaching experience, but worked as a teaching assistant in college and a tutor in community programs, as well as solid credentials in computers and as an employee in financial work for a retail store and a bank.

What should be apparent is that it does *NOT* matter which candidate you choose. The principles and qualifications will be written in such a way that you can write in favor of *EITHER* candidate. Make your choice. Stick to it. Don't worry about the other candidate. What your readers will be looking for are clarity, consistency, relevance, and correctness of grammar and usage. Since you have only one-half hour to read the topic, plan, and write your essay, you will not be expected to write a long or a subtle essay. But you must write on the topic clearly and correctly.

The questions will make clear the sort of audience you are writing for and you can be sure that this audience is literate and informed about the issues in your paper. In the math teacher topic, for example, the assumed audience is whoever is to hire the math teacher. You do not need to tell this audience what he already knows, but you do want to make him focus upon the issues that support your case. Let us assume you are making the case for the experienced teacher with some computer training. Your essay should stress the obvious qualifications—her teaching experience and computer training. Where you have no direct evidence of expertise, you can invent, so long as you do so plausibly and work from details that are given in the question. You could, for example, argue that although there are two criteria, the computer issue is really the more important since the students will not be able to find good work-study projects in the community until they have a greater knowledge of computers.

Assume you have chosen the second candidate. Your essay should focus upon her strengths (for example, her experience in business will help her in setting up a business-related program for the students). Where her qualifications are weaker (her lack of high-school teaching experience), your essay can make something of the other kind of teaching experience she has had. Do not be afraid to introduce details to support your argument that are your own ideas. Just be sure that when you do present additional information, it is consistent with and arises plausibly from the information on the test.

So far, the writing topics have used two slightly different forms. The first (the math teachers) used two sentences, one for each of two equally weighted criteria, and then described the two equally qualified candidates. The sample topic in the LSAT Bulletin also uses two sentences to describe the principles, but the first contains two criteria, and the second sentence elaborates on one of them. For example, the two principles might be: (1) Lifeguards are promoted on the basis of years of service and community acitivities. (2) Community activities include lifesaving clinics, talks to school children, waterfront safety seminars, and high school swimming team coaching. The biographies would then describe two candidates whose years of service differ slightly, and each of whom has some strength in the areas listed under (2). Since you are not told which of the two criteria is the more important, nor which of the various sorts of community service is most important, you can decide for yourself how to weight them, so long as you do so plausibly. You cannot contradict the question—for example, by saying length of service is not important—but you can argue that, although your candidate's length of service is slightly less than that of his competition, his overwhelming superiority in community service is more important.

Here is a suggested plan for approaching any writing sample of this sort.

PHASE 1 — PREWRITING

1. Read the two statements of policy or criteria at least twice, *actively.* (Circle or mark the essential points of the topic.) Are they equally weighted? If not, clarify the difference.

2. Read the biographies or descriptions at least twice, *actively.* Test them; carefully against the policy or criteria statements.

3. Choose your candidate or item. Again set the qualifications or qualities beside those of the statements. Decide exactly what his or her greatest strengths are. What are the limitations? Think about how these limitations can be invalidated or turned into strengths.

4. Outline your essay. It should be two or three paragraphs long. If you are selecting a candidate, paragraph one might focus on the obvious strengths of the candidate that meet the given criteria. Paragraph two, or two and three, might deal with how he or she also shows promise of fulfilling the other requirements.

PHASE 2 — WRITING

1. Do *not* waste time with a fancy opening paragraph on an irrelevant topic like the importance of math teachers or lifeguards in this complex modern world.
2. Start with a direction. Your first sentence should serve a purpose.
3. Support your argument with examples or other specifics.
4. Do *not* write a closing paragraph which simply repeats what you have already said.
5. Write legibly. Write clearly. Write naturally. Do *not* use big words for their own sake. Do not try to be cute or ironic or funny.
6. Remember the assumed purpose of this paper is to convince a reader to prefer one candidate to another. Your real purpose, of course, is to show a law school that you can follow instructions and write an essay that is well organized, to the point, and grammatically correct.

PHASE 3 — READING

1. Allow sufficient time to proofread your essay. At this point, add any information that is vital, and delete any information that seems confusing or out of place.
2. Don't make extensive changes that will make your writing less readable.
3. Check each sentence for mechanical errors (spelling, punctuation, grammar). Some common types of errors are:
  A. using pronouns with no clear reference
  B. lack of agreement between subject and verb
  C. using the wrong verb tense
  D. faulty parallelism in a series of items
  E. misplaced or dangling modifiers
  F. adjective–adverb confusion
  G. misuse of comparative terms or comparisons

TWO COMPLETED WRITING SAMPLES

Following are two handwritten versions of the essay we have just discussed, written on LSAT Writing Sample booklet-type pages. Notice that these two sample "model" essays are each written from a different perspective.

These samples are written on the same topic given in the Diagnostic Mini-Exam on page 15.

WRITING SAMPLE

SAMPLE TOPIC:

Read the following descriptions of Bergquist and Kretchmer, applicants for the job of Assistant Director on a major motion picture. *Then, in the space provided, write an argument for hiring either Bergquist or Kretchmer.* The following criteria are relevant to your decision:

1. In addition to working closely with and advising the Director on creative decisions, the Assistant Director must work with all types of individuals—from stars to Teamster truck drivers—and elicit the best from every cast and crew member for the good of the motion picture.
2. The Assistant Director is responsible for all the planning and organization—including paperwork, travel itinerary, meals, etc.—of the entire film project. He/she lays the groundwork for a successful "shoot."

BERGQUIST began her career in films as an Administrative Assistant to the president of a major film studio. As such, she often accompanied her employer in his wining and dining of stars, or to the set when problems arose. She doublechecked contracts, shooting schedules, cast and crew checks, and kept a close eye on the budget of several multimillion-dollar films. When her boss was subsequently fired due to a poor season of films, Bergquist was able to secure a position as Assistant Editor at the studio, helping several highly respected film editors "cut" feature films. It was here that she learned about the creative end of the business, and soon after became the chief editor of an hour-long studio documentary, which won several awards. After two years, Bergquist was accepted into the Assistant Directors Training Program, and is presently a candidate for Assistant Director of this new $15,000,000 motion picture.

KRETCHMER was a principal/teacher for 12 years before embarking on a film career. Not only did she teach math at the New York School for the Creative Arts, but she worked with parents in the community, the board of education, and local government representatives in securing financing for the $20,000,000 school building. As Chairperson of the New Building Committee, she worked closely with architects, townspeople, contractors, and even children to understand their needs for the building. Today the building stands as a model for such schools everywhere. Eight years ago Kretchmer came to Hollywood and, through persistence and charm, secured a studio position and worked her way up to Chief Auditor, where she oversaw budgets on several multimillion-dollar films. She enrolled in the Assistant Directors Training Program, which she recently completed, and is now the other candidate being considered for the postion of Assistant Director of this new film.

As administrative assistant to the studio president, Bergquist obtained the essential grounding in the budgeting and paperwork aspects of motion pictures, a necessary part of the Assistant Director's tasks. However, Bergquist has more than the needed requirements. She has something special: an understanding of and experience in the creative elements of filmmaking.

An Assistant Director must advise the Director in many key creative decisions: who to cast in important supporting roles, how to best structure and order the shooting schedule (not only for the budget) but to enhance the actors' grasp of their roles, where to place the camera to best highlight an actor, a scene, or a mood. While the ultimate decision rests with the Director, the Assistant Director's input is vital. She is like the caddy advising a golfer of the distance and terrain of the course. Thus, her knowledge of the creative elements of filmmaking greatly enhances her ability in these tasks. Since the success of a film rests on these creative decisions of the Director, the Assistant Director's contributions in this regard can often make or break a film.

After learning the logistics of film-making, Bergquist became an assistant editor to many respected editors. She learned how a film is cut together, how the pieces must fit to make a smooth and consistent whole. With this creative knowledge, she later "cut" her own film and won several awards. Since an editor's creative contribution is a ~~was~~ major element in a film, these honors reflect her ability to understand and make essential creative choices.

This special knowledge of how a film ultimately fits together - how it is paced, how shots must match, how moods and shots build ~~your~~ upon each other - will significantly enhance Bergquist's ability to advise her Director. With her enlightened input into the all-important creative decisions, Bergquist can play a major role in insuring the final success of the film. If I were the Director, I would eagerly seek Bergquist as my Assistant Director.

Second Sample Essay

Though Bergquist may have adequate qualifications for the position of Assistant Director, Kretchmer is by far the more qualified of the two candidates. Not only thoroughly experienced in the day-to-day logistics and paperwork of motion-picture budgeting, she has what Bergquist seriously lacks — the experience and ability to work well with all kinds of people — a crucial skill in the collaborative art/business of filmmaking.

Any movie goer sitting through the final credits of a modern motion picture has to be impressed with the huge number of people contributing talent to the film effort. From lighting technicians to laborers to art designers to stunt people to musicians — literally hundreds of different artists and craftspeople work closely with the Director (and the Assistant Director) to produce a finished film. As the Director's right-hand person, the Assistant Director must help orchestrate that effort. She must know how to "read" the personality of each individual, how to appeal to each ego and drive, how to garner the best from each. A less-than-best effort from any "link in the chain" weakens the finished product.

During her term as Chairperson of the

New Building Committee, Kretchmer worked closely with dozens of different personalities in pursuit of a common goal, not unlike a film project. She carefully elicited the best input from taxpayers, architects, contractors, children—many individuals often at odds with each other—to successfully complete a $20,000,000 project. She settled arguments, mediated differences, and gently avoided impasses, any of which could have prevented the completion of the building. In working with such diverse personalities, Kretchmer had to have a keen understanding of other people's needs, desires and even short comings, and be able to work within those constraints. This is precisely her most important task as a motion picture Assistant Director.

In the great collaboration called film making, the day-in and day-out pressures of working closely on the set with hundreds of personalities requires a specially skilled individual. As her experience has shown, Kretchmer _is_ that special person.

REVIEW OF GENERAL TIPS

1. Read the topic question at least twice, *actively:* circle or mark the essential points of the question. Note the main question or parts to be discussed, the audience you are addressing, and the persona or position from which you are writing.

2. Remember to *prewrite,* or plan before you write. Spend at least five minutes organizing your thoughts by jotting notes, outlining, brainstorming, clustering, etc.

3. As you write, keep the flow of your writing going. Don't stop your train of thought to worry about the spelling of a word. You can fix little things later.

4. Leave a few minutes to reread and edit your paper after you finish writing. A careful reread will often catch careless mistakes and errors in punctuation, spelling, etc., that you didn't have time to worry about as you wrote.

5. Remember a good essay will be
- on-topic/
- well organized/
- well developed with examples/
- grammatically sound with few errors/
- interesting to read with a variety of sentence types/
- clear, neat, and easy to read.

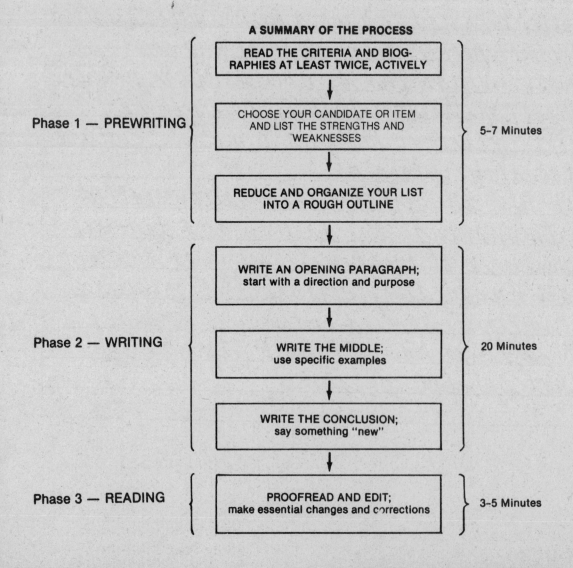

A SUMMARY OF THE PROCESS

Phase 1 — PREWRITING	READ THE CRITERIA AND BIOGRAPHIES AT LEAST TWICE, ACTIVELY
	CHOOSE YOUR CANDIDATE OR ITEM AND LIST THE STRENGTHS AND WEAKNESSES
	REDUCE AND ORGANIZE YOUR LIST INTO A ROUGH OUTLINE

5–7 Minutes

Phase 2 — WRITING
- WRITE AN OPENING PARAGRAPH; start with a direction and purpose
- WRITE THE MIDDLE; use specific examples
- WRITE THE CONCLUSION; say something "new"

20 Minutes

Phase 3 — READING
- PROOFREAD AND EDIT; make essential changes and corrections

3–5 Minutes

PRACTICE: WRITING SAMPLE

After reviewing the completed essays, try some practice on your own. We have provided sample questions and sample essay booklets. The first two topics are of the most recent format, with the remaining topics of the standard type.

Try following the steps we have suggested, varying them slightly, if necessary, to suit your personal style. Have an honest critic read and respond to each practice essay you complete.

WRITING SAMPLE TOPIC 1

Read the following description of Arbit and Blatas, candidates for your party's nomination to the city council. Write an argument for nominating either Arbit or Blatas. Use the information in this description and assume that two general policies guide your party's decisions on nomination:

    1. Nominations are based upon a combination of the probable success in the election and party service.

    2. Party service includes seniority, committee work, and fund-raising.

Arbit, a Rumanian-American, has lived in the district and worked for the party for fifteen years. He is chairman of two key party committees and a member of two others. His fund-raising picnic, begun ten years ago, now raises at least $10,000 every year. Arbit is 47, a trial lawyer, with no prior experience in elective office. Twenty percent of the district is Rumanian-American, almost all of whom support the party in every election.

Blatas, of Hungarian background, moved to the district seven years ago. She has worked for the party for seven years as a member of several party committees, and as Arbit's assistant in arranging the fund-raising picnic. A graduate of law school, she is 35, and was recently promoted to director of the city's real estate research office. She narrowly lost an election for city assessor two years ago. Thirty-five percent of the voters in the district are Hungarian-American.

WRITING SAMPLE TOPIC 2

Read the following descriptions of Arnot and Brecht, applicants for the position of head chef at *Chez Moi,* a highly successful New York restaurant. Write an argument for hiring either Arnot or Brecht. The following criteria are relevant to your decision:

1. The chef at *Chez Moi* must be able to socialize freely and to discuss each day's menu with the patrons.
2. *Chez Moi's* reputation depends upon the remarkable range and originality of its seafood and its desserts.

Chef ARNOT was born in Normandy and trained in Paris. For fifteen years he has been the head chef at major international restaurants in Paris and Marseilles. While in Paris, he won competition among the city's pastry chefs four times. In Marseilles, his speciality was Mediterranean seafood. He is among the most respected chefs in the world, known equally for his inventive recipes for fish and his short temper. His English is competent, but slow and heavily accented. He has, for the first time, agreed to accept a position outside of France.

Chef BRECHT was born in Berlin and trained in Paris, London, and Rome. For the last five years, she has been the head chef in one of Chicago's most successful restaurants. Through her books and her television cooking programs, she has become the most widely known and most popular chef in America. She is especially renowned for her recipes for ice creams and sherbets. She has agreed to apply for the position at *Chez Moi* because of the restaurant's reputation and because it is located in New York, a center of the publishing and television industries.

SAMPLE TOPIC: It has recently been argued that, despite this nation's growing need for cheap sources of energy, the disastrous consequences of an accident involving nuclear power should convince the government to pursue other, less dangerous types of energy. Solar energy and wind energy are among the alternatives suggested in lieu of developing more nuclear power plants. Proponents of nuclear power, however, maintain that the possibility of accidents should not stop the development of this very valuable and available source of energy. Imagine that a nuclear power plant is about to be proposed for construction on the edge of your community. A town hall meeting has been called so that citizens may address the issue and present their views. This meeting is very important, as the citizens of your community will vote and decide whether construction will, in fact, take place. In the space provided, express and support your position as you would in addressing your fellow citizens.

SAMPLE TOPIC: It has recently been argued that the government should pursue a course of action. Write an essay in which you develop a position on whether the government should pursue a course of action. Some people believe the government should pursue a nuclear power plant. Proponents of nuclear power argue that the possibility of a major accident at a nuclear power plant is too remote to warrant concern. Opponents argue that should pursue their plans.

Use the space provided to enter your response to the question.

WRITING SAMPLE TOPIC 4

SAMPLE TOPIC: As state-supported universities begin to feel the effects of inflation, many are asking students who are state residents to pay tuition, just as out-of-state students do. Local students, for whom a college education was relatively free, are now complaining that even minimal tuition is an unfair burden. Write an article for the college newspaper in which you develop an argument for or against tuition for all state university students.

WRITING SAMPLE TOPIC 5

SAMPLE TOPIC: Faced with budget cuts, your local high school has decided to eliminate competitive sports from its curriculum. The school officials argue that competitive sports have always fostered unhealthy aggression in team members, and they welcome ideas for inexpensive recreational activities in which there are no winners or losers. Write a letter to the school officials responding to their position.

WRITING SAMPLE TOPIC 6

SAMPLE TOPIC: Imagine that your application to law school has been rejected, and that the law school's only criterion was your LSAT score. Compose a letter to the law school explaining strengths of yours that are relevant to success in law school, strengths that are *not* measured by the LSAT.

SAMPLE TOPIC: A major university has recently announced that, in order to graduate, students must now fulfill certain "Living Skills Requirements" before they will be issued their diplomas. These "Living Skills Requirements" (LSRs) include knowing not only basic auto mechanics, plumbing, electrical skills, sewing, nutrition, and first aid, but also how to swim and stay afloat. The president of the university endorses the new LSR curriculum, stating that too many graduates know only how to read and write, and little else. She hopes the new requirements and courses will better prepare students for life after graduation. Imagine that you are an alumna or alumnus of this university and have just been asked to make a financial contribution which would help support the LSR program. In addition to asking your financial help, the university has invited you to write a letter to fellow graduates expressing your personal views on this unique curriculum requirement. Your letter will appear in the *Alumni Weekly Magazine* which is read by thousands of university graduates. In the space below, write your letter, either supporting or opposing the new requirement.

PART THREE

PRACTICE
Mastering Time Pressures
and Problem Types

7

Model Test One

This chapter contains full-length Model Test One. It is geared to the format of the LSAT and it is complete with answers and explanations. It is equivalent to the LSAT in question structure, number of questions, level of difficulty, and time allotments. (The questions used are not taken directly from the LSAT, as those questions are copyrighted and may not be reproduced.)

Model Test One should be taken under strict test conditions. The test begins with a 30-minute Writing Sample which is not scored. Thereafter each section is 35 minutes in length.

Section	Description	Number of Questions	Time Allowed
	Writing Sample		30 minutes
I	Reading Comprehension	30	35 minutes
II	Analytical Reasoning	25	35 minutes
III	Evaluation of Facts	35	35 minutes
IV	Logical Reasoning	26	35 minutes
V	Reading Comprehension	28	35 minutes
VI	Analytical Reasoning	26	35 minutes
TOTALS:		170	240 minutes

Now please turn to the next page, remove your answer sheets, and begin Model Test One.

ANSWER SHEET—MODEL TEST ONE
LAW SCHOOL ADMISSION TEST (LSAT)

Section I:
Reading Comprehension

1. Ⓐ Ⓑ Ⓒ Ⓓ Ⓔ
2. Ⓐ Ⓑ Ⓒ Ⓓ Ⓔ
3. Ⓐ Ⓑ Ⓒ Ⓓ Ⓔ
4. Ⓐ Ⓑ Ⓒ Ⓓ Ⓔ
5. Ⓐ Ⓑ Ⓒ Ⓓ Ⓔ
6. Ⓐ Ⓑ Ⓒ Ⓓ Ⓔ
7. Ⓐ Ⓑ Ⓒ Ⓓ Ⓔ
8. Ⓐ Ⓑ Ⓒ Ⓓ Ⓔ
9. Ⓐ Ⓑ Ⓒ Ⓓ Ⓔ
10. Ⓐ Ⓑ Ⓒ Ⓓ Ⓔ
11. Ⓐ Ⓑ Ⓒ Ⓓ Ⓔ
12. Ⓐ Ⓑ Ⓒ Ⓓ Ⓔ
13. Ⓐ Ⓑ Ⓒ Ⓓ Ⓔ
14. Ⓐ Ⓑ Ⓒ Ⓓ Ⓔ
15. Ⓐ Ⓑ Ⓒ Ⓓ Ⓔ
16. Ⓐ Ⓑ Ⓒ Ⓓ Ⓔ
17. Ⓐ Ⓑ Ⓒ Ⓓ Ⓔ
18. Ⓐ Ⓑ Ⓒ Ⓓ Ⓔ
19. Ⓐ Ⓑ Ⓒ Ⓓ Ⓔ
20. Ⓐ Ⓑ Ⓒ Ⓓ Ⓔ
21. Ⓐ Ⓑ Ⓒ Ⓓ Ⓔ
22. Ⓐ Ⓑ Ⓒ Ⓓ Ⓔ
23. Ⓐ Ⓑ Ⓒ Ⓓ Ⓔ
24. Ⓐ Ⓑ Ⓒ Ⓓ Ⓔ
25. Ⓐ Ⓑ Ⓒ Ⓓ Ⓔ
26. Ⓐ Ⓑ Ⓒ Ⓓ Ⓔ
27. Ⓐ Ⓑ Ⓒ Ⓓ Ⓔ
28. Ⓐ Ⓑ Ⓒ Ⓓ Ⓔ
29. Ⓐ Ⓑ Ⓒ Ⓓ Ⓔ
30. Ⓐ Ⓑ Ⓒ Ⓓ Ⓔ

Section II:
Analytical Reasoning

1. Ⓐ Ⓑ Ⓒ Ⓓ Ⓔ
2. Ⓐ Ⓑ Ⓒ Ⓓ Ⓔ
3. Ⓐ Ⓑ Ⓒ Ⓓ Ⓔ
4. Ⓐ Ⓑ Ⓒ Ⓓ Ⓔ
5. Ⓐ Ⓑ Ⓒ Ⓓ Ⓔ
6. Ⓐ Ⓑ Ⓒ Ⓓ Ⓔ
7. Ⓐ Ⓑ Ⓒ Ⓓ Ⓔ
8. Ⓐ Ⓑ Ⓒ Ⓓ Ⓔ
9. Ⓐ Ⓑ Ⓒ Ⓓ Ⓔ
10. Ⓐ Ⓑ Ⓒ Ⓓ Ⓔ
11. Ⓐ Ⓑ Ⓒ Ⓓ Ⓔ
12. Ⓐ Ⓑ Ⓒ Ⓓ Ⓔ
13. Ⓐ Ⓑ Ⓒ Ⓓ Ⓔ
14. Ⓐ Ⓑ Ⓒ Ⓓ Ⓔ
15. Ⓐ Ⓑ Ⓒ Ⓓ Ⓔ
16. Ⓐ Ⓑ Ⓒ Ⓓ Ⓔ
17. Ⓐ Ⓑ Ⓒ Ⓓ Ⓔ
18. Ⓐ Ⓑ Ⓒ Ⓓ Ⓔ
19. Ⓐ Ⓑ Ⓒ Ⓓ Ⓔ
20. Ⓐ Ⓑ Ⓒ Ⓓ Ⓔ
21. Ⓐ Ⓑ Ⓒ Ⓓ Ⓔ
22. Ⓐ Ⓑ Ⓒ Ⓓ Ⓔ
23. Ⓐ Ⓑ Ⓒ Ⓓ Ⓔ
24. Ⓐ Ⓑ Ⓒ Ⓓ Ⓔ
25. Ⓐ Ⓑ Ⓒ Ⓓ Ⓔ

Section III:
Evaluation of Facts

1. Ⓐ Ⓑ Ⓒ Ⓓ
2. Ⓐ Ⓑ Ⓒ Ⓓ
3. Ⓐ Ⓑ Ⓒ Ⓓ
4. Ⓐ Ⓑ Ⓒ Ⓓ
5. Ⓐ Ⓑ Ⓒ Ⓓ
6. Ⓐ Ⓑ Ⓒ Ⓓ
7. Ⓐ Ⓑ Ⓒ Ⓓ
8. Ⓐ Ⓑ Ⓒ Ⓓ
9. Ⓐ Ⓑ Ⓒ Ⓓ
10. Ⓐ Ⓑ Ⓒ Ⓓ
11. Ⓐ Ⓑ Ⓒ Ⓓ
12. Ⓐ Ⓑ Ⓒ Ⓓ
13. Ⓐ Ⓑ Ⓒ Ⓓ
14. Ⓐ Ⓑ Ⓒ Ⓓ
15. Ⓐ Ⓑ Ⓒ Ⓓ
16. Ⓐ Ⓑ Ⓒ Ⓓ
17. Ⓐ Ⓑ Ⓒ Ⓓ
18. Ⓐ Ⓑ Ⓒ Ⓓ
19. Ⓐ Ⓑ Ⓒ Ⓓ
20. Ⓐ Ⓑ Ⓒ Ⓓ
21. Ⓐ Ⓑ Ⓒ Ⓓ
22. Ⓐ Ⓑ Ⓒ Ⓓ
23. Ⓐ Ⓑ Ⓒ Ⓓ
24. Ⓐ Ⓑ Ⓒ Ⓓ
25. Ⓐ Ⓑ Ⓒ Ⓓ
26. Ⓐ Ⓑ Ⓒ Ⓓ
27. Ⓐ Ⓑ Ⓒ Ⓓ
28. Ⓐ Ⓑ Ⓒ Ⓓ
29. Ⓐ Ⓑ Ⓒ Ⓓ
30. Ⓐ Ⓑ Ⓒ Ⓓ
31. Ⓐ Ⓑ Ⓒ Ⓓ
32. Ⓐ Ⓑ Ⓒ Ⓓ
33. Ⓐ Ⓑ Ⓒ Ⓓ
34. Ⓐ Ⓑ Ⓒ Ⓓ
35. Ⓐ Ⓑ Ⓒ Ⓓ

ANSWER SHEET—MODEL TEST ONE
LAW SCHOOL ADMISSION TEST (LSAT)

Section IV:
Logical Reasoning

1. Ⓐ Ⓑ Ⓒ Ⓓ Ⓔ
2. Ⓐ Ⓑ Ⓒ Ⓓ Ⓔ
3. Ⓐ Ⓑ Ⓒ Ⓓ Ⓔ
4. Ⓐ Ⓑ Ⓒ Ⓓ Ⓔ
5. Ⓐ Ⓑ Ⓒ Ⓓ Ⓔ
6. Ⓐ Ⓑ Ⓒ Ⓓ Ⓔ
7. Ⓐ Ⓑ Ⓒ Ⓓ Ⓔ
8. Ⓐ Ⓑ Ⓒ Ⓓ Ⓔ
9. Ⓐ Ⓑ Ⓒ Ⓓ Ⓔ
10. Ⓐ Ⓑ Ⓒ Ⓓ Ⓔ
11. Ⓐ Ⓑ Ⓒ Ⓓ Ⓔ
12. Ⓐ Ⓑ Ⓒ Ⓓ Ⓔ
13. Ⓐ Ⓑ Ⓒ Ⓓ Ⓔ
14. Ⓐ Ⓑ Ⓒ Ⓓ Ⓔ
15. Ⓐ Ⓑ Ⓒ Ⓓ Ⓔ
16. Ⓐ Ⓑ Ⓒ Ⓓ Ⓔ
17. Ⓐ Ⓑ Ⓒ Ⓓ Ⓔ
18. Ⓐ Ⓑ Ⓒ Ⓓ Ⓔ
19. Ⓐ Ⓑ Ⓒ Ⓓ Ⓔ
20. Ⓐ Ⓑ Ⓒ Ⓓ Ⓔ
21. Ⓐ Ⓑ Ⓒ Ⓓ Ⓔ
22. Ⓐ Ⓑ Ⓒ Ⓓ Ⓔ
23. Ⓐ Ⓑ Ⓒ Ⓓ Ⓔ
24. Ⓐ Ⓑ Ⓒ Ⓓ Ⓔ
25. Ⓐ Ⓑ Ⓒ Ⓓ Ⓔ
26. Ⓐ Ⓑ Ⓒ Ⓓ Ⓔ

Section V:
Reading Comprehension

1. Ⓐ Ⓑ Ⓒ Ⓓ Ⓔ
2. Ⓐ Ⓑ Ⓒ Ⓓ Ⓔ
3. Ⓐ Ⓑ Ⓒ Ⓓ Ⓔ
4. Ⓐ Ⓑ Ⓒ Ⓓ Ⓔ
5. Ⓐ Ⓑ Ⓒ Ⓓ Ⓔ
6. Ⓐ Ⓑ Ⓒ Ⓓ Ⓔ
7. Ⓐ Ⓑ Ⓒ Ⓓ Ⓔ
8. Ⓐ Ⓑ Ⓒ Ⓓ Ⓔ
9. Ⓐ Ⓑ Ⓒ Ⓓ Ⓔ
10. Ⓐ Ⓑ Ⓒ Ⓓ Ⓔ
11. Ⓐ Ⓑ Ⓒ Ⓓ Ⓔ
12. Ⓐ Ⓑ Ⓒ Ⓓ Ⓔ
13. Ⓐ Ⓑ Ⓒ Ⓓ Ⓔ
14. Ⓐ Ⓑ Ⓒ Ⓓ Ⓔ
15. Ⓐ Ⓑ Ⓒ Ⓓ Ⓔ
16. Ⓐ Ⓑ Ⓒ Ⓓ Ⓔ
17. Ⓐ Ⓑ Ⓒ Ⓓ Ⓔ
18. Ⓐ Ⓑ Ⓒ Ⓓ Ⓔ
19. Ⓐ Ⓑ Ⓒ Ⓓ Ⓔ
20. Ⓐ Ⓑ Ⓒ Ⓓ Ⓔ
21. Ⓐ Ⓑ Ⓒ Ⓓ Ⓔ
22. Ⓐ Ⓑ Ⓒ Ⓓ Ⓔ
23. Ⓐ Ⓑ Ⓒ Ⓓ Ⓔ
24. Ⓐ Ⓑ Ⓒ Ⓓ Ⓔ
25. Ⓐ Ⓑ Ⓒ Ⓓ Ⓔ
26. Ⓐ Ⓑ Ⓒ Ⓓ Ⓔ
27. Ⓐ Ⓑ Ⓒ Ⓓ Ⓔ
28. Ⓐ Ⓑ Ⓒ Ⓓ Ⓔ

Section VI:
Analytical Reasoning

1. Ⓐ Ⓑ Ⓒ Ⓓ Ⓔ
2. Ⓐ Ⓑ Ⓒ Ⓓ Ⓔ
3. Ⓐ Ⓑ Ⓒ Ⓓ Ⓔ
4. Ⓐ Ⓑ Ⓒ Ⓓ Ⓔ
5. Ⓐ Ⓑ Ⓒ Ⓓ Ⓔ
6. Ⓐ Ⓑ Ⓒ Ⓓ Ⓔ
7. Ⓐ Ⓑ Ⓒ Ⓓ Ⓔ
8. Ⓐ Ⓑ Ⓒ Ⓓ Ⓔ
9. Ⓐ Ⓑ Ⓒ Ⓓ Ⓔ
10. Ⓐ Ⓑ Ⓒ Ⓓ Ⓔ
11. Ⓐ Ⓑ Ⓒ Ⓓ Ⓔ
12. Ⓐ Ⓑ Ⓒ Ⓓ Ⓔ
13. Ⓐ Ⓑ Ⓒ Ⓓ Ⓔ
14. Ⓐ Ⓑ Ⓒ Ⓓ Ⓔ
15. Ⓐ Ⓑ Ⓒ Ⓓ Ⓔ
16. Ⓐ Ⓑ Ⓒ Ⓓ Ⓔ
17. Ⓐ Ⓑ Ⓒ Ⓓ Ⓔ
18. Ⓐ Ⓑ Ⓒ Ⓓ Ⓔ
19. Ⓐ Ⓑ Ⓒ Ⓓ Ⓔ
20. Ⓐ Ⓑ Ⓒ Ⓓ Ⓔ
21. Ⓐ Ⓑ Ⓒ Ⓓ Ⓔ
22. Ⓐ Ⓑ Ⓒ Ⓓ Ⓔ
23. Ⓐ Ⓑ Ⓒ Ⓓ Ⓔ
24. Ⓐ Ⓑ Ⓒ Ⓓ Ⓔ
25. Ⓐ Ⓑ Ⓒ Ⓓ Ⓔ
26. Ⓐ Ⓑ Ⓒ Ⓓ Ⓔ

EXAMINATION

WRITING SAMPLE

Time—30 Minutes

Directions:

You have 30 minutes to write an essay in response to a given topic. Take a few minutes to plan your work before you begin writing. DO NOT WRITE ON A TOPIC OF YOUR OWN CHOICE. ESSAYS THAT DO NOT ADDRESS THE GIVEN TOPIC ARE UNACCEPTABLE.

The quality of your writing is more important than the length of your response or the content. Pay attention to organization, appropriate diction, and correct usage. You will not be expected to display any specialized knowledge in your response, nor will you be expected to write a "perfect" essay; law schools understand that you are writing under a time constraint, and will allow for the minor lapses in writing ability that might occur under this circumstance.

Only the lined area in your booklet will be reproduced for the law schools, so do not write outside this space. *Do not* skip lines or use wide margins. These precautions, along with careful planning and legible handwriting that is not unduly large, will keep you within the allowed space.

SAMPLE TOPIC

Read the following descriptions of Jackson and Brown. *Then, in the space provided, write an argument for deciding which of the two should be assigned the responsibility of hiring teachers for the Hapsville School System.* The following criteria are relevant to your decision:

1. The tax payers want educators who can instill in students the desire to learn and an excitement for knowledge, something that has been lacking in their schools.
2. A majority of students' parents believe that their children should be equipped, upon graduation, to earn a living, and thus favor a more trade-oriented (rather than academic) approach to schooling.

JACKSON was appointed as Superintendent of Schools by the Hapsville School Board, which was elected by the community's taxpayers. As a 30-year resident of Hapsville (population 45,000), Jackson is unique in that he not only holds a doctorate in administration, but also a master's degree in education. He taught in the Hapsville schools for 16 years until he served on the state Commission on Education. He has always favored a progressive approach to education, although it may not always have been popular with the town's population. Through the years he has brought many fine teachers to the faculty, because of his willingness to encourage new classroom techniques.

BROWN is a 52-year resident of Hapsville, having been born in the same house in which he now lives. He was elected to the School Board 13 years ago, and continues to win nearly unanimous reelection every two years. As the foremost developer in the Four Counties area, Mr. Brown has had the opportunity to build hundreds of new homes in the six housing developments he's planned and actualized, and, in the interim, has employed hundreds of Hapsville residents as carpenters, electricians, plumbers, architects, landscapers, groundskeepers, etc. As such, he is held in high esteem by most of the town, not only for his providing livelihoods for many, but also for his fair and realistic outlook on life, Mr. Brown feels strongly that the key to life is having a marketable skill.

SECTION I
READING COMPREHENSION

Time—35 Minutes
30 Questions

Directions:
Read the passages and answer the questions following each passage by blackening the appropriate space on the answer sheet. You may refer back to the passages when answering the questions. Answer all questions on the basis of what is stated or implied.

Passage 1

Although different plants have varying environmental requirements because of physiological differences, there are certain plant species that are found associated with relatively extensive geographical areas. The distribution of plants depends upon a number of factors among which are (1) length of daylight and darkness, (2) temperature means and extremes, (3) length of growing season, and (4) precipitation amounts, types, and distribution.

Daylight and darkness are the keys by which a plant regulates its cycle. It is not always obvious how the triggering factor works, but experiments have shown day length to be a key. A case in point is that many greenhouse plants bloom only in the spring without being influenced by outside conditions other than light. Normally, the plants keyed to daylight and darkness phenomena are restricted to particular latitudes.

In one way or another, every plant is affected by temperature. Some species are killed by frost; others require frost and cold conditions to fruit. Orange blossoms are killed by frost, but cherry blossoms will develop only if the buds have been adequately chilled for an appropriate time. Often the accumulation of degrees or the direction of temperatures above or below a specific figure critically affects plants. Plant distributions are often compared with isotherms to suggest the temperature limits and ranges for different species. The world's great vegetation zones are closely aligned with temperature belts.

Different plant species adjust to seasonal changes in different ways. Some make the adjustment by retarding growth and arresting vital functions during winter. This may result in the leaf fall of middle latitude deciduous trees. Other plants disappear entirely at the end of the growing season and only reappear through their seeds. These are the *annuals*, and they form a striking contrast to the *perennials*, which live from one season to another.

Precipitation supplies the necessary soil water for plants, which take it in at the roots. All plants have some limiting moisture stress level beyond which they must become inactive or die. Drought-resistant plants have a variety of defenses against moisture deficiencies, but *hygrophytes*, which also are adapted to humid environments, have hardly any defense against a water shortage.

1. According to the passage, the temperature belts aligned with the world's great vegetation zones may be characterized by
   (A) extreme frost
   (B) either frost or warmth
   (C) extreme cold, but not frost
   (D) the accumulation of degrees
   (E) directed temperatures

2. From this passage we must conclude that a long drought striking a humid environment must inevitably
   (A) render most plants inactive
   (B) result in legislation aimed at building new canals
   (C) reduce or extinguish the hygrophytes

(D) affect the plant's responses to daylight and darkness
(E) produce a corresponding change in drainage conditions

3. The passage implies that plants affected by length of day are normally located
   (A) in random locations
   (B) in regions where nights are longer
   (C) in regions where days are longer
   (D) in certain regions east or west of the prime meridian
   (E) in certain regions north or south of the equator

4. The behavior of annuals may be compared to
   (A) senility   (B) eternal life   (C) reincarnation   (D) exfoliation   (E) hibernation

5. According to the passage, the phrase "distribution of plants" (paragraph 1) refers to
   (A) factors too numerous to be listed in this brief passage
   (B) the marketing of plants in areas conducive to further germination and reproduction
   (C) the varieties of size, shape, and color among plants
   (D) the locations in which plants grow and thrive
   (E) certain species only

6. As the author discusses each of the factors affecting the distribution of plants, the overall implication that he does not stress is that
   (A) each of the factors produces notable effects
   (B) no one of these factors operates independently of the others
   (C) soil conditions have one of the most pronounced effects upon plant life
   (D) environmental factors either promote or retard growth
   (E) isotherms affect every factor surveyed

Passage 2

More than two thousand years ago, Aristotle utilized two major criteria in classifying governments. One was the *number of persons* in which governing authority is vested; the other, the *primary purpose* toward which the exercise of governmental powers is directed.

In terms of the first criterion Aristotle distinguished three forms of government, viz., government by the one, by the few, and by the many. The second basis of classification, i.e, purpose, led him to differentiate "true" from "perverted" forms. True forms of government are characterized by the exercise of governmental authority for the benefit of all members of the body politic, whereas *perverted* types are featured by the use of governing power to promote the special and selfish interests of the ruling personnel. Government by the one for the benefit of all is *kingship* or *royalty;* government by the one for his private advantage is *tyranny*. Government by the few, if conducted for the purpose of promoting the common welfare, constitutes *aristocracy*. If the few rule in furtherance of their own selfish interests, the government is an *oligarchy*. The dominant few are likely to be men of property interested in increasing their wealth. Finally, government by the many (the citizens at large) for the benefit of all was identified as *polity* or *constitutional government*, whereas government by the many, usually the poor or the needy, for the purpose of promoting their selfish interests, was named *democracy*, a perverted form of government.

Unlike Aristotle, contemporary political scientists usually classify forms of government without introducing a test of purpose or motivation with respect to the use of governmental powers. Definitions of democracy, for instance, seldom include stipulations concerning the objectives to be attained by a government of the democratic type. However, an underlying assumption, even though unstated, seems to be that democratic processes of government probably will result in promotion of the common welfare.

Aristotle conceived of government by the many, whether of the true or perverted variety, as involving direct action by the body of qualified citizens in the formulation and adoption of policies. Hamilton and Madison, in their comments about democracy in the Federalist Papers, revealed a like conception of the nature of democracy. Thus Madison distinguished between a republic (representative government) and pure democracy. In his words a pure democracy is "a society consisting of a small number of citizens, who assemble and administer the government in person." A distinction is still drawn between direct and indirect democracy, but emphasis now is placed on the latter form, that is, democracy of the representative variety. Although direct democracy survives in a few small communities, e.g., New England towns and some of the cantons of Switzerland, representative democracy prevails in communities of large size. Consequently, the term *democracy* as used today almost always signifies a democratic government of the indirect or representative type.

7. According to the author's understanding of Aristotle, democracy is a "perverted" form of government because
   (A) the poor comprise a special interest group
   (B) the needs of the poor are sought through perverted behavior
   (C) the poor comprise a larger group than the citizens at large
   (D) the needs of the poor are less pure than those of other groups
   (E) excessive poverty is the prelude to tyranny

8. In his discussion of pure democracy, the author is not explicit about
   (A) Madison's conception of pure democracy
   (B) the typical modern definition of democracy
   (C) why pure democracy on a large scale is unwieldy
   (D) the distinction between direct and indirect democracy
   (E) why the views of Hamilton and Madison are similar to those of Aristotle

9. The author's primary purpose in this passage is
   (A) to compare American and Greek philosophies
   (B) to judge the relative worth of various forms of government
   (C) to discuss the relationship of Aristotle's conception to later theory and practice
   (D) to praise the foresight of Aristotle
   (E) to develop an absolute definition of democracy

10. The author says that a modern democracy would regard the promotion of the common welfare as
   (A) a partial result
   (B) a probable result
   (C) a certain result
   (D) a questionable result
   (E) a unique result

11. The author seems to presume that Aristotle
   (A) would have supported the American Revolution
   (B) utilized more than two major criteria in classifying governments
   (C) is the one figure from antiquity whose political analyses are especially relevant to a discussion of modern government
   (D) was studied by Hamilton and Madison
   (E) was a philosopher who scarcely recognized the human potential for democratic government

12. The author's reliance on conceptions of government which are many centuries old suggests his belief that
   (A) governments since antiquity have been obeying Aristotle's classification scheme
   (B) conceptions of government change little through the ages
   (C) political scientists have no need for new definitions
   (D) later political theorists had read Aristotle before formulating their theories
   (E) ancient definitions of government are analogous but not identical to current conceptions

Passage 3

From this day natural philosophy, and particularly chemistry, in the most comprehensive sense of the word, became nearly my sole occupation. I read with ardour those works so full of genius and discrimination, which modern enquirers have written on these subjects. I attended the lectures, and cultivated the acquaintance of the men of science at the university.

My application was at first fluctuating and uncertain; it gained strength as I proceeded, and soon became so ardent and eager, that the stars often disappeared in the light of morning whilst I was yet engaged in my laboratory. As I applied so closely, it may be easily conceived that my progress was rapid.

. . . One of the phenomena which had peculiarly attracted my attention was the structure of the human frame, and, indeed, any animal endued with life. Whence, I often asked myself, did the principle of life proceed? It was a bold question, and one which has ever been considered as a mystery; yet with how many things are we on the brink of becoming acquainted, if cowardice or carelessness did not restrain our enquiries. I revolved these circumstances in my mind, and determined thenceforth to apply myself more particularly to those branches of natural philosophy which relate to physiology. Unless I had been animated by an almost supernatural enthusiasm, my application to this study would have been irksome, and almost intolerable. To examine the causes of life, we must observe the natural decay and corruption of the human body. In my education my father had taken the greatest precautions that my mind should be impressed with no supernatural horrors. I do not ever remember to have trembled at a tale of superstition, or to have feared the apparition of a spirit. Darkness had no effect upon my fancy; and a churchyard was to me merely the receptacle of bodies deprived of life, which, from being the seat of beauty and strength, had become food for the worm. Now I was led to examine the cause and progress of this decay, and forced to spend days and nights in vaults and charnel houses. My attention was fixed upon every object the most insupportable to the delicacy of the human feelings. I saw how the fine form of man was degraded and wasted; I beheld the corruption of death succeed to the blooming cheek of life; I saw how the worm inherited the wonders of the eye and brain. I paused, examining and analyzing all the minutiae of causation, as exemplified in the change from life to death, and death to life, until from the midst of this darkness a sudden light broke in upon me—a light so brilliant and wondrous, yet so simple, that while I became dizzy with the immensity of the prospect which it illustrated, I was surprised, that among so many men of genius who had directed their enquiries towards the same science, I alone should be reserved to discover so astonishing a secret.

13. The statement "I saw how the worm inherited the wonders of the eye and brain" is a figurative expression of which of the following literal statements?
    (A) I watched a despicable relative inherit wonderful things.
    (B) I saw worms become more clear-sighted and intelligent.
    (C) I saw men humiliated and executed.
    (D) I studied the organs of sight and intellect in corpses.
    (E) I saw the ways in which death caused blindness and mental illness.

14. We may infer that the two academic subjects which contributed most to the narrator's final discovery were
    (A) natural philosophy and the occult
    (B) chemistry and physiology
    (C) life and death
    (D) courage and care
    (E) psychology and religion

15. From the preceding details, we may conclude that the astonishing discovery which the narrator makes is related to
    (A) his sensitivity to human feelings
    (B) contact with the spirit world

(C) overcoming his fear of superstition
(D) the principle of life
(E) beauty and strength

16. The passage is written in the style of a
(A) scientific treatise   (B) personal journal   (C) soliloquy   (D) confession
(E) drama

17. By stressing that he does not acknowledge or fear "supernatural horrors" the narrator implies that he practices
(A) obedience to his father
(B) a systematic devotion to the occult
(C) the analysis of nocturnal phenomena
(D) scientific objectivity
(E) natural philosophy

18. In the second paragraph, the narrator is using "application" to mean
(A) experiments that affect the stars themselves
(B) attendance at lectures
(C) study of chemistry
(D) insomnia
(E) checklist of chemical reactions

Passage 4

The nomads who inhabit the deserts of the Middle East make up about five percent of the people of the area. They are known as *bedouins* and they live in tribes. Their time is spent moving through the desert in search of water and grass for their herds of sheep, goats, and camels.

Because he is always on the move, the nomad has few goods besides his cooking pots, his loose flowing clothes, his rugs, and his blankets. He lives in a tent and sleeps and eats on rugs. The men and boys live in one half of the tent, and the women and girls live in the other half.

The animals provide the nomad with most of his needs. Goat's milk and cheese are his main foods. He rarely eats meat. His blankets, his tent, and most of his clothes are woven from the hair of goats and camels. Leather from the hides of the animals is used to make baskets and sandals.

Whatever his animals do not supply, the nomad buys when he reaches an *oasis*. (An oasis is a place in the desert where there is water and vegetation. The water comes from underground streams.) In this way the nomads are dependent on the farms and cities that lie beyond the desert. Part of the nomad's diet consists of flour, dates, and fruits that come from the farms and groves. From the towns and cities he obtains his utensils, cloth, coffee, tea, and sugar. The bedouins in turn provide the farmers and city people with animals and animal products.

Duties and responsibilities among the bedouins have always been divided according to sex. It is the man's duty to fight and look after the camels, while the woman takes care of the other animals, the household, and the children, and sees to it that the family has enough water.

The bedouins are very proud individuals who believe in equality and do not like to be ruled by other people. Nevertheless, the family, clan, and tribe (which is composed of clans) claim the loyalty of individual members.

Since humans are so helpless in the desert, there is complete dependence of man upon other men. Generosity is an important quality among bedouins. A guest is treated as well as or better than one's own family. No bedouin may refuse another man protection from an enemy. He must admit the pursued man to his tent and offer him food and a place to sleep for three days, even though he is a stranger. The enemy cannot attack the person during the time that he is being sheltered in someone's tent.

In the past, the herders of the desert were the rulers of the Middle East. They crossed and recrossed borders as they pleased. They were able to attack the village swiftly on their horses and camels. The bedouins policed the desert and protected the caravans that crossed it. Today, as a result of changes in transportation and communication, the bedouins have come under the control of the governments in the cities. As a result, their whole way of life has changed. Thousands have left the desert to take jobs in the oil industry—especially in Iraq and Saudi Arabia. Others have become soldiers. Large numbers have settled down on the oases and in the cities. Many of the tribal chiefs are now rich landowners. Those living on land where oil has been discovered have adopted a way of life that is totally different from that of their fellow bedouins in the desert.

19. Just as "duties and responsibilities among the bedouins have always been divided according to sex" (paragraph 5), so have (has)
(A) weapons   (B) water   (C) food   (D) living space   (E) sleeping space

20. The tendency of nomads to protect visitors may be compared to the Medieval European practice of
(A) Catholicism   (B) sanctuary   (C) treachery   (D) barter   (E) agrarian reform

21. We may infer that ninety-five percent of the Middle East populace
(A) is not dependent upon an oasis
(B) disdains life in tents
(C) does not live in tribes
(D) has established nonmobile residences
(E) opposes the practice of the nomads

22. We may infer that the total number of bedouin clans in the Middle East
(A) is larger than the number of tribes
(B) is equal to the number of families
(C) is more significant than the number of tribes
(D) is proportional to the number of tribes
(E) includes families that are not members of tribes

23. According to the passage, the nomad's diet almost never includes
(A) fruit   (B) milk   (C) cheese   (D) meat   (E) coffee

24. The author's purpose in this passage is to provide
(A) a narrative of events
(B) an argument
(C) a controversial viewpoint
(D) an innovative point of view
(E) simple information

Passage 5

Naturalism differs from realism in several aspects, none of which is clear-cut and definitive. It tends to be more doctrinaire in its exposition of pseudoscientific principles, it is less interested in character and more in the conflict of social forces, and it is concerned to a greater extent with the sordid, the shocking, and the depressing sides of existence. By these criteria, however, there are naturalistic elements in Dostoevsky; and Galsworthy, Hemingway, and Scott Fitzgerald demonstrate many qualities of typical realists. Some further suggested qualities of literary naturalism are as follows:

(a) Naturalism is scientific or pseudoscientific in its approach; it attempts to treat human beings as biological pawns rather than agents of free will. The author does not attempt to judge his characters or to comment on their actions; he merely inserts them into a crucial situation and then pretends to stand back and watch them with the impassivity of the scientists. Although Zola applied this principle with some success, it has generally remained a synthetic theory and has only infrequently been applied to actual literary works.

(b) The naturalist attempts to make literature into a document of society. He writes "novel cycles" purporting to cover every aspect of modern life, or creates characters who are personifications of various social classes. Many naturalists gather copious data from actual life and include it in their literary works: they write novels around specific occupations such as railroading or textile manufacturing in which they utilize technical details of the trade for story-interest. This aspect of naturalism represents an attempt to remove literature from the realm of the fine arts into the field of the social sciences.

(c) Because of the above-described documentary nature of naturalism, the technique often involves the conscious suppression of the poetic elements in literature. The prose style is flat, objective, and bare of imagery; it includes copious details and explanations, and is wary of highly literary metaphors. Like the pseudoscientific dogma described in (a) above, this quality is often more theoretical than practical. The best naturalists are those who do not totally abandon the literary traditions of the past. On the other hand some naturalists are merely writers lacking in the poetic instinct; they avoid a highly literary prose because they have little feeling for style and imagery. Others like Hardy are essentially poets who achieve highly poetic effects in their prose.

(d) Naturalistic literature tends to be concerned with the less elegant aspects of life; its typical settings are the slum, the sweatshop, the factory, or the farm. Where the romantic author selects the most pleasant and idealistic elements in his experience, the naturalistic author often seems positively drawn toward the brutal, the sordid, the cruel, and the degraded. This tendency is in part a reaction against earlier literature, especially against the sentimentalism of the Dumas school where vice is invariably made to appear romantic. The real motivating forces in a naturalistic novel are not religion, hope, or human idealism; they are alcohol, filth, disease, and the human instinct toward bestiality. It will be seen immediately that there are important exceptions to this principle. Galsworthy's scenes are middle-class, and Scott Fitzgerald prefers to do his slumming at the Ritz.

25. The passage implies that one reason for calling naturalism "pseudoscientific" rather than "scientific" is that
    (A) a scientist would acknowledge the existence of free will
    (B) Zola's theory has been infrequently applied
    (C) biological pawns are not amenable to study
    (D) Zola did not meet with total success
    (E) the author's scientific perspective is a pretense

26. In paragraph (c), the author turns from description to
    (A) documentary   (B) evaluation   (C) praise   (D) disdain   (E) naturalism

27. A naturalist suppressing highly literary metaphors might avoid which of the following?
    (A) The sunset was full of reds and yellows.
    (B) His nemesis was iron-willed.
    (C) The community regarded Frank as a tower of strength.
    (D) The President describes the period of military laxity as a "window of vulnerability."
    (E) Marriage is a sad, sober beverage.

28. The passage suggests that the naturalist behaves most like a scientist when he
    (A) gathers details from life
    (B) transforms fact into fiction
    (C) de-emphasizes the importance of character
    (D) writes history or biography rather than actual literary works
    (E) restricts his subject matter

29. In the first paragraph the author is careful not to make
    (A) suggestions
    (B) absolute pronouncements
    (C) any useful distinctions between naturalism and realism
    (D) his examples too noteworthy
    (E) any references to arts other than literature

30. We may infer that the naturalist novel is unlikely to contain
    (A) a rural setting
    (B) an acknowledgment of human woes
    (C) a romantic hero
    (D) a social crisis
    (E) an urban setting

STOP

IF YOU FINISH BEFORE TIME HAS ELAPSED, CHECK YOUR WORK ON THIS SECTION OF THE TEST ONLY. DO NOT GO ON TO THE NEXT SECTION OF THE TEST UNTIL TIME IS UP FOR THIS SECTION.

SECTION II
ANALYTICAL REASONING

Time—35 Minutes
25 Questions

Directions:
In this section you will be given groups of questions based on different sets of conditions. Drawing a simple diagram may be helpful in answering some of the questions. You are to choose the best answer and mark the corresponding space on your answer sheet.

Questions 1–6

(1) Six friends—three boys (Tom, Fred, and Simon) and three girls (Jan, Lynn, and Enola)—are going to the movies.
(2) All six sit in the same row, which has only six seats.
(3) No friends of the same sex sit next to each other.
(4) Tom will not sit next to Lynn.
(5) Fred has friends on each side of him.
(6) Lynn sits between Fred and Simon, and next to each of them.
(7) Enola sits in the first seat and Simon sits in the last seat.

  1. It can be deduced from statements 1, 2, and 7 that
    (A) Lynn sits next to Simon
    (B) Simon does not sit next to Tom
    (C) Fred sits between two friends
    (D) Jan sits next to Enola
    (E) None of the above

2. It can be deduced from statements 1, 2, 6, and 7 that

   I. Fred sits next to Jan
  II. Tom doesn't sit next to Simon
(A) I only   (B) II only   (C) Both I and II   (D) Neither I nor II
(E) Either I or II, but not both

3. Which of the original statements can be deduced solely from statement 7?
(A) 1   (B) 3   (C) 4   (D) 5   (E) None of them

4. Which of the following statements MUST be true?
(A) Enola sits between Tom and Fred.
(B) Fred sits between Jan and Lynn, but not next to either one.
(C) Tom sits next to Enola, and next to Jan.
(D) Lynn sits next to Fred, but not Simon.
(E) Jan sits between Tom and Simon, and next to each.

5. Which of the following MUST be false?
(A) Tom sits next to Jan.
(B) Enola sits next to only one friend.
(C) Lynn sits next to Tom.
(D) Fred sits next to Lynn.
(E) Lynn sits between Enola and Simon.

6. The friends could sit in which order?
(A) Enola, Tom, Jan, Fred, Lynn, Simon
(B) Enola, Fred, Jan, Tom, Lynn, Simon
(C) Simon, Lynn, Tom, Jan, Fred, Enola
(D) Simon, Tom, Lynn, Fred, Jan, Enola
(E) Fred, Lynn, Simon, Enola, Tom, Jan

Questions 7–10

Do, Rey, Mi, and Fa are children.
Do is Rey's brother.
Rey is Mi's sister.
Mi is Fa's brother.

7. Which of the following MUST be true?

   I. Do is a boy.
  II. Fa is a girl.
  III. Mi is a boy.
(A) I   (B) II   (C) III   (D) I and III   (E) II and III

8. Which of the following MUST be false?

   I. Fa is Rey's brother.
  II. Do is Mi's brother.
(A) I only   (B) II only   (C) Both I and II   (D) Either I or II, but not both
(E) Neither I nor II

9. Which of the following could be true?

   I. Fa is Rey's sister.
  II. Fa is Do's brother.
(A) I only   (B) II only   (C) Both I and II   (D) Either I or II, but not both
(E) Neither I nor II

10. If Fa is a girl, then
    (A)   Do is her brother
    (B)   Rey is her brother
    (C)   Mi is her sister
    (D)   Two of the above
    (E)   None of the above

Questions 11–19

    (1)   Alpha combines with Beta, giving Zeta.
    (2)   Theta combines with Zeta, giving Beta.
    (3)   Zeta combines with Beta, giving Alpha.
    (4)   Beta combines with Theta, giving Omega.
    (5)   Theta is formed only when Alpha and Zeta combine.
    (6)   Alpha combines with Theta, giving Zeta.
    (7)   The order of the combinations makes no difference in their outcome.

11. Which of the following MUST be true?

    I.   Theta can be formed without Alpha.
    II. Beta can be formed without Zeta.
    (A) I only   (B) II only   (C) Both I and II   (D) Either I or II, but not both
    (E) Neither I nor II

12. Alpha combining with any other will not give
    (A) Zeta   (B) Theta   (C) Alpha   (D) Beta   (E) two of these

13. Omega may be formed from a combination of
    (A)   Theta and Beta
    (B)   Alpha and Beta
    (C)   Beta and Zeta
    (D)   Theta and Zeta
    (E)   Alpha and Theta

14. Beta may be involved in the combination if the outcome is
    (A)   Alpha or Theta
    (B)   Alpha, Omega, or Zeta
    (C)   Beta
    (D)   Beta, Theta, or Zeta
    (E)   None of the above

15. If Omega combines with Zeta, the outcome is
    (A) Alpha   (B) Beta   (C) Theta   (D) Zeta   (E) cannot be determined from the
information given

16. Which of the following MUST be true?

    I.   Zeta can be formed in at least two different ways.
    II. Omega can be formed in two different ways.
    (A) I only   (B) II only   (C) Both I and II   (D) Either I or II, but not both
    (E) Neither I nor II

17. Which of the following MUST be true?

    I.   Zeta and Theta combine to give Beta.
    II. Beta and Zeta combine to give Omega.
    III. Alpha and Beta combine to give Theta.
    (A) I   (B) II   (C) III   (D) I and II   (E) II and III

18. If the outcome of Alpha and Beta combine with the outcome of Alpha and Zeta, the result is
(A) Alpha   (B) Beta   (C) Omega   (D) Theta   (E) Zeta

19. If Omega combines with Theta, the outcome is Zeta or Theta. Then the outcome of a combination of Omega and Theta is similar to the outcome of
(A) Alpha with any other
(B) Beta with any other
(C) Theta with any other
(D) Zeta with any other
(E) two of these

Questions 20–25

In a certain culture, people have either blue eyes or green eyes; also, they have either red hair or brown hair.
All males have either blue eyes or brown hair, or both.
All females have either green eyes or red hair, or both.
Male children always retain both of the father's characteristics for eyes and hair.
All female children retain only one of their father's traits and the other of their mother's traits for eyes and hair.

20. If all the children born of a blue-eyed, brown-haired male each have blue eyes and red hair, then which of the following MUST be true?

I.   They have a red-haired mother.
II. Their mother has green eyes.
III. They are all girls.
(A) I   (B) II   (C) III   (D) I and III   (E) I, II, and III

21. A blue-eyed, brown-haired male and a blue-eyed, red-haired female marry (1st generation) and many years later are blessed with one grandchild. This grandchild (3rd generation) has red hair and green eyes. Which of the following MUST be true?

I.   The child of the 1st generation is a female.
II. The father from the 2nd generation has green eyes.
III. The grandchild is a female.
(A) I   (B) II   (C) III   (D) I and III   (E) I, II, and III

22. A blue-eyed, brown-haired male and a green-eyed, red-haired female have a child. All of the following are possible characteristics of the child except
(A) green eyes, brown hair
(B) red hair, blue eyes
(C) green eyes, red hair
(D) blue eyes, brown hair
(E) all are possible

23. A green-eyed male

I.   may have red hair
II. may have brown hair
III. must have red hair
IV. must have brown hair
(A) I only   (B) II only   (C) III only   (D) IV only   (E) I and II

24. Two blue-eyed people get married. If their child has red hair, it MUST be true that
(A) the child has brown eyes
(B) the mother has red hair

    (C)   the child is a male
    (D)   the child is a female
    (E)   none of the above must be true

25. All of the children of a couple have brown hair, and the children are both boys and girls. Therefore, the mother
    (A)   must have brown hair
    (B)   must have red hair
    (C)   must have blue eyes
    (D)   must have green eyes
    (E)   none of the above

STOP

IF YOU FINISH BEFORE TIME HAS ELAPSED, CHECK YOUR WORK ON THIS SECTION OF THE TEST ONLY. DO NOT GO ON TO THE NEXT SECTION OF THE TEST UNTIL TIME IS UP FOR THIS SECTION.

SECTION III
EVALUATION OF FACTS

Time—35 Minutes
35 Questions

Directions:
This section consists of several sets; each set presents a factual statement, the description of a dispute, and two rules. In some sets, the rules will be conflicting. Be sure that you consider each rule independently and not as an exception to the other. Following each set are questions; select from four choices (given below) the one that best categorizes each question, based upon the relationship of one or both of the rules to the dispute. Darken the appropriate space on your answer sheet.

    (A)   **A relevant question which you can only answer by choosing between the rules.**
    (B)   **A relevant question which you cannot answer because you need more information or additional rules, but which does not require a choice between the rules.**
    (C)   **A relevant question which you can answer by referring to the facts or rules, or both.**
    (D)   **An irrelevant question or one which is only remotely relevant to the outcome of the dispute.**

Set 1

FACTS
    Having won one hundred dollars at the horse races on Sunday, Scarlet decided to buy an expensive perfume. When the retailer was unable to supply the perfume she wanted in a shatter-proof purse flask, she bought a little-known, man-catching aphrodisiacal perfume in a glass bottle. She put it in her pocket, intending to use it on her date that evening. But while she was horseback riding that afternoon, the perfume shattered against the saddle because of a defective bottle, and spilled all over the horse. Scarlet was not hurt. That night when the horse was back in the stable, he broke down the stable door and impregnated several of the female horses. As a consequence, Scarlet had to pay the stables for the medical care of the female horses.

DISPUTE

Scarlet sued the retail seller. The seller contested.

RULE I

One who is in the business of selling products is liable to any buyer for all damages and injuries occurring because of the use of that product, provided that the product was used as intended by the seller during the time of injury.

RULE II

A retail seller is responsible for all injuries or damages occurring because of the use of his product.

Questions

1. Was the perfume used as intended by the seller?

2. Why did the bottle shatter?

3. Will Scarlet win the suit?

4. If Scarlet had planned to use the perfume on the horses, will she win the suit?

5. If the perfume was intended for use on horses, will Scarlet win the suit?

Set 2

FACTS

Mrs. Zee, a widow with six children, supports her family through her job as a bank teller. Occasionally on Sunday mornings, if she has time, she bakes three or four loaves of poppyseed bread for her children to sell, at $1 each, to sympathetic neighbors. However, Mrs. Zee no longer sees too well, and, one day, instead of using poppyseed, she used large grains of black pepper. As a result, anyone eating even one piece of bread would require hospitalization. Michael, a very overweight 2-year-old who was a compulsive eater, ate a whole loaf by himself. Michael's mother had to rush him to the hospital to have his stomach pumped when he began to pass out from the overdose of pepper. The injuries were minor.

DISPUTE

Michael's mother sued Mrs. Zee for injuries. Mrs. Zee contested.

RULE I

One who manufactures a product is liable for all personal injuries to the user of the product, arising from the use of that product.

RULE II

The manufacturer of a product is not liable for injuries from the product caused by accidental negligence of the manufacturer.

Questions

6. Was Michael injured?

7. Will Michael's mother win the suit?

8. If Mrs. Zee had intentionally used the pepper, would she win the suit?

9. How much pepper was in the bread?

10. If the bread was given to Mrs. Zee and she did not manufacture it, but merely gave it to Michael, would she be liable?

Set 3

FACTS

Laura owned an apartment building in Boston. She rented one of her apartments to Tanya, with an oral agreement that on the first of each month Tanya would pay $500 to Laura for the use of the apartment during that calendar month. After paying the January rent and moving in on January 1, Tanya became aware that overhead aircraft caused a noise problem in the apartment. Tanya decided to leave and found a new place which she could move into on February 10. On January 6, Tanya informed Laura that she intended to vacate the apartment on February 10, and paid Laura an additional $200. Laura accepted the payment; but when she was unable to relet the premises during February, Laura called Tanya and demanded the balance of the February rent ($300). Tanya refused.

DISPUTE

Laura sued Tanya for the balance of the February rent. Tanya contested.

RULE I

Where premises are occupied without a written lease, notice must be given by the tenant before the premises are vacated. The notice must be received at least 30 days before the date on which the succeeding rental payment is due.

RULE II

When, through no fault of the tenant, a disturbance regularly occurs that prevents a tenant from enjoying leased premises, the tenant is not responsible for rent accruing after his departure from the premises.

Questions

11. How often did planes fly over the apartment building?

12. Was Laura aware of the overhead aircraft noise problem when she purchased the building?

13. If the airplane noises kept Tanya awake each night, and she told Laura of this on January 6 when she informed her of her intention to move, how will Laura's case be decided?

14. Was the $200 an adequate rent for the length of time Tanya occupied the apartment in February?

Set 4

FACTS

When the Rutledges decided to take their children to Disneyland during spring vacation, they asked a neighbor's son, Herman, to feed their cat and water the houseplants while they were gone. When they left, they gave Herman the house keys. Herman suspected there was money in the house, but to avert suspicion, he broke into the house through a back window late at night. He searched for the money but could find none. Frustrated, he rampaged about the house, overturning and breaking furniture and appliances. As Herman opened the front door and stepped outside, he was arrested by the police, who had been summoned by neighbors alerted by the commotion.

DISPUTE

Herman was charged with burglary. He contested.

RULE I

Burglary constitutes the breaking and entering into the residence of another for the purpose of stealing property.

RULE II

During the evening hours, only one who obtains possession of another's property by unlawful means has committed a burglary.

Questions

15. If Herman had broken into the house in the morning, would he be found guilty of burglary?

16. Is breaking furniture considered obtaining possession of property?

17. If Herman had found money in the house, would he be found guilty of burglary?

18. If Herman had intended to steal property but obtained possession of none, would he be found guilty?

19. Should the neighbors have alerted the police?

20. How did Herman get into the house?

Set 5

FACTS

Linda Jenkins wished to buy a second-hand car. She went to Ronstat Motors, where she told the salesman, Morris, that she wanted a trouble-free compact. Morris showed her a used compact; and though he knew the car required some minor repairs, he assured her it would perform without trouble for a long, long time. Linda agreed to buy the car under Ronstat Motors' time-purchase plan. Paragraph 3 of the loan agreement read as follows:

"There are no expressed or implied warranties, the Buyer agreeing to take the vehicle which is the subject of this contract without any recourse against Seller for any repairs or service."

Linda signed the contract. Two weeks later, the engine of the car burst into flame while Linda was driving. Linda escaped unhurt, but the car was virtually a total wreck.

DISPUTE

Linda sues Ronstat Motors and Morris for the return of her down payment. Ronstat Motors and Morris contest.

RULE I

A seller is liable for defective goods if his oral warranty is based on a factually false affirmation or a false promise, not on a statement representing merely the seller's evaluation of his goods.

RULE II

Written disclaimers are binding in cases where the customer's knowledge of the written disclaimer can be assured.

Questions

21. Did Linda read the contract before she signed?

22. If Morris knew the car to be defective and if Linda signed the contract assuming it to contain only the schedule of her payment dates, how will the case be resolved?

23. Did Morris have any training in automotive mechanics?

24. If Linda read the contract carefully before she signed, how will the case be resolved?

25. If Linda had been injured in the accident, would she be more likely to win the suit?

Set 6

FACTS

The city of Topsy has grown in a quaint but rather unregulated way. Midtown tenement houses are built right up to the edges of their lots. But as the taller buildings are next to either vacant lots or buildings of only one story, they enjoy good light and air. Since these buildings have no central heating or central air-conditioning, many tenants have installed electric heaters and window air conditioners. A number of the tenants grow geraniums on their window ledges, and several keep small pets in their apartments. Tower Builders, Inc. (TBI) announces plans for an ultramodern, windowless, 40-floor office building, to be erected just 12 inches from a 70-year-old, 15-floor, tenement-type apartment building owned by Slim Lord.

DISPUTE

Slim sues to restrain TBI from going ahead with construction. TBI contests.

RULE I

Owners of multiple-unit residential property, which has been substantially benefited by sunlight passing through space rising vertically from adjacent unimproved land for over 21 years, acquire a permanent easement or right of enjoyment of sunlight for that property.

RULE II

Owners of vacant land may block sunlight from adjacent existing residential buildings.

Questions

26. How long had Slim owned the property?

27. If Slim's building had substantially benefited from the sunlight, would TBI be allowed to build?

28. If Slim's building has substantially benefited from the sunlight for 25 years, and TBI's lot is now vacant, who will win the suit?

29. If the TBI building would block the sunlight that had been unobstructed for 25 years, and if the TBI land was not vacant, would Slim win the suit?

Set 7

FACTS

Thomas owned a large parcel of rural land, which encompassed a marshy area. Thomas wanted to fill the marsh, so that he could begin construction of a shopping center on the land. Since the nearest large shopping mall was forty-five miles away, Thomas believed that the shopping center would be beneficial to the entire area. An environmental group, however, objected to Thomas' plans to fill the marsh. They pointed out that three species of salamander and several species of butterfly now lived in the marsh and that it was the source of numerous streams which were vital to the environment of that entire region. Thomas applied to the county for a variance to allow him to fill the marsh and build on the land.

DISPUTE

The environmentalists brought suit to prevent Thomas from getting a variance and filling the marsh. Thomas contested.

RULE I

A landowner may not obtain a variance when the consequences would be detrimental to the environment of the region.

RULE II

Zoning variances pertaining to rural areas will be granted only when the result will be beneficial to the surrounding region.

Questions

30. If the streams were vital to the environment of the entire region and if the shopping center would be beneficial to the entire region, would Thomas obtain the variance?

31. If the plans were not detrimental to the environment of the region, would Thomas obtain the variance?

32. Would the shopping center be beneficial to the area?

33. Were the environmentalists correct in evaluating the streams as vital to the region?

34. If Thomas' land was not rural and the marsh was the source of streams vital to the environment of the region, would he get the variance?

35. How many streams were emanating from the marsh?

STOP

IF YOU FINISH BEFORE TIME HAS ELAPSED, CHECK YOUR WORK ON THIS SECTION OF THE TEST ONLY. DO NOT GO ON TO THE NEXT SECTION OF THE TEST UNTIL TIME IS UP FOR THIS SECTION.

SECTION IV
LOGICAL REASONING

Time—35 Minutes
26 Questions

Directions:
In this section you will be given brief statements or passages and will be required to evaluate the reasoning involved. In some instances, more than one choice will appear to be a possible answer. You are to choose the *best* answer. Use common sense and reasonableness in making your selection; then mark the proper space on the answer sheet.

Questions 1–2 refer to the following passage.

Chariots of Fire may have caught some professional critics off guard as the Motion Picture Academy's choice for an Oscar as the year's best film, but it won wide audience approval as superb entertainment.

Refreshingly, *Chariots of Fire* features an exciting story, enchanting English and Scottish scenery, a beautiful musical score, and appropriate costumes.

All of these attractions are added to a theme that extols traditional religious values—without a shred of offensive sex, violence, or profanity.

Too good to be true? See *Chariots of Fire* and judge for yourself.

Those who condemn the motion picture industry for producing so many objectionable films can do their part by patronizing wholesome ones, thereby encouraging future Academy Award judges to recognize and reward decency.

1. The author of the above passage implicitly defines which of the following terms?
   (A) objectionable   (B) appropriate   (C) patronizing   (D) Oscar   (E) professional

2. Which of the following is a basic assumption underlying the final sentence of the passage?
   (A) Academy judges are not decent people.
   (B) The popularity of a film influences academy judges.
   (C) Future academy judges will be better than past ones.
   (D) There are those who condemn the motion picture industry.
   (E) *Chariots of Fire* is a patronizing film.

3. *Andy*: All teachers are mean.
Bob: That is not true. I know some doctors who are mean too.

Bob's answer demonstrates that he thought Andy to mean that
(A) all teachers are mean
(B) some teachers are mean
(C) doctors are meaner than teachers
(D) teachers are meaner than doctors
(E) only teachers are mean

4. Theodore Roosevelt was a great hunter. He was the mighty Nimrod of his generation. He had the physical aptitude and adventurous spirit of the true frontiersman. "There is delight," he said, "in the hardy life of the open; in long rides, rifle in hand; in the thrill of the fight with dangerous game." But he was more than a marksman and tracker of beasts, for he brought to his sport the intellectual curiosity and patient observation of the natural scientist.

Which of the following would most weaken the author's concluding contention?
(A) Theodore Roosevelt never studied natural science.
(B) Actually, Theodore Roosevelt's sharpshooting prowess was highly exaggerated.
(C) Theodore Roosevelt always used native guides when tracking game.
(D) Theodore Roosevelt was known to leave safaris if their first few days were unproductive.
(E) Theodore Roosevelt's powers of observation were significantly hampered by his near-sightedness.

5. The following is an excerpt from a letter sent to a law school applicant:

"Thank you for considering our school to further your education. Your application for admission was received well before the deadline and was processed with your admission test score and undergraduate grade report.

"We regret to inform you that you cannot be admitted for the fall semester. We have had to refuse admission to many outstanding candidates due to the recent cut in state funding of our program.

"Thank you for your interest in our school and we wish you success in your future endeavors."

Which of the following can be deduced from the above letter?
(A) The recipient of the letter did not have a sufficiently high grade point average to warrant admission to this graduate program.
(B) The recipient of the letter was being seriously considered for a place in the entering class.
(C) The law school sending the letter could not fill all the places in its entering class due to a funding problem.
(D) Criteria other than test scores and grade reports were used in determining the size of the entering class.
(E) The school sending the letter is suffering severe financial difficulties.

Questions 6–7 refer to the following passage.

At birth we have no self-image. We cannot distinguish anything from the confusion of light and sound around us. From this beginning of no-dimension, we gradually begin to differentiate our body from our environment and develop a sense of identity, with the realization that we are a separate and independent human being. We then begin to develop a conscience, the sense of right and wrong. Further, we develop social consciousness, where we become aware that we live with other people. Finally, we develop a sense of values, which is our overall estimation of our worth in the world.

6. Which of the following would be the best completion of this passage?
   (A) The sum total of all these developments we call the self-image or the self-concept.
   (B) This estimation of worth is only relative to our value system.
   (C) Therefore, our social consciousness is dependent on our sense of values.
   (D) Therefore, our conscience keeps our sense of values in perspective.
   (E) The sum total of living with other people and developing a sense of values makes us a total person.

7. The author of this passage would most likely agree with which of the following?
   (A) Children have no self-dimension.
   (B) Having a conscience necessitates the ability to differentiate between right and wrong.
   (C) Social consciousness is our most important awareness.
   (D) Heredity is predominant over environment in development.
   (E) The ability to distinguish the difference between moral issues depends on the overall dimension of self-development.

8. Opportunity makes the thief.
   Without thieves there would be no crime.
   Without opportunity there would be no crime.

   The preceding statements fail to consider that

   I.   thieves make opportunities
   II. without crime there would be no opportunity
   III. thieves are not the only criminals
   (A) I only   (B) II only   (C) I and III only   (D) I and II only   (E) II and III only

Questions 9–10 refer to the following passage.

In a report released last week, a government-funded institute concluded that there is "overwhelming" evidence that violence on television leads to criminal behavior by children and teenagers.

The report, based on an extensive review of several hundred research studies conducted during the 1970s, is an update of a 1972 Surgeon General's report that came to similar conclusions.

9. Which of the following is the most convincing statement in support of the argument in the first paragraph above?
   (A) A 50-state survey of the viewing habits of prison inmates concluded that every inmate watches at least 2 hours of violent programming each day.
   (B) A 50-state survey of the viewing habits of convicted adolescents shows that each of them had watched at least 2 hours of violent programming daily since the age of 5.
   (C) One juvenile committed a murder that closely resembled a crime portrayed on a network series.
   (D) The 1972 Surgeon General's report was not nearly as extensive as this more recent study.
   (E) Ghetto residents who are burglarized most often report the theft of a television set.

10. The argument above is most weakened by its vague use of the word
   (A) violence   (B) government   (C) aggressive   (D) update   (E) overwhelming

Questions 11–12 require you to complete the missing portions of the following passage by selecting from five alternatives the one that best fits the context of the passage.

It may be that sensation is the most primitive nervous activity, that in the evolutionary process certain sensations or combinations of sensations may develop the intensities which we know as affects and that those affects when connected with observed causes, or more properly with observations that are taken to be causes, become in the higher animals the complex patterns we know as (11) ——————————————. If such is the case, then an emotion is simply an intense sensation complex with a logical component. This would imply that only a symbol-using animal can have emotions. Of course, his symbols may be private symbols and even (12) ——————————.

11. This sentence would be best completed with the words
(A) emotional intentions   (B) emotional behavior   (C) unintentional reactions
(D) unconquerable fears   (E) emotional sensation

12. This sentence would be best completed with the word
(A) unintelligible   (B) illogical   (C) nonlingual   (D) irrational   (E) nonsensical

13.   The study of village communities has become one of the fundamental methods of discussing the ancient history of institutions. It would be out of the question here to range over the whole field of human society in search for communal arrangements of rural life. It will be sufficient to confine the present inquiry to the varieties presented by nations of Aryan race, not because greater importance is to be attached to these nations than to other branches of humankind, although this view might also be reasonably urged, but principally because the Aryan race in its history has gone through all sorts of experiences, and the data gathered from its historical life can be tolerably well ascertained. Should the road be sufficiently cleared in this particular direction, it will not be difficult to connect the results with similar researches in other racial surroundings.

Which of the following, if true, most weakens the author's conclusion?
(A)   Information about the Aryan race is no more conclusive than information about any other ethnic group.
(B)   The experiences and lifestyle of Aryans are uniquely different from those of other cultures.
(C)   The Aryan race is no more important than any other race.
(D)   The historical life of the Aryans dates back only 12 centuries.
(E)   Aryans lived predominantly in villages, while today 90 percent of the world population live predominantly in or around major cities.

14. Although any reasonable modern citizen of the world must abhor war and condemn senseless killing, we must also agree that honor is more valuable than life. Life, after all, is transient, but honor is ——————————.

Which of the following most logically completes the passage above?
(A) sensible   (B) real   (C) eternal   (D) of present value   (E) priceless

Questions 15–16 refer to the following statements.

Bill said, "All dogs bark. This animal does not bark. Therefore, it is not a dog."

15. Which of the following most closely parallels the logic of this statement?
   (A) All rocks are hard. This lump is hard. Therefore, it may be a rock.
   (B) All foreign language tests are difficult. This is not a foreign language test. Therefore, it is not difficult.
   (C) All Blunder automobiles are poorly built. Every auto sold by Joe was poorly built. Therefore, Joe sells Blunder automobiles.
   (D) Rocks beat scissors, scissors beat paper, and paper beats rocks. Therefore, it is best to choose paper.
   (E) All paint smells. This liquid does not smell. Therefore, it is not paint.

16. Which of the following would weaken Bill's argument the most?
   (A) Animals other than dogs bark.
   (B) Some dogs cannot bark.
   (C) Dogs bark more than cockatiels.
   (D) You can train a dog not to bark.
   (E) You can train birds to bark.

17. No one cheats on all the exams he takes. Some people cheat on most of the exams they take. Most cheat on some of the exams they take. Everyone has cheated on at least one exam he has taken. Cheating is wrong.

Which of the following is inconsistent with the preceding facts?
   (A) Joe has never been caught cheating.
   (B) Cheating is an acceptable procedure.
   (C) Jack is never wrong.
   (D) More people cheat on none of the exams they have taken than cheat on all of the exams they have taken.
   (E) More people cheat on some of the exams they have taken than cheat on most of the exams they have taken.

Questions 18–19 refer to the following sentence.

Everyone is ignorant, only on different subjects.

18. This sentence can have more than one meaning. Which of the following implies at least one of its meanings?

   I.   Everybody is ignorant.
   II. Frank is not ignorant about life.
   III. Frank and Hal cannot be ignorant on the same subject.
   IV. Hal can be ignorant on more than one subject.
   (A) I, II, and IV only   (B) II and III only   (C) I, III, and IV only   (D) III and IV only
   (E) I and IV only

19. The author of this sentence would most likely be a
   (A) politician   (B) philosopher   (C) satirist   (D) actor   (E) attorney

20. The law of parsimony urges a strict economy upon us; it requires that we can never make a guess with two or three assumptions in it if we can make sense with one.

The author means:
   (A) Complications arise from economy.
   (B) Simplify terminology whenever possible.
   (C) Don't complicate a simple issue.
   (D) Assumptions are necessarily simple in nature.
   (E) Excess assumptions never clarify the situation.

21. You can use a bottle opener to open the new beer bottles.
You do not need to use a bottle opener to open the new beer bottles.

Which of the following most closely parallels the logic of these statements?
(A) You must turn on the switch to light the lamp. If you turn on the switch, the lamp may not light.
(B) A cornered rattlesnake will strike, so do not corner a rattlesnake.
(C) If you do not study you will fail the test. If you do study, you may fail the test.
(D) Every candidate I voted for in the election lost his race. I must learn to vote better.
(E) I can move the sofa with my brother's help. If my brother is not available, I'll get a neighbor to help me.

22. To be admitted to Bigshot University, you must have a 3.5 grade-point average (GPA) and a score of 800 on the admissions test, a 3.0 GPA and a score of 1000 on the admissions test, or a 2.5 GPA and a score of 1200 on the admissions test. A sliding scale exists for other scores and GPAs.

Which of the following is inconsistent with the above?
(A) The higher the GPA, the lower the admissions test score needed for admission.
(B) Joe was admitted with a 2.7 GPA and a score of 1100 on the admissions test.
(C) No student with a score of less than 800 on the admissions test and a 3.4 GPA will be admitted.
(D) More applicants had a GPA of 3.5 than had a GPA of 2.5
(E) Some students with a score of less than 1200 on the admissions test and a GPA of less than 2.5 were admitted.

23. The Census Bureau's family portrait of America may remind us of the problems we face as a nation, but it also gives us reason to take heart in our ability to solve them in an enlightened way. The 1980 census was the first in history to show that the majority of the population in every state has completed high school. And the percentage of our people with at least 4 years of college rose from 11% in 1970 to 16.3% in 1980. That's progress—where it really counts.

Which of the following assumptions underlies the author's conclusion in the above passage?
(A) Greater numbers of high school and college degrees coincide with other firsts in the 1980 census.
(B) Greater numbers of high school and college degrees coincide with greater numbers of well-educated people.
(C) Greater numbers of high school and college degrees coincide with a great commitment to social progress.
(D) Greater numbers of high school and college degrees coincide with a better chance to avoid national catastrophe.
(E) Greater numbers of high school and college degrees coincide with the 1980 census.

24. Add No-NOCK to your car and watch its performance soar. No-NOCK will give it more get-up-and-go and keep it running longer. Ask for No-NOCK when you want better mileage!

According to the advertisement above, No-NOCK claims to do everything *except*
(A) improve your car's performance
(B) increase your car's life
(C) improve your car's miles per gallon
(D) cause fewer breakdowns
(E) stop the engine from knocking

So many arrogant and ill-tempered young men have dominated the tennis courts of late that we had begun to fear those characteristics were prerequisites for championship tennis.

Tennis used to be a gentleman's game. What is sad is not just that the game has changed. With so much importance placed on success, it may be that something has gone out of the American character—such things as gentleness and graciousness.

25. Which of the following statements, if true, would most weaken the above argument?
(A) The American character is a result of American goals.
(B) Tennis has only recently become a professional sport.
(C) Some ill-tempered tennis players are unsuccessful.
(D) The "gentlemen" of early tennis often dueled to the death off the court.
(E) Some even-tempered tennis players are successful.

26. *Dolores*: To preserve the peace, we must be prepared to go to war with any nation at any time, using either conventional or nuclear weapons.
Fran: Which shall it be, conventional weapons or nuclear weapons?

Fran mistakenly concludes that the "either . . . or" phrase in Dolores' statement indicates
(A) fear   (B) indecision   (C) a choice   (D) a question   (E) a refusal

STOP

IF YOU FINISH BEFORE TIME HAS ELAPSED, CHECK YOUR WORK ON THIS SECTION OF THE TEST ONLY. DO NOT GO ON TO THE NEXT SECTION OF THE TEST UNTIL TIME IS UP FOR THIS SECTION.

SECTION V
READING COMPREHENSION

Time—35 Minutes
28 Questions

Directions:
Read the passages and answer the questions following each passage by blackening the appropriate space on the answer sheet. You may refer back to the passages when answering the questions. Answer all questions on the basis of what is stated or implied.

Passage 1

Moviemakers have always been interested in politicians, and vice-versa. As early as 1912, Raoul Walsh followed Pancho Villa around, filming his ambushes and executions. Villa even delayed them by two to three hours so Walsh would have enough light to shoot the scenes.

In Russia, Sergei Eisenstein made several films at Stalin's request, including *Alexander Nevski* in 1938 and *Ivan the Terrible* in 1945, both of which made the new regime appear to be the heir of a glorious revolutionary tradition. In Germany, the "Mabuse" series from 1922 to 1933 sketched the portrait of a budding dictator, but when Goebbels as propaganda minister asked Fritz Lang to become the Third Reich's official film maker, Lang refused.

Hitler himself charged Leni Riefenstahl to film the Nazi rallies at Nuremberg in 1934. The result was *The Triumph of Will*, which took two years to make and included oceans of swastika flags, miles of military parades, stylized eagles, rolling drums, and an omnipresent Hitler whose profile stood out against the sky.

But the movies soon helped create a political style less stridently heroic and melodramatic than that inspired by the theater and opera. At the beginning, of course, early cinema techniques encouraged the leader to pantomime heavily with excessive gestures and expressions. The result was similar to expressionist theater. But it soon became clear that the cinema offered possibilities unknown on the stage; for example, the close-up, which abolished the distance between the actor and the audience and made exaggerated gestures unnecessary. With the actor's image enlarged on the screen, even a trembling of the lips or batting of the eyelids would be magnified.

When the talkies appeared, the theatrical delivery of lines was no longer the rule. A conversational tone—even a whisper—was easily heard by the audience, making actors adopt a more natural style.

Political leaders have adapted their style to this evolution of the dramatic arts. The hero leader necessarily has a style more suited to the theater or silent movies and is less able to use the new tone required by cinema and television, which js more sober, allusive, and elliptical. In this sense, de Gaulle was of the theater generation while Giscard d'Estaing belongs to the cinema and television generation that understands the need for a more nuanced "stage presence."

Another result of the cinema has been to make actors more influential as models to imitate, since they are so much more visible. It was this that gave rise to the star system, which for a long time was virtually the basis of the movie industry.

In a sense, the era of the star system can be broken down into three phases, each corresponding to three main types of stars. Each offered different models to the audience—and to political leaders.

The first phase was from 1920 to 1932, when stars were inaccessible, marmoreal, and inimitable. These were the idols, surrounded by an aura of myth. In short, they were the cinema equivalent of the hero leader.

Then, during the 1930s and 1940s, the star became more human. He or she, though still shining brightly, was less exceptional, a bit more like the rest of us. The star became a model that could be imitated—like the charm leader.

The third phase was in the 1950s and 1960s, when stars became virtually the reflection of the spectator if not, indeed, his double. It became more difficult to imitate a star, since he or she was already like everyone else. This corresponded to the political Mr. Everyman.

1. Franklin Roosevelt's "Fireside Chats" (seemingly informal radio talks with his constituency) might have been mentioned in this passage as an example of
   (A) the same mode of propaganda practiced by the Germans and Russians
   (B) the unpopularity of excessive theatricality during the 1930s and 1940s
   (C) the use of a new medium for political communications
   (D) the more natural style of presentation that developed in both movies and politics
   (E) the mastery of nuance

2. Overall, the passage develops a comparison between
   (A) bandits and political leaders
   (B) actors and politicians
   (C) moviemakers and politicians
   (D) Nazis and Communists
   (E) de Gaulle and d'Estaing

3. The author's attitude toward the factualness of the two films mentioned that Eisenstein made for Stalin is
   (A) enthusiastic   (B) satiric   (C) angry   (D) skeptical   (E) ambiguous

4. The author might agree that the exaggerated gestures in Hitler's speeches were influenced by
   (A) the Führer's desire to outdo Russian propaganda
   (B) Leni Riefenstahl's direction
   (C) the style of movie heroes
   (D) the dramatic style of the theater and opera
   (E) Hitler's effort to stress profile features

5. Which of the following is the most appropriate title for this passage?
   (A) "The Movies Invade Politics"
   (B) "The Waning of Expressionist Theater"
   (C) "Propaganda as Entertainment"
   (D) "Four Countries and Theatricality"
   (E) "Government as Cinema"

6. According to the passage, after 1932 both actors and politicians began to seem
   (A) less like mirror images of each other
   (B) less introverted
   (C) more popular
   (D) less unique
   (E) more involved in each other's profession

7. The literary technique that the author employs throughout this passage is
   (A) synthesis   (B) synecdoche   (C) analysis   (D) analogy   (E) metonymy

Passage 2

Mary Hamilton, a twenty-eight-year-old black field secretary for the Congress of Racial Equality (CORE), participated in a demonstration in Gasden, Alabama, in 1963. White police officers arrested her, along with fellow demonstrators. Believing their arrests to be unlawful, the group petitioned the Circuit Court of Etowah County for release on a writ of habeas corpus. The hearing on the petition was held on June 25, before Judge Cunningham, a white judge, assisted by white court clerks and bailiffs.

Black attorneys Charles Conley and Norman Amaker represented the petitioners and white Solicitor Rayburn spoke for the state. Mr. Rayburn followed the southern establishment practice of addressing each black witness by his or her first name, despite objections from the opposing counsel.

When Mary Hamilton completed her direct testimony, Solicitor Rayburn began his cross-examination by asking, "What is your name, please?"

"Miss Mary Hamilton."

"Mary, . . . who were you arrested by?"

"My name is Miss Hamilton. Please address me correctly," she said.

"Who were you arrested by, Mary?" the solicitor asked again, deliberately.

"I will not answer a question—" she began, and Attorney Amaker interjected, "The witness's name is Miss Hamilton."

"— your question until I am addressed correctly," she finished.

"Answer the question," Judge Cunningham ordered.

Miss Hamilton would not be intimidated. "I will not answer them unless I am addressed correctly."

"You are in contempt of court," ruled the judge.

"Your Honor—your Honor—" Attorney Conley began, but the judge paid no attention.

"You are in contempt of this court," he went on, "and you are sentenced to five days in jail and a fifty-dollar fine."

Miss Hamilton was taken to jail then and there, and served the five days. Since she did not intend to pay the fine, and therefore would be subject to another twenty days in jail, she was allowed out on bond to appeal the contempt conviction.

On July 25, she petitioned the Alabama Supreme Court to review the contempt citation on two grounds. Her lawyers contended that the solicitor's manner of addressing black witnesses violated the equal protection clause of the Fourteenth Amendment. Finding no cases on this point, they relied on logic, history, and etiquette. They rejected the state's reliance on Emily Post and Amy Vanderbilt because their books did not discuss the use of first names in a racial situation. They also reminded the court that Miss Hamilton's contempt conviction violated the due process clause because she was summarily sentenced without even being given a trial— an opportunity to present a defense to the charge. (Remember the Red Queen in *Alice in Wonderland*—"sentence first, trial afterward"?)

The Alabama Supreme Court found, however, that "the question was a lawful one and the witness invoked no valid legal exemption to support her refusal to answer it. The record conclusively shows that petitioner's name is Mary Hamilton, not Miss Mary Hamilton. Many witnesses are addressed by various titles, but one's own name is an acceptable appellation at law. . . . In the cross-examination of witnesses, a wide latitude is allowed resting in the sound discretion of the trial court and unless the discretion is grossly abused, the ruling of the court will not be overturned. . . . We hold that the trial court did not abuse its discretion and the record supports the summary punishment inflicted."

The NAACP Legal Defense and Educational Fund then took the case up to the United States Supreme Court for review. The defense lawyers relied on long-standing principles governing the conduct of prosecuting attorneys: as quasi-judicial officers of the court they are under a duty not to prejudice a party's case through overzealous prosecution or to detract from the impartiality of courtroom atmosphere. The defense presented historical and sociological proof that the forms of address used by Solicitor Rayburn were a distinct part of a "racial caste system" that deprived black citizens of equal protection of the laws. They also quoted from novels by Richard Wright, James Baldwin, and Lillian Smith.

8. By objecting to being addressed by her first name, Mary Hamilton implies that such an address is
   (A) illegal
   (B) not appropriate in a Southern court
   (C) incorrect
   (D) demeaning
   (E) unfortunate

9. By alluding to *Alice in Wonderland*, the author seems to brand the judge as
   (A)   a literary artifact
   (B)   an absurd tyrant
   (C)   childish
   (D)   an intimidating legislator
   (E)   both B and D

10. We must presume that the author of this passage was

   I.   present at the trial of Mary Hamilton
   II.   able to secure a transcript of the court proceedings
   III. able to secure a paraphrase of the court proceedings
   (A) I and II   (B) I or II   (C) II only   (D) I only   (E) I, II, and III

11. The question raised but left unanswered in this passage is which of the following?
   (A)   Is impartiality possible?
   (B)   What did the U.S. Supreme Court decide?
   (C)   Is Mary Hamilton still politically active?
   (D)   Can a court ruling be made without precedent?
   (E)   Are Emily Post and Amy Vanderbilt recognized authorities?

12. By stressing that the judge and the court staff were white, the author implies which of the following questions?
   (A)   Was the court biased against Mary Hamilton?
   (B)   Should the legal profession in Alabama be integrated?
   (C)   Should Mary Hamilton have been tried in another court?
   (D)   Is the race of judges less crucial today?
   (E)   Is the race of the judge more important than that of the arresting officers?

13. The author suggests that the judge's response to Miss Hamilton was an effort to
   (A)   intimidate the witness
   (B)   demonstrate that only the judge should be formally addressed
   (C)   cut short the cross examination
   (D)   elicit an answer that would help decide the case
   (E)   offer a popular ruling

14. The overall tone of the author in this passage is
   (A) frivolous   (B) presumptuous   (C) messianic   (D) humorous   (E) none of these

Passage 3

   Alain Robbe-Grillet is not as cerebral a writer as Nathalie Sarraute or Michel Butor. But he has been more popular, particularly in America. Perhaps that is one reason. There are others. He relies even more heavily than his fellow novelists on the *roman policier* for basic structure, and detective stories have a built-in popular fascination. Most of his characters, so far as we can determine, seem to be psychopathological. He is there fore a kind of Alfred Hitchcock of the novel. He has also devoted himself to film writing and film making in association with the *Nouvelle Vague*. His cinema-novels as he called them, rather than film-scripts, *L'Année Dernière à Marienbad* (1961) and *L'Immortelle* (1963), have certainly brought him a wider public exposure than would have been possible with the novels alone. Furthermore his novels have had wide paperback distribution in English translation. But he is an authentic New Novelist and therefore disturbing but not easy. He is reported to have said that he *wants* his readers to feel disappointed (in their expectation of clarification, presumably), that if they feel disappointed he knows he has succeeded in what he was trying to do. At least one critic has placed Robbe-Grillet at "the most advanced point of evolution of the twentieth-century novel and film."

LIFE: Alain Robbe-Grillet was born August 18, 1922, in Brest on the seacoast of Brittany, the son of Gaston and Yvonne Robbe-Grillet, who had moved there from the Jura. As a child he was intrigued by the lichens and rock plants of the coast (perhaps observing their tropisms while Nathalie Sarraute was writing in these terms) and by the gulls on the cliffs of Finistère (which may reappear in *The Voyeur*). Educated at the Lycée Buffon, the Lycée St. Louis, and the Institut National Agronomique in Paris, he became a professional agronomic engineer in the years 1949 to 1951 at the Institute des Fruits Tropicaux in Guinea, Morocco, Martinique, and Guadaloupe; but his interests turned increasingly toward writing, which eventually became his full-time career. The banana plantations, verandas, and fronds of Martinique return in *La Jalousie*. Robbe-Grillet's first novel, *Les Gommes* (*The Erasers*), appeared in 1953; his second, *Le Voyeur*, in 1955; and his career was well launched. In 1957 he married Catherine Rstakian and published his third novel, *La Jalousie*, followed two years later by a fourth, *Dans le Labyrinthe* (*In the Labyrinth*).

His attention then turned to the cinema, at first in collaboration with the film director Alain Resnais. In 1961 *L'Année Dernière à Marienbad* hit the movie world with an originality that for a time usurped the attention customarily given to the Italian films of Fellini or the Swedish films of Bergman. *Last Year at Marienbad* played long runs in the art film houses in New York and across the United States. Bruce Morrissette in a critique of the film pointed out to less perceptive critics that it represented a continuation of techniques established in the earlier novels: "False scenes and objectified hypothesis as in *The Voyeur*, a subjective universe converted into objective perceptions as in *Jealousy*—with its detemporalization of mental states, its mixture of memories (true and false), of desire images and affective projections—the 'dissolves' found in *The Labyrinth*: all these reach a high point in Marienbad. . . . The spectator's work, like that of the reader, becomes an integral part of the cinematic or novelistic creation." The viewer like the reader was expected to collaborate in creating meaning. *Marienbad* takes place at an ornate Bavarian palace; the action is circular (like *Finnegans Wake*, says Morrissette) beginning with "Once more" as the camera moves through Freudian corridors, empty rooms and a formal garden (with a return at the end); characters emerge as a young woman, A, an older man, M (presumably her jealous husband), and a persistent lover, X. Fantasies of seduction, resistance, desire, fear, rape, and even murder are projected; but whose they are, A's or M's or X's, is never clear. You take your choice.

15. We may assume that the plot of a *roman policier* involves
   (A) French characters
   (B) a crime
   (C) psychopathological characters
   (D) an omniscient narrator
   (E) the collaboration of other novelists

16. According to the passage, the viewer of *Last Year at Marienbad* is a
   (A) participant in the clearly delineated fantasy
   (B) fan of triangular love relationships
   (C) detached spectator
   (D) reader as well
   (E) partner in constructing the plot

17. According to the passage, one might finish a successful Robbe-Grillet novel feeling
   (A) more intelligent
   (B) in the mood to read the novel
   (C) as if he had seen an Alfred Hitchcock film
   (D) wondering "Who dunnit?"
   (E) disappointed

18. According to the passage, Robbe-Grillet's literary work indicated his familiarity with
  (A) the habits of gulls
  (B) jealousy
  (C) farming
  (D) French life
  (E) insoluble problems

19. The "that" in line 2 refers to which of the following?
  (A) the cerebral quality of most French fiction
  (B) the contention that Robbe-Grillet's work does not appeal only to the intellect
  (C) the brainlessness of Robbe-Grillet's work
  (D) Robbe-Grillet's reliance on emotional effects
  (E) a fact apparently discussed elsewhere

20. A prominent stylistic feature of the first sentence of the second paragraph is
  (A) the factuality of its terms
  (B) the realization that Robbe-Grillet is no longer a young man
  (C) its discontinuity with the first paragraph, because of the absence of transitional terms
  (D) the colon following *LIFE*
  (E) the naming of Robbe-Grillet's parents

21. We may conclude that Nathalie Sarraute and Michel Butor are
  (A) interested in Robbe-Grillet
  (B) masters of detective fiction
  (C) contemporaries of Robbe-Grillet
  (D) antagonistic to Robbe-Grillet
  (E) comparable to Robbe-Grillet

Passage 4

"Shalom!" he said finally out loud.

"Shalom to you." So it was what I had heard, who would have thought so? We both relaxed, looking at opposite sides of the street.

The taxi driver sat in his shirt sleeves on a cool June day, not more than 55° Fahrenheit. He was a man in his thirties who looked as if what he ate didn't fully feed him—in afterthought a discontented type, his face on the tired side; not bad-looking—now that I'd studied him a little, even though the head seemed pressed a bit flat by somebody's heavy hand although protected by a mat of healthy hair. His face, as I said, veered to Slavic: round; broad cheekbones, small firm chin; but he sported also a longish nose and a distinctive larynx on a slender hairy neck; a mixed type, it appeared. At any rate, the shalom had seemed to alter his appearance, even of the probing eyes. He was dissatisfied for certain this fine June day—his job, fate, appearance—what? And a sort of indigenous sadness hung on him, coming God knows from where; nor did he seem to mind if who he was was immediately visible; not everybody could do that or wanted to. This one showed himself. Not too prosperous, I would say, yet no underground man. He sat firm in his seat, all of him driving, a touch frantically. I have an experienced eye for such details.

"Israeli?" he asked in a whisper.

"Americansky." I know no Russian, just a few polite words.

He dug into his shirt pocket for a thin pack of cigarettes and swung his arm over the seat, the Volga swerving to avoid a truck making a turn.

"Take care!"

I was thrown sideways—no apologies. Extracting a Bulgarian cigarette I wasn't eager to smoke—too strong—I handed him his pack. I was considering offering my prosperous American cigarettes in return but didn't want to affront him.

"Feliks Levitansky," he said. "How do you do? I am the taxi driver." His accent was strong, verging on fruity, but redeemed by fluency of tongue.

"Ah, you speak English? I sort of thought so."

"My profession is translator—English, French." He shrugged sideways.

"Howard Harvitz is my name. I'm here for a short vacation, about three weeks. My wife died not so long ago, and I'm traveling partly to relieve my mind."

My voice caught, but then I went on to say that if I could manage to dig up some material for a magazine article or two, so much the better.

In sympathy Levitansky raised both hands from the wheel.

"Watch out, for God's sake!"

"Horovitz?" he asked.

I spelled it for him. "Frankly, it was Harris after I entered college but I changed it back recently. My father had it legally changed after I graduated from high school. He was a doctor, a practical sort."

"You don't look to me Jewish."

"If so why did you say shalom?"

"Sometimes you say." After a minute he asked, "For which reason?"

"For which reason what?"

"Why you changed back your name?"

"I had a crisis in my life."

"Existential? Economic?"

"To tell the truth I changed it back after my wife died."

"What is the significance?"

"The significance is I am closer to my true self."

The driver popped a match with his thumbnail and lit the cigarette.

"I am marginal Jew," he said, "although my father—Avrham Isaakovich Levitansky—was Jewish. Because my mother was gentile woman I was given choice, but she insisted me to register for internal passport with notation of Jewish nationality in respect for my father. I did so."

"You don't say."

"My father died in my childhood. I was rised—raised?—to respect Jewish people and religion but I went my own way. I am atheist. This is almost inevitable."

"You mean Soviet life?"

Levitansky smoked without replying as I grew embarrassed by my question. I looked around to see if I knew where we were. In afterthought he asked, "to which destination?"

I said, still on the former subject, that I had been not much of a Jew myself. "My mother and father were totally assimilated."

"By their choice?"

"Of course by their choice."

"Do you wish," he then asked, "to visit Central Synagogue on Arkhipova Street? Very interesting experience."

"Not just now," I said, "but take me to the Chekhov Museum on Sadovaya Kudrinskaya."

At that the driver, sighing, seemed to take heart.

22. The narrator's indication of the temperature suggests that he assumes
    (A) that the temperature is cool
    (B) that the driver works under adverse conditions
    (C) that it is related to the taxi driver's personality
    (D) that some of his readers measure temperature in Centigrade units
    (E) both A and C

23. The narrator implies that his "true self" is
    (A) marginal   (B) a writer   (C) a widower   (D) Russian   (E) Jewish

24. What is certain about the taxi driver's apparel?
    (A) He is not wearing a jacket.
    (B) He is wearing a government uniform.
    (C) He is past thirty.
    (D) It is unusual.
    (E) It is of a mixed type.

25. The narrator mentions that Levitansky neither acknowledges nor apologizes for
    (A) the death of his wife
    (B) strong cigarettes
    (C) careless driving
    (D) poor English
    (E) being Jewish

26. When the narrator says, "So it was what I had heard" (line 2), he suggests that
    (A) he is hard of hearing
    (B) he had thought he heard a previous "shalom"
    (C) he had never heard "shalom" before
    (D) "shalom" is a dangerous greeting
    (E) he has become more relaxed

27. The narrator's attitude toward his own powers of observation is
    (A) confident   (B) uncertain   (C) ambiguous   (D) sad   (E) skeptical

28. When the narrator says "in afterthought a discontented type," he probably means that
    (A) the taxi driver becomes discontented after thinking heavily
    (B) there are many other discontents in the city
    (C) Slavic types are normally discontent
    (D) the driver is discontented with his passenger
    (E) his perception of the taxi driver's discontent did not occur to him when they first met

STOP

IF YOU FINISH BEFORE TIME HAS ELAPSED, CHECK YOUR WORK ON THIS SECTION OF THE TEST ONLY. DO NOT GO ON TO THE NEXT SECTION OF THE TEST UNTIL TIME IS UP FOR THIS SECTION.

SECTION VI
ANALYTICAL REASONING

Time—35 Minutes
26 Questions

Directions:
In this section you will be given groups of questions based on different sets of conditions. Drawing a simple diagram may be helpful in answering some of the questions. You are to choose the best answer and mark the corresponding space on your answer sheet.

Questions 1–6

   (1)   Three bakers, Juan, Karen, and Leslie, each has a speciality. One bakes cookies, one bakes bread, and one bakes pies. One works at the Uptown Bakery, one works at the Midtown Bakery, and one works at the Downtown Bakery. Each bakery bakes only one thing, either cookies, bread, or pies.

   (2)   The Uptown Bakery bakes only cookies.

   (3)   Leslie does not work at Uptown.

   (4)   Karen does not work at Downtown.

   (5)   Pies are not baked at Midtown.

   (6)   Karen does not bake cookies.

1. Which statements are necessary to determine whether Leslie bakes cookies?
   (A) 1, 3, and 4   (B) 1, 2, and 3   (C) 1, 3, and 6   (D) 1, 2, and 6
   (E) 1, 2, 4, and 6

2. Using only statements 1, 2, and 5, which of the following can be deduced?

   I.   Bread is baked at Midtown.
   II.   Pies are baked at Downtown.
   III.   Cookies are baked at Uptown.
   (A) II only   (B) III only   (C) I and III   (D) II and III   (E) I, II, and III

3. Using only statements 1, 2, 3, 5, and 6, which of the following can be deduced?

   I.   Juan bakes cookies.
   II.   Leslie works at either Midtown or Downtown.
   III.   Karen does not work at Downtown.
   (A) I and II   (B) I and III   (C) II and III   (D) I, II, and III   (E) None of the above

4. Which of the following MUST be true about pies?

   I.   Pies are baked at Downtown.
   II.   Juan bakes pies.
   III.   Karen does not bake pies.
   (A) I only   (B) II only   (C) III only   (D) I and III   (E) II and III

5. Which of the following MUST be true?

   I.   Leslie does not bake cookies.
   II.   Karen bakes bread.
   III.   Juan does not bake cookies.
   (A) I and II   (B) II and III   (C) I and III   (D) I, II, and III   (E) None of the above

6. How many of the above statements (1–6) are necessary to determine whether bread is baked at Downtown?
   (A) Two   (B) Three   (C) Four   (D) Five   (E) Six

Questions 7–10

   (1)   Team 1 consists of players A, B, and C.
   (2)   Team 2 consists of players D, E, and F.
   (3)   Team 3 consists of players G, H, and K.
   (4)   Another team of six players is to be chosen from the above teams with two players coming from each of the three teams.
   (5)   B refuses to play with D.
   (6)   If C plays, K must play.
   (7)   G and H refuse to play together.

7. If A is not chosen, then how many members of the team are determined?
(A) Two   (B) Three   (C) Four   (D) Five   (E) Six

8. If D is chosen, then three of the other players could be

  I. A, G, K
  II. B, C, G
  III. C, E, K
(A) I only   (B) II only   (C) III only   (D) Two of these   (E) All of these

9. Which of the following is (are) true?

  I. C must play.
  II. If A plays, then so must F.
  III. If B plays, then so must E.
(A) I only   (B) II only   (C) III only   (D) Two of these   (E) All of these

10. In addition to facts 1, 2, 3, and 4, which of the facts lead(s) to the conclusion that K must play?
(A) 6 and 7   (B) 6   (C) 7   (D) 5, 6, and 7   (E) K does not have to play

Questions 11–14

Eight people—A, B, C, D, E, F, G, H—are to be seated at a square table, two people on each side.
B must sit directly across from H.
A must sit between and next to F and G.
C cannot sit next to F.

11. Which of the following MUST be true?

  I. C sits next to either B or H.
  II. H must sit next to G.
  III. F sits next to D or E.
(A) I and II   (B) I and III   (C) II and III   (D) One of these   (E) All of these

12. If B does not sit next to G, then which of the following is (are) possible?

  I. If C sits next to B, then D could sit directly across from F.
  II. If C sits next to D, then E could sit directly across from G.
  III. C could sit next to G.
(A) I and II   (B) I and III   (C) II and III   (D) One of these   (E) All of these

13. If C sits directly across from F, who could sit next to H?

  I. C
  II. D
  III. E
  IV. G
(A) One of these   (B) Two of these   (C) Three of these   (D) None of these
(E) All of these

14. How many different people could be seated directly across from A?
(A) One   (B) Two   (C) Three   (D) Four   (E) Five

Questions 15–19

Eight busts of American Presidents are to be arranged on two shelves, left to right. Each shelf accommodates exactly four busts. One shelf is directly above the other shelf. The busts are of John Adams, George Washington, Abraham Lincoln, Thomas Jefferson, James Monroe, John Kennedy, Theodore Roosevelt and Franklin Delano Roosevelt.
The Roosevelt busts may not be directly one above the other.
The bust of Kennedy must be adjacent to the bust of a Roosevelt.
The bust of Jefferson must be directly above the bust of John Adams.
The busts of Monroe, Adams, Kennedy and Franklin Delano Roosevelt must be on the bottom shelf.
The bust of Monroe must be third from the left.

15. If the bust of Theodore Roosevelt is second from the left on one shelf, which MUST be true?
    (A) The bust of Adams must be first on a shelf.
    (B) The bust of Adams must be third on a shelf.
    (C) The bust of Kennedy must be first on a shelf.
    (D) The bust of Kennedy must be second on a shelf.
    (E) The bust of Kennedy must be third on a shelf.

16. Which of the following MUST be true about the bust of Monroe?
    (A) It is next to the bust of Adams.
    (B) It is next to the bust of Kennedy.
    (C) It is next to the bust of Franklin Delano Roosevelt.
    (D) It is directly under the bust of Lincoln.
    (E) It is directly under the bust of Theodore Roosevelt.

17. If the bust of Washington is first, directly above Kennedy's, all of the following MUST be true except
    (A) the bust of Jefferson is fourth
    (B) the bust of Theodore Roosevelt is third
    (C) the bust of Franklin Delano Roosevelt is second
    (D) the bust of Lincoln is third
    (E) the bust of Adams is fourth

18. Which of the following are possible orders for the busts on the top shelf?
    I.   Washington, Lincoln, Theodore Roosevelt, Jefferson
    II. Lincoln, Washington, Theodore Roosevelt, Jefferson
    III. Theodore Roosevelt, Lincoln, Washington, Jefferson
    IV. Lincoln, Theodore Roosevelt, Washington, Jefferson
    (A) I and II   (B) I and III   (C) I, II, and III
    (D) I, II, and IV   (E) I, II, III, and IV

19. If the bust of Lincoln is next to the bust of Jefferson, all of the following are true except
    (A) if the bust of Kennedy is first, the bust of Theodore Roosevelt is also first
    (B) if the bust of Washington is first, the bust of Franklin Delano Roosevelt is also first
    (C) if the bust of Washington is second, the bust of Kennedy is also second
    (D) if the bust of Kennedy is second, the bust of Theodore Roosevelt is also second
    (E) if the bust of Washington is second, the bust of Franklin Delano Roosevelt is also second

Questions 20–26

For a dinner party, a hostess needs several different three-bean salads.
Each salad is to contain three types of beans, chosen from garbanzos, chili beans, wax beans,

lima beans, and kidney beans.
Chili beans and lima beans do not taste good together and therefore are never used in the same salad.
Lima beans and kidney beans do not look good together and therefore are never used in the same salad.

20. How many different salads (using the above ingredients) could the hostess serve that contain lima beans?
(A) Zero   (B) One   (C) Two   (D)Three   (E) Four

21. How many different salads could she serve that do not contain chili beans?
(A) Zero   (B) One   (C) Two   (D)Three   (E) Four

22. How many different salad combinations could she serve at the party?
(A) Four   (B) Five   (C) Six   (D) Seven   (E) Eight

23. Which beans will occur most often in the salad combinations that could be served at the party?
(A)   chili and garbanzos
(B)   chili and limas
(C)   limas and wax beans
(D)   kidney and limas
(E)   garbanzos and wax beans

24. If there are only enough wax beans to go into two salads, what is the total number of salads that can be served?
(A) One   (B) Two   (C) Three   (D) Four   (E) Five

25. If the hostess discovers the garbanzos have gone bad, how many three-bean combinations can she serve without using the rotten garbanzos?
(A) Zero   (B) One   (C) Two   (D) Three   (E) Four

26. If there were no restrictions on any three-bean combinations, the number of salads she could serve at the party with her given ingredients would increase by
(A) one   (B) two   (C) three   (D) five   (E) ten

STOP

END OF EXAMINATION. IF YOU FINISH BEFORE TIME HAS ELAPSED, CHECK YOUR WORK ON THIS SECTION ONLY. DO NOT GO BACK TO ANY OTHER SECTION OF THE EXAMINATION.

ANSWER KEY

Section I:
Reading Comprehension

1. B	7. A	13. D	19. D	25. E
2. C	8. C	14. B	20. B	26. B
3. E	9. C	15. D	21. D	27. E
4. C	10. B	16. B	22. A	28. A
5. D	11. C	17. D	23. D	29. B
6. B	12. E	18. C	24. E	30. C

Section IV:
Logical Reasoning

1. A	7. B	12. C	17. D	22. E
2. B	8. C	13. B	18. C	23. B
3. E	9. B	14. C	19. C	24. E
4. D	10. E	15. E	20. C	25. D
5. D	11. B	16. B	21. E	26. B
6. A				

Section II:
Analytical Reasoning

1. C	6. A	11. E	16. A	21. E
2. B	7. D	12. E	17. A	22. C
3. E	8. E	13. A	18. B	23. D
4. C	9. D	14. B	19. A	24. B
5. C	10. A	15. E	20. D	25. D

Section V:
Reading Comprehension

1. D	7. D	13. A	19. B	24. A
2. B	8. D	14. E	20. C	25. C
3. D	9. B	15. B	21. E	26. B
4. D	10. B	16. E	22. D	27. A
5. E	11. B	17. E	23. E	28. E
6. D	12. A	18. C		

Section III:
Evaluation of Facts

1. C	8. C	15. C	22. C	29. C
2. D	9. D	16. B	23. D	30. A
3. A	10. B	17. B	24. A	31. C
4. A	11. B	18. A	25. D	32. B
5. C	12. D	19. D	26. D	33. B
6. C	13. A	20. C	27. B	34. C
7. A	14. D	21. B	28. A	35. D

Section VI:
Analytical Reasoning

1. B	6. B	11. D	16. A	21. C
2. E	7. D	12. E	17. D	22. B
3. A	8. D	13. E	18. E	23. E
4. D	9. C	14. C	19. C	24. C
5. A	10. C	15. D	20. B	25. B
				26. D

MODEL TEST ANALYSIS

Doing model exams and understanding the explanations afterwards are of course important in acquainting you with typical LSAT question types and successful approaches to the questions. However, another benefit of carefully analyzing these model tests is to understand the kinds of errors you are making and thus work to minimize them. For instance, if a very high percentage of your incorrect answers is due to "careless error" or "misread problem," then perhaps you are working much too fast and should slow your pace accordingly. If your incorrect answers are due primarily to "lack of knowledge," then a careful rereading and reworking of the appropriate question-type chapter may be in order. Or if you find that you aren't completing a large number of questions because of lack of time, you may need to either increase your speed or learn to use the "one-check, two-check" technique more effectively.

This kind of analysis of the model tests will enable you to identify your particular weaknesses and thus remedy them.

Model Test One Analysis

Section	Total Number of Questions	Number Correct	Number Incorrect	Number Unanswered*
I: Reading Comprehension	30			
II: Analytical Reasoning	25			
III: Evaluation of Facts	35			
IV: Logical Reasoning	26			
V: Reading Comprehension	28			
VI: Analytical Reasoning	26			
TOTALS:	170			

*At this stage in your preparation, you should not be leaving any unanswered answer spaces. At least fill in a guess, as there is no penalty for a wrong answer.

Reasons for Incorrect Answers

You may wish to evaluate the explanations before completing this chart.

Section	Total Number Incorrect	Lack of Knowledge	Misread Problem	Careless Error	Unanswered or Wrong Guess
I: Reading Comprehension					
II: Analytical Reasoning					
III: Evaluation of Facts					
IV: Logical Reasoning					
V: Reading Comprehension					
VI: Analytical Reasoning					
TOTALS:					

EXPLANATIONS OF ANSWERS

Section I

Passage 1

1. **B** Paragraph 3 states, "Some species are killed by frost; others require frost and cold conditions to fruit."

2. **C** Paragraph 5 tells that hygrophytes have little defense against a water shortage.

3. **E** The final sentence in paragraph 2 aligns plants affected by light and darkness with "particular latitudes," that is, particular regions north or south of the equator.

4. **C** Reincarnation (C) might be associated with *annuals*, which disappear and reappear again through new seeds ("new life").

5. **D** The factors that account for distribution are all related to geographic location, and all affect the plant's growth and sustenance; this becomes more obvious through the remainder of the passage. (A) must be eliminated because, although the author may have left other factors unmentioned, she does not acknowledge their existence within the passage.

6. **B** Each of the factors is accorded a separate paragraph, and although we must reasonably suppose that such factors must coexist, the author does not express interrelationships among factors. (E) is not stressed in the passage, but neither is it implied. Each of the other choices is an expressed fact.

Passage 2

7. **A** Aristotle's democracy had the poor "promoting their selfish interests." (D) may be considered, but must be eliminated because no clear relationship exists between "selfish interests" and the *purity* of one's needs.

8. **C** By mentioning small countries in which pure democracy is viable, the author implies that large countries cannot administer pure democracy, but he does not detail the difficulties of direct representation on a large scale. Each of the other choices is explicitly mentioned in the paragraph.

9. **C** After explaining Aristotle's theory, the author compares it to later conceptions. This overall purpose implies the praise of Aristotle's foresight (D), but the passage as a whole informs much more than it praises.

10. **B** The common welfare is an "underlying assumption" of modern democracy, says the author, one that "probably will result" (paragraph 3).

11. **C** A presumption is the taking of something for granted. By citing Aristotle only, the author seems to presume his singular relevance to modern democracy. (B) and (D) are not matters taken for granted, and (A) and (E) are irrelevant to the passage.

12. **E** The author's stress on how "democracy" has changed since Aristotle's time helps us to eliminate (B) and (C). (A) and (D) are neither expressed nor implied. (E) summarizes the belief that motivates the whole discussion.

MODEL TEST ONE

Passage 3

13. **D** The statement follows the narrator's admission that he is spending time in "vaults and charnel houses," that is, studying corpses. "Wonders of the eye and brain," explicitly refers to sight and intellect. Only (D) mentions corpses.

14. **B** The narrator stresses his interest in chemistry in the first sentence, and later stresses his interest in physiology. He also mentions anatomy, but that subject is not offered as a choice. (A), (C), and (D) are not *academic* subjects.

15. **D** The central question that motivates his research is "Whence . . . did the principle of life proceed?"

16. **B** The narration of personal experiences is appropriate in a personal journal. A "soliloquy" is a dramatic mode in which a character speaks privately, without acknowledging an audience.

17. **D** The narrator's comment on his lack of superstition immediately precedes his scientific investigation of the dead and thus verifies the objectivity of that investigation. His lack of superstition was, admittedly, influenced by his father, but is not described as a species of obedience (A).

18. **C** The first paragraph introduces his interest in chemistry, and the second paragraph describes "application . . . in my laboratory," clearly the further pursuit of scientific (chemical) study.

Passage 4

19. **D** Paragraph 2 explicitly states that the men and boys live in half the tent, and the women and girls live in the other half. (E) is also correct, but not as complete as (D).

20. **B** As commonly understood, sanctuary was shelter (within the church) for a criminal in flight. The other choices might be eliminated simply because they are not exclusively Medieval practices.

21. **D** The nomads, always on the move, comprise five percent of the populace; presumably, the rest have stationary residences (see paragraph 1).

22. **A** In paragraph 6, a parenthetical remark states that tribes are comprised of clans; this means, of course, that *several* clans make up *one* tribe. (D) is possible, but not verified in the passage.

23. **D** In paragraph 3 we are told, "He rarely eats meat."

24. **E** The passage consists of fact after fact, simply presented in plain language. The author is objective, and never presents information that seems, on the face of it, biased or controversial.

Passage 5

25. **E** Paragraph (a) tells us that the author only "pretends" to watch with the "impassivity of the scientists."

26. **B** Halfway through paragraph (c), the author begins generalizing about the "best naturalists," distinguishing them from "mere" naturalists. This section is a mixture of both praise and disdain.

27. **E** Each of the other choices is either factual or a commonplace expression not regarded as literary, or a quite nonliterary use of metaphor (D). (E) compares marriage to a beverage and produces an unusual, highly subjective metaphor that departs from the dispassionate objectivity of the most conservative naturalism.

28. **A** Paragraph (b), which aligns naturalism with social science, stresses the writer's attention to "data from actual life." (C) is generally true of naturalism, but deemphasized character does not receive so close a comparison with scientific research.

29. **B** Note the author's emphasis that differences between realism and naturalism are not "clear-cut and definitive," and his enumeration of tendencies rather than unquestionable facts. He does not refer to arts other than literature (E), but this is not because he is "careful" not to, but simply because he excludes the subject. His lack of absolutism, however, comes across through careful wording.

30. **C** Throughout the passage the author stresses the "real life" quality of naturalism. In the final paragraph he explicitly distinguishes between the "romantic" author and the "naturalistic" one, and enumerates factors mentioned in (A), (B), (D), and (E) as aspects of naturalism.

Section II

Answers 1–6

1. **C** From statements 1, 2, and 7 we can only deduce that Fred must sit between two people because the end seats are already taken.

2. **B** From statements 1, 2, 6, and 7 we can construct the following chart:

E			F	L	S

We now know that Tom cannot sit next to Simon because Lynn already occupies that seat.

3. **E** None of the original statements can be deduced solely from statement 7. For instance, we cannot deduce that Fred will have people on each side of him because we do not know whether all the boys and girls sit in the same row.

4. **C** From all the information given, the following chart can be constructed:

E	T	J	F	L	S

Thus, Tom sits next to Enola and next to Jan.

5. **C** From the chart we can see that Lynn sits next to Fred and Simon, not next to Tom. Note that (E) is still true ("Lynn sits between Enola and Simon") even though Lynn doesn't necessarily sit next to them.

6. **A** From the information given, the friends could sit only in this order: Enola, Tom, Jan, Fred, Lynn, Simon.

Answers 7–10

Constructing the following chart would be helpful in answering the questions:

$$\mathbf{DO}$$
$$\text{(brother of)} \longrightarrow \mathbf{REY}$$
$$\text{(sister of)} \longrightarrow \mathbf{MI}$$
$$\text{(brother of)} \longrightarrow \mathbf{FA}$$

7. **D** Statements I and III must be true. Since Do is Rey's brother, then Do must be a boy (I). Since Mi is Fa's brother, then Mi must be a boy (III). We have no knowledge, however, as to the sex of Fa.

8. **E** Neither I nor II *must* be false. We do know that Rey is the sister of Mi, and Mi is the brother of Fa, so we therefore know that Rey and Fa are related. But since we do not know whether Fa is a boy or a girl, I ("Fa is Rey's brother") could possibly be true. Statement II ("Do is Mi's brother"), on the other hand, is definitely true, since Do is the brother of Rey, and Rey is the sister of Mi. (Be careful of the wording in these types of questions. Look for the words "MUST be true" and "could be true," two very different situations.)

9. **D** Either I or II could be true, but not both. We know that Do, Rey, Mi, and Fa are all siblings (since Do is Rey's brother, Rey is Mi's sister, and Mi is Fa's brother). But we do not know Fa's sex. If Fa is a girl, I is true. If Fa is a boy, II is true. So either I or II *could* be true, but not both at the same time.

10. **A** If Fa is a girl, then we now know the sex of all the siblings. Of the choices, the only correct answer then is (A)—Do is her brother.

Answers 11–19

Constructing the following chart from the information given would be helpful in answering the questions:

	A	B	T	Z
A	?	Z	Z	T
B	Z	?	O	A
T	Z	O	?	B
Z	T	A	B	?

11. **E** Neither I nor II *must* be true. We do not know of any definite way to form Theta without Alpha. Nor do we know of any definite way to form Beta without Zeta. Therefore neither statement *must* be true.

12. **E** From our chart we can see that, when Alpha forms with any other, the result is either Zeta or Theta. Therefore, it will not give Alpha or Beta.

13. **A** This answer may be derived directly from statement 4: Beta combines with Theta, giving Omega.

14. **B** From our chart we can see that, if Beta is involved, then the outcome may be Alpha, Omega, or Zeta.

15. **E** We have no information about the results if Omega combines with anything.

16. **A** Only I must be true. From our chart we can see that Zeta may be formed by the combinations of Alpha with Theta, or Alpha with Beta. (It may also be formed by the combinations of Alpha with itself, Beta with itself, etc.) So we know that Zeta can be formed in at least two different ways. But we know of only one definite way that Omega may be formed (Theta with Beta). So only I *must* be true.

17. **A** From the chart we can see that only I is true: Zeta and Theta combine to give Beta.

18. **B** The outcome of Alpha and Beta is Zeta. The outcome of Alpha and Zeta is Theta. Thus, if the two outcomes (Zeta and Theta) combine, the result will then be Beta.

19. **A** Alpha with any other (with the exception of Omega, which we do not know) produces either Zeta or Theta, which is similar to the outcome of Omega with Theta.

Answers 20–25

A simple chart may help to answer each question.

20. **D** For this question your chart may look like this:

FATHER
blue eyes
brown hair

MOTHER
?

CHILDREN
blue eyes
red hair

First, note that, if all the children have red hair, then all must be girls, since a boy would take both of the father's characteristics. Therefore, III is true. And the children would thus have to get their red hair from their mother (I). Statement II is not necessarily true as their red-haired mother could have blue eyes.

21. **E** This is a difficult problem. Your chart should look like this:

1ST GENERATION: **FATHER** **MOTHER**
blue eyes blue eyes
brown hair red hair

2ND GENERATION: **IF MALE CHILD** **IF FEMALE CHILD** **CHILD'S SPOUSE**
blue eyes blue eyes ?
brown hair red hair

3RD GENERATION: **GRANDCHILD**
red hair
green eyes

Since the grandchild has red hair and green eyes, she must be a girl (III). And since she is a girl, she must get one characteristic from each of her parents (the 2nd generation). Therefore, the only person from whom she could get green eyes would be the other spouse of the second generation (II). The red hair must thus come from the 2nd generation female (I).

22. **C** Only girls can have both green eyes and red hair. But any girl from a blue-eyed, brown-haired father must have at least one of his characteristics. Therefore, green eyes and red hair are not possible characteristics of his child.

23. **D** Every male must have *at least one* of the following characteristics: blue eyes, brown hair. Therefore, a green-eyed male *must* have brown hair.

24. **B** If two blue-eyed people get married, the female *must* have red hair because all females have *at least one* of the following characteristics: green eyes and/or red hair. Note that the father could also have blue eyes and red hair; therefore, the child could be either a boy or girl.

25. **D** If all the children of a couple have brown hair, then the girls must have green eyes, brown hair. Thus, if the girls get their brown hair from their mother, then the other characteristic of their mother *must* be green eyes (since all females have at least one of green eyes/red hair). Or the girls could get their green eyes from their mother. Either way, their mother must have green eyes.

Section III

Set 1

1. **C** This is a relevant question that can be answered from the facts. No, Scarlet was not using the man-catching perfume as intended.

2. **D** This question is irrelevant.

3. **A** To answer this relevant question, you must choose between the two rules. Each rule will give you a different answer. By Rule I, Scarlet will not win the suit, as the product was not used as intended by the seller. By Rule II, she will win the suit, since the retail seller is responsible for all injuries or damages occurring because of the use of his product.

4. **A** To answer this relevant question, you must choose between the two rules. Each rule will give you a different answer. By Rule I, Scarlet will not win the suit, as the product was not used as intended by the seller during the time of injury. Scarlet's intentions have no bearing on the rules. By Rule II, she will win the suit since the retail seller is responsible.

5. **C** This relevant question can be answered by applying the rules. By Rule I, if the perfume was originally meant for horses, then Scarlet will win the suit since she was using the perfume as intended by the seller. By Rule II also, she will win the suit.

Set 2

6. **C** This relevant question can be answered from the facts. Yes, he was injured.

7. **A** To answer this relevant question, you must choose between the two rules. Each rule will give you a different answer. By Rule I, Michael's mother will win the suit as Mrs. Zee is liable. By Rule II, she will not win because the negligence was accidental.

8. **C** This relevant question can be answered by applying Rule I. By Rule I, Mrs. Zee would be guilty. Rule II does not apply because the negligence was not accidental.

9. **D** This question is irrelevant.

10. **B** To answer this relevant question, you need additional rules. Since Mrs. Zee was not the manufacturer, Rules I and II do not apply.

Set 3

11. **B** To answer this relevant question, you need additional information. Since Rule II calls for a disturbance that occurs "regularly," more information is required about the frequency of the aircraft noise.

12. **D** This question is irrelevant.

13. **A** To answer this relevant question, you must choose between the two rules. Each rule gives a different outcome. If the noise kept Tanya awake each night, Rule II would support her; but since her notice to leave was not given 30 days before February 1, Rule I supports Laura.

14. **D** This question is irrelevant.

Set 4

15. **C** This relevant question can be answered by applying Rule I, since Herman broke into the house for the purpose of stealing property. Rule II does not apply since he broke into the house in the morning.

16. **B** To answer this relevant question you need additional rules. Since possession of another's property is a major part of Rule II, this question is highly relevant.

17. **B** To answer this relevant question you need additional information. Even if Herman found money in the house, you do not know that he took it.

18. **A** To answer this relevant question you need to choose between the rules. Each rule will give a different outcome. By Rule I, Herman would be guilty. By Rule II, he would not be guilty.

19. **D** This question is irrelevant.

20. **C** This relevant question can be readily answered from the facts. Herman broke a back window and slid into the house.

Set 5

21. **B** To answer this relevant question, you need additional information. The facts do not make clear whether or not Linda's knowledge of the written disclaimer can be established.

22. **C** This relevant question can be answered by applying the rules. If Morris knew of the car defects, Linda will win according to Rule I. If Linda did not know of the disclaimer, Rule II will not apply.

23. **D** This question is irrelevant. The facts make it clear that Morris falsely affirmed the reliability of the car.

24. **A** To answer this relevant question, you must choose between the two rules. Each rule gives a different outcome. According to Rule I, Linda will win; according to Rule II, she will not.

25. **D** This question is irrelevant. Personal injury has no relevance to the rules of this case.

Set 6

26. **D** This question is irrelevant. Length is not an issue.

27. **B** To answer this relevant question you need additional information. You need to know the length of time that the sunlight was unobstructed to see whether Rule I applies.

28. **A** To answer this relevant question you must choose between the rules. Each rule gives a different outcome. By Rule I, Slim will win. By Rule II, TBI will win.

29. **C** This relevant question can be answered by applying Rule I. By Rule I, Slim would win the suit. Rule II does not apply if the land was not vacant.

Set 7

30. **A** To answer this relevant question you must choose between the rules. Each rule will give you a different outcome. By Rule I, since the consequences would be detrimental to the environment of the region, Thomas would not obtain the variance. By Rule II, since the result would be beneficial to the surrounding region, he would get the variance.

31. **C** This relevant question can be answered by applying the rules. If the shopping center would not be detrimental and would be beneficial, then Thomas would get the variance.

32. **B** To answer this relevant question you need more information. You do not know whether the shopping center would be beneficial to the area, only that Thomas believes that it would.

33. **B** To answer this relevant question you need more information concerning the evaluation process used by the environmentalists. Knowing whether the streams are vital to the region is relevant to Rule I.

34. **C** This relevant question can be answered by applying Rule I. If the streams are vital to the environment, then Thomas would not get the variance. Rule II does not apply because the land was not rural.

35. **D** This question is irrelevant.

Section IV

1. **A** By criticizing "offensive sex, violence, or profanity" in the third paragraph, the author implicitly defines "objectionable" as used in the fifth paragraph. (C), (D), and (E) are common enough terms so that no explicit or implicit definition is required here, and (B), "appropriate," is left largely undefined in the passage.

2. **B** By urging moviegoers to patronize films *in order to* influence academy judges, the author reveals his assumption that the academy will be influenced by the number of people paying to see a movie.

3. **E** Bob's answer shows that he thinks that people other than teachers are mean. His thought was that Andy meant otherwise.

4. **D** The author's concluding contention is that Roosevelt was not only a good marksman, but also an intellectually curious and patient man. If Roosevelt was known to leave safaris which were not immediately productive, this fact would substantially weaken the author's contention about Roosevelt's "patient observation."

5. **D** "Due to a recent cut in state funding of our program" indicates that other criteria were used in determining entering class size besides candidates' scores and grades, namely the financial situation of the college. The words *seriously* in choice (B) and *severe* in choice (E) are not necessarily supported by the passage, and thus make those choices incorrect. Since grade point average is only one of several criteria for admission, we cannot deduce (A) with certainty.

6. **A** This sentence not only fits well stylistically but completes the thought of the passage by tying it into the opening statement.

7. **B** The author of this passage actually defines conscience as the ability to sense right and wrong.

8. **C** "Opportunity makes the thief" fails to take into account that some people were already thieves, before the opportunity arose. "Without opportunity there would be no crime" fails to consider that thievery is not the only type of crime.

9. **B** This choice offers the most thorough and comprehensive evidence that the viewing of violent television precedes criminal behavior. (A) is not the best choice because it describes viewing habits that follow rather than precede criminal behavior.

10. **E** The use of "overwhelming" leaves the evidence unspecified, thus opening to challenge the extent and nature of the report's data.

11. **B** The mention of "emotion" in two of the sentences following (11) narrows your choices to (A), (B), or (E). Since the passage is about the "affects" of sensations, (A) or (E) would be inaccurate.

12. **C** An emotion has a *logical* component, so the passage says. All choices except (C) are "illogical" terms.

13. **B** If the experiences and lifestyle of the Aryan race are uniquely different from those of other cultures, it would seriously weaken the author's conclusion that studying the Aryan race will be helpful in understanding the experiences and life styles of other races. That its communal arrangements are *unique* would make comparison between the Aryan race and other cultures impossible.

14. **C** The author presents a *contrast* between life and honor: in particular, the final sentence suggests that life and honor have opposite qualities. Of the choices, the only opposite of *transient* is *eternal*.

15. **E** The logic of this statement goes from the general absolute ("all") to the specific ("this animal"), concluding with specific to specific. Symbolically, if *P* implies *Q*, then *not Q* implies *not P*. (E) goes from general absolute ("all") to specific ("this liquid"), concluding with specific to specific. Notice how and where the inverse ("not") is inserted. Using symbols, we have that, if *P* implies *Q*, then *not Q* implies *not P*.

16. **B** This is a close one. (B) and (D) both weaken the argument by pointing out that all dogs do not always bark, but (B) is absolute. (D) is tentative, since a dog trained not to bark might do so by accident.

17. **D** (D) is the correct answer, since it states "cheat on *none* of the exams," while the passage states, "Everyone has cheated on *at least* one exam." (A) is incorrect, since it says nothing about what Joe actually did. (B) is incorrect, since, although we are told that cheating is "wrong," we do not know what is "acceptable" and what is not. Do not make subjective answers. (C) is not a good choice, since Jack may never have taken an exam. (E) is incorrect, since it just restates two of the given conditions.

18. **C** Statement I repeats the first part of the sentence, and III and IV demonstrate the second part of the sentence—ignorance of *different* subjects. But since the sentence singles out no *one* subject, II is incorrect.

19. **C** The sentence criticizes people, and a satirist is such a critic.

20. **C** (A) contradicts the statement's urging of economy. (B) introduces an irrelevant word, "terminology." (D) and (E) are *absolute* statements about assumptions, but the statement itself is *relative*, urging us only to simplify our assumptions *if one such simplification is possible; in other words, "If an issue is simple, don't complicate it."*

21. **E** The question demonstrates a solution and the fact that an alternative exists.

22. **E** (A) is obviously true. (B) also satisfies the conditions. (C) is correct, since 3.5 was required with a score of 800. (D) is correct, since we do not know anything about numbers of appli-

cants. (E) is inconsistent, since a score of 1200 is required with a GPA of 2.5. (E) specifies a score *less than* 1200. Therefore, a GPA greater than (*not less than*) 2.5 would be required for admittance.

23. **B** To speak in positive terms about the increase in school degrees, the author must assume that the degrees indicate what they are supposed to indicate, that is, well-educated individuals. (A) and (E) are empty statements; (C) and (D) are altogether unsubstantiated by either expressed or implied information.

24. **E** Although the brand name is No-NOCK, the advertisement makes no claim to stop the engine from knocking. All the other claims are contained in the advertisement.

25. **D** This choice repudiates the suggestion that gentleness and graciousness were once part of the American character. (B), another choice worth considering, is not best because it does not address the temperament of tennis players as directly as does (D).

26. **B** By asking Dolores to choose between conventional and nuclear weapons, Fran has concluded that Dolores' statement calls for a decision. (C), worth considering, is not best because Fran supposes that Dolores has *not* made a choice—hence her question.

Section V

Passage 1

1. **D** A conversational tone is mentioned as part of the "natural style" that developed coincidentally with Roosevelt's administration in the 1930s (paragraph 5). Roosevelt's own radio "conversations" would seem to be examples of this natural style. (C) is an irrelevant point; (E) seems unrelated to the limitations of radio; (A) is not supported by a characterization of American politics as propaganda; (B) refers to theatricality, a characteristic largely unrelated to Roosevelt's chats.

2. **B** This is an explicit and repeated point.

3. **D** The author's skepticism is expressed when he says that the Russian films "made the new regime *appear* to be the heir of a glorious revolutionary tradition"; he calls into question the facts by labeling them as merely *apparent*.

4. **D** The author's persistent point, that the style of popular entertainment affects the style of politics, indicates this choice. He associates excessive gestures with early cinema and expressionist theater (paragraph 4); only (D) accounts for at least one of these media. (C) refers to the style of movie *heroes*, a style not necessarily associated with exaggerated gestures.

5. **E** All other choices are either inaccurate or too specific. The author's repeated comparison of politics and government to popular entertainment (mainly movies) indicates (E).

6. **D** We are told toward the end of the passage that during the 1930s and 1940s the isolated, idolized, one-of-a-kind stars became "more human" and could be imitated. The eventual result of their influence was "the political Mr. Everyman."

7. **D** Analogy occurs when one phenomenon is compared point by point with another. In this case, politics is compared to show business. Synecdoche (B) and metonomy (E) are the only other terms that describe *literary* techniques. Synecdoche uses a part to stand for the whole

(all *hands* on deck); and metonomy is the emblematic substitution of one term for another ("the King" being called "the Crown").

Passage 2

8. **D** Miss Hamilton explicitly states that the use of her first name is "incorrect," and since this question asks for what she implies, you should eliminate (C). (B) is also an explicitly stated fact. Her later petition indicates the implication of her objection; she cites "equal protection" and "etiquette" in her favor. Both are related to the "demeaning" quality of her court experience.

9. **B** The Red Queen in *Alice* is an absurd tyrant, as you should realize either through familiarity with the book, or by recognizing that "sentence first, trial afterward" is both absurd and tyrannical.

10. **B** The author's ability to *quote* the court participants indicates that he was either at the hearing or privy to a direct transcript.

11. **B** Only (B) is a question that is both raised and not answered in the passage. Other choices are either questions that are answered or questions that are never raised.

12. **A** (C) is irrelevant to the race of *this* judge and staff; (B) refers to the legal profession in general rather than the officers of the court in particular; (D) should be eliminated because the present racial situation is not addressed; and (E) should be eliminated because the race of the arresting officers is never mentioned.

13. **A** In the midst of recounting the court dialogue, the author says, "Miss Hamilton would not be intimidated," thus suggesting the judge's purpose.

14. **E** The narrator writes seriously, so we may eliminate (A) and (D). He is not openly contemptuous of the court (B), although he does not support their position. And he is not explicitly messianic (C), that is, he does not advertise himself as a savior or liberator.

Passage 3

15. **B** Directly following the mention of a *roman policier*, we have a coordinate statement about detective stories; the indication is that a *roman policier* is a detective story. Also, note that *policier* suggests the English word "police." Altogether, it appears that a *roman policier* centers on the investigation of a crime.

16. **E** After enumerating the possible components of the plot of *Marienbad,* the author says, "You take your choice"; earlier he notes that "the spectator's work" becomes part of the "creation." (D) is possibly but not necessarily true.

17. **E** The first paragraph states that he "*wants* his readers to feel disappointed," and that their disappointment tells him he has been successful.

18. **C** In the second paragraph we are told that Robbe-Grillet's first novel contained descriptions stemming from his work as an agronomic (farming) engineer. (D) is probably true, but quite vague. (A) refers to an observation from childhood, but we are not told that he is *familiar* with the *habits* of the birds.

19. **B** The first and second sentence imply a connection between popularity and less cerebral (intellectual) work, and the only logical antecedent to "that" is the initial statement that Robbe-Grillet is less cerebral.

20. **C** Paragraph 2 begins abruptly with *LIFE*, and introduces biographical details apart from the preceding discussion of Robbe-Grillet's writing. (B), (D), and (E) do not describe stylistic features.

21. **E** In the mention of Sarraute and Butor at the beginning of the passage, the author declares only that they can be compared to Robbe-Grillet. All other choices require more information than is given.

Passage 4

22. **D** We are looking for an underlying *assumption*, that is, an unstated but suggested belief. To stress Fahrenheit is to clarify the nature of the measurement and distinguish it from Centigrade. (A) is true, but it is an explicit fact, not an assumption.

23. **E** (B) and (C) are explicit facts rather than implications. The taxi driver, not the narrator, calls himself a "marginal Jew," (A). The narrator has recently changed his name back to its more Jewish version—Harvitz—and it is the significance of this change that he associates with his "true self."

24. **A** The first long paragraph says, "The taxi driver sat in his shirt sleeves." (B), (D), and (E) are not certain, and (C) does not refer to apparel.

25. **C** While riding, the narrator is "thrown sideways," and notes that the driver offers "no apologies."

26. **B** The "it" clearly refers to "Shalom," and the author's amazement ("who would have thought so?"), suggests that he had dismissed an earlier "shalom" as an impossibility.

27. **A** At the end of the first long paragraph, the narrator says of his description, "I have an experienced eye for such details." He clearly expresses confidence.

28. **E** The narrator is here describing the driver's physical features. The "afterthought" is sandwiched between two dashes, stressing its nature as an *extra* detail occurring to the narrator apart from the earlier, already established perceptions. Other choices present specific conclusions about the driver that are neither expressed nor implied.

Section VI

Answers 1–6

1. **B** Since statement 2 says that only cookies are baked at Uptown, and statement 3 says that Leslie does not work at Uptown, then she does not bake cookies.

2. **E** From statement 2 we know that cookies are baked at Uptown. Statement 5 eliminates pies from Midtown. Since we know that cookies are baked at Uptown, this means that bread must be baked at Midtown, and pies are baked at Downtown. Thus, I, II, and III are all true.

3. **A** Using only statements 1, 2, 3, 5, and 6, we can construct the following chart to answer the question:

	Pies Downtown	Bread Midtown	Cookies Uptown
J	X	X	✓
K			X
L			X

Thus we know that Juan bakes cookies at Uptown, and that Leslie works at either Midtown or Downtown.

4. **D** From all the statements we can construct a chart as follows:

	Pies Downtown	Bread Midtown	Cookies Uptown
J	X	X	✓
K	X	✓	X
L	✓	X	X

Thus, pies are baked at Downtown, and Karen does not bake pies.

5. **A** From the above chart, we see that I and II are true and III is false.

6. **B** Only three are needed. Statements 1, 2, and 5 are sufficient, as shown in Question 2.

Answers 7–10

From the information given, it would be helpful to construct the following chart to answer the questions:

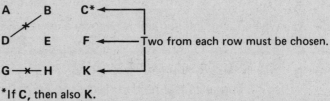

*If **C**, then also **K**.

7. **D** If A is not chosen, then B and C are chosen. Since C is chosen, K is chosen too. Since B is chosen, D is not chosen. Thus, E and F are chosen. So, if A is not chosen, B, C, E, F, and K must be chosen.

8. **D** If D is chosen, then B is not chosen. Thus, A and C are chosen. If C is chosen, then so is K. E *or* F is chosen. G *or* H is chosen. Thus I and III are possible.

9. **C** If B is chosen, then D is not chosen. Thus, E and F are chosen. Notice that statement 6 is not two-directional.

10. **C** Since G and H do not play together, only one will be chosen. Thus, K must be chosen.

Answers 11–14

From the information given, it would be helpful to construct a diagram to answer the questions.
NOTE: When more than one letter appears at a seat, those letters represent all the possible occupants of that seat.

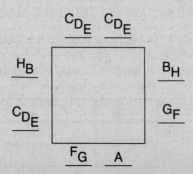

11. **D** From the diagram, C must sit next to B or H; therefore I is true. Taking a second look at the diagram, we can see that H doesn't have to sit next to G, and F doesn't have to sit next to D or E; therefore, II and III are not necessarily true.

12. **E** If B does not sit next to G, then we should adjust the diagram as follows:

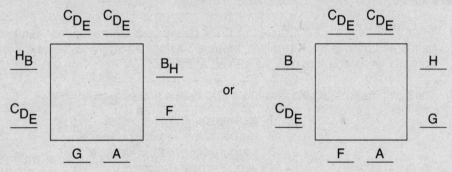

From these diagrams, it can be seen that all three statements are possible. (I) If C sits next to B, then D could sit directly across from F. (II) If C sits next to D, then E could sit directly across from G. (III) C could sit next to G.

13. **E** If C sits across from F, then H could sit next to any of these four (C, D, E, G) depending on the positions of B and H.

14. **C** B and H can't, since they must sit opposite each other. F and G can't, since they must sit next to A. That leaves only C, D, and E.

Answers 15–19

Drawing a simple diagram, below, will help answer the questions.

```
                                                    TR
                                                     *
        _____  _____  _____   __J__       FDR

M, A, K, FDR  →  _____  _____  __M__  __A__   K - FDR or FDR - K
```

Note that, once Madison is placed in position 3 on the bottom, Adams must go in position 4 in order to leave spots for Kennedy to be adjacent to Franklin Delano Roosevelt.

15. **D** If Theodore Roosevelt is second from the left (on top), then Franklin Delano Roosevelt must be first on the bottom since one Roosevelt may not be above the other. Therefore, Kennedy must be second on the bottom.

16. **A** Adams must go to the far right on the bottom to allow Kennedy to be adjacent to Franklin Delano Roosevelt.

17. **D** If Washington and Kennedy are both first on their shelves, then Franklin Delano Roosevelt must be second on the lower shelf. Therefore, Theodore Roosevelt cannot be second on the top shelf and therefore must be third. Thus, statement D cannot be true.

18. **E** I, II, III, and IV. All of the orders listed are possible for the top shelf.

19. **C** If Lincoln is next to Jefferson, that leaves Theodore Roosevelt and Washington for the first two positions on the top shelf. All of the choices are therefore true except (C) because that choice would place one Roosevelt above the other, which is not permitted.

Answers 20–26

20. **B** Since lima beans will not go with kidney beans or chili beans, they can go only with wax beans and garbanzos. Therefore, there is only one salad (limas + wax + garbanzos) that contains limas and that may be served at the party.

21. **C** The combinations of salads without chili beans are as follows:

1. garbanzos + wax + limas
2. garbanzos + limas + kidneys
3. garbanzos + wax + kidneys
4. wax + limas + kidneys

But remember that the *servable* salads may not include limas with kidneys or chili beans, thus reducing the number to two: garbanzos + wax + kidneys, and garbanzos + wax + limas.

22. **B** Without any restrictions there are 10 possible ways to choose three ingredients from a total of five:

CGW   GWL   WLK
CGL   GLK
CGK   GWK
CWL
CWK
CLK

However, the imposed restrictions (lima beans do not go with kidney beans or chili beans) narrow the servable salads down to five:

CGW   GWL   ~~WLK~~
~~CGL~~   ~~GLK~~
CGK   GWK
~~CWL~~
CWK
~~CLK~~

23. **E** From the chart above, we can see that garbanzos and wax beans appear more times in the servable salads. The other ingredients do not appear as often.

24. **C** From our chart we can see that having only enough wax beans for two salads will eliminate two of the four wax bean salads. Therefore, instead of five servable salads, there will now be only three.

25. **B** Again from our chart, if we eliminate the servable salads with garbanzos, we are left with only one servable salad: chili + wax + kidneys.

26. **D** With restrictions, our chart shows five servable three-bean salads. However, if there were no restrictions, we would have 10 three-bean salads. Thus the number would increase by five.

Chapter

8

Model Test Two

This chapter contains full-length Model Test Two. It is geared to the format of the LSAT, and it is complete with answers and explanations. It is equivalent to the LSAT in question structure, number of questions, level of difficulty, and time allotments. (The questions used are not taken directly from the LSAT, as those questions are copyrighted and may not be reproduced.)

Model Test Two should be taken under strict test conditions. The test begins with a 30-minute Writing Sample which is not scored. Thereafter each section is 35 minutes in length.

Section	Description	Number of Questions	Time Allowed
	Writing Sample		30 minutes
I	Logical Reasoning	26	35 minutes
II	Reading Comprehension	30	35 minutes
III	Analytical Reasoning	26	35 minutes
IV	Logical Reasoning	26	35 minutes
V	Evaluation of Facts	36	35 minutes
VI	Reading Comprehension	28	35 minutes
TOTALS:		172	240 minutes

Now please turn to the next page, remove your answer sheets, and begin Model Test Two.

ANSWER SHEET—MODEL TEST TWO
LAW SCHOOL ADMISSION TEST (LSAT)

Section I:
Logical Reasoning

1. Ⓐ Ⓑ Ⓒ Ⓓ Ⓔ
2. Ⓐ Ⓑ Ⓒ Ⓓ Ⓔ
3. Ⓐ Ⓑ Ⓒ Ⓓ Ⓔ
4. Ⓐ Ⓑ Ⓒ Ⓓ Ⓔ
5. Ⓐ Ⓑ Ⓒ Ⓓ Ⓔ
6. Ⓐ Ⓑ Ⓒ Ⓓ Ⓔ
7. Ⓐ Ⓑ Ⓒ Ⓓ Ⓔ
8. Ⓐ Ⓑ Ⓒ Ⓓ Ⓔ
9. Ⓐ Ⓑ Ⓒ Ⓓ Ⓔ
10. Ⓐ Ⓑ Ⓒ Ⓓ Ⓔ
11. Ⓐ Ⓑ Ⓒ Ⓓ Ⓔ
12. Ⓐ Ⓑ Ⓒ Ⓓ Ⓔ
13. Ⓐ Ⓑ Ⓒ Ⓓ Ⓔ
14. Ⓐ Ⓑ Ⓒ Ⓓ Ⓔ
15. Ⓐ Ⓑ Ⓒ Ⓓ Ⓔ
16. Ⓐ Ⓑ Ⓒ Ⓓ Ⓔ
17. Ⓐ Ⓑ Ⓒ Ⓓ Ⓔ
18. Ⓐ Ⓑ Ⓒ Ⓓ Ⓔ
19. Ⓐ Ⓑ Ⓒ Ⓓ Ⓔ
20. Ⓐ Ⓑ Ⓒ Ⓓ Ⓔ
21. Ⓐ Ⓑ Ⓒ Ⓓ Ⓔ
22. Ⓐ Ⓑ Ⓒ Ⓓ Ⓔ
23. Ⓐ Ⓑ Ⓒ Ⓓ Ⓔ
24. Ⓐ Ⓑ Ⓒ Ⓓ Ⓔ
25. Ⓐ Ⓑ Ⓒ Ⓓ Ⓔ
26. Ⓐ Ⓑ Ⓒ Ⓓ Ⓔ

Section II:
Reading Comprehension

1. Ⓐ Ⓑ Ⓒ Ⓓ Ⓔ
2. Ⓐ Ⓑ Ⓒ Ⓓ Ⓔ
3. Ⓐ Ⓑ Ⓒ Ⓓ Ⓔ
4. Ⓐ Ⓑ Ⓒ Ⓓ Ⓔ
5. Ⓐ Ⓑ Ⓒ Ⓓ Ⓔ
6. Ⓐ Ⓑ Ⓒ Ⓓ Ⓔ
7. Ⓐ Ⓑ Ⓒ Ⓓ Ⓔ
8. Ⓐ Ⓑ Ⓒ Ⓓ Ⓔ
9. Ⓐ Ⓑ Ⓒ Ⓓ Ⓔ
10. Ⓐ Ⓑ Ⓒ Ⓓ Ⓔ
11. Ⓐ Ⓑ Ⓒ Ⓓ Ⓔ
12. Ⓐ Ⓑ Ⓒ Ⓓ Ⓔ
13. Ⓐ Ⓑ Ⓒ Ⓓ Ⓔ
14. Ⓐ Ⓑ Ⓒ Ⓓ Ⓔ
15. Ⓐ Ⓑ Ⓒ Ⓓ Ⓔ
16. Ⓐ Ⓑ Ⓒ Ⓓ Ⓔ
17. Ⓐ Ⓑ Ⓒ Ⓓ Ⓔ
18. Ⓐ Ⓑ Ⓒ Ⓓ Ⓔ
19. Ⓐ Ⓑ Ⓒ Ⓓ Ⓔ
20. Ⓐ Ⓑ Ⓒ Ⓓ Ⓔ
21. Ⓐ Ⓑ Ⓒ Ⓓ Ⓔ
22. Ⓐ Ⓑ Ⓒ Ⓓ Ⓔ
23. Ⓐ Ⓑ Ⓒ Ⓓ Ⓔ
24. Ⓐ Ⓑ Ⓒ Ⓓ Ⓔ
25. Ⓐ Ⓑ Ⓒ Ⓓ Ⓔ
26. Ⓐ Ⓑ Ⓒ Ⓓ Ⓔ
27. Ⓐ Ⓑ Ⓒ Ⓓ Ⓔ
28. Ⓐ Ⓑ Ⓒ Ⓓ Ⓔ
29. Ⓐ Ⓑ Ⓒ Ⓓ Ⓔ
30. Ⓐ Ⓑ Ⓒ Ⓓ Ⓔ

Section III:
Analytical Reasoning

1. Ⓐ Ⓑ Ⓒ Ⓓ Ⓔ
2. Ⓐ Ⓑ Ⓒ Ⓓ Ⓔ
3. Ⓐ Ⓑ Ⓒ Ⓓ Ⓔ
4. Ⓐ Ⓑ Ⓒ Ⓓ Ⓔ
5. Ⓐ Ⓑ Ⓒ Ⓓ Ⓔ
6. Ⓐ Ⓑ Ⓒ Ⓓ Ⓔ
7. Ⓐ Ⓑ Ⓒ Ⓓ Ⓔ
8. Ⓐ Ⓑ Ⓒ Ⓓ Ⓔ
9. Ⓐ Ⓑ Ⓒ Ⓓ Ⓔ
10. Ⓐ Ⓑ Ⓒ Ⓓ Ⓔ
11. Ⓐ Ⓑ Ⓒ Ⓓ Ⓔ
12. Ⓐ Ⓑ Ⓒ Ⓓ Ⓔ
13. Ⓐ Ⓑ Ⓒ Ⓓ Ⓔ
14. Ⓐ Ⓑ Ⓒ Ⓓ Ⓔ
15. Ⓐ Ⓑ Ⓒ Ⓓ Ⓔ
16. Ⓐ Ⓑ Ⓒ Ⓓ Ⓔ
17. Ⓐ Ⓑ Ⓒ Ⓓ Ⓔ
18. Ⓐ Ⓑ Ⓒ Ⓓ Ⓔ
19. Ⓐ Ⓑ Ⓒ Ⓓ Ⓔ
20. Ⓐ Ⓑ Ⓒ Ⓓ Ⓔ
21. Ⓐ Ⓑ Ⓒ Ⓓ Ⓔ
22. Ⓐ Ⓑ Ⓒ Ⓓ Ⓔ
23. Ⓐ Ⓑ Ⓒ Ⓓ Ⓔ
24. Ⓐ Ⓑ Ⓒ Ⓓ Ⓔ
25. Ⓐ Ⓑ Ⓒ Ⓓ Ⓔ
26. Ⓐ Ⓑ Ⓒ Ⓓ Ⓔ

ANSWER SHEET—MODEL TEST TWO
LAW SCHOOL ADMISSION TEST (LSAT)

Section IV:
Logical Reasoning

1. Ⓐ Ⓑ Ⓒ Ⓓ Ⓔ
2. Ⓐ Ⓑ Ⓒ Ⓓ Ⓔ
3. Ⓐ Ⓑ Ⓒ Ⓓ Ⓔ
4. Ⓐ Ⓑ Ⓒ Ⓓ Ⓔ
5. Ⓐ Ⓑ Ⓒ Ⓓ Ⓔ
6. Ⓐ Ⓑ Ⓒ Ⓓ Ⓔ
7. Ⓐ Ⓑ Ⓒ Ⓓ Ⓔ
8. Ⓐ Ⓑ Ⓒ Ⓓ Ⓔ
9. Ⓐ Ⓑ Ⓒ Ⓓ Ⓔ
10. Ⓐ Ⓑ Ⓒ Ⓓ Ⓔ
11. Ⓐ Ⓑ Ⓒ Ⓓ Ⓔ
12. Ⓐ Ⓑ Ⓒ Ⓓ Ⓔ
13. Ⓐ Ⓑ Ⓒ Ⓓ Ⓔ
14. Ⓐ Ⓑ Ⓒ Ⓓ Ⓔ
15. Ⓐ Ⓑ Ⓒ Ⓓ Ⓔ
16. Ⓐ Ⓑ Ⓒ Ⓓ Ⓔ
17. Ⓐ Ⓑ Ⓒ Ⓓ Ⓔ
18. Ⓐ Ⓑ Ⓒ Ⓓ Ⓔ
19. Ⓐ Ⓑ Ⓒ Ⓓ Ⓔ
20. Ⓐ Ⓑ Ⓒ Ⓓ Ⓔ
21. Ⓐ Ⓑ Ⓒ Ⓓ Ⓔ
22. Ⓐ Ⓑ Ⓒ Ⓓ Ⓔ
23. Ⓐ Ⓑ Ⓒ Ⓓ Ⓔ
24. Ⓐ Ⓑ Ⓒ Ⓓ Ⓔ
25. Ⓐ Ⓑ Ⓒ Ⓓ Ⓔ
26. Ⓐ Ⓑ Ⓒ Ⓓ Ⓔ

Section V:
Evaluation of Facts

1. Ⓐ Ⓑ Ⓒ Ⓓ
2. Ⓐ Ⓑ Ⓒ Ⓓ
3. Ⓐ Ⓑ Ⓒ Ⓓ
4. Ⓐ Ⓑ Ⓒ Ⓓ
5. Ⓐ Ⓑ Ⓒ Ⓓ
6. Ⓐ Ⓑ Ⓒ Ⓓ
7. Ⓐ Ⓑ Ⓒ Ⓓ
8. Ⓐ Ⓑ Ⓒ Ⓓ
9. Ⓐ Ⓑ Ⓒ Ⓓ
10. Ⓐ Ⓑ Ⓒ Ⓓ
11. Ⓐ Ⓑ Ⓒ Ⓓ
12. Ⓐ Ⓑ Ⓒ Ⓓ
13. Ⓐ Ⓑ Ⓒ Ⓓ
14. Ⓐ Ⓑ Ⓒ Ⓓ
15. Ⓐ Ⓑ Ⓒ Ⓓ
16. Ⓐ Ⓑ Ⓒ Ⓓ
17. Ⓐ Ⓑ Ⓒ Ⓓ
18. Ⓐ Ⓑ Ⓒ Ⓓ
19. Ⓐ Ⓑ Ⓒ Ⓓ
20. Ⓐ Ⓑ Ⓒ Ⓓ
21. Ⓐ Ⓑ Ⓒ Ⓓ
22. Ⓐ Ⓑ Ⓒ Ⓓ
23. Ⓐ Ⓑ Ⓒ Ⓓ
24. Ⓐ Ⓑ Ⓒ Ⓓ
25. Ⓐ Ⓑ Ⓒ Ⓓ
26. Ⓐ Ⓑ Ⓒ Ⓓ
27. Ⓐ Ⓑ Ⓒ Ⓓ
28. Ⓐ Ⓑ Ⓒ Ⓓ
29. Ⓐ Ⓑ Ⓒ Ⓓ
30. Ⓐ Ⓑ Ⓒ Ⓓ
31. Ⓐ Ⓑ Ⓒ Ⓓ
32. Ⓐ Ⓑ Ⓒ Ⓓ
33. Ⓐ Ⓑ Ⓒ Ⓓ
34. Ⓐ Ⓑ Ⓒ Ⓓ
35. Ⓐ Ⓑ Ⓒ Ⓓ
36. Ⓐ Ⓑ Ⓒ Ⓓ

Section VI:
Reading Comprehension

1. Ⓐ Ⓑ Ⓒ Ⓓ Ⓔ
2. Ⓐ Ⓑ Ⓒ Ⓓ Ⓔ
3. Ⓐ Ⓑ Ⓒ Ⓓ Ⓔ
4. Ⓐ Ⓑ Ⓒ Ⓓ Ⓔ
5. Ⓐ Ⓑ Ⓒ Ⓓ Ⓔ
6. Ⓐ Ⓑ Ⓒ Ⓓ Ⓔ
7. Ⓐ Ⓑ Ⓒ Ⓓ Ⓔ
8. Ⓐ Ⓑ Ⓒ Ⓓ Ⓔ
9. Ⓐ Ⓑ Ⓒ Ⓓ Ⓔ
10. Ⓐ Ⓑ Ⓒ Ⓓ Ⓔ
11. Ⓐ Ⓑ Ⓒ Ⓓ Ⓔ
12. Ⓐ Ⓑ Ⓒ Ⓓ Ⓔ
13. Ⓐ Ⓑ Ⓒ Ⓓ Ⓔ
14. Ⓐ Ⓑ Ⓒ Ⓓ Ⓔ
15. Ⓐ Ⓑ Ⓒ Ⓓ Ⓔ
16. Ⓐ Ⓑ Ⓒ Ⓓ Ⓔ
17. Ⓐ Ⓑ Ⓒ Ⓓ Ⓔ
18. Ⓐ Ⓑ Ⓒ Ⓓ Ⓔ
19. Ⓐ Ⓑ Ⓒ Ⓓ Ⓔ
20. Ⓐ Ⓑ Ⓒ Ⓓ Ⓔ
21. Ⓐ Ⓑ Ⓒ Ⓓ Ⓔ
22. Ⓐ Ⓑ Ⓒ Ⓓ Ⓔ
23. Ⓐ Ⓑ Ⓒ Ⓓ Ⓔ
24. Ⓐ Ⓑ Ⓒ Ⓓ Ⓔ
25. Ⓐ Ⓑ Ⓒ Ⓓ Ⓔ
26. Ⓐ Ⓑ Ⓒ Ⓓ Ⓔ
27. Ⓐ Ⓑ Ⓒ Ⓓ Ⓔ
28. Ⓐ Ⓑ Ⓒ Ⓓ Ⓔ

EXAMINATION

WRITING SAMPLE

Time—30 Minutes

Directions:
You have 30 minutes to write an essay in response to a given topic. Take a few minutes to plan your work before you begin writing. DO NOT WRITE ON A TOPIC OF YOUR OWN CHOICE. ESSAYS THAT DO NOT ADDRESS THE GIVEN TOPIC ARE UNACCEPTABLE.

The quality of your writing is more important than the length of your response or the content. Pay attention to organization, appropriate diction, and correct usage. You will not be expected to display any specialized knowledge in your response, nor will you be expected to write a "perfect" essay; law schools understand that you are writing under a time constraint, and will allow for the minor lapses in writing ability that might occur under this circumstance.

Only the lined area in your booklet will be reproduced for the law schools, so do not write outside this space. *Do not* skip lines or use wide margins. These precautions, along with careful planning and legible handwriting that is not unduly large, will keep you within the allowed space.

SAMPLE TOPIC

Read the following descriptions of Thomas and Peters, candidates for the position of head coach of the Ventura Vultures professional football team. *Then, in the space provided, write an argument for appointing either Thomas or Peters.* Use the information in this description and assume that the two general policies below equally guide the Vultures' decision on the appointment:

1. The head coach should possess the ability to work with players and coaching staff toward achieving a championship season.
2. The head coach should successfully manage the behind-the-scenes activities of recruiting, analyzing scouting reports, and handling the media and fans in order to enhance the public relations and image of the team.

THOMAS has been General Manager of the Vultures for the past ten years. A physical education major with a masters in psychology, he knows the player personnel as well as anyone, including the coaching staff. His on-target assessment of player skills and weaknesses has been instrumental in building a more balanced team over the past decade, through his skillful trading and recruitment of college athletes. As the chief managing officer, he has also enhanced the team's image by his careful press relationship and understated approach when negotiations with star players reached an impass. He rarely alienates players, coaches, press, or fans with his even-handed (though sometimes unemotional) attitude, and the Vulture owners feel fortunate that they were able to entice him away from his high-school coaching position, which he loved 10 years ago. Although he has never played either pro or college ball, he is one candidate for the head coach position.

PETERS, the other candidate for head coach, is presently a wide receiver and defensive end for the Vultures. A one-time star, Peters has played both offense and defense for the Vultures since their inception in the league 14 years ago, a remarkable feat equalled by few in the game. He was elected captain of the team the past five years due to his charisma, although he occasionally angers management and fellow players with his strong comments about his philosophy of the game. His only experience in the front office was leading a player charity benefit for the Vultures, which raised more than $2,000,000 for abused Ventura County children. Although a high school dropout, Peters is a self-made man who firmly believes the key to life is having a strong educational background, even though he sometimes feels uncomfortable around college-educated athletes. The Vulture owners believe Peters may provide the emotional charge the team needs at its helm to win its first championship.

SECTION I:
LOGICAL REASONING

Time—35 Minutes
26 Questions

Directions:

In this section you will be given brief statements or passages and will be required to evaluate the reasoning involved. In some instances, more than one choice will appear to be a possible answer. You are to choose the *best* answer. Use common sense and reasonableness in making your selection; then mark the proper space on the answer sheet.

Questions 1–2 refer to the following passage.

Probability is a curiously unstable concept. Semantically speaking, it is an assumption, a pure artifice, a concept that may or may not be true, but nevertheless facilitates a logical process. It is not a hypothesis because, by its very nature, it cannot be proved. Suppose we flip a coin that has a distinguishable head and tail. In our ignorance of the coming result, we say that the coin has one chance in two of falling heads up, or that the probability of a head turning up is one-to-two. Here it must be understood that the one-to-two is not "true" but is merely a species of the genus probability.

1. The author of this passage assumes that
   (A) nothing about our coin influences its fall in favor of either side or that all influences are counterbalanced by equal and opposite influences
   (B) probability can be dealt with without the use of logic
   (C) an assumption must be plausible
   (D) the probability of the coin's landing on an edge is counterbalanced by the probability of its not landing on an edge
   (E) probability can be precisely calculated

2. The last sentence implies that

   I. probability is not absolute
   II. one-to-two is merely a guess
   III. one-to-two is a worthless ratio
   (A) I only   (B) II only   (C) I and II only   (D) I and III only   (E) II and III only

3. Self-confidence is a big factor in success. The person who thinks he can, will master most of the things he attempts. The person who thinks he can't, may not try.

   The author of these statements would agree that
   (A) nothing is impossible
   (B) no task is too large
   (C) success relies on effort
   (D) self-confidence is of most importance
   (E) trying is half the battle

4. Booker T. Washington was criticized by members of his own race for rationalizing the fate of black people with the following assertion: "No race shall prosper 'til it learns there is as much dignity in tilling a field as in writing a poem."

Which of the following, if true, would strengthen the criticism of Washington's assertion?

(A) Most black people during Washington's time were denied access to a liberal arts education.
(B) Black landowners who worked hard running a farm were often able to pay for the artistic or professional education of their children.
(C) White people had respect for both black poets and black farmers.
(D) The economically dominant countries of the world are mainly agricultural.
(E) Most of Washington's critics had never tilled a field.

5. If no test has no easy questions, then which of the following MUST be true?

  I. Every test has some easy questions.
  II. Some tests have some easy questions.
  III. No test has all hard questions.

(A) I only   (B) II only   (C) III only   D Two of the above   (E) I, II, and III

Questions 6–7 require you to complete the missing portions of the following passage by selecting from the five alternatives the one that best fits the context of the passage.

Relations are spiritual or mental things that inhabit the world of consciousness. We may call them holy ghosts if they have to do with the relation between the finite and infinite, the limited and the limitless, the conceivable and the inconceivable. Thus it is the very contrary of stupidity to say that you cannot be (6) _____ of one thing and one only. In order to have one, you must have three: a thing, a relation, and another thing. The meaning of one of them is determined by your (7) _____.

6. (A) unaware   (B) considerate   (C) conscious   (D) knowledgeable   (E) stupid

7. (A) momentary awareness of the other two
  (B) momentary unawareness of the other two
  (C) overall knowledge of the other relation
  (D) complete mastery of the relationship
  (E) identification of the ambiguity of the statement

Questions 8–10 refer to the following statements.

(A) The President is not well. He must therefore miss his appointment.
(B) Imagine what would happen if you tried to raise geraniums in a dark room. Plants must have light to survive.
(C) His tardiness was probably the key factor in his failure to be prompt, according to his supervisor.
(D) Arnold's disability was apparent. He winced during the examination of his knee.
(E) Kermit and I kept a dozen trophies; otherwise we would have nothing to show for our years of playing sports.

8. Which of the above statements is an example of the use of *specific instance* to support a point?

9. Which of the above statements is an example of *circular reasoning* to support a point?

10. Which of the above statements uses *hypothetical example* to support a point?

Questions 11–13 refer to the following passage.

Sixty percent of the American people, according to the latest polls, now believe that inflation is the nation's most important problem. This problem of inflation is closely related to rising prices.

The inflation rate has been 10 percent or more most of this year. Undoubtedly, our gluttonous appetite for high-priced foreign oil has been a major factor. We have been shipping billions of dollars overseas, more than foreigners can spend or invest here. Dollars are selling cheaply and this has forced the value of the dollar down. Government programs now being inaugurated to slow this trend are at best weak, but deserve our support, as they appear to be the best our government can produce. Hopefully, they won't fail as they have in the past.

11. The author of this passage implies that
    (A) inflation cannot be stopped or slowed, because of a weak government
    (B) the fear of inflation is not only unwarranted, but also detrimental
    (C) 40% of non-Americans believe inflation is not the most important problem
    (D) foreign oil is the sole reason for the sudden increase in inflation
    (E) the present programs will probably not slow inflation

12. Which of the following contradicts something in the preceding passage?
    (A) Foreign oil is actually underpriced.
    (B) The inflation rate has not risen for most of this year.
    (C) Overseas investors are few and far between.
    (D) Our government is trying a new approach to end inflation.
    (E) The weakness of the programs stems from lack of support.

13. The author of this passage would agree that

    I. our government is giving its utmost
    II. the latest polls are giving false information
    III. oil independence could help slow the trend
    (A) I only   (B) II only   (C) III only   (D) I and II only   (E) I and III only

14. No one reads *Weight-Off* magazine unless he is fat. Everyone reads *Weight-Off* magazine unless he eats chocolate.

    Which of the following is inconsistent with the above?

    I. Everyone is fat.
    II. No one is fat and only some people eat chocolate.
    III. Some people are fat and no one eats chocolate.
    (A) II only   (B) III only   (C) I and II only   (D) II and III only   (E) I, II, and III

15. *Jerry*: Every meal my wife cooks is fantastic.
    Dave: I disagree. Most of my wife's meals are fantastic, too.

    Dave's response shows that he understood Jerry to mean that
    (A) Dave's wife does not cook fantastic meals
    (B) only Jerry's wife cooks fantastic meals
    (C) every one of Jerry's wife's meals is fantastic
    (D) not every one of Jerry's wife's meals is fantastic
    (E) no one cooks fantastic meals all the time

Questions 16–17 refer to the following quotation.

    "Before a man can be in any capacity to speak on the subject, it is necessary he be acquainted with it; or else it is as foolish to set him to discourse of it as to set a blind man to talk of colors, or a deaf man of music."—*Dewey*

16. This passage is discussing
    (A) scientific methods
    (B) biological behavior
    (C) sociological foundations

(D) education practices
(E) legal implications

17. The author of this passage would most likely be a
(A) lawyer   (B) chemist   (C) philosopher   (D) poet   (E) minister

18. Mike will talk to Joe if Joe will talk to Henry.
If Henry does not talk to Dave, then Mike will not talk to Joe.

Which of the following are true (based on the above conditions)?

I.   If Mike won't talk to Joe, then Joe won't talk to Henry.
II. If Henry talks to Dave, then Mike will talk to Joe.
III. If Mike talks to Joe, then Henry will talk to Dave.
(A) I and II only   (B) II and III only   (C) I and III only   (D) I, II, and III
(E) None of the above

19. X: "We discover new knowledge by the syllogistic process when we say, for example, 'All men are mortal; Socrates is a man; therefore Socrates is mortal.' "
Y: "Yes, but the fact is that if all men are mortal we cannot tell whether Socrates is a man until we have determined his mortality—in other words, until we find him dead. Of course, it's a great convenience to assume that Socrates is a man because he looks like one, but that's just a deduction. If we examine its formulation—'Objects that resemble men in most respects are men; Socrates resembles men in most respects; therefore Socrates is a man'—it's obvious that if he is a man, he resembles men in *all* necessary respects. So it's obvious we're right back where we started."
X: "Yes. We must know all the characteristics of men, and that Socrates has all of them, before we can be sure."

Which of the following best expresses X's concluding observation?
(A) In deductive thinking we are simply reminding ourselves of the implications of our generalizations.
(B) It is often too convenient to arrive at conclusions simply by deduction instead of induction.
(C) Socrates' mortality is not the issue; the issue is critical thinking.
(D) Socrates' characteristics do not necessarily define his mortality.
(E) The key to the syllogistic process is using theoretical, rather than practical, issues of logic.

20. It takes a good telescope to see the moons of Neptune. I can't see the moons of Neptune with my telescope. Therefore, I do not have a good telescope.

Which of the following most closely parallels the logic of this statement?
(A) It takes two to tango. You are doing the tango. Therefore, you have a partner.
(B) If you have a surfboard, you can surf. You do not have a surfboard. Therefore, you cannot surf.
(C) You need gin and vermouth to make a martini. You do not have any gin. Therefore, you cannot make a martini.
(D) If you know the area of a circle, you can find its circumference. You cannot figure out the circumference. Therefore, you do not know the area.
(E) You can write a letter to your friend with a pencil. You do not have a pencil. Therefore, you cannot write the letter.

Questions 21–22 refer to the following passage.

Over 90% of our waking life depends on habits which for the most part we are unconscious of, from brushing our teeth in the morning, to the time and manner in which we go to sleep at night. Habits are tools which serve the important function of relieving the conscious mind for more important activities. Habits are stored patterns of behavior which are found to serve the needs of the individual that has them and are formed from what once was conscious behavior which over years of repetition can become an automatic behavior pattern of the unconscious mind.

21. It can be inferred that the author bases his beliefs on
(A) the testimony of a controlled group of students
(B) biblical passages referring to the unconscious state
(C) an intense psychological research
(D) extensive psychological research
(E) recent findings of clinical psychologists

22. The last sentence implies that
(A) all repetitious patterns become unconscious behavior
(B) conscious behavior eventually becomes habit
(C) the unconscious mind causes repetitive behavior
(D) automatic behavior patterns of the conscious mind are not possible
(E) habits can be good or bad

Questions 23–24 refer to the following passage.

It should be emphasized that only one person in a thousand who is bitten by a disease-carrying mosquito develops symptoms that require hospitalization, according to Dr. Reeves. But it is a potentially serious disease that requires close collaboration by citizens and local government to prevent it from reaching epidemic proportions.

Citizens should fill or drain puddles where mosquitoes breed. They should repair leaking swamp coolers and be sure swimming pools have a good circulating system. Make sure drain gutters aren't clogged and holding rainwater. Keep barrels and other water-storage containers tightly covered. Use good window screens.

23. Which of the following statements, if true, would most strengthen the advice given in the second paragraph above?
(A) Leaking swamp coolers are the primary cause of mosquito infestation.
(B) It is possible to completely eliminate mosquitoes from a neighborhood.
(C) No one can completely protect herself from being bitten by a mosquito.
(D) Tightly covered water containers do not ensure the purity of the water in all cases.
(E) Window screens seldom need to be replaced.

24. What additional information would strengthen the clarity of the second sentence above?
(A) The names of some local governments that have fought against disease.
(B) The name of the disease under discussion.
(C) The names of those bitten by disease-carrying mosquitoes.
(D) The full name of Dr. Reeves.
(E) A description of the symptoms that a bitten person might develop.

25. That which is rare is always more valuable than that which is abundant. And so we are continually frustrated in our attempts to teach young people how to use time wisely; they have too much of it to appreciate its value.

Which of the following statements, if true, would most weaken the argument above?
(A) Appreciation is not the same as obedience.
(B) "Abundant" is a term whose definition varies widely.
(C) Currency that is based on rare metals is more valuable than currency that is not.
(D) Many young people possess an intuitive knowledge of what time it is, a knowledge they lose around middle age.
(E) The leisure time of people aged 18–24 has decreased by 80% over the last 10 years.

26.   Many theorists now believe that people cannot learn to write if they are constantly worrying about whether their prose is correct or not. When a would-be writer worries about correctness, his ability for fluency is frozen.

With which of the following statements would the author of the above passage probably agree?
(A) Writing theorists are probably wrong.
(B) Writing prose is different from writing poetry.
(C) Literacy is a function of relaxation.
(D) Fear blocks action.
(E) Most good writers are careless.

STOP

IF YOU FINISH BEFORE TIME HAS ELAPSED, CHECK YOUR WORK ON THIS SECTION OF THE TEST ONLY. DO NOT GO ON TO THE NEXT SECTION OF THE TEST UNTIL TIME IS UP FOR THIS SECTION.

SECTION II
READING COMPREHENSION

Time—35 Minutes
30 Questions

Directions:
Read the passages and answer the questions following each passage by blackening the appropriate space on the answer sheet. You may refer back to the passages when answering the questions. Answer all questions on the basis of what is stated or implied.

Passage 1

In many ways, the Supreme Court is the worst place to win a human rights case—even when an Earl Warren is sitting as Chief Justice. It takes a large amount of money and a long time to get a case to the Court. Even when a party wins, he may not come out with a clear victory. The decisions are seldom unanimous, and a five-to-four or six-to-three split tends to weaken the impact of a majority opinion. A Supreme Court decision may have a tremendous effect in the long run, but it seldom brings about immediate major changes.

Most cases do not get to the Supreme Court anyway. This is especially true of human rights disputes, where the parties usually cannot afford to appeal, and their lawyers will never get paid even if they win because a monetary award seldom goes with a victory on principle.

Most disputes never even become lawsuits. People don't tend to go to a lawyer when they think they have been treated unfairly. They may not know a lawyer they trust; they may not have the money to pay a fee; and they don't think it will help to go to court anyway.

This means that for most people the highest court, the supreme court of the land, is the policeman on the beat, the highway patrolman, the parent, the priest, the landlord, the boss, the creditor, or the voter registrar. A decision by the Supreme Court guaranteeing human rights has no meaning until these people around the country know about and decide to follow it.

Of course, all the courts and government agencies in the country are required to follow Supreme Court decisions, too. But "the Court's authority—possessed of neither the purse nor the sword—ultimately rests on sustained public confidence in its moral sanction," as Justice Frankfurter put it so succinctly. And compliance with Warren Court opinions was certainly not automatic.

Studying the development of human rights law through the landmark decisions of the Warren Court can lead to increased respect for our legal system. At the same time it can lead to the opposite conclusion: that the best time to win a human rights case is at the beginning, the best place is where the case starts, the best judge and jury are the participants, and the best method is without a lawsuit. In other words, the best protectors of human rights are not the courts but rather citizens who know and insist on their own rights and who act to guarantee the rights of others to freedom, justice, and equality.

Citizens concerned about human rights who were raised during the Warren Court era came to depend on the Court to right the wrongs created by acts of Congress, executive orders, and lower court decisions, and by the actions of government officials, private citizens, and groups. The Court did not always fulfill this function, but it did so more often than any previous Supreme Court—and perhaps more often than any Court of the near future. To the extent it followed and advanced the development of human rights law, it was the Camelot of courts. To the extent it disarmed the people by suggesting reliance on the courts rather than on their own collective action, it led to disillusionment when Earl Warren stepped down. It is necessary to reassess the opportunities for progress through the judicial system.

1. The passage calls the Warren Court the "Camelot of courts"; this implies that
   (A) it made decisions we usually see only in the movies
   (B) like King Arthur's court, it valued justice and mercy
   (C) Earl Warren was the king and the other justices were knights
   (D) its decisions were mythical
   (E) its decisions were chivalric

2. More often than not, human rights cases
   (A) do not get to the Supreme Court
   (B) are appealed
   (C) result in a split decision
   (D) require high-principled judges
   (E) flounder

3. According to the passage, a human rights case may be won in the Supreme Court, but the winner should not expect his victory to bring about
   (A) a unanimous response
   (B) an executive decision
   (C) a clear victory
   (D) immediate major changes
   (E) the approval of the Chief Justice

4. Once the Supreme Court makes a decision, the enforcement of that decision rests largely upon
   (A) a national requirement
   (B) the people's confidence in the Court
   (C) automatic obedience
   (D) the Court's authority
   (E) the support of parents, priests, policemen, and landlords

5. According to the passage, citizens who wish to preserve their human rights must be
   (A) aggressive, knowledgeable, and insistent
   (B) law-abiding and humble
   (C) rich and arrogant
   (D) friends of the Court
   (E) energetic and tenacious

Passage 2

Yesterday's announcement that Monarch Steel plans to close three mills, thereby eliminating three hundred jobs, came as a surprise. Things have been going badly at Monarch for some time now, and this latest news bears out what we all have suspected for some time now—that the situation isn't improving.

The net effect is that three hundred more people will soon be added to the approximately seven hundred already on layoff. The culprit, according to a Monarch spokesperson, is the increasing influx of low-cost foreign steel into the United States and increased labor and material costs.

The situation at Monarch makes all too clear an economic fact of life that we in the United States seem reluctant to accept: that our country is no longer an economic "island unto itself." No longer can we go about merrily doing as we please, living lavishly with no care for tomorrow, relying on the economic strength and abundant wealth of the United States to carry us.

There was a point in time—and it wasn't so long ago—when the wealth of our country was so great that we were virtually self-contained. We could overcome any obstacle, surmount any problem, because as a nation we were, quite simply, very rich.

But that time has now passed, and while our country is a little less rich, the rest of the world, generally speaking, is a little more rich. Now, other countries have improved technology and production methods, and are capable of manufacturing numerous products more cheaply than we do. Unfortunately, steel is one of those products.

Another fact of economic life which must be accepted if we are to continue to prosper is that the day when everyone "bought American" is over, just as the day when everyone shopped exclusively with his or her local community merchants is over. Say what we will, people nowadays go where the prices are best and the quality greatest; it is a truism that holds for the local housewife as well as for giant manufacturing concerns.

While we may condemn others for not buying American-made products, how many of us drive foreign cars, own foreign televisions, or any of the hundreds of other foreign products which have proliferated in our markets? The simple truth is that we all want the best quality and performance at the lowest possible price, and the vendor who offers them is the one who gets our dollar.

Before any significant progress can be made in solving the problem of foreign imports, both management and labor are going to have to accept these economic facts and act accordingly. Once they recognize that they must compete not only with other U.S. industries engaged in a similar activity, but also with those same type industries in other countries, they can begin to develop a strategy for competing.

Perhaps management, labor, and stockholders will all discover that they must accept a little less and lower their expectations in order to get back into the economic mainstream, but it's a small price to pay when compared with the alternative: annihilation.

The problems at Monarch aren't going to go away quickly, though, and in the near term we can only hope that the displaced workers can be put back on the payroll somewhere else. According to one company spokesman, the chances of the three mills being reopened are "nonexistent," so if the three hundred workers can't be placed in other jobs, the community loses, the company loses, but, worst of all, the former employees lose.

6. According to the author, the U.S. economy is suffering from
    (A) overactive exuberance
    (B) being less rich than the rest of the world
    (C) economic annihilation
    (D) complacent isolationism
    (E) having three mills too many

7. A reason for the closure of three steel mills is
    (A) Monarch's authoritarian policy
    (B) the appealing cost of foreign steel
    (C) too many workers who "bought American"

    (D)   a rift between management and labor
    (E)   too many displaced workers on the payroll

8. The truism with which the author agrees is that
    (A)   consumers favor low prices and high quality
    (B)   the vendor is the one who gets our dollar
    (C)   the local housewife holds with giant manufacturing concerns
    (D)   the alternative to lowered expectations is economic annihilation
    (E)   the chances of the three mills being reopened are nonexistent

9. Not so long ago, according to the author,
    (A)   the proliferation of foreign products was inevitable
    (B)   some strategy for competing was not necessary
    (C)   a net loss of a thousand workers would not be tolerated
    (D)   steel was not in demand in this country
    (E)   the United States was wealthier than it is today

10. The author implies that American consumers who chastise the buyers of foreign goods are
    (A) insensitive   (B) tightfisted   (C) largely members of management   (D) traitorous
    (E) hypocritical

11. Faced with a definition of *laissez-faire* economics, the author of this passage would probably
    (A)   modify it
    (B)   approve it
    (C)   sanction it
    (D)   misunderstand it
    (E)   annihilate it

12. The layoffs at Monarch Steel
    (A)   came as no surprise
    (B)   continued a discouraging trend
    (C)   reversed an encouraging trend
    (D)   portend starvation for many families
    (E)   are strictly temporary

Passage 3

    Taxonomy, the science of classifying and ordering organisms, has an undeserved reputation as a harmless, and mindless, activity of listing, cataloguing, and describing—consider the common idea of a birdwatcher, up at 5:30 in the morning with his binoculars, short pants, and "life list" of every bird he has seen. Even among fellow scientists, taxonomy is often treated as "stamp collecting," while its practitioners are viewed much as the Biblical hyraxes—"a feeble folk that dwelleth among the rocks."

    It was not always so. During the eighteenth and early nineteenth centuries, taxonomy was in the forefront of the sciences. The greatest biologists of Europe were professional taxonomists—Linnaeus, Cuvier, Lamarck. Darwin's major activity during the twenty years separating his Malthusian insights from the publication of his evolutionary theory was a three-volume work on the taxonomy of barnacles. Thomas Jefferson took time out from the affairs of state to publish one of the great taxonomic errors in the history of paleontology—he described a giant sloth claw as a lion three times the size of Africa's version. These heady days were marked by discovery as naturalists collected the fauna and flora of previously uncharted regions. They were also marked by the emergence of intellectual structure, as coherent classifications seemed to mirror the order of God's thought.

    A Species of Eternity is an account of America's part in this great epoch of natural history. We often forget that 150 years ago much of our continent was as unknown and potentially hazardous as any place on earth. During the eighteenth century, when most naturalists denied the possibility of extinction, explorers expected to find mammoths and other formidable fossil creatures alive in the American West.

Kastner's theme is discovery and the American frontier. His book is a series of short biographies, chronologically arranged, of the dozen or so passionate, single-minded iconoclasts who fought the hostility of the wilderness, and often of urban literary people, to disclose the rich fauna and flora of America. For the most part, they worked alone, with small support from patrons or government. The Lewis and Clark expedition is the only official trip treated here—and its primary purpose was not natural history. We may now look upon tales of frontier toughness and perseverance as the necessary mythology of a nation too young to have real legends. But there is often a residue of truth in such tales, and Kastner's dozen are among the genuine pioneers.

In his stories about them they appear as eccentric, undaunted. Alexander Wilson walked from New England to Charleston peddling subscriptions to his *American Ornithology*. Thomas Nuttall seems dottily heroic—oblivious to danger, a Parsifal under a lucky star, vanquishing every Klingsor in the woods, he discovered some of the rarest, most beautiful, and most useful of American plants. We find J. J. Audubon lying and drinking his way across Europe but selling his beautiful pictures of birds to lords and kings. Charles Willson Peale, the great promoter of natural history, was snubbed as an old man and excluded from the ceremonies honoring Lafayette on his triumphal return to Philadelphia in 1824. While Peale stood as a spectator on the steps of Independence Hall Lafayette saw his old companion, rushed over to embrace him, and stood by him through all the official homages. John Lawson, captured by Tuscarora Indians, met the following fate according to an eyewitness: "They stuck him full of fine small splinters or torchwoods like hog's bristles and so set them gradually afire." David Douglas fell into a pit trap for wild cattle and was stomped to death by a bull.

13. This passage is largely a
   (A) description of the modern bias against taxonomy
   (B) comparison of Wilson to Kastner
   (C) book review
   (D) history of taxonomy
   (E) species of eternity

14. Parsifal and Klingsor were probably a
   (A) German taxonomist and his nemesis
   (B) man and a plant
   (C) taxonomist and a fauna
   (D) flora and a fauna
   (E) knight and a monster

15. As Jefferson showed, a flaw that the careful taxonomist should avoid is
   (A) presumption   (B) intellectualization   (C) foolhardiness   (D) mindless activity
   (E) cataloguing

16. Taxonomy was considered to be an important science from about
   (A) 1800 to 1930   (B) 1700 to 1830   (C) 1818 to 1918   (D) 1700 to 1800
   (E) 1700 to 1950

17. The last story in Kastner's book probably describes incidents that occurred
   (A) in the nineteenth century
   (B) recently in the American West
   (C) in 1824 in Philadelphia
   (D) when homesteading was not enforced
   (E) when fossil creatures were alive

18. The scope of Kastner's book does not include
- (A) Meriweather Lewis
- (B) Linnaeus and Cuvier
- (C) Charles Peale
- (D) the Tuscarora Indians
- (E) the Marquis de Lafayette

Passage 4

In a sense, no intelligent person in his lifetime can entirely escape at least some informal speculation. In the form of a dilemma, Aristotle presented this truth in the fragment of one of his lost treatises, *Protreptikos:* "You say one must philosophize. Then you must philosophize. You say one should not philosophize. Then to prove your contention you must philosophize. In any case you must philosophize." To abandon philosophy altogether is itself a philosophical decision. In spite of some incurious or inept minds, the human intellect is naturally philosophical: it has a quenchless thirst for knowledge, not merely for data but for their explorations, justifications, and proofs; it tries to grasp its findings in an ultimate understanding of reality. Man's search is always for truth; he even proves truth by truth. In a popular sense, every thinking person is philosophizing.

Philosophy in the strict, technical sense, however, is quite different from the popular use of the term. The philosophizing of the common man is superficial, vague, haphazard, unconscious, uncritical, and subjective; but philosophy in the strict sense is a conscious, precise, critical, objective, and systematic study of all things.

Etymologically, the term "philosophy" derives from two Greek words: *philia* ("love") and *sophia* ("wisdom"). According to Cicero and Diogenes Laërtius, the term "philosophy" goes back to Pythagoras, one of the Seven Wise Men of ancient Greece, who allegedly repudiated the arrogant name of "sage" (*sophos*) by which contemporary thinkers had designated themselves. Pythagoras claimed, "No man, but only God, is wise"; since the goal of perfect wisdom is beyond the attainment of mortal men, he wanted to be called a *philosophos,* a "lover of wisdom."

Originally the term *sophia* designated the carpenter's art, the art of making pontoons, the art of navigation and guessing riddles. Later it meant talent in poetry and excellence in any art, music in particular. In ancient Greece a wise man was a person characterized by common sense or by great skill and outstanding performance in any art. Not until the time of Aristotle, though, did the term "philosophy" assume a technical meaning, distinguishing it from the other branches of learning.

Wisdom in the strict sense, as an intellectual virtue, is the certain and evident knowledge of all things through the ultimate reasons, principles, and causes. Philosophy, then, the loving quest for wisdom, is, according to its essential definition, the supreme science of all things through the ultimate reasons, principles, and causes acquired by means of natural human reason.

Science in general is universal, certain, evidenced, and systematized knowledge of things through their causes. Scientific knowledge is organized according to the intrinsic principles proper to its subject, thus making demonstrable its conclusions. Science does not desire a mere enumeration of facts, since the phenomena of nature are not isolated and independent; it seeks rather to discover the laws behind these facts in order to explain them and arrange them into a comprehensive system of knowledge. Philosophy goes beyond this purpose; it unites the findings of the various sciences into the highest system possible to the human intellect. Philosophy is not to be identified with any of the special sciences either singly or together; it is the unification and systematization of all important knowledge within the realm of reason. Philosophy is a universal science in the sense that it investigates and inquires into everything: knowledge itself and its methods, being in general, particular types of being both inanimate and animate, finite beings, and the Infinite Being. Its universal character, however, must not be understood in the sense that it is the sole science of mankind, absorbing all the special sciences, being merely their supreme synthesis. Philosophy is the supreme science, for it is not content with just the intermediate principles of truth, but also studies things in their ultimate aspects. It is preoccupied with the totalization of knowledge; it integrates the multiplicity of reality into a total and fundamental unity.

The main objects of philosophy, those that best indicate its meaning, are speculation and criticism. Concerning speculation, philosophy looks upon things from the broadest possible perspective; as for criticism, it has the twofold role of questioning and judging everything that pertains either to the foundations or to the superstructure of human thinking. [It is interesting to note that the English word "speculation" comes from the Latin verb *specere* ("to see"), but its immediate origin is in the noun *specula,* indicating a "watch tower" or, metonymically, a "hill." Just as one can see the wide horizon from a tower or a hilltop, so he obtains through philosophy a broad view of reality.] In short, philosophy is the science of beings in search of their ultimate reasons, causes, and principles.

As a science of beings, philosophy is concerned with everything that is or becomes or is known. Whereas the special sciences are looking for the proximate causes of things, philosophy searches for the ultimate explanations and causes of being.

19. Which of the following occupations was not associated with the term for wisdom by the ancient Greeks who preceded Aristotle?
(A) fortune-telling   (B) navigation   (C) making pontoons   (D) guessing riddles
(E) carpentry

20. According to the passage, one cannot escape philosophizing, because
(A)   Aristotle could not
(B)   antiphilosophy is superficial and vague
(C)   to decide not to philosophize is itself a philosophical decision
(D)   all human beings are intelligent during their lifetimes
(E)   one is obliged to pursue the systematic study of all things

21. The author of this passage would probably call philosophy
(A)   the province of the Greeks
(B)   one of the best of the practical·arts
(C)   an essential definition
(D)   a supreme study, encompassing all things
(E)   an indeterminate but highly rewarding pursuit

22. *Philosophos* is derived from which of the following sources?
(A) Greek   (B) Pythagoras   (C) Cicero   (D) Diogenes   (E) etymology

23. The main point of the sixth paragraph is emphasized through which of the following processes?
(A) subtlety   (B) repetition   (C) deduction   (D) induction   (E) elimination

24. The "desire" of philosophy, according to the passage, is to
(A)   systematize and enumerate causal phenomena
(B)   make intrinsic properties demonstrable
(C)   create universal tenets
(D)   synthesize all knowledge
(E)   publish the immediate principles of truth

25. According to the passage, the very fact that man thinks means that he is
(A)   following in the tradition of the ancient Greeks
(B)   tending toward a strict philosophical practice
(C)   an informal philosopher
(D)   a sage
(E)   beyond the attainment of perfect wisdom

Passage 5

It is deemed a necessity to understand clearly the nature of science in a time commonly known as the "scientific age." Of significance is the student's ability to see that biology, for example, is a science and to relate it to other sciences like chemistry or physics. While compartmentalizing knowledge into biology, chemistry, geology, or anthropology is a convenience, there is danger in that we can easily overlook how these seemingly unrelated fields actually complement one another.

The word *science* is heard so often in modern times that almost everybody has some notion of its meaning. On the other hand, its definition is difficult for many people. The meaning of the term is confused because many endeavors masquerading under the name of science do not have any valid connection with it. Therefore everyone should understand its import and objectives. Just to make the explanation as simple as possible, suppose science is defined as classified knowledge (facts). An example that adequately meets the requirements is astronomy. On the other hand, astrology, regardless of how sincerely it is believed by some, must be excluded since it is not based on fact.

Even in the true sciences distinguishing fact from fiction is not always easy. For this reason great care should be taken to distinguish between beliefs and truths. There is no danger as long as a clear difference is made between temporary and proved explanations. For example, hypotheses (tentative theories) and theories are attempts to explain natural phenomena. From these tentative positions the scientist continues to experiment and observe until they are proved or discredited. The exact status of any explanation should be clearly labeled to avoid confusion.

The objectives of science are primarily the discovery and the subsequent understanding of the unknown. Man cannot be satisfied with recognizing that secrets exist in nature or that questions are unanswerable; he must solve them. Toward that end specialists in the field of biology and related fields of interest are directing much of their time and energy. A beginning student should understand the motivation of science and acquire the spirit of inquiry. That kind of spirit, plus practice in the methods of science, should make a course more meaningful.

Actually, two basic approaches lead to the discovery of new information. One, aimed at satisfying curiosity, is referred to as *pure* science. The other is aimed at using knowledge for specific purposes—for instance, improving health, raising standards of living, or creating new consumer products. In this case knowledge is put to economic use. Such an approach is referred to as *applied* science.

Sometimes practical-minded people miss the point of pure science in thinking only of its immediate utilization for economic rewards. One can see that an extraordinary amount of knowledge about chemistry is necessary before one can possibly understand functions of protoplasm like respiration or photosynthesis. Chemists responsible for many of the discoveries could hardly have anticipated that their findings would one day result in applications of such a practical nature as those directly related to life and health. Furthermore, geneticists working on insects could not foresee all the possible applications of their findings to the improvement of plants and animals through selective breeding. The discovery of one bit of information opens the door to the discovery of another. Some discoveries seem so simple that one is amazed they were not made years ago; however, one should remember that the construction of the microscope had to precede the discovery of the cell, and a knowledge of the chemical nature of oxygen and carbon dioxide had to come before a breakthrough in the understanding of photosynthesis. The host of scientists dedicating their lives to pure science are not apologetic about ignoring the practical side of their discoveries; they know from experience that most knowledge is eventually applied. Probably one can safely say that even from a practical point of view all discoveries will eventually be used.

26. To define science, we may simply call it
   (A) the complementation of unrelated fields
   (B) the convergence of unrelated fields
   (C) biology, chemistry, geology, physics, and anthropology
   (D) biology, chemistry, geology, and anthropology
   (E) classified knowledge

27. According to the passage, which of the following cannot be classified as a science?
    (A) phrenology   (B) astronomy   (C) astrology   (D) chemistry   (E) botany

28. Pure science, leading to the construction of a microscope,
    (A) may lead to antiscientific, "impure" results
    (B) necessarily precedes applied science, leading to the discovery of a cell
    (C) is not always pure
    (D) comes largely from the efforts of eccentric scientists
    (E) necessarily results from applied science and the discovery of a cell

29. A scientist interested in adding to our general knowledge about oxygen would probably call his approach
    (A) applied science   (B) beginning science   (C) agricultural science   (D) pure science   (E) botanical science

30. The best title for this passage is
    (A) "Manifestations and Relationships of Life"
    (B) "Biology and the Scientific Age"
    (C) "The Nature of Science and Scientists"
    (D) "Organisms and Their Environments"
    (E) "Changing Life"

STOP

IF YOU FINISH BEFORE TIME HAS ELAPSED, CHECK YOUR WORK ON THIS SECTION OF THE TEST ONLY. DO NOT GO ON TO THE NEXT SECTION OF THE TEST UNTIL TIME IS UP FOR THIS SECTION.

SECTION III
ANALYTICAL REASONING

Time—35 Minutes
26 Questions

Directions:
In this section you will be given groups of questions based on different sets of conditions. Drawing a simple diagram may be helpful in answering some of the questions. You are to choose the best answer and mark the corresponding space on your answer sheet.

Questions 1–7

There are five flagpoles in a row.
Each flagpole flies one flag and one pennant.
The flags are either red, white, or blue.
The pennants are either green, white, or blue.
On a given flagpole, the pennant and the flag cannot be the same color.
Two adjacent flagpoles cannot fly the same color flags.
Two adjacent flagpoles cannot fly the same color pennants.
No more than two of any color flag or pennant may fly at one time.

1. If the 2nd and 5th pennants are blue, the 2nd and 5th flags are red, and the 3rd flag is white, then which of the following MUST be true?

   I.   The 4th flag is blue.
   II.   The 3rd pennant is green.
   III.   If the 1st flag is white, then the 1st pennant is green.
(A) I and II   (B) I and III   (C) II and III   (D) I, II, and III   (E) None of these

2. If the 1st flag is red and the 2nd pennant is blue, then which of the following is not necessarily true?
(A)   The 2nd flag is white.
(B)   If the 5th flag is red, then the 3rd flag is blue.
(C)   If the 4th pennant is green, then the 1st pennant is white.
(D)   If the 1st and 5th flags are the same color, then the 3rd flag is blue.
(E)   If the 4th pennant is green and the 5th pennant is white, then the 1st and 3rd pennants are different colors.

3. If the 1st and 3rd flags are white and the 2nd and 4th pennants are blue, then which of the following is false?
(A)   The 4th flag is red.
(B)   The 1st pennant is green.
(C)   The 3rd pennant is not red.
(D)   The 5th pennant is green.
(E)   There is one blue flag.

4. If the 1st and 4th flags are blue and the 3rd pennant is white, then which of the following MUST be true?

   I.   If the 5th pennant is white, then the 1st pennant is green.
   II.   If the 1st pennant is green, then the 5th pennant is white.
   III.   The 2nd flag is white.
(A) I and II   (B) I and III   (C) I, II, and III   (D) II only   (E) III only

5. If the 1st and 3rd flags are blue and the 1st and 4th pennants are white, then which of the following MUST be true?

   I.   The 2nd pennant is blue.
   II.   The 5th flag is white.
   III.   The 2nd flag is red.
(A) I and II   (B) I and III   (C) II and III   (D) I, II, and III   (E) II only

6. If the 2nd flag is red and the 3rd flag is white, and the 4th pennant is blue, then which of the following MUST be true?
(A)   If the 5th flag is white, then two of the pennants are blue.
(B)   If the 1st flag is white, then the 2nd flag is white.
(C)   If the 1st pennant is blue, then the 5th pennant is green.
(D)   If the 1st pennant is green, then the 5th flag is not blue.
(E)   If the 1st and 5th flags are the same color, then the 1st and 5th pennants are not the same color.

7. If the 1st flag and the 2nd pennant are the same color, the 2nd flag and the 3rd pennant are the same color, the 3rd flag and the 4th pennant are the same color, and the 4th flag and the 5th pennant are the same color, then which of the following MUST be true?

   I.   The 1st pennant is white.
   II.   The 2nd flag is not white.
   III.   The 5th flag is red.
(A) I only   (B) II only   (C) III only   (D) I and III   (E) I, II, and III

Questions 8–14

There are 10 books standing next to each other on a shelf.
There are two math books, two science books, three English books, and three poetry books.
There is a math book on one end and an English book on the other end.
The two math books are never next to each other.
The two science books are always next to each other.
The three English books are always next to each other.

8. If the 8th book is a math book, then which of the following could be true about the 4th book?

   I.   It is a poetry book.
   II. It is next to an English book.
   III. If it is not a poetry book, then it is a math book.
   (A) I only   (B) II only   (C) III only   (D) I and II   (E) I and III

9. If the 9th book is an English book and the 5th and 6th books are poetry books, then which of the following MUST be true?
   (A) There is a math book next to a poetry book.
   (B) The 2nd book is a science book.
   (C) The 3 poetry books are all next to one another.
   (D) The 7th book is a math book.
   (E) The 4th book is not a poetry book.

10. If the first book is a math book and the 7th book is a science book, then which of the following COULD be false?

   I.   Both math books are next to poetry books.
   II. All three poetry books are next to each other.
   III. The 2nd book is a poetry book..
   (A) I and II   (B) I and III   (C) I only   (D) II only   (E) III only

11. If the 4th book is a math book and the 5th book is a science book, then which of the following MUST be true?

   I.   If the 8th book is an English book, then the 2nd book is a poetry book.
   II. If a math book is next to an English book; then all three poetry books are next to one another.
   III. If the 7th book is a poetry book, then the 3rd book is an English book.
   (A) I only   (B) II only   (C) I and II   (D) I and III   (E) II and III

12. If no two poetry books are next to each other, then which of the following MUST be true?

   I.   The 2nd or the 4th book is a poetry book.
   II. A poetry book is next to an English book.
   III. Each science book is next to a poetry book.
   (A) I and II   (B) I and III   (C) II and III   (D) I, II, and III   (E) None of these

13. If a science book is next to an English book, but not next to a poetry book, then which of the following MUST be true?
   (A) The 7th book is a poetry book.
   (B) The 3rd book is an English book or a math book.
   (C) The 5th or the 6th book is a math book.
   (D) The three poetry books are not next to each other.
   (E) The 7th or the 10th book is a math book.

14. If the 7th and 8th books are poetry books, how many different arrangements are there for the 10 books?
(A) One   (B) Two   (C) Three   (D) Four   (E) Five

Questions 15–21

The following restrictions apply to freshmen taking courses at State College:

Each freshman must take either Latin or Greek, or both.
Enrollment in the Sex Lab requires concurrent enrollment in Marriage/Family Relations.
Enrollment in Marriage/Family Relations does not require concurrent enrollment in the Sex Lab.
Freshmen may not enroll in American History and Latin at the same time.
Anyone enrolled in Roman History must also be enrolled in Greek.
A freshman must enroll in at least three classes.
The above-listed courses are the only ones offered to freshmen.

15. What is the maximum number of courses that a freshman can take?
(A) Three   (B) Four   (C) Five   (D) Six   (E) Cannot be determined from the given facts.

16. If a freshman wishes to enroll in American History and the Sex Lab, then which of the following is true?
(A)   She must enroll in at least four classes.
(B)   She cannot enroll in Marriage/Family Relations.
(C)   She may enroll in Latin.
(D)   She cannot enroll in Roman History.
(E)   She must enroll in Roman History.

17. If a freshman does not enroll in Greek, what is the maximum number of classes he can take?
(A) One   (B) Two   (C) Three   (D) Four   (E) Five

18. If a freshman enrolls in Latin, which of the following classes MUST be taken in addition to Latin?

I.   Marriage/Family Relations
II.   Sex Lab
III.   Roman History
(A) I and II   (B) I and III   (C) II and III   (D) I only   (E) None of these

19. If a freshman does not take Latin or the Sex Lab, how many different classes can she voluntarily choose from?
(A) One   (B) Two   (C) Three   (D) Four   (E) Five

20. If a freshman does not wish to take American History or Greek, what is the maximum number of classes he can take?
(A) One   (B) Six   (C) Three   (D) Four   (E) Five

21. If a freshman enrolls in Latin, which of the following MUST be true?

I.   He enrolls in only three classes.
II.   He enrolls in the Sex Lab.
III.   He may choose from four classes.
(A) I and III   (B) I only   (C) III only   (D) I and II   (E) I, II, and III

Questions 22–26

Four teams (Red, Blue, Green, and Yellow) participate in the Junior Olympics, in which there are five events. In each event participants place either 1st, 2nd, 3rd, 4th, or 5th. First place is awarded a gold medal, 2nd place is awarded a silver medal, and 3rd place is awarded a bronze medal. There are no ties and each team enters one contestant in each event. All contestants finish each event.

The results of the Junior Olympics are:
No team wins gold medals in two consecutive events.
No team fails to win a medal within two consecutive events.
The Blue team wins only two medals, neither of them gold.
The Red team wins only three gold medals.

22. If the green team wins only one gold medal, then which MUST be true?
    (A) The yellow team wins two gold medals.
    (B) The red team wins only two bronze medals.
    (C) The yellow team wins only one gold medal.
    (D) The yellow team wins only silver medals.
    (E) The green team wins only bronze medals.

23. Which of the following MUST be true?
    (A) The yellow team wins only bronze and gold medals.
    (B) The yellow team wins five medals.
    (C) The green team cannot win a silver medal.
    (D) The yellow team cannot win a bronze medal.
    (E) The green team wins exactly three medals.

24. If the yellow team wins five silver medals, then the green team MUST win
    I. two gold medals
    II. three bronze medals
    III. two bronze medals
    (A) I   (B) II   (C) III   (D) I and II   (E) I and III

25. All of the following MUST be true except:
    (A) the green team wins five medals
    (B) the yellow team wins five medals
    (C) if the green team wins one gold medal, the yellow team wins one gold medal
    (D) if the green team wins only one silver medal, the yellow team wins only one silver medal
    (E) if the yellow team wins only silver medals, the green team cannot win a silver medal

26. If a sixth team, Orange, enters all events and wins only three consecutive silver medals, which of the following MUST be true?
    (A) If green wins a gold in the 2nd event, it also wins a bronze in the 3rd event.
    (B) If green wins a gold in the 2nd event, it also wins a gold in the 4th event.
    (C) If yellow wins a gold in the 2nd event, green wins a bronze in the 3rd event.
    (D) If yellow wins a gold in the 2nd event, blue wins a silver in the 3rd event.
    (E) If red wins a gold in the 1st event, orange wins a silver in the last event.

STOP

IF YOU FINISH BEFORE TIME HAS ELAPSED, CHECK YOUR WORK ON THIS SECTION OF THE TEST ONLY. DO NOT GO ON TO THE NEXT SECTION OF THE TEST UNTIL TIME IS UP FOR THIS SECTION.

SECTION IV
LOGICAL REASONING

Time—35 Minutes
26 Questions

Directions:
In this section you will be given brief statements or passages and will be required to evaluate the reasoning involved. In some instances, more than one choice will appear to be a possible answer. You are to choose the *best* answer. Use common sense and reasonableness in making your selection; then mark the proper space on the answer sheet.

Questions 1–2 refer to the following passage.

The spate of bills in the Legislature dealing with utility regulation shows that our lawmakers recognize a good political issue when they see one. Among the least worthy is a proposal to establish a new "Consumers Utility Board" to fight proposed increases in gas and electric rates.

It is hardly a novel idea that consumers need representation when rates are set for utilities which operate as monopolies in their communities. That's exactly why we have a state Public Utilities Commission.

Supporters of the proposed consumer board point out that utility companies have the benefit of lawyers and accountants on their payrolls to argue the case for rate increases before the PUC. That's true. Well, the PUC has the benefit of a $40 million annual budget and a staff of 900—all paid at taxpayer expense—to find fault with these rate proposals if there is fault to be found.

1. Which of the following is the best example to offer in support of this argument against a Consumers Utility Board?
   (A) the percentage of taxpayer dollars supporting the PUC
   (B) the number of lawyers working for the Consumers Utility Board
   (C) the number of concerned consumers
   (D) a PUC readjustment of rates downward
   (E) the voting record of lawmakers supporting the board

2. Which of the following would most seriously weaken the above argument?
   (A) Private firms are taking an increasing share of the energy business.
   (B) Water rates are also increasing.
   (C) The PUC budget will be cut slightly, along with other state agencies.
   (D) Half of the PUC lawyers and accountants are also retained by utilities.
   (E) More tax money goes to education than to the PUC.

3. Most of those who enjoy music play a musical instrument; therefore, if Maria enjoys music, she probably plays a musical instrument.

   Which of the following most closely parallels the reasoning in the statement above?
   (A) The majority of those who voted for Smith in the last election oppose abortion; therefore, if the residents of University City all voted for Smith, they probably oppose abortion.
   (B) If you appreciate portrait painting you are probably a painter yourself; therefore, your own experience is probably the cause of your appreciation.
   (C) Most of those who join the army are male; therefore, if Jones did not join the army, Jones is probably female.
   (D) Over 50% of the high school students polled admitted hating homework; therefore, a majority of high school students do not like homework.
   (E) If most workers drive to work, and Sam drives to work, then Sam must be a worker.

4. "To be a good teacher, one must be patient. Some good teachers are good administrators."

Which of the following can be concluded from the above statement?
(A) Some good teachers are not patient.
(B) All good administrators are patient.
(C) Some good administrators are patient.
(D) Only good administrators are patient.
(E) Many good administrators are patient.

5. "Good personnel relations of an organization depend upon mutual confidence, trust, and good will. The basis of confidence is understanding. Most troubles start with people who do not understand each other. When the organization's intentions or motives are misunderstood, or when reasons for actions, practices, or policies are misconstrued, complete cooperation from individuals is not forthcoming. If management expects full cooperation from employees, it has a responsibility of sharing with them the information which is the foundation of proper understanding, confidence, and trust. Personnel management has long since outgrown the days when it was the vogue to 'treat them rough and tell them nothing.' Up-to-date personnel management provides all possible information about the activities, aims, and purposes of the organization. It seems altogether creditable that a desire should exist among employees for such information which the best-intentioned executive might think would not interest them and which the worst-intentioned would think was none of their business."

The above paragraph implies that one of the causes of the difficulty that an organization might have with its personnel relations is that its employees
(A) have not expressed interest in the activities, aims, and purposes of the organization
(B) do not believe in the good faith of the organization
(C) have not been able to give full cooperation to the organization
(D) do not recommend improvements in the practices and policies of the organization
(E) can afford little time to establish good relations with their organization

6. Of all psychiatric disorders, depression is the most common; yet, research on its causes and cures is still far from complete. As a matter of fact, very few facilities offer assistance to those suffering from this disorder.

The author would probably agree that
(A) depression needs further study
(B) further research will make possible further assistance to those suffering from depression
(C) most facilities are staffed by psychiatrists whose speciality is not depression
(D) those suffering from depression need to know its causes and cures
(E) depression and ignorance go hand in hand

7. No brown-eyed people have red hair. Some short people have red hair.

Based on the foregoing information, which of the following MUST also be true?
  I. There are short people who do not have brown eyes.
  II. There are people without brown eyes who are short.
  III. Some brown-eyed people are short.
(A) I only   (B) II only   (C) III only   (D) I and II only   (E) II and III only

8. *Ivan:* What the Church says is true because the Church is an authority.
  Mike: What grounds do you have for holding that the Church is a genuine authority?
  Ivan: The authority of the Church is implied in the Bible.
  Mike: And why do you hold that the Bible is true?
  Ivan: Because the Church holds that it is true.

The argument present in the foregoing dialogue is best described as
(A) vague   (B) pointed   (C) undeniable   (D) taboo   (E) circular

9. *Mary:*   All Italians are great lovers.
Kathy: That is not so. I have met some Spaniards who were magnificent lovers.

Kathy's reply to Mary indicates that she has misunderstood Mary's remark to mean that
(A)   every great lover is an Italian
(B)   Italians are best at the art of love
(C)   Spaniards are inferior to Italians
(D)   Italians are more likely to be great lovers than are Spaniards
(E)   there is a relationship between nationality and love

Questions 10–11 refer to the following passage.

Mr. Dimple: Mrs. Wilson's qualifications are ideal for the position. She is intelligent, forceful, determined, and trustworthy. I suggest we hire her immediately.

10. Which of the following, if true, would most weaken Mr. Dimple's statement?
(A)   Mrs. Wilson is not interested in being hired.
(B)   There are two other applicants whose qualifications are identical to Mrs. Wilson's.
(C)   Mrs. Wilson is currently working for a rival company.
(D)   Mr. Dimple is not speaking directly to the hiring committee.
(E)   Mrs. Wilson is older than many of the other applicants.

11. Which of the following, if true, offers the strongest support of Mr. Dimple's statement?
(A)   All the members of the hiring committee have agreed that intelligence, trustworthiness, determination, and forcefulness are important qualifications for the job.
(B)   Mr. Dimple holds exclusive responsibility for hiring new employees.
(C)   Mr. Dimple has known Mrs. Wilson longer than he has known any of the other applicants.
(D)   Mrs. Wilson is a member of Mr. Dimple's family.
(E)   Mrs. Dimple is intelligent, forceful, determined, and trustworthy.

12. American publisher Horace Greeley said, ''The illusion that times that were are better than those that are has probably pervaded all ages.''

Which of the following expresses at least one of the meanings of Greeley's words?
(A)   The grass is always greener on the other side.
(B)   Life is full of sound and fury, signifying nothing.
(C)   Beauty is in the eyes of the beholder.
(D)   Live for today.
(E)   All ages look at the world through rose-colored glasses.

13.   When a dental hygienist cleans your teeth, you may not see much evidence that she is supervised by a dentist. Hygienists often work pretty much on their own, even though they are employed by dentists. Then why can't hygienists practice independently, perhaps saving patients a lot of money in the process? The patients would not have to pay the steep profit that many dentists make on the hygienists' labors.

Which of the following statements weaken(s) the argument above?

I.   A dentist should be on hand to inspect a hygienist's work to make sure the patient has no problems that the hygienist is unable to detect.
II.   Some patients might be less inclined to go to a dentist regularly if they could get their teeth cleaned otherwise.
III.   Some dentists do not employ dental hygienists.
(A) I and II   (B) II and III   (C) III only   (D) I and III   (E) II only

14.   There are those of us who, determined to be happy, are discouraged repeatedly by social and economic forces that cause us nothing but trouble. And there are those of us who are blessed with health and wealth and still grumble and complain about almost everything.

Which of the following can be a point to which the author is leading?

I.   Happiness is both a state of mind and a state of affairs.
II. Both personal and public conditions can make happiness difficult to attain.
III. No one can be truly happy.
(A) I   (B) II   (C) III   (D) I and II   (E) I, II, and III

15. "Keep true, never be ashamed of doing right; decide on what you think is right and stick to it."—
George Eliot

If one were to follow Eliot's advice,

I.   he would never change his mind
II. he would do what is right
III. he might never know what is right
(A) I   (B) II   (C) III   (D) I and II   (E) II and III

16.   To paraphrase Oliver Wendell Holmes, taxes keep us civilized. Just look around you, at well-paved superhighways, air-conditioned schools, and modernized prisons, and you cannot help but agree with Holmes.

Which of the following is the strongest criticism of the statement above?
(A)   The author never actually met Holmes.
(B)   The author does not acknowledge those of us who do not live near highways, schools, and prisons.
(C)   The author does not assure us that he has been in a modernized prison.
(D)   The author does not offer a biographical sketch of Holmes.
(E)   The author does not define "civilized."

Questions 17–18 refer to the following passage.

Information that is published is part of the public record. But information that a reporter collects, and sources that he contacts, must be protected in order for our free press to function free of fear.

17. The above argument is most severely weakened by which of the following statements?
(A)   Public information is usually reliable.
(B)   Undocumented evidence may be used to convict an innocent person.
(C)   Members of the press act ethically in most cases.
(D)   The sources that a reporter contacts are usually willing to divulge their identity.
(E)   Our press has never been altogether free.

18. Which of the following statements is consistent with the argument above?
(A)   Privileged information has long been an important and necessary aspect of investigative reporting.
(B)   Not all the information a reporter collects becomes part of the public record.
(C)   Tape-recorded information is not always reliable.
(D)   The victim of a crime must be protected at all costs.
(E)   The perpetrator of a crime must be protected at all costs.

Questions 19–21 refer to the following passage.

A federal court ruling that San Diego County can't sue the government for the cost of medical care of illegal aliens is based upon a legal technicality that ducks the larger moral question. But the U.S. Supreme Court's refusal recently to review this decision has closed the last avenue of legal appeal.

The medical expenses of indigent citizens or legally resident aliens are covered by state and federal assistance programs. The question of who is to pay when an undocumented alien falls ill remains unresolved, however, leaving California counties to bear this unfair and growing burden.

19. The author implies that
   (A) the U.S. Supreme Court has refused to review the federal court ruling
   (B) the burden of medical expenses for aliens is growing
   (C) the larger moral question involves no legal technicalities
   (D) San Diego should find another avenue of appeal
   (E) the federal government is dodging the moral issue

20. Which of the following arguments, if true, would most seriously weaken the argument above?
   (A) There are many cases of undocumented aliens being denied medical aid at state hospitals.
   (B) A private philanthropic organization has funded medical aid programs that have so far provided adequate assistance to illegal aliens nationwide.
   (C) Illegal aliens do not wish federal or state aid, because those accepting aid risk detection of their illegal status and deportation.
   (D) Undocumented aliens stay in California only a short time before moving east.
   (E) Judges on the Supreme Court have pledged privately to assist illegal aliens with a favorable ruling once immigration laws are strengthened.

21. Which of the following changes in the above passage could strengthen the author's argument?
   (A) adding interviews with illegal aliens
   (B) a description of the stages that led to a rejection by the Supreme Court
   (C) a clarification with numbers of the rate at which the burden of medical expenses is growing
   (D) the naming of those state and federal assistance programs that aid indigent citizens
   (E) the naming of those California counties that do not participate in medical aid to illegal aliens

22.   History is strewn with the wreckage of experiments in communal living, often organized around farms and inspired by religious or philosophical ideals. To the more noble failures can now be added Mao Tse-tung's notorious Chinese communes. The current rulers of China, still undoing the mistakes of the late Chairman, are quietly allowing their agricultural communes to _____.

Which of the following is the most logical completion of the passage above?
(A) evolve   (B) increase   (C) recycle   (D) disintegrate   (E) organize

23. *Sal:*   Herb is my financial planner.
    Keith: I'm sure he's good; he's my cousin.

Which of the following facts is Keith ignoring in his response?
(A) Financial planning is a professional, not a personal, matter.
(B) Sal is probably flattering Keith.
(C) Professional competence is not necessarily a family trait.

(D) "Good" is a term with many meanings.
(E) Sal's financial planner is no one's cousin.

24. Many very effective prescription drugs are available to patients on a "one time only" basis. Suspicious of drug abuse, physicians will not renew a prescription for a medicine that has worked effectively for a patient. This practice denies a patient her right to health.

Which of the following is a basic assumption made by the author?
(A) A new type of medicine is likely to be more expensive.
(B) Physicians are not concerned with a patient's health.
(C) Most of the patients who need prescription renewals are female.
(D) Most physicians prescribe inadequate amounts of medicine.
(E) Patients are liable to suffer the same ailment repeatedly.

Questions 25–26 refer to the following passage.

Forty years ago, hardly anybody thought about going to court to sue somebody.

A person could bump a pedestrian with his Chrysler Airflow and the victim would say something like, "No harm done," and walk away. Ipso facto. No filing of codicils, taking of depositions or polling the jury. Attorneys need not apply.

25. Which of the following sentences most logically continues the above passage?
(A) The Chrysler Airflow is no longer the harmless machine it used to be.
(B) Fortunately, this is still the case.
(C) Unfortunately, times have changed.
(D) New legislation affecting the necessity for codicils is a sign of the times.
(E) But now, as we know, law schools are full of eager young people.

26. Which of the following details, if true, would most strengthen the above statement?
(A) There were fewer courthouses then than now.
(B) The marked increase in pedestrian accidents is a relatively recent occurrence.
(C) Most citizens of 40 years ago were not familiar with their legal rights.
(D) The number of lawsuits filed during World War II was extremely low.
(E) Most young attorneys were in the armed forces 40 years ago.

STOP

IF YOU FINISH BEFORE TIME HAS ELAPSED, CHECK YOUR WORK ON THIS SECTION OF THE TEST ONLY. DO NOT GO ON TO THE NEXT SECTION OF THE TEST UNTIL TIME IS UP FOR THIS SECTION.

SECTION V
EVALUATION OF FACTS

Time—35 Minutes
36 Questions

Directions:
This section consists of several sets; each set presents a factual statement, the description of a dispute, and two rules. In some sets, the rules will be conflicting. Be sure that you consider each rule independently and not as an exception to the other. Following each set are questions; select from four choices (given below) the one that best categorizes each question, based upon the relationship of one or both of the rules to the dispute. Darken the appropriate space on your answer sheet.

(A) A relevant question which you can only answer by choosing between the rules.
(B) A relevant question which you cannot answer because you need more information or additional rules, but which does not require a choice between the rules.
(C) A relevant question which you can answer by referring to the facts or rules, or both.
(D) An irrelevant question or one which is only remotely relevant to the outcome of the dispute.

Set 1

FACTS

Leo Lemon, a used-car dealer, had been unsuccessfully trying to sell an old green Buick for the past year. He had purchased the car from an elderly couple who were unaware that the engine was bad. About one day before Leo was going to take the car to the junk yard, Jack and Jill Hill came onto the lot and showed interest in buying the car. Leo, realizing that this was his big chance to sell the car, explained that it was in perfect condition, but that they would have to return the next day for a test drive. In the meantime, Leo had a mechanic adjust the engine so that it would run perfectly for one week. After the test drive, Jack and Jill bought the car, signing a bill of sale. Six days later, the radiator overheated, the transmission failed, and the brakes locked. The Hills had the car towed immediately to Leo's lot, and demanded a refund. Leo refused.

DISPUTE

The Hills sued Leo for the return of their money; Leo contested.

RULE I

Misrepresentation occurs when intentional verbal false representation of a material fact is sufficiently significant so that one would act in reliance upon it. Misrepresentation invalidates a contract and is punishable by a $500 fine.

RULE II

The consumer is obligated to carefully inspect all materials before purchase and cannot hold the seller liable after 10 days following the transaction.

Questions

1. Will Jack and Jill get their money returned?

2. Is the elderly couple guilty of misrepresentation?

3. Was the agreement a valid contract?

4. If the elderly couple was aware of the poor condition of the car engine, could Leo get his money back?

5. If the Hills had not returned with the car for 3 weeks, would they have been eligible for a refund?

6. Was Leo trying to deceive the Hills?

7. Should the elderly couple have taken better care of the car?

Set 2

FACTS

Maloney and Stevenson lived on the same floor of a residential hotel. One night Stevenson noticed that he had exhausted his supply of cigarettes. He left the room to get some from the store on the corner but neglected to close the door on his departure. As Maloney was returning to his room, he noticed the open door to Stevenson's empty room. He decided to see whether there was anything of value that he could steal. Maloney entered, closed the door behind him, and began to search the apartment. Hoping to find cash, he carefully removed the clothes from the two drawers of the dresser. Finding nothing, he opened the door to exit but found his path blocked by an enraged Stevenson.

DISPUTE

Maloney was charged with burglary. He contested.

RULE I

No burglary occurs unless property is actually removed from another's premises.

RULE II

One who enters another's premises with the intent of theft is guilty of burglary.

Questions

8. Did Maloney take anything from Stevenson's apartment?

9. Will Maloney be found guilty of burglary?

10. If Maloney had not intended to steal anything, would he be found guilty of burglary?

11. Did Maloney know Stevenson?

Set 3

FACTS

Estelle, a novelist who needed absolute quiet to do her work, moved from the city to a quiet suburb. Two months later the Smiths, a family with three active children, moved in next door. Despite Estelle's repeated polite requests for quiet, the Smith children played noisily in the street near her house. One afternoon when she saw the children pass on their way to the playground, Estelle called the Smiths and said, "This is the police calling. Your children are in Park Emergency Hospital. They have been critically injured by an automobile. Hurry, please. There's not much time." Estelle made up the story in order to frighten the Smiths into keeping their children off the street. The shock did great harm to Mrs. Smith's nervous system and Mr. Smith's heart. Both needed hospitalization.

DISPUTE

The Smiths sued Estelle for intentional infliction of emotional distress. Estelle contested.

RULE I

One who communicates a falsehood is liable for the harm he causes only if the communicator does not identify himself at the time of the communication.

RULE II

One who frightens others with false stories is liable in damages for the injuries caused by the fright.

Questions

12. Was the communication a falsehood?

13. If the children's noise had prevented her from practicing her profession, was Estelle justified in making the call?

14. Will Estelle be found guilty?

15. If Estelle had identified herself, would she be found guilty?

Set 4

FACTS

Phil, Judy, Hall, and Jamie belonged to the Blue Ribbon Running Club. All four entered the Flag Day ten-kilometer run. Because the route of the race was not clearly marked, the sponsors of the event urged all entrants to familiarize themselves with the course on the weekend before the race. Of the four Blue Ribbon runners, only Hall went to the practice run. In the race, Phil was well ahead of all the other runners when he accidentally ran off the course. Realizing his mistake, he backtracked, got on the right course, and continued. Hall, who was far behind, ran off the course taking a shortcut, and Jamie who was close behind Hall, followed him. Hall crossed the finish line first, followed closely by Jamie. The sponsors declared Hall the winner and Jamie second.

DISPUTE

The runners from the Victory Running Club, who had observed Hall's leaving the course, contested the awards of first and second place.

RULE I

A runner who accidentally runs off the course will not be disqualified if he returns and continues from his point of departure.

RULE II

A runner who runs off the course will be disqualified.

Questions

16. Will Hall be disqualified?

17. Will Jamie win the race if Hall is disqualified?

18. Who will be declared the winner?

19. Should the course have been more clearly marked?

20. If Phil finished directly behind Jamie, will he be considered the winner?

21. Where did Hall leave the course?

Set 5

FACTS

The YMCA in Twalama City has three conference rooms which are available for rent. On Thursday evening, three groups were meeting: the Twilight Years Investment Club in the Green Room, the Polka Club in the Blue Room, and the Barker Gang in the Red Room. While the Investment Club members were discussing tax-free bonds, the Gang was quietly planning a forceable entry and robbery of a nearby bank. The Polka Club was debating the introduction of disco dancing at their annual polka ball, and the disagreement became extremely noisy and dangerously violent. An elderly member of the Investment Club summoned the police. When the police arrived, they entered the Red Room by mistake and, recognizing a man wanted for questioning in a recent robbery, arrested the Gang. Five minutes later, though by this time the noise had abated, they also arrested the members of the Polka Club.

DISPUTE

The members of both the Polka Club and the Barker Gang contested their arrests, pleading not guilty.

RULE I

A meeting of more than five people that unreasonably disturbs the peace is called unlawful assembly and is punishable by a maximum of 30 days in jail or a $100 fine, or both.

RULE II

A meeting of more than two people with a plan to commit a crime by force is conspiracy and is punishable by up to 2 years in prison.

Questions

22. If all 15 members of the Polka Club were in attendance at the meeting, will they be found guilty of unlawful assembly?

23. If the Barker Gang proves in court that it had not planned to use force, will it be convicted of conspiracy?

24. Will the Polka Club members be fined or go to jail?

25. Could the Gang have escaped?

26. Was the nearby bank an easy target for the planned robbery?

27. If eight members of the Barker Gang were arrested, will all the members of the Gang be found guilty of conspiracy?

28. Should the police have come earlier?

29. If the Polka Club was also planning to forcibly rob a nearby bank, would it be fined?

30. Will the Gang be found guilty of unlawful assembly?

31. If only three members of the Gang were present, could they go to prison?

Set 6

FACTS

Mr. Bona was owner of a small department store in Agoura, California. One day he noticed Sue, a female customer, acting rather suspiciously. Bona observed Sue until finally he thought he saw her put a pack of cigarettes into her pocketbook. Bona then rushed toward Sue, grabbed her by the arm as she reached the sidewalk, and said, "Come with me!" Sue, not knowing that Bona managed the store and unaware of his reasons for accosting her, broke away from Bona's grip and ran into the crowded street, screaming, "Help! Help! A madman is after me!"

To escape Bona's pursuit, Sue jumped on an unoccupied bicycle that was parked outside the store and peddled into the crowded street. Bona gave chase for about three blocks before finally catching her in front of the local police station. Bona dragged Sue into the station.

DISPUTE

Bona charged Sue with petty theft; Sue contested and charged Bona with assault.

RULE I

An assault occurs when one person causes another to believe that the former is about to make a physical attack upon the latter.

RULE II

A person may use reasonable force to recover property that has been taken from his premises without consent.

Questions

32. Did Sue steal the cigarettes?

33. If Sue did not take the cigarettes, will Bona be guilty of assault?

34. If Sue had taken the cigarettes without consent, would Bona be guilty of assault?

35. Will Sue be charged with theft for taking the bicycle?

36. Where did Bona finally catch Sue?

STOP

IF YOU FINISH BEFORE TIME HAS ELAPSED, CHECK YOUR WORK ON THIS SECTION OF THE TEST ONLY. DO NOT GO ON TO THE NEXT SECTION OF THE TEST UNTIL TIME IS UP FOR THIS SECTION.

SECTION VI
READING COMPREHENSION

Time—35 Minutes
28 Questions

Directions:
Read the passages and answer the questions following each passage by blackening the appropriate space on the answer sheet. You may refer back to the passages when answering the questions. Answer all questions on the basis of what is stated or implied.

Passage 1

Now then, you have the facts. You know what the human race enjoys, and what it doesn't enjoy. It has invented a heaven, out of its own head, all by itself: guess what it is like! In fifteen hundred eternities you couldn't do it. The ablest mind known to you or me in fifty million aeons couldn't do it. Very well, I will tell you about it.

1. First of all, I recall to your attention the extraordinary fact with which I began. To wit, that the human being, like the immortals, naturally places sexual intercourse far and away above all other joys—yet he has left it out of his heaven! The very thought of it excites him; opportunity sets him wild, in this state he will risk life, reputation, everything—even his queer heaven itself—to make good that opportunity and ride it to the overwhelming climax. From youth to middle age all men and all women prize copulation above all other pleasures combined, yet it is actually as I have said: it is not in their heaven; prayer takes its place.

2. In man's heaven *everybody sings*! The man who did not sing on earth sings there; the man who could not sing on earth is able to do it there. This universal singing is not casual, not occasional, not relieved by intervals of quiet; it goes on, all day long, and every day, during a stretch of twelve hours. And *everybody stays*; whereas on the earth the place would be empty in two hours. The singing is of hymns alone. Nay, it is of *one* hymn alone. The words are always the same, in number they are only about a dozen, there is no rhyme, there is no poetry: "Hosannah, hosannah, hosannah, Lord God of Sabaoth, 'rah! 'rah! 'rah! siss!—boom! . . . a-a-ah!"

3. Meantime, every person is playing on a harp—those millions and millions!—whereas not more than twenty in the thousand of them could play an instrument on the earth, or ever wanted to.

Consider the deafening hurricane of sound—millions and millions of harps gritting their teeth at the same time! I ask you: is it hideous, is it odious, is it horrible?

4. The inventor of their heaven empties into it all the nations of the earth, in one common jumble. All are on an equality absolute, no one of them ranking another; they have to be "brothers"; they have to mix together, pray together, harp together, hosannah together—whites, blacks, Jews, everybody—there's no distinction. Here on the earth all nations hate each other. Yet every pious person adores that heaven and wants to get into it. He really does. And when he is in a holy rapture he thinks he thinks that if he were only there he would take all the populace to his heart, and hug, and hug, and hug!

He is a marvel—man is! I would I knew who invented him.

5. Every man on the earth possesses some share of intellect, large or small; and be it large or be it small he takes pride in it. Also his heart swells at mention of the names of the majestic intellectual chiefs of his race, and he loves the tale of their splendid achievements. For he is of their blood, and in honoring themselves they have honored him. Lo, what the mind of man can do! he cries; and calls the roll of the illustrious of all the ages; and points to the imperishable literatures they have given to the world, and the mechanical wonders they have invented, and the glories wherewith they have clothed science and the arts; and to them he uncovers, as to kings, and gives to them the profoundest homage, and the sincerest, his exultant heart can furnish—thus exalting intellect above all things else in his world, and enthroning it there under the arching skies in a supremacy unapproachable. And then he contrives a heaven that hasn't a rag of intellectuality in it anywhere!

Make a note of it: in man's heaven there are no exercises for the intellect, nothing for it to live upon. It would rot there in a year—rot and stink. Rot and stink—and at that stage become holy. A blessed thing: for only the holy can stand the joys of that bedlam.

1. The primary purpose of the passage is to
   (A) satirize the human conception of eternal life
   (B) encourage the reader to prepare for heaven
   (C) encourage the reader to become sinful
   (D) attack the moral guidelines of the late nineteenth century
   (E) reveal human stupidity

2. Which of the following is probably one of the author's beliefs relative to racism, as indicated in the passage?
   (A) Bigotry and prejudice does not occur among females.
   (B) Everybody has to hate somebody.
   (C) He expects racism to continue in heaven.
   (D) He accepts and condones racism on earth.
   (E) None of the above.

3. According to the author, the inventor of heaven is
   (A) a single capable intellect
   (B) an immortal
   (C) God
   (D) the author himself
   (E) the human race

4. We may infer that the author views the human intellect as
  (A) a blessed thing
  (B) an essential characteristic of humankind
  (C) something people don't really want
  (D) an earthly contrivance
  (E) unrelated to the artistic, industrial, and scientific achievements of the ages

5. The human attitude toward sexual intercourse, as understood by the author, might be summarized as follows:
  (A) Sexual intercourse is only for the young.
  (B) Sexual intercourse is only for the holy.
  (C) Sexual intercourse is prized on earth, and excluded from heaven.
  (D) The joy of sex is equivalent to the joy of heaven.
  (E) Middle-aged sex is less "heavenly" than that enjoyed by the young.

6. The author's conclusion that harp playing in heaven must be horrible is based upon which of the following assumptions?
  (A) The harp is not a pleasant instrument.
  (B) Most heavenly harpists would not be competent musicians.
  (C) The same song, heard over and over, becomes intolerable.
  (D) Most inhabitants of heaven sing as they play.
  (E) Harps in heaven have teeth.

7. We may infer that the author is a
  (A) skeptic   (B) dissenter   (C) Roman Catholic   (D) socialist   (E) Christian

Passage 2

   In ancient Rome "orient" meant the direction toward the rising sun because "orient" means "rising" in Latin. For us it may mean as much as to tell what we are, where we are, whither we would go, and how we propose to get there. Here, then, is our orientation: we are English-speaking human beings; we live in a world full of conflict and distrust; we go in pursuit of the good life, which is liberty and happiness; and we set forth believing that the best way to do it is to use our heads, and to use them as a competent engineer might use a delicate instrument with appropriate care and skill. If you proposed to be a mechanical engineer, you would accept the challenge of the mathematical discipline as a matter of course; you would acknowledge the extreme utility of the slide rule and all it represents. The principles and procedures we invite you to consider stand in the same vital relationship to you if you would be civilized and free. They appear to us to offer the only solid ground upon which free men may ultimately stand between their loved homes and war's desolation—be the war within these homes or on distant shores or hilltops.
   We have commented thus emphatically upon what seems to us the desperately important connection between freedom and language because we wish to make it clear at the start that this connection presents a philosophy of life as well as a system for controlling the most characteristically human activity in it.
   Now as language is the most characteristic sort of human behavior, so it is the most imitative, the most conventional, of all behavior. We might, therefore, study it as a social discipline. Of words we might ask many questions: "What do other people do with them?" "How do others arrange them—particularly the 'best people'?" "What is 'correct'?" "What are the 'rules'?" This is etiquette. It is critically important sometimes and has to do with such things as usage and grammar, "split" infinitives and the agreement of nouns and verbs; it frowns upon comma faults and misspellings. People call it "composition-rhetoric." You scorn it at your peril.
   But in a democracy science is more vital than etiquette. Progress takes precedence over protocol. We shall leave important tasks undone or even unattempted if we dally overlong in getting democrats to say "pre-SEED-ence" instead of "PRESS-a-dence." We believe that the psychological approach to language study is more worthy than the conventional one, but we

also know that if you become genuinely interested in the wonderful phenomena of linguistic behavior, much knowledge of the etiquette will come to you.

Be this as it may, our approach is the engineer's approach. We study not rhetoric or philology but linguistic engineering. We shall not be content with the mere description of language behavior or even the fascinating story of its historical development; we seek rather to make our language behave. Our study is really a branch of applied psychology; and like most other practical activities, it is an art which calls for a sound working knowledge of the anatomy and physiology of the subject. In our case, that subject is the conscious mind, which we here define as the highest function of the brain.

8. The primary purpose of this passage is to
  (A)   establish psychological rules for language
  (B)   develop the connection between freedom and language
  (C)   establish the author's orientation
  (D)   set aside the rules of grammar and usage
  (E)   replace mechanical engineering with language study

9. The author believes that the ability most essential for attaining the "good life" is
  (A)   intellectual ability
  (B)   skill in elocution
  (C)   familiarity with the principles and procedures of one's chosen field
  (D)   the ability to remain free
  (E)   scientific ability

10. Which of the following is consistent with the statement in the second paragraph?
  (A)   Speaking freely is related to speaking philosophically.
  (B)   Understanding how language works helps one to attain liberty and to think philosophically.
  (C)   Those who are most adept at language are most free.
  (D)   Those who can control the language of others are most free.
  (E)   Wars are based on ignorance.

11. The author creates an analogy between
  (A)   psychology and linguistics
  (B)   freedom and language
  (C)   correctness and pronunciation
  (D)   the mechanical engineer and the linguistic engineer
  (E)   etiquette and democracy

12. We may infer from the passage that the study of language is related to
  (A)   the study of the brain
  (B)   the study of diverse practical activities
  (C)   the study of politics
  (D)   the study of ancient cultures
  (E)   the study of liberty and happiness

13. The author concludes that learning the etiquette of language is a result of
  (A)   imitating others
  (B)   accepting social discipline
  (C)   becoming interested in linguistic behavior
  (D)   studying the practice of the "best people"
  (E)   taking a course in composition-rhetoric

14. One of the reasons for taking a psychological rather than a conventional approach to language study is

(A)   the psychological approach is an art rather than a skill
(B)   the conventional approach is not interesting
(C)   correct usage is unrelated to utility
(D)   conventions are always changing
(E)   conventional study concentrates on correctness at the expense of progress

Passage 3

No sooner had the British forces in June 1944 carried out their part in the Allied invasion of Germany than they were faced with the fact that among the prisoners of war captured there were Russians in German uniforms. By the time the war in Europe ended, between two and three million Soviet citizens had passed through Allied hands. This extraordinary situation, certainly never before known in the history of war, was the consequence of the policy of both the Soviet and the German regimes. On the Soviet side, the very existence of prisoners of war was not recognized: the Soviet government refused to adhere to the Geneva Convention, and washed its hands of the millions who fell into German power.

The Germans, in turn, treated their Soviet prisoners with such callous brutality that only a relatively small number of them survived. For a Soviet prisoner in German hands to enlist in the German armed forces was about the only way open to him of saving his life. There were also Soviet citizens whose hatred of the Communist regime was so strong that they were prepared to fight alongside the Germans in order to overthrow Stalin: nominally headed by General Andrey Vlasov, they saw little combat until the end of the war, largely because of Hitler's suspicion of Vlasov's claims to maintain his political independence of the National Socialist regime even as a prisoner of war. There were also some other combat units composed of Russians, some of them noted for their savagery. Then there were hordes of civilians in German hands—some compulsorily swept into the German labor mobilization drive, many more borne along the wave of the German retreat from Russia and thereafter drafted for labor duties. These civilians included many women and children.

The problem facing the British government from the outset was what policy to adopt toward this mass of humanity that did not fall into any of the accepted categories thrown up by war. Quite apart from the logistic problems, there existed a well-established tradition in Britain which refused to repatriate against their will people who found themselves in British hands and the nature of whose reception by their own government was, to say the least, dubious. The first inclination of the Cabinet—to send all captured Russians back to the Soviet Union—was challenged by the minister of economic warfare, Lord Selborne, who was moved by the fact that the Russians in British hands had only volunteered to serve in German uniforms as an alternative to certain death; and that it would therefore be inhuman to send them back to be shot or to suffer long periods of forced labor. Winston Churchill was also swayed by this argument.

15. The primary purpose of this passage is
    (A)   to explain one of the problems facing British forces near the end of World War II
    (B)   to reveal the savagery of both the German and the Russian forces
    (C)   to stress America's noninvolvement
    (D)   to detail a "war within a war"
    (E)   to give evidence for Churchill's position

16. "Repatriate" in paragraph 3 means
    (A)   to send back to the country of birth
    (B)   to send back to the country of allegiance
    (C)   to send back to the victorious country
    (D)   to reinstill patriotism
    (E)   to reinstill British patriotism

17. The author's position is
(A) pro-Russian   (B) anti-Russian   (C) pro-British   (D) pro-German   (E) neutral

18. The problem in World War II concerning the disposition of Soviet prisoners of war was very similar to
(A) the plight of Armenian refugees
(B) Hitler's own loss of identity after 1944
(C) the plight of British prisoners of war
(D) no previous situation
(E) several instances in the history of war

19. Lord Selborne's opinion disregards which of the following facts?
(A) The Soviet Union posed a nuclear threat to the United States.
(B) Traditionally, repatriation was not imposed by Great Britain.
(C) Certain Soviet citizens wanted to overthrow Stalin.
(D) General Andrey Vlasov was politically independent.
(E) Soviet prisoners were treated brutally.

20. The German labor mobilization drive consisted partly of
(A) women and children
(B) retreating German soldiers
(C) followers of General Andrey Vlasov
(D) savage combat units
(E) those born during the retreat

21. The Soviet policy toward their prisoners of war was one of
(A) nonrecognition   (B) nonaggression   (C) nonproliferation   (D) noncontempt
(E) nonadherence

Passage 4

"A sad spectacle!" exclaimed Thomas Carlyle, contemplating the possibility that millions of planets circle other suns. "If they be inhabited, what a scope for pain and folly; and if they be not inhabited, what a waste of space!"

Much more is now known about the universe than in Carlyle's time, but the question of whether ETI (a fashionable new acronym for Extraterrestrial Intelligence) exists is as open as it ever was. However, one incredible new fact has entered the picture. For the first time in history we have the technology for maybe answering the question. This mere possibility is so overwhelming in its implications that a new science called "exobiology" has already been named even though its entire subject matter may not exist.

We do know that our Milky Way galaxy contains more than 200 billion suns, and that there are billions of other galaxies. Are there other planets? Fifty years ago the two most popular theories about the origin of the solar system each made such planetary systems so unlikely that top astronomers believed that ours was the only one in the galaxy. After flaws were found in both theories, astronomers returned to a model proposed by Immanuel Kant (later by Laplace) in which solar systems are so likely that most of the Milky Way's stars must have them. The wobblings of a few nearby suns suggest big planets close to them, but no one really knows.

If solar systems are plentiful, our galaxy could contain billions of planets earthlike enough to support carbon-based life. Biologists have a strong case for confining life to carbon compounds (silicon and boron are the next best bets), but no one has any notion of how earthlike a planet must be to permit carbon life to arise. Our two nearest neighbors, Venus and Mars, were probably formed the same time the earth was; yet their atmospheres are strikingly different from each other and from ours. Even if a planet goes through an early history exactly like our earth's, no one knows the probability that life on its surface can get started. If it does start, no one knows the probability that it will evolve anything as intelligent as a fish.

Our probes of Mars have been great disappointments in SETI (Search for ETI). I can still recall the tingling of my spine when as a boy I read on the first page of H. G. Wells' *War of the Worlds*:

> Yet across the gulf of space, minds that are to our minds as ours are to those of the beasts that perish, intellects vast and cool and unsympathetic, regarded this earth with envious eyes, and slowly and surely drew their plans against us.

Not even Wells guessed how quickly the Martians would vanish from science fiction.

22. The primary purpose of this passage is
    (A) to describe the space program
    (B) to disprove the existence of Martians
    (C) to discuss the possibility of ETI
    (D) to provide conclusive evidence about ETI
    (E) to point our the folly of Carlyle and Wells

23. Thomas Carlyle was probably H. G. Wells's
    (A) contemporary   (B) predecessor   (C) colleague   (D) nemesis   (E) friend

24. ETI is an acronym for
    (A) something fashionable and new
    (B) exobiology
    (C) a model proposed by Immanuel Kant
    (D) Extraterrestrial Intelligence
    (E) the situation described in *War of the Worlds*

25. The quote from H.G. Wells suggests that
    (A) the Martians would vanish from science fiction
    (B) we were being scrutinized by superior aliens
    (C) an intergalactic war would be imminent
    (D) our intellect is comparatively similar to beasts
    (E) it would take a long time for earth to be invaded

26. The passage implies that the intelligence of a fish is
    (A) equal to man's   (B) equal to that on Venus and Mars   (C) carbon-based
    (D) small   (E) confined to water

27. The naming of a new science, exobiology, contradicts the fact that
    (A) its subject matter may not exist
    (B) the name is probably inappropriate
    (C) the name fits no corresponding acronym
    (D) carbon-based life is not necessarily biological
    (E) there is no literary precedent for the name

28. The question "Are there other planets?" refers only to
    (A) planets outside our own solar system
    (B) planets outside our own galaxy
    (C) planets within our own solar system and outside our own galaxy
    (D) planets outside our own solar system and within our own galaxy
    (E) nongalactic planets

STOP

END OF EXAMINATION. IF YOU FINISH BEFORE TIME HAS ELAPSED, CHECK YOUR WORK ON THIS SECTION ONLY. DO NOT GO BACK TO ANY OTHER SECTION OF THE EXAMINATION.

ANSWER KEY

Section I:
Logical Reasoning

1. A	7. A	12. D	17. C	22. B
2. A	8. D	13. E	18. C	23. B
3. D	9. C	14. A	19. A	24. B
4. A	10. B	15. B	20. D	25. E
5. E	11. E	16. D	21. D	26. D
6. C				

Section IV:
Logical Reasoning

1. D	7. D	12. A	17. B	22. D
2. D	8. E	13. A	18. A	23. C
3. A	9. A	14. D	19. E	24. E
4. C	10. B	15. B	20. B	25. C
5. B	11. A	16. E	21. C	26. D
6. B				

Section II:
Reading Comprehension

1. B	7. B	13. C	19. A	25. C
2. A	8. A	14. E	20. C	26. E
3. D	9. E	15. A	21. D	27. C
4. B	10. E	16. B	22. A	28. B
5. A	11. A	17. A	23. B	29. D
6. D	12. B	18. B	24. D	30. C

Section V:
Evaluation of Facts

1. C	9. A	16. C	23. C	30. C
2. D	10. C	17. C	24. B	31. C
3. C	11. D	18. B	25. D	32. B
4. D	12. C	19. D	26. D	33. C
5. A	13. D	20. A	27. B	34. A
6. C	14. C	21. D	28. D	35. D
7. D	15. A	22. C	29. B	36. D
8. C				

Section III:
Analytical Reasoning

1. D	6. A	11. C	16. A	21. C
2. C	7. C	12. D	17. C	22. C
3. D	8. D	13. C	18. E	23. B
4. B	9. A	14. B	19. C	24. D
5. A	10. D	15. C	20. C	25. D
				26. C

Section VI:
Reading Comprehension

1. A	7. A	13. C	19. C	24. D
2. E	8. C	14. E	20. A	25. B
3. E	9. A	15. A	21. A	26. D
4. B	10. B	16. A	22. C	27. A
5. C	11. D	17. E	23. B	28. A
6. B	12. A	18. D		

MODEL TEST ANALYSIS

Doing model exams and understanding the explanations afterwards are of course important in acquainting you with typical LSAT question types and successful approaches to the questions. However, another benefit of carefully analyzing these model tests is to understand the kinds of errors you are making and thus work to minimize them. For instance, if a very high percentage of your incorrect answers is due to "careless error" or "misread problem," then perhaps you are working much too fast and should slow your pace accordingly. If your incorrect answers are due primarily to "lack of knowledge," then a careful rereading and reworking of the appropriate question-type chapter may be in order. Or if you find that you aren't completing a large number of questions because of lack of time, you may need to either increase your speed or learn to use the "one-check, two-check" technique more effectively.

This kind of analysis of the model tests will enable you to identify your particular weaknesses and thus remedy them.

Model Test Two Analysis

Section	Total Number of Questions	Number Correct	Number Incorrect	Number Unanswered*
I: Logical Reasoning	26			
II: Reading Comprehension	30			
III: Analytical Reasoning	26			
IV: Logical Reasoning	26			
V: Evaluation of Facts	36			
VI: Reading Comprehension	28			
TOTALS:	172			

*At this stage in your preparation, you should not be leaving any unanswered answer spaces. At least fill in a guess, as there is no penalty for a wrong answer.

Reasons for Incorrect Answers

You may wish to evaluate the explanations before completing this chart.

Section	Total Number Incorrect	Lack of Knowledge	Misread Problem	Careless Error	Unanswered or Wrong Guess
I: Logical Reasoning					
II: Reading Comprehension					
III: Analytical Reasoning					
IV: Logical Reasoning					
V: Evaluation of Facts					
VI: Reading Comprehension					
TOTALS:					

EXPLANATIONS OF ANSWERS

Section I

1. **A** The author must assume "that nothing about our coin influences its fall in favor of either side or that all influences are counterbalanced by equal and opposite influences"; otherwise "our ignorance of the coming result" is untrue. Also, he mentions that the chances are one out of two that the coin will fall heads up; this would not be correct if the coin had been weighted or tampered with.

2. **A** I is implied by the author's statement that one-to-two is not "true." II and III are not implied and would not follow from the passage.

3. **D** The author is actually pointing out that self-confidence is of most importance. (C) and (E) focus on behavior, while the author is focusing on mental attitude.

4. **A** (A) stresses that farmwork is a fate rather than a privilege, and therefore strengthens the criticism of Washington's positive attitude toward labor. (B), (C), and (D) weaken the criticism, and (E) is irrelevant.

5. **E** If no test has no easy questions, then all tests have at least one easy question. Thus, I, II, and III are all possible.

6. **C** "Considerate" (B) and "knowledgeable" (D) both roughly fit the meaning of the passage, but "considerate" carries too many other connotations, and "knowledgeable" is not idiomatic.

7. **A** This is the only statement that is consistent with the information in sentence 4.

8. **D** Arnold's wincing during his knee examination is a specific instance supporting the statement that his disability was apparent.

9. **C** "Failure to be prompt" is a phrase which simply repeats the meaning of the term "tardiness." Nothing new is added to the sentence.

10. **B** The consequences of raising geraniums is a hypothetical situation—an event that is being "imagined," that has not actually occurred.

11. **E** The author states that the present programs are at best weak and hopefully won't fail as they have in the past.

12. **D** The statement that "Hopefully, they won't fail as they have in the past" tells us that our government is *not* trying a new approach to end inflation. (A) is close, but the passage states that foreign oil is "high-priced," not "overpriced." "High-priced" tells us the relative cost, not the actual comparative value.

13. **E** The author clearly states that he feels we should support our government's programs, as they appear to be the best the government can produce. He also states that the major factor in this trend is our dependence on oil from foreign countries.

14. **A** Three possibilities exist:
    (a) You read *Weight-Off* magazine, are fat, and do not eat chocolate.
    (b) You are fat, eat chocolate, but do not read *Weight-Off* magazine.
    (c) You eat chocolate, are not fat, and do not read *Weight-Off* magazine.

Thus,
I is not inconsistent if (c) is void of people.
II is inconsistent by (a) and (b).
III is not inconsistent if (b) and (c) are void of people.
Thus, I and III are possible if everyone is fat and reads *Weight-Off* magazine.

15. **B** Dave felt that Jerry implied that no one except Jerry's wife cooks fantastic meals.

16. **D** "Acquainting" people with subjects is synonymous with educating them.

17. **C** Because the author speaks of general, rather than specific, relationships between men and knowledge, he is most likely to be a philosopher.

18. **C** (a) Joe talks to Henry implies that Mike talks to Joe.
(b) Henry does not talk to Dave implies that Mike does not talk to Joe.
Thus,
I is true based on (a).
II is false based on (b).
III is true based on (b).
Thus, I and III are true. (Technically, *if x implies y, then "not y" implies "not x."*)

19. **A** X's new realization is expressed in his final sentence: "We must know all the characteristics of men, and that Socrates has all of them, before we can be sure." The "characteristics of men" are what is implied by the generalization "man," in "Socrates is a man." Therefore, deductive thinking is simply reminding ourselves of the particular specifics implied by generalizations.

20. **D** Symbolically, A is necessary to have B (a good telescope to see moons of Neptune). You do not have B (can't see moons with my telescope). Therefore, you cannot have A (a good telescope). (D) is the only choice that follows this line of reasoning. Symbolically, A is necessary to have B (knowing area of circle to find circumference). You do not have B (can't figure out circumference). Therefore, you cannot have A (area of circle).

21. **D** Extensive psychological research would most likely give the information that the author discusses. (E) limits the research to clinical psychologists and to recent findings.

22. **B** "Conscious behavior eventually becomes habit" is indirectly stated in the last sentence. (A) is a close answer, but that absolute word "all" is inconsistent with the words "can become" in the last sentence. This does not imply that they *must* become unconscious behavior.

23. **B** The given advice would be strengthened by the assurance that such measures are effective. Each of the other choices either weakens the advice, or addresses only a portion of the paragraph.

24. **B** The disease under discussion is termed "it," and thus its identity is unclear. The other choices either are not applicable to the second sentence or refer to terms that require no further definition.

25. **E** (E) weakens the argument that young people have abundant time. The other choices are only tangentially relevant to the argument.

26. **D** The passage says that worrying about writing unfortunately keeps one from writing at all; (D) summarizes this viewpoint. (B) and (C) are irrelevant notions; (A) contradicts the author's implied support for writing theorists; and (E) is an unreasonable, unsupported conclusion.

Section II

Passage 1

1. **B** Paragraph 7 says that the Warren Court was a Camelot insofar as it advanced human rights; a concern with human rights is consistent with both justice and mercy.

2. **A** "Most [human rights] cases do not get to the Supreme Court anyway" (paragraph 2).

3. **D** "A Supreme Court decision . . . seldom brings about immediate major changes" (paragraph 1).

4. **B** Paragraph 5 says that "the Court's authority . . . ultimately rests on sustained public confidence."

5. **A** Paragraph 6 says that "the best protectors of human rights are . . . citizens who know and insist on their own rights and who act to guarantee the rights of others."

Passage 2

6. **D** The author says that "our country is no longer an economic 'island unto itself' " and later urges business to develop strategies for competing with foreign concerns; in other words, our country can no longer sit back, disregarding the rest of the economic world, and grow rich.

7. **B** This answer is stated explicitly in the second paragraph: "The culprit . . . is the increasing influx of low-cost foreign steel." There are other reasons for the steel mill closure, but the question asks only for *a* reason.

8. **A** Only this choice is explicitly called a "truism" in the passage (paragraph 6).

9. **E** This choice is stated explicitly in paragraph 4. None of the other choices is mentioned or implied in the paragraph.

10. **E** In paragraph 7 the point is made that, although "we may condemn others for not buying American-made products, how many of us drive foreign cars . . ."; in other words, how many of us are hypocrites! However, the passage does not condemn such foreign buying by implying that it is "traitorous" (D). Nor does it even go so far as to label price-conscious U.S. consumers as "tightfisted" (B).

11. **A** *Laissez-faire* economics advocates noninterference; it recommends that industries do as they please without government regulation. This author would probably modify *laissez-faire*, for although he does not explicitly advocate government interference, he does prescribe change, saying that we can no longer go about "doing as we please." (B) and (C) are synonymous, and inconsistent with the author's opinion. (D) is inconsistent with his obvious knowledge of economics, and (E) implies a sort of anger not present in the passage.

12. **B** Paragraphs 1 and 2 demonstrate that layoffs have been going on at Monarch "for some time now."

Passage 3

13. **C** Paragraph 3 begins commenting upon *A Species of Eternity*, and this commentary/review continues to the end of the passage.

14. **E** In paragraph 5, the author refers to Nuttall as "oblivious to danger." Implied then is a comparison between his bravery and that of a knight (Parsifal), who faces and vanquishes the danger of a monster (Klingsor).

15. **A** Paragraph 2 states that Jefferson mistakenly *presumed* "a giant sloth claw as a lion."

16. **B** Paragraph 2 says, "During the eighteenth and early nineteenth centuries, taxonomy was in the forefront of the sciences."

17. **A** Kastner's book is "chronologically arranged" (paragraph 4), so that the last story is probably not located in the early years of taxonomy—the eighteenth century. "The nineteenth century" is a probable answer. (B) and (C) are too specific, not directly supported by the passage.

18. **B** Kastner's book discusses the "American frontier," so foreign taxonomists are not within his scope.

Passage 4

19. **A** Paragraph 4 mentions (B), (C), (D), and (E) as the arts designated by the term for wisdom.

20. **C** The correct answer is a paraphrase of the quotation from Aristotle in paragraph 1.

21. **D** Paragraph 6 states, "Philosophy is the supreme science . . . preoccupied with the totalization of knowledge."

22. **A** *Philosophos* was chosen as a label by Pythagoras, but the word was *derived* from Greek *(philia + sophia)*.

23. **B** The last paragraph mainly defines philosophy and does so through repetition of this definition in different words. "Philosophy is a universal science . . . it is the sole science of mankind . . . philosophy is the supreme science."

24. **D** Unlike the "desire" of science, philosophy works toward the "unification and systematization of all important knowledge" (paragraph 6).

25. **C** Paragraph 1 states, "In a popular sense, every thinking person is philosophizing." Such informal, popular philosophizing is opposed to "philosophy in the strict, technical sense" (paragraph 2).

Passage 5

26. **E** Paragraph 2 says, ". . . suppose science is defined as classified knowledge."

27. **C** Paragraph 2 specifically excludes astrology as a science (last sentence).

28. **B** Paragraph 6 compares pure science to applied science, stating, "The discovery of one bit of information opens the door to the discovery of another."

29. **D** This example of pure science is mentioned in paragraph 6.

30. **C** Clearly, the passage is a general discussion of the characteristics of science and scientists. The other choices are science-related but deal with other, more specific aspects of science.

Section III

Answers 1–7

UPPER-case letters denote colors given in the problem, and lower-case letters denote deduced colors.

1. **D**

1	2	3	4	5	
b/w	R	W	b	R	(flag)
w/g	B	g	w	B	(pennant)

The 3rd pennant cannot be blue or white, so therefore it is green. The 4th flag cannot be white or red, so it must be blue. The 4th pennant cannot be green or blue, so it must be white. The 1st flag cannot be red, so it is either blue or white. The 1st pennant cannot be blue, so it must be green or white. Thus statement I is true, statement II is true, and statement III is true.

2. **C**

1	2	3	4	5	
R	w	r/b			(flag)
g/w	B	g/w			(pennant)

(A) is clearly true. If the 5th flag is red, then the 3rd flag cannot be, since the 1st flag is red and we can have only two of any one color. Thus, (B) is true. If the 4th pennant is green, then the 3rd pennant must be white. But that does not determine the color of the 1st pennant. Thus, (C) is not necessarily true. (D) is the same as (A) and is also true. If the 4th pennant is green, this implies that the 3rd pennant must be white. If the 5th pennant is white, then the 1st pennant cannot be. Therefore (E) is true.

3. **D**

1	2	3	4	5	
W	r	W	r	b	(flag)
g	B	g	B	w	(pennant)

The facts in this problem determine the complete configuration of flags and pennants. (D) is the one statement that is false.

4. **B**

1	2	3	4	5	
B	w	r	B		(flag)
	W	g			(pennant)

Statement I is true since the 1st pennant cannot be blue or white. Statement II is false since the 5th pennant could be blue or white. Statement III is true; the 2nd flag cannot be blue since two other flags are already blue, and it cannot be red since the 3rd flag must be red.

5. **A**

1	2	3	4	5	
B	r/w	B	r	w	(flag)
W	b	g	W	g/b	(pennant)

Since the 3rd flag is blue and the 4th pennant is white, the 3rd pennant must be green and the 4th flag must be red. Since the 1st pennant is white, the 2nd pennant must be blue; thus I is true. Since the 1st and 3rd flags are blue, the 5th flag cannot be blue. Since the 4th flag is red, the 5th flag must be white; thus II is true. Since the 2nd flag could be red or white, III is false.

6. **A**

1	2	3	4	5	
R	W	r			(flag)
	g	B			(pennant)

If the 5th flag is white, then the 5th pennant must be green. Thus the 1st and 2nd pennants cannot be green and cannot be the same color, so one of them is blue. Therefore, (A) is true. All the other statements are false.

7. **C**

1	2	3	4	5		1	2	3	4	5
W	B	W	B	r	(flag)	B	W	B	W	r
g	W	B	W	B	(pennant)	g	B	W	B	W

Since blue and white are the two common colors between flags and pennants, the above are the only two arrangements possible. In both cases, the 5th flag is red and the 1st pennant is green. Thus III is the only statement that MUST be true.

Answers 8–14

8. **D**

1	2	3	4	5	6	7	8	9	10
E	E	E					M		M

If the 8th book is a math book, then the three English books must be in positions 1, 2, and 3, since they cannot be in positions 8, 9, and 10. Thus the other math book is in position 10. Statement II is always true. Statement I could be true. Statement III is false since the two math books are in positions 8 and 10.

9. **A**

1	2	3	4	5	6	7	8	9	10
M				P	P		E	E	E

If the 9th book is an English book, then so are the 8th and 10th books. Thus there is a math book in position 1. The science books must be in positions 2 and 3 *or* 3 and 4. This leaves only positions 4 and 7 for the other math book. Thus (A) is always true. (C) could be true, but does not have to be true. The 3rd poetry book could be in position 2.

10. **D**

1	2	3	4	5	6	7	8	9	10
M					S	S	E	E	E

If the 1st book is a math book, then the 8th, 9th, and 10th books must be the English books. If the 7th book is a science book, so must be the 6th book. This means that the other math book must be either the 3rd, the 4th, or the 5th book. The remainder of the books are poetry books, including the 2nd book. Thus, I and III must be true, and II could be false.

11. **C**

1	2	3	4	5	6	7	8	9	10
M	P	P	M	S	S	P	E	E	E
				or					
E	E	E	M	S	S	P	P	P	M

If the 4th book is a math book and the 5th book is a science book, then the 6th book is also a science book. This leaves two possible arrangements for the remaining books, as shown above. From this diagram we see that I and II are true. Statement III is false since the 3rd book and the 7th book could both be poetry books.

12. **D**

1	2	3	4	5	6	7	8	9	10
E	E	E	P					P	M

or

M	P					P	E	E	E

The poetry books must be in positions 4 and 9 *or* 2 and 7, depending on whether the math book is in position 1 or 10. See diagrams above. For example, let us assume that the math book is the 10th book. In order for no two poetry books to be next to each other, the 4th and 9th books must be poetry books, with the 3rd poetry book in either position 6 or 7, depending on the positions of the science books. The same argument holds if the 1st book is a math book. Thus, all three statements are true.

13. **C**

1	2	3	4	5	6	7	8	9	10
E	E	E	S	S	M	P	P	P	M

and

M	P	P	P	M	S	S	E	E	E

These are the two possible arrangements. We see that (A) is false, (B) could be false, (D) is false, and (E) could be false. Only (C) is always true.

14. **B**

1	2	3	4	5	6	7	8	9	10
E	E	E	M	S	S	P	P	P	M

and

E	E	E	S	S	M	P	P	P	M

These are the only two possible combinations; thus, (B) is the correct answer.

Answers 15–21

A simple chart, as follows, will help to answer the questions:

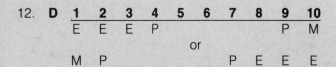

15. **C** From the chart we can see that a freshman can take everything except Latin (if he takes American History), or take everything except American History (if he takes Latin).

16. **A** In order to enroll in American History and the Sex Lab, a freshman must take Marriage/Family Relations plus Greek. Therefore, only (A) is true.

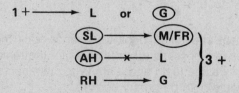

17. **C** If a freshman does not enroll in Greek, he can take only Latin, Sex Lab, and Marriage/Family Relations.

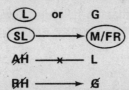

18. **E** If a freshman enrolls in Latin, his course load could consist of Latin, Greek, and Roman History; or it could consist of Latin, Sex Lab, and Marriage/Family Relations; or it could consist of Latin, Greek, and Marriage/Family Relations. Therefore, none of the above *must* necessarily be taken in addition to Latin.

19. **C** If a freshman does not take Latin or the Sex Lab, she must take Greek. Then she can choose Marriage/Family Relations, American History, or Roman History to round out her schedule.

20. **C** If a freshman does not take Greek or American History, he must take Latin, and cannot take Roman History (because Roman History requires taking Greek). Therefore, the other two courses left for him to take are Sex Lab and Marriage/Family Relations.

21. **C** If a freshman enrolls in Latin, he may choose from any of the classes except American History. Thus, he may choose from Greek, Sex Lab, Marriage/Family Relations, and Roman History—a total of four. Only III *must* be true.

Answers 22–26

Drawing a diagram, below, will help answer the questions.

| | **EVENTS** | | | | |
	1	2	3	4	5
RED	G	—	G	—	G
BLUE	—	B/S	–	B/S	—
GREEN					
YELLOW					

Since the red team wins only 3 gold medals, it must win gold medals in events 1, 3, and 5, since no team wins gold medals in consecutive events. Also, note that since blue wins only two medals (neither of them gold), it must have won medals in events 2 and 4, so that it didn't fail to win a medal within two consecutive events. Be aware then that green and yellow, therefore, must each have won medals in all five events.

22. **C** If the green team wins only one gold medal, there remains only one gold medal, which the yellow team must win.

23. **B** Since three medals are given for each event, and, according to our diagram from the facts, red and blue already account for their total awards with one medal in each event, the other two medals in each event must go to yellow and green. Thus, yellow and green will each be awarded five medals.

24. **D** By completing the chart such that the yellow team wins five silver medals, we can see that green must win two gold and three bronze medals.

	1	2	3	4	5
RED	G	—	G	—	G
BLUE	—	B/S	—	B/S	—
GREEN					
YELLOW	S	S	S	S	S

25. **D** We know choices (A) and (B) are both true: both the green and yellow teams each must win five medals. Therefore (E) is also true. Choice (C) is true because three of the gold medals are already won by the red team; since blue doesn't win gold, if green wins one gold, yellow wins the remaining gold medal. Choice (D) is not true: if the green team wins only one silver medal, the yellow team must win at least two silver medals.

26. **C** If a sixth team enters all events and wins only three consecutive silver medals, it must win the silver in events 2, 3, and 4, so that it does not fail to win a medal within two consecutive events.
Therefore our diagram would look like this:

	1	2	3	4	5
RED	G	—	G	—	G
BLUE	—	B	—	B	—
GREEN					
YELLOW					
ORANGE	—	S	S	S	—

Therefore, if yellow wins a gold in the 2nd event, green must win a medal in the 3rd event (since no team fails to win a medal within two consecutive events). Thus, green must win a bronze in the 3rd event.

Section IV

1. **D** This choice provides the most direct evidence of the effectiveness of the PUC consumer action. Each of the other choices is only tangentially related to the argument.

2. **D** This choice most seriously weakens the author's contention that the PUC acts in the public interest. (C) is a weaker choice, especially because "slightly" softens the statement.

3. **A** This choice parallels both the reasoning and the structure of the original. The original reasoning may be summarized as follows: most $X \rightarrow Y$; therefore $X \rightarrow Y$ (probably).

4. **C** The reasoning goes as follows: All good teachers are patient (rephrasing of the first statement); some good teachers (patient) are good administrators; therefore, some good administrators are patient. To use a term of degree other than *some* requires assumptions beyond the information given.

5. **B** Since good personnel relations of an organization, according to the passage, rely upon "mutual confidence, trust and good will," one of the causes of personnel difficulties would most certainly be the employees' not believing in the good faith of the organization.

6. **B** In the second sentence, the author implies that the lack of facilities is related to the lack of research mentioned in the first sentence. In any case, the passage reveals the author's concern with both research and assistance, and therefore agrees more fully with (B) than with (A), which mentions research only.

7. **D** Since some short people have red hair, and since anyone with red hair can't have brown eyes, I is true: there are short people who do not have brown eyes. Likewise, since there are some short people with red hair, and those red-haired people cannot have brown eyes, II is true: there are people without brown eyes who are short.
   Or, by using Venn diagrams, three groupings can be drawn that satisfy the given conditions:

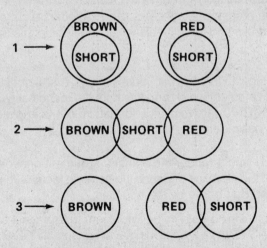

   Notice that, based on alternative **3**, III need not be true.

8. **E** The correct answer is "circular." The argument that what the Church says is true is ultimately based upon this same assertion.

9. **A** Kathy believes Mary to have meant that *only Italians* are great lovers. Therefore, Kathy takes issue with this and points out in her reply that there are non-Italians who are great lovers. (A), if replaced for Mary's statement, would make Kathy's reply a reasonable one.

10. **B** Only (B) addresses Dimple's assumption that Mrs. Wilson is the *only* applicant whose qualifications are ideal. Other choices are irrelevant to the *argument*, although some may be relevant to the implied situation.

11. **A** Only (A) addresses the substance of Dimple's argument.

12. **A** Greeley suggests that we are always comparing what we have with what we don't have. Therefore, (A) is correct. None of the other choices makes a *comparison*.

13. **A** The author of the argument skirts the issue of *quality*; therefore, statements that raise that issue stress the incompleteness of the pro-hygienist position, and weaken it. Statement III is irrelevant.

14. **D** The passage describes two types of obstacles to happiness: exterior forces and personal attitude. Both these factors are mentioned in I and II. Statement III requires the assumption that the two categories discussed by the author are the *only* categories.

15. **B** Statement I may be eliminated because changing one's mind need not involve issues of right and wrong (in the moral sense that Eliot implies). Statement III may be eliminated because it refutes the underlying assumption of Eliot's words, that one can tell what is right.

16. **E** Without an implied or explicit definition of "civilized," the relevance of the examples is vague, at best. (A) and (D) are irrelevant considerations, and (B) and (C), although possibly relevant, do not address the most apparent weakness of the passage.

17. **B** (A) and (C) strengthen the argument. Although (D) and (E) partially weaken certain aspects of the argument, only (B) introduces a situation which suggests that freedom of the press may have harmful consequences.

18. **A** (B) and (C) are irrelevant to the argument. (D) and (E) contradict the implied assertion that a free press must be protected at all costs. Only (A) offers a statement both favorable to the concept of a free press and directly relevant to the subject discussed: the use of privileged information.

19. **E** By stating that "a legal technicality . . . ducks the . . . moral question," the author is implying that the federal government which benefits from the technicality is associated with dodging the issue. (A) and (B) restate explicit information; (C) is implausible; and (D) contradicts information in the passage.

20. **B** Private medical aid would render the author's argument unnecessary. (C), a choice worth considering, is not the best one because the author's focus is less on the aliens' needs than on the monetary burden borne by the counties.

21. **C** By documenting the rate at which the medical expense burden grows, the author could strengthen the argument that the situation he describes is indeed a burden.

22. **D** The passage talks about communes as failures. Therefore, the most logical completion must be a negative term consistent with failure. The only negative choice is (D).

23. **C** By linking Herb's ability with his "cousinhood," Herb is assuming that the latter determines the former; therefore, he is ignoring (C). (B) is irrelevant. (A) is too vague to be the best answer. (D) is inapplicable, because Keith uses "good" in a context that makes its meaning clear. Finally, (E) refers to contradictory information.

24. **E** In order to argue for the value of renewable prescriptions, the author must first assume that more medicine may be necessary, or, in other words, that the patient may suffer a relapse. Without the possibility of relapse, a call for more medicine that has already effected a cure ("worked effectively") is illogical.

25. **C** The passage consistently implies a difference between the past and the present, and (C) makes this contrast explicit. (B) contradicts the implication of the passage, while (A) and (D) narrow the focus unnecessarily, and (E) is irrelevant.

26. **D** This fact would strengthen the merely impressionistic evidence that lawsuits were less prevalent 40 years ago. It is the only choice dealing directly with the implied subject of the passage—lawsuits.

Section V

Set 1

1. **C** This question can be answered by applying the rules and facts. Yes, they will get their money returned, as Rule I invalidates the contract and they did return before the deadline of 10 days in Rule II.

2. **D** This is irrelevant to the outcome of the dispute.

3. **C** This question can be answered by applying Rule I: Leo is guilty of misrepresentation; therefore, the contract is not valid.

4. **D** This is irrelevant to the outcome of the dispute.

5. **A** To answer this question, you must choose between the two rules. Each rule will give you a different answer. By Rule I, the Hills would have been eligible for a refund because misrepresentation had taken place. By Rule II, had the Hills returned after 3 weeks, they would have exceeded the specified time limit, and therefore would not have been able to hold the seller liable. Thus they would not have been eligible for a refund.

6. **C** The facts clearly indicate that Leo was trying to deceive the Hills; therefore, the question is answerable.

7. **D** This issue is irrelevant.

Set 2

8. **C** This relevant question can be readily answered from the facts. No, Maloney took nothing.

9. **A** To answer this relevant question you must choose between the rules. Each rule gives you a different outcome. By Rule I, Maloney is not guilty, as he took nothing. By Rule II, he is guilty, as he entered with the intent to steal.

10. **C** This relevant question can be readily answered by applying Rule I. No, he would not be guilty since he did not remove any property. If he had not intended to steal anything, Rule II would not apply.

11. **D** This is an irrelevant question.

Set 3

12. **C** This relevant question can be readily answered from the facts. Yes, the communication was a falsehood.

13. **D** This question is irrelevant to the dispute as governed by the rules.

14. **C** This relevant question can be answered by applying the facts and rules. By Rule I, she will be found guilty since she did not identify herself and did communicate a falsehood. By Rule II she will also be guilty because she frightened others with false stories.

15. **A** To answer this relevant question, you must choose between the rules. Each rule gives a different outcome. By Rule I, she would not be guilty if she identified herself. By Rule II, she would be guilty.

Set 4

16. **C** This can be determined by applying the rules. Since Hall intentionally ran off the course, he will be disqualified according to Rules I and II.

17. **C** This can also be determined by applying the rules. Even though Jamie left the course accidentally, she did not return to her point of departure and therefore would be disqualified by Rule I. Rule II disqualifies anyone who runs off the course.

18. **B** More information is necessary to answer this question because we do not know how many other runners were entered in the race and when they crossed the finish line. We do know that Jamie or Hall will not be the winner.

19. **D** This is irrelevant.

20. **A** To answer this question, you must choose between the two rules. Each rule will give you a different answer. By Rule I, Phil will win the race because Hall and Jamie were disqualified, but Phil will not be disqualified. According to Rule II, Phil will also be disqualified.

21. **D** This is an unimportant issue.

Set 5

22. **C** This question can be answered by application of the facts to Rule I. If all 15 members of the Polka Club were in attendance and they were unruly and extremely noisy, then they will be found guilty of unlawful assembly.

23. **C** This question can be answered by the facts and some logical reasoning. Since the Gang was not planning to use force (Rule II), it cannot be convicted of conspiracy.

24. **B** To answer this question, you would need to know how many members of the Polka Club were present at the meeting. Otherwise, Rule I cannot be applied.

25. **D** This is irrelevant to the case and rules as given.

26. **D** This is also irrelevant.

27. **B** To answer this question you would need to know the total number of members in the Gang. Since only eight members were present at the meeting, only eight members could be found guilty by Rule II.

28. **D** This is an unimportant issue.

29. **B** To answer this question, you would need to know how many members of the Polka Club were present at the meeting. Otherwise, neither rule can be applied. Therefore, more information is needed.

30. **C** This question can be answered by application of the facts to Rule I. From the facts, the Gang was not unreasonably disturbing the peace; therefore, it would not be found guilty of unlawful assembly.

31. **C** This question can be answered by using Rule II and applying the facts. If three members of the Gang were present (Rule II still applies), and they were planning to commit a crime by force, then they could go to prison.

Set 6

32. **B** To answer this relevant question you need more information. Bona thought he observed Sue put a pack of cigarettes into her pocketbook, but he didn't know for sure.

33. **C** This relevant question can be answered by applying Rule I. Yes, Bona will be guilty as he did cause Sue to believe she was about to be physically attacked. Since Sue did not take the cigarettes, Rule II does not apply.

34. **A** To answer this relevant question, you must choose between the rules. Each rule will give you a different outcome. By Rule I, Bona would be guilty; by Rule II, he would not be guilty.

35. **D** This question is irrelevant.

36. **D** This question is irrelevant.

Section VI

Passage 1

1. **A** Obviously, the author is poking fun at the heaven that was "invented" by the human race; he suggests his intention to do so in the first paragraph. Although (E) is also a possible answer, it is much less specific than (A), and therefore not best.

2. **E** In item 4 the author criticizes the belief that racism and bigotry will disappear in the hereafter; this explicit criticism eliminates (C). In the midst of his criticism the author does not explicitly indicate his own attitude toward racism and bigotry; rather, he stresses that it does exist and will continue to prevail widely. Because his own attitude is not expressed or implied, (A), (B), and (D) are eliminated.

3. **E** This is stated explicitly in the first paragraph.

4. **B** In item 5, the author lists the many accomplishments of the intellect, in the areas of science, art, and industry; and later he associates a realm without intellect with rotting, stinking, and bedlam. These comments are enough to establish the intellect as essential. (A) should be eliminated because "blessed" has religious connotations inappropriate to the author's view of human achievements; (C) contradicts the author's catalogue of intellectual pride and achievements, as does (E); and (D) is true about the human conception of heaven, but not about the human intellect.

5. **C** This choice summarizes the argument of item 1; all other choices contradict some part of that item.

6. **B** The author states (item 3) that "not more than twenty in the thousand of them could play an instrument on the earth," and then goes on to describe the terrible sound in heaven, suggesting a connection between musical incompetence on earth and its continuance in heaven. (C) is more precisely applicable to his comments about singing in heaven, discussed in item 2.

7. **A** All other choices denote particular religious or political positions that are not indicated in the passage. We may conclude that the author is a skeptic because he doubts and questions commonly accepted conceptions.

Passage 2

8. **C** The author begins with several definitions of "orient" and "orientation," and then goes on to discuss the orientation (direction and purpose) of his own study. (A), (B), and (D) are mentioned in the passage, but constitute subsidiary points rather than a primary purpose. (E) contradicts the analogy between engineering and language study made explicit in the final paragraph.

9. **A** In the first paragraph, the author proposes that we believe that the good life will result from "using our heads." He joins in this belief by associating his own (intellectual) study with freedom and happiness during the course of the passage. (E) is not as strong a choice because it is not as comprehensive as (A).

10. **B** The second paragraph emphasizes the connection between freedom and language and a "philosophy of life." All other choices draw conclusions that are neither explicitly nor implicitly supported in the paragraph: to pick one of these choices requires "reading into" the paragraph, a poor test-taking strategy.

11. **D** In the final paragraph, the author calls his approach "linguistic engineering," thus creating an analogy by recalling the mechanical engineer he introduced in the first paragraph. None of the other choices is, strictly speaking, an analogy.

12. **A** The final two sentences stress the connection between the author's study, applied psychology, the conscious mind, and the brain. The other choices are not so explicitly relevant as this one, and therefore are weaker.

13. **C** In the fourth paragraph the author states that interest in linguistic behavior will result in knowledge of language "etiquette."

14. **E** The fourth paragraph stresses that concentration on the rules of language will cause us to "leave important tasks undone," and that in a democracy "progress" is preferred to "protocol."

Passage 3

15. **A** The passage discusses the past and present facts contributing to the British problem with captured Russians.

16. **A** The final paragraph discusses at length the question of whether to send Russians back to Russia despite their lack of allegiance to Russia. This is the repatriation question and is consistent with the dictionary definition of *repatriate*—to send back to the country of birth.

17. **E** The author does not himself argue for or against a particular position or nationality. He simply presents facts and the arguments of others. His comments in paragraph 2 might be called anti-German, but this attitude is not one of the choices.

18. **D** Paragraph 1 states, "This extraordinary situation [was] . . . never before known in the history of war."

19. **C** Selborne argued that Russians served the Germans only "as an alternative to certain death" (paragraph 3). But paragraph 2 states that some Russians fought with the Germans "in order to overthrow Stalin."

20. **A** Paragraph 2 says that "the German labor mobilization drive. . . included many women and children."

21. **A** Paragraph 1 states, "On the Soviet side, the very existence of prisoners of war was not recognized."

Passage 4

22. **C** The theories of Carlyle and Wells are treated with respect, so (E) should be eliminated. (D) is also incorrect, because the evidence given is incomplete and tentative, not conclusive. (A) and (B) are irrelevant to the purpose of the passage, which is well described by (C).

23. **B** Since Wells's style is more modern than Carlyle's, and since Wells imagines extraterrestrial life while Carlyle merely wonders about it, we may conclude that Wells is a more modern thinker than is Carlyle.

24. **D** This is defined in paragraph 2: "ETI (a fashionable new acronym for Extraterrestrial Intelligence)."

25. **B** The phrase, "intellects vast and cool and unsympathetic, regarded this earth with envious eyes . . . " suggests that earth was being scrutinized by superior aliens. The quote also indicates that some sort of plan against us may be imminent ("they drew their plans against us"), but choice (C) is incorrect, as Wells does not necessarily imply an "intergalactic war."

26. **D** Paragraph 4 discusses the development of ETI and says that even planets which are similar to earth are not certain to develop life as advanced as we know it, perhaps not even life as "intelligent as a fish."

27. **A** Paragraph 2 states, " 'Exobiology' has already been named even though its entire subject matter may not exist."

28. **A** The first sentence of paragraph 3 mentions both the 200 billion *other* suns in our galaxy and the billions of other galaxies outside our own. The following question, "Are there other planets?" refers directly to planets surrounding these suns and galaxies outside our own solar system.

Chapter

9

Model Test Three

This chapter contains full-length Model Test Three. It is geared to the format of the LSAT, and it is complete with answers and explanations. It is equivalent to the LSAT in question structure, number of questions, level of difficulty, and time allotments. (The questions used are not taken directly from the LSAT, as those questions are copyrighted and may not be reproduced.)

Model Test Three should be taken under strict test conditions. The test begins with a 30-minute Writing Sample which is not scored. Thereafter each section is 35 minutes in length.

Section	Description	Number of Questions	Time Allowed
	Writing Sample		30 minutes
I	Analytical Reasoning	25	35 minutes
II	Evaluation of Facts	35	35 minutes
III	Reading Comprehension	28	35 minutes
IV	Analytical Reasoning	25	35 minutes
V	Logical Reasoning	26	35 minutes
VI	Evaluation of Facts	37	35 minutes
TOTALS:		176	240 minutes

Now please turn to the next page, remove your answer sheets, and begin Model Test Three.

ANSWER SHEET—MODEL TEST THREE
LAW SCHOOL ADMISSION TEST (LSAT)

Section I:
Analytical Reasoning

1. Ⓐ Ⓑ Ⓒ Ⓓ Ⓔ
2. Ⓐ Ⓑ Ⓒ Ⓓ Ⓔ
3. Ⓐ Ⓑ Ⓒ Ⓓ Ⓔ
4. Ⓐ Ⓑ Ⓒ Ⓓ Ⓔ
5. Ⓐ Ⓑ Ⓒ Ⓓ Ⓔ
6. Ⓐ Ⓑ Ⓒ Ⓓ Ⓔ
7. Ⓐ Ⓑ Ⓒ Ⓓ Ⓔ
8. Ⓐ Ⓑ Ⓒ Ⓓ Ⓔ
9. Ⓐ Ⓑ Ⓒ Ⓓ Ⓔ
10. Ⓐ Ⓑ Ⓒ Ⓓ Ⓔ
11. Ⓐ Ⓑ Ⓒ Ⓓ Ⓔ
12. Ⓐ Ⓑ Ⓒ Ⓓ Ⓔ
13. Ⓐ Ⓑ Ⓒ Ⓓ Ⓔ
14. Ⓐ Ⓑ Ⓒ Ⓓ Ⓔ
15. Ⓐ Ⓑ Ⓒ Ⓓ Ⓔ
16. Ⓐ Ⓑ Ⓒ Ⓓ Ⓔ
17. Ⓐ Ⓑ Ⓒ Ⓓ Ⓔ
18. Ⓐ Ⓑ Ⓒ Ⓓ Ⓔ
19. Ⓐ Ⓑ Ⓒ Ⓓ Ⓔ
20. Ⓐ Ⓑ Ⓒ Ⓓ Ⓔ
21. Ⓐ Ⓑ Ⓒ Ⓓ Ⓔ
22. Ⓐ Ⓑ Ⓒ Ⓓ Ⓔ
23. Ⓐ Ⓑ Ⓒ Ⓓ Ⓔ
24. Ⓐ Ⓑ Ⓒ Ⓓ Ⓔ
25. Ⓐ Ⓑ Ⓒ Ⓓ Ⓔ

Section II:
Evaluation of Facts

1. Ⓐ Ⓑ Ⓒ Ⓓ
2. Ⓐ Ⓑ Ⓒ Ⓓ
3. Ⓐ Ⓑ Ⓒ Ⓓ
4. Ⓐ Ⓑ Ⓒ Ⓓ
5. Ⓐ Ⓑ Ⓒ Ⓓ
6. Ⓐ Ⓑ Ⓒ Ⓓ
7. Ⓐ Ⓑ Ⓒ Ⓓ
8. Ⓐ Ⓑ Ⓒ Ⓓ
9. Ⓐ Ⓑ Ⓒ Ⓓ
10. Ⓐ Ⓑ Ⓒ Ⓓ
11. Ⓐ Ⓑ Ⓒ Ⓓ
12. Ⓐ Ⓑ Ⓒ Ⓓ
13. Ⓐ Ⓑ Ⓒ Ⓓ
14. Ⓐ Ⓑ Ⓒ Ⓓ
15. Ⓐ Ⓑ Ⓒ Ⓓ
16. Ⓐ Ⓑ Ⓒ Ⓓ
17. Ⓐ Ⓑ Ⓒ Ⓓ
18. Ⓐ Ⓑ Ⓒ Ⓓ
19. Ⓐ Ⓑ Ⓒ Ⓓ
20. Ⓐ Ⓑ Ⓒ Ⓓ
21. Ⓐ Ⓑ Ⓒ Ⓓ
22. Ⓐ Ⓑ Ⓒ Ⓓ
23. Ⓐ Ⓑ Ⓒ Ⓓ
24. Ⓐ Ⓑ Ⓒ Ⓓ
25. Ⓐ Ⓑ Ⓒ Ⓓ
26. Ⓐ Ⓑ Ⓒ Ⓓ
27. Ⓐ Ⓑ Ⓒ Ⓓ
28. Ⓐ Ⓑ Ⓒ Ⓓ
29. Ⓐ Ⓑ Ⓒ Ⓓ
30. Ⓐ Ⓑ Ⓒ Ⓓ
31. Ⓐ Ⓑ Ⓒ Ⓓ
32. Ⓐ Ⓑ Ⓒ Ⓓ
33. Ⓐ Ⓑ Ⓒ Ⓓ
34. Ⓐ Ⓑ Ⓒ Ⓓ
35. Ⓐ Ⓑ Ⓒ Ⓓ

Section III:
Reading Comprehension

1. Ⓐ Ⓑ Ⓒ Ⓓ Ⓔ
2. Ⓐ Ⓑ Ⓒ Ⓓ Ⓔ
3. Ⓐ Ⓑ Ⓒ Ⓓ Ⓔ
4. Ⓐ Ⓑ Ⓒ Ⓓ Ⓔ
5. Ⓐ Ⓑ Ⓒ Ⓓ Ⓔ
6. Ⓐ Ⓑ Ⓒ Ⓓ Ⓔ
7. Ⓐ Ⓑ Ⓒ Ⓓ Ⓔ
8. Ⓐ Ⓑ Ⓒ Ⓓ Ⓔ
9. Ⓐ Ⓑ Ⓒ Ⓓ Ⓔ
10. Ⓐ Ⓑ Ⓒ Ⓓ Ⓔ
11. Ⓐ Ⓑ Ⓒ Ⓓ Ⓔ
12. Ⓐ Ⓑ Ⓒ Ⓓ Ⓔ
13. Ⓐ Ⓑ Ⓒ Ⓓ Ⓔ
14. Ⓐ Ⓑ Ⓒ Ⓓ Ⓔ
15. Ⓐ Ⓑ Ⓒ Ⓓ Ⓔ
16. Ⓐ Ⓑ Ⓒ Ⓓ Ⓔ
17. Ⓐ Ⓑ Ⓒ Ⓓ Ⓔ
18. Ⓐ Ⓑ Ⓒ Ⓓ Ⓔ
19. Ⓐ Ⓑ Ⓒ Ⓓ Ⓔ
20. Ⓐ Ⓑ Ⓒ Ⓓ Ⓔ
21. Ⓐ Ⓑ Ⓒ Ⓓ Ⓔ
22. Ⓐ Ⓑ Ⓒ Ⓓ Ⓔ
23. Ⓐ Ⓑ Ⓒ Ⓓ Ⓔ
24. Ⓐ Ⓑ Ⓒ Ⓓ Ⓔ
25. Ⓐ Ⓑ Ⓒ Ⓓ Ⓔ
26. Ⓐ Ⓑ Ⓒ Ⓓ Ⓔ
27. Ⓐ Ⓑ Ⓒ Ⓓ Ⓔ
28. Ⓐ Ⓑ Ⓒ Ⓓ Ⓔ

ANSWER SHEET—MODEL TEST THREE
LAW SCHOOL ADMISSION TEST (LSAT)

Section IV:
Analytical Reasoning

1. (A) (B) (C) (D) (E)
2. (A) (B) (C) (D) (E)
3. (A) (B) (C) (D) (E)
4. (A) (B) (C) (D) (E)
5. (A) (B) (C) (D) (E)
6. (A) (B) (C) (D) (E)
7. (A) (B) (C) (D) (E)
8. (A) (B) (C) (D) (E)
9. (A) (B) (C) (D) (E)
10. (A) (B) (C) (D) (E)
11. (A) (B) (C) (D) (E)
12. (A) (B) (C) (D) (E)
13. (A) (B) (C) (D) (E)
14. (A) (B) (C) (D) (E)
15. (A) (B) (C) (D) (E)
16. (A) (B) (C) (D) (E)
17. (A) (B) (C) (D) (E)
18. (A) (B) (C) (D) (E)
19. (A) (B) (C) (D) (E)
20. (A) (B) (C) (D) (E)
21. (A) (B) (C) (D) (E)
22. (A) (B) (C) (D) (E)
23. (A) (B) (C) (D) (E)
24. (A) (B) (C) (D) (E)
25. (A) (B) (C) (D) (E)

Section V:
Logical Reasoning

1. (A) (B) (C) (D) (E)
2. (A) (B) (C) (D) (E)
3. (A) (B) (C) (D) (E)
4. (A) (B) (C) (D) (E)
5. (A) (B) (C) (D) (E)
6. (A) (B) (C) (D) (E)
7. (A) (B) (C) (D) (E)
8. (A) (B) (C) (D) (E)
9. (A) (B) (C) (D) (E)
10. (A) (B) (C) (D) (E)
11. (A) (B) (C) (D) (E)
12. (A) (B) (C) (D) (E)
13. (A) (B) (C) (D) (E)
14. (A) (B) (C) (D) (E)
15. (A) (B) (C) (D) (E)
16. (A) (B) (C) (D) (E)
17. (A) (B) (C) (D) (E)
18. (A) (B) (C) (D) (E)
19. (A) (B) (C) (D) (E)
20. (A) (B) (C) (D) (E)
21. (A) (B) (C) (D) (E)
22. (A) (B) (C) (D) (E)
23. (A) (B) (C) (D) (E)
24. (A) (B) (C) (D) (E)
25. (A) (B) (C) (D) (E)
26. (A) (B) (C) (D) (E)

Section VI:
Evaluation of Facts

1. (A) (B) (C) (D)
2. (A) (B) (C) (D)
3. (A) (B) (C) (D)
4. (A) (B) (C) (D)
5. (A) (B) (C) (D)
6. (A) (B) (C) (D)
7. (A) (B) (C) (D)
8. (A) (B) (C) (D)
9. (A) (B) (C) (D)
10. (A) (B) (C) (D)
11. (A) (B) (C) (D)
12. (A) (B) (C) (D)
13. (A) (B) (C) (D)
14. (A) (B) (C) (D)
15. (A) (B) (C) (D)
16. (A) (B) (C) (D)
17. (A) (B) (C) (D)
18. (A) (B) (C) (D)
19. (A) (B) (C) (D)
20. (A) (B) (C) (D)
21. (A) (B) (C) (D)
22. (A) (B) (C) (D)
23. (A) (B) (C) (D)
24. (A) (B) (C) (D)
25. (A) (B) (C) (D)
26. (A) (B) (C) (D)
27. (A) (B) (C) (D)
28. (A) (B) (C) (D)
29. (A) (B) (C) (D)
30. (A) (B) (C) (D)
31. (A) (B) (C) (D)
32. (A) (B) (C) (D)
33. (A) (B) (C) (D)
34. (A) (B) (C) (D)
35. (A) (B) (C) (D)
36. (A) (B) (C) (D)
37. (A) (B) (C) (D)

EXAMINATION

WRITING SAMPLE

Time—30 Minutes

Directions:
You have 30 minutes to write an essay in response to a given topic. Take a few minutes to plan your work before you begin writing. DO NOT WRITE ON A TOPIC OF YOUR OWN CHOICE. ESSAYS THAT DO NOT ADDRESS THE GIVEN TOPIC ARE UNACCEPTABLE.

The quality of your writing is more important than the length of your response or the content. Pay attention to organization, appropriate diction, and correct usage. You will not be expected to display any specialized knowledge in your response, nor will you be expected to write a "perfect" essay; law schools understand that you are writing under a time constraint, and will allow for the minor lapses in writing ability that might occur under this circumstance.

Only the lined area in your booklet will be reproduced for the law schools, so do not write outside this space. *Do not* skip lines or use wide margins. These precautions, along with careful planning and legible handwriting that is not unduly large, will keep you within the allowed space.

SAMPLE TOPIC:

Your local Parent-Teacher Association recently formed a special committee to evaluate the necessity and importance of letter grades (A, B, C, D, etc.) for elementary school students. Some on the committee believe that grades should be eliminated entirely at the elementary school level. The committee plans to hear all arguments—for and against—by first eliciting written statements from concerned citizens, and then allowing those who wrote the best essays to speak before the group.

Imagine that you are a citizen wishing to be heard by the committee. Write a clear and concise statement of your argument, providing several reasons why you either support or oppose letter grades for elementary school students.

SECTION I
ANALYTICAL REASONING

Time—35 Minutes
25 Questions

Directions:
In this section you will be given groups of questions based on different sets of conditions.
Drawing a simple diagram may be helpful in answering some of the questions. You are to
choose the best answer and mark the corresponding space on your answer sheet.

Questions 1–7

To get into Buldonia you need a blue card.
To get a blue card you need a yellow ticket and a blue ticket.
To get a blue ticket you need a green hat or a yellow card.
You can trade a yellow card for either a blue ticket or a yellow ticket.
You can trade a red ticket for either a green hat or a yellow card.
You can trade a red card for a yellow ticket.

1. Which of the following will NOT get you into Buldonia?
   (A) a red ticket and a red card
   (B) a yellow ticket and a green hat
   (C) a blue ticket and a yellow card
   (D) a red card and a yellow ticket
   (E) a green hat and a red ticket

2. Which of the following will get you into Buldonia?

   I.   Two red tickets
   II. Two yellow cards
   III. Two green hats
   (A) I and II   (B) I and III   (C) II and III   (D) I, II, and III   (E) Only one of the above

3. Which of the following, when used in combination with a yellow card, will NOT get you into
   Buldonia?
   (A) green hat   (B) red card   (C) red ticket   (D) yellow ticket
   (E) Any of these will get you in.

4. If you could trade a yellow hat for a green hat, then which of the following would NOT get you into
   Buldonia?

   I.   A yellow hat and a blue ticket
   II. A yellow hat and a red card
   III. A green hat and a yellow hat
   (A) I and II   (B) I and III   (C) II and III   (D) I only   (E) III only

5. If the price of a blue card is two blue tickets and one yellow ticket, then which of the following will
   get you into Buldonia?

   I.   A yellow card, a red card, and a green hat
   II. Two red cards and a green hat
   III. Three red tickets
   (A) I and II   (B) I and III   (C) II and III   (D) I only   (E) II only

6. If the price of a blue card is two yellow tickets and one blue ticket, then which of the following will NOT get you into Buldonia?

 I. A red ticket and two green hats
 II. A green hat and two blue tickets
 III. A yellow card and two red cards

(A) I and II   (B) I and III   (C) II and III   (D) I only   (E) I, II, and III

7. If a green ticket will get you a yellow ticket, then which of the following will NOT get you into Buldonia?
(A) a red ticket and a green ticket
(B) a red card and a red ticket
(C) a green ticket and a red card
(D) a green hat and a red card
(E) a yellow ticket and a red ticket

Questions 8–14

Four judges (George, Harriet, Irving, and Josephine) vote for three show pigs (Porky, Shmorky, and Corky) at the state fair competition.
(1) Each judge has five points he/she must distribute among the three pigs.
(2) Harriet was impressed by Porky and gave him 4 points.
(3) Shmorky had an off day, receiving only 1 total point, which was from Josephine.
(4) George awarded the same number of points to Porky that Irving gave to Corky.
(5) No pig received all 5 points from one judge.
(6) Irving awarded Porky 3 points.
(7) Porky won the competition by 1 point.

8. From statements 1, 3, 4, and 6, how many points did George award Porky?
(A) 0   (B) 1   (C) 2   (D) 3   (E) 4

9. From statements 1, 2, and 3, how many points did Harriet give Corky?
(A) 0   (B) 1   (C) 2   (D) 3   (E) 4

10. Which judge gave all contestants at least 1 point each?

 I. George
 II. Josephine
 III. Irving

(A) I   (B) II   (C) III   (D) I and II   (E) I and III

11. How many points did Josephine award Corky?
(A) 0   (B) 1   (C) 2   (D) 3   (E) 4

12. Which contestant(s) received the same number of votes from both George and Josephine?

 I. Porky
 II. Shmorky
 III. Corky

(A) I   (B) II   (C) III   (D) I and II   (E) I and III

13. Which contestant(s) received at least 2 points from every judge?
(A) Porky   (B) Corky   (C) Shmorky   (D) Two of these   (E) None of these

14. Which of the statements above is either irrelevant or may be deduced from the others?
(A) 6   (B) 2   (C) 3   (D) 4   (E) 5

Questions 15–18

(1) Axel, Benty, and Carmen are sitting around a table. Each is a member of one of the following clubs: the YES Club, the NO Club, and the MAYBE Club. Each belongs to a different club.
(2) A YES always tells the truth.
(3) A NO always tells a lie.
(4) A MAYBE, answering 2 or more questions, tells the truth and lies alternately; however, the first answer may be either a lie or the truth.
(5) Axel answered his first question: "I am a MAYBE."
(6) Axel answered his second question: "Benty is a YES."
(7) Axel answered his third question: "Carmen is a NO."

15. From statements 1, 2, 3, 4, and 5 it can be determined that

  I.   Axel is telling the truth
  II. Axel is telling a lie
  III. Axel is not a YES
  (A) I only   (B) II only   (C) III only   (D) Two of these   (E) None of these

16. If Benty were asked the question, "Who are you?", what would his reply be?

  I.   I am a YES.
  II. I am a NO.
  III. I am a MAYBE.
  (A) I or II   (B) II or III   (C) I or III   (D) I, II, or III   (E) III only

17. Which of the following MUST be true?

  I.   Axel is not a MAYBE.
  II. Benty is not a NO.
  III. Carmen is not a YES.
  (A) I only   (B) II only   (C) III only   (D) Two of these   (E) All of these

18. If Carmen were asked the question about membership in the club, which of the following could be the response?
  (A) Benty is not a NO.
  (B) Axel is not a YES.
  (C) I am not a MAYBE.
  (D) Two of these.
  (E) All of these.

Questions 19–25

(1) Six people sat equally spaced around a circular table with six seats. Their first names were Albert, Beatrice, Clyde, Dexter, Eileen, and Frances. Their last names were Truckner, Upland, Williams, Xymer, Youngton, and Zipley (not necessarily in that order). They all faced toward the center of the table.
(2) Xymer sat two places to the left of Clyde.
(3) Frances sat two places to the right of Youngton.
(4) Williams sat on Albert's left, and Eileen sat on Albert's right.
(5) Dexter sat on Upland's right, and Truckner sat on Upland's left.
(6) Zipley sat directly across from Frances.
(7) Beatrice sat one seat away from Eileen.
(8) Dexter's last name is Williams.

19. Which of the following can be deduced from facts 1, 3, and 6?

I. Youngton sat on Zipley's right.
II. Zipley sat directly across from Youngton.
III. There were two seats between Frances and Zipley.
(A) I and II   (B) I and III   (C) II and III   (D) I only   (E) I, II, and III

20. Which of the following cannot be deduced from facts 1, 4, 5, and 8?
(A) Upland sat two places to the left of Albert.
(B) Eileen sat directly across from Upland.
(C) Truckner sat directly across from Albert.
(D) Truckner sat two places to the left of Eileen.
(E) Upland sat next to Williams.

21. What is Truckner's first name?
(A) Albert   (B) Beatrice   (C) Clyde   (D) Dexter   (E) Eileen

22. Which of the following MUST be true?

I. Upland is Frances' last name.
II. Zipley is Eileen's last name.
III. Frances sat next to Dexter.
(A) I and II   (B) I and III   (C) I only   (D) II only   (E) I, II, and III

23. Which of the following MUST be false?

I. Clyde sat directly across from Dexter.
II. Eileen sat directly across from Frances.
III. Clyde sat next to Eileen.
(A) I only   (B) II only   (C) I and III   (D) All of the above   (E) None of the above

24. What is Clyde's last name?
(A) Truckner   (B) Upland   (C) Xymer   (D) Youngton   (E) Zipley

25. Which of the following MUST be true?

I. Xymer sat two places to the left of Upland.
II. Zipley sat next to Youngton.
III. Youngton sat directly across from Dexter.
(A) I and II   (B) I and III   (C) II and III   (D) I, II, and III   (E) One of the above

STOP

IF YOU FINISH BEFORE TIME HAS ELAPSED, CHECK YOUR WORK ON THIS SECTION OF THE TEST ONLY. DO NOT GO ON TO THE NEXT SECTION OF THE TEST UNTIL TIME IS UP FOR THIS SECTION.

SECTION II
EVALUATION OF FACTS

Time—35 Minutes
35 Questions

Directions:
This section consists of several sets; each set presents a factual statement, the description of a dispute, and two rules. In some sets, the rules will be conflicting. Be sure that you consider each rule independently and not as an exception to the other. Following each set are questions; select from four choices (given below) the one that best categorizes each question, based upon the relationship of one or both of the rules to the dispute. Darken the appropriate space on your answer sheet:

(A) A relevant question which you can only answer by choosing between the rules.
(B) A relevant question which you cannot answer because you need more information or additional rules, but which does not require a choice between the rules.
(C) A relevant question which you can answer by referring to the facts or rules, or both.
(D) An irrelevant question or one which is only remotely relevant to the outcome of the dispute.

Set 1

FACTS

Fred Wilson and his two sons were out riding their motorcycles when they came upon a hilly off-road. The road was fenced off, and a sign posted read "NO TRESPASSING." Wilson felt that this would be a good place to ride, pried the gate open, and rode in with his sons. After riding for about 2 hours, the younger Wilson noticed a man approaching the front gate. The man, Mr. Tam, who was the owner of the property, yelled out, "Get off my property! Can't you read? It says NO TRESPASSING!" Upon hearing this, Wilson and his sons attempted to drive out the gate very quickly. But in doing so, the youngest son, Carl, accidentally hit the gate, crashing his motorcycle and breaking a leg. Mr. Tam, who was standing by the gate, was knocked over.

DISPUTE

Mr. Tam sued for trespassing, while Mr. Wilson countersued for injuries to Carl. Both contested the suits.

RULE I

One is guilty of trespassing when one enters the property of another that is marked "NO TRES-PASSING." A trespasser cannot sue for injuries.

RULE II

The owner of the property is liable to trespassers for any injuries occurring on the property unless he took reasonable precautions to ensure that the property was secure from entrance.

Questions

1. If Mr. Tam's precautions were reasonable, is he liable for Carl's injury?

2. If there had been no sign posted, would the Wilsons have been trespassing?

3. If there had been no fence around the property, would Mr. Tam be liable for Carl's injury?

4. Did the Wilson boys have valid licenses to drive the motorcycles?

5. Had the property not been secured, could Carl recover damages from Mr. Tam?

Set 2

FACTS

Helen and Arthur Rosen were on their way to their annual skiing trip in the High Sierra. As they proceeded, it became evident that they would have to put snow chains on their tires. The Rosens stopped at Joe's Chainery, a small shop that rented chains. The Rosens had their car fitted with chains by Joe, the owner. They gave a deposit and rental fee and then proceeded into the hills. As they got closer to their destination, the Rosens heard a clanking noise. Checking the chains, they noticed that one of the rear chains had slipped, ruining their tire and, at the same time, denting their fender. Mr. Rosen attempted to alleviate the situation by taking off the rear chain, but this did not help. The car would not move without the chain. While attempting to replace the chain, Mr. Rosen broke it and could not replace it. Finally the car had to be towed down the hill to Joe's Chainery.

DISPUTE

The Rosens complained about the chains and demanded reimbursement for the tire. They also stated that they should not have to pay for the chain rental. Joe disagreed, adding that they should pay for the chain.

RULE I

The rentor (one who rents equipment to others) is liable for damages caused by any equipment that he rents that occur due to faulty equipment, or damages for his negligence.

RULE II

It is the rentee's (one who rents from another) obligation to inspect all rental property before leaving the premises of the rentor, after which the rentor is not liable for any equipment malfunction.

Questions

6. If the chain was defective, will the Rosens be reimbursed for the tire?

7. Was the chain defective?

8. Will Mr. Rosen have to pay for the broken chain?

9. Could the Rosens have driven the car back?

10. Was Joe negligent?

11. Was this the Rosens' first trip to the High Sierra?

12. If the Rosens had inspected the chains before leaving the premises and found that a defective chain had damaged their rear tire, would Joe have been liable?

13. Should the Rosens have put on snow chains?

Set 3

FACTS

Dino Paneno and Lena Genst had been living together for 3 years. In that time, they had made a number of joint investments, including purchase of a large house and surrounding property. Lena's personal savings, which she had accumulated before the relationship, were used for the down payment, but Dino was the primary contributor to their income and house payments. Lena, realizing that this relationship was not leading toward marriage, decided to go out with Jordan, the local florist. Upon learning of this, Dino wanted to break up the relationship immediately. Lena agreed but wanted her share of the accumulated investments, house, and property.

DISPUTE

Dino and Lena disagreed on the splitting of property and went to court.

RULE I

Property acquired during a nonmarital relationship must be divided evenly between the parties involved after termination of the relationship.

RULE II

Upon termination of a relationship, the primary contributor to the income retains all property purchased only if the relationship existed for more than 2 years.

Questions

14. Will Dino get only half of the property?

15. If Lena and Dino were married, who would get the property when they broke up?

16. If Lena and Dino had lived together for 1½ years, would Lena get the house?

17. Was Lena the primary contributor to the income?

18. Should Jordan have dated Lena?

Set 4

FACTS

After the Hatfields and McCoys had been feuding for many years, it finally appeared that they would become friends. To iron out their differences, the Hatfields invited the McCoys to their newly purchased house for dinner, and the McCoys accepted. That evening the McCoys were warmly welcomed, and they all enjoyed a sumptuous buffet. After the dinner, as the McCoys were leaving, Grandpa McCoy slipped on a roller skate that had been accidentally left in the hallway by one of the younger Hatfields. The McCoys became enraged. They claimed that the placement of the skate was intentional. In retaliation, Mrs. McCoy pushed Mrs. Hatfield, who flipped over the couch and landed on her coffee table, smashing it to pieces. The police arrived just in time to prevent further damage.

DISPUTE

The McCoys sued for damages, and the Hatfields contested and countersued.

RULE I

The property owner is liable for all injuries and damages occurring on his property.

RULE II

One who intentionally causes harm to another or damage to property, either directly or indirectly, is liable.

Questions

19. Was Grandpa McCoy injured?

20. If Grandpa McCoy was injured, would the Hatfields be liable for his injury?

21. Will Mrs. McCoy be liable for her action?

22. If the table was broken by accident, would Mrs. McCoy be liable?

23. Should the McCoys have invited the Hatfields?

Set 5

FACTS

As part of its fitness program, the Ivanhoe Elementary School held a junior Olympics day. Among the events was a weightlifting contest for the boys in the sixth grade. The three finalists were Bob, Tom, and George. Bob lifted 90 pounds over his head with both hands, three times. Tom lifted 40 pounds over his head four times, using only one hand. George lifted 150 pounds once, but not over his head. The school principal, who did not know all of the established rules for the event, declared George the winner.

DISPUTE

Tom and Bob contested the decision, each claiming victory.

RULE I

The winner is the person who lifts the most weight over his head on one lift.

RULE II

The winner is the one who lifts the most weight on one lift.

Questions

24. Will George win the contest?

25. Will the rules settle the dispute?

26. Will Bob be the winner?

27. Can Tom declare himself the winner?

28. How well did the principal know the three boys?

29. If Bob attempted to lift 160 pounds on his second try, would he be declared the winner?

Set 6

FACTS

Shelly, Phil, and Tina were participants in a TV game show. Cash prizes were awarded for the total number of points won in each game. Shelly had never played before but when the program ended, she had won three games by a total of 50 points. Phil won the first two games, which was one-third as many as he had won the previous day. When the announcer called "Time is up" and stopped the show, Tina was leading in total games and was invited back, along with Phil, for the next day. Only two people can be invited back the next day, but the invitation to return is determined by the rules of the game.

DISPUTE

After the show, Shelly complained to the announcer that she had the most total points and should have been invited back for the next day. Phil and Tina disagreed.

RULE I

A player must win at least five games to be invited back the next day.

RULE II

The player with the most games won will be invited back the next day.

Questions

30. Will Shelly be invited back for the next day?

31. Did Phil win the most games the previous day?

32. Did Phil win five games or more?

33. Was this Tina's first appearance on a game show?

34. If Shelly won three more games, would she be invited back?

35. If Tina won four games, and if Phil won three games, will Tina be invited back?

STOP

IF YOU FINISH BEFORE TIME HAS ELAPSED, CHECK YOUR WORK ON THIS SECTION OF THE TEST ONLY. DO NOT GO ON TO THE NEXT SECTION OF THE TEST UNTIL TIME IS UP FOR THIS SECTION.

SECTION III
READING COMPREHENSION

Time—35 Minutes
28 Questions

Directions:
Read the passages and answer the questions following each passage by blackening the appropriate space on the answer sheet. You may refer back to the passages when answering the questions. Answer all questions on the basis of what is stated or implied.

Passage 1

In the fall of 1946, President Truman asked for a comprehensive study of Soviet-American relations, which he knew would be the central problem of American foreign policy. The result was an important state paper prepared through the secretary of state, the secretary of war, the attorney general, the secretary of the navy, Fleet Admiral Leahy (who had been Roosevelt's chief military adviser), the joint chiefs of staff, Ambassador Edwin W. Pauley (in charge of negotiating postwar reparations), the director of central intelligence, and other persons with special knowledge of foreign affairs. The document was imposing in its scope and depth, comprising nearly a hundred thousand words and divided into an introduction and six sections. It dealt with Soviet foreign policy, Soviet-American agreements, Soviet violations of its agreements with the U.S., conflicting views on reparations, Soviet activities affecting American security, and U.S. policy toward the Soviet Union.

This study Truman asked for was drafted on the premise that only through an accurate understanding of the Soviet Union would the U.S. be able to make and carry out policies that would reestablish international order and protect the U.S. at all times. The key, according to the study, was to realize that Moscow's leaders adhered to the Marxian theory of ultimate destruction of capitalist states by communist states but that they sought to postpone the inevitable conflict while they strengthened and prepared the Soviet Union for its clash with the Western democracies. The study said Moscow's main concern regarding the other nations of Western Europe was to prevent the formation of a Western bloc. It noted, too, that Red Army troops and Russian planes in combat readiness outnumbered American units opposite them in Germany, Austria, and Korea in overwhelming strength, placing U.S. forces literally at the mercy of the Soviet government.

1. The passage associates President Truman with
   (A) peace with honor
   (B) anti-Communist sentiment
   (C) the long-standing Cold War
   (D) Western imperialism
   (E) sympathy for U.S. forces

2. The author's attitude toward Truman seems to be
   (A) supportive   (B) skeptical   (C) cynical   (D) worshipful   (E) hostile

3. Evidence in the passage allows us to conclude that the study described in this passage was notable for its
   (A) far-reaching effects
   (B) controversial wording
   (C) literary quality
   (D) objectivity
   (E) completeness

4. The passage implies that U.S. forces in 1946 needed to
- (A) engage in a new sort of training
- (B) increase
- (C) come home
- (D) confront Soviet forces
- (E) retrain

5. The state paper described in this passage did not deal with
- (A) agreements between the U.S.S.R. and the U.S.A.
- (B) those Russian activities relevant to U.S. security
- (C) the Truman policy of containment
- (D) the respective views of the United States and the USSR concerning reparations
- (E) the foreign policy of the Russians

6. A Russian government official might argue that "accurate" (paragraph 2, line 1) is an imprecise term because
- (A) accuracy is an unattainable goal
- (B) Truman never visited Russia
- (C) the anti-Soviet conclusions in the study were biased
- (D) Communism is not concerned with accuracy
- (E) English is an imprecise language

7. The branch of government not participating in the preparation of the described document was
- (A) the legislative
- (B) the judicial
- (C) both (A) and (B)
- (D) not stated or implied
- (E) the executive

Passage 2

OF STUDIES—*Francis Bacon*
(1597 Version)

Studies serve for pastimes, for ornaments, and for abilities. Their chief use for pastime is in privateness and retiring; for ornament is in discourse; and for ability is in judgment. For expert men can execute, but learned men are fittest to judge or censure.

(5)   To spend too much time in them is sloth; to use them too much for ornament is affectation; to make judgment wholly by their rules is the humour of a scholar. They perfect Nature, and are perfected by experience. Crafty men contemn them, simple men admire them, wise men use them: for they teach not their own use, but that is a wisdom without them, and above them, won by observation. Read not to contradict, nor to believe, but to weigh and consider. Some books are to be tasted, others to be swallowed, and some few to be chewed and digested: that is,

(10)   some books are to be read only in parts; others to be read, but cursorily; and some few to be read wholly and with diligence and attention. Reading maketh a full man, conference a ready man, and writing an exact man. And therefore if a man write little, he had need have a great memory; if he confer little, he had need have a present wit; and if he read little, he had need have much cunning, to seem to know that he doth not. Histories make men wise, poets witty; the

(15)   mathematics subtle, natural philosophy deep; moral grave, logic and rhetoric able to contend.

(1625 Version: Additions/Changes Underlined)

Studies serve for delight, for ornament, and for ability. Their chief use for delight, is in privateness and retiring; for ornament, is in discourse; and for ability, is in the judgment and disposition of business. For expert men can execute, and perhaps judge of particulars, one by

(5) one; but the general counsels, and the plots and marshalling of affairs, come best from those that are learned. To spend too much time in studies is sloth; to use them too much for ornament is affectation; to make judgment wholly by their rules, is the humour of a scholar. They perfect nature, and are perfected by experience: for natural abilities are like natural plants, that need pruning by study; and studies themselves do give forth directions too much at large, except they be bounded in by experience. Crafty men contemn studies, simple men admire them, and wise

(10) men use them; for they teach not their own use; but that is a wisdom without them, and above them, won by observation. Read not to contradict and confute; nor to believe and take for granted; nor to find talk and discourse; but to weigh and consider. Some books are to be tasted, others to be swallowed, and some few to be chewed, and digested; that is, some books are to read only in parts; others to be read, but not curiously; and some few to be ready wholly, and

(15) with diligence and attention. Some books also may be read by deputy, and extracts made of them by others; but that would be only in the less important arguments, and the meaner sort of books; else distilled books are like common distilled waters, flashy things. Reading maketh a full man; conference a ready man; and writing an exact man. And therefore, if a man write little, he had need have a great memory; if he confer little, he had need have a present wit; and if he read

(20) little, he had need have much cunning, to seem to know that he doth not. Histories make men wise; poets witty; the mathematics subtle; natural philosophy deep; moral grave; logic and rhetoric able to contend. Abeunt studia in mores. Nay, there is no stond or impediment in the wit, but may be wrought out by fit studies: like as diseases of the body may have appropriate exercises. Bowling is good for the stone and reins; shooting for the lungs and breast; gentle

(25) walking for the stomach; riding for the head, and the like. So if a man's wit be wandering, let him study the mathematics; for in demonstrations, if his wit be called away ever so little, he must begin again. If his wit be not apt to distinguish and find differences, let him study the schoolmen, for they are cymini sectores. If he be not apt to beat over matters, and to call up one thing to prove and illustrate another, let him study the lawyers' cases. So every defect of the mind may

(30) have a special receipt.

8. The primary purpose of both the 1597 version and the 1625 version is
   (A) to ornament commonplace ideas about studies
   (B) to distinguish crafty men, wise men, and simple men
   (C) to justify Bacon's own studies
   (D) to explain the relative value of studies
   (E) to explain the absolute value of studies

9. It can be inferred from the second passage that the author regards "distilled books" (line 17) as
   (A) negative
   (B) not established
   (C) not the same way he regarded them in 1597
   (D) not important to him
   (E) mean

10. It can be inferred from the later passage that punctuation
   (A) is a casual concern of the author
   (B) is a significant concern of the author
   (C) does not vary when the 1625 version matches the 1597 one
   (D) obeys consistent rules in the author's use
   (E) defies analysis

11. Both passages state which of the following about reading?
   (A) Readers have little humor.
   (B) Reading cultivates the habit of exactness.
   (C) Extracts from books are of questionable value.
   (D) Few books are worth close, careful reading.
   (E) Practice in reading influences ability in writing.

12. Which of the following terms most nearly describes the type of addition that Bacon made in the 1625 edition?

(A) evidence   (B) amplification   (C) analogy   (D) contradiction   (E) correction

13. From the later passage, we may conclude that "studies" do not include

(A) reading   (B) conversation   (C) writing   (D) sports   (E) judgment

14. In both passages, "moral grave" (line 15 in 1597; line 21 in 1625) is a shorthand way of expressing which of the following ideas?

(A) Morals are grave.
(B) The study of morals makes men grave.
(C) Histories make men wise and assure them a moral grave.
(D) Natural philosophy is deep, moral, and grave.
(E) Either (A) or (B).

Passage 3

The American, though he dresses like an Englishman, and eats roast beef with a silver fork—or sometimes with a steel knife—as does an Englishman, is not like an Englishman in his mind, in his aspirations, in his tastes, or in his politics. In his mind he is quicker, more universally intelligent, more ambitious of general knowledge, less indulgent of stupidity and ignorance in others, harder, sharper, brighter with the surface brightness of steel, than is an Englishman; but he is more brittle, less enduring, less malleable, and I think less capable of impressions. The mind of the Englishman has more imagination, but that of the American more incision. The American is a great observer, but he observes things material rather than things social or picturesque. He is a constant and ready speculator; but all speculations, even those which come of philosophy, are with him more or less material. In his aspirations the American is more constant than an Englishman—or I should rather say he is more constant in aspiring. Every citizen of the United States intends to do something. Every one thinks himself capable of some effort. But in his aspirations he is more limited than an Englishman. The ambitious American never soars so high as the ambitious Englishman. He does not even see up to so great a height; and when he has raised himself somewhat above the crowd becomes sooner dizzy with his own altitude. An American of mark, though always anxious to show his mark, is always fearful of a fall. In his tastes the American imitates the Frenchman. Who shall dare to say that he is wrong, seeing that in general matters of design and luxury the French have won for themselves the foremost name? I will not say that the American is wrong, but I cannot avoid thinking that he is so. I detest what is called French taste; but the world is against me. When I complained to a landlord of a hotel out in the West that his furniture was useless; that I could not write at a marble table whose outside rim was curved into fantastic shapes; that a gold clock in my bedroom which did not go would give me no aid in washing myself; that a heavy, immovable curtain shut out the light; and that *papier-maché* chairs with small fluffy velvet seats were bad to sit on—he answered me completely by telling me that his house had been furnished not in accordance with the taste of England, but with that of France. I acknowledged the rebuke, gave up my pursuits of literature and cleanliness, and hurried out of the house as quickly as I could. All America is now furnishing itself by the rules which guided that hotel-keeper. I do not merely allude to actual household furniture—to chairs, tables, and detestable gilt clocks. The taste of America is becoming French in its conversation, French in its comforts and French in its discomforts, French in its eating, and French in its dress, French in its manners, and will become French in its art. There are those who will say that English taste is taking the same direction. I do not think so. I strongly hope that it is not so. And, therefore, I say that an Englishman and an American differ in their tastes.

15. The primary purpose of this passage is

(A) to explain America to a foreign audience
(B) to recount the travels of an Englishman in America

(C) to compare and contrast Englishmen and Americans
(D) to insult the French
(E) to argue that Englishmen are better than Americans

16. The author believes that, although Americans are "constant" in their aspirations, they are also
(A) cautious   (B) dizzy   (C) speculative   (D) incapable   (E) unimaginative

17. Relative to the popularity of French taste, the author believes that he constitutes
(A) an advocacy
(B) a minority
(C) a new viewpoint
(D) a moral alternative
(E) both (C) and (D)

18. Of the four contrasting characteristics that the author mentions in the first sentence, the one he says no more about is
(A) mind   (B) aspirations   (C) tastes   (D) politics   (E) eating style

19. The author claims that America is becoming "French in its comforts and French in its discomforts." The comforts resulting from French taste are
(A) marble tables
(B) gilt clocks
(C) porcelain wash basins
(D) heavy curtains
(E) not mentioned

20. From the last four sentences, we may infer that the English and the Americans will continue to differ in taste as long as
(A) English furniture retains its utilitarian character
(B) the English stay out of America
(C) Englishmen continue to pursue "literature and cleanliness"
(D) English taste does not move closer to French taste
(E) the French populate America

21. When he says that "a gold clock in my bedroom which did not go would give me no aid in washing myself," the author is stressing
(A) the lack of cleanliness in the American West
(B) the French preference for decoration over utility
(C) his frustration at not knowing the time
(D) the taste of France
(E) the weakness of American hotel-keepers

Passage 4

In science, as elsewhere, we meet the assumptions of convenience and expedience, such as equations that assume frictionless machines or chemicals in a pure state. But by far the most important function of language in the development of scientific understanding and control of the world about us is the use of a kind of assumption called *hypothesis* at first, *theory* in a more developed state, and *law* when its implications have been extensively corroborated. A hypothesis resembles other assumptions in that it may be either true or false and may be used as the premise of rational action; otherwise it differs radically as to function and purpose. Hypotheses are employed experimentally in the search for truth. Without them the so-called scientific method is not possible. The reason for this is not always readily grasped and will now be illustrated in some detail.

Suppose, for example, that you are about to prepare an account of some fairly complex subject, such as the history of marriage. As soon as you have arrived at a clear working definition of your topic, you begin the collection of data. Now a *datum* is an item of some sort regarded as relevant to your problem. But everything is in some way related to everything else, and since you cannot possibly consider all the facts related to marriage, you must limit the field of relevance in some practical, arbitrary manner. Let us assume that you are at work on the status of marriage in modern urban society; perhaps you may attempt to discover to what extent the institution persists because it is biologically useful, economically expedient, socially convenient, religiously compulsory, or merely psychologically traditional. To proceed thus is to set up a fivefold hypothesis that enables you to gather from the innumerable items cast up by the sea of experience upon the shores of your observation only the limited number of relevant data—relevant, that is, to one or more of the five factors of your hypothesis. The hypothesis (the reference of the symbol *hypothesis*) is like a light by means of which we search for truth; but it is a colored light that may render invisible the very object we seek. That is why, after a fair trial, we must not hesitate to abandon one color for another. When our hypothesis possesses the proper color and intensity, it will reveal some of the facts as data, which may then be further studied and verified as signs of truth.

As the evidence in favor of a hypothesis (the thing again, not the word) accumulates to a convincing degree, we frequently symbolize the fact with the term *theory*. Thus, semantically, a theory is the name of a hypothesis that has outgrown its experimental short pants. With Charles Darwin, *biological evolution* was a hypothesis; in contemporary science it is a theory that no rational observer, however cautious, hesitates to accept.

When predictions based on the implications of a theory are continually borne out by observation, the relation symbolized is still further elevated to the status of a *law or natural law*. The abstraction "law" is a dangerous one to employ because it implies that the mind has finally arrived at the truth, ultimate and eternal. Thus, the eyes of science become myopic and lose the power to discover old errors and discern new truths.

22. The author's primary purpose is
    (A) to note the progress in understanding since Darwin's time
    (B) to define and discuss some basic scientific terms
    (C) to develop a hypothesis
    (D) to argue for the value of scientific truth
    (E) to criticize the scientific method

23. We may infer that the author would have difficulty accepting which of the following statements?
    (A) The discovery of old errors may lead to new truths.
    (B) The Darwinian theory was once a hypothesis.
    (C) The establishment of natural laws is the final goal of science.
    (D) It is sometimes advisable to abandon a hypothesis.
    (E) A hypothesis may be either true or false.

24. On two occasions, the author follows the word "hypothesis" with a parenthetical remark that serves to
    (A) diminish the value of scientific hypotheses
    (B) stress the value of symbolism in science
    (C) demonstrate that the term presents semantic problems
    (D) stress the difference between a hypothesis and a theory
    (E) stress the difference between the term and what it stands for

25. According to the passage, the factor that distinguishes a hypothesis from a theory is
    (A) the passage of time
    (B) the goal of the scientist
    (C) the method of the scientist
    (D) the relevance of the investigation
    (E) the convincingness of the evidence

26. The author would agree with which of the following statements?
(A) Hypotheses and truth are mutually exclusive.
(B) "Hypothesis," "theory," and "law" are synonymous terms.
(C) Language hinders the development of scientific understanding.
(D) Hypotheses are more important for science than are equations.
(E) Most people understand the importance of hypotheses to the scientific method.

27. We may infer from the passage that a hypothesis is always
(A) objective   (B) subjective   (C) the wrong color   (D) fivefold   (E) useful

28. The author assumes that the relationship between hypotheses and the scientific method is
(A) only a theory
(B) not commonly understood
(C) not significant
(D) a product of evolution
(E) apparent to most people

STOP

IF YOU FINISH BEFORE TIME HAS ELAPSED, CHECK YOUR WORK ON THIS SECTION OF THE
TEST ONLY. DO NOT GO ON TO THE NEXT SECTION OF THE TEST UNTIL TIME IS UP FOR THIS
SECTION.

SECTION IV
ANALYTICAL REASONING

Time—35 Minutes
25 Questions

Directions:
In this section you will be given groups of questions based on different sets of conditions.
Drawing a simple diagram may be helpful in answering some of the questions. You are to
choose the best answer and mark the corresponding space on your answer sheet.

Questions 1–7

Kelly, Clyde, Roland, Fred, and Harriet are a lawyer, an accountant, a doctor, a police officer, and
a cab driver, not necessarily in that order.
1. Kelly is not the doctor or the accountant.
2. If Fred is the accountant, then Kelly is the doctor.
3. Roland is not the police officer.
4. If Clyde is the doctor, then Harriet is the lawyer.
5. If Harriet is the cab driver, then Kelly is not the police officer.
6. Harriet is the cab driver.

1. If the accountant, the doctor, and the police officer meet for lunch, which three people get to-
gether?
(A) Kelly, Fred, and Clyde
(B) Roland, Fred, and Kelly
(C) Roland, Clyde, and Kelly
(D) Roland, Fred, and Clyde
(E) None of these

2. Clyde cannot be the

    I.   accountant
    II. police officer
    III. doctor
    (A) I only   (B) II only   (C) III only   (D) I and III   (E) II and III

3. If Roland is the doctor, then Clyde is the
    (A)   police officer
    (B)   accountant
    (C)   lawyer
    (D)   none of these
    (E)   not enough information to tell

4. If Clyde is NOT the accountant, then

    I.   Roland is the accountant
    II. Clyde is the police officer
    III. Fred is the doctor
    (A) I only   (B) II only   (C) III only   (D) I and III   (E) I, II, and III

5. If Fred is the police officer, then
    (A)   Roland could be the doctor
    (B)   Roland must be the accountant
    (C)   Clyde must be the accountant
    (D)   Clyde could be the lawyer
    (E)   Clyde must be the doctor

6. The doctor could be

    I.   Clyde
    II. Roland
    III. Fred
    (A) I only   (B) II only   (C) III only   (D) I and III   (E) II and III

7. If the cab driver picks up the lawyer and the accountant, which three people could be in the cab?

    I.   Harriet
    II. Fred
    III. Roland
    IV. Kelly
    (A) I, II, and III   (B) II, III, and IV   (C) I, II, and IV   (D) I, III, and IV   (E) None of these

Questions 8–14.

Eleven people stand single file in a straight line. There are four women, three men, two boys and two girls.
The children are all next to each other.
Three of the women stand next to each other at one end of the line.
No man stands next to another man.

8. If a child is in the sixth place, which of the following MUST be true?
    (A)   A woman is in the first place.
    (B)   A woman is in the second place.
    (C)   A woman is in the seventh place.
    (D)   A woman is in the eighth place.
    (E)   A woman is in the ninth place.

9. Which of the following MUST be true?

(A) A woman is either first or third.
(B) A woman is either second or tenth.
(C) A woman is either sixth or seventh.
(D) A woman is fourth.
(E) A woman is seventh.

10. All of the following MUST be true except

(A) if a man is first, a woman is last
(B) if a child is second, a man is sixth
(C) if a child is sixth, a woman is tenth
(D) if a man is fourth, a child is eighth
(E) if a woman is third, a man is sixth

11. If a girl is second and a boy is third, which of the following MUST be true?

(A) The two boys are next to each other.
(B) The two boys are not next to each other.
(C) The two girls are not next to men.
(D) The two girls are not next to each other.
(E) A boy is next to a woman.

12. If a boy is eighth, which of the following could be true?

I. A man is third.
II. A man is last.
III. A girl is tenth.

(A) I only (B) II ONLY (C) III only (D) I and III (E) II and III

13. If a man is fourth, a woman MUST be

I. first
II. second
II. fifth
IV. tenth

(A) I (B) II (C) I and II (D) I and III (E) I and IV

14. If each man is next to at least one woman, which of the following MUST be true?

(A) A man is first.
(B) A woman is second.
(C) A woman is third.
(D) A child is fourth.
(E) A man is eighth.

Questions 15–18.

(1) June and Kathy (two girls) and Aaron and Bryan (two boys) have last names of Sands, Townsend, Williams, and Zakey, not necessarily in that order. Their ages, not necessarily in order, are 6, 7, 8, and 9.
(2) Sands told his mother that Williams said she would send him a valentine.
(3) Aaron and the 9-year-old boy live next door to each other.
(4) Townsend is younger than Kathy and older than June.
(5) Zakey is the youngest.

15. What are the last names of the two girls?

(A) Sands and Williams
(B) Sands and Zakey
(C) Townsend and Zakey
(D) Townsend and Williams
(E) Williams and Zakey

16. What are the ages of the two boys?

(A) 6 and 8 (B) 7 and 9 (C) 7 and 8 (D) 6 and 9 (E) 8 and 9

17. Which of the following can be deduced from statements 1, 3, and 4?

I. Kathy is 8.
II. Zakey is 6.
III. Aaron is 9.

(A) I only (B) II only (C) I and II (D) I and III (E) II and III

18. Which of the following MUST be true?
 I. Kathy is younger than Bryan.
 II. Townsend is older than June.
 III. Aaron is younger than Williams.
 (A) I and II   (B) I and III   (C) II and III   (D) One of these   (E) All of these

Questions 19-25
(1) Bill is taller than Ann.
(2) Drew is shorter than Bill.
(3) Clem is taller than Drew, but shorter than Ann.
(4) Ellen is taller than Clem, but shorter than Bill.
(5) Fran is taller than Ellen.
(6) Gina is shorter than Ann.

19. If Ann is 5 feet tall, then which of the following could not be true?

 I. Fran is 4 feet 10 inches tall.
 II. Ellen is 5 feet 10 inches tall.
 III. Drew is 5 feet 10 inches tall.
 (A) I only   (B) II only   (C) III only   (D) Two of the above   (E) None of the above

20. Which of the following could not be true?
 (A) Drew is shorter than Ann.   (D) Fran is shorter than Clem.
 (B) Ellen is 4 feet tall.   (E) Drew is 4 feet tall.
 (C) Bill is taller than Fran.

21. If Ellen is taller than Ann, then which of the following MUST be true about Fran?

 I. Fran is taller than Ann.
 II. Fran is taller than Bill.
 III. Fran is taller than Drew.
 (A) I and II   (B) I and III   (C) II and III   (D) II only   (E) III only

22. Which statement is redundant and repeats information obtainable from the other statements?
 (A) 1   (B) 2   (C) 3   (D) 4   (E) 5

23. If Clem is 5 feet tall, which of the following could be true?

 I. Gina is taller than Fran.
 II. Gina is 4 feet tall.
 III. Ellen is taller than Gina.
 (A) I and II   (B) I and III   (C) II and III   (D) I, II, and III   (E) III only

24. If Hank joins the group, and if he is shorter than Gina, then which of the following MUST be true?
 (A) Hank is taller than Drew.
 (B) Clem is shorter than Hank.
 (C) Hank is shorter than Ellen.
 (D) Hank is taller than Ann.
 (E) Bill is taller than Hank.

25. If Fran and Ann are the same height, then which of the following MUST be true?

 I. Ann is taller than Ellen.
 II. Gina is taller than Ellen.
 III. Gina is shorter than Fran.

 (A) I and II   (B) I and III   (C) II and III   (D) I, II, and III   (E) Only one of the above

STOP

IF YOU FINISH BEFORE TIME HAS ELAPSED, CHECK YOUR WORK ON THIS SECTION OF THE TEST ONLY. DO NOT GO ON TO THE NEXT SECTION OF THE TEST UNTIL TIME IS UP FOR THIS SECTION.

SECTION V
LOGICAL REASONING

Time—35 Minutes
26 Questions

Directions:
In this section you will be given brief statements or passages and will be required to evaluate the reasoning involved. In some instances, more than one choice will appear to be a possible answer. You are to choose the *best* answer. Use common sense and reasonableness in making your selection; then mark the proper space on the answer sheet.

Questions 1–3 refer to the following passage.

It has long been apparent that the nation's violent crime problem is disproportionately a juvenile crime problem. Those under age 18 constitute a fifth of the population, but account for nearly half of the arrests for the seven major crimes on which the FBI maintains national statistics. The statistical trend lines suggest the problem is growing; the number of juveniles arrested for murder and aggravated assault rose 82 percent and 91 percent respectively from 1967 to 1976. Yet, under the laws of most states, courts are obliged to treat these young hard-core hoodlums as if they were little worse than wayward delinquents.

1. The author of this passage would argue that
   (A)   crime has increased because of juveniles
   (B)   young hard-core hoodlums account for nearly 50 percent of the seven major crimes
   (C)   our legal system is biased in favor of hardened criminals
   (D)   arrests for aggravated assault are growing more rapidly than those for murder
   (E)   a fifth of our population is comprised of wayward delinquents

2. The author of this passage assumes that

   I.   statistical trend lines are accurate predictors
   II.   1967 to 1976 were not abnormal years
   III.   the laws of most states are consistent involving juveniles
   (A) I only   (B) II only   (C) I and II only   (D) II and III only   (E) I, II, and III

3. This argument would be weakened most by pointing out that
   (A)   the laws in each state are different concerning juveniles
   (B)   the population has shifted to juveniles
   (C)   there are eight major crimes
   (D)   the FBI's national statistics are inaccurate
   (E)   statistical trend lines are poor predictors

4. Some of Mike's chores take less than 1 hour to complete.
   Some of Mike's chores take more than 1 hour to complete.
   It will take Mike at least 2 hours to complete his chores.

   Which of the following additional conditions are necessary to make the third statement valid?

   I.   More of Mike's chores take at least 1 hour to complete than take less than 1 hour to complete.
   II.   All chores, except one, take less than 1 hour to complete.
   III.   All chores, except one, take at least 1 hour to complete.
   (A) I only   (B) II only   (C) III only   (D) Two of these   (E) I, II, and III

5. Ten marbles are split among Juan, Maria, and Alvin. If Maria gives her marbles to Juan, then Juan will have more marbles than Alvin. Alternatively, if Alvin gives his marbles to Maria, then Maria will have more marbles than Juan.

Which of the following may be true?

   I. Maria has six marbles.
   II. Alvin has four marbles.
   III. Juan has six marbles.
   (A) I and II only   (B) I and III only   (C) II and III only   (D) I, II, and III
   (E) None of these

Questions 6–7 refer to the following statement.

Recent studies show that the height of the average American has increased 2 inches in the past 10 years, lending support to the view that modern foods stimulate growth.

6. The argument would be strengthened by pointing out that
   (A) statistical studies were done on which foods were eaten
   (B) modern foods are unhealthy
   (C) all average heights are increasing
   (D) comparisons have been studied in control groups
   (E) there is no such thing as an average American

7. This argument would be weakened most by pointing out that
   (A) statistics don't lie
   (B) there are too many variables in this type of study
   (C) the genetic background of the subjects was not investigated
   (D) the sample group used was small
   (E) some people's height decreased

Questions 8 and 9 refer to the following passage.

A glance at the five leading causes of death in 1900, 1910, and 1945, years representing in some measure the early and late practice of physicians still active, shows a significant trend. In 1900 these causes were (1) tuberculosis, (2) pneumonia, (3) enteritis, typhoid fever, and other acute intestinal diseases, (4) heart diseases, and (5) cerebral hemorrhage and thrombosis. Ten years later the only change was that heart disease had moved from fourth to first place, tuberculosis now being second, and pneumonia third. In 1945, however, the list had changed profoundly. Heart diseases were far out in front; cancer, which had come up from eighth place, was second; and cerebral hemorrhage and thrombosis, third. Fatal accidents, which had been well down the list, were now fourth, and nephritis was fifth. All of these are, of course, composites rather than single diseases, and it is significant that, except for accidents, they are characteristic of the advanced rather than the early or middle years of life.

8. Which of the following is the most logical conclusion from the passage above?
   (A) A cure for cancer will be found within the decade.
   (B) Many of the medical problems of today are problems of the gerontologist (specialist in medical problems of old age).
   (C) Older persons are more accident-prone than are younger persons.
   (D) Tuberculosis has been all but eliminated.
   (E) Heart disease has never been a real threat to the aged.

9. Which of the following is not indicated by the passage?
   (A) As one grows older he is more subject to disease.
   (B) Pneumonia is no longer among the five most common causes of death.

(C) Compared to mortality rates for acute intestinal diseases, the mortality rate for cancer has increased.
(D) The incidence of heart disease has increased.
(E) Fatal accidents today claim more lives than ever.

10. Bitter it is, indeed, in human fate, when life's supreme temptation comes too late.

—John Masefield

Which of the following is neither implied nor expressed in the above quotation?
(A) the specific nature of the temptation
(B) the time of life during which the supreme temptation occurs
(C) the effect of the supreme temptation coming late in life
(D) the role of fate
(E) the importance of the temptation

Questions 11–12 refer to the following passage.

Within the unconscious realm of the mind, of which we are normally unaware, lie our basic drives and the coordination and control of our bodily functions and chemistry. This dark area of the mind constitutes about 90 percent of our mind and is responsible for about 95 percent of our behavior. We are dimly aware of its existence through our dreams, spontaneous recall of forgotten memories, and slips of speech.

11. Which of the following is not implied in the passage?

I. Ninety-five percent of our behavior is controlled by 90 percent of our mind.
II. Five percent of our behavior is uncontrolled.
III. Dreams, spontaneous recall, and slips of speech constitute about 90 percent of our behavior.
(A) I only   (B) II only   (C) III only   (D) I and II only   (E) I, II, and III

12. The author of this passage assumes that
(A) all humans have the same bodily functions and chemical balance
(B) it is difficult to define the unconscious realm of the mind
(C) behavior modification could not take place in the conscious realm of the mind
(D) our basic drives and the coordination and control of our bodily functions take place in the same half of the brain
(E) a small part of our mind controls a small part of our behavior

13. All teachers like some of their students. No teacher likes all of his or her students.

If these statements are true, then which of the following MUST be true?

I. Most teachers like most of their students.
II. All teachers dislike some of their students.
III. No teacher dislikes all of his or her students.
(A) I and II only   (B) II and III only   (C) I and III only   (D) I, II, and III
(E) Only one of the three

Questions 14–15 refer to the following passage.

There seems to be no way of accounting for the fundamental and widespread misunderstanding of the relation between language and thought unless the reason be the one quoted from Aristotle, that the mind is characteristically blind to things that are at once (14) ————————.
Be this as it may, the most important thing to know about language, regardless of any of its particular functions, is the principle of (15) ————————.

14. This sentence would be best completed by the words
- (A) logical and obscure
- (B) irrelevant and complex
- (C) linguistic and cerebral
- (D) important and obvious
- (E) simplistic and subjective

15. This sentence would be best completed by the word
- (A) ambiguity (B) clarity (C) unity (D) logic (E) communication

16. On-the-job training alone, of course, cannot solve the unemployment problem. The national economic recession is basically responsible for the recent surge in unemployment. The administration is pinning its chief hope for full employment on its program for revitalizing the economy.

Which of the following topics would most logically precede the passage above?
- (A) successful economic plans of the past
- (B) government policies preceding the administration
- (C) the motives of the administration
- (D) causes of the recession
- (E) opportunities for on-the-job training

17. On the one hand, "little white lies" are sinful; on the other hand, when we lie in order to save a friend from unnecessary pain, the "whiteness" of our lie becomes more apparent. Those who tell the whole truth all of the time are sure to leave misery in their wake.

The author makes which of the following arguments?
- (A) Lying is either sinful or virtuous.
- (B) Truthtellers are sure to be miserable.
- (C) Little white lies are the only justifiable lies.
- (D) It is good to lie in order to avoid hurting someone.
- (E) Pain is the result of truth.

18. CLEENUP SOAP will scour your pots and pans while it whitens your sink. You'll want Cleenup for all your clean-up chores, especially the hard jobs around the house.

The advertisement above implies that
- (A) Cleenup Soap is better than the rest.
- (B) Cleenup Soap is the best soap for household clean-up chores.
- (C) Cleenup Soap can be used for many cleaning jobs.
- (D) Cleenup Soap is economically the best buy.
- (E) Cleenup Soap can be used only for jobs around the house.

19. *Landlord*: When are you going to pay last month's rent?
Renter: First, I've already paid it. Second, I don't owe you anything. Third, not until you fix the heater.

The weakness in the renter's response is best expressed by which of the following?
- (A) He contradicts himself.
- (B) He dislikes his landlord.
- (C) He assumes the landlord has a poor memory.
- (D) He repeats himself.
- (E) He makes no sense.

Questions 20–21 refer to the following passage.

It is a common belief that a thing is desirable because it is scarce and thereby has ostentation value. The notion that such a standard of value is an inescapable condition of settled social existence rests on one of two implicit assumptions. The first is that the attempt to educate the human race so that the desire to display one's possessions is not a significant feature of man's social behavior, is an infringement against personal freedom. The greatest obstacle to lucid discourse in these matters is the psychological anti-vaccinationist who uses the word freedom to signify the natural right of men and women to be unhappy and unhealthy through scientific ignorance instead of being healthy and happy through the knowledge which science confers. Haunted by a perpetual fear of the dark, the last lesson which man learns in the difficult process of growing up is "Ye shall know the truth, and the truth shall make you free." The professional economist who is too sophisticated to retreat into the obscurities of this curious conception of liberty may prefer to adopt the second assumption, that the truth does not and cannot make us free because the need for ostentation is a universal species characteristic, and all attempts to eradicate the unconscionable nuisance and discord which arise from overdeveloped craving for personal distinction artificially fostered by advertisement, propaganda and so-called good breeding are therefore destined to failure. It may be earnestly hoped that those who entertain this view have divine guidance. No rational basis for it will be found in textbooks of economics. Whatever can be said with any plausibility in the existing state of knowledge rests on the laboratory materials supplied by anthropology and social history.

20. According to the writer, the second assumption
    (A) is fostered by propaganda and so-called good breeding
    (B) is basically opposite to the view of the psychological antivaccinationist
    (C) is not so curious a conception of liberty as is the first assumption
    (D) is unsubstantiated
    (E) is a religious explanation of an economic phenomenon

21. The author's purpose in writing this paragraph is most probably to
    (A) denounce the psychological anti-vaccinationists
    (B) demonstrate that the question under discussion is an economic rather than a psychological problem
    (C) prove the maxim "Ye shall know the truth, and the truth shall make you free"
    (D) suggest that ostentation is not an inescapable phenomenon of settled social existence
    (E) prove the inability of economics to account for ostentation

22. You do not succeed unless you take a gamble. Gambling is foolish. Therefore, only fools succeed.

    Which of the following would weaken the conclusion the most?
    (A) Most fools gamble.
    (B) Most fools do not succeed.
    (C) Some succeed without gambling.
    (D) Most successful gamblers are not foolish.
    (E) A fool and his money are soon parted.

23. Christopher Lasch is, in one sense, a modern-day Aesop. The ancient Greek philosopher once said, "Self-conceit may lead to self-destruction," and this warning is echoed by Lasch in his best-selling study, *The Culture of Narcissism.*

    Which of the following excerpts from the above passage is least relevant to a comparison between Lasch and Aesop?
    (A) "warning is echoed"   (B) "ancient Greek philosopher"   (C) "modern-day Aesop"
    (D) "best-selling" (E) "in one sense"

24. In the Soviet Union, it is a crime for anyone to offer religious instruction to a person under the age of 18. The overtly religious are systematically excluded from any higher education, or position of professional responsibility. By definition, every person holding official power is an atheist. And religious activists, most especially those who share Dr. Graham's evangelical spirit, are prime candidates for the torment of life in the Gulag Archipelago.

Which of the following assumptions does the author of the above passage necessarily make about his readers?
(A) They know who Dr. Graham is.
(B) They are enemies of the Soviet Union.
(C) They are not religious activists.
(D) They have been offered religious instruction.
(E) They may become evangelical themselves.

25. There is something sinister about progress. Just look at the folks who cling to the past, and whom do you find?—friendly, neighborly types who respect traditional religious and moral values and who fear a machine age that will replace the leisurely back-fence conversation with instantaneous "telephonatronics."

With which of the following would the author be likely to agree?
(A) Progress is our most important product.
(B) We have nothing to fear except fear itself.
(C) Lack of progress coincides with a migration from the cities.
(D) The enemies of the future are always the very nicest people.
(E) The best people own no machines.

26. Far too often today, concern about nuclear weapons is focused exclusively on the superpowers. The issue of nuclear proliferation is, at best, considered secondary. Yet more and more nations are moving to the threshold of the nuclear club. The search for ways to curb nuclear proliferation deserves as much attention as the quest for arms control between the U.S. and the USSR.

Which of the following statements, if true, would weaken the argument above?
(A) Nuclear proliferation is given more attention than human rights.
(B) All nations, including the United States and the USSR, have promised not to abuse their nuclear technology.
(C) An arms reduction by the United States and the USSR will result in an overall arms reduction by other countries.
(D) Two adversary middle-Eastern countries have aimed nuclear missiles at each other.
(E) Arms control in general has never before received as much attention as it has in this decade.

STOP

IF YOU FINISH BEFORE TIME HAS ELAPSED, CHECK YOUR WORK ON THIS SECTION OF THE TEST ONLY. DO NOT GO ON TO THE NEXT SECTION OF THE TEST UNTIL TIME IS UP FOR THIS SECTION.

SECTION VI
EVALUATION OF FACTS

Time—35 Minutes
37 Questions

Directions:
This section consists of several sets; each set presents a factual statement, the description of a dispute, and two rules. In some sets, the rules will be conflicting. Be sure that you consider each rule independently and not as an exception to the other. Following each set are questions; select from four choices (given below) the one that best categorizes each question, based upon the relationship of one or both of the rules to the dispute. Darken the appropriate space on your answer sheet.

(A) A relevant question which you can only answer by choosing between the rules.
(B) A relevant question which you cannot answer because you need more information or additional rules, but which does not require a choice between the rules.
(C) A relevant question which you can answer by referring to the facts or rules, or both.
(D) An irrelevant question or one which is only remotely relevant to the outcome of the dispute.

Set 1

FACTS

Sara wanted a skateboard. Her father thought she was too young to have one, but Sara's persistent complaints wore him down. Trying to save money, her father bought her a skateboard that the manufacturers had sold to the retailer at a very low price because of a defect in the wheels. While riding her new skateboard Sara fell and broke three teeth. She left the skateboard by the front steps while she went with her mother to the dentist. Her father tripped over the skateboard, fell down the steps, and dislocated his shoulder.

DISPUTE

Sara's father sued the skateboard retailer for his and his daughter's injuries. The seller contested.

RULE I

The seller of merchandise is liable for injuries resulting from the product only if the injury was directly due to the product's being defective.

RULE II

The seller of a product is liable for all injuries occurring because of the use of the product only if the product was used as intended by the seller during the time of injury.

QUESTIONS

1. Was the father's injury directly due to the defect?

2. Was the skateboard defective?

3. If the suit was only for Sara's injuries, will her father win?

4. When was the skateboard purchased?

5. If the board was not defective, will the father win a suit for his injuries?

6. Did the seller know of the manufacturing defect when he sold the skateboard?

7. If the skateboard was intended for use by a teenager, will the father win a suit for Sara's injury?

Set 2

FACTS

J.R., a wealthy businessman, had made his fortune through shady dealings and backstabbing. A former partner of his, S.L., had discovered evidence that clearly showed that J.R. had cheated her out of a large sum of money two years earlier. S.L. decided to press charges. As S.L. was on her way to the court hearing, a newspaperman cornered her and pressured her for a comment. S.L. stated, "J.R. is a cheat and will get what's coming to him!" In the excitement of the interview, S.L.'s husband, who was there, added, "And J.R.'s been cheating on his taxes, too!" J.R., who heard these words while entering the courtroom, yelled in reply, "You should talk! You spent two years in prison for tax evasion!"

DISPUTE

Hearing this reply, S.L. and her husband decided to add defamation to the charges, as neither of them had ever been in prison. J.R. contested and also sued for defamation.

RULE I

One is liable for defamation if one falsely verbally demeans another to a third party. This is called "slander."

RULE II

The defamation of a person must be in writing and is punishable by a minimum fine of $500. This is called "libel."

Questions

8. If they charged J.R. with slander, were S.L. and her husband justified in adding the charge of defamation?

9. Did S.L. slander J.R.?

10. Did S.L.'s husband slander J.R.?

11. Will J.R. be convicted of defamation?

12. Should S.L.'s husband have been at the interview?

13. If J.R. had never cheated on his taxes, will S.L.'s husband be found guilty of defamation in a suit?

14. Could J.R. have cheated his other partners?

15. If J.R. had written his reply about tax evasion and mailed it to the newspapers, would he have been guilty of libel?

Set 3

FACTS

Apex Corporation and Beverly Hills Cadillac Company wished to enter into a written contract whereby Apex would buy ten cars and pay $6,000 for each of them. Delivery was to be made within one month, and payment was to be made by Apex within 90 days of delivery. Prior to signing the contract, Cadillac requested a financial statement from Apex. Not wanting to incur the expense of retaining an accountant, Apex simply changed the date on a financial statement which had been prepared for it three years ago. While that statement showed net assets of $50,000, Apex's present net assets were $25,000. Apex delivered the statement, both parties signed the contract, and the cars were delivered. Three weeks later, however, Cadillac learned that Apex's financial statement was three years out of date.

DISPUTE

Cadillac sought to recover the cars immediately, stating that the contract was invalid. Apex refused to return the cars.

RULE I

A written contract for over $50,000 signed by both parties is a valid and binding contract.

RULE II

A contract entered into because of a knowingly false representation by one party is not a valid contract.

Questions

16. If Cadillac took Apex to court, who would win?

17. If the contract was not in writing, will Apex have to return the cars?

18. Were the cars delivered on time?

19. Was the contract valid?

20. If Apex unknowingly sent Cadillac an old financial statement, was the contract valid?

Set 4

FACTS

For more than two decades, Milton and Judy had been competitors. Milton, on a dare from Judy, had scaled a five-story office building, and Judy had completed a woman's marathon. One summer, Milton decided to vacation in the Grand Canyon. As he was admiring the beautiful sunset in the canyon, Milton suddenly spotted Judy. He shouted across the canyon to her, "Hey, Judy! I'll give you a $1,000 bill if you will walk that tightrope across this gorge and come over to me and get it!" Judy, never backing down from a dare, walked across the gorge on the tightrope and demanded the money. Milton refused to give it to her, insisting, "There was no contract!"

DISPUTE

Judy sued to get the $1000 from Milton. Milton contested.

RULE I

Before there can be a legally enforceable contract, there must be an offer by one party and subsequent acceptance by the other. This acceptance can be in the form of a performance.

RULE II

A legally enforceable contract of more than $800 must be in writing.

Questions

21. Was the contract in writing?

22. Will Judy win the suit?

23. If Milton offered Judy $500 to walk the tightrope, will she win?

24. Did Judy accept?

25. Did Milton have the $1000 bill?

Set 5

FACTS

Ned falsely told Sally that his painting, "Still Life with Chrysanthemums," was a genuine Renoir but that he would sell it to her for a small amount because he needed the money. Sally was led to believe that the painting must be worth thousands and asked Al, her father, to buy it. Al, who would do anything to please Sally, went to Ned's place, pointed to the painting that fit Sally's description of it, and said, "If that's a genuine Renoir, I'll buy it." Ned, who knew that it was not genuine, said, "Yes. Sold," took Al's money, and gave him the painting. One year later, when an art expert saw the painting in Sally's house, the painting was declared to be inauthentic. Sally gave the painting to Al, who took it back to Ned to recover his money. Ned said, "Sorry, no refunds after 90 days."

DISPUTE

Al sued for fraud to recover his money. Ned contested.

RULE I

One who intentionally misrepresents the facts is guilty of fraud.

RULE II

One is not guilty of fraud if his misrepresentation causes loss of money or property valued at under $100.

Questions

26. What did Al pay for the painting?

27. If Al paid $50 for the painting, will Ned be found guilty of fraud?

28. Was the painting a good copy?

29. If Al paid $150 for the painting, will Ned be found guilty of fraud?

30. Did Ned intentionally misrepresent the facts?

Set 6

FACTS

Kid and Bud were on parole. Kid's violent temper had got him into trouble many times, but for almost a year he had not been in a fight. Walking down the street, Bud and Kid were minding their own business. They passed by three boys who were older and bigger. Jack, one of the older boys, called out, "Punk Kid!" Bud turned to Kid and said loudly, "You're not going to take that from him, are you?" Kid rushed at Jack, punched him, and knocked him down. The older boy then got up and returned the blow. A nasty fight ensued, in which Jack was seriously hurt.

DISPUTE

In a suit by Jack against Kid for battery, Kid claimed that he acted in self-defense.

RULE I

Adequate provocation justifies physical force which constitutes self-defense. Self-defense precludes battery.

RULE II

The first person to use physical force cannot claim self-defense and is liable for battery.

Questions

31. If Kid was adequately provoked, will he be guilty of battery?

32. If the court decided that Kid was not provoked, who will win the suit?

33. What is adequate provocation?

34. Who won the fight?

35. If Jack threw the first punch but missed, would Kid win the suit?

36. Did Kid use physical force first?

37. Could Bud be convicted of battery?

STOP

END OF EXAMINATION. IF YOU FINISH BEFORE TIME HAS ELAPSED, CHECK YOUR WORK ON THIS SECTION ONLY. DO NOT GO BACK TO ANY OTHER SECTION OF THE EXAMINATION.

ANSWER KEY

Section I:
Analytical Reasoning

1. D	6. A	11. D	16. D	21. B
2. A	7. C	12. C	17. D	22. E
3. E	8. C	13. E	18. E	23. E
4. B	9. B	14. E	19. B	24. D
5. B	10. B	15. C	20. D	25. C

Section IV:
Analytical Reasoning

1. D	6. E	11. D	16. B	21. B
2. C	7. D	12. E	17. A	22. B
3. B	8. B	13. C	18. E	23. D
4. E	9. B	14. B	19. C	24. E
5. C	10. E	15. E	20. D	25. B

Section II:
Evaluation of Facts

1. C	8. B	15. C	22. C	29. B
2. C	9. D	16. B	23. D	30. C
3. B	10. B	17. C	24. A	31. D
4. D	11. D	18. D	25. C	32. C
5. A	12. C	19. B	26. A	33. D
6. A	13. D	20. C	27. C	34. B
7. B	14. A	21. A	28. D	35. A

Section V:
Logical Reasoning

1. B	7. B	12. E	17. D	22. C
2. E	8. B	13. B	18. C	23. D
3. D	9. A	14. D	19. A	24. A
4. A	10. A	15. A	20. D	25. D
5. A	11. E	16. E	21. D	26. C
6. D				

Section III:
Reading Comprehension

1. B	7. D	13. D	19. E	24. E
2. A	8. D	14. B	20. D	25. E
3. E	9. D	15. C	21. B	26. D
4. B	10. B	16. A	22. B	27. B
5. C	11. D	17. B	23. C	28. B
6. C	12. B	18. D		

Section VI:
Evaluation of Facts

1. C	9. C	17. C	24. C	31. A
2. C	10. B	18. D	25. D	32. C
3. C	11. A	19. A	26. B	33. B
4. D	12. D	20. C	27. A	34. D
5. C	13. A	21. C	28. D	35. B
6. D	14. D	22. A	29. C	36. C
7. B	15. C	23. C	30. C	37. D
8. C	16. A			

MODEL TEST ANALYSIS

Doing model exams and understanding the explanations afterwards are of course important in acquainting you with typical LSAT question types and successful approaches to the questions. However, another benefit of carefully analyzing these model tests is to understand the kinds of errors you are making and thus work to minimize them. For instance, if a very high percentage of your incorrect answers is due to "careless error" or "misread problem," then perhaps you are working much too fast and should slow your pace accordingly. If your incorrect answers are due primarily to "lack of knowledge," then a careful rereading and reworking of the appropriate question-type chapter may be in order. Or if you find that you aren't completing a large number of questions because of lack of time, you may need to either increase your speed or learn to use the "one-check, two-check" technique more effectively.

This kind of analysis of the model tests will enable you to identify your particular weaknesses and thus remedy them.

Model Test Three Analysis

Section	Total Number of Questions	Number Correct	Number Incorrect	Number Unanswered*
I: Analytical Reasoning	25			
II: Evaluation of Facts	35			
III: Reading Comprehension	28			
IV: Analytical Reasoning	25			
V: Logical Reasoning	26			
VI: Evaluation of Facts	37			
TOTALS:	176			

*At this stage in your preparation, you should not be leaving any unanswered answer spaces. At least fill in a guess, as there is no penalty for a wrong answer.

Reasons for Incorrect Answers

You may wish to evaluate the explanations before completing this chart.

Section	Total Incorrect	Lack of Knowledge	Misread Problem	Careless Error	Unanswered or Wrong Guess
I: Analytical Reasoning					
II: Evaluation of Facts					
III: Reading Comprehension					
IV: Analytical Reasoning					
V: Logical Reasoning					
VI: Evaluation of Facts					
TOTALS:					

EXPLANATIONS OF ANSWERS

Section I

Answers 1–7

A diagram will help you to organize the information.

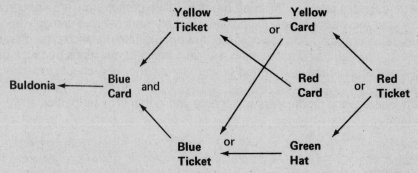

1. **D** From the diagram, a red card will get you a yellow ticket (which you already have), but you need a blue ticket with the yellow ticket to get a blue card to get into Buldonia. You have no way of getting a blue ticket.

2. **A** Statement II is true because you can use one yellow card to get a yellow ticket and the other yellow card to get a blue ticket. With both a yellow ticket and a blue ticket you can get a blue card and get into Buldonia. Statement I is true since you could trade both red tickets for yellow cards and proceed as above. Statement III is false since you have no way of getting a yellow ticket.

3. **E** Since a yellow card will get you either a blue ticket or a yellow ticket, and each of (A)–(D) will get you either a blue ticket or a yellow ticket, the combination will get you into Buldonia.

4. **B** Pair II is the only pair that will get you into Buldonia. The red card will get you a yellow ticket, and a yellow hat will get you a green hat, which will get you a blue ticket. With both a blue ticket and a yellow ticket you can get a blue card and get into Buldonia. Pairs I and III will not get you both a yellow ticket and a blue ticket.

5. **B** Choice II will get you two yellow tickets and one blue ticket instead of the other way around. Choices I and III can get you two blue tickets and one yellow ticket.

6. **A** Only III will give you two yellow tickets and one blue ticket. The two red cards will get you the two yellow tickets, and the yellow card will get you the blue ticket.

7. **C** A green ticket and a red card will each get you a yellow ticket. You have no way of getting a blue ticket.

Answers 8–14

8. **C** Statements 1, 3, 4, and 6 allow us to fill in a chart looking like this:

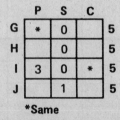

Therefore, George must have awarded Corky 2 points.

9. **B** Statements 1, 2, and 3 allow us to fill in a chart looking like this:

	P	S	C	
G		0		5
H	4	0		5
I		0		5
J		1		5

Thus, Harriet must have given her remaining 1 point to Corky.

10. **B** Since statement 3 tells us that Shmorky's only point was given to him by Josephine, we can conclude (since there isn't a "none of these" answer choice) that only Josephine gave all contestants at least 1 point each.

11. **D** To determine how many points Josephine awarded Corky, a chart may be constructed using the information given. After statement 6 your chart should look like this:

	P	S	C	
G	2	0	3	5
H	4	0	1	5
I	3	0	2	5
J		1		

Now, since statement 7 says that Porky won by 1 point, Josephine must have awarded 1 point to Porky and 3 points to Corky, so that Porky finished with 10 points, and Corky finished with 9 points. (Note that this can also be deduced from the fact that Shmorky finished with only 1 total point, leaving 19 to be divided between Porky and Corky.)

12. **C** From our chart we can see that only Corky received the same number of points (3) from both George and Josephine.

13. **E** From our chart we can see that none of the contestant pigs received at least 2 points from each judge.

14. **E** Statement 5 adds nothing helpful to complete our chart, and may be finally derived when the chart is complete.

Answers 15–18

15. **C** If Axel were a YES, he would tell the truth and would say he was a YES. Since he said he was a MAYBE, he cannot be a YES.

16. **D** If Axel were a MAYBE, he would tell the truth and lie alternately. Since he said he was a MAYBE, his first response would be truthful. Thus, his third response must also be the truth. Thus, Carmen is a NO. His second response then has to be a lie. This means that Benty must be something other than a YES, which could not be possible since they all must belong to different clubs. Therefore, Axel is not a MAYBE. Since Axel is not a YES or a MAYBE, he must be a NO. Therefore, Benty is not a YES. This leaves the MAYBE as the only other alternative for Benty. Thus, Carmen is the YES. So Benty, being a MAYBE, could give a true or false answer to his question. Thus, any of the alternatives are possible.

17. **D** I and II are true. This follows from the above explanation.

18. **E** This follows from the above explanation.

	YES	NO	MAYBE
A		x	
B			x
C	x		

Answers 19–25

19. **B** From diagram 1 below, we see that I and III are true and II is false.

20. **D** From diagram 2, we see that only (D) is false. Truckner sat two places to the *right* (not left) of Eileen.

21. **B** From diagram 2 and fact 7, we see that Beatrice must be Truckner's first name, giving diagram 3.

22. **E** From diagram 3 and fact 6, the only place for Frances is between Beatrice and Dexter. Thus Upland's first name is Frances and Eileen's last name is Zipley. Therefore, all three statements are true.

23. **E** There is only one seat left for Clyde. In diagram 5, we see that all three statements are true; thus, none is false.

24. **D** Using either fact 2 or fact 3, we can complete the seating arrangement, as shown in diagram 6.

25. **C** Statements II and III are true. Statement I is false since Xymer sat two places to the *right* of Upland.

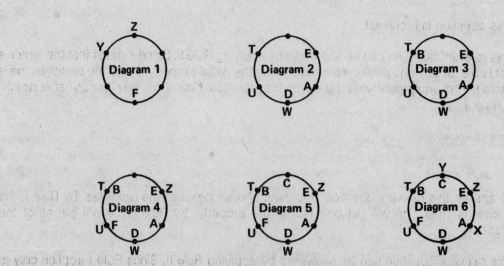

Section II

Set 1

1. **C** This relevant question can be reasonably answered from the facts and rules. Since Mr. Tam took reasonable precautions to secure the property from entrance and did have a "NO TRESPASSING" sign posted, he is not liable.

2. **C** This relevant question can be reasonably answered from the facts and Rule I. If there had been no sign posted, the Wilsons would not have been trespassing.

3. **B** This question is relevant, but to answer it, you need more information. We do not know whether Mr. Tam took other reasonable precautions to secure the property from entrance.

4. **D** This is irrelevant.

5. **A** To answer this relevant question, you need to choose between the two rules. By Rule I, Carl could not recover damages as he was a trespasser. By Rule II, he could recover damages.

Set 2

6. **A** To answer this relevant question, you must choose between the two rules. By Rule I, they will be reimbursed, as Joe was liable. By Rule II, since the Rosens left the premises, Joe was not liable.

7. **B** To answer this relevant question, you need more information. We do not know whether the chain was defective.

8. **B** To answer this relevant question, you need more information. Since Mr. Rosen was trying to alleviate a situation that was possibly caused by Joe's Chainery, we need more rules to determine whether he is liable.

9. **D** This question is irrelevant.

10. **B** This is a relevant question because it ties in to Rule I. But we need more information to answer the question.

11. **D** This question is irrelevant.

12. **C** This relevant question can be answered by applying Rule II. Since it states that the rentor is not liable for any equipment malfunction after the rental property leaves the premises, he is liable for the equipment while it is still on the premises. Notice the "key" words "after which" in Rule II.

13. **D** This is irrelevant.

Set 3

14. **A** To answer this relevant question, you must choose between the two rules. By Rule I, the answer is "yes," he will get only half of the property. By Rule II, he will get all of the property.

15. **C** This relevant question can be answered by applying Rule II. Since Rule I applies only to nonmarital relationships, by Rule II Dino would get the property.

16. **B** This relevant question cannot be answered without additional information. If Lena and Dino had lived together for only 1½ years, Rule II does not apply. But even the application of Rule I does not tell us who gets the house.

17. **C** This question is relevant, as it ties into the rules, and can be readily answered from the facts. No, she was not the primary contributor.

18. **D** This question is irrelevant.

Set 4

19. **B** This relevant question cannot be answered without additional facts.

20. **C** This relevant question can be answered by the application of Rule I. Yes, the Hatfields would be liable. Rule II refers to intentionally causing harm or damage and therefore would not apply.

21. **A** To answer this relevant question, you must choose between the two rules. By Rule I, the property owner is liable. By Rule II, Mrs. McCoy will be liable.

22. **C** This relevant question can be answered by applying Rule II. Because the breaking of the table was unintentional, Mrs. McCoy would not be liable.

23. **D** This question is irrelevant.

Set 5

24. **A** To answer this relevant question, you must choose between the two rules. By Rule I, George will not win, because he did not lift the weight over his head. By Rule II, George will win, because he lifted the most weight.

25. **C** You can answer this relevant question from the facts and rules. Since the rules are conflicting, they will not end the dispute.

26. **A** To answer this relevant question, you must choose between the two rules. By Rule I, Bob will be declared the winner, but by Rule II, he will not.

27. **C** This relevant question can be answered from the facts and rules. Tom cannot be the winner by either Rule I or Rule II.

28. **D** This is irrelevant.

29. **B** To answer this relevant question, you need more information. The question said Bob "attempted" to lift 160 pounds. We do not know whether he lifted it.

Set 6

30. **C** This relevant question can be reasonably answered from the facts and application of the rules. Since the rules specifically deal with only games won, and do not consider total points, Shelly will not be invited back.

31. **D** This question is irrelevant.

32. **C** This relevant question can be answered by using the facts and rules. Since Phil was invited back, and since Tina won the most games, then, by Rule I, the only way Phil could have been invited back was by winning five games or more.

33. **D** This question is irrelevant.

34. **B** To answer this relevant question, you need more information. If Shelly won three more games, then she has won at least six games, but we do not know how many games the others won.

35. **A** To answer this relevant question, you must choose between the two rules. By Rule I, Tina will not be invited back, as you need to win at least five games; but by Rule II, she would have won the most games and therefore should be invited back.

Section III

Passage 1

1. **B** (A) and (E) are implied in the passage: "Peace with honor" is implicitly related to two of the desired goals—"international order" and the protection of the United States; "sympathy for U.S. forces" is implied by the final sentence, which says that U.S. forces are outnumbered. However, the *best* answer is (B) because anti-Communist sentiment is explicitly described and associated with the overall conclusions of the passage.

2. **A** The terms describing the state paper are positive; it is called "important" and "imposing"; such terms imply praise of Truman, who is responsible for the project. (D) is unsupported by extensive and extremely positive remarks. The passage expresses or implies no negative judgments, so (B), (C), and (E) should be eliminated.

3. **E** In the first paragraph we are told, "The document was imposing in its scope and depth," and we are given details supporting this idea. A possible choice, (D), may be eliminated because the conclusions of the study are clearly subjective—anti-Soviet in sentiment.

4. **B** The final sentence stresses that U.S. forces are outnumbered, thus implying the value of an increase; otherwise, they are "literally at the mercy of the Soviet government."

5. **C** All other choices are mentioned in the passage. The Truman containment policy is a real historical phenomenon, but is not mentioned or implied in the passage.

6. **C** The "understanding" of the Soviets that is described in this passage is one that cites no positive qualities, and characterizes the Russians as threatening enemies. A Russian would certainly not accept such a characterization as accurate.

7. **D** Many people were involved in the drafting of the document, including "other persons with special knowledge of foreign affairs"; such persons could be affiliated with any or no branch of government.

Passage 2

8. **D** The title, as well as the first sentence of each version, highlights studies as the primary subject; their relative value emerges in each passage when studies are discussed relative to other pastimes. Also, studies themselves are given relative value; for instance, spending too much time studying is "sloth."

9. **D** Distilled books are compared to distilled water, "flashy" but not substantial. No opinion on the subject is expressed in the earlier version, so (C) may be eliminated.

10. **B** Many of the changes that the author makes in the second version are changes in punctuation; it is apparent that he makes such changes quite deliberately. (E) is incorrect because the intended function of the chosen punctuation marks may be easily analyzed.

11. **D** See the statement between lines 8 and 11 in the earlier version, and between lines 12 and 15 in the later version. Both assert that few books are to be "chewed and digested." Other choices are either not mentioned in either passage, or mentioned in only one or the other.

12. **B** The later version is *expanded;* the only choice which indicates expansion is *amplification.* The second version does contain more evidence than the first, but evidence is a type of amplification, as are so many of the other sorts of changes.

13. **D** The later passage concludes by mentioning bowling and shooting as very different activities from studying. All other choices are mentioned in conjunction with studies.

14. **B** This phrase occurs in a list of phrases that begins with "Histories *make men* wise" and continues mentioning only the subject and its effect in each subsequent phrase, so that "make(s) men" continues to be understood but not expressed.

Passage 3

15. **C** Although the passage discusses French taste to an extent, this is done only to further expand and clarify the overall comparison between Englishmen and Americans. The author does not really argue that Englishmen are better than Americans (E); he mentions the good and bad points of both nationalities.

16. **A** When the author talks of American aspirations, he notes that Americans are always "fearful of a fall." When he calls aspiring Americans "dizzy" (B), he is speaking metaphorically rather than literally.

17. **B** The author explicitly "detests" French taste, but notes that "the world is against me."

18. **D** The passage ends with a discussion of taste, the third of four contrasting characteristics introduced. Politics is not discussed. Each of the other choices is a characteristic mentioned in the passage.

19. **E** Each of the other choices in the passage is associated with a *discomfort* of French taste.

20. **D** In this final section, the author justifies his assertion that the English and Americans differ in tastes by stressing that English taste is not taking the "direction" of American taste, that is, closer to French taste. (C) is a characteristic mentioned at an earlier point in the passage.

21. **B** The author is obviously implying that his room lacks supplies for *washing,* such as a washbowl. Such supplies are *useful,* but the gold clock seems rather useless in the author's view.

Passage 4

22. **B** The passage discusses the terms *hypothesis, theory, law,* and, to a lesser extent, *datum,* all to examine the function of language "in the development of scientific understanding." The second paragraph discusses the method of developing a hypothesis, but does not itself develop one, so (C) is not a good answer.

23. **C** Toward the end of the passage, the author expresses his skepticism about *natural law:* it is a term "dangerous . . . to employ." All other choices are agreeable to the author.

24. **E** The author's parenthetical remarks in paragraphs 2 and 3 emphasize that hypothesis is a *word,* a *symbol,* which stands for (in reference to) an action. He is pointing out the difference between language and what it stands for.

25. **E** In the third paragraph we learn that "As the evidence in favor of a hypothesis . . . accumulates to a convincing degree," it often becomes a theory.

26. **D** All other choices are explicitly refuted in the passage. The author begins the passage by mentioning scientific assumptions such as equations, and then states that the hypothesis is a much more important function.

27. **B** The long second paragraph describing the development of a hypothesis stresses that a hypothesis is a "colored light," that is, subjective and subject to question. The author's claim that a hypothesis may be abandoned suggests that not all hypotheses are useful (E).

28. **B** This is stated at the end of the first paragraph: hypotheses are "not always readily grasped."

Section IV

Answers 1–7

From the information given, the following chart may be drawn to help you to answer the questions:

	L	A	Dr.	P.O.	C.D.
Kelly	✓	X	X	X	X
Clyde	X		X		X
Roland	X			X	X
Fred	X	X			X
Harriet	X	X	X	X	✓

Note the following: In statement 2, since Kelly is *not* the doctor (see statement 1), then Fred cannot be the accountant. And in statement 4, since Harriet is not the lawyer (see statement 6), then Clyde cannot be the doctor.

1. **D** From our chart we can see that the only persons left to be the accountant, the doctor, and the police officer are Clyde, Roland, and Fred.

2. **C** From the chart we can see that Clyde is not the lawyer, the doctor, or the cab driver.

3. **B** If Roland is the doctor, then from our chart we can see that Fred must be the police officer, and thus Clyde must be the accountant.

4. **E** If Clyde is not the accountant, he must be the police officer. Therefore Fred must be the doctor, leaving Roland to be the accountant. Thus all of I, II, and III are true.

5. **C** If Fred is the police officer, then Clyde must be the accountant.

6. **E** The doctor could be either Roland or Fred.

7. **D** If the cab driver, the lawyer, and the accountant are in the cab, then Harriet (cab driver) and Kelly (lawyer) are definitely in the cab. Since the accountant is either Clyde or Roland, then either of them *could* possibly be also in the cab. Thus, the answer is Harriet, Roland, and Kelly (I, III, and IV).

Answers 8-14.

Drawing a simple diagram will help answer the questions. Note, however, that there are several possible diagrams. First, since three of the women are together at one end of the line, these women could be at either the beginning or the end:

W	W	W								
1	2	3	4	5	6	7	8	9	10	11
								W	W	W

Then note that, since a man never stands next to another man, there can only be two possible arrangements of men for each of the above arrangements of women:

W	W	W	M	W/C	M/C	C/C	C/C	C/M	C/W	M
1	2	3	4	5	6	7	8	9	10	11
M	W/C	M/C	C/C	C/C	C/M	C/W	M	W	W	W

Now the questions are more easily answered.

8. **B** Note that if a child is in the sixth place (the middle four possible arrangements) then a woman must be in the second place.

9. **B** Since the rules state that three of the women stand next to each other at one end of the line, then a woman must be either second or tenth (second to last).

10. **E** All of the choices must be true except choice (E). If a woman is third, a child could be sixth, as in the second arrangement.

11. **D** If a girl is second and a boy is third, it can only be the fourth arrangement (the bottom arrangement) because that is the only time children are in the second and third positions. Since the other two children are in the fourth and fifth positions, the two girls cannot be next to each other.

12. **E** If a boy is eighth, we may consider both the first and second arrangements. Therefore, a man could be last (in fact, he must be last) and a girl could be tenth.

13. **C** If a man is fourth, we may consider the first and second arrangements. Therefore, women *must* be in the first and second positions.

14. **B** If each man is next to at least one woman, we may rule out the first and fourth arrangements. Therefore, considering the other two arrangements, only that a woman is second must necessarily be true.

Answers 15-18

The following ordering of information might have been helpful:

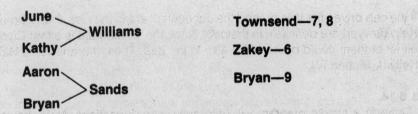

June
Kathy ⟩ Williams

Aaron
Bryan ⟩ Sands

Townsend—7, 8

Zakey—6

Bryan—9

15. **E** From statement 2 we know that Sands is a boy and Williams is a girl. From statement 4 Townsend must be a boy. Thus the girls' names are Williams and Zakey.

16. **B** From statement 3 Bryan is the 9-year-old. From statement 4 Townsend is the other boy, and his age is between the ages of the two girls. So his age must be 7, and his first name is Aaron. Thus, the boys' ages are 7 and 9. Since Townsend is Aaron and Williams and Zakey are girls, Bryan must be Sands.

17. **A** From statement 3 Bryan is 9, so Aaron cannot be 9. From statement 4, Kathy must be 8 and June must be 6. Statement 5 tells us that Zakey is the youngest, or 6.

18. **E** From statement 4, Kathy is older than June, so Kathy is 8 and June is 6. From statement 5, Zakey must be June, leaving Kathy to be Williams.

Answers 19–25

19. **C** First we draw a diagram to show the height comparisons:

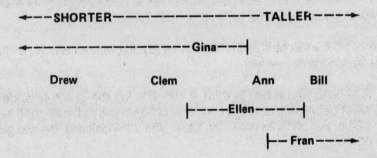

←——SHORTER——————————— TALLER——→

←———————————— Gina——⊣

Drew   Clem   Ann   Bill

⊢————Ellen————⊣

⊢— Fran ————→

We see that Drew is shorter than Ann. Thus III is false. Statements I and II could be true.

20. **D** Since Fran is taller than Ellen and Ellen is taller than Clem, Fran is taller than Clem.

21. **B** Since Fran is taller than Ellen, and if Ellen is taller than Ann, then Fran must be taller than Ann. Thus I is true. Since Ann is taller than Drew, Fran must be taller than Drew. Thus, III is true. Statement II could be true, but does not have to be.

22. **B** From statement 3 Drew is shorter than Ann. From statement 1 Ann is shorter than Bill. It follows that Drew is shorter than Bill.

23. **D** All three statements could be true.

24. **E** (A), (B), (C), and (D) are false by inspecting the chart. Only (E) can be deduced.

25. **B** Since Fran is taller than Ellen, Ann must also be taller than Ellen. Therefore I is true. Since Gina is shorter than Ann, Gina must be shorter than Fran too. Thus, III is true. Statement II could be true but does not have to be, since there is an overlap in heights between Gina and Ellen.

Section V

1. **B** The passage states, "Those under . . . 18 . . . account for nearly half of the arrests for the seven major crimes . . . yet . . . courts are obliged to treat these young hard-core hoodlums . . . ." (A) is a close answer; however, the author is not pointing out that crime has increased, but that violent crime has become more disproportionate.

2. **E** All of these are assumed by the author. He would not rely on statistical trend lines if they were not accurate predictors (I). If the years from 1967 to 1976 *were* abnormal years, his statistics would be suspect (II). He finally makes a statement grouping the laws in most states as handling juveniles in the same manner, therefore assuming that the laws are consistent involving juveniles (III).

3. **D** If the FBI's national statistics are inaccurate, then violent juvenile crime may not be disproportionate, thus nullifying the argument. (E) is a close answer, as this would also weaken the argument, but not as significantly as (D).

4. **A** Condition II will not help, since, with only one chore taking at least 1 hour, the entire job could be completed in less than 2 hours. Condition III will not help, since Mike may have only two chores. Condition I implies at least two 1-hour chores.

5. **A** If Juan ends up with more marbles than Alvin, that means that Alvin must have less than five marbles. If Maria can end up with more marbles than Juan, then Juan must also have less than five marbles. We do not know how many marbles Maria has. Thus, I and II may be true, but III is false.

6. **D** (B) and (E) weaken the argument, (A) repeats the argument, and (C) makes no sense, since "average height" is a *single* composite of all heights.

7. **B** Pointing out that "there are too many variables in this type of study" weakens the argument tremendously, because isolating the reason for the growth increase now becomes very difficult. Thus, we could not deduce that modern foods stimulate growth. (D) is close, as it also weakens the argument, but it isn't specific enough. If (D) were "*too* small," then it would be an excellent answer.

8. **B** The information in (B) directly corresponds to the "significant" conclusion in the paragraph's final sentence. (A) is beyond the time scope of the paragraph; (C) is untenable because the final sentence states that accidents are not characteristic of advanced years. There is no evidence in the paragraph which supports (D) or (E).

9. **A** All of the statements except (A) are solidly supported by a comparison of the "cause lists" for 1900, 1910, and 1945. (A) is a conclusion that may be true, but it is not an issue the paragraph raises.

10. **A** We are not provided with an implicit or explicit clue to what the temptation is, but we are told that it occurs late (B), has a bitter effect (C), is caused by fate (D), and is "supremely" important (E).

11. **E** The passage states that 90 percent of our mind controls 95 percent of our behavior, thus implying that the other 10 percent of our mind controls 5 percent of our behavior. The

passage does not state or imply that "dreams, spontaneous recall, and slips of speech constitute about 90 percent of our behavior."

12. **E** The passage states that 90 percent of our mind controls 95 percent of our behavior; therefore, a small part of our mind controls a small part of our behavior, as the other 10 percent of our mind must control 5 percent of our behavior.

13. **B** I may be false, since nothing was said about the majority of students. II and III must be true.

14. **D** (B), "irrelevant," and (E), "simplistic," are inconsistent with the implied importance of the statement. (C) does not advance the argument; it merely supplies obvious synonyms for language and thought. (A) is self-contradictory; something is not likely to be at once logical *and* obscure.

15. **A** Since the passage is all about the unsolved misunderstanding of the relation between language and thought, its subject remains, of course, ambiguous.

16. **E** The passage begins with a sentence about the value of on-the-job training, but leaves that topic rather than developing it. The implication of this first sentence is that on-the-job training has just been discussed, thus allowing a transition to consequent topics.

17. **D** This choice summarizes the argument of the paragraph. (A) contradicts the "two-sidedness" of lying that the author explains; (B) and (E) are unsupported conclusions; and (C) is an overstatement because it employs "only."

18. **C** Neither (A) nor (B) is implied, because no comparison is made with other brands of soap. Nor is (D) correct because there is no implication regarding what is economically the best value or price. And though the advertisement states that Cleenup is good for household jobs, it doesn't infer that household chores are its only range. That Cleenup Soap may be used for scouring pots and pans, whitening the sink, and performing other household chores indicates that it can be used for many cleaning jobs (C).

19. **A** The renter's third statement contradicts his second statement.

20. **D** The notion that "the need for ostentation is a universal species characteristic" has "no rational basis." According to the professional economist, "the craving for personal distinction" is fostered by propaganda and so-called good breeding (A) and its effects cannot be eradicated. The writer does not imply that the economist's assumption is fostered by the same influences.

21. **D** The author sets out to demonstrate this thesis by attacking the validity of the two assumptions made by those who oppose his view and who believe ostentation is either a natural right or an unavoidable impulse in man.

22. **C** (C) is the choice, since it contradicts the original statement. (A), (D), and (E) are obviously incorrect. They do not have anything to do with the problem. (B) would tend to strengthen the argument.

23. **D** The fact that Lasch's book is a best-seller has nothing to do with his similarity to Aesop, at least not in the context of this passage. Each of the other choices reinforces or clarifies the comparison.

24. **A** Dr. Graham is not given a full name, and we are not told anything beyond the mention of his evangelical spirit. Therefore, we must conclude that the author is writing to an audience

already familiar with the identity and significance of Dr. Graham. Each of the other choices is a possible but not necessary underlying assumption.

25. **D** The author stresses the nice qualities of "folks who cling to the past" (in other words, "the enemies of the future"). (A) contradicts the author's viewpoint, and the other choices provide irrelevant or unsubstantiated conclusions.

26. **C** This choice ties reduced nuclear proliferation to arms reduction by the United States and the USSR, thus weakening the author's argument that proliferation and arms control are separate issues. (D) strengthens the argument. (A), (B), and (E) are tangential if not irrelevant.

Section VI

Set 1

1. **C** This relevant question can be answered from the facts. No, the father's injury was indirectly related to the defect.

2. **C** This relevant question can be readily answered from the facts. Yes, the skateboard was defective.

3. **C** This relevant question can be answered from the facts and the rules. By Rule I, Sara's father will win because the injury was directly due to the defect. By Rule II, Sara's father will again win, this time because Sara was using the skateboard as intended.

4. **D** This question is irrelevant.

5. **C** This relevant question can be answered from the facts and rules. If the board was not defective, by Rule I, the seller is not liable. By Rule II, since the board was not used as intended when the father's injuries were incurred, the seller is not liable. No, Sara's father will not win the suit for his injuries.

6. **D** This question is irrelevant.

7. **B** To answer this relevant question, you need more information. You need to know Sara's age to see whether Rule II applies.

Set 2

8. **C** This relevant question can be reasonably answered from the facts. Since S.L. and her husband had not been to prison, this was clearly slander and they were justified.

9. **C** Since S.L. did not falsely verbally demean J.R., by application of Rule I, she did not slander him.

10. **B** To answer this relevant question, you need more information. We do not know whether S.L.'s husband's accusations are false; therefore, we cannot apply Rule I.

11. **A** To answer this relevant question, you must choose between the two rules. Each rule will give you a different answer. By Rule I, J.R. is guilty of defamation as he did falsely verbally demean another to a third party. But Rule II states that defamation must be in writing; therefore, J.R. is not guilty.

12. **D** This is irrelevant.

13. **A** To answer this relevant question, you must choose between the two rules. Each rule will give you a different answer. By Rule I, S.L.'s husband will be found guilty of defamation; by Rule II, he will not.

14. **D** This is irrelevant.

15. **C** This relevant question can be answered by applying Rule II. If the reply were in writing, then J.R. would have been guilty of libel.

Set 3

16. **A** To answer this relevant question, you must choose between the rules. Each rule gives you a different outcome. By Rule I, Apex would win, because a written contract is binding. By Rule II, Cadillac would win because of the knowingly false representation.

17. **C** This relevant question can be answered by applying Rule II. Rule I does not apply if the contract was not in writing. By Rule II, the contract is invalid; therefore, the cars will have to be returned.

18. **D** This question is irrelevant, even though it can be readily answered.

19. **A** To answer this relevant question, you must choose between the rules. Each rule gives you a different outcome. By Rule I, since the contract was in writing and was for over $50,000, the contract was valid. But by Rule II, the contract was not valid, since it was entered into because of knowingly false representation.

20. **C** This relevant question can be answered by applying Rule I. Since the contract was in writing and was for over $50,000, the contract was valid. If Apex unknowingly sent an old financial statement, Rule II does not apply.

Set 4

21. **C** This relevant question can be answered from the facts. No, the contract was not in writing.

22. **A** To answer this relevant question, you must choose between the rules. Each rule gives you a different outcome. By Rule I, Judy will win. By Rule II, she will lose, since the contract was not in writing.

23. **C** This relevant question can be answered by applying Rule I. By Rule I, Judy will win. Rule II does not apply if the offer was for less than $800.

24. **C** This relevant question can be answered from the facts and Rule I. Judy's acceptance was in the form of her performance.

25. **D** This question is irrelevant.

Set 5

26. **B** To answer this relevant question you need more information. The actual price is not stated in the facts.

27. **A** To answer this relevant question you must choose between the rules. Each rule gives a different outcome. By Rule I, Ned is guilty of fraud. By Rule II, since the value was under $100, Ned is not guilty.

28. **D** This question is irrelevant.

29. **C** This relevant question can be answered by applying Rule I. By Rule I, Ned will be found guilty. If the amount paid was $150, Rule II does not apply.

30. **C** This relevant question can be answered from the facts. Yes, Ned did intentionally misrepresent the facts.

Set 6

31. **A** To answer this relevant question, you must choose between the rules. Each rule gives a different outcome. By Rule I, Kid will not be guilty, since he was adequately provoked. By Rule II, he will be guilty, since he was the first person to use physical force.

32. **C** This relevant question can be answered by the rules and facts. Rule I does not apply if Kid was not provoked. By Rule II, he will be guilty since he used physical force first.

33. **B** To answer this relevant question you need another rule.

34. **D** This question is irrelevant.

35. **B** To answer this relevant question, you need more information. You don't know whether throwing the first punch was adequate provocation.

36. **C** This relevant question can be readily answered from the facts. Yes, Kid used physical force first.

37. **D** This question is irrelevant.

Chapter

10

Model Test Four

This chapter contains full-length Model Test Four. It is geared to the format of the LSAT, and it is complete with answers and explanations. It is equivalent to the LSAT in question structure, number of questions, level of difficulty, and time allotments. (The questions used are not taken directly from the LSAT, as those questions are copyrighted and may not be reproduced.)

Model Test Four should be taken under strict test conditions. The test begins with a 30-minute Writing Sample which is not scored. Thereafter each section is 35 minutes in length.

Section	Description	Number of Questions	Time Allowed
	Writing Sample		30 minutes
I	Reading Comprehension	28	35 minutes
II	Analytical Reasoning	26	35 minutes
III	Evaluation of Facts	36	35 minutes
IV	Logical Reasoning	26	35 minutes
V	Analytical Reasoning	23	35 minutes
VI	Logical Reasoning	26	35 minutes
TOTALS:		165	240 minutes

Now please turn to the next page, remove your answer sheets, and begin Model Test Four.

ANSWER SHEET—MODEL TEST FOUR
LAW SCHOOL ADMISSION TEST (LSAT)

Section I:
Reading Comprehension

1. Ⓐ Ⓑ Ⓒ Ⓓ Ⓔ
2. Ⓐ Ⓑ Ⓒ Ⓓ Ⓔ
3. Ⓐ Ⓑ Ⓒ Ⓓ Ⓔ
4. Ⓐ Ⓑ Ⓒ Ⓓ Ⓔ
5. Ⓐ Ⓑ Ⓒ Ⓓ Ⓔ
6. Ⓐ Ⓑ Ⓒ Ⓓ Ⓔ
7. Ⓐ Ⓑ Ⓒ Ⓓ Ⓔ
8. Ⓐ Ⓑ Ⓒ Ⓓ Ⓔ
9. Ⓐ Ⓑ Ⓒ Ⓓ Ⓔ
10. Ⓐ Ⓑ Ⓒ Ⓓ Ⓔ
11. Ⓐ Ⓑ Ⓒ Ⓓ Ⓔ
12. Ⓐ Ⓑ Ⓒ Ⓓ Ⓔ
13. Ⓐ Ⓑ Ⓒ Ⓓ Ⓔ
14. Ⓐ Ⓑ Ⓒ Ⓓ Ⓔ
15. Ⓐ Ⓑ Ⓒ Ⓓ Ⓔ
16. Ⓐ Ⓑ Ⓒ Ⓓ Ⓔ
17. Ⓐ Ⓑ Ⓒ Ⓓ Ⓔ
18. Ⓐ Ⓑ Ⓒ Ⓓ Ⓔ
19. Ⓐ Ⓑ Ⓒ Ⓓ Ⓔ
20. Ⓐ Ⓑ Ⓒ Ⓓ Ⓔ
21. Ⓐ Ⓑ Ⓒ Ⓓ Ⓔ
22. Ⓐ Ⓑ Ⓒ Ⓓ Ⓔ
23. Ⓐ Ⓑ Ⓒ Ⓓ Ⓔ
24. Ⓐ Ⓑ Ⓒ Ⓓ Ⓔ
25. Ⓐ Ⓑ Ⓒ Ⓓ Ⓔ
26. Ⓐ Ⓑ Ⓒ Ⓓ Ⓔ
27. Ⓐ Ⓑ Ⓒ Ⓓ Ⓔ
28. Ⓐ Ⓑ Ⓒ Ⓓ Ⓔ

Section II:
Analytical Reasoning

1. Ⓐ Ⓑ Ⓒ Ⓓ Ⓔ
2. Ⓐ Ⓑ Ⓒ Ⓓ Ⓔ
3. Ⓐ Ⓑ Ⓒ Ⓓ Ⓔ
4. Ⓐ Ⓑ Ⓒ Ⓓ Ⓔ
5. Ⓐ Ⓑ Ⓒ Ⓓ Ⓔ
6. Ⓐ Ⓑ Ⓒ Ⓓ Ⓔ
7. Ⓐ Ⓑ Ⓒ Ⓓ Ⓔ
8. Ⓐ Ⓑ Ⓒ Ⓓ Ⓔ
9. Ⓐ Ⓑ Ⓒ Ⓓ Ⓔ
10. Ⓐ Ⓑ Ⓒ Ⓓ Ⓔ
11. Ⓐ Ⓑ Ⓒ Ⓓ Ⓔ
12. Ⓐ Ⓑ Ⓒ Ⓓ Ⓔ
13. Ⓐ Ⓑ Ⓒ Ⓓ Ⓔ
14. Ⓐ Ⓑ Ⓒ Ⓓ Ⓔ
15. Ⓐ Ⓑ Ⓒ Ⓓ Ⓔ
16. Ⓐ Ⓑ Ⓒ Ⓓ Ⓔ
17. Ⓐ Ⓑ Ⓒ Ⓓ Ⓔ
18. Ⓐ Ⓑ Ⓒ Ⓓ Ⓔ
19. Ⓐ Ⓑ Ⓒ Ⓓ Ⓔ
20. Ⓐ Ⓑ Ⓒ Ⓓ Ⓔ
21. Ⓐ Ⓑ Ⓒ Ⓓ Ⓔ
22. Ⓐ Ⓑ Ⓒ Ⓓ Ⓔ
23. Ⓐ Ⓑ Ⓒ Ⓓ Ⓔ
24. Ⓐ Ⓑ Ⓒ Ⓓ Ⓔ
25. Ⓐ Ⓑ Ⓒ Ⓓ Ⓔ
26. Ⓐ Ⓑ Ⓒ Ⓓ Ⓔ

Section III:
Evaluation of Facts

1. Ⓐ Ⓑ Ⓒ Ⓓ
2. Ⓐ Ⓑ Ⓒ Ⓓ
3. Ⓐ Ⓑ Ⓒ Ⓓ
4. Ⓐ Ⓑ Ⓒ Ⓓ
5. Ⓐ Ⓑ Ⓒ Ⓓ
6. Ⓐ Ⓑ Ⓒ Ⓓ
7. Ⓐ Ⓑ Ⓒ Ⓓ
8. Ⓐ Ⓑ Ⓒ Ⓓ
9. Ⓐ Ⓑ Ⓒ Ⓓ
10. Ⓐ Ⓑ Ⓒ Ⓓ
11. Ⓐ Ⓑ Ⓒ Ⓓ
12. Ⓐ Ⓑ Ⓒ Ⓓ
13. Ⓐ Ⓑ Ⓒ Ⓓ
14. Ⓐ Ⓑ Ⓒ Ⓓ
15. Ⓐ Ⓑ Ⓒ Ⓓ
16. Ⓐ Ⓑ Ⓒ Ⓓ
17. Ⓐ Ⓑ Ⓒ Ⓓ
18. Ⓐ Ⓑ Ⓒ Ⓓ
19. Ⓐ Ⓑ Ⓒ Ⓓ
20. Ⓐ Ⓑ Ⓒ Ⓓ
21. Ⓐ Ⓑ Ⓒ Ⓓ
22. Ⓐ Ⓑ Ⓒ Ⓓ
23. Ⓐ Ⓑ Ⓒ Ⓓ
24. Ⓐ Ⓑ Ⓒ Ⓓ
25. Ⓐ Ⓑ Ⓒ Ⓓ
26. Ⓐ Ⓑ Ⓒ Ⓓ
27. Ⓐ Ⓑ Ⓒ Ⓓ
28. Ⓐ Ⓑ Ⓒ Ⓓ
29. Ⓐ Ⓑ Ⓒ Ⓓ
30. Ⓐ Ⓑ Ⓒ Ⓓ
31. Ⓐ Ⓑ Ⓒ Ⓓ
32. Ⓐ Ⓑ Ⓒ Ⓓ
33. Ⓐ Ⓑ Ⓒ Ⓓ
34. Ⓐ Ⓑ Ⓒ Ⓓ
35. Ⓐ Ⓑ Ⓒ Ⓓ
36. Ⓐ Ⓑ Ⓒ Ⓓ

ANSWER SHEET—MODEL TEST FOUR
LAW SCHOOL ADMISSION TEST (LSAT)

Section IV:
Logical Reasoning

1. Ⓐ Ⓑ Ⓒ Ⓓ Ⓔ
2. Ⓐ Ⓑ Ⓒ Ⓓ Ⓔ
3. Ⓐ Ⓑ Ⓒ Ⓓ Ⓔ
4. Ⓐ Ⓑ Ⓒ Ⓓ Ⓔ
5. Ⓐ Ⓑ Ⓒ Ⓓ Ⓔ
6. Ⓐ Ⓑ Ⓒ Ⓓ Ⓔ
7. Ⓐ Ⓑ Ⓒ Ⓓ Ⓔ
8. Ⓐ Ⓑ Ⓒ Ⓓ Ⓔ
9. Ⓐ Ⓑ Ⓒ Ⓓ Ⓔ
10. Ⓐ Ⓑ Ⓒ Ⓓ Ⓔ
11. Ⓐ Ⓑ Ⓒ Ⓓ Ⓔ
12. Ⓐ Ⓑ Ⓒ Ⓓ Ⓔ
13. Ⓐ Ⓑ Ⓒ Ⓓ Ⓔ
14. Ⓐ Ⓑ Ⓒ Ⓓ Ⓔ
15. Ⓐ Ⓑ Ⓒ Ⓓ Ⓔ
16. Ⓐ Ⓑ Ⓒ Ⓓ Ⓔ
17. Ⓐ Ⓑ Ⓒ Ⓓ Ⓔ
18. Ⓐ Ⓑ Ⓒ Ⓓ Ⓔ
19. Ⓐ Ⓑ Ⓒ Ⓓ Ⓔ
20. Ⓐ Ⓑ Ⓒ Ⓓ Ⓔ
21. Ⓐ Ⓑ Ⓒ Ⓓ Ⓔ
22. Ⓐ Ⓑ Ⓒ Ⓓ Ⓔ
23. Ⓐ Ⓑ Ⓒ Ⓓ Ⓔ
24. Ⓐ Ⓑ Ⓒ Ⓓ Ⓔ
25. Ⓐ Ⓑ Ⓒ Ⓓ Ⓔ
26. Ⓐ Ⓑ Ⓒ Ⓓ Ⓔ

Section V:
Analytical Reasoning

1. Ⓐ Ⓑ Ⓒ Ⓓ Ⓔ
2. Ⓐ Ⓑ Ⓒ Ⓓ Ⓔ
3. Ⓐ Ⓑ Ⓒ Ⓓ Ⓔ
4. Ⓐ Ⓑ Ⓒ Ⓓ Ⓔ
5. Ⓐ Ⓑ Ⓒ Ⓓ Ⓔ
6. Ⓐ Ⓑ Ⓒ Ⓓ Ⓔ
7. Ⓐ Ⓑ Ⓒ Ⓓ Ⓔ
8. Ⓐ Ⓑ Ⓒ Ⓓ Ⓔ
9. Ⓐ Ⓑ Ⓒ Ⓓ Ⓔ
10. Ⓐ Ⓑ Ⓒ Ⓓ Ⓔ
11. Ⓐ Ⓑ Ⓒ Ⓓ Ⓔ
12. Ⓐ Ⓑ Ⓒ Ⓓ Ⓔ
13. Ⓐ Ⓑ Ⓒ Ⓓ Ⓔ
14. Ⓐ Ⓑ Ⓒ Ⓓ Ⓔ
15. Ⓐ Ⓑ Ⓒ Ⓓ Ⓔ
16. Ⓐ Ⓑ Ⓒ Ⓓ Ⓔ
17. Ⓐ Ⓑ Ⓒ Ⓓ Ⓔ
18. Ⓐ Ⓑ Ⓒ Ⓓ Ⓔ
19. Ⓐ Ⓑ Ⓒ Ⓓ Ⓔ
20. Ⓐ Ⓑ Ⓒ Ⓓ Ⓔ
21. Ⓐ Ⓑ Ⓒ Ⓓ Ⓔ
22. Ⓐ Ⓑ Ⓒ Ⓓ Ⓔ
23. Ⓐ Ⓑ Ⓒ Ⓓ Ⓔ

Section VI:
Logical Reasoning

1. Ⓐ Ⓑ Ⓒ Ⓓ Ⓔ
2. Ⓐ Ⓑ Ⓒ Ⓓ Ⓔ
3. Ⓐ Ⓑ Ⓒ Ⓓ Ⓔ
4. Ⓐ Ⓑ Ⓒ Ⓓ Ⓔ
5. Ⓐ Ⓑ Ⓒ Ⓓ Ⓔ
6. Ⓐ Ⓑ Ⓒ Ⓓ Ⓔ
7. Ⓐ Ⓑ Ⓒ Ⓓ Ⓔ
8. Ⓐ Ⓑ Ⓒ Ⓓ Ⓔ
9. Ⓐ Ⓑ Ⓒ Ⓓ Ⓔ
10. Ⓐ Ⓑ Ⓒ Ⓓ Ⓔ
11. Ⓐ Ⓑ Ⓒ Ⓓ Ⓔ
12. Ⓐ Ⓑ Ⓒ Ⓓ Ⓔ
13. Ⓐ Ⓑ Ⓒ Ⓓ Ⓔ
14. Ⓐ Ⓑ Ⓒ Ⓓ Ⓔ
15. Ⓐ Ⓑ Ⓒ Ⓓ Ⓔ
16. Ⓐ Ⓑ Ⓒ Ⓓ Ⓔ
17. Ⓐ Ⓑ Ⓒ Ⓓ Ⓔ
18. Ⓐ Ⓑ Ⓒ Ⓓ Ⓔ
19. Ⓐ Ⓑ Ⓒ Ⓓ Ⓔ
20. Ⓐ Ⓑ Ⓒ Ⓓ Ⓔ
21. Ⓐ Ⓑ Ⓒ Ⓓ Ⓔ
22. Ⓐ Ⓑ Ⓒ Ⓓ Ⓔ
23. Ⓐ Ⓑ Ⓒ Ⓓ Ⓔ
24. Ⓐ Ⓑ Ⓒ Ⓓ Ⓔ
25. Ⓐ Ⓑ Ⓒ Ⓓ Ⓔ
26. Ⓐ Ⓑ Ⓒ Ⓓ Ⓔ

EXAMINATION

WRITING SAMPLE

Time—30 Minutes

Directions:
You have 30 minutes to write an essay in response to a given topic. Take a few minutes to plan your work before you begin writing. DO NOT WRITE ON A TOPIC OF YOUR OWN CHOICE. ESSAYS THAT DO NOT ADDRESS THE GIVEN TOPIC ARE UNACCEPTABLE.

The quality of your writing is more important than the length of your response or the content. Pay attention to organization, appropriate diction, and correct usage. You will not be expected to display any specialized knowledge in your response, nor will you be expected to write a "perfect" essay; law schools understand that you are writing under a time constraint, and will allow for the minor lapses in writing ability that might occur under this circumstance.

Only the lined area in your booklet will be reproduced for the law schools, so do not write outside this space. *Do not* skip lines or use wide margins. These precautions, along with careful planning and legible handwriting that is not unduly large, will keep you within the allowed space.

SAMPLE TOPIC:

Newscasters, political scientists, and sociologists have recently begun debating the merits of election polls. Some maintain that such polls are a disservice to democracy and to the American voter. This position holds that, if citizens learn from pre-election polls that "their" candidate hasn't even a slim chance to win, these potential voters will stay home instead of going to vote. And in a recent national election, television news exit polls predicted the winner of the American presidential race long *before* voting booths closed on the West coast. Voters in California, Oregon, Washington, Hawaii, etc., thus felt that their votes were meaningless. Though the networks have since agreed not to predict winners in future elections until after the electorate in all national regions have voted, the implication of election polls are still unclear.

Imagine that you are a trustee on the board of advisers of a national news organization, and you are faced with establishing guidelines for your news agency's election polls.

In the space provided, present and support your position on the guidelines you would recommend for such activity.

SECTION I
READING COMPREHENSION

Time—35 Minutes
28 Questions

Directions:
Read the passages and answer the questions following each passage by blackening the appropriate space on the answer sheet. You may refer back to the passages when answering the questions. Answer all questions on the basis of what is stated or implied.

Passage 1

Literary periods are slippery concepts. When dates are established and cultural developments are outlined, predecessors and successors have a way of making them dissolve. One discovers that the Romantic Period in English literature so comfortably introduced as extending from 1800 to 1830 has a long Pre-Romantic development and that it really isn't over yet. The same thing is true of American literary history, perhaps more so. But if there is one date that seems to make a decisive cut in the continuity of twentieth-century America, it is probably the stock market crash at the end of October 1929. By 1930 reassessment was forced on the American consciousness.

The Twenties have a character of their own, an individualized and particularized decade for which there has come to be felt considerable nostalgia among the older generation. Clear memories can hardly regard these years as the good old days (this was the era of prohibition and gangsters), but one of the blessings of the human condition is the tendency to forget unpleasantness and remember what one chooses to remember. Perhaps even the Sixties will become a happy recollection in the twenty-first century.

Three major designations arose in the Twenties to define the Twenties as a cultural phenomenon: the Jazz Age, the Lost Generation, and the Wasteland—all with significant literary associations. Of them all the Jazz Age, as represented best in F. Scott Fitzgerald's fiction, was most clearly cut off by the stock market collapse and the ensuing depression. It is the period of the Twenties alone. But the Lost Generation (as proclaimed in the double epigraph from *Ecclesiastes* and Gertrude Stein in the 1926 *The Sun Also Rises*—"You are all a lost generation."— Gertrude Stein in conversation) continued to be lost in the Thirties. The uprootedness and disillusionment of the post-World War I fiction writers, many of whom had participated in that war and perhaps particularly of the Paris expatriate group including Hemingway, Elliot Paul, Henry Miller, and others, pursued them into the depression and beyond. The third term, the Wasteland, established by T. S. Eliot in his 1922 poem, had perhaps an even longer life; it has come to represent an age extending from the Twenties to 1945 and may indeed suggest the central features of the landscape of this larger period. The Wasteland poets, including Ezra Pound, Eliot himself, and possibly William Carlos Williams, Archibald MacLeish, and e. e. cummings, although many of them had written distinctive poetry even before 1920 and certainly before 1930, continued to develop and sharpen both their verse and their ideas into the Thirties and Forties. The Wasteland runs into and disappears in the Age of Anxiety.

This is one reason for the inclusion of such American writers as Gertrude Stein, Ezra Pound, T. S. Eliot, Williams, cummings, and Hemingway in the post-1930 Canon rather than in the pre-1930 one. They had all certainly made a mark in the literary world before 1930, but they were ahead of their time and made a larger and deeper mark after that date. This is true even for Gertrude Stein, who had only sixteen more years to live and who had begun her serious writing in the first decade of the twentieth century with *Things as They Are* (originally *Quod Erat Demonstrandum*) and *Three Lives* (1909). *Tender Buttons*, among her stylistically most radical work, appeared in 1914, and even *Four Saints in Three Acts* had been written and published in *transition* by 1929. But although she had been read and sought out by other writers like Sherwood Anderson and Hemingway, her initial impact on the public, even the most literate portion of it, probably did not come until the Thirties (and production of the Stein-Virgil Thomson opera, *Four Saints in Three Acts*) when people began to make fun of "A rose is a rose is a rose is a rose is" (often misquoting the lovely verse from *The World is Round*, a book for children) and the phrase from *Four Saints*, "Pigeons on the grass, alas." Gertrude Stein was alway avant-garde and probably still is. Although T. S. Eliot became the most important single literary influence on Hart Crane, whose major creative period was over by 1930, again his greatest impact on a more general public had hardly begun. That half or third of his creative effort in verse drama did not get under way until the mid-Thirties.

It is in this fashion that American literature approaches the period which begins in 1930, trailing clouds of several impulses—some would say glory—as it comes. Realism and naturalism are by this time established as dominant modes, but antirealistic frames of reference like expressionism, surrealism, psychology, and religious ideology are also operative.

1. When the author says in the third paragraph, "It is the period of the Twenties alone," he probably means that
   (A) the Jazz Age was a phenomenon of the Twenties only
   (B) he will discuss the 1920s only
   (C) "it" is a synonym for "period"
   (D) the stock market crash and the depression occurred in the 1920s
   (E) the 1920s alone constituted a cultural phenomenon

2. At the beginning of paragraph 4, the term "Canon" probably means
   (A) canyon in the Wasteland
   (B) literary weaponry
   (C) catalogue
   (D) a list of saints
   (E) partnership

3. We may conclude that the author regards the 1960s as
   (A) a worse decade than the 1920s
   (B) a replica of the 1920s
   (C) a happy recollection
   (D) not the best of times
   (E) a political and artistic disaster

4. The author's extensive attention to Gertrude Stein is intended to stress that
   (A) she wrote much before her death in 1946
   (B) although many of her major works preceded 1930, her fame reached its height after 1930
   (C) she was a versatile writer, even in her youth
   (D) she lived until the age of 46
   (E) she was not a public figure

5. In view of the author's skepticism in the first paragraph about the strict demarcation of literary and historical periods, he would probably agree with which of the following statements about the stock market crash?
   (A) Economics did not impinge upon the Romantic Age.
   (B) The stock market crash affected economic history but not literary history.
   (C) The crash was the focus of a series of events that both preceded it and followed it.
   (D) The crash was not a welcome phenomenon.
   (E) The crash motivated a wave of new poems and novels.

6. According to the author, the literature of the 1930s was dominated by
   (A) no particular mode or frame of reference
   (B) realism

(C) impressionism
(D) expressionism
(E) surrealism

7. In the final sentence of paragraph 3, the term "the Wasteland" is used
(A) malignantly   (B) sloppily   (C) ambiguously   (D) literally   (E) figuratively

Passage 2

Article I, Section 4, of the Constitution provides: "The Times, Places and Manner of holding Elections for Senators and Representatives shall be prescribed in each State by the Legislature thereof; but the Congress may at any time by Law make or alter such Regulations, except as to the Places of chusing Senators."

At first Congress exercised its power to supervise apportionment by simply specifying in the statutes how many representatives each state was to have. From 1842 until the 1920s, it went further and required that the districts be relatively compact (not scattered areas) and relatively equal in voting population.

Major shifts in population occurred in the twentieth century: large numbers of farmers could no longer maintain small farms and moved to the cities to find employment; rapidly growing industries, organized in factory systems, attracted rural workers; and many blacks who could no longer find work in southern agriculture moved to the North to get better jobs and get away from strict Jim Crow living conditions. The rural areas of the country became more sparsely populated while the city populations swelled.

As these changes were occurring, Congress took less interest in its reapportionment power, and after 1929 did not reenact the requirements. In 1946, voters in Illinois asked the Supreme Court to remedy the serious malapportionment of their state congressional districts. Justice Frankfurter, writing for the Court in *Colegrove v. Green*, said the federal courts should stay out of "this political thicket." Reapportionment was a "political question" outside the jurisdiction of these courts. Following the *Colgrove* holding, malapportionment grew more severe and widespread in the United States.

In the Warren Court era, voters again asked the Court to pass on issues concerning the size and shape of electoral districts, partly out of desperation because no other branch of government offered relief, and partly out of hope that the Court would reexamine old decisions in this area as it had in others, looking at basic constitutional principles in the light of modern living conditions.

Once again the Court had to work through the problem of separation of powers, which had stood in the way of court action concerning representation. In this area, too, the Court's rulings were greeted by some as shockingly radical departures from "the American way," while others saw them as a reversion to the democratic processes established by the Constitution, applied to an urbanized setting.

8. The primary purpose of the passage is
(A) to criticize public apathy concerning apportionment
(B) to describe in general the history of political apportionment
(C) to argue for the power of the Supreme Court
(D) to describe the role of the Warren Court
(E) to stress that reapportionment is essentially a congressional concern

9. The author implies which of the following opinions about federal supervision of apportionment?
(A) Federal supervision is unnecessary.
(B) Federal supervision is necessary.
(C) Apportionment should be regulated by the Court.
(D) Apportionment should be regulated by Congress.
(E) Court rulings on apportionment violate "the American way."

10. In paragraph 4, "malapportionment" refers to
- (A) the influx of farmers into the city
- (B) the Jim Crow phenomenon
- (C) the shift from rural to urban populations
- (D) the distribution of voters in Illinois
- (E) the unfair size and shape of congressional districts

11. We may infer that during the Warren Court era
- (A) the most dissatisfied voters lived in cities
- (B) the constituency was dissatisfied
- (C) the separation of powers became important for the first time
- (D) the public turned its attention away from issues of apportionment
- (E) a ballot issue concerning electoral apportionment passed

12. The passage provides answers to which of the following questions?

I. Does the Constitution delegate authority for supervising apportionment?
II. Do population shifts intensify racism?
III. Should the Constitution still be consulted, even though times have changed?
- (A) I only   (B) II only   (C) I and II   (D) II and III   (E) I, II, and III

13. We may conclude that Justice Frankfurter
- (A) was a member of the Warren Court
- (B) was not a member of the Warren Court
- (C) is opposed to reapportionment
- (D) was skeptical about the separation of powers
- (E) was too attached to outmoded interpretations of the Constitution

14. In the passage the author is primarily concerned with
- (A) summarizing history
- (B) provoking a controversy
- (C) suggesting a new attitude
- (D) reevaluating old decisions
- (E) challenging constitutional principles

Passage 3

Seventy-five years after the death of Louis XIV, the French Revolution enlarged considerably the dimensions of the government show, organizing mass demonstrations with grandiose staging. The national holiday on July 14, 1790, attracted 200,000 people to the Champs de Mars. There were Memorial Day on August 26, 1792, to honor those who died on August 10, Unity of the Republic Day and the solemn funeral for Marat in 1793, and the Feast of the Supreme Being on June 8, 1794, organized by the painter David, "grand master of holidays of the Republic."

Robespierre held the main role as president of the Convention. While choirs intoned a specially composed hymn entitled "Father of the Universe, Supreme Intelligence," he lighted the flame before a statue of Atheism. Then, marching at the head of the column of members of the Convention, with each member carrying a bouquet of flowers and ears of wheat, he proceeded from the Tuileries Gardens to the Champs de Mars, where a symbolic hillock topped with the Tree of Freedom had been erected.

The objective of these vast liturgical assemblies? To strike the public imagination, mobilize it and involve it in a collective ritual. Later, mass demonstrations in Red Square or Tien An-men Square would be held for the same reason. Participation in such rituals has become an act of allegiance to official beliefs.

Other regimes, like facism or Nazism, aim not only at raising the consciousness of the people, but at creating a "mass psychology" by using gigantic demonstrations, whether in Rome or in the stadium at Nuremberg.

Here, following Durkheim's theory, the demonstration has the double aspect of ceremony-spectacle and diversion. It is diversion also in the sense of diverting attention away from true problems and realities. The public lives in a surrealistic atmosphere of festivals and games, like plebians during the Roman empire.

Other political systems also mix show business and politics in a minor way. American elections are the occasion for confetti, parades, and majorettes, and each national political convention has a show business style orchestra. At the Democratic National Convention in 1976, Peter Duchin's orchestra, perched on the bleachers behind the official rostrum, played the traditional hymn, "Happy Days Are Here Again." At the Republican National Convention, Manny Harmon's orchestra, presented by former actor and senator George Murphy, played "God Bless America." Mrs. Betty Ford, presented to the public by Cary Grant, even danced the bump with Tony Orlando.

For that matter, political rallies are often held in places generally reserved for shows or sports events like Madison Square Garden in New York, where the Democratic Convention was held, or the Walnut Street Theater in Philadelphia, where the first Ford-Carter debate was held.

So it can be seen that politics does have its play function. Indeed, we often speak of the "political game," as if politics also constituted entertainment, amusement, recreation.

And, as with a show, we speak of the "public" to designate the people. Some refer to what they consider to be the public's taste for theatricalization, arguing that politics must use star system techniques to save it from the public's lack of interest, to adapt it to "mass culture."

From the moment when the television viewer can choose between his president, a film, and a variety show, the president has to become an entertainer to compete effectively with show business professionals and keep his popularity rating. In short, to compete with stars, political stars have to use their methods and personalize their "performances."

15. The author of this passage would agree that
   (A) Durkheim's theory is unrelated to the alignment of politics with show business
   (B) the "surrealistic atmosphere of festivals and games" occurred only in Ancient Rome
   (C) politics consistently stresses serious public problems
   (D) the theatricality of present-day politics has no historical precedent
   (E) a show-business atmosphere has pervaded the politics of democratic as well as totalitarian regimes

16. The primary purpose of this passage is
   (A) to compare Ancient Rome to modern America
   (B) to argue that show business and politics have converged throughout history
   (C) to show that politics diverts attention from real problems
   (D) to establish Robespierre as the first political "star"
   (E) to demonstrate that television has sustained the politician as celebrity

17. Which of the following is the most appropriate substitute for "liturgical assemblies" (paragraph 3)?
   (A) political circuses
   (B) political conventions
   (C) spectacles of worship
   (D) human dramas
   (E) religious holidays

18. The author's attitude toward politicians who are deliberately entertaining would most likely be
   (A) sympathetic   (B) skeptical   (C) supportive   (D) unconcerned   (E) hostile

19. The author implies that citizens who are attracted by entertaining politicians are
   (A) too obedient
   (B) not facing reality
   (C) television addicts

(D) not interested in politics
(E) victims of a totalitarian regime

20. The author strengthens his argument through the use of which of the following techniques?
(A) the acknowledgement that he might be mistaken
(B) a profusion of references to experts
(C) a profusion of historical facts
(D) an appeal to the "official beliefs" of his readers
(E) the use of specialized terminology

21. Which of the following would be an additional example of the sort of politics the author describes?
(A) Ronald Reagan's speaking at the Academy Awards
(B) Nancy Reagan's preference for the color red
(C) Edward Kennedy's New England accent
(D) Rich Little's impersonation of Richard Nixon
(E) Richard Nixon's purchase of a Park Avenue penthouse

Passage 4

The largest manufacturing belt in the world is within the quadrilateral bounded by Baltimore, Boston, Minneapolis-St. Paul, and Kansas City. In the United States a number of manufacturing regions of considerable significance are located outside this quadrilateral. Centers such as those focused in southern California, the San Francisco Bay region, the Seattle-Portland axis, Dallas-Ft. Worth, the Galveston Bay area, and the Atlanta region are of considerable importance.

The principal advantages of the manufacturing belt are: (1) the principal market for commodities in the country; (2) a great variety and abundance of raw materials; (3) large quantities of high quality, low cost bituminous coal; (4) access to large quantities of electric power; (5) access to supplies of petroleum and natural gas; (6) excellent transportation facilities; (7) a large and skilled labor supply.

Just across the border in Canada in the Ontario Peninsula and St. Lawrence River Valley is an extension of the American manufacturing belt. The principal advantages of this region are essentially the same as those on the American side of the border. The accident of international boundaries separates what is essentially a single region with great significance in manufacturing.

Another major manufacturing region is located in western and northwestern Europe. This region served as a focus for the Industrial Revolution, and the advantages of an early start have persisted. Manufacturing was assisted early by the presence of important coal and iron deposits. Several districts in the United Kingdom, the Saar Basin, the Sambre-Meuse coal districts, and the Ruhr Valley all spawned coal demanding industries. The presence of ore in several areas of the United Kingdom and the Lorraine deposits of France and Luxembourg were additional spurs to early industrial development. Heavy industries, such as iron and steel, chemicals, rolling mills, metal fabrication plants, and others, developed and flourished. The United Kingdom, the Federal Republic of Germany (West Germany), the Benelux (Belgium, Netherlands, and Luxembourg) nations, and France were involved in these early developments. Expansion of industrial activities into most other urbanized areas of Europe has accelerated in the interval after World War II.

The population of Europe enjoys a stimulating climate, and is, in itself, a huge market. Excellent transportation facilities, availability of power, and coal are significant advantages of the region. Exploration for, and development of, oil and natural gas in the North Sea has been an added benefit and spur to industry in countries which rim it. This region rivals the industrial might of North America and is one of the great manufacturing regions of the world.

The Soviet Union has become a massive industrial power, and her wealth of resources has contributed mightily to her industrial might. She has become a leading producer of coal, and her production of oil exceeds national needs. Clusters of industrial facilities, such as those in the Ukraine, around Moscow, in the Urals, and in Soviet middle Asia have typically had a major local resource and power base. Strategic considerations along with governmental considerations have obviously been of major concern in plant location. It's clear that recent thaws in relationships with the West have come to open the door for the infusion of new technologies and equipment from capitalist states.

22. The author provides information to answer which of the following questions?

    I. Are there manufacturing belts in Asian countries south of Russia?
    II. Did the Industrial Revolution influence the growth of manufacturing belts?
    III. What is manufactured in the large American "quadrilateral" belt?
    (A) I only   (B) II only   (C) II and III   (D) III only   (E) I and III

23. "Strategic considerations," mentioned in the final paragraph, probably refers to which of the following?
    (A) the relationship of a plant to the West
    (B) the vulnerability of a plant to military attack
    (C) the receptivity of a plant to new technologies
    (D) the efficiency of a plant's facilities
    (E) the marketing of excess oil

24. Which of the following is the most appropriate substitute for "spurs to" (fourth paragraph)?
    (A) impulses over   (B) cleats on   (C) reasons of   (D) matters for
    (E) none of the above

25. The primary purpose of the passage is
    (A) to compare North America, Europe, and the Soviet Union
    (B) to reveal the advantages of manufacturing
    (C) to argue for the dominance of the United States as a manufacturer
    (D) to survey the locations and characteristics of manufacturing belts
    (E) to describe the influence of the Industrial Revolution on manufacturing

26. The author believes which of the following about the Industrial Revolution?
    (A) It created manufacturing belts.
    (B) Its effects on the United States were negligible.
    (C) It afforded western Europe a head start in manufacturing.
    (D) It did not take effect in Europe until after World War II.
    (E) It encouraged the presence of coal and iron deposits.

27. Which of the following is NOT a principal advantage of a manufacturing belt?
    (A) availability of energy
    (B) good highways
    (C) a temperate climate
    (D) availability of trained workers
    (E) a market for the manufactured goods

28. In general, this passage discusses the relationship between manufacturing and
    (A) geography   (B) history   (C) energy   (D) political pressure   (E) capitalism

STOP

IF YOU FINISH BEFORE TIME HAS ELAPSED, CHECK YOUR WORK ON THIS SECTION OF THE TEST ONLY. DO NOT GO ON TO THE NEXT SECTION OF THE TEST UNTIL TIME IS UP FOR THIS SECTION.

SECTION II
ANALYTICAL REASONING

Time—35 Minutes
26 Questions

Directions:
In this section you will be given groups of questions based on different sets of conditions. Drawing a simple diagram may be helpful in answering some of the questions. You are to choose the best answer and mark the corresponding space on your answer sheet.

Questions 1-7

1. Four brothers (Aaron, Bryan, Clifford, and David) all sing in a barbershop quartet, which consists of a bass, a baritone, a tenor, and an alto. Each brother also plays a different infield position on a local softball team (one plays first base; one plays second base; one plays third base; and one plays shortstop).
2. Aaron sings bass.
3. The baritone plays first base.
4. Clifford is not the tenor.
5. Bryan is not the shortstop.
6. Aaron is not the third baseman.
7. David is not the baritone or the second baseman.
8. Clifford is not the first baseman.
9. Bryan is not the alto.
10. The tenor is not the third baseman.

1. From statements 1, 2, and 7, which of the following can be deduced?

   I.   The tenor could be the second baseman.
  II. The bass is not the third baseman.
 III. The bass is not the shortstop.
(A) I only   (B) II only   (C) III only   (D) I and III   (E) II and III

2. From statements 1, 3, 4, and 8, which of the following can be deduced?

   I.   Clifford could be the third baseman.
  II. Clifford is not the baritone.
 III. Clifford could be the bass.
(A) I only   (B) I and II   (C) II and III   (D) I and III   (E) I, II, and III

3. From all the statements, who is the first baseman?
   (A) Aaron   (B) Bryan   (C) Clifford   (D) David   (E) Cannot be determined

4. From all the statements, which of the following MUST be true?

   I.   David is either the alto or the tenor.
  II. Aaron is either the first baseman or the second baseman.
 III. Bryan is either the first baseman or the tenor.
(A) I only   (B) II only   (C) III only   (D) Two of the above   (E) All of the above

5. From all the statements, which of the following MUST be true about David?

    I.   He is the tenor.
    II. He is not the first baseman.
    III. He is not the bass.
    IV. He is the shortstop.
    (A) I and III   (B) II and IV   (C) II and III   (D) I, II, III, and IV   (E) None of the above

6. From all the statements, who is the third baseman?
    (A) Aaron   (B) Bryan   (C) Clifford   (D) David   (E) Cannot be determined

7. If Aaron and Bryan switch playing positions on the softball team, how many of the original statements are false?
    (A) One   (B) Two   (C) Three   (D) Four   (E) Five

Questions 8–14

    1. All A's, B's, and C's are D's.
    2. All B's are A's.
    3. All E's are B's.
    4. All A's are G's.
    5. No C's are B's.
    6. Some, but not all, C's are A's.

8. From the conditions given above, which of the following statements MUST be true?

    I.   Some C's are G's.
    II. All C's are G's.
    III. All E's are G's.
    (A) I   (B) II   (C) III   (D) I and III   (E) II and III

9. Which of the following statements MUST be false?
    (A) All A's are D's.
    (B) All E's are A's.
    (C) All G's are D's.
    (D) No E's are C's.
    (E) Some C's are B's.

10. If all D's are G's, then

    I.   all C's are G's
    II. all G's are C's
    (A) I only   (B) II only   (C) Both I and II   (D) Either I or II, but not both
    (E) Neither I nor II

11. If Q is within C, then Q MUST also be within
    (A) A   (B) B   (C) G   (D) D   (E) E

12. All G's MUST be

    I.   D's
    II. C's
    III. E's
    (A) I and II   (B) II and III   (C) I and III   (D) I, II, and III   (E) None of the above

13. If all J's are B's, then all J's MUST be
  I.   A's
  II. D's
  III. E's
  IV. C's
  (A) I   (B) I and II   (C) I, II, and III   (D) I, II, III, and IV   (E) none of these choices

14. If some D's are Q's, then Q's MUST be
  (A) C's   (B) A's   (C) B's   (D) G's   (E) none of these

Questions 15–20

  1. A, B, C, D, and E are contestants in a talent show, and are ranked 1st through 5th with no ties.
  2. Contestant A places ahead of contestant B.
  3. Contestant C places 1st or last.
  4. Contestant D places 1st or last.

15. If E finishes ahead of A, then which of the following MUST be true?
  I.   B finishes ahead of D.
  II. B finishes 4th.
  III. E finishes 2nd.
  (A) I and II   (B) II and III   (C) II only   (D) III only   (E) I, II, and III

16. If C finishes ahead of B, then which of the following MUST be false?
  (A) D is 5th.
  (B) E is 2nd.
  (C) B is 4th.
  (D) A finishes ahead of D.
  (E) None of these

17. If B finishes ahead of E, then which of the following MUST be true?
  (A) A is 2nd.
  (B) B is 4th.
  (C) E finishes ahead of D.
  (D) C is 1st.
  (E) D is not 1st.

18. If C and B finish in consecutive positions, then which of the following MUST be true?
  I.   D finishes 1st.
  II. E finishes ahead of A.
  III. B finishes ahead of E.
  (A) I and II   (B) I and III   (C) I, II, and III   (D) I only   (E) II only

19. If a sixth contestant, F, places 4th, and B finishes behind F, then which of the following MUST be false?
  (A) A and E finish consecutively.
  (B) A must place ahead of D.
  (C) B is 5th.
  (D) B and E do not finish consecutively.
  (E) All of these are true.

20. If E finishes 2nd and F, a sixth contestant, finishes next to C, then which of the following MUST be true?
  I.   B is 4th.
  II. F finishes ahead of B.
  III. A is 3rd.
  (A) I and II   (B) I and III   (C) II and III   (D) I only   (E) I, II, and III

Questions 21-26.

Along the coast of Zambatania there are four major cities, X, Y, Z, and Q. Each of these cities lies on a straight road that runs from east to west.
1. City X is 30 miles from city Y.
2. City Z is 40 miles from city Y.
3. City Q is 2 miles from city Z.

21. Which of the following could be true?
(A) City Z is 30 miles from city X.
(B) City Z is 40 miles from city X.
(C) City Z is 10 miles from city X.
(D) City Y is 50 miles from city Z.
(E) City Q is 80 miles from City Z.

22. All of the following could be true except
(A) city Q is 38 miles from city Y
(B) city Q is 42 miles from city Y
(C) city Q is 68 miles from city X
(D) city Q is 8 miles from city X
(E) city Q is 38 miles from city X

23. If city Q is 12 miles from city X, then
(A) city Z is 70 miles from city X
(B) city Q is 38 miles from city Y
(C) city Q is 8 miles from city Y
(D) city Q is 18 miles from city Y
(E) city Z is 10 miles from city X

24. Each of the following is a possible order of cities along the coast road except
(A) XYQZ
(B) XYZQ
(C) QZYX
(D) XQZY
(E) QZXY

25. If a traveller takes the coast road, beginning his trip at X and ending at Q, he must travel
(A) through city Y
(B) through both Y and Z
(C) through Z
(D) at least 10 miles
(E) under none of the above conditions, necessarily

26. If a fifth city, M, is located on the same straight coast road, and M is 5 miles from city Y, all of the following could be true except
(A) M is 35 miles from city X
(B) M is 35 miles from city Z
(C) M is 45 miles from city Z
(D) M is 49 miles from city Q
(E) M is 47 miles from city Q

STOP

IF YOU FINISH BEFORE TIME HAS ELAPSED, CHECK YOUR WORK ON THIS SECTION OF THE TEST ONLY. DO NOT GO ON TO THE NEXT SECTION OF THE TEST UNTIL TIME IS UP FOR THIS SECTION.

SECTION III
EVALUATION OF FACTS

Time—35 Minutes
36 Questions

Directions:
This section consists of several sets; each set presents a factual statement, the description of a dispute, and two rules. In some sets, the rules will be conflicting. Be sure that you consider each rule independently and not as an exception to the other. Following each set are questions; select from four choices (given below) the one that best categorizes each question, based upon the relationship of one or both of the rules to the dispute. Darken the appropriate space on your answer sheet:

(A) A relevant question which you can only answer by choosing between the rules.
(B) A relevant question which you cannot answer because you need more information or additional rules, but which does not require a choice between the rules.
(C) A relevant question which you can answer by referring to the facts or rules, or both.
(D) An irrelevant question or one which is only remotely relevant to the outcome of the dispute.

Set 1

FACTS

Ena owns and manages the Summer Breeze Ice Cream Store, which manufactures and sells homemade ice cream, sherbet and frozen yoghurt. State law provides that a product may not be labeled ice cream unless it contains a minimum of 18% real cream; frozen yoghurts must contain 22% real cream and sherbet at least 20% milk. One day, as Ena is manufacturing her ice cream, she runs short of cream and uses some milk. The finished product contains only 17½% real cream, but tastes exactly like the product containing 18% real cream, so she labels it ice cream. Mitch, an inspector for the State Agriculture Department, purchases and tests the product.

DISPUTE

Mitch, on behalf of the state, sues Ena for misrepresentation. Ena contests.

RULE I

A seller is liable to the state for misrepresentation, regardless of intent, if state law is violated.

RULE II

A seller who does not intentionally misrepresent to a buyer is not liable for misrepresentation.

Questions

1. Was state law violated?

2. If Ena accidentally used milk instead of cream and thus did not realize that the product contained less than 18% real cream, will she win the suit?

3. If Ena knew that the product did not contain 18% real cream, but thought that no one would catch her, will Mitch win the suit?

4. Were the state standards fair?

Set 2

FACTS

Jim Corn was a well-known practical joker. In his community he was famous for such practical jokes as borrowing everyone's left shoe from the municipal pool, painting the City Hall lawn red, and posting "Free Food" signs at the local exit from the interstate highway. No one in his community took Jim Corn seriously. One evening, Jim went to the Palace Theatre to see the film "Towering Inferno." He sat in the front row of the balcony, and from time to time dropped popcorn on the audience below him. At the climax of the film, Jim yelled "Fire!" Most in the theater knew Jim and did nothing, but Sally, visiting her aunt for the first time, panicked. She ran screaming from the theater, fell, and broke her leg.

DISPUTE

Sally sues Jim for negligence. Jim contests.

RULE I

Anyone causing, or whose acts cause intentional or unintentional injury to another, is guilty of negligence and is liable.

RULE II

One who causes, or whose acts cause injury to another, is negligent only if the acts causing the injury were premeditated and intended to cause injury.

Questions

5. If Jim had intended to cause injury and the act was premeditated, will Sally win the suit?

6. If the act was not premeditated, will Jim win the suit?

7. Was Sally severely injured?

8. Was Jim's cry premeditated?

9. Should Jim have yelled "Fire" at the show?

Set 3

FACTS

Adams rented an unfurnished apartment in his building to Lincoln for one year beginning June 1, 1982. On June 1, Lincoln was unable to move in because the apartment was still occupied by Billings, whose lease had expired May 31. Billings eventually moved out on June 30, and Lincoln moved in on July 1. During early July, a hailstorm broke two windowpanes in the apartment. Lincoln demanded that Adams replace the windowpanes, but Adams refused. Rain coming in through the broken panes caused damage to the floors, which began to warp and ruined Lincoln's new furniture. Lincoln became furious, vacated the premises on August 31, and refused to pay the last month's rent, claiming that the apartment was not habitable.

DISPUTE

Adams brought suit, and Lincoln contested.

RULE I

If leased premises fall below habitable standards and the landlord knowingly fails to correct the situation, the tenant is entitled to vacate the premises and is not liable for the last month's rent.

RULE II

A tenant is responsible for all rent payments due to the landlord if the tenant has occupied the premises for at least 30 days.

Questions

10. If Lincoln had vacated on July 28, and if the premises had fallen below habitable standards, would he be liable for the last month's rent?

11. If the premises fell below habitable standards, will Lincoln have to pay the last month's rent?

12. If Adams was unaware of the broken windowpanes, who will win the suit?

13. Was the hailstorm severe?

14. What constitutes habitable standards?

15. If Lincoln moved into the apartment on July 1, but left on vacation after staying only 2 weeks and returned on August 31, will he be liable?

Set 4

FACTS

Danny, age 12, wanted desperately to join the 47th Street Club, a gang of teenagers in his neighborhood. When he finally got up the courage to ask Rick, the leader of the gang, about becoming a member, Rick laughed and told Danny that membership requirements consisted of shooting somebody in the 8th Avenue Sluggers, their rival gang across town. Rick then offered Danny a loaded revolver, which Danny quickly accepted. Rick sent Danny across town and instructed him to empty the gun into the crowd of teenagers that hung out behind the 8th Avenue Pool Hall. Danny went alone to 8th Avenue and fired four shots. One member of the 8th Avenue Sluggers was wounded, and a postman, delivering mail at the building next door, was killed.

DISPUTE

Danny and Rick were arrested and charged with killing someone. They contested.

RULE I

Anyone under 14 years of age is not liable for his or her actions and may not be punished or imprisoned in any way.

RULE II

One who kills another or is involved in the killing of another is liable for his or her actions and may be punished or imprisoned.

Questions

16. Will Rick be convicted of killing another?

17. How old is Danny?

18. Who owned the revolver?

19. Will Danny be convicted of killing another?

20. If Rick was 14 years old and was involved in the killing, will he be convicted of killing another person?

21. If Rick was 13 years of age and was involved in the killing, will he be liable for his actions?

22. Had Danny been a member of the 8th Avenue Sluggers?

Set 5

FACTS

For a Christmas present, Albert purchased for his daughter, Darla, and his son-in-law, Sammy, a new Brite Eye color television. At the Ace TV Store Albert and the salesperson, Jack, discussed only the picture quality, the cash price of the set, and the question of whether it could be delivered to the home of Sammy and Darla on Christmas Eve. Agreement was reached, and the set arrived on Christmas Eve at Sammy and Darla's home. Sammy removed the set from its box, filed the warranty papers, which were also in the box, and plugged in the television set. On New Year's Day, during a football bowl game broadcast, the picture tube exploded because of a manufacturing defect. Everyone who was watching the television—Sammy, Darla, Otis (a neighbor), and Albert—was seriously injured.

DISPUTE

Sammy, Darla, Albert, and Otis each sued the TV manufacturer for damages and injuries. The TV manufacturer contested.

RULE I

A manufacturer is liable for any damages or injuries incurred because of manufacturing defects, provided that the item costs over $300.

RULE II

A manufacturer is liable only to the purchaser of a product and to no one else, provided that the warranty papers were filed. Otherwise the manufacturer is not liable.

Questions

23. If the TV set cost $350, will Sammy win his suit?

24. If the TV set cost $250, will Albert win his suit?

25. If the warranty papers were not filed, and the TV set cost $400, will Darla win her suit?

26. Were the warranty papers filed on time?

27. What was the cost of the TV set?

28. If the TV set cost $400, will Otis win the suit?

29. Did Sammy plug in the set correctly?

Set 6

FACTS

Sal and his brother, Hal, had been planning the kidnapping of a well-known movie star, Scarlet Starlet, for the past six months. As the day approached, Sal and Hal borrowed their cousin's van for the job. They did not know that their cousin's son, Tim, had hidden in the back of the van in an attempt to hide out and run away from home. The kidnapping went as planned. Scarlet Starlet and her boyfriend were forced into the van while leaving a grocery store and were taken to another country. Her boyfriend was dropped off before the group left the country. When they were captured by police upon entering the new country, Tim was discovered hiding in the van.

DISPUTE

Sal and Hal were charged with kidnapping and contested the charge.

RULE I

A kidnapping has occurred only when one is forcibly abducted from a country and taken to another country.

RULE II

When one is intentionally falsely imprisoned and moved, the perpetrator and accomplices are guilty of kidnapping.

Questions

30. Should Sal have borrowed his cousin's van?

31. Was Sal guilty of kidnapping Scarlet?

32. Was Tim kidnapped?

33. Was Hal guilty of kidnapping Scarlet's boyfriend?

34. If Scarlet had not been taken out of the country, would Sal have been guilty of kidnapping?

35. When did Tim get into the van?

36. If Hal was not involved in the planning, and did not show up on the day of the kidnapping, would he be found guilty?

STOP

IF YOU FINISH BEFORE TIME HAS ELAPSED, CHECK YOUR WORK ON THIS SECTION OF THE TEST ONLY. DO NOT GO ON TO THE NEXT SECTION OF THE TEST UNTIL TIME IS UP FOR THIS SECTION.

SECTION IV
LOGICAL REASONING

Time—35 Minutes
26 Questions

Directions:
In this section you will be given brief statements or passages and will be required to evaluate the reasoning involved. In some instances, more than one choice will appear to be a possible answer. You are to choose the *best* answer. Use common sense and reasonableness in making your selection; then mark the proper space on the answer sheet.

1. Recent studies show that the reduction in the maximum speed limit from 65 mph to 55 mph substantially reduces the number of highway fatalities.

   The preceding statement would be most weakened by establishing that
   (A) most fatal car accidents occur at night
   (B) most accidents occurring at speeds between 45 and 55 mph are nonfatal
   (C) few fatal accidents involve only one vehicle
   (D) prior to this reduction, 97% of fatal accidents occurred below 45 mph
   (E) prior to the reduction, 97% of fatal accidents occurred between 55 and 65 mph

2.   Board member Smith will vote for the busing of students if she is reelected to the board. If the busing of students is passed by the board, then Smith was not reelected to the board. Smith was reelected to the board.

   Given the foregoing information, which of the following can be concluded?
   (A) Smith assisted in the passage of student busing.
   (B) The passage of busing carried Smith to a reelection victory.
   (C) Smith voted against busing; however, it still passed.
   (D) Busing was defeated despite Smith's vote in favor of it.
   (E) Student busing was voted down by a majority of the board.

3. Daniel Webster said, "Falsehoods not only disagree with truths, but usually quarrel among themselves."

Which of these would follow from Webster's statement?
(A) Quarreling is endemic to American political life.
(B) Truth and falsehood can be distinguished from one another.
(C) Liars often quarrel with each other.
(D) Those who know the truth are normally silent.
(E) Truth and falsehood are emotional, rather than intellectual, phenomena.

4. A recording industry celebrity observed: "I am not a star because all my songs are hits; all my songs are hits because I am a star."

Which of the following most nearly parallels this reasoning?
(A) A college professor noted: "I am the final word in the classroom not because my judgment is always correct, but my judgment in the classroom is always correct because I am the instructor."
(B) A nurse observed: "I am not competent in my duties because I am a nurse, but I am competent in my duties because of my training in nursing."
(C) A dance instructor noted: "I am not the instructor because I know all there is about dance; rather I am an instructor because of my ability to teach dancing."
(D) A recording industry celebrity observed: "I am not wealthy because I am a star; I am wealthy because so many people buy my recordings."
(E) A recording industry celebrity observed: "I am not a star because my every song is enjoyed; I am a star because people pay to watch me perform."

5. The enzyme Doxin cannot be present if the bacterium *Entrox* is absent.

Given the foregoing condition, which of the following would also be true?

I. *Entrox* may be present without the presence of Doxin.
II. Doxin and *Entrox* may be present together.
III. Doxin may be present without *Entrox*.
IV. There may be a case in which neither Doxin nor *Entrox* is present.
(A) II only   (B) IV only   (C) II and IV only   (D) I, II, and III only   (E) I, II, and IV only

6.   If a speaker were highly credible, would an objectively irrelevant personal characteristic of the speaker influence the effectiveness of her communication? For example, if a Nobel prize-winning chemist were speaking on inorganic chemistry, would she induce a lesser change in the opinions of an audience if she were known to be a poor cook? Would the speaker's effectiveness be different if she were obese rather than trim, sloppy rather than neat, ugly rather than attractive?
    By failing to consider irrelevant aspects of communicator credibility, studies in communication science have unknowingly implied that audiences are composed of individuals who are responsive only to objectively relevant aspects of a speaker.

Which of the following represent(s) assumptions upon which the foregoing passage is based?

I. Audiences are composed of people who are responsive only to objectively relevant aspects of a communicator.
II. Objectively irrelevant personal characteristics have a bearing on a speaker's effectiveness.
III. Some characteristics of a communicator are of greater relevance than others.
(A) I only   (B) II only   (C) III only   (D) I and II only   (E) I, II, and III only

Questions 7–8 refer to the following passage.

I read with interest the statements of eminent archaeologists that the presence of a crude snare in an early Neolithic grave indicates that man of this period subsisted by snaring small mammals. I find this assertion open to question. How do I know the companions of the deceased did not toss the snare into the grave with the corpse because it had proved to be totally useless?

7. The author employs which of the following as a method of questioning the archaeologists' claims?
   (A) evidence that contradicts the conclusion drawn by the archaeologists
   (B) a doubtful tone about the motives of the archaeologists
   (C) a body of knowledge inconsistent with that employed by the archaeologists
   (D) an alternative to the conclusion drawn by the archaeologists
   (E) the suggestion that archaeological studies are of little use

8. Which of the following best expresses the author's criticism of the archaeologists whose statements he questions?
   (A) They have not subjected their conclusions to scientific verification.
   (B) They have stressed one explanation and ignored others.
   (C) They have drawn a conclusion that does not fit the evidence upon which it was based.
   (D) They failed to employ proper scientific methods in arriving at their conclusion.
   (E) They have based their conclusion on behaviors exhibited by more modern humans.

9. Semanticists point out that words and phrases often acquire connotations tinged with emotions. Such significances are attached because of the context, the history of the usage of the expression, or the background of the person reading or listening. Thus, "the hills of home" may evoke a feeling of nostalgia or a pleasant sensation; but "Bolshevik" may arouse derision or disgust in the minds of many people.

The term "progressive education" has gone through several stages in the connotative process. At one time progressive education was hailed as the harbinger of all that was wise and wholesome in classroom practice, such as the recognition of individual differences and the revolution against formalized dictatorial procedures. However, partly because of abuses on the fanatical fringe of the movement, many people began to associate progressive schools with frills, fads, and follies. What had been discovered and developed by Froebel in Germany, by Pestalozzi in Switzerland, by Montessori in Italy, and by men like Parker and Dewey in the United States was muddled in a melange of mockery and misunderstanding and submerged in satirical quips. As a result, many educators have recently avoided the expression and have chosen to call present educational practices "new" or "modern" rather than "progressive."

Which of the following would most seriously weaken the author's argument?
   (A) In a recent poll of American voters, 76 percent responded that they would certainly not vote for the Progressive Labor Party.
   (B) Open classrooms have recently fallen out of the educational limelight.
   (C) New techniques in teaching cognitive skills, called "Progressive Learning" have recently met with widespread approval in middle class public schools.
   (D) Parker and Dewey were well respected by academicians and educational theorists.
   (E) Every new advance in education is first denounced as a "fad."

10. *Bill*: Professor Smith has been late for class almost every morning.
   Dave: That can't be true; he was on time yesterday.

Dave apparently believes that Bill has said which of the following?
   (A) Professor Smith is seldom late.
   (B) Professor Smith does not enjoy teaching.

(C) Professor Smith has been late every day without exception.
(D) Professor Smith was late yesterday.
(E) Professor Smith informs Bill of his whereabouts.

11. Sunbathers do not usually spend much time in the shade. Shade prevails during most of June in La Jolla. It is June 14.

Which of the following would be a logically defensible conclusion based upon the foregoing premises?

I. There are probably few sunbathers in La Jolla at present.
II. There may be sunbathers in La Jolla at present.
III. La Jolla is the site of frequent sunbathing.

(A) I only   (B) II only   (C) III only   (D) I and II only   (E) II and III only

12. Although American politicians disagree about many things, none of them disagrees with Wendell Willkie's assertion that "the Constitution does not provide for first- and second-class citizens."

Willkie's statement implies that
(A) the Constitution provides for third- and fourth-class citizens
(B) first-class citizens don't need to be provided for
(C) there is no such thing as a second-class citizen
(D) the Constitution makes no class distinctions
(E) none of these

13.   Recently, psychologists have proposed that American productivity is dropping because workers spend much of their time creating excuses for their laziness instead of focusing on assigned tasks. Although such workers sometimes experience "good" days when they labor efficiently and productively, such days are rare, and wasted time is the rule.

Which of the following proverbs best summarizes the argument above?
(A) As ye sow, so shall ye reap.
(B) Don't count your chickens before they hatch.
(C) A stitch in time saves nine.
(D) He that is good for making excuses is seldom good for anything else.
(E) You can fool some of the people all of the time.

14. Nothing can come of nothing; nothing can go back to nothing.

Which of the following follows most logically from the above statement?
(A) Something can come out of something; something can go back to something.
(B) Something can come out of nothing; something can go back to nothing.
(C) Nothing can come out of something; nothing can go back to something.
(D) Something must come out of something; something must go back to something.
(E) Something must come out of something; nothing can go back to nothing.

15. The President has vowed in speeches across the country that there will be no increase in taxes and no reduction in defense; he has repeatedly challenged Congress to narrow the deficit through deeper spending cuts. Congressional critics have responded with labored comparisons between a bloated Pentagon and the nation's poor being lacerated by merciless budget cutters. In Democratic cloakrooms, laments about the "intolerable deficit" are code words for higher taxes.

Which of the following additions to the passage would make clear the author's position on the budget issue?

(A) Everyone agrees that the President's budget deficit of around 100 billion is highly undesirable, to say the least.

(B) Everyone agrees that the President's budget deficit is both undesirable and unavoidable.

(C) Everyone agrees that this will be a summer of hot debate in Congress over the President's budget proposal.

(D) Everyone agrees that the partisan disagreement over the President's budget proposal will be won by those who create the most persuasive terminology.

(E) Everyone agrees that the President's budget proposal is a product of careful, honest, but sometimes misguided analysis.

16.   *The average wage in this plant comes to exactly $7.87 per working day.* In this statement *average* has the strict mathematical sense. It is the quotient obtained by dividing the sum of all wages for a given period by the product of the number of workers and the number of days in the period.

Which of the following is the most logical implication of the passage above?

(A) More workers in the plant earn $7.87 per day than those who do not earn $7.87 per day.

(B) Any particular worker in the plant receives $7.87 per day.

(C) There must be workers in the plant who earn far more than $7.87 per day.

(D) If some workers in the plant earn more than $7.87 per day, there must be others in the plant who earn less than $7.87 per day.

(E) There must be workers in the plant who earn exactly $7.87 per day.

17.   *Magazine article:* Davy "Sugar" Jinkins is one of the finest boxers to have ever fought. Last week Davy announced his retirement from the ring, but not from the sport. Davy will continue in boxing as the trainer of "Boom Boom" Jones. With Jinkins handling him, we are sure that Boom Boom will become a title contender in no time.

The foregoing article is based upon which of the following assumptions?

  I. Boxers who have a good trainer can do well.
 II. Jinkins did well as a boxer.
III. Those who were good boxers can be fine trainers.

(A) I only   (B) II only   (C) III only   (D) I and II only   (E) I and III only

18.   Motivation implies action, but the motivated individual will pursue certain goals and avoid others. The types of goals pursued and avoided have been determined by a statistical study of the (18) ——————————————— and deterrents, satisfactions and dissatisfactions, and rewards and punishments described by a number of motivated individuals.

Which of the following represents the most likely completion of the foregoing passage?

(A) incentives   (B) discouragements   (C) rewards   (D) avoidances   (E) goals

19.   The stores are always crowded on holidays. The stores are not crowded; therefore, it must not be a holiday.

Which of the following most closely parallels the kind of reasoning used in the above sentences?

(A) The stores are always crowded on Christmas. The stores are crowded; therefore, it must be Christmas.

(B) Reptiles are present on a hot day in the desert. Reptiles are absent in this desert area; therefore, this cannot be a hot desert day.

(C) There is a causal relationship between the occurrence of holidays and the number of people in stores.

(D) The voting places are empty; therefore, it is not an election day.
(E) The stores are always empty on Tuesdays. It is Tuesday; therefore, the stores will be empty.

Questions 20–21 refer to the following passage.

For one to be assured of success in politics, one must have a sound experiential background, be a polished orator, and possess great wealth. Should an individual lack any one of these attributes, he most certainly will be considered a dark horse in any campaign for public office. Should an individual be without any two of these attributes, he cannot win an election. If Nelson Nerd is to win the Presidency, he must greatly improve his ability as a public speaker. His extraordinary wealth is not enough.

20. The author of the above passage appears to believe that

  I. Nerd is the wealthiest candidate
  II. Nerd is a sufficiently experienced politician
  III. being a good public speaker alone can win one a high public office
  (A) I only   (B) II only   (C) III only   (D) I and II only   (E) I and III only

21. Which of the following would most weaken the speaker's claims?
  (A) Nerd is not the wealthiest candidate running for President.
  (B) The incumbent President had little relevant experience before coming into office and has always been a poor public speaker.
  (C) Of the individuals elected to public office, 0.001% have lacked either oratory skill, experience, or money.
  (D) Nerd failed in his last bid for the Presidency.
  (E) The incumbent President, who is running for reelection, is as wealthy as Nerd.

22. Since this car is blue, it must not accelerate quickly.

The foregoing conclusion can be properly drawn if it is also known that
  (A) all red cars accelerate quickly
  (B) there are some slow blue cars
  (C) all blue cars may not accelerate slowly
  (D) all cars that accelerate quickly are red
  (E) all slow cars are red

Questions 23–24 refer to the following passage.

As almost everyone is painfully aware, the federal government has butted into almost every sector of human existence in recent years. But this manic intrusiveness isn't always the government's fault. Sometimes there is a compulsion to enlist Uncle Sam as a superbusybody.

23. Which of the following is one of the author's basic assumptions?
  (A) Most of his readers have suffered government intrusion.
  (B) All government intrusion is unwarranted.
  (C) Government intrusion is always government-initiated.
  (D) All memories of government intrusion are painful memories.
  (E) At no time has the federal government practiced nonintrusiveness.

24. Which of the following most nearly restates the final sentence?
  (A) Most of the time government is responsible for government intrusion.
  (B) Sometimes government does more than intrude; it compels intrusion.
  (C) Sometimes Uncle Sam himself enlists in the ranks of the intruders.
  (D) Sometimes Uncle Sam is compulsive rather than merely symbolic.
  (E) Sometimes the government itself is not responsible for government intrusion.

25. Those who dictate what we can and cannot see on television are guilty of falsely equating knowledge with action. They would have us believe that to view violent behavior is to commit it.

On the basis of the content of the above passage, we may infer that the author would believe which of the following?
(A) Knowing how to manufacture nuclear weapons leads to nuclear war.
(B) Those guilty of committing a crime were not necessarily influenced by an awareness that such crimes occurred.
(C) Media censorship is based upon logical justification.
(D) Know your enemy.
(E) The truth shall set you free.

26. In 1975, the U.S. Supreme Court ruled that the federal government has exclusive rights to any oil and gas resources on the Atlantic Outer Shelf beyond the 3-mile limit.

Which of the following must be true in order for this ruling to be logical?
(A) The U.S. Supreme Court has met recently.
(B) The Atlantic Outer Shelf may possibly contain oil and gas resources.
(C) No oil and gas resources exist within the 3-mile limit.
(D) In 1977, the Court reversed this ruling.
(E) Oil and gas on the Atlantic Shelf has not been explored for in the past 3 years.

STOP

IF YOU FINISH BEFORE TIME HAS ELAPSED, CHECK YOUR WORK ON THIS SECTION OF THE TEST ONLY. DO NOT GO ON TO THE NEXT SECTION OF THE TEST UNTIL TIME IS UP FOR THIS SECTION.

SECTION V
ANALYTICAL REASONING

Time—35 Minutes
23 Questions

Directions:
In this section you will be given groups of questions based on different sets of conditions. Drawing a simple diagram may be helpful in answering some of the questions. You are to choose the best answer and mark the corresponding space on your answer sheet.

Questions 1–5

(1) Six people are seated around a circular table. There are no empty seats. Each person is wearing a colored shirt and a colored hat.
(2) Three people are wearing red shirts, two are wearing blue shirts, and one is wearing a green shirt.
(3) Two people are wearing blue hats, two are wearing red hats, and two are wearing green hats.
(4) One person is wearing a matching hat and shirt.
(5) No two people with the same color hats are sitting next to each other.
(6) No two people with the same color shirts are sitting next to each other.
(7) The one person who is wearing the green shirt is sitting between and next to the two people wearing the blue hats.
(8) The two people wearing the blue shirts are wearing the green hats.

1. Which of the following statements MUST be true?

    I.   A green hat is worn by a person in a red shirt.
    II. A blue hat is worn by a person in a blue shirt.
    III. Both blue hats are worn by people in red shirts.
    (A) I only   (B) II only   (C) III only   (D) II and III   (E) I and III

2. If the green shirt should turn red, then how many of the above conditions would no longer be true?
    (A) 1   (B) 2   (C) 3   (D) 4   (E) 5

3. If the two blue shirts turned green, then which of the following MUST be true?

    I.   Three people would be wearing a matching shirt and hat.
    II. Red and green shirts would alternate around the table.
    III. Except for the people wearing blue hats, everyone is wearing a matching hat and shirt.
    (A) I and II   (B) I and III   (C) II and III   (D) One of these   (E) All of these

4. If each person passed his hat two people to the left, how many people would end up with the same color hat they started with?
    (A) One   (B) Two   (C) Three   (D) Four   (E) Cannot be determined

5. If each person passed his hat three people to the right, then which of the following would be true?

    I.   Three people would now be wearing matching shirts and hats.
    II. No one wearing a red shirt would be wearing a blue hat.
    III. The two people wearing green hats would be wearing red shirts.
    (A) I and II   (B) I and III   (C) II and III   (D) I, II, and III   (E) Only one of these

Questions 6–10

    (1) Caryn, Dave, Ellen, and Frank have nicknames of Shorty, Peaches, King Kong, and Tiny—of course, not necessarily in that order.
    (2) Caryn is younger than Peaches and older than Tiny.
    (3) Tiny is older than Frank and younger than Shorty.

6. If Frank's nickname is not Peaches, then which of the following statements MUST be true?

    I.   Caryn's nickname is Shorty.
    II. Dave's nickname is not King Kong.
    III. Ellen's nickname is not Peaches.
    (A) I and II   (B) I and III   (C) II and III   (D) One of these   (E) All of these

7. If Shorty is older than King Kong, then which of the following MUST be true?

    I.   Shorty is older than Tiny.
    II. Caryn's nickname is not Shorty.
    III. Frank is younger than King Kong.
    (A) I and II   (B) I and III   (C) II and III   (D) One of these   (E) All of these

8. If Ellen's nickname is not Tiny, then Dave's nickname is
    (A) Shorty   (B) Peaches   (C) King Kong   (D) Tiny   (E) Cannot be determined

9. Who is the oldest?
    (A) Caryn   (B) Dave   (C) Ellen   (D) Frank   (E) Cannot be determined

10. Who is the youngest?
    (A) Caryn   (B) Dave   (C) Ellen   (D) Frank   (E) Cannot be determined

Questions 11–15

Flit Flies, which can mate on the day they are born, are insects capable of quick reproduction. Therefore, they are commonly used in laboratory experiments.

(1) Flit Flies mate only if three of four conditions are met: the presence of *agar-agar* (1) in a *petri dish* (2) at *78° temperature* (3) at *normal barometric pressure* (4).

(2) There is a 5-day interval from the time when Flit Flies mate to the birth of the offspring, during which time the Flit Flies may continue to mate.

(3) Flit Flies mate only once within any 24-hour period.

(4) Flit Flies are placed in a petri dish on June 1.

11. If a 2nd generation of Flit Flies is born, then which of the following MUST be true?

   I.   The temperature was 78°.
   II. Agar-agar was present.
   (A) I only   (B) II only   (C) Both I and II   (D) Either I or II, but not both
   (E) Either I or II or both

12. From June 1 to June 4, if agar-agar is present at 78° at normal barometric pressure, then which of the following MUST be true?
   (A)   The Flit Flies will mate.
   (B)   The Flit Flies will mate twice in one day.
   (C)   Offspring will not appear.
   (D)   The Flit Flies will not mate once daily.
   (E)   Offspring will mate.

13. If a 3rd generation of Flit Flies appears on June 15, which of the following MUST be true?

   I.   The 1st generation didn't begin mating until after June 5.
   II.   The 2nd generation didn't begin mating until after June 5.
   III. The 2nd generation didn't begin mating until after June 10.
   (A) I   (B) II   (C) III   (D) I and II   (E) I, II, and III

14. If a second set of 2nd generation Flit Flies appears on June 13, all of the following could be true except
   (A)   a first set of 2nd generation Flit Flies appeared on June 7
   (B)   a first set of 3rd generation Flit Flies appears on June 13
   (C)   the petri dish contained agar-agar at 78° temperature
   (D)   a first set of 3rd generation Flit Flies appeared on June 9
   (E)   a first set of 2nd generation Flit Flies mated on June 8

15. If suddenly Flit Flies are discovered to be dangerous to produce, what steps MUST the governor take to eliminate the Flit Fly population?

   I.   Destroy all petri dishes
   II. Confiscate all agar-agar
   III. Destroy all 1st generation Flit Flies
   (A) I   (B) II   (C) III   (D) Either I or II   (E) Both I and II

Questions 16–23

Crimes against people, habitation, society, or property may be divided into two types: felonies and misdemeanors. Felonies are the more serious crimes, punishable by death, or forfeiture of property and/or freedom for an extended period of time.

(1) Murder, manslaughter, rape, robbery, and kidnapping are felonies against people.

(2) Burglary and arson are crimes involving habitation, and are of the same level.

(3) Assault and battery are crimes against people that are not felonies.

(4) Crimes involving property are larceny, embezzlement, forgery, and the receiving of stolen goods; only one of these is always a felony.

(5) Embezzlement and larceny are the only crimes that can be either a felony or misdemeanor, depending on severity.

(6) Burglary and robbery are the same level of crime, but receiving stolen goods is not.

(7) Adultery, incest, bigamy, and prostitution are moral offenses, only two of which are felonies.

(8) Adultery and prostitution are not the same level as arson, but incest and bigamy are the same level as forgery.

Using only the statements above and commonsense reasoning, answer the following questions.

16. Which of the following MUST be felonies?

   I. Rape
  II. Arson
 III. Larceny
(A) I only   (B) II only   (C) I and II only   (D) I and III only   (E) II and III only

17. How many crimes can be classified as either felonies or misdemeanors?
(A) One   (B) Two   (C) Three   (D) Four   (E) More than four

18. Which of the following could be misdemeanors?
(A) Embezzlement, prostitution, and receiving stolen property
(B) Larceny, forgery, and adultery
(C) Prostitution, larceny, and murder
(D) Burglary, embezzlement, and receiving stolen property
(E) Bigamy, incest, and adultery

19. If all felonious crimes against people were punishable by death, then
(A) arson and burglary would not be punishable by death
(B) murder, rape, manslaughter, robbery and kidnapping would be punishable by death
(C) assault and battery would be punishable by death
(D) some of the felonious crimes against people would be punishable by loss of freedom
(E) none of the above

20. The most abundant crimes are
(A) crimes against people
(B) crimes against habitation
(C) crimes against society
(D) crimes against property
(E) not determinable by these statements

21. Which of the following can be deduced from the statements and MUST be true?

   I. Burglary is a felony.
  II. Larceny is a misdemeanor.
 III. Receiving stolen property is the same level of crime as adultery.
(A) I only   (B) II only   (C) III   (D) I and III   (E) II and III

22. If indecent exposure is a crime against society, then what MUST it be?
(A) a misdemeanor
(B) a crime against people

    (C)   punishable by forfeiture of property
    (D)   a felony
    (E)   cannot be determined

23. According to statements 1–8, there are
    (A)   more felonies than misdemeanors committed each year
    (B)   seven sorts of crimes against people
    (C)   no two crimes that can be committed at the same time
    (D)   three sorts of moral offenses that are felonies
    (E)   less than two crimes that can be felonies or misdemeanors

STOP

IF YOU FINISH BEFORE TIME HAS ELAPSED, CHECK YOUR WORK ON THIS SECTION OF THE TEST ONLY. DO NOT GO ON TO THE NEXT SECTION OF THE TEST UNTIL TIME IS UP FOR THIS SECTION.

SECTION VI
LOGICAL REASONING

Time—35 Minutes
26 Questions

Directions:
In this section you will be given brief statements or passages and will be required to evaluate the reasoning involved. In some instances, more than one choice will appear to be a possible answer. You are to choose the *best* answer. Use common sense and reasonableness in making your selection; then mark the proper space on the answer sheet.

Questions 1–2 refer to the following passage.

    Lotteries are a socially expensive form of generating revenues. They attract those least able to afford it, and thus become a form of regressive taxation. A six-month study conducted in 1979 in New Castle County, Delaware, found that poor persons bet three times as much on a regular basis as did those from upper-middle income areas. In fact, most lottery machines were located in the poorest areas of the county, areas where unemployment is highest and the standard of living lowest. By contrast, not a single lottery machine was located in the high-income neighborhood of the county. Maryland's instant lottery came under such severe criticism that it was soaking the poor that the government finally scrapped it several weeks ago.

1. Which of the following facts would be most useful in judging the effectiveness of the details offered to support the author's criticism of lotteries?
    (A)   The name of the group that conducted the 6-month survey.
    (B)   A comparison of the amounts bet by the poor, the middle class, and the upper class.
    (C)   A discussion of the gambling activity of upper-class citizens.
    (D)   The rationale for locating the lottery machines in poor neighborhoods.
    (E)   A discussion of the revenue-generating programs that preceded the lottery in Delaware.

2. Which of the following, if true, would be the best refutation of the argument above?
(A)   Many of the poor have enjoyed the opportunity to gamble.
(B)   The high-income neighborhood is exclusively residential.
(C)   Money from the lottery is generated more from the middle-class areas.
(D)   The study conducted in New Castle has been duplicated elsewhere, but other lotteries continue to operate.
(E)   The upper-class citizens shoulder 10% of the tax burden.

3. Every movie star I have read about lives in an expensive home. They must all live in such places.

Which of the following most nearly parallels the logic of the foregoing argument?
(A)   All movie producers must be demanding, probably because of the stresses placed upon them.
(B)   This piece of matter must be a rock, since it does not fit any other description in the textbook.
(C)   All the paintings by Visson in the library are bright. Every one of his works must be bright.
(D)   All paint has noxious odor. This liquid has such an odor and, therefore, must be paint.
(E)   Inasmuch as all pine trees are evergreen and this tree has not lost its needles, it is likely to be a pine.

4.   The San Diego Chargers practice expertly for long hours every day and keep a written log of their errors.

The above fact is an example of which of the following assumptions?
(A)   Practice makes perfect.
(B)   To err is human.
(C)   People make mistakes; that's why they put erasers on pencils.
(D)   Practice is what you know, and it will help to make clear what now you do not know.
(E)   Writing is a mode of learning.

5.   I.   Pine trees may be taller than any other tree.
   II.   Pines are never shorter than the shortest palms, and some palms may exceed the height of some pines.
   III.   Pepper trees are always taller than palm trees.
   IV.   Peach trees are shorter than pepper trees but not shorter than all palms.

Given the foregoing, which of the following would be true?
(A)   Peach trees may be shorter than pine trees.
(B)   Pepper trees may be shorter than some peach trees.
(C)   Every pine is taller than every palm.
(D)   A particular palm could not be taller than a particular pine.
(E)   Now and then a peach tree may be taller than a pepper.

Questions 6–7 refer to the following passage.

With so many opportunities for true reform that would save the taxpayers' money, there is reason to look askance at proposals by legislators that would make life easier for them with public funds. Only last year, the Assembly, after a considerable public outcry, finally ruled out a bill whereby only 25 percent of campaign spending reports filed by legislative candidates would be audited instead of 50 percent under current law.

6. Which of the following is the most logical continuation of this passage?
   (A) Clearly, it is through increased auditing of campaign spending that we will secure honest representation.
   (B) Must we consider every "gift" the legislator offers us as a Trojan horse, filled with traitors bent on destroying the state?
   (C) Who are they trying to kid?
   (D) We must bemoan the fact that there are no opportunities for true reform, only for white-collar fraud.
   (E) Is it any wonder, then, that citizens should be as wary of legislators bearing election reforms as the adage warns one to be of Greeks bearing gifts?

7. The author is arguing that
   (A) legislators often act in their own best interests
   (B) public outcry is more effective than the ballot box
   (C) more than half of campaign expenditures are unwarranted
   (D) legislators are not aware of opportunities for true reform
   (E) this year, reform is more possible than it was last year

8. A few mimes are sad.
   All mimes are funny.
   Children cannot be sad and funny at the same time.

   Given that the foregoing are true, which of the following MUST be true?

   I.   There are no sad children.
   II. No child is a mime.
   III. No sad mimes are children.
   (A) I only   (B) II only   (C) III only   (D) I and II only   (E) II and III only

9. I. Everyone who is a slow runner either does not engage in any track and field event or does poorly in such events.
   II. Everyone who does not engage in any track and field event is a slow runner.

   Which of the following best indicates the relationship between the two statements above?
   (A) If II is true, then I is true.
   (B) If II is true, then I is most likely false.
   (C) If II is true, then I can be either true or false.
   (D) If I is true, the II is true.
   (E) If I is false, then II is most likely false.

10. Given that this rock is white in color, it must be quartz.

   The foregoing conclusion can be properly drawn if it is true that
   (A) only quartz rocks are white in color
   (B) quartz rocks are generally white in color
   (C) other white rocks have proved to be quartz
   (D) few other types of rocks are white in color
   (E) all quartz rocks are white in color

11. During the last 50 years, the majority of individuals receiving awards for their humanitarian works have been blonde. Therefore, having blonde hair is the cause of humanitarianism.

   Each of the following, if true, *weakens* the preceding conclusion *except*
   (A) these people who received such honors are not representative of all humanitarians
   (B) a physical condition not caused by having blonde hair, but more prevalent among blondes than among others, causes humanitarian behavior
   (C) during the last 100 years fewer blondes than others received humanitarian honors

(D) the total population contains a higher percentage of blondes than others at any given time

(E) the total population contains a far smaller percentage of blondes than does the subpopulation consisting of those individuals having received honors for humanitarian endeavors

12. Operation of nuclear reactor-driven power plants does not adversely affect small game hunting within nearby public ranges. The Fertile Crescent Nuclear Facility began operating this year, and a number of squirrels caught nearby set a five-season high.

All of the following statements, if true, are valid objections to the foregoing argument *except*
(A) radiation from such reactors renders certain species of rodents sterile
(B) radiation from such reactors reduces the mortality rate among immature squirrels
(C) factors having nothing to do with the well-being of squirrels may have a marked impact on the number of animals taken in a given season
(D) radioactivity emanating from power plant reactors interferes with the growth of various forms of vegetation consumed by squirrels
(E) squirrels are only one of numerous species of small game that may be affected by the presence of a nuclear reactor

13. If the poodle was reared at Prince Charming Kennels, then it is a purebred.

The foregoing statement can be deduced logically from which of the following statements?
(A) Every purebred poodle is reared at Prince Charming Kennels or another AKC approved kennel.
(B) The poodle in question was bred at either Prince Charming Kennels or at another AKC approved kennel.
(C) The poodle in question either is a purebred or looks remarkably like a purebred.
(D) The majority of poodles reared at Prince Charming Kennels are purebred.
(E) There are no dogs reared at Prince Charming Kennels that are not purebred.

14. There is no reason to eliminate the possibility of an oil field existing beneath the Great Salt Lake. Therefore, we must undertake the exploration of the Salt Lake's bottom.

The foregoing argument assumes which of the following?
(A) Exploration of the Salt Lake's bottom has not been previously proposed.
(B) An oil field located beneath the lake would be easy to identify.
(C) The Great Salt Lake is the only large inland body of water beneath which an oil field may lie.
(D) The quest for oil is a sufficient motive to undertake exploration of the Salt Lake's bottom.
(E) An oil field exists beneath the Great Salt Lake.

15. Most popular paperback novels are of low intellectual quality; therefore, *Splendor Behind the Billboard*, an unpopular paperback novel, is probably of high intellectual quality.

The foregoing argument is most like which of the following?
(A) Most locusts inhabit arid places; therefore, locusts are probably found in all deserts.
(B) Most acts of criminal violence have declined in number during the past few years; therefore, law enforcement during this period has improved.
(C) Most people who stop drinking gain weight; therefore, if Carl does not cease drinking, he will probably not gain weight.
(D) Most nations run by autocratic governments do not permit a free press; therefore the country of Endorff, which is run by an autocratic government, probably does not have a free press.
(E) Most new motor homes are equipped with air conditioning; therefore, Jim's new motor home may not be equipped with air conditioning.

16.   The greatest danger to a society ruled by a monarchy is the increasing bureaucratization of the ruling process. As the bureaucracy becomes more entrenched, it becomes less responsive to both the ruler and the ruled. There is a threshold beyond which the result is governance by technocracy.

It can be inferred from the foregoing that the author believes that
(A)   bureaucracy should be curbed
(B)   monarchy is doomed
(C)   bureaucracies are more efficient than monarchies
(D)   bureaucrats are hostile to those they serve
(E)   bureaucracy is a superior form of governance

17. All medications are habit forming.
Everything habit forming soothes pain.
Nothing nonaddictive soothes pain.

Given that the foregoing are true, which of the following MUST be *false*?

  I.   Some medications are nonaddictive.
  II. All medications soothe pain.
  III. Aspirins are habit forming and nonaddictive.
(A) I only   (B) II only   (C) III only   (D) I and II only   (E) I and III only

Questions 18–19 refer to the following statement.

Jane states, "All mammals have hair. This creature possesses no hair. Therefore, it is not a mammal."

18. Which of the following most closely parallels the logic of Jane's statement?
(A)   All reptiles have scales. This creature possesses scales. Therefore, it is a reptile.
(B)   All physics tests are difficult. This is not a physics test. Therefore, it is not difficult.
(C)   All American cars are poorly constructed. Every car sold by Fred was poorly constructed. Therefore, Fred sells only American cars.
(D)   All mammals do not have hair. This creature possesses hair. Therefore, it may be a mammal.
(E)   All lubricants smell. This liquid does not have an odor. Therefore, it is not a lubricant.

19. Which of the following, if true, would most weaken Jane's argument?
(A)   Animals other than mammals have hair.
(B)   Some mammals do not have hair.
(C)   Mammals have more hair than nonmammals.
(D)   One could remove the hair from a mammal.
(E)   Reptiles may have hair.

Questions 20–22 refer to the missing portions of the following passage. For each question, select the insertion that best fits the meaning of the passage.

Psychoanalytical theory asserts that by attributing (projecting) his own consciously unacceptable motivations to those around him, the individual is able to avoid recognizing them as being his own. Inasmuch as social prejudices involve the ascription of undesirable traits and motives to various groups or classes, they would seem to be particularly attractive to those individuals who employ projection as a technique for (20) ——————————————their perception of their own consciously unacceptable motivations. The fact that the undesirable traits ascribed to groups or classes in which the target of prejudice often includes motives of greed and mistrust (motives commonly (21) ——————————————by those who have them) supports the theory that these attributions of traits are, in fact, projections by individuals who (22) —————————————— their own motivations of the same nature.

20. (A) validating   (B) strengthening   (C) proving   (D) avoiding   (E) clarifying

21. (A) desired   (B) rejected   (C) held   (D) projected   (E) accepted

22. (A) repress   (B) reject   (C) accept   (D) project   (E) recognize

23. When we approach land, we usually sight birds. The lookout has just sighted birds.

Which of the following represents the most logical conclusion based upon the foregoing statements?
(A)   The conjecture that we are approaching land is strengthened.
(B)   Land is closer than it was before the sighting of the birds.
(C)   We are approaching land.
(D)   We may or may not be approaching land.
(E)   We may not be approaching land.

24. The presence of the gas Nexon is a necessary condition, but not a sufficient condition, for the existence of life on the planet Plex.

On the basis of the foregoing, which of the following would also be true?

 I.   If life exists on Plex, then only the gas Nexon is present.
 II.   If life exists on Plex, then the gas Nexon may or may not be present.
 III.   If life exists on Plex, then the gas Nexon is present.
(A) I only   (B) II only   (C) III only   (D) I and II only   (E) I and III only

25. The absence of the liquid Flennel is a sufficient condition for the cessation of life on the planet Fluke, but it is not a necessary condition.

On the basis of the foregoing, which of the following would also be true?

 I.   If life on Fluke ceased to exist, there would have to have been an absence of the liquid Flennel.
 II.   If all liquid Flennel were removed from Fluke, life there would surely perish.
 III.   If all liquid Flennel were removed from Fluke, life there might or might not cease.
(A) I only   (B) II only   (C) III only   (D) I and II only   (E) I, II, and III

26. None but fools would do that.

Which of the following has the same meaning as the preceding statement?

 I.   All of those who would do that are fools.
 II.   Every one who would do that is a fool.
 III.   All fools do that.
(A) I only   (B) II only   (C) I and II only   (D) I and III only   (E) II and III only

STOP

END OF EXAMINATION. IF YOU FINISH BEFORE TIME HAS ELAPSED, CHECK YOUR WORK ON THIS SECTION ONLY. DO NOT GO BACK TO ANY OTHER SECTION OF THE EXAMINATION.

ANSWER KEY

Section I:
Reading Comprehension

1. A	7. E	13. B	19. B	24. E
2. C	8. B	14. A	20. C	25. D
3. D	9. B	15. E	21. A	26. C
4. B	10. E	16. B	22. B	27. C
5. C	11. E	17. C	23. B	28. A
6. B	12. A	18. B		

Section IV:
Logical Reasoning

1. D	7. D	12. D	17. E	22. D
2. D	8. B	13. D	18. A	23. A
3. C	9. C	14. D	19. B	24. E
4. A	10. C	15. A	20. B	25. B
5. E	11. D	16. D	21. B	26. B
6. C				

Section II:
Analytical Reasoning

1. A	7. A	13. B	19. B	23. E
2. E	8. D	14. E	20. B	24. D
3. B	9. E	15. B	21. C	25. E
4. E	10. A	16. E	22. E	26. D
5. D	11. D	17. A		
6. C	12. E	18. D		

Section V:
Analytical Reasoning

1. C	6. A	11. E	16. C	20. E
2. D	7. D	12. C	17. B	21. D
3. A	8. D	13. B	18. A	22. E
4. B	9. E	14. D	19. B	23. B
5. D	10. D	15. E		

Section III:
Evaluation of Facts

1. C	9. D	16. B	23. A	30. D
2. A	10. C	17. C	24. C	31. C
3. C	11. A	18. D	25. A	32. C
4. D	12. C	19. A	26. D	33. A
5. C	13. D	20. C	27. B	34. A
6. A	14. B	21. A	28. A	35. D
7. D	15. B	22. D	29. D	36. B
8. B				

Section VI:
Logical Reasoning

1. B	7. A	12. B	17. E	22. A
2. C	8. C	13. E	18. E	23. A
3. C	9. C	14. D	19. B	24. C
4. D	10. A	15. C	20. D	25. B
5. A	11. E	16. A	21. B	26. C
6. E				

MODEL TEST ANALYSIS

Doing model exams and understanding the explanations afterwards are of course important in acquainting you with typical LSAT question types and successful approaches to the questions. However, another benefit of carefully analyzing these model tests is to understand the kinds of errors you are making and thus work to minimize them. For instance, if a very high percentage of your incorrect answers is due to "careless error" or "misread problem," then perhaps you are working much too fast and should slow your pace accordingly. If your incorrect answers are due primarily to "lack of knowledge," then a careful rereading and reworking of the appropriate question-type chapter may be in order. Or if you find that you aren't completing a large number of questions because of lack of time, you may need to either increase your speed or learn to use the "one-check, two-check" technique more effectively.

This kind of analysis of the model tests will enable you to identify your particular weaknesses and thus remedy them.

Model Test Four Analysis

Section	Total Number of Questions	Number Correct	Number Incorrect	Number Unanswered*
I: Reading Comprehension	28			
II: Analytical Reasoning	26			
III: Evaluation of Facts	36			
IV: Logical Reasoning	26			
V: Analytical Reasoning	23			
VI: Logical Reasoning	26			
TOTALS:	165			

*At this stage in your preparation, you should not be leaving any unanswered answer spaces. At least fill in a guess, as there is no penalty for a wrong answer.

Reasons for Incorrect Answers

You may wish to evaluate the explanations before completing this chart.

Section	Total Incorrect	Lack of Knowledge	Misread Problem	Careless Error	Unanswered or Wrong Guess
I: Reading Comprehension					
II: Analytical Reasoning					
III: Evaluation of Facts					
IV: Logical Reasoning					
V: Analytical Reasoning					
VI: Logical Reasoning					
TOTALS					

EXPLANATIONS OF ANSWERS

Section I

Passage 1

1. **A** In the preceding sentence of the third paragraph, the author states that the Jazz Age ended with the 1929 depression, thus stressing that it was a phenomenon of the 1920s only. Recognizing that "it" stands for "Jazz Age," and refers to the preceding sentence, you must choose (A).

2. **C** The sentence indicates that the "Canon" consists of a group of writers and their works; the only choice that suggests a group or collection is (C).

3. **D** The 1960s are mentioned at the end of the second paragraph, just after the author has noted the human tendency to "forget unpleasantness." The '60s may become a happy recollection, we are told, but not until the twenty-first century. This speculation suggests that the author presently regards the '60s as an unhappy time that may be recalled more pleasantly after the passage of a few decades.

4. **B** The long assessment of Gertrude Stein in paragraph 4 follows the author's statement that she is one who made a deep impact after 1930, although many of her works were written before 1930. She, along with others, was "ahead of her time." (A), (C), and (D) are all true, but state subordinate facts rather than stressed points.

5. **C** Although the author acknowledges the importance of the stock market crash as an event that makes a "decisive cut" in literary history, he also stresses, "When dates are established, . . . predecessors and successors have a way of making them dissolve," thus suggesting that the crash cannot be isolated as a demarcation point without accounting for the events that led up to it and followed it. (D) and (E) are supported by the passage, but irrelevant to this particular question.

6. **B** In the final paragraph of the passage, the author states that in the 1930s "realism and naturalism are by this time established as dominant modes."

7. **E** Earlier in the third paragraph, we are told that the Wasteland "represents" a view of the '20s, '30s, and '40s. Therefore, the term does not literally describe an actual wasteland (D), but rather stands for a point of view that artists held about this era; it is a *figurative* term.

Passage 2

8. **B** Each of the other choices is too specific and/or not indicative of the *neutral* rather than argumentative *tone* of the passage.

9. **B** In the fourth paragraph, the author notes that after Congress had stopped enacting its reapportionment power, "serious malapportionment" problems ensued; the author thus implies that federal supervision is necessary. (C), (D), and (E) are issues on which the author does not imply an opinion.

10. **E** A clue to this answer occurs in paragraph 5, in which "malapportionment" is replaced by "the size and shape of electoral districts." Each of the other choices *may contribute* to malapportionment, but each is too specific to be the best choice.

11. **E** In the fifth paragraph we learn that the *voters* asked the Warren Court to rule on apportionment issues; therefore, we must assume that a ballot was taken that expressed the voters' opinions.

12. **A** Question I is answered in the first paragraph. The other questions, although they may be implied as *issues* in the passage, are not answered.

13. **B** Justice Frankfurter did not declare his opinion about reapportionment per se, but did declare that the Supreme Court should not address the issue; the Warren Court, on the other hand, did deliberate over the reapportionment issue. Therefore, we may conclude that Frankfurter was not a member of the Warren Court.

14. **A** The passage is a summary of events that occurred through the century, relative to apportionment. Each of the other choices has the author writing a passage calculated to persuade rather than to inform.

Passage 3

15. **E** The passage mentions diverse forms of government, from totalitarian Rome to modern American democracy, in each instance stressing the theatrical nature of political assemblies. The other choices are explicitly contradicted in the passage.

16. **B** Each of the other choices describes a subsidiary point of the passage. In general, the passage demonstrates that, in many governments at many times, politics has been a theatrical enterprise.

17. **C** The author uses "spectacle" at other points in the passage to describe the same sort of assembly he mentions here; we can call the "liturgical assembly" a "spectacle of worship," because the definition of "liturgical" is "connected with public worship."

18. **B** Although the author does not overtly and angrily criticize politics-as-show-business, he certainly calls into question through his descriptions of theatrical frivolity the worth of a politician who is "entertaining." If it seemed to you that the author was objective and neutral, your only possible choice would be (D), "unconcerned," which certainly contradicts the author's detailed interest in the phenomenon he describes.

19. **B** In the fifth paragraph, the author says that the diversion of political entertainment takes attention "away from true problems and realities."

20. **C** Each of the other choices may be eliminated easily, and it is quite obvious that historical facts occur repeatedly throughout the passage.

21. **A** Only (A) is an example of a politician taking part in show business; this example stresses the convergence of politics and show business that is the subject of the whole passage.

Passage 4

22. **B** Asian countries south of Russia are not mentioned in the passage, and neither are the products of the large American quadrilateral belt; therefore I and III may be eliminated.

23. **B** With the common knowledge that the USSR and the United States are military rivals (knowledge stressed in the final sentence of the passage), we may conclude that strategic considerations are military ones. Each of the other choices is either not related to a *strategic* consideration or not related to the issue of *location*.

24. **E** None of the choices connotes *motivation,* which is relevant to the meaning of "spur" in this context.

25. **D** Although North America, Europe, and the Soviet Union are compared during the course of the passage, (A) is not best because it does not specify the nature of the comparison, and is therefore too vague. (D) is both comprehensive and precise.

26. **C** This is stated explicitly in the fourth paragraph. (A), (B), and (D) are contradicted in the passage, and (E) is illogical.

27. **C** The advantages are listed in paragraph 2, and climate is not one of them.

28. **A** Although each of the other choices is touched upon in the passage, the overall survey is geographical.

Section II

Answers 1–7

1. **A** From statements 1, 2, and 7, we know that Aaron sings bass, and that David is not the baritone or the second baseman. Therefore, the tenor could be the second baseman (I). However, these statements do not specify whether Aaron, the bass player, is or is not the third baseman or the shortstop. Therefore, II and III cannot be deduced.

2. **E** From statements 1, 3, 4, and 8, we know that Clifford is not the tenor or the first baseman, and that the baritone plays first base. Therefore, (I), the tenor could be the second baseman; (II), Clifford is not the baritone (since he is not the first baseman and the baritone plays first base); and (III), Clifford could be the bass.

3. **B** Using all the statements, we may construct two charts:

	A	B	C	D
1st			X	
2nd				X
3rd	X			
SS		X		

Bar = 1st
Ten ≠ 3rd

	A	B	C	D
Bass	√	X	X	X
Bar	X			X
Ten	X		X	
Al	X	X		

Now notice that the baritone can only be either Bryan or Clifford. Since Clifford is not the first baseman, and the first baseman is the baritone, Bryan must be the baritone.

Now the charts will look like this:

	A	B	C	D
1st	X	√	X	X
2nd		X		X
3rd	X	X		
SS		X		

	A	B	C	D
Bass	√	X	X	X
Bar	X	√	X	X
Ten	X	X	X	
Al	X	X		

This will now allow us to complete the rest of the Barbershop Quartet Chart (since David must be the tenor, then Clifford must be the alto). And since the tenor (David) is not the third baseman (statement 10), we may complete the softball chart:

	A	B	C	D
1st	X	✓	X	X
2nd	✓	X	X	X
3rd	X	X	✓	X
SS	X	X	X	✓

	A	B	C	D
Bass	✓	X	X	X
Bar	X	✓	X	X
Ten	X	X	X	✓
Al	X	X	✓	X

Thus, Bryan is the first baseman.

4. **E** From the completed charts we can see that all of the statements are true.

5. **D** Since David is the tenor and the shortstop, all of the statements are true.

6. **C** Clifford is the third baseman.

7. **A** If Aaron and Bryan switch playing positions on the softball team, only statement 3 ("The baritone plays first base,") is false.

Answers 8–14

The following Venn diagram may be constructed from the information to help you answer the questions:

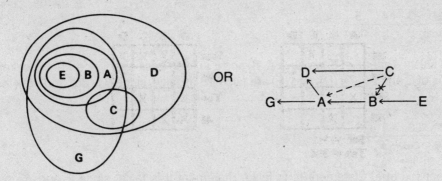

Note that the circles indicate all the possibilities that may exist.

8. **D** If some C's are A's, and all A's are G's (from statements 6 and 4), then logically some C's are G's. Since all E's are B's, and all B's are A's, then all E's are G's.

9. **E** Since statement 5 tells us no C's are B's, then "some C's are B's" must be false. Note that (C) may be false, but not necessarily must be false.

10. **A** If all D's are G's, then from statement 1 we can conclude that all A's, B's, and C's are also G's. Thus I is true. There is no statement, however, that would lead us to believe II to be true.

11. **D** Since all C's are D's (statement 1), then, if Q is within C, Q must also be within D.

12. **E** There are no statements telling us what G's are. Therefore we can conclude none of the above statements. Notice that our diagram shows G may exist *outside* any of the other circles.

13. **B** If all J's are B's, then all J's must lie within A's and D's. Therefore only I and II *must* be true. Note that III *may* be true.

14. **E** If some D's are Q's, then Q's could possibly exist within circle D but not within any of the other circles. Therefore, though Q's *may* be C's, A's, B's, or G's, they are not necessarily any of these.

Answers 15–20

Note: UPPER-case letters denote fixed positions. Lower-case letters denote various possibilities.

15. **B**

1	2	3	4	5
c/d	E	A	B	d/c

Since E, A, and B cannot be 1st or 5th, their places are fixed. Since we do not know whether D finished 1st or 5th, I is false. Statements II and III follow from the diagram.

16. **E**

1	2	3	4	5
C	e	a	b	D
	a	e	b	
	a	b	e	

(A) is always true. (B) could be true. (C) could be true. (D) is always true. Thus the answer is (E).

17. **A**

1	2	3	4	5
c/d	A	B	E	d/c

Since B finishes ahead of E, we have A, B, and E in fixed positions. Since we do not know the positions of C and D, (C), (D), and (E) are false. (B) is false, since B is 3rd and not 4th. (A) is true.

18. **D**

1	2	3	4	5
D	a/e	e/a	B	C

Statement I is true. Statement III is false. Statement II is false, since E and A could be reversed at any time.

19. **B**

1	2	3	4	5	6
c/d	a/e	e/a	F	B	d/c

(A), (C), and (D) are all true from observation. (B) is false since we cannot determine the exact positions of C and D.

20. **B**

1	2	3	4	5	6
D	E	A	B	F	C

This is the only possible arrangement based on the facts. Thus, I and III are true and II is false.

Answers 21–26.

Drawing the simple diagram below will help answer the questions.

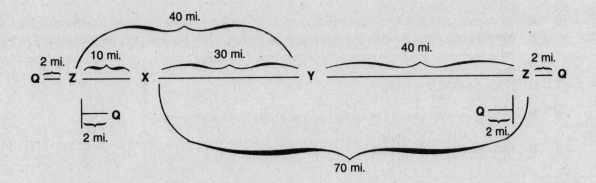

21. **C** Since Z is 40 miles from Y, and X is 30 miles from Y, Z could be 10 miles from X (left side of diagram).

22. **E** Q may be either 38 or 42 miles from Y, and either 68 or 8 miles from X. City Q may not be 38 miles from city X.

23. **E** If city Q is 12 miles from X, Q must be situated at the extreme left side of the diagram above. Therefore Z must be 10 miles from city X.

24. **D** XQZY may not be a possible order because Q may not come between X and Y.

25. **E** If a traveler begins at X and ends at Q, he may possibly only travel 8 miles, directly to Q without passing through any other city.

26. **D** By adding M 5 miles on either side of Y, all of the choices could be true, with the exception of E.

Section III

Set 1

1. **C** This relevant question can be answered from the facts. Since ice cream must have a minimum of 18% real cream, and Ena's had 17½% real cream, then she violated state law.

2. **A** To answer this relevant question you must choose between the rules. Each rule gives a different outcome. By Rule I, she is liable and will lose the suit. By Rule II, if the use of milk was an accident, then she is not liable and will win the suit.

3. **C** This relevant question is answerable by applying the facts to the rules. By Rule I, she is liable and Mitch will win the suit. Rule II does not apply.

4. **D** This question is irrelevant.

Set 2

5. **C** This relevant question can be answered by applying the facts to the rules. By Rules I and II, if Jim had intended to cause injury and the act was premeditated, then he is liable and Sally will win the suit.

6. **A** To answer this relevant question you must choose between the rules. Each rule gives a different outcome. By Rule I, Jim will lose. By Rule II, if the act was not premeditated, Jim will win.

7. **D** This question is irrelevant.

8. **B** To answer this relevant question you need additional information.

9. **D** This question is irrelevant.

Set 3

10. **C** This relevant question can be answered from the facts and rules. By Rule I, Lincoln would win because the premises fell below habitable standards and the landlord failed to correct the situation. Rule II does not apply since the premises were occupied for less than 30 days.

11. **A** To answer this relevant question, you will have to choose between the rules. Each rule gives a different outcome. By Rule I, Lincoln will not have to pay the last month's rent. By Rule II, since he occupied the premises for at least 30 days, he will have to pay the last month's rent.

12. **C** This relevant question can be answered by applying Rule II, since Rule I would not apply. By Rule II, Adams will win the suit.

13. **D** This question is irrelevant.

14. **B** To answer this relevant question you need additional rules.

15. **B** To answer this relevant question you need additional rules defining occupancy and habitable standards.

Set 4

16. **B** To answer this relevant question you need additional information. You need to know Rick's age and a definition for "involved in the killing" (Rule II).

17. **C** This relevant question can be readily answered from the facts. Danny is 12 years old.

18. **D** This question is irrelevant.

19. **A** To answer this relevant question you must choose between the rules. Each rule gives a different outcome. By Rule I, Danny is not liable and will not be convicted because he is under 14 years of age. By Rule II, he will be convicted, regardless of his age.

20. **C** This relevant question can be answered by applying the facts and rules. By Rule I, Rick could be guilty. By Rule II, he is guilty, since he was involved.

21. **A** To answer this relevant question you must choose between the rules. Each rule gives a different outcome. By Rule I, he will not be guilty because of his age. By Rule II, since he was involved, he will be guilty.

22. **D** This question is irrelevant.

Set 5

23. **A** To answer this relevant question you must choose between the rules. Each gives a different outcome. By Rule I, Sammy will win his suit, as the manufacturer is liable. By Rule II, the manufacturer is liable only to the purchaser; therefore Sammy will not win.

24. **C** This relevant question can be answered by applying the facts and Rule II. By Rule II, Albert will win his suit, since he was the purchaser and the warranty papers were filed. Rule I does not apply if the set cost under $300.

25. **A** To answer this relevant question you must choose between the rules. Each rule gives a different outcome. By Rule I, if the set cost $400, then Darla will win her suit. By Rule II, if the warranty papers were not filed, then the manufacturer is not liable. Even if they were filed, the manufacturer would be liable only to the purchaser, not Darla.

26. **D** This question is irrelevant.

27. **B** To answer this relevant question you need additional information. The cost of the TV set is important.

28. **A** To answer this relevant question you must choose between the rules. Each rule gives a different outcome. By Rule I, Otis will win his suit. By Rule II, Otis will not win, as the manufacturer is liable only to the purchaser.

29. **D** This question is irrelevant.

Set 6

30. **D** This is an unimportant issue.

31. **C** This relevant question can be answered by applying Rule II. Yes, Sal was guilty because he did forcibly take Scarlet to another country. Rule I is more general, but would still give the same answer.

32. **C** This relevant question can be answered by using the facts and the rules. Since Tim was not intentionally or forcibly imprisoned or moved, he was not kidnapped.

33. **A** To answer this relevant question, you must choose between the two rules. Each rule will give you a different answer. By Rule I, Hal is not guilty because Scarlet's boyfriend never left the country. By Rule II, Hal is guilty.

34. **A** To answer this relevant question, you must choose between the two rules. Each rule will give you a different answer. By Rule I, Sal is not guilty because Scarlet never left the country. By Rule II, Sal is guilty.

35. **D** This is irrelevant.

36. **B** To answer this relevant question you need additional rules. You need to know whether Hal is still considered an accomplice.

Section IV

1. **D** If 97% of fatalities occurred *below 45 mph*, then a reduction in the maximum speed from 65 to 55 mph would have little impact, no more than a 3% reduction (if we assume that all other fatalities occurred between 55 and 65 mph). (A) and (C) are not relevant, (B) provides no conclusive data, and (E) *strengthens* the argument.

2. **D** The information states:
    1. If busing passes, then Smith was not reelected.
    2. Smith was reelected.
    Therefore, busing failed.
    3. If Smith is reelected she will vote for busing.
    4. Smith was reelected.
    Therefore, Smith voted for busing.

    (A) and (B) are wrong, because busing failed. (C) is wrong because Smith voted for busing. (E) is wrong because there are insufficient data to support it.

3. **C** Webster is stating that not only do lies disagree with truth, but they usually also disagree with other lies. Thus, it would follow that liars often quarrel with other liars.

4. **A** The given argument can be reduced to:
    is <u>not</u> S (star) because H (hit)
    <u>is</u>   H   because S

    (A) exhibits the structure closest to that of the given argument:
    is <u>not</u> F (final word) because C (correct)
    <u>is</u>   C (correct)   because F ("Instructor" is the final word.)

5. **E** *Setting aside the condition given* in the question, there are four possible states that could exist:

	Doxin	*Entrox*
1.	Present	Present
2.	Present	Absent
3.	Absent	Present
4.	Absent	Absent

    The condition contained in the question rules out state 2 only. I (state 3), II (state 1), and IV (state 4) are true. III (state 2) is false.

6. **C** The discussion points out that I is an implication (rather than an assumption) of the studies. Statement II is also not an assumption but is a restatement of the discussion's central issue. In order to consider speaker characteristics as either relevant or irrelevant, the author must assume that such a distinction exists; that assumption is expressed by III only.

7. **D** The final sentence of the passage offers an alternative explanation of the phenomenon introduced in the first sentence.

8. **B** The author, by offering an alternative explanation, stresses the scientists' unwillingness to consider such alternatives. (A), a choice worth considering, should be eliminated because the alternative suggested by the author is no more verifiable than the assertion he criticizes.

9. **C** The author argues that the term "progressive" is avoided by educators because of abuses in the progressive education movement, and that therefore, recently new, educational practices have avoided being tagged with the name "progressive." If choice (C) were true—that "Progressive Learning" has recently met with approval in middle class public schools—it would contradict the author's statement about the connotation of the word "progressive" and seriously weaken his argument.

10. **C** The misunderstanding arises from Dave's assumption that Bill has said *every* morning, not *almost* every morning. (D), although worth considering, is not best because it does not address the scope of Bill's remark.

11. **D** Because the first two statements are not absolute, we may conclude that sunbathing is unlikely but not impossible. Choices I and II reinforce this conclusion. Choice III is a conclusion requiring more information than is contained in the passage.

12. **D** (A) and (B) are, by commonsense standards, implausible. (C) might be a valid statement, but it is not implied by Wilkie's assertion, which makes no distinction between first- and second-class citizens, and so implies (D).

13. **D** Although several of the choices mention or imply the virtue of productivity, only (D) links a decline in productivity with a reliance on excuses.

14. **D** If *nothing* produces only nothing, then the production of something *must* require something. (A) makes the production of something from something a possibility; however, the original statement implies that the something/something relationship is imperative.

15. **A** Only (A) makes an unqualified negative assessment; each of the other choices is either a neutral statement or one that attempts to balance positive and negative terms.

16. **D** The term *average* in the passage implies that if some workers earned more than $7.87 per day, others must have earned less. In choice (C) the words *far more than* make that choice not necessarily true.

17. **E** The magazine is sure that Jones will be a contender soon, and all that is offered to support this is the fact that Jinkins will train him. Therefore, III and I are the assumptions motivating the passage. Choice II is not an assumption, but rather a statement made explicitly in the article.

18. **A** Note the relationship between the words in the pairs used in the concluding portion of the paragraph—they are sets of opposites, positive versus negative terms. The only choice that offers a positive/negative pairing of opposites is (A).

19. **B** The structure of question 19 may be simplified as follows:
C (crowded) whenever H (holiday)
Not C; therefore, not H

(B) is most nearly parallel to the relationships presented in the question:
R (reptiles) whenever D (hot desert day)
Not R (absent); therefore, not D.

20. **B** Choice I is not a strong choice. The author indicates only that Nerd is *very* wealthy. The author does not compare Nerd's wealth to that of the other candidates. Choice III contradicts the third sentence of the author's statement. Since the author tells us that Nerd has the necessary wealth and should acquire skill as a speaker, the author must believe that the third attribute (experience) is not an issue. In other words, the author believes that Nerd has satisfactory experience.

21. **B** (A) would not weaken the argument, since being wealthy, but not necessarily wealthiest, is all that is called for. (D) and (E) are consistent with the expressed or implied information in the argument. Although (C) is a possible answer choice, (B) is superior; it directly contradicts the author's assertions.

22. **D** The given statement tells us only that the car is blue. For us to be *assured* that it is slow we must know either that *every* blue car is slow *or* that no blue car accelerates quickly. (D) restricts quick acceleration to red cars.

23. **A** The argument obviously avoids absolute terms, relying instead on words such as "almost" and "sometimes." Therefore, it would seem consistent that a basic assumption would also avoid absolute terms; only (A) does so. In addition, (A) makes explicit the assumption underlying the first sentence of the passage.

24. **E** The second sentence diminishes the government's "fault," and the final sentence continues this idea; the only restatement that takes into account extragovernmental responsibility for intrusion is (E).

25. **B** The key phrase in the author's remarks is *"falsely* equating knowledge [viewing] with action [crime]." (A) is poor because it links knowledge with action. (C) is poor because the author indicates that those who dictate what we see (in other words, the censors) are guilty of drawing false (illogical) relationships. (D) and (E) are not relevant to the author's argument. (B) is consistent with the author's position that knowledge and action do not necessarily go hand in hand.

26. **B** A ruling on resources must at least presume the possibility that such resources exist; otherwise it is absurd. All other choices are irrelevant to the ruling.

Section V

Answers 1–5

From the statements we can construct a chart as follows, using statements 2, 3, and 8:

HATS:				G	G	
SHIRTS:	R	R	R	B	B	G

Now, from statement 7 we know that the person wearing the green shirt is not wearing a blue hat. Therefore, we get:

HATS:		B	B	G	G	
SHIRTS:	R	R	R	B	B	G

which leaves the two red hats to complete the chart:

HATS:	R	B	B	G	G	R
SHIRTS:	R	R	R	B	B	G

Now, placing the people around the table, using first statement 7 and then statement 6, gives:

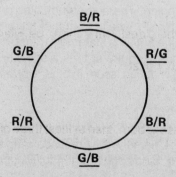

Now all the questions can be easily answered.

1. **C** Only III is true.

2. **D** If the green shirt should suddenly turn red, then statements 2, 4, 6, and 7 would no longer be true.

3. **A** If the two blue shirts turned green, then three people would be wearing matching hats and shirts, making I true and III false. Statement II is also true.

4. **B** One of the two people who started with a green hat would still have a green hat, and one of the two people who started with a blue hat would still have a blue hat.

5. **D** All three statements are true.

Answers 6–10

6. **A** Make a grid, showing names versus nicknames, and a chart, showing relative ages. From statement 2, Caryn is not Peaches or Tiny. From statement 3, Frank is not Shorty or Tiny. Using the relative age chart, from statements 2 and 3, Frank is not Peaches. Thus, Frank must be King Kong. Thus, Caryn is not King Kong. Also, neither Dave nor Ellen is King Kong. But if Caryn is not King Kong, then she must be Shorty. You do not know the nicknames of Dave and Ellen.

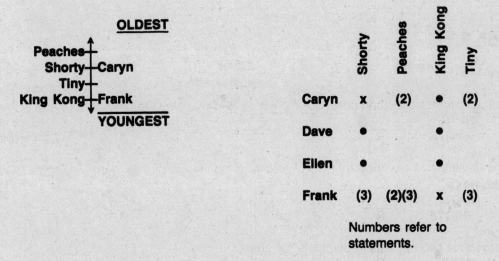

	Shorty	Peaches	King Kong	Tiny
Caryn	x	(2)	●	(2)
Dave	●		●	
Ellen	●		●	
Frank	(3)	(2)(3)	x	(3)

Numbers refer to statements.

7. **D** Only I is correct. First, III is false since Frank *is* King Kong, and II is false since Caryn *is* Shorty. From the relative age chart, we see that Shorty is older than Tiny.

8. **D** Since the two nicknames Tiny and Peaches must go with Ellen and Dave, and if Ellen is not Tiny, then Dave must be.

9. **E** We know that Peaches is the oldest, but it might be Ellen or Dave.

10. **D** Frank (King Kong) is the youngest.

Answers 11–15

11. **E** If a 2nd generation of Flit Flies is born, then at least three of the four conditions necessary for Flit Flies to mate must be met, namely, the presence of *agar-agar* in a *petri dish* at 78° and at *normal barometric pressure*. Since statement 4 fulfills one condition (petri dish), then only

one of the other remaining three conditions may be deleted (but not necessarily has to be). Therefore *at least* one of conditions I and II must be present, but both could also be present. Therefore the answer is (E): either I or II or both.

12. **C** Since three of the conditions are met (agar-agar, petri dish, and 78°), then conditions are sufficient for Flit Flies to mate, but they don't necessarily have to. (Thus we eliminate (A).) (B) is blatantly incorrect, as it is against the rules. (C) is correct, since 5 days must intervene between mating and birth of the offspring. (D) could be true, but not necessarily must be. And (E) must be incorrect because offspring will not have appeared by June 4.

13. **B** No matter when a 3rd generation appears, a 2nd generation cannot start mating until 5 days after the beginning of the experiment, since 5 days must intervene before the 2nd generation offspring are born (II). If I and III were to be true, then a 3rd generation could not appear on June 15.

14. **D** The earliest a 2nd generation could have appeared would be on June 6 (June 1 + 5 days); thus, the earliest a 3rd generation could appear would be June 11 (June 6 + 5 days). Therefore, a 3rd generation could not have appeared on June 9.

15. **E** Simply destroying 1st generation Flit Flies will not solve the problem, as the 2nd or 3rd or 4th generation may continue to reproduce. If, however, the governor eliminates two of the four necessary conditions for Flit Fly reproduction, then the species will not be able to reproduce and will, in fact, become extinct.

Answers 16–23

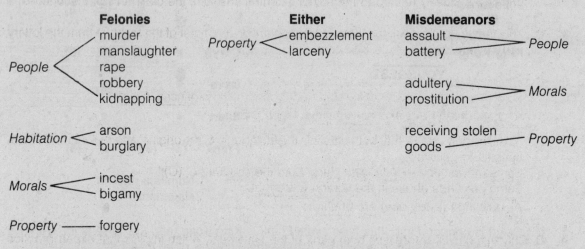

A COMMON MISTAKE IS TO *OVERCHART*, THAT IS, TO MAKE YOUR CHART TOO COMPLEX OR TOO COMPLETE, AND NOT HAVE ENOUGH TIME FOR THE QUESTIONS. KEEP YOUR CHART SIMPLE AND EASY TO READ.

16. **C** Rape and arson must be felonies, according to the chart. If we refer to the statements, statement 1 tells us that rape is a felony; statement 6 tells us that burglary and robbery are the same level of crime—therefore, by statement 1, burglary is a felony; and statement 2 tells us that arson and burglary are the same level—thus arson is also a felony.

17. **B** Embezzlement and larceny are the only two crimes that are stated (statement 5) as having the possibility of being one or the other.

18. **A** The chart shows that embezzlement, prostitution, and receiving stolen goods could be misdemeanors. If we do not use the chart: embezzlement (statement 5) could be a misde-

meanor; prostitution, not being the same level as arson (statement 8), must be a misdemeanor (arson was deduced as a felony in question 16); and receiving stolen goods must be a misdemeanor (statement 6), as it is also not the same level as arson.

19. **B** If all felonious crimes against people were punishable by death, then murder, rape, manslaughter, robbery, and kidnapping would be punishable by death, because they are felonious crimes against people (statement 1 or chart).

20. **E** The most abundant crimes are not determinable by these statements. They never refer to the number of crimes.

21. **D** That burglary is a felony and that receiving stolen property is the same level as adultery can be deduced, using the chart.

22. **E** Cannot be determined. None of the choices *must* be true.

23. **B** According to the statements, there are seven sorts of crimes against people. This can be seen in the chart.

Section VI

1. **B** The author's criticism of lotteries is based on the contention that poor persons are spending more than they can afford. However, the details he offers in support of this contention mention the frequency of betting without specifying the amount gambled. The effectiveness of the *frequency* detail could be better judged if the *amount* were given. None of the other choices is closely related to the author's central criticism, the costliness of the lotteries.

2. **C** This fact severely weakens the author's contention that most of the revenue from the lottery comes from the lower class or poor.

3. **C** The given argument may be reduced to:
Some <u>stars</u> (those the speaker has read about) <u>have</u> <u>expensive</u> <u>homes</u>.
<u>All</u> <u>stars</u> (they) <u>have</u> <u>expensive</u> <u>homes</u> (such places).

(C) is the only choice that both parallels the faulty logic of the original and retains the pattern, specific to general:
Some movie stars → All movie stars. Note the structure of (C):
Some <u>paintings</u> (those in the library) <u>are</u> <u>bright</u>.
<u>All</u> <u>paintings</u> (every one) <u>are</u> <u>bright</u>.

4. **D** Only this choice addresses both parts of the statement, which implies that expert practice helps identify errors. (B) and (C) stress error only; (A) stresses practice only; and (E) stresses writing only.

5. **A** Refer to the following diagram:

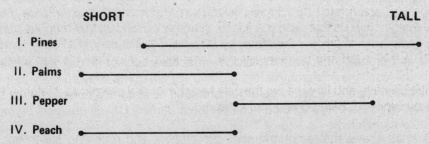

SHORT   TALL

I. Pines

II. Palms

III. Pepper

IV. Peach

On the basis of the foregoing diagram, (B), (C), (D), and (E) are false.

6. **E** (A) is a *nonsequitur*; the passage does not align honesty with auditing. (B) is weaker than (E) because it mentions destroying the state, an extreme not expressed or implied in the passage. (C) is too vague. (D) introduces a new subject, fraud.

7. **A** The author explicitly opposes legislative proposals that would "make life easier for them [the legislators]."

8. **C** On the basis of the first and second statements, *all sad* mimes are *also funny*. From the third statement, we conclude that no child can be both sad and funny; therefore, III must be true, that is, no sad mimes are children. Statements I and II need not be true.

9. **C** Statement I, whether true or false, tells only about slow runners. If everyone who does not engage in track and field is *slow*, then the converse (implied by part of I) *may* also be true. In other words, "all nontrack competitors are slow" does not guarantee that "all slow runners are nontrack competitors," but does not exclude this possibility. Because there is no certain or likely relationship between the two converse statements, the other choices (which require certainty or likelihood) are weak.

10. **A** The conclusion can be properly drawn only if the condition, "*being white*," is sufficient to rule out all but quartz. (A) allows the conclusion, "*must* be quartz," to be reached.

11. **E** (E) may be restated: "The group consisting of humanitarians who received honors contains a much higher proportion of blondes than that which exists in the total population." Such a condition increases the credibility of the conclusion. (A), (B), (C), and (D) all reduce the probability of the conclusion.

12. **B** Reducing the mortality rate among squirrels would result in an increase in the squirrel (small game) population. (B) is the only answer that does not point out an ill effect of the reactor—(A), (D)—or a weakness in the argument presented—(C), (E).

13. **E** The statement presented can be logically made only if being reared at Prince Charming Kennels assures that a poodle is purebred. (E) provides such assurance. (A) does not state that only purebreds are reared and, therefore, does not assure that any given poodle from the kennels is pure.

14. **D** (A) may be eliminated because the argument does not rule out a possible previous proposal. (B) may be eliminated as no suggestion of easy identification or the necessity of easy identification is presupposed. (C) may be eliminated because the argument is independent of any comparison between the Great Salt Lake and any other body of water. (E) can be eliminated because the argument presents the weaker claim of the *possibility* of oil. (D) allows, if true, the *possibility* of oil to be sufficient cause for exploration.

15. **C** The structure of the given argument may be simplified:
Most are <u>popular</u> and <u>low</u>.
Splendor is <u>not</u> popular and high (<u>not low</u>).

(C) parallels this structure:
Most who <u>stop</u> do <u>gain</u>.
Carl does <u>not stop</u> and will <u>not gain</u>.

16. **A** (B) is inappropriate because the argument speaks only of a "danger" and a "threshold beyond which" the monarchy is lost. (C) and (E) are completely contrary to the argument. (D) is inappropriate because the argument does not address bureau*crats* or suggest any hostility. (A) is the proper choice because the argument clearly presents bureaucracy as a threat to monarchy.

17. **E** Since all medications are habit forming and everything habit forming soothes pain, then all medications make one feel better (II is true). Since nothing nonaddictive soothes pain and all medications soothe pain, then no medications can be nonaddictive (I and III are false).

18. **E** The statement given can be simplified:
All <u>have</u> <u>hair</u>   (mammal).
<u>This</u> does <u>not</u> have <u>hair</u>.
<u>It</u> is <u>not</u> (mammal).

Only (E) can be reduced to this same form:
All <u>have</u> <u>smell</u> (lubricants).
<u>This</u> does <u>not</u> have <u>smell</u>.
<u>It</u> is <u>not</u> (lubricant).

19. **B** (A) has no bearing because the argument is concerned only with mammals. (C) is not relevant; the argument does not address the amount of hair. (E) is likewise outside the argument's subject. (D) is a possible answer because the claim is that the absence of hair indicates a nonmammal. However, (B) is a better choice. (D) is a possibility—"One *could* remove." (B) points out that, without any other intervention, there *are* creatures with no hair that are also mammals.

20. **D** The first portion of the passage discusses projection as a method for avoiding the personal recognition of unacceptable motivations. (A), (B), (C), and (E) are inappropriate conclusions because they suggest the employment of projections as a technique for substantiating unacceptable motivations.

21. **B** (A) and (E) illogically condone greed and mistrust. (D) is poor given the balance of the sentence, which stresses repression. (C) is poor because "held" is vague and does not contribute to the final meaning of the sentence. (B) is consistent with the beginning of the discussion and supports the conclusion drawn.

22. **A** (B) does not fit the sentence structure. (C) and (E) are inconsistent with the discussion. (D) would be redundant. (A) is the logical and appropriate insertion.

23. **A** The key word in the statements given is "usually." "Usually" suggests a frequent or regular phenomenon. It implies that an event may be normally expected and allows one to draw a conclusion *stronger than* those contained in (D) and (E). "Usually" does not mean "with certainty." Therefore, the categorical conclusions of (B) and (C) are not appropriate.

24. **C** Statement I is not true, since Nexon is not a *sufficient condition* for life, that is, Nexon alone is not enough. Statement II is not true because Nexon must be present if there is life (*necessary condition*). Statement III is true; Nexon must be present (it is a necessary condition). Statement III does not suggest the absence of things other than Nexon and, therefore, does not contradict the original statement.

25. **B** Statement I need not be true, because absence of Fennel is *not a necessary condition*, that is, there can be other conditions that result in the end of life. Statement III is not true, because the absence of Fennel *is sufficient* to end life (one cannot say life "may not" cease). Statement II is true, given that absence of Fennel is sufficient to end life.

26. **C** The statement means that *only* fools would do that. This is the same as both I and II. It does not mean, however, that *all* fools would do that (III)—just *only* fools.

PART FOUR

FINAL TOUCHES
Reviewing the Important Techniques

Chapter

11

A Summary of Strategies

DIRECTIONS AND STRATEGIES

GENERAL TIPS

- Use the "one-check, two-check" system, doing the easier questions first, and saving the time-consuming and difficult questions for later.
- Don't leave any blank answer spaces. At least guess on your unanswered questions.
- Eliminate unreasonable or irrelevant answers immediately, marking them out on your question booklet.
- Highlight key words and phrases by marking right in your question booklet. Use the margins to draw diagrams, set up charts, and so on.
- Mark "T" and "F" (for "True" and "False") alongside the Roman numeral statements in "multiple-multiple-choice" questions. Often these will allow you to immediately eliminate incorrect answer choices.

REVIEW OF LSAT AREAS

Writing Sample

Directions:
You have 30 minutes to write an essay in response to a given topic. Take a few minutes to plan your work before you begin writing. DO NOT WRITE ON A TOPIC OF YOUR OWN CHOICE. ESSAYS THAT DO NOT ADDRESS THE GIVEN TOPIC ARE UNACCEPTABLE.

The quality of your writing is more important than the length of your response or the content. Pay attention to organization, appropriate diction, and correct usage. You will not be expected to display any specialized knowledge in your response, nor will you be expected to write a "perfect" essay; law schools understand that you are writing under a time constraint, and will allow for the minor lapses in writing ability that might occur under this circumstance.

Only the lined area in your booklet will be reproduced for the law schools, so do not write outside this space. *Do not* skip lines or use wide margins. These precautions, along with careful planning and legible handwriting that is not unduly large, will keep you within the allowed space.

Strategies:
- First list ideas and examples relevant to the topic on the scratch paper provided.
- Reduce and organize your list into a rough outline.
- Write an opening paragraph stating your general thesis and points you intend to cover.
- Write the middle, using concrete examples.
- Write the conclusion, saying something "new."
- Proofread and edit your essay.

Reading Comprehension

Directions:
Read the passages and answer the questions following each passage by blackening the appropriate space on the answer sheet. You may refer back to the passages when answering the questions.

Strategies:
- Skim the questions first, marking key words and phrases. (Don't read the answer choices.)
- Skim the passage (optional). Read and mark the first sentence of each paragraph.
- Read actively, marking the passage. In particular, look for answer spots, repeat spots, intuition spots.
- Answer the questions. Skip if necessary. Eliminate weak choices. Don't "read into" the passage.

Analytical Reasoning

Directions:
In this section you will be given groups of questions based on different sets of conditions. Drawing a simple diagram may be helpful in answering some of the questions. You are to choose the best answer and mark the corresponding space on your answer sheet.

Strategies:
- No formal logic is required.
- Make simple charts or diagrams.

- Fill in as much of the diagram as possible, but don't worry if you cannot complete it.
- Look for the framework of the diagram that would be most effective.
- Apply evidence in both directions, that is, also use what you know is *not* true.
- Use question marks for information that is variable.
- Sometimes looking at the questions can tip off the framework of the diagram that would be most helpful.
- Sometimes no standard chart will apply. Then simply pull out information or use simple notes.

Evaluation of Facts

Directions:

This section consists of several sets; each set presents a factual statement, the description of a dispute, and two rules. In some sets, the rules will be conflicting. Be sure that you consider each rule independently and not as an exception to the other. Following each set are questions; select from four choices (given below) the one that best categorizes each question, based upon the relationship of one or both of the rules to the dispute. Darken the appropriate space on your answer sheet:

(A) A relevant question which you can only answer by choosing between the rules.
(B) A relevant question which you cannot answer because you need more information or additional rules, but which does not require a choice between the rules.
(C) A relevant question which you can answer by referring to the facts or rules, or both.
(D) An irrelevant question or one which is only remotely relevant to the outcome of the dispute.

Strategies:

- The facts and rules do not presuppose any specific legal knowledge.
- The rules may be conflicting; do not automatically assume that one rule takes precedence over the other rule.
- Technical or legal terms will be defined for you.
- Do not bring in specific legal knowledge.
- Some of the facts and conflicts may deal with games, quiz shows, and so on; do not bring in specialized knowledge in these situations.
- Each question must be evaluated independently of the other questions.
- Read actively, marking important facts.
- Pay special attention to such words as *if, only, all, and, or, provided that, otherwise, only when,* and *unless.* These words give directions to the rules and relationships.
- Note the difference between the two rules.
- Remember that you are being asked to classify the questions, not to answer them.

Logical Reasoning

Directions:

In this section you will be given brief statements or passages and will be required to evaluate the reasoning involved. In some instances, more than one choice will appear to be a possible answer. You are to choose the *best* answer. Use common sense and reasonableness in making your selection; then mark the proper space on the answer sheet.

Strategies:

- Read the question first; then go back and read the argument or statement. This will give insight into what is going to be asked.

- Watch for items in the answer choices that are irrelevant or not addressed in the given information. Eliminate these immediately.
- Notice the overall tone of the question: Positive or negative? Agreeing and strengthening the author's argument or criticizing or weakening the statement?
- Important words to watch for are *some, all, none, only, one, few, no, could, must, each, except.*

A FINAL CHECKLIST

A Few Days before the Test
- Review the test directions and strategies for each area.
- Become familiar with the test site; visit it if necessary.
- Follow your normal daily routine; don't make drastic changes.

The Night before the Test
- Review briefly, but don't cram.
- Get a normal night's sleep; don't go to bed too early or too late.

On the Day of the Test
- Eat a high-protein breakfast, unless you never eat breakfast.
- Arrive on time, equipped with No. 2 pencils, an eraser, identifications, your admissions ticket (with your photograph inserted), and a watch.
- Read the test directions carefully.
- Use the "one-check, two-check" system.
- Read *actively*.
- Look at all choices before marking your answer.
- Guess at any problem you cannot solve.

PART FIVE

ABOUT THE LAW SCHOOLS

Chapter

12

An Overall View of ABA-Approved Law Schools

The graduates of ABA-approved law schools have completed the education requirements necessary for admission to the bar anywhere in the United States. Graduates of non-ABA-approved law schools, on the other hand, are generally qualified to take the bar examination only in the state in which the school is located.

The table on the following pages presents a brief overall look at ABA-approved law schools; all of these schools require the LSAT.

The enrollment figures are in terms of head count. The figures beneath the name of the school show the enrollment by each class or year and by division. Students are classified for purposes of the enrollment statistics on the basis of whether they are carrying a full load in the division in which they are enrolled. Minority group enrollment is the total enrollment of students who classify themselves as Black, not of Hispanic Origin; American Indian or Alaskan Native; Asian or Pacific Islander; Mexican American; Puerto Rican; and other Hispano-American. Puerto Rican law students enrolled in the three approved law schools in Puerto Rico are not classified as minority students.

The "Degrees Awarded" column gives the total number of each of the specified degrees awarded by each school since the start of the 1982–83 academic year, including the 1983 summer session. The number of degrees awarded to graduates of each division is stated separately.

The next column lists full-time and part-time teachers engaged in the school's teaching program. The dean, librarian with academic rank, and those associate and assistant deans who teach are not included in the count of full-time teachers. They are shown separately in the next column.

Under the heading "Annual Tuition and Fees," "r" stands for resident and "nr" stands for nonresident. If the amount is not followed by a symbol, it is the same for both resident and nonresident. The figure given shows what each student was required to pay for the 1983–84 academic year, excluding summer session, and includes both tuition and fees.

The number of academic years of college study required for admission to each approved law school is indicated by a number where a degree is not required and by "D" where a baccalaureate degree is required for admission. The letter "s" after the number of weeks indicates the school is on a semester basis. The letter "q" indicates the school is on a quarterly basis. The next column states the minimum number of weeks required to complete the full-time program of law study. Weeks of class and examination are included, but weeks of vacation and registration are excluded in this statement.

In the next column, "Yes" is indicated where a school will accept transfer credit for courses successfully completed by students in summer sessions at other institutions and where a school permits students to accelerate their graduation by attending summer sessions at other institutions. "No" indicates the school does not do so.

"Joint Degrees" indicates whether the law school, in conjunction with some other college or school, offers a program leading to a joint degree. "MPA," for example, indicates that the law school offers with another college a joint Juris Doctor–Master of Public Administration degree. The figure following the letters indicates the number of each of these degrees awarded during the 1982–83 academic year. Where the school reported that it had no joint degree program, this is indicated by "No." Where there is a joint degree program but no degrees were awarded that year, this is indicated by a "0." Following is a list of abbreviations used in reporting the joint degrees:

MAd. . . . . Master of Administration
MALD . . . . Master of Arts in Law and Diplomacy
MALIR . . . . Masters in Labor and Industrial Relations
MBA . . . . Master of Business Administration
MBT . . . . Master of Business Taxation
MCP . . . . Master of Civil Planning
MCRP . . . . Master of City and Regional Planning
MD . . . . Doctor of Medicine
MDiv. . . . . Master of Divinity
MHA . . . . Master of Health Administration
MILR . . . . Master of Industrial and Labor Relations
MLS . . . . Master of Library Science
MSL . . . . Master of Studies in Law (non JD)
MLT . . . . Master of Law in Taxation
MPA . . . . Master of Public Administration
MPH . . . . Master of Public Health
MPIA . . . . Master of Law and Public and International Affairs
MPP . . . . Master of Public Planning
MPPM . . . . Master of Public and Private Planning
MSFS . . . . Master of Science in Foreign Service
MSW . . . . Master of Social Work
MTA . . . . Master of Tax Accounting
MTh. . . . . Master of Theology
MUP . . . . Master of Urban Planning
PAA . . . . Master of Public Affairs Administration
RUP . . . . Master of Regional Urban Planning
MSJA . . . . Master of Science in Judicial Administration
MSLS . . . . Master of Science in Library Science
Acct. . . . . Accounting
Agri. Econ. . . . . Agricultural Economics
Am. St. . . . . American Studies
Anth. . . . . Anthropology
Arch. . . . . Architecture
Art & Sc. . . . . . . Art and Science
Asian St. . . . . . . Asian Studies
Comm. . . . . Communications

This explanation and the table on the following pages are reprinted by permission from *A Review of Legal Education in the United States, Fall, 1983, Law Schools and Bar Admission Requirements*. Published by the American Bar Association Section of Legal Education and Admissions to the Bar.

Comp. Lit. . . . . . Comparative Literature
Comp. Sc. . . . . . Computer Science
Crim. Jus. . . . . . Criminal Justice
E. Asian St. . . . . East Asian Studies
East. Lang. . . . . Eastern Languages
Econ. . . . . Economics
Ed. . . . . Education
Ed. Adm. . . . . . . Education Administration
Ed. Lead. . . . . . . Educational Leadership
Eng. . . . . Engineering
Engl. . . . . English
Env. St. . . . . Environmental Studies
Est. Adm. . . . . . . Estate Administration
Fin. . . . . Finance
For. . . . . Forestry, Forest Services
For. Ser. . . . . Foreign Services
Genetics
Gov. . . . . Government
Gov. & For.
    Aff. . . . . Government and Foreign Affairs
Health Ad. . . . . . Health Services Administration
Hist. . . . . History
Hist. Pres. . . . . . . Historical Preservation
Hum. . . . . Humanities
Inf. Sci. . . . . Information Sciences
Intl. Aff. . . . . International Affairs
Intl. St. . . . . International Studies
Intl. R. . . . . International Relations
Journ. . . . . Journalism
Jud. St. . . . . Judicial Studies
Jur. St. . . . . Juridical Studies
Juris. & Soc.
    Pol. . . . . Jurisdiction and Social Policy
Lab. & Ind. . . . . . Labor and Industrial Relations
Lat. Am. St. . . . . Latin American Studies
Law & Ec. . . . . . . Law and Economics
Law & Ed. . . . . . Law and Education
Law & Psy. . . . . . Law and Psychology
Law & Soc. Sc. . Law and Social Sciences
M. Com. . . . . . . Mass Communications
M.E. St. . . . . Mid Eastern Studies
Man. . . . . Management
Mar. Aff. . . . . Marine Affairs
Med. . . . . Medicine
Min. Econ. . . . . . Mineral Economics
Mod. Letters . . . . Modern Letters
Nat. Res. . . . . Natural Resources
Org. Bio. . . . . Organic Biology
Phil. . . . . Philosophy
Phys. . . . . Physics
Pol. Sc. . . . . Political Science
Policy St. . . . . Policy Studies
Pres. St. . . . . Preservation Studies
Pro. Psy. . . . . Professional Psychology
Psy. . . . . Psychology

Pub. Com. . . . . . . Public Communications
Pub. Man. . . . . . . Public Management
Pub. Pol. . . . . Public Policy
Rhet. . . . . Rhetoric
Rus. St. . . . . Russian Studies
Soc. . . . . Sociology
Soc. Sc. . . . . Social Science
Tax. . . . . Taxation
Tax Acct. . . . . Tax Accounting
Telecom. . . . . Telecommunications
Tech. & Hum.
    Aff. . . . . Technology and Human Affairs
Urb. Aff. . . . . Urban Affairs Studies
Urb. Plan. . . . . . . Urban Planning
World Pol. . . . . . . World Politics

"Total Hard Copy Volumes" refers to the total number of volumes of law and law-related books held by the law school at the end of the 1982–83 fiscal year. "Hard Copy Volume" means a physical unit of any printed, typewritten, handwritten, mimeographed, or processed work contained in one binding or portfolio, hardbound or paperbound, which has been catalogued, classified, or made ready for use.

"Microform Volume Equivalents" are also reported as the total number held at the end of the 1982–83 fiscal year. The U.S. Department of Education, National Center for Educational Statistics, has not yet achieved general agreement among librarians on a definition. In the interim, law librarians were instructed to use the following method for determining volume equivalents of microform materials:

(1) If the original material (hard copy) was in countable volumes, use that number as volume equivalents. The number of volumes of the original material is usually available from the bibliographic description.

(2) If the original material was not in countable volumes, figure 800 pages of original material as the equivalent of one volume.

For additional information, please contact:

James P. White, Consultant on Legal Education to the American Bar Association, Indiana University School of Law–Indianapolis, 735 West New York Street, Indianapolis, IN 46202, 317/264-8071;

or

Frederick R. Franklin, Staff Director, Section of Legal Education and Admissions to the Bar, American Bar Association, 750 North Lake Shore Drive, Chicago, IL 60611, 312/988-5581.

Law Schools on the 1983 Approved List of the American Bar Association

ALABAMA

Samford University
Cumberland School of Law
800 Lakeshore Drive
Birmingham, Alabama 35229
205/870-2701
(Approved in 1949; Private)

University of Alabama
School of Law
P.O. Box 1435
University, Alabama 35486
205/348-5117
(Approved in 1926; Public)

ARIZONA

Arizona State University
College of Law
Tempe, Arizona 85287
602/965-6181
(Approved in 1969; Public)

		Total	Women	Minorities	Total	Women	Minorities	Total	Women	Minorities
1st Year Enrollment	Full-Time	275	63	4	176	65	12	148	75	26
	Part-Time	None			None			None		
2nd Year Enrollment	Full-Time	251	61	3	149	58	11	139	55	18
	Part-Time	None			None			None		
3rd Year Enrollment	Full-Time	259	75	3	164	58	9	141	62	15
	Part-Time	None			None			None		
4th Year Enrollment	Full-Time									
	Part-Time	None			None			None		
Graduate Enrollment	Full-Time	None			None			None		
	Part-Time	None			55	10	1	None		
Other Enrollment	Full-Time	None			None			10	4	0
	Part-Time	None			7	2	0	None		
Fall, 1983, Enrollment	Full-Time	785	199	10	489	181	32	438	196	59
	Part-Time				62	12	1			
	Total	**785**	**199**	**10**	**551**	**193**	**33**	**438**	**196**	**59**
Degrees Awarded through Summer, 1983	Full-Time	JD 230	57	4	JD 165	49	2	JD 133	55	22
	Part-Time				LLM 18	2	0			
Teachers	Full-Time	28	5	0	19	2	0	20	1	2
	Part-Time	14	0	0	9	1	1	3	1	0
Full-time Teaching Deans and Librarians		5	2	0	4	2	0	3	0	0
Tuition and Fees	Full-Time	$4,930			$1,604 r	$2,919 nr		$850 r	$3,515 nr	
	Part-Time				$ 752 r	$1,240 nr				
College Required—Degree or 3 years		D			D			D		
Weeks Required	Full-Time	96			102			95		
	Part-Time									
Credits Required semester (s) or quarter (q)		88s			90s			87s		
Summer Programs	Accepts summer credit from other schools	Yes			Yes			Yes		
	Allows acceleration of graduation by attending summer sessions	Yes			Yes			Yes		
Joint Degrees		MBA 0			MBA 4	MPA 0	MTA 0	None		
Library	Total Hard Copy Volumes	117,174			177,776			178,414		
	Microform Volume Equivalents	51,748			3,636			23,008		

Law Schools on the 1983 Approved List of the American Bar Association

ARKANSAS

University of Arizona
College of Law
Tucson, Arizona 85721
602/621-1373
(Approved in 1930; Public)

University of Arkansas
School of Law
Fayetteville, Arkansas 72701
501/575-5601
(Approved in 1926; Public)

University of Arkansas at Little Rock
School of Law
400 West Markham
Little Rock, Arkansas 72201
501/371-1071
(Approved in 1926; Public)

		Total	Women	Minorities	Total	Women	Minorities	Total	Women	Minorities
1st Year Enrollment	Full-Time	145	72	25	146	39	10	87	40	7
	Part-Time	None			None			79	31	7
2nd Year Enrollment	Full-Time	150	69	18	131	35	5	74	22	6
	Part-Time	None			None			25	7	0
3rd Year Enrollment	Full-Time	139	52	12	115	32	7	69	33	5
	Part-Time	None			None			20	6	0
4th Year Enrollment	Full-Time									
	Part-Time	None			None			18	6	0
Graduate Enrollment	Full-Time	None			11	3	0	None		
	Part-Time	None			None			None		
Other Enrollment	Full-Time	None			None			2	2	0
	Part-Time	None			None			16	7	0
Fall, 1983, Enrollment	Full-Time	434	193	55	403	109	22	232	97	18
	Part-Time							158	57	7
	Total	**434**	**193**	**55**	**403**	**109**	**22**	**390**	**154**	**25**
Degrees Awarded through Summer, 1983	Full-Time	JD 127	47	9	JD 155 LLM 2	29 1	3 0	JD 61	26	3
	Part-Time							JD 36	6	2
Teachers	Full-Time	21	3	0	24	4	2	17	3	1
	Part-Time	9	4	1	7	0	0	9	1	1
Full-time Teaching Deans and Librarians		2	0	0	1	0	0	1	0	0
Tuition and Fees	Full-Time	$850 r	$3,515 nr		$1,100 r	$2,360 nr		$1,120 r	$2,380 nr	
	Part-Time							$75/cr.hr. r	$138/cr.hr. nr	
College Required—Degree or 3 years		D			D			D		
Weeks Required	Full-Time	94			98			90		
	Part-Time							120		
Credits Required semester (s) or quarter (q)		85s			84s			87s		
Summer Programs	Accepts summer credit from other schools	Yes			Yes			Yes		
	Allows acceleration of graduation by attending summer sessions	Yes			Yes			Yes		
Joint Degrees		Ph.D./Phil. 1			MBA 0			MBA 0		
Library	Total Hard Copy Volumes	158,452			152,975			103,015		
	Microform Volume Equivalents	53,916			24,363			41,420		

Law Schools on the 1983 Approved List of the American Bar Association

CALIFORNIA

California Western School of Law
350 Cedar Street
San Diego, California 92101
619/239-0391
(Approved in 1926; Private)*

Golden Gate University
School of Law
536 Mission Street
San Francisco, California 94105
415/442-7250
(Approved in 1956; Private)

Loyola Law School
1441 West Olympic Boulevard
Los Angeles, California 90015
213/736-1000
(Approved in 1935; Private)

		Total	Women	Minorities	Total	Women	Minorities	Total	Women	Minorities
1st Year Enrollment	Full-Time	230	60	17	157	71	16	295	134	57
	Part-Time	None			113	60	11	109	50	20
2nd Year Enrollment	Full-Time	215	53	8	159	84	24	281	130	41
	Part-Time	None			82	41	9	95	37	17
3rd Year Enrollment	Full-Time	210	58	12	161	76	10	318	147	48
	Part-Time	None			59	20	3	92	38	15
4th Year Enrollment	Full-Time									
	Part-Time	None			78	37	17	83	34	5
Graduate Enrollment	Full-Time	None			17	6	2	None		
	Part-Time	None			70	20	15	None		
Other Enrollment	Full-Time	None			None			25	8	0
	Part-Time	None			17	7	0	4	1	0
Fall, 1983, Enrollment	Full-Time	655	171	37	494	237	52	919	419	146
	Part-Time				419	185	55	383	160	57
	Total	**655**	**171**	**37**	**913**	**422**	**107**	**1,302**	**579**	**203**
Degrees Awarded through Summer, 1983	Full-Time	JD 208	53	13	JD 149 LLM 11	76 3	17 0	JD 269	117	24
	Part-Time				JD 75 LLM 7	38 3	10 1	JD 117	45	14
Teachers	Full-Time	25	8	1	25	6	3	43	12	1
	Part-Time	25	7	0	10	1	0	12	1	2
Full-time Teaching Deans and Librarians		3	0	1	1	0	0	4	1	0
Tuition and Fees	Full-Time	$6,415			$6,168			$6,448		
	Part-Time				$4,656			$4,061		
College Required—Degree or 3 years		D			D			D		
Weeks Required	Full-Time	96			90			90		
	Part-Time				120			136		
Credits Required semester (s) or quarter (q)		88s			84s			87s		
Summer Programs	Accepts summer credit from other schools	Yes			Yes			Yes		
	Allows acceleration of graduation by attending summer sessions	Yes			Yes			Yes		
Joint Degrees		None			MBA 0	MPA 0	MS/Tax. 0	None		
Library	Total Hard Copy Volumes	87,491			114,008			185,061		
	Microform Volume Equivalents	45,119			63,884			89,530		

* Independent law school, not affiliated with a university.

AN OVERALL VIEW OF ABA-APPROVED LAW SCHOOLS

Law Schools on the 1983 Approved List of the American Bar Association		Pepperdine University School of Law Malibu, California 90265 213/456-4611 (Approved in 1972; Private)			Southwestern University School of Law 675 South Westmoreland Avenue Los Angeles, California 90005 213/738-6700 (Approved in 1970; Private)			Stanford Law School Stanford, California 94305 415/497-2465 (Approved in 1923; Private)		
		Total	Women	Minorities	Total	Women	Minorities	Total	Women	Minorities
1st Year Enrollment	Full-Time Part-Time	256 None	92	18	302 127	112 50	20 20	170 None	65	36
2nd Year Enrollment	Full-Time Part-Time	179 None	51	12	247 117	100 57	25 14	168 None	57	23
3rd Year Enrollment	Full-Time Part-Time	214 None	68	7	291 137	115 54	19 16	182 None	58	34
4th Year Enrollment	Full-Time Part-Time	None			86	33	11	None		
Graduate Enrollment	Full-Time Part-Time	None None			None None			8 None	4	3
Other Enrollment	Full-Time Part-Time	None None			None None			8 None	4	0
Fall, 1983, Enrollment	Full-Time Part-Time Total	649 — 649	211 — 211	37 — 37	840 467 1,307	327 194 521	64 61 125	536 — 536	188 — 188	96 — 96
Degrees Awarded through Summer, 1983	Full-Time	JD 195	57	9	JD 267	99	21	JD 168 JM 1 JSD 1 JSM 3	52 0 0 2	32 0 0 0
	Part-Time				JD 92	35	9			
Teachers	Full-Time Part-Time	22 10	2 0	0 0	42 19	34 4	2 3	33 4	4 0	2 0
Full-time Teaching Deans and Librarians		2	0	0	11	10	0	None		
Tuition and Fees	Full-Time Part-Time	$7,540			$6,580 $4,182			$9,228		
College Required—Degree or 3 years		D			3			D		
Weeks Required	Full-Time Part-Time	90			96 128			108		
Credits Required semester (s) or quarter (q)		88s			87s			86s		
Summer Programs	Accepts summer credit from other schools	Yes			Yes			Yes		
	Allows acceleration of graduation by attending summer sessions	Yes			Yes			Yes		
Joint Degrees		None			None			MBA 13 MA/Econ. 0 MA/Hist. 0	MA/Pol.Sc. 0 MA/Psy. 0 Ph.D./Econ. 0	MA/Lat.Am.St. 0 MA/Health Ad. 0
Library	Total Hard Copy Volumes	84,150			150,856			286,608		
	Microform Volume Equivalents	86,898			67,643			12,433		

* Independent law school, not affiliated with a university.

Law Schools on the 1983 Approved List of the American Bar Association

		University of California School of Law 221 Boalt Hall Berkeley, California 94720 415/642-1741 (Approved in 1923; Public)			University of California School of Law King Hall Davis, California 95616 916/752-0243 (Approved in 1968; Public)			University of California School of Law 405 Hilgard Avenue Los Angeles, California 90024 213/825-4841 (Approved in 1950; Public)		
		Total	Women	Minorities	Total	Women	Minorities	Total	Women	Minorities
1st Year Enrollment	Full-Time Part-Time	270 None	117	66	157 None	79	55	306 None	127	89
2nd Year Enrollment	Full-Time Part-Time	289 None	110	73	147 None	72	42	308 None	123	105
3rd Year Enrollment	Full-Time Part-Time	293 None	104	69	189 None	98	49	317 None	129	80
4th Year Enrollment	Full-Time Part-Time	None			None			None		
Graduate Enrollment	Full-Time Part-Time	20 None	3	8	None None			10 None	2	3
Other Enrollment	Full-Time Part-Time	40 None	13	4	None None			21 None	7	11
Fall, 1983, Enrollment	Full-Time Part-Time **Total**	912 **912**	347 **347**	220 **220**	493 **493**	249 **249**	146 **146**	962 **962**	388 **388**	288 **288**
Degrees Awarded through Summer, 1983	Full-Time	JD 328 LLM 13 JSD 2	132 2 0	65 7 1	JD 166	73	33	JD 348 LLM 8	130 1	103 2
	Part-Time									
Teachers	Full-Time Part-Time	39 22	4 3	2 2	23 6	7 1	2 1	41 3	4 1	3 1
Full-time Teaching Deans and Librarians		5	0	0	2	0	0	2	1	0
Tuition and Fees	Full-Time Part-Time	$1,451 r	$4,811 nr		$1,383 r	$4,743 nr		$1,451 r	$4,811 nr	
College Required—Degree or 3 years		D			D			D		
Weeks Required	Full-Time Part-Time	90			96			90		
Credits Required semester (s) or quarter (q)		81s			84s			87s		
Summer Programs	Accepts summer credit from other schools	No			Yes			Yes		
	Allows acceleration of graduation by attending summer sessions	No			Yes			No		
Joint Degrees		MBA 17 MA/Pub.Pol. 5 Ph.D./Journ. 1	MCRP 4 MA/Ed. 1	MLS 0 MA/Econ. 1	None			MBA 17 RUP 0	MLS 0 MA/Law Ed. 1	MPH 0
Library	Total Hard Copy Volumes	441,026			191,824			283,808		
	Microform Volume Equivalents	58,417			41,390			11,313		

**Law Schools on the
1983 Approved List
of the American
Bar Association**

		University of California Hastings College of the Law 200 McAllister Street San Francisco, California 94102-4978 415/557-0448 (Approved in 1934; Public)			University of the Pacific McGeorge School of Law 3200 Fifth Avenue Sacramento, California 95817 916/739-7121 (Approved in 1969; Private)			University of San Diego School of Law Alcala Park San Diego, California 92110 619/293-4527 (Approved in 1961; Private)		
		Total	Women	Minorities	Total	Women	Minorities	Total	Women	Minorities
1st Year Enrollment	Full-Time Part-Time	490 None	231	118	354 174	108 56	24 13	244 86	102 35	17 9
2nd Year Enrollment	Full-Time Part-Time	472 None	212	70	258 202	77 68	19 19	249 47	92 22	9 4
3rd Year Enrollment	Full-Time Part-Time	512 None	221	133	204 149	69 43	11 7	225 42	85 13	12 0
4th Year Enrollment	Full-Time Part-Time	None			160	58	14	46	20	1
Graduate Enrollment	Full-Time Part-Time	None None			27 47	·5 10	2 3	27 72	4 11	5 6
Other Enrollment	Full-Time Part-Time	15 None	4	1	None None			5 9	2 3	0 0
Fall, 1983, Enrollment	Full-Time Part-Time Total	1,489 1,489	668 668	322 322	843 732 1,575	259 235 494	56 56 112	750 302 1,052	285 104 389	43 20 63
Degrees Awarded through Summer, 1983	Full-Time	JD 476	205	59	JD 210 LLM 25	67 6	8 1	JD 221 LLM 7 MCL 10	71 1 2	20 1 2
	Part-Time				JD 150 LLM 22	43 2	11 0	JD 40 LLM 32	12 6	1 1
Teachers	Full-Time Part-Time	42 26	5 3	2 1	44 14	9 0	1 2	38 14	6 1	3 1
Full-time Teaching Deans and Librarians		5	2	1	6	2	2	4	1	0
Tuition and Fees	Full-Time Part-Time	$1,470 r	$4,830 nr			$6,583 $3,904			$6,320 $4,495	
College Required—Degree or 3 years		D			D			D		
Weeks Required	Full-Time Part-Time	90			111 161			84 120		
Credits Required semester (s) or quarter (q)		87s			129q			85s		
Summer Programs	Accepts summer credit from other schools	Yes			Yes			Yes		
	Allows acceleration of graduation by attending summer sessions	Yes			No			Yes		
Joint Degrees		MBA 4			MBA 1 MA/Acct. 0	MPA 0	MA/Inf.Sci. 0	MBA 0	MA/Intl.R. 0	
Library	Total Hard Copy Volumes	272,569			132,120			137,049		
	Microform Volume Equivalents	92,719			81,550			70,625		

Law Schools on the 1983 Approved List of the American Bar Association

		University of San Francisco School of Law Ignatian Heights San Francisco, California 94117-1080 415/666-6307 (Approved in 1935; Private)			University of Santa Clara School of Law Santa Clara, California 95053 408/984-4361 (Approved in 1937; Private)			University of Southern California The Law Center University Park Los Angeles, California 90089-0071 213/743-6473 (Approved in 1924; Private)		
		Total	Women	Minorities	Total	Women	Minorities	Total	Women	Minorities
1st Year Enrollment	Full-Time	173	81	47	210	83	27	175	61	19
	Part-Time	50	21	5	57	24	2	None		
2nd Year Enrollment	Full-Time	162	72	33	237	105	23	210	85	33
	Part-Time	55	25	9	48	25	2	None		
3rd Year Enrollment	Full-Time	197	98	23	237	95	34	232	82	29
	Part-Time	57	15	6	45	26	3	None		
4th Year Enrollment	Full-Time									
	Part-Time	64	30	10	46	16	7	None		
Graduate Enrollment	Full-Time	None			None			None		
	Part-Time	None			None			None		
Other Enrollment	Full-Time	None			1	0	0	None		
	Part-Time	None			5	1	0	None		
Fall, 1983, Enrollment	Full-Time	532	251	103	685	283	84	617	228	81
	Part-Time	226	91	30	201	92	14			
	Total	758	342	133	886	375	98	617	228	81
Degrees Awarded through Summer, 1983	Full-Time	JD 161	72	12	JD 244	98	30	JD 186	77	30
	Part-Time	JD 34	12	7	JD 39	11	5			
Teachers	Full-Time	24	6	2	27	7	4	27	2	1
	Part-Time	16	2	1	11	2	0	12	0	0
Full-time Teaching Deans and Librarians		3	2	0	2	0	0	3	0	0
Tuition and Fees	Full-Time	$6,372			$6,376			$8,936		
	Part-Time	$232/unit			$4,498					
College Required—Degree or 3 years		D			D			D		
Weeks Required	Full-Time	90			90			84		
	Part-Time	120			120					
Credits Required semester (s) or quarter (q)		82s			86s			88s		
Summer Programs	Accepts summer credit from other schools	Yes			Yes			No		
	Allows acceleration of graduation by attending summer sessions	Yes			Yes			No		
Joint Degrees		None			MBA 18			MBA 4 MA/Econ. 1	MPA 0 MBT 1	MSW 0
Library	Total Hard Copy Volumes	99,796			107,328			193,656		
	Microform Volume Equivalents	77,527			55,281			74,980		

Law Schools on the 1983 Approved List of the American Bar Association

COLORADO

		Whittier College School of Law 5353 West Third Street Los Angeles, California 90020 213/938-3621 (Approved in 1978; Private) **			University of Colorado School of Law Campus Box 401 Boulder, Colorado 80309 303/492-8047 (Approved in 1923; Public)			University of Denver College of Law 200 West 14th Avenue Denver, Colorado 80204 303/753-2395 (Approved in 1929; Private)		
		Total	Women	Minorities	Total	Women	Minorities	Total	Women	Minorities
1st Year Enrollment	Full-Time	125	31	12	160	75	17	204	83	26
	Part-Time	49	15	8	None			95	49	12
2nd Year Enrollment	Full-Time	117	37	10	176	81	21	206	80	14
	Part-Time	53	18	6	None			97	51	11
3rd Year Enrollment	Full-Time	52	20	5	151	72	12	219	95	13
	Part-Time	34	16	5	None			73	32	10
4th Year Enrollment	Full-Time									
	Part-Time	29	16	2	None			67	33	3
Graduate Enrollment	Full-Time	None			None			10	8	1
	Part-Time	None			None			49	16	2
Other Enrollment	Full-Time	None			None			33	20	2
	Part-Time	None			None			None		
Fall, 1983, Enrollment	Full-Time	294	88	27	487	228	50	692	286	56
	Part-Time	165	65	21				381	181	38
	Total	459	153	48	487	228	50	1,073	467	94
Degrees Awarded through Summer, 1983	Full-Time	JD 31	13	6	JD 152	66	9	JD 179 LLM 20	83 4	12 2
	Part-Time	JD 34	22	2				JD 71 LLM 20	37 5	6 0
Teachers	Full-Time	18	5	0	26	3	1	31	4	1
	Part-Time	7	0	0	7	3	0	18	2	0
Full-time Teaching Deans and Librarians		3	0	0	1	0	0	6	2	0
Tuition and Fees	Full-Time		$6,480		$1,546 r	$5,036 nr			$6,673	
	Part-Time		$3,896						$5,005	
College Required—Degree or 3 years			D			D			D	
Weeks Required	Full-Time		96			90			90	
	Part-Time		152						120	
Credits Required semester (s) or quarter (q)			87s			86s			130q	
Summer Programs	Accepts summer credit from other schools		Yes			Yes			Yes	
	Allows acceleration of graduation by attending summer sessions		Yes			Yes			Yes	
Joint Degrees			MBA 0			None		MBA 13 MA/Anth. 0 MA/Psy. 1 MSLS 0	MSW 0 MA/Econ. 0 MA/Soc. 0 MS/Min.Econ.2	RUP 0 MA/Intl.St. 5 MSJA 0 MS/Pro.Psy. 0
Library	Total Hard Copy Volumes		70,935			163,562			129,235	
	Microform Volume Equivalents		42,501			20,717			58,908	

** Provisionally approved, status of graduates and students equal to that of fully approved law schools.

Law Schools on the 1983 Approved List of the American Bar Association

CONNECTICUT

University of Bridgeport
School of Law
303 University Avenue
Bridgeport, Connecticut 06601
203/576-4041
(Approved in 1979; Private)

University of Connecticut
School of Law
West Hartford, Connecticut 06117
203/241-4633
(Approved in 1933; Public)

Yale Law School
P.O. Box 401A Yale Station
New Haven, Connecticut 06520-7397
203/436-8895
(Approved in 1923; Private)

		Total	Women	Minorities	Total	Women	Minorities	Total	Women	Minorities
1st Year Enrollment	Full-Time	168	57	3	141	72	16	178	69	33
	Part-Time	92	29	4	78	38	2	None		
2nd Year Enrollment	Full-Time	187	56	2	146	64	12	183	69	32
	Part-Time	85	31	5	57	22	2	None		
3rd Year Enrollment	Full-Time	134	47	0	153	71	11	189	61	23
	Part-Time	71	23	4	60	27	5	None		
4th Year Enrollment	Full-Time							None		
	Part-Time	31	9	0	47	19	2			
Graduate Enrollment	Full-Time	None			None			52	14	20
	Part-Time	29	6	1	None			None		
Other Enrollment	Full-Time	None			6	6	0	23	12	3
	Part-Time	None			6	2	1	None		
Fall, 1983, Enrollment	Full-Time	489	160	5	446	213	39	625	225	111
	Part-Time	308	98	14	248	108	12			
	Total	**797**	**258**	**19**	**694**	**321**	**51**	**625**	**225**	**111**
Degrees Awarded through Summer, 1983	Full-Time	JD 125	43	2	JD 142	63	13	JD 183 LLM 30 SJD 2 MSL 8	59 14 0 3	26 5 0 1
	Part-Time	JD 34	11	1	JD 45	22	2			
Teachers	Full-Time	26	6	2	30	6	2	41	4	3
	Part-Time	9	0	0	20	3	0	18	0	1
Full-time Teaching Deans and Librarians		4	0	0	None			None		

Tuition and Fees	Full-Time	$6,655	$2,090 r	$4,390 nr	$9,050
	Part-Time	$5,555	$75/cr.hr. r	$75/cr.hr. nr	
College Required—Degree or 3 years		D	D		D
Weeks Required	Full-Time	90	93		99
	Part-Time	120	139		
Credits Required semester (s) or quarter (q)		86s	86s		81s
Summer Programs — Accepts summer credit from other schools		Yes	Yes		No
Summer Programs — Allows acceleration of graduation by attending summer sessions		Yes	Yes		No

Joint Degrees	MBA 0	MBA 2 MSW 3	MLS 0 MA/Pub.Pol. 0	MPA 0	M.Div. 0 MA/For. 0 MA/Pol.Sc. 1 Ph.D./Pol.Sc.0 — MPPM 3 MA/Hist. 0 Ph.D./Econ. 0 Ph.D./Am.St.1 — MA/Am.St. 0 MA/East.Lang. 1 Ph.D./Hist. 1 Ph.D./Phil. 2

Library				
	Total Hard Copy Volumes	92,034	168,749	617,948
	Microform Volume Equivalents	59,981	61,154	43,449

Law Schools on the 1983 Approved List of the American Bar Association

DELAWARE

Delaware Law School
Widener University
P.O. Box 7474
Concord Pike
Wilmington, Delaware 19803
302/478-3000
(Approved in 1975; Private)

DISTRICT OF COLUMBIA

American University
Washington College of Law
4400 Massachusetts Avenue, N.W.
Washington, D.C. 20016
202/686-2620
(Approved in 1940; Private)

Antioch School of Law
2633 16th Street, N.W.
Washington, D.C. 20009
202/639-2600
(Approved in 1973; Private)

		Total	Women	Minorities	Total	Women	Minorities	Total	Women	Minorities
1st Year Enrollment	Full-Time	186	63	3	260	120	23	158	78	55
	Part-Time	91	35	4	78	42	5	None		
2nd Year Enrollment	Full-Time	217	59	3	283	129	17	168	86	60
	Part-Time	84	26	9	57	35	5	None		
3rd Year Enrollment	Full-Time	152	44	1	186	91	20	151	72	53
	Part-Time	71	27	5	58	26	4	None		
4th Year Enrollment	Full-Time							None		
	Part-Time	63	21	8	62	30	5			
Graduate Enrollment	Full-Time	None			None			None		
	Part-Time	None			27	11	13	None		
Other Enrollment	Full-Time	2	2	0	None			33	7	7
	Part-Time	2	0	0	22	9	2	None		
Fall, 1983, Enrollment	Full-Time	557	168	7	729	340	60	510	243	175
	Part-Time	311	109	26	304	153	34			
	Total	**868**	**277**	**33**	**1,033**	**493**	**94**	**510**	**243**	**175**
Degrees Awarded through Summer, 1983	Full-Time	JD 149	29	1	JD 248	114	8	JD 139	68	63
	Part-Time	JD 70	17	2	JD 46 LLM 11	21 2	3 6			
Teachers	Full-Time	26	1	1	31	6	2	17	7	4
	Part-Time	22	1	0	None			9	2	0
Full-time Teaching Deans and Librarians		2	0	0	4	0	1	1	0	0
Tuition and Fees	Full-Time	$5,150			$7,340			$6,330		
	Part-Time	$3,860			$268/cr.hr.			$250/cr.hr.		
College Required—Degree or 3 years		D			D			D		
Weeks Required	Full-Time	94			84			94		
	Part-Time	126			120					
Credits Required semester (s) or quarter (q)		87s			84s			92s		
Summer Programs	Accepts summer credit from other schools	Yes			Yes			Yes		
	Allows acceleration of graduation by attending summer sessions	Yes			Yes			Yes		
Joint Degrees		MBA 3			MBA 0 MA/Intl.St. 0			None		
Library	Total Hard Copy Volumes	110,806			117,218			60,500		
	Microform Volume Equivalents	50,148			82,901			4,597		

Law Schools on the 1983 Approved List of the American Bar Association

		Catholic University of America School of Law Washington, D.C. 20064 202/635-5144 (Approved in 1925; Private)			Georgetown University Law Center 600 New Jersey Avenue, N.W. Washington, D.C. 20001 202/624-8000 (Approved in 1924; Private)			George Washington University The National Law Center Washington, D.C. 20052 202/676-6592 (Approved in 1923; Private)		
		Total	Women	Minorities	Total	Women	Minorities	Total	Women	Minorities
1st Year Enrollment	Full-Time	196	88	6	512	219	101	344	150	36
	Part-Time	68	34	11	125	71	32	127	67	3
2nd Year Enrollment	Full-Time	186	64	12	478	209	68	323	139	41
	Part-Time	66	29	14	114	60	23	109	43	5
3rd Year Enrollment	Full-Time	192	82	6	498	203	93	331	151	38
	Part-Time	63	30	7	91	42	21	93	42	7
4th Year Enrollment	Full-Time									
	Part-Time	63	26	5	123	50	36	96	37	13
Graduate Enrollment	Full-Time	None			162	50	20	61	15	10
	Part-Time	None			357	96	37	176	36	6
Other Enrollment	Full-Time	2	1	0	9	7	0	4	1	1
	Part-Time	15	2	7	120	42	20	26	5	2
Fall, 1983, Enrollment	Full-Time	576	235	24	1,659	688	282	1,063	456	126
	Part-Time	275	121	44	930	361	169	627	230	36
	Total	851	356	68	2,589	1,049	451	1,690	686	162

Degrees Awarded through Summer, 1983

Full-Time		JD 172	77	18	JD 466	200	77	JD 340	138	41
					LLM 6	0	0	LLM 46	7	3
					MCL 10	1	2	MCL 22	4	13
					MLT 43	5	3	SJD 4	0	2
					MLSR 2	0	0			
					MLIC 12	3	4			
					MLL 7	2	2			
					MLA 7	4	0			
Part-Time		JD 44	17	6	JD 114	47	20	JD 81	28	8
					LLM 9	2	0	LLM 34	9	1
					MLT 86	16	4	MCL 7	2	3
					MLSR 7	1	0	SJD 1	0	0
					MLL 9	3	0			
					MLIC 13	4	1			

Teachers	Full-Time	24	6	0	61	13	3	44	8	2
	Part-Time	25	3	1	106	6	1	41	4	1
Full-time Teaching Deans and Librarians		1	0	0	6	1	0	3	0	0

		Catholic University			Georgetown University			George Washington University		
Tuition and Fees	Full-Time	$6,750			$8,310			$8,100 1st yr. $7,200 upper		
	Part-Time	$240/cr.hr.			$283/cr.hr.			$290/cr. 1st yr. $257/cr. upper		
College Required—Degree or 3 years		D			D			D		
Weeks Required	Full-Time	90			90			102		
	Part-Time	120			120			136		
Credits Required semester (s) or quarter (q)		84s			83s			84s		
Summer Programs	Accepts summer credit from other schools	Yes			Yes			Yes		
	Allows acceleration of graduation by attending summer sessions	Yes			No			Yes		
Joint Degrees		MSW 0 MA/Phil. 0 MA/Hist. 0 MA/Econ. 0 MA/Psy. 0 MA/Pol.Sc. 0 MA/Acct. 0 MSLS 0			MBA 0 MSFS 8			MAd 0 MBA 0 MPA 0		
Library	Total Hard Copy Volumes	98,608			222,403			229,579		
	Microform Volume Equivalents	30,288			156,551			84,544		

Law Schools on the 1983 Approved List of the American Bar Association

FLORIDA

		Howard University School of Law 2900 Van Ness Street, N. W. Washington, D.C. 20008 202/686-6837 (Approved in 1931; Private)			Florida State University College of Law Tallahassee, Florida 32306 904/644-3400 (Approved in 1968; Public)			Nova University Center for the Study of Law 3100 Southwest 9th Avenue Fort Lauderdale, Florida 33315 305/522-2300 (Approved in 1975; Private)		
		Total	Women	Minorities	Total	Women	Minorities	Total	Women	Minorities
1st Year Enrollment	Full-Time Part-Time	186 None	88	161	221 None	92	20	265 None	105	19
2nd Year Enrollment	Full-Time Part-Time	190 None	97	172	211 None	84	20	211 None	84	16
3rd Year Enrollment	Full-Time Part-Time	176 None	96	156	208 None	65	24	197 None	81	23
4th Year Enrollment	Full-Time Part-Time	None			None			None		
Graduate Enrollment	Full-Time Part-Time	22 None	4	22	None None			None None		
Other Enrollment	Full-Time Part-Time	None None			None None			None None		
Fall, 1983, Enrollment	Full-Time Part-Time Total	574 574	285 285	511 511	640 640	241 241	64 64	673 673	270 270	58 58
Degrees Awarded through Summer, 1983	Full-Time	JD 178 MCJ 10	77 2	160 10	JD 198	66	14	JD 221	77	20
	Part-Time									
Teachers	Full-Time Part-Time	24 16	4 1	22 12	21 4	3 0	0 1	25 24	4 8	0 0
Full-time Teaching Deans and Librarians		5	2	5	5	2	1	5	3	0
Tuition and Fees	Full-Time Part-Time	$3,215			$1,193 r	$3,353 nr		$5,285		
College Required—Degree or 3 years		D			D			D		
Weeks Required	Full-Time Part-Time	101			90			90		
Credits Required semester (s) or quarter (q)		88s			88s			87s		
Summer Programs	Accepts summer credit from other schools	Yes			Yes			Yes		
	Allows acceleration of graduation by attending summer sessions	No			Yes			Yes		
Joint Degrees		MBA 0			MBA 3 MA/Intl.Aff. 1	MPA 0 MS/Econ. 0	RUP 0	None		
Library	Total Hard Copy Volumes	161,493			132,742			100,829		
	Microform Volume Equivalents	51,390			97,601			124,172		

Law Schools on the 1983 Approved List of the American Bar Association

		Stetson University College of Law 1401 61st Street South St. Petersburg, Florida 33707 813/345-1300 (Approved in 1930; Private)			University of Florida College of Law Spessard L. Holland Law Center Gainesville, Florida 32611 904/392-0421 (Approved in 1930; Public)			University of Miami School of Law P.O. Box 248087 Coral Gables, Florida 33124 305/284-2392 (Approved in 1941; Private)		
		Total	Women	Minorities	Total	Women	Minorities	Total	Women	Minorities
1st Year Enrollment	Full-Time Part-Time	195 None	85	15	453 2	163 2	18 2	359 84	137 30	49 17
2nd Year Enrollment	Full-Time Part-Time	137 None	66	7	306 None	104	38	310 63	132 26	51 18
3rd Year Enrollment	Full-Time Part-Time	203 None	64	9	191 None	72	24	343 26	123 4	34 4
4th Year Enrollment	Full-Time Part-Time	None			None			13	6	3
Graduate Enrollment	Full-Time Part-Time	None None			95 10	15 3	1 0	85 74	17 20	12 15
Other Enrollment	Full-Time Part-Time	5 None	1	0	10 None	4	0	7 2	2 1	3 1
Fall, 1983, Enrollment	Full-Time Part-Time Total	540 540	216 216	31 31	1,055 12 1,067	358 5 363	81 2 83	1,104 262 1,366	411 87 498	149 58 207
Degrees Awarded through Summer, 1983	Full-Time	JD 171	63	11	JD 422 LLM 60	126 10	33 0	JD 288 LLM 56 MCL 5	108 3 3	13 4 4
	Part-Time				LLM 4	2	0	JD 39 LLM 11 MCL 5	11 2 0	11 0 5
Teachers	Full-Time Part-Time	16 17	4 1	1 1	43 3	5 1	3 0	35 44	4 6	1 0
Full-time Teaching Deans and Librarians		4	0	1	2	0	0	2	0	0
Tuition and Fees	Full-Time Part-Time		$5,160		$966 r	$2,694 nr			$6,886 $5,083	
College Required—Degree or 3 years			D			D			D	
Weeks Required	Full-Time Part-Time		100			90			96 96	
Credits Required semester (s) or quarter (q)			86s			86s			88s	
Summer Programs	Accepts summer credit from other schools		No			Yes			Yes	
	Allows acceleration of graduation by attending summer sessions		Yes			Yes			Yes	
Joint Degrees			None		MBA 2	MPA 3	RUP 0		None	
Library	Total Hard Copy Volumes		145,264			239,813			244,359	
	Microform Volume Equivalents		47,485			116,083			30,679	

Law Schools on the 1983 Approved List of the American Bar Association

GEORGIA

		Emory University School of Law Atlanta, Georgia 30322 404/329-6815 (Approved in 1923; Private)			Mercer University Walter F. George School of Law Macon, Georgia 31207 912/744-2601 (Approved in 1925; Private)			University of Georgia School of Law Athens, Georgia 30602 404/542-7140 (Approved in 1930; Public)		
		Total	Women	Minorities	Total	Women	Minorities	Total	Women	Minorities
1st Year Enrollment	Full-Time Part-Time	212 None	93	19	180 1	56 1	11 0	216 None	67	13
2nd Year Enrollment	Full-Time Part-Time	269 None	109	16	150 None	48	3	243 None	76	15
3rd Year Enrollment	Full-Time Part-Time	218 None	94	12	164 1	50 1	14 0	200 None	42	8
4th Year Enrollment	Full-Time Part-Time	None			None			None		
Graduate Enrollment	Full-Time Part-Time	19 72	5 10	1 2	None None			10 None	2	3
Other Enrollment	Full-Time Part-Time	12 None	7	0	None None			3 None	1	1
Fall, 1983, Enrollment	Full-Time Part-Time Total	730 72 802	308 10 318	48 2 50	494 2 496	154 2 156	28 0 28	672 672	188 188	40 40
Degrees Awarded through Summer, 1983	Full-Time	JD 223 LLM 10	75 1	6 0	JD 140	38	9	JD 208 LLM 1	72 0	12 0
	Part-Time	LLM 18	3	0						
Teachers	Full-Time Part-Time	29 14	2 0	1 0	17 7	3 1	0 0	27 1	1 0	3 0
Full-time Teaching Deans and Librarians		2	0	0	4	1	0	4	1	0
Tuition and Fees	Full-Time Part-Time	$6,920			$5,652			$1,482 r	$3,930 nr	
College Required—Degree or 3 years		D			3			D		
Weeks Required	Full-Time Part-Time	96			90			84		
Credits Required semester (s) or quarter (q)		88s			88s			88s		
Summer Programs	Accepts summer credit from other schools	Yes			Yes			No		
	Allows acceleration of graduation by attending summer sessions	Yes			Yes			Yes		
Joint Degrees		MBA 13	MTH 0		MBA 1			MBA 2	MA/Acct. 1	
Library	Total Hard Copy Volumes	161,838			102,865			288,087		
	Microform Volume Equivalents	18,999			44,872			59,476		

Law Schools on the 1983 Approved List of the American Bar Association		HAWAII University of Hawaii William S. Richardson School of Law 2515 Dole Street Honolulu, Hawaii 96822 808/948-7966 (Approved in 1974; Public)			IDAHO University of Idaho College of Law Moscow, Idaho 83843 208/885-6422 (Approved in 1925; Public)			ILLINOIS DePaul University College of Law 25 East Jackson Boulevard Chicago, Illinois 60604 312/321-7700 (Approved in 1925; Private)		
		Total	Women	Minorities	Total	Women	Minorities	Total	Women	Minorities
1st Year Enrollment	Full-Time Part-Time	81 None	37	62	89 None	22	4	246 89	98 29	22 11
2nd Year Enrollment	Full-Time Part-Time	78 None	37	59	107 None	25	6	254 72	108 30	10 8
3rd Year Enrollment	Full-Time Part-Time	88 None	33	55	82 None	22	0	205 75	84 21	9 2
4th Year Enrollment	Full-Time Part-Time	None			None			87	32	9
Graduate Enrollment	Full-Time Part-Time	None None			None None			None 119	28	8
Other Enrollment	Full-Time Part-Time	None None			None None			None None		
Fall, 1983, Enrollment	Full-Time Part-Time Total	247 247	107 107	176 176	278 278	69 69	10 10	705 442 1,147	290 140 430	41 38 79
Degrees Awarded through Summer, 1983	Full-Time	JD 69	33	53	JD 92	24	1	JD 263 LLM 1	98 0	22 0
	Part-Time							JD 73 LLM 31	22 5	4 1
Teachers	Full-Time Part-Time	13 8	4 1	2 1	9 6	1 2	0 0	37 32	11 4	2 6
Full-time Teaching Deans and Librarians		1	0	0	4	1	0	1	1	0
Tuition and Fees	Full-Time Part-Time	$1,040 r	$3,310 nr		$1,066 r	$3,066 nr		$6,275 $4,975		
College Required—Degree or 3 years		D			D			D		
Weeks Required	Full-Time Part-Time	99			96			102 136		
Credits Required semester (s) or quarter (q)		89s			84s			86s		
Summer Programs	Accepts summer credit from other schools	Yes			Yes			Yes		
	Allows acceleration of graduation by attending summer sessions	Yes			Yes			Yes		
Joint Degrees		MBA 1 MSW 1 MA/Asian St. 1 Ph.D./Hist. 1	MCRP 1 RUP 1 MA/Arch. 1	MPH 1 MA/Am.St. 1 MA/Ed.Adm. 1	None			MBA 4		
Library	Total Hard Copy Volumes	60,447			81,076			131,815		
	Microform Volume Equivalents	78,031			15,926			74,532		

Law Schools on the 1983 Approved List of the American Bar Association		Illinois Institute of Technology Chicago-Kent College of Law 77 South Wacker Drive Chicago, Illinois 60606 312/567-5000 (Approved in 1936; Private)			The John Marshall Law School 315 South Plymouth Court Chicago, Illinois 60604 312/427-2737 (Approved in 1951; Private)			Loyola University of Chicago School of Law 1 East Pearson Street Chicago, Illinois 60611 312/670-2920 (Approved in 1925; Private)		
		Total	Women	Minorities	Total	Women	Minorities	Total	Women	Minorities
1st Year Enrollment	Full-Time	240	84	13	336	104	10	146	71	7
	Part-Time	95	31	8	154	53	8	75	32	7
2nd Year Enrollment	Full-Time	227	73	10	311	97	16	214	104	16
	Part-Time	82	22	6	139	31	7	51	20	1
3rd Year Enrollment	Full-Time	210	59	10	309	92	8	126	60	3
	Part-Time	68	13	5	128	38	9	53	19	3
4th Year Enrollment	Full-Time									
	Part-Time	60	17	4	104	31	7	58	22	2
Graduate Enrollment	Full-Time	None			None			None		
	Part-Time	59	15	2	128	27	7	None		
Other Enrollment	Full-Time	2	1	0	None			4	3	0
	Part-Time	10	3	0	11	4	2	7	1	2
Fall, 1983, Enrollment	Full-Time	679	217	33	956	293	34	490	238	26
	Part-Time	374	101	25	664	184	40	244	94	15
	Total	1,053	318	58	1,620	477	74	734	332	41
Degrees Awarded through Summer, 1983	Full-Time	JD 216 MSL 1	58 0	4 0	JD 277	75	11	JD 140	76	10
	Part-Time	JD 57 LLM 1	23 1	4 0	JD 128 LLM 74	24 9	3 6	JD 17	5	0
Teachers	Full-Time	31	6	0	40	4	0	21	5	1
	Part-Time	81	12	5	34	5	1	43	9	0
Full-time Teaching Deans and Librarians		1	0	0	1	0	0	3	1	0
Tuition and Fees	Full-Time	$6,334			$5,090			$5,661		
	Part-Time	$4,234			$4,010			$4,220		
College Required—Degree or 3 years		D			D			D		
Weeks Required	Full-Time	90			102			90		
	Part-Time	120			136			120		
Credits Required semester (s) or quarter (q)		90s			86s			86s		
Summer Programs	Accepts summer credit from other schools	Yes			Yes			Yes		
	Allows acceleration of graduation by attending summer sessions	Yes			Yes			Yes		
Joint Degrees		MBA 1			MBA 3			MSW 0 MA/Pol.Sc. 0		
Library	Total Hard Copy Volumes	146,834			128,470			86,994		
	Microform Volume Equivalents	89,024			76,091			32,114		

* Independent law school, not affiliated with a university.

Law Schools on the 1983 Approved List of the American Bar Association

		Northern Illinois University College of Law DeKalb, Illinois 60115 815/753-1067 (Approved in 1978; Public)			Northwestern University School of Law 357 East Chicago Avenue Chicago, Illinois 60611 312/649-8462 (Approved in 1923; Private)			Southern Illinois University School of Law Carbondale, Illinois 62901 618/536-7711 (Approved in 1974; Public)		
		Total	Women	Minorities	Total	Women	Minorities	Total	Women	Minorities
1st Year Enrollment	Full-Time Part-Time	94 None	28	6	189 None	85	21	114 None	28	6
2nd Year Enrollment	Full-Time Part-Time	92 1	38 1	4 1	198 None	89	22	109 None	31	4
3rd Year Enrollment	Full-Time Part-Time	65 1	20 0	6 0	197 None	86	22	102 None	27	4
4th Year Enrollment	Full-Time Part-Time	13	6	1	None			None		
Graduate Enrollment	Full-Time Part-Time	None None			10 None	1	5	None None		
Other Enrollment	Full-Time Part-Time	None None			10 None	8	1	1 None	0	0
Fall, 1983, Enrollment	Full-Time Part-Time **Total**	251 15 **266**	86 7 **93**	16 2 **18**	604 **604**	269 **269**	71 **71**	326 **326**	86 **86**	14 **14**
Degrees Awarded through Summer, 1983	Full-Time	JD 49	13	3	JD 167 LLM 5	76 1	19 0	JD 79	24	0
	Part-Time	JD 31	7	2						
Teachers	Full-Time Part-Time	18 3	3 0	0 0	35 4	5 3	1 2	19 4	2 1	1 1
Full-time Teaching Deans and Librarians		4	0	0	None			4	2	0
Tuition and Fees	Full-Time Part-Time	$2,441 $112/cr.hr.			$9,560			$1,465 r	$3,577 nr	
College Required—Degree or 3 years		D			D			D		
Weeks Required	Full-Time Part-Time	90 120			95			90		
Credits Required semester (s) or quarter (q)		85s			90s			90s		
Summer Programs	Accepts summer credit from other schools	Yes			Yes			Yes		
	Allows acceleration of graduation by attending summer sessions	Yes			Yes			Yes		
Joint Degrees		MBA 0			MBA 15	Ph.D./Law & Soc.Sc. 0		MBA 0	MPA 0	MA/Acct. 2
Library	Total Hard Copy Volumes	68,457			397,360			125,891		
	Microform Volume Equivalents	51,521			37,655			89,872		

Law Schools on the 1983 Approved List of the American Bar Association

INDIANA

		University of Chicago Law School 1111 East 60th Street Chicago, Illinois 60637 312/962-9494 (Approved in 1923; Private)			University of Illinois College of Law 504 East Pennsylvania Avenue Champaign, Illinois 61820 217/333-0931 (Approved in 1923; Public)			Indiana University School of Law Bloomington, Indiana 47405 812/335-8885 (Approved in 1923; Public)		
		Total	Women	Minorities	Total	Women	Minorities	Total	Women	Minorities
1st Year Enrollment	Full-Time Part-Time	173 None	55	7	206 None	70	22	182 9	72 7	23 0
2nd Year Enrollment	Full-Time Part-Time	179 None	63	8	219 None	82	10	180 2	60 1	26 0
3rd Year Enrollment	Full-Time Part-Time	170 None	56	13	201 None	65	10	193 1	56 1	24 0
4th Year Enrollment	Full-Time Part-Time	None			None			None		
Graduate Enrollment	Full-Time Part-Time	None None			29 None	8	0	16 None	4	4
Other Enrollment	Full-Time Part-Time	7 None	1	0	None None			2 19	1 10	0 0
Fall, 1983, Enrollment	Full-Time Part-Time **Total**	529 **529**	175 **175**	28 **28**	655 **655**	225 **225**	42 **42**	573 31 **604**	193 19 **212**	77 0 **77**
Degrees Awarded through Summer, 1983	Full-Time	JD 163 LLM 1	50 0	12 0	JD 191 LLM 9 MCL 16 SJD 1	51 3 5 0	7 0 0 0	JD 176 LLM 5	58 1	24 1
	Part-Time							LLM 1	1	0
Teachers	Full-Time Part-Time	24 3	3 0	0 0	25 2	2 0	1 0	23 1	3 0	1 0
Full-time Teaching Deans and Librarians		None			2	0	0	1	0	0
Tuition and Fees	Full-Time Part-Time	$9,528			$2,030 r	$5,234 nr		$1,722 r $62/cr.hr. r	$4,718 nr $169/cr.hr. nr	
College Required—Degree or 3 years		3			D			D		
Weeks Required	Full-Time Part-Time	90			90			96		
Credits Required semester (s) or quarter (q)		140q			90s			82s		
Summer Programs	Accepts summer credit from other schools	No			Yes			Yes		
	Allows acceleration of graduation by attending summer sessions	No			Yes			Yes		
Joint Degrees		MBA 10 Ph.D./Econ. 0	MPP 1	MA/Econ. 0	MBA 6 MA/Acct. 1 Ph.D./Ed. 0	MPA 2 MA/Ed. 1 MALIR 5	RUP 0 JD/MD 0	MBA 7 Ph.D./Law & Soc.Sc. 0	MPA 1	MS/Env.St. 0
Library	Total Hard Copy Volumes	407,876			403,501			218,691		
	Microform Volume Equivalents	19,598			26,910			27,542		

Law Schools on the 1983 Approved List of the American Bar Association

Indiana University
School of Law–Indianapolis
735 West New York Street
Indianapolis, Indiana 46202
317/264-8523
(Approved in 1936; Public)

University of Notre Dame
Law School
Notre Dame, Indiana 46556
219/239-6627
(Approved in 1925; Private)

Valparaiso University
School of Law
Valparaiso, Indiana 46383
219/464-5436
(Approved in 1929; Private)

		Total	Women	Minorities	Total	Women	Minorities	Total	Women	Minorities
1st Year Enrollment	Full-Time	153	64	6	160	59	18	153	52	6
	Part-Time	88	37	6	7	4	1	None		
2nd Year Enrollment	Full-Time	149	59	3	156	48	6	120	36	10
	Part-Time	98	41	6	None			None		
3rd Year Enrollment	Full-Time	171	65	6	163	47	14	96	31	7
	Part-Time	170	62	3	None			None		
4th Year Enrollment	Full-Time									
	Part-Time	None			None			None		
Graduate Enrollment	Full-Time	None			None			None		
	Part-Time	None			None			None		
Other Enrollment	Full-Time	None			20	10	0	None		
	Part-Time	6	3	2	None			None		
Fall, 1983, Enrollment	Full-Time	473	188	15	499	164	38	369	119	23
	Part-Time	362	143	17	7	4	1			
	Total	**835**	**331**	**32**	**506**	**168**	**39**	**369**	**119**	**23**
Degrees Awarded through Summer, 1983	Full-Time	JD 143 LLB 1	46 1	2 0	JD 165	51	10	JD 118	43	4
	Part-Time	JD 75	23	4						
Teachers	Full-Time	28	6	1	23	5	2	17	2	0
	Part-Time	1	0	0	10	1	0	3	1	0
Full-time Teaching Deans and Librarians		7	3	0	5	1	0	1	0	0

		Indiana	Notre Dame	Valparaiso
Tuition and Fees	Full-Time	$1,850 r $5,060 nr	$6,487	$6,005
	Part-Time	$1,235 r $3,375 nr		
College Required—Degree or 3 years		D	D	D
Weeks Required	Full-Time	90	90	96
	Part-Time	120		
Credits Required semester (s) or quarter (q)		85s	90s	85s
Summer Programs	Accepts summer credit from other schools	Yes	Yes	Yes
	Allows acceleration of graduation by attending summer sessions	Yes	No	No
Joint Degrees		MBA 2 MHA 0 MPA 0	MBA 1 MTH 0	None
Library	Total Hard Copy Volumes	239,550	126,139	83,013
	Microform Volume Equivalents	81,782	5,775	54,019

Law Schools on the 1983 Approved List of the American Bar Association

IOWA

Drake University
Law School
Des Moines, Iowa 50311
515/271-2824
(Approved in 1923; Private)

University of Iowa
College of Law
Iowa City, Iowa 52242
319/353-5742
(Approved in 1923; Public)

KANSAS

The University of Kansas
School of Law
Lawrence, Kansas 66045
913/864-4550
(Approved in 1923; Public)

		Total	Women	Minorities	Total	Women	Minorities	Total	Women	Minorities
1st Year Enrollment	Full-Time	170	53	11	229	78	13	185	68	17
	Part-Time	4	2	1	None			None		
2nd Year Enrollment	Full-Time	152	50	10	226	85	19	176	57	6
	Part-Time	None			None			None		
3rd Year Enrollment	Full-Time	175	55	8	186	68	22	189	67	8
	Part-Time	None			None			None		
4th Year Enrollment	Full-Time									
	Part-Time	None			None			None		
Graduate Enrollment	Full-Time	None			5	1	2	None		
	Part-Time	None			None			None		
Other Enrollment	Full-Time	19	2	1	6	2	1	None		
	Part-Time	None			None			None		
Fall, 1983, Enrollment	Full-Time	516	160	30	652	234	57	550	192	31
	Part-Time	4	2	1						
	Total	520	162	31	652	234	57	550	192	31
Degrees Awarded through Summer, 1983	Full-Time	JD 158	36	8	JD 209 MCL 1	77 0	17 0	JD 174	51	11
	Part-Time									
Teachers	Full-Time	19	2	0	36	6	2	22	2	1
	Part-Time	12	0	0	5	0	0	7	2	0
Full-time Teaching Deans and Librarians		3	0	1	7	3	2	4	1	0

Tuition and Fees	Full-Time Part-Time	$6,250	$1,384 r $3,410 nr	$1,202 r $2,856 nr
College Required—Degree or 3 years		D	D	D
Weeks Required	Full-Time Part-Time	102	96	90
Credits Required semester (s) or quarter (q)		90s	90s	90s
Summer Programs	Accepts summer credit from other schools	Yes	Yes	Yes
	Allows acceleration of graduation by attending summer sessions	Yes	Yes	Yes
Joint Degrees		MBA 3 MPA 0 MA/M.Com. 0 MA/Pol.Sc. 0 MA/Agri.Econ. 0	MA/Acct. 1 MBA 4 RUP 1 MA, MS, and Ph.D. offered in 30 subject areas	MBA 3 MPA 2 RUP 0 MA/Econ. 0 MA/Phil. 0
Library	Total Hard Copy Volumes	116,449	370,125	185,120
	Microform Volume Equivalents	19,280	52,658	23,983

Law Schools on the 1983 Approved List of the American Bar Association		Washburn University of Topeka School of Law 1700 College Topeka, Kansas 66621 913/295-6660 (Approved in 1923; Private)			**KENTUCKY** Northern Kentucky University Salmon P. Chase College of Law Highland Heights, Kentucky 41076 606/572-5340 (Approved in 1954; Public)			University of Kentucky College of Law Lexington, Kentucky 40506-0048 606/257-1678 (Approved in 1923; Public)		
		Total	Women	Minorities	Total	Women	Minorities	Total	Women	Minorities
1st Year Enrollment	Full-Time Part-Time	210 None	65	11	72 69	22 20	2 7	146 None	60	3
2nd Year Enrollment	Full-Time Part-Time	187 None	65	8	61 34	27 8	1 2	157 None	69	4
3rd Year Enrollment	Full-Time Part-Time	206 None	67	10	64 47	20 17	0 2	151 None	57	5
4th Year Enrollment	Full-Time Part-Time	None			50	15	0	None		
Graduate Enrollment	Full-Time Part-Time	None None			None None			None None		
Other Enrollment	Full-Time Part-Time	None None			3 1	1 1	0 0	6 None	1	0
Fall, 1983, Enrollment	Full-Time Part-Time **Total**	603 **603**	197 **197**	29 **29**	200 201 **401**	70 61 **131**	3 11 **14**	460 **460**	187 **187**	12 **12**
Degrees Awarded through Summer, 1983	Full-Time	JD 183	44	7	JD 72	20	0	JD 147	51	3
	Part-Time				JD 44	9	2			
Teachers	Full-Time Part-Time	24 13	4 0	4 0	18 6	2 1	0 0	21 5	4 0	1 0
Full-time Teaching Deans and Librarians		2	0	0	2	1	0	3	0	1
Tuition and Fees	Full-Time Part-Time	$2,630 r	$3,350 nr		$1,399 r $1,059 r	$3,499 nr $2,643 nr		$1,468 r	$3,568 nr	
College Required—Degree or 3 years		D			D			D		
Weeks Required	Full-Time Part-Time	92			90 135			90		
Credits Required semester (s) or quarter (q)		90s			88s			87s		
Summer Programs	Accepts summer credit from other schools	Yes			Yes			Yes		
	Allows acceleration of graduation by attending summer sessions	Yes			No			Yes		
Joint Degrees		None			None			None		
Library	Total Hard Copy Volumes	106,239			110,945			180,403		
	Microform Volume Equivalents	36,434			50,520			64,903		

Law Schools on the 1983 Approved List of the American Bar Association

LOUISIANA

		University of Louisville School of Law Belknap Campus Louisville, Kentucky 40292 502/588-6358 (Approved in 1931; Public)			Louisiana State University The Paul M. Hebert Law Center Baton Rouge, Louisiana 70803 504/388-8491 (Approved in 1926; Public)			Loyola University School of Law 6363 Loyola Avenue New Orleans, Louisiana 70118 504/865-2261 (Approved in 1931; Private)		
		Total	Women	Minorities	Total	Women	Minorities	Total	Women	Minorities
1st Year Enrollment	Full-Time Part-Time	111 55	50 16	3 3	290 None	98	10	176 73	76 33	8 7
2nd Year Enrollment	Full-Time Part-Time	105 45	49 19	2 3	208 None	74	7	151 48	77 18	15 4
3rd Year Enrollment	Full-Time Part-Time	102 21	37 5	0 0	223 None	66	3	154 33	69 13	13 4
4th Year Enrollment	Full-Time Part-Time	34	14	0	None			41	17	4
Graduate Enrollment	Full-Time Part-Time	None None			4 None	0	1	None None		
Other Enrollment	Full-Time Part-Time	2 1	2 0	0 0	7 None	1	1	1 None	0	0
Fall, 1983, Enrollment	Full-Time Part-Time Total	320 156 476	138 54 192	5 6 11	732 732	239 239	22 22	482 195 677	222 81 303	36 19 55
Degrees Awarded through Summer, 1983	Full-Time	JD 126	51	2	JD 215 LLM 1	55 0	7 1	JD 138	58	6
	Part-Time	JD 44	7	1				JD 43	15	5
Teachers	Full-Time Part-Time	27 12	4 0	1 0	22 13	2 0	2 0	20 11	3 1	1 0
Full-time Teaching Deans and Librarians		3	2	0	3	0	0	2	0	0
Tuition and Fees	Full-Time Part-Time	$1,479 r	$3,579 nr		$1,380 r $998 r	$3,050 nr $2,286 nr			$4,943 $3,643	
College Required—Degree or 3 years			D			D			3	
Weeks Required	Full-Time Part-Time		90 120			109			90 129	
Credits Required semester (s) or quarter (q)			90s			97s			90s	
Summer Programs	Accepts summer credit from other schools		Yes			Yes			Yes	
	Allows acceleration of graduation by attending summer sessions		Yes			No			No	
Joint Degrees			M.Div. 0			MPA 1			MBA 1	
Library	Total Hard Copy Volumes		123,385			302,659			106,426	
	Microform Volume Equivalents		14,397			72,252			33,520	

Law Schools on the 1983 Approved List of the American Bar Association		Southern University School of Law Southern Branch Post Office Baton Rouge, Louisiana 70813 504/771-2552 (Approved in 1953; Public)			Tulane University School of Law 6801 Freret Street New Orleans, Louisiana 70118 504/865-5939 (Approved in 1925; Private)			**MAINE** University of Maine School of Law 246 Deering Avenue Portland, Maine 04102 207/780-4340 (Approved in 1962; Public)		
		Total	Women	Minorities	Total	Women	Minorities	Total	Women	Minorities
1st Year Enrollment	Full-Time Part-Time	124 None	36	80	269 None	119	30	86 2	31 0	0 0
2nd Year Enrollment	Full-Time Part-Time	100 None	35	62	251 None	97	13	77 1	27 1	0 0
3rd Year Enrollment	Full-Time Part-Time	90 None	18	55	221 None	86	16	75 None	26	0
4th Year Enrollment	Full-Time Part-Time	None			None			None		
Graduate Enrollment	Full-Time Part-Time	None None			65 20	14 6	24 2	None None		
Other Enrollment	Full-Time Part-Time	None None			None None			1 None	1	0
Fall, 1983, Enrollment	Full-Time Part-Time Total	314 314	89 89	197 197	806 20 826	316 6 322	83 2 85	239 3 242	85 1 86	0 0 0
Degrees Awarded through Summer, 1983	Full-Time	JD 125	34	91	JD 250 LLM 94 SJD 5	82 14 0	14 28 4	JD 64	27	0
	Part-Time				LLM 5	1	0			
Teachers	Full-Time Part-Time	12 8	2 0	8 4	26 8	2 0	2 1	13 5	3 1	1 0
Full-time Teaching Deans and Librarians		2	0	2	5	1	1	3	0	0
Tuition and Fees	Full-Time Part-Time	$692 r	$1,412 nr		$7,350 $393/cr.hr.			$2,252 r $74/cr.hr. r	$5,582 nr $185/cr.hr. nr	
College Required—Degree or 3 years			D			3			D	
Weeks Required	Full-Time Part-Time		90			96			90 150	
Credits Required semester (s) or quarter (q)			96s			90s			89s	
Summer Programs	Accepts summer credit from other schools		Yes			Yes			Yes	
	Allows acceleration of graduation by attending summer sessions		No			No			Yes	
Joint Degrees			None		MBA 5 MA/Lat.Am.St. 0	MPH 1	MSW 0		None	
Library	Total Hard Copy Volumes		101,909			187,233			141,730	
	Microform Volume Equivalents		51,605			116,753			43,862	

Law Schools on the 1983 Approved List of the American Bar Association

MARYLAND

University of Baltimore
Law School
1420 North Charles Street
Baltimore, Maryland 21201
301/625-3000
(Approved in 1972; Public)

University of Maryland
School of Law
500 West Baltimore Street
Baltimore, Maryland 21201
301/528-7214
(Approved in 1930; Public)

MASSACHUSETTS

Boston College
Law School
885 Centre Street
Newton, Massachusetts 02159
617/552-4340
(Approved in 1932; Private)

		Total	Women	Minorities	Total	Women	Minorities	Total	Women	Minorities
1st Year Enrollment	Full-Time	184	93	20	192	103	40	270	111	46
	Part-Time	130	50	17	63	38	15	2	1	0
2nd Year Enrollment	Full-Time	172	70	5	190	93	32	314	150	38
	Part-Time	117	40	16	61	33	26	None		
3rd Year Enrollment	Full-Time	149	66	10	186	77	31	253	125	38
	Part-Time	102	27	7	57	23	14	None		
4th Year Enrollment	Full-Time									
	Part-Time	89	35	3	53	23	10	None		
Graduate Enrollment	Full-Time	None			None			None		
	Part-Time	None			None			None		
Other Enrollment	Full-Time	None			13	7	2	None		
	Part-Time	6	1	0	None			None		
Fall, 1983, Enrollment	Full-Time	505	229	35	581	280	105	837	386	122
	Part-Time	444	153	43	234	117	65	2	1	0
	Total	949	382	78	815	397	170	839	387	122
Degrees Awarded through Summer, 1983	Full-Time	JD 146	47	1	JD 239	107	27	JD 253	101	47
	Part-Time	JD 78	30	5						
Teachers	Full-Time	33	8	0	37	5	3	29	5	1
	Part-Time	9	0	0	37	6	0	13	2	2
Full-time Teaching Deans and Librarians		3	2	0	2	1	0	4	1	0
Tuition and Fees	Full-Time	$2,445 r	$4,445 nr		$2,479 r	$4,511 nr		$7,460		
	Part-Time	$79/cr.hr. r	$159/cr.hr. nr		$1,828 r	$3,350 nr		$355/cr.hr.		
College Required—Degree or 3 years		D			3			D		
Weeks Required	Full-Time	90			90			90		
	Part-Time	120			120					
Credits Required semester (s) or quarter (q)		84s			84s			85s		
Summer Programs	Accepts summer credit from other schools	Yes			Yes			No		
	Allows acceleration of graduation by attending summer sessions	Yes			Yes			No		
Joint Degrees		MBA 1 MA/Crim.Jus. 0	ML&T 0	MPA 0	MBA 2 Ph.D./Law& Psy. 0	MSW 0	MA/Policy St. 1	MALD 0 MA/Pol.Sc 0	MBA 1	MCRP 3
Library	Total Hard Copy Volumes	87,385			189,496			139,396		
	Microform Volume Equivalents	37,139			18,255			40,982		

Law Schools on the 1983 Approved List of the American Bar Association

		Boston University School of Law 765 Commonwealth Avenue Boston, Massachusetts 02215 617/353-3112 (Approved in 1925; Private)			Harvard University Law School Cambridge, Massachusetts 02138 617/495-3100 (Approved in 1923; Private)			New England School of Law 154 Stuart Street Boston, Massachusetts 02116 617/451-0010 (Approved in 1969; Private)*		
		Total	Women	Minorities	Total	Women	Minorities	Total	Women	Minorities
1st Year Enrollment	Full-Time Part-Time	469 None	180	15	549 None	190	104	186 140	83 53	15 8
2nd Year Enrollment	Full-Time Part-Time	446 None	166	29	550 None	187	97	171 114	66 38	4 6
3rd Year Enrollment	Full-Time Part-Time	423 1	175 0	29 0	540 None	177	91	164 93	63 38	5 2
4th Year Enrollment	Full-Time Part-Time	None			None			102	26	4
Graduate Enrollment	Full-Time Part-Time	76 274	16 86	2 2	123 None	35	0	None None		
Other Enrollment	Full-Time Part-Time	None None			46 None	7	1	3 None	0	0
Fall, 1983, Enrollment	Full-Time Part-Time Total	1,414 275 **1,689**	537 86 **623**	75 2 **77**	1,808 **1,808**	596 **596**	293 **293**	524 449 **973**	212 155 **367**	24 20 **44**
Degrees Awarded through Summer, 1983	Full-Time	JD 375 LLM 79	140 19	11 3	JD 530 LLM 106 SJD 6	154 27 1	70 1 2	JD 241	95	5
	Part-Time	LLM 69	15	0				JD 83	29	0
Teachers	Full-Time Part-Time	48 26	9 1	1 2	56 11	6 0	3 2	28 34	5 10	2 0
Full-time Teaching Deans and Librarians		3	1	0	4	0	0	2	0	0
Tuition and Fees	Full-Time Part-Time	$8,400 $260/cr.hr.			$8,258 $494/cr.hr.			$5,345 $4,035		
College Required—Degree or 3 years		D			D			D		
Weeks Required	Full-Time Part-Time	90			93			90 120		
Credits Required semester (s) or quarter (q)		84s			83s			84s		
Summer Programs	Accepts summer credit from other schools	No			No			Yes		
	Allows acceleration of graduation by attending summer sessions	No			No			No		
Joint Degrees		MBA 4 MCRP 3 MPH 0 MA/Hist.Pres. 1 MS/M.Comm. 0			MALD 0 MBA 12 MCRP 0 M. Div. 0 MPA 1 MPP 8 MCP 1			None		
Library	Total Hard Copy Volumes	197,860			1,391,311			111,796		
	Microform Volume Equivalents	108,387			40,241			59,990		

* Independent law school, not affiliated with a university.

Law Schools on the 1983 Approved List of the American Bar Association

		Northeastern University School of Law 400 Huntington Avenue Boston, Massachusetts 02115 617/437-4931 (Approved in 1969; Private)			Suffolk University Law School 41 Temple Street Boston, Massachusetts 02114 617/723-4700 (Approved in 1953; Private)			Western New England College School of Law 1215 Wilbraham Road Springfield, Massachusetts 01119 413/782-3111 (Approved in 1974; Private)		
		Total	Women	Minorities	Total	Women	Minorities	Total	Women	Minorities
1st Year Enrollment	Full-Time	145	86	28	299	133	13	187	75	11
	Part-Time	None			204	66	6	97	51	2
2nd Year Enrollment	Full-Time	137	78	17	312	131	21	175	74	7
	Part-Time	None			174	72	2	69	33	3
3rd Year Enrollment	Full-Time	160	96	13	295	129	16	166	57	2
	Part-Time	None			147	61	4	76	28	0
4th Year Enrollment	Full-Time									
	Part-Time	None			153	52	5	84	33	3
Graduate Enrollment	Full-Time	None			None			None		
	Part-Time	None			None			None		
Other Enrollment	Full-Time	1	0	0	None			2	1	0
	Part-Time	None			24	11	0	5	1	0
Fall, 1983, Enrollment	Full-Time	443	260	58	906	393	50	530	207	20
	Part-Time				702	262	17	331	146	8
	Total	443	260	58	1,608	655	67	861	353	28
Degrees Awarded through Summer, 1983	Full-Time	JD 138	69	18	JD 317	139	7	JD 210	79	7
	Part-Time				JD 174	68	7	JD 81	24	4
Teachers	Full-Time	13	2	2	47	6	1	27	4	0
	Part-Time	11	2	2	28	0	1	26	3	1
Full-time Teaching Deans and Librarians		1	0	0	4	0	0	2	0	0
Tuition and Fees	Full-Time	$7,950/1st yr. $6,500/upper			$5,355			$5,760		
	Part-Time				$4,020			$3,650		
College Required—Degree or 3 years		D			D			D		
Weeks Required	Full-Time	78			90			96		
	Part-Time				120			128		
Credits Required semester (s) or quarter (q)		99q			90s			88s		
Summer Programs	Accepts summer credit from other schools	No			Yes			Yes		
	Allows acceleration of graduation by attending summer sessions	No			Yes			No		
Joint Degrees		MA/Policy St. 0			MPA 0			None		
Library	Total Hard Copy Volumes	85,308			144,012			115,916		
	Microform Volume Equivalents	11,750			39,637			60,135		

Law Schools on the 1983 Approved List of the American Bar Association

MICHIGAN

		Detroit College of Law 130 East Elizabeth Street Detroit, Michigan 48201 313/965-0150 (Approved in 1941; Private)*			Thomas M. Cooley Law School 217 South Capitol Avenue P. O. Box 13038 Lansing, Michigan 48901 517/371-5140 (Approved in 1975; Private)*			University of Detroit School of Law 651 East Jefferson Avenue Detroit, Michigan 48226 313/961-5444 (Approved in 1933; Private)		
		Total	Women	Minorities	Total	Women	Minorities	Total	Women	Minorities
1st Year Enrollment	Full-Time Part-Time	156 125	54 33	5 16	None 484	153	18	133 73	44 23	12 13
2nd Year Enrollment	Full-Time Part-Time	128 107	49 36	11 12	None 388	110	6	105 52	46 19	2 2
3rd Year Enrollment	Full-Time Part-Time	133 86	44 24	5 10	9 275	2 74	1 8	137 63	46 31	8 5
4th Year Enrollment	Full-Time Part-Time	104	27	10	None			44	14	4
Graduate Enrollment	Full-Time Part-Time	None None			None None			None None		
Other Enrollment	Full-Time Part-Time	None None			None None			None None		
Fall, 1983, Enrollment	Full-Time Part-Time Total	417 422 **839**	147 120 **267**	21 48 **69**	9 1,147 **1,156**	2 337 **339**	1 32 **33**	375 232 **607**	136 87 **223**	22 24 **46**
Degrees Awarded through Summer, 1983	Full-Time	JD 144	46	10	JD 8	0	0	JD 112	52	7
	Part-Time	JD 98	24	3	JD 326	79	10	JD 44	15	2
Teachers	Full-Time Part-Time	26 24	5 1	0 1	25 40	4 11	1 4	22 10	4 1	1 0
Full-time Teaching Deans and Librarians		4	0	1	1	1	1	2	1	1
Tuition and Fees	Full-Time Part-Time	$4,370 $3,275			$4,725 $157/cr.hr.			$5,597 $4,193		
College Required—Degree or 3 years		D			3			D		
Weeks Required	Full-Time Part-Time	96 128			90 120			90 120		
Credits Required semester (s) or quarter (q)		85s			90s			86s		
Summer Programs	Accepts summer credit from other schools	Yes			No			Yes		
	Allows acceleration of graduation by attending summer sessions	No			No			Yes		
Joint Degrees		None			None			MBA 0		
Library	Total Hard Copy Volumes	69,573			75,803			109,430		
	Microform Volume Equivalents	75,172			56,307			59,070		

* Independent law school, not affiliated with a university.

Law Schools on the 1983 Approved List of the American Bar Association

MINNESOTA

University of Michigan
Law School
625 South State Street
Ann Arbor, Michigan 48109-1215
313/764-1358
(Approved in 1923; Public)

Wayne State University
Law School
468 West Ferry
Detroit, Michigan 48202
313/577-3930
(Approved in 1936; Public)

Hamline University
School of Law
1536 Hewitt Avenue
St. Paul, Minnesota 55104
612/641-2400
(Approved in 1975; Private)

		Total	Women	Minorities	Total	Women	Minorities	Total	Women	Minorities
1st Year Enrollment	Full-Time	375	137	49	241	101	20	170	58	2
	Part-Time	None			85	39	16	None		
2nd Year Enrollment	Full-Time	367	125	45	237	103	20	167	56	2
	Part-Time	None			62	26	7	None		
3rd Year Enrollment	Full-Time	372	122	38	225	102	18	142	53	4
	Part-Time	None			47	19	5	None		
4th Year Enrollment	Full-Time									
	Part-Time	None			73	24	9	None		
Graduate Enrollment	Full-Time	26	1	0	3	0	0	None		
	Part-Time	None			148	25	0	None		
Other Enrollment	Full-Time	None			3	2	0	None		
	Part-Time	None			3	2	0	None		
Fall, 1983, Enrollment	Full-Time	1,140	385	132	709	308	58	479	167	8
	Part-Time				418	135	37			
	Total	1,140	385	132	1,127	443	95	479	167	8
Degrees Awarded through Summer, 1983	Full-Time	JD 376 LLM 21 MCL 6	114 5 1	38 0 0	JD 178 LLM 1	77 0	10 0	JD 180	61	4
	Part-Time				JD 76 LLM 21	21 4	17 1			
Teachers	Full-Time	48	2	1	28	2	1	23	4	0
	Part-Time	6	0	0	21	4	0	11	1	1
Full-time Teaching Deans and Librarians		2	0	0	2	0	0	2	0	0
Tuition and Fees	Full-Time	$3,742 r	$7,850 nr		$3,104 r	$6,660 nr			$5,600	
	Part-Time				$2,240 r	$4,780 nr				
College Required—Degree or 3 years		D			D			D		
Weeks Required	Full-Time	96			90			102		
	Part-Time									
Credits Required semester (s) or quarter (q)		84s			86s			88s		
Summer Programs — Accepts summer credit from other schools		Yes			Yes			Yes		
Summer Programs — Allows acceleration of graduation by attending summer sessions		Yes			Yes			Yes		
Joint Degrees		None			MA/Hist. 1			None		
Library — Total Hard Copy Volumes		520,938			195,091			103,806		
Library — Microform Volume Equivalents		51,330			70,301			58,470		

Law Schools on the 1983 Approved List of the American Bar Association

MISSISSIPPI

		University of Minnesota Law School 285 Law Center Minneapolis, Minnesota 55455 612/373-2717 (Approved in 1923; Public)			William Mitchell College of Law 875 Summit Avenue St. Paul, Minnesota 55105 612/227-9171 (Approved in 1938; Private) *			Mississippi College School of Law 151 East Griffith Street Jackson, Mississippi 39201 601/944-1950 (Approved in 1980; Private) **		
		Total	Women	Minorities	Total	Women	Minorities	Total	Women	Minorities
1st Year Enrollment	Full-Time Part-Time	250 None	103	24	171 140	76 60	9 6	106 20	28 6	7 3
2nd Year Enrollment	Full-Time Part-Time	229 None	94	20	145 170	49 70	8 6	73 24	22 7	3 1
3rd Year Enrollment	Full-Time Part-Time	233 None	92	18	None 184	90	9	60 14	16 4	4 1
4th Year Enrollment	Full-Time Part-Time	None			300	94	5	17	5	2
Graduate Enrollment	Full-Time Part-Time	None None			None None			None None		
Other Enrollment	Full-Time Part-Time	11 None	5	0	None None			None 2	1	1
Fall, 1983, Enrollment	Full-Time Part-Time Total	723 723	294 294	62 62	316 794 1,110	125 314 439	17 26 43	239 77 316	66 23 89	14 8 22
Degrees Awarded through Summer, 1983	Full-Time	JD 232 LLM 1	87 0	14 0				JD 25	10	2
	Part-Time				JD 277	98	2	JD 9	1	0
Teachers	Full-Time Part-Time	31 15	4 2	1 0	29 160	6 44	1 3	13 3	3 0	0 0
Full-time Teaching Deans and Librarians		2	0	1	5	0	0	2	1	0
Tuition and Fees	Full-Time Part-Time	$2,444 r	$4,650 nr		$5,262 $3,602			$4,496 $2,748		
College Required—Degree or 3 years		D			3			D		
Weeks Required	Full-Time Part-Time	102			90 120			90 120		
Credits Required semester (s) or quarter (q)		88s			88s			88s		
Summer Programs	Accepts summer credit from other schools	Yes			Yes			Yes		
	Allows acceleration of graduation by attending summer sessions	No			Yes			Yes		
Joint Degrees		None			None			None		
Library	Total Hard Copy Volumes	445,718			88,500			74,819		
	Microform Volume Equivalents	58,584			79,260			69,790		

* Independent law school, not affiliated with a university.

** Provisionally approved, status of graduates and students equal to that of fully approved law schools.

Law Schools on the 1983 Approved List of the American Bar Association		University of Mississippi School of Law University, Mississippi 38677 601/232-7361 (Approved in 1930; Public)			**MISSOURI** St. Louis University School of Law 3700 Lindell Boulevard St. Louis, Missouri 63108 314/658-2800 (Approved in 1924; Private)			University of Missouri—Columbia School of Law Tate Hall Columbia, Missouri 65211 314/882-6487 (Approved in 1923; Public)		
		Total	Women	Minorities	Total	Women	Minorities	Total	Women	Minorities
1st Year Enrollment	Full-Time Part-Time	188 None	49	12	235 None	81	19	148 None	48	11
2nd Year Enrollment	Full-Time Part-Time	214 None	48	9	221 None	84	13	123 None	37	9
3rd Year Enrollment	Full-Time Part-Time	88 None	23	5	203 None	76	9	143 None	44	10
4th Year Enrollment	Full-Time Part-Time	None			None			None		
Graduate Enrollment	Full-Time Part-Time	1 None	0	0	None None			None None		
Other Enrollment	Full-Time Part-Time	2 None	1	0	None None			5 None	2	0
Fall, 1983, Enrollment	Full-Time Part-Time **Total**	493 **493**	121 **121**	26 **26**	659 **659**	241 **241**	41 **41**	419 **419**	131 **131**	30 **30**
Degrees Awarded through Summer, 1983	Full-Time Part-Time	JD 144	37	7	JD 208	74	12	150	44	9
Teachers	Full-Time Part-Time	20 2	1 0	1 1	23 7	4 1	1 0	21 3	3 0	0 0
Full-time Teaching Deans and Librarians		5	0	1	3	2	0	3	1	0
Tuition and Fees	Full-Time Part-Time	$1,641 r $55/cr.hr. r	$2,617 nr $104/cr.hr. nr		$5,850 $220/cr.hr.			$1,915 r $69/cr.hr. r	$4,491 nr $161/cr.hr. nr	
College Required—Degree or 3 years		D			D			3		
Weeks Required	Full-Time Part-Time	96			96			96		
Credits Required semester (s) or quarter (q)		90s			84s			88s		
Summer Programs	Accepts summer credit from other schools	Yes			Yes			Yes		
	Allows acceleration of graduation by attending summer sessions	Yes			Yes			Yes		
Joint Degrees		MBA 2	MPA 0		MBA 9 MHA 4 MPA 1 MSW 0 MA/Urb.Aff. 0			MBA 0		
Library	Total Hard Copy Volumes	110,738			185,632			160,496		
	Microform Volume Equivalents	52,299			43,798			25,732		

Law Schools on the 1983 Approved List of the American Bar Association		University of Missouri—Kansas City 5100 Rockhill Road Kansas City, Missouri 64110 816/276-1644 (Approved in 1936; Public)			Washington University School of Law Campus Box 1120 St. Louis, Missouri 63130 314/889-6400 (Approved in 1923; Private)			MONTANA University of Montana School of Law Missoula, Montana 59812 406/243-4311 (Approved in 1923; Public)		
		Total	Women	Minorities	Total	Women	Minorities	Total	Women	Minorities
1st Year Enrollment	Full-Time Part-Time	154 None	66	6	219 None	72	8	76 None	35	1
2nd Year Enrollment	Full-Time Part-Time	146 1	59 1	9 0	184 None	68	10	67 None	32	1
3rd Year Enrollment	Full-Time Part-Time	152 1	63 0	8 0	192 None	71	9	73 None	29	1
4th Year Enrollment	Full-Time Part-Time	None			None			None		
Graduate Enrollment	Full-Time Part-Time	6 23	1 4	1 0	19 35	6 12	1 0	None None		
Other Enrollment	Full-Time Part-Time	None 31	9	0	None None			None None		
Fall, 1983, Enrollment	Full-Time Part-Time Total	458 56 **514**	189 14 **203**	24 0 **24**	614 35 **649**	217 12 **229**	28 0 **28**	216 **216**	96 **96**	3 **3**
Degrees Awarded through Summer, 1983	Full-Time	JD 144 LLM 6	63 2	10 0	JD 218 LLM 12	92 1	9 1	JD 76	21	4
	Part-Time	JD 8	1	1						
Teachers	Full-Time Part-Time	20 3	3 0	1 0	27 7	3 0	1 0	12 6	1 1	0 0
Full-time Teaching Deans and Librarians		3	0	0	None			1	1	0
Tuition and Fees	Full-Time Part-Time	$2,358 r $86/cr.hr. r	$4,934 nr grad. scale/cr.hr. nr		$7,700 $325/cr.hr.			$1,533 r	$3,081 nr	
College Required—Degree or 3 years		3			D			D		
Weeks Required	Full-Time Part-Time	96			90			96		
Credits Required semester (s) or quarter (q)		90s			86s			90s		
Summer Programs	Accepts summer credit from other schools	Yes			Yes			Yes		
	Allows acceleration of graduation by attending summer sessions	Yes			Yes			No		
Joint Degrees		None			MBA 7 MHA 0 MSW 2 MA/Pol.Sc. 0 MA/Tech.& Ph.D./ MA/Arch. 1 Hum.Aff. 0 Comp.Lit. 1 Ph.D./JSD 0 MS/Econ. 0 MS/Jur.St. 0			MPA 0		
Library	Total Hard Copy Volumes	115,837			200,812			100,313		
	Microform Volume Equivalents	15,829			84,102			3,928		

Law Schools on the 1983 Approved List of the American Bar Association

NEBRASKA

Creighton University
School of Law
2500 California Street
Omaha, Nebraska 68178
402/280-2872
(Approved in 1924; Private)

University of Nebraska
College of Law
Lincoln, Nebraska 68583 0902
402/472-2161
(Approved in 1923; Public)

NEW HAMPSHIRE

Franklin Pierce Law Center
2 White Street
Concord, New Hampshire 03301
603/228-1541
(Approved in 1974; Private)*

		Total	Women	Minorities	Total	Women	Minorities	Total	Women	Minorities
1st Year Enrollment	Full-Time	205	59	8	164	62	8	123	49	2
	Part-Time	1	0	1	None			None		
2nd Year Enrollment	Full-Time	144	39	9	141	54	5	102	47	4
	Part-Time	2	2	2	None			None		
3rd Year Enrollment	Full-Time	171	55	8	158	56	4	125	48	5
	Part-Time	1	1	1	None			None		
4th Year Enrollment	Full-Time									
	Part-Time	None			None			None		
Graduate Enrollment	Full-Time	None			None			None		
	Part-Time	None			None			None		
Other Enrollment	Full-Time	4	2	0	None			None		
	Part-Time	None			None			None		
Fall, 1983, Enrollment	Full-Time	524	155	25	463	172	17	350	144	11
	Part-Time	4	3	4						
	Total	528	158	29	463	172	17	350	144	11
Degrees Awarded through Summer, 1983	Full-Time	JD 169	57	10	JD 148	46	5	JD 118	41	1
	Part-Time	JD 1	0	0						
Teachers	Full-Time	18	3	0	19	0	0	13	3	0
	Part-Time	9	2	0	10	3	0	9	1	0
Full-time Teaching Deans and Librarians		4	2	0	1	0	0	5	2	0
Tuition and Fees	Full-Time	$5,020			$1,312 r	$3,248 nr		$5,800		
	Part-Time	$251/cr.hr.								
College Required—Degree or 3 years		D			3			D		
Weeks Required	Full-Time	90			90			96		
	Part-Time									
Credits Required semester (s) or quarter (q)		90s			96s			84s		
Summer Programs	Accepts summer credit from other schools	Yes			Yes			No		
	Allows acceleration of graduation by attending summer sessions	No			Yes			No		
Joint Degrees		MBA 2			MBA 0 Ph.D./Ed.Adm. 1 Ph.D./Psy. 1			None		
Library	Total Hard Copy Volumes	110,742			133,890			90,070		
	Microform Volume Equivalents	20,995			21,401			28,437		

* Independent law school, not affiliated with a university.

Law Schools on the 1983 Approved List of the American Bar Association

NEW JERSEY

Rutgers—The State University of
New Jersey School of Law
Fifth and Penn Streets
Camden, New Jersey 08102
609/757-6398
(Approved in 1951; Public)

Rutgers—The State University of
New Jersey School of Law
S.I. Newhouse Center for Law & Justice
15 Washington Street
Newark, New Jersey 07102
201/648-5561
(Approved in 1941; Public)

Seton Hall University
School of Law
111 Raymond Boulevard
Newark, New Jersey 07102
201/642-8500
(Approved in 1951; Private)

		Total	Women	Minorities	Total	Women	Minorities	Total	Women	Minorities
1st Year Enrollment	Full-Time	207	92	30	181	95	48	267	115	20
	Part-Time	37	11	7	63	27	17	110	40	5
2nd Year Enrollment	Full-Time	190	79	23	183	104	42	253	107	14
	Part-Time	38	12	6	68	27	16	109	38	6
3rd Year Enrollment	Full-Time	194	96	9	179	91	37	241	97	13
	Part-Time	27	10	1	64	25	17	84	23	5
4th Year Enrollment	Full-Time									
	Part-Time	34	12	1	44	19	8	117	39	8
Graduate Enrollment	Full-Time	None			None			None		
	Part-Time	None			None			None		
Other Enrollment	Full-Time	2	1	0	3	0	2	None		
	Part-Time	1	0	0	None			None		
Fall, 1983, Enrollment	Full-Time	593	268	62	546	290	129	761	319	47
	Part-Time	137	45	15	239	98	58	420	140	24
	Total	**730**	**313**	**77**	**785**	**388**	**187**	**1,181**	**459**	**71**
Degrees Awarded through Summer, 1983	Full-Time	JD 161	68	10	JD 164	88	34	JD 245	98	14
	Part-Time	JD 24	9	3	JD 36	10	6	JD 94	32	12
Teachers	Full-Time	33	4	2	33	5	4	31	5	5
	Part-Time	12	3	0	15	2	0	25	0	0
Full-time Teaching Deans and Librarians		2	0	0	3	2	0	3	0	0
Tuition and Fees	Full-Time	$2,585 r	$3,565 nr		$2,582 r	$3,562 nr			$5,800	
	Part-Time	$99/cr.hr. r	$140/cr.hr. nr		$99/cr.hr. r	$140/cr.hr. nr			$4,335	
College Required—Degree or 3 years			D			D			D	
Weeks Required	Full-Time		96			96			90	
	Part-Time		136			128			120	
Credits Required semester (s) or quarter (q)			84s			84s			84s	
Summer Programs	Accepts summer credit from other schools		Yes			Yes			Yes	
	Allows acceleration of graduation by attending summer sessions		Yes			No			Yes	
Joint Degrees		MBA 0	MCRP 0	MS/Pol.Sc. 0	MCRP 0	MA/Crim.Jus. 0			MBA 0	
Library	Total Hard Copy Volumes		258,364			274,137			133,686	
	Microform Volume Equivalents		39,308			49,200			70,959	

Law Schools on the 1983 Approved List of the American Bar Association

NEW MEXICO

University of New Mexico
School of Law
1117 Stanford, N.E.
Albuquerque, New Mexico 87131
505/277-2146
(Approved in 1948; Public)

NEW YORK

Brooklyn Law School
250 Joralemon Street
Brooklyn, New York 11201
212/625-2200
(Approved in 1937; Private)*

Columbia University
School of Law
435 West 116th Street
New York, New York 10027
212/280-2675
(Approved in 1923; Private)

		Total	Women	Minorities	Total	Women	Minorities	Total	Women	Minorities
1st Year Enrollment	Full-Time	123	64	49	249	103	26	313	114	70
	Part-Time	None			96	49	13	None		
2nd Year Enrollment	Full-Time	109	58	38	296	129	22	315	109	40
	Part-Time	None			81	26	13	None		
3rd Year Enrollment	Full-Time	118	59	43	281	136	25	315	98	70
	Part-Time	None			94	40	18	None		
4th Year Enrollment	Full-Time									
	Part-Time	None			107	47	12	None		
Graduate Enrollment	Full-Time	None			None			62	21	15
	Part-Time	None			None			None		
Other Enrollment	Full-Time	None			10	5	1	9	3	7
	Part-Time	None			7	1	2	None		
Fall, 1983, Enrollment	Full-Time	350	181	130	836	373	74	1,014	345	212
	Part-Time				385	163	58			
	Total	**350**	**181**	**130**	**1,221**	**536**	**132**	**1,014**	**345**	**212**
Degrees Awarded through Summer, 1983	Full-Time	JD 109	57	36	JD 282	138	16	JD 282	101	0
								LLM 46	10	0
								SJD 3	0	0
	Part-Time				JD 106	37	11			
Teachers	Full-Time	27	5	5	37	12	1	47	5	2
	Part-Time	5	2	0	30	6	2	13	3	3
Full-time Teaching Deans and Librarians		2	0	0	3	0	0	None		
Tuition and Fees	Full-Time	$776 r	$2,570 nr		$6,660			$10,038		
	Part-Time				$5,010					
College Required—Degree or 3 years		D			D			3		
Weeks Required	Full-Time	90			90			90		
	Part-Time				120					
Credits Required semester (s) or quarter (q)		86s			85s			83s		
Summer Programs	Accepts summer credit from other schools	Yes			Yes			No		
	Allows acceleration of graduation by attending summer sessions	No			No			No		
Joint Degrees		MBA 1	MPA 0		MBA 1	MCRP 1	MLS 0	MBA 0	MPA 1	MA/Intl.St. 0
					MPA 0			MA/Hist. 0	MA/Pol. Sc. 0	MA/Phil. 0
								MS/Journ. 1	Ph.D./Pol.Sc. 0	
Library	Total Hard Copy Volumes	172,500			165,885			659,213		
	Microform Volume Equivalents	60,975			54,453			73,094		

* Independent law school, not affiliated with a university.

Law Schools on the 1983 Approved List of the American Bar Association

Cornell Law School
Myron Taylor Hall
Ithaca, New York 14853
607/256-3626
(Approved in 1923; Private)

Fordham University
School of Law
140 West 62nd Street
New York, New York 10023
212/841-5193
(Approved in 1936; Private)

Hofstra University
School of Law
Hempstead, New York 11550
516/560-6600
(Approved in 1971; Private)

		Total	Women	Minorities	Total	Women	Minorities	Total	Women	Minorities
1st Year Enrollment	Full-Time	184	64	19	233	84	21	258	125	15
	Part-Time	None			139	51	6	None		
2nd Year Enrollment	Full-Time	187	67	19	287	117	12	255	105	12
	Part-Time	None			88	32	8	None		
3rd Year Enrollment	Full-Time	173	63	20	306	125	14	247	97	7
	Part-Time	None			83	42	3	None		
4th Year Enrollment	Full-Time									
	Part-Time	None			94	37	8	None		
Graduate Enrollment	Full-Time	20	2	11	None			None		
	Part-Time	None			None			None		
Other Enrollment	Full-Time	3	2	1	None			None		
	Part-Time	None			None			None		
Fall, 1983, Enrollment	Full-Time	567	198	70	826	326	47	760	327	34
	Part-Time				404	162	25			
	Total	**567**	**198**	**70**	**1,230**	**488**	**72**	**760**	**327**	**34**
Degrees Awarded through Summer, 1983	Full-Time	JD 174 LLM 17	58 7	11 10	JD 255	100	12	JD 247	104	18
	Part-Time				JD 75	31	4			
Teachers	Full-Time	21	2	0	34	6	0	25	5	2
	Part-Time	8	0	0	34	6	1	9	0	0
Full-time Teaching Deans and Librarians		2	1	0	2	0	0	2	0	0
Tuition and Fees	Full-Time	$9,270			$6,900			$6,390		
	Part-Time				$5,200					
College Required—Degree or 3 years		3			D			D		
Weeks Required	Full-Time	96			96			96		
	Part-Time				128					
Credits Required semester (s) or quarter (q)		84s			82s			85s		
Summer Programs	Accepts summer credit from other schools	Yes			Yes			Yes		
	Allows acceleration of graduation by attending summer sessions	No			Yes			Yes		
Joint Degrees		MBA 5 MPA 0 Ph.D./Phil. 0	MCRP 0 MS/MILR 0 Ph.D./Econ. 0	MHA 0 MA/Phil. 0 Ph.D./Hist. 0	None			MBA 1		
Library	Total Hard Copy Volumes	352,597			228,464			162,490		
	Microform Volume Equivalents	21,837			65,804			62,549		

**Law Schools on the
1983 Approved List
of the American
Bar Association**

		New York Law School 57 Worth Street New York, New York 10013 212/431-2100 (Approved in 1954; Private)*			New York University School of Law 40 Washington Square South New York, New York 10012 212/598-2511 (Approved in 1930; Private)			Pace University School of Law 78 North Broadway White Plains, New York 10603 914/681-4200 (Approved in 1978; Private)		
		Total	Women	Minorities	Total	Women	Minorities	Total	Women	Minorities
1st Year Enrollment	Full-Time Part-Time	273 99	108 44	46 21	375 None	185	37	153 102	83 43	11 4
2nd Year Enrollment	Full-Time Part-Time	291 96	100 31	38 23	382 None	185	56	153 93	75 43	6 4
3rd Year Enrollment	Full-Time Part-Time	383 124	120 39	39 15	373 None	163	57	187 57	112 19	5 3
4th Year Enrollment	Full-Time Part-Time	129	39	19	None			86	37	3
Graduate Enrollment	Full-Time Part-Time	None None			298 847	77 227	0 0	None None		
Other Enrollment	Full-Time Part-Time	10 18	4 7	0 1	11 None	6	0	5 2	4 2	2 0
Fall, 1983, Enrollment	Full-Time Part-Time **Total**	957 466 **1,423**	332 160 **492**	123 79 **202**	1,439 847 **2,286**	616 227 **843**	150 0 **150**	498 340 **838**	274 144 **418**	24 14 **38**
Degrees Awarded through Summer, 1983	Full-Time	JD 311	130	40	JD 355 LLM 273 MCS 33 SJD 1	172 48 5 0	62 8 0 0	JD 135	70	5
	Part-Time	JD 98	31	8	LLM 182	34	4	JD 82	33	5
Teachers	Full-Time Part-Time	44 53	6 4	3 0	61 64	15 6	3 2	25 19	7 1	0 0
Full-time Teaching Deans and Librarians		5	1	0	4	1	0	2	0	0
Tuition and Fees	Full-Time Part-Time	$6,300 $4,750			$9,300 $388/cr.hr.			$6,200 $4,650		
College Required—Degree or 3 years		D			D			D		
Weeks Required	Full-Time Part-Time	90 120			96			90 120		
Credits Required semester (s) or quarter (q)		85s			82s			84s		
Summer Programs	Accepts summer credit from other schools	No			Yes			Yes		
	Allows acceleration of graduation by attending summer sessions	Yes			Yes			Yes		
Joint Degrees		MBA 2	MPA 0		MBA 3 MA/Econ. 0	MPA 3 MA/Pol.Sc. 0	RUP 0 MA/Soc. 0	MBA 3		
Library	Total Hard Copy Volumes	150,951			593,732			95,919		
	Microform Volume Equivalents	97,775			70,457			59,762		

* Independent law school, not affiliated with a university.

Law Schools on the 1983 Approved List of the American Bar Association

St. John's University
School of Law
Fromkes Hall
Grand Central and Utopia Parkways
Jamaica, New York 11439
212/990-6161
(Approved in 1937; Private)

State University of New York at Buffalo
John Lord O'Brian Hall
Amherst Campus
Buffalo, New York 14260
716/636-2061
(Approved in 1936; Public)

Syracuse University
College of Law
E. I. White Hall
Syracuse, New York 13210
315/423-2524
(Approved in 1923; Private)

		Total	Women	Minorities	Total	Women	Minorities	Total	Women	Minorities
1st Year Enrollment	Full-Time	250	112	22	255	95	28	228	82	21
	Part-Time	110	36	9	None			7	3	0
2nd Year Enrollment	Full-Time	217	86	12	262	99	17	223	81	10
	Part-Time	98	29	5	None			7	4	0
3rd Year Enrollment	Full-Time	290	109	8	293	118	20	187	52	5
	Part-Time	89	30	4	None			4	2	0
4th Year Enrollment	Full-Time				None			None		
	Part-Time	93	36	1						
Graduate Enrollment	Full-Time	None			None			None		
	Part-Time	None			None			None		
Other Enrollment	Full-Time	None			None			None		
	Part-Time	None			None			2	2	0
Fall, 1983, Enrollment	Full-Time	757	307	42	810	312	65	638	215	36
	Part-Time	390	131	19				20	11	0
	Total	1,147	438	61	810	312	65	658	226	36
Degrees Awarded through Summer, 1983	Full-Time	JD 253	96	9	JD 286	114	24	JD 223	90	6
	Part-Time	JD 94	28	3				JD 2	1	0
Teachers	Full-Time	38	4	4	27	5	1	25	3	0
	Part-Time	15	0	0	19	1	1	12	2	1
Full-time Teaching Deans and Librarians		3	0	0	3	0	0	2	0	0
Tuition and Fees	Full-Time	$6,738			$3,213 r	$4,813 nr		$7,480		
	Part-Time	$5,018			$132/cr.hr. r	$198/cr.hr. nr		$6,459		
College Required—Degree or 3 years		D			3			3		
Weeks Required	Full-Time	96			90			90		
	Part-Time	128			105			120		
Credits Required semester (s) or quarter (q)		83s			86s			86s		
Summer Programs	Accepts summer credit from other schools	Yes			Yes			Yes		
	Allows acceleration of graduation by attending summer sessions	No			Yes			Yes		
Joint Degrees		None			MBA 12 Ph.D./Policy St. 1 Ph.D./Econ. 0 Ph.D./Pol.Sc. 4 Ph.D./Soc. 1 Ph.D./Hist. 0 Ph.D./Phil. 1			MBA 6 MLS 0 MPA 5 MA/Ph.D./Econ. 1 MA/Ph.D./Hist. 0 MA/Ph.D./Intl.R. 0 MA/Ph.D./Phil. 0 MA/Ph.D./Pol.Sc. 0 MS/Acct. 1 MS/Ph.D./Env.St. 3 MS/Telecom. 3		
Library	Total Hard Copy Volumes	177,050			220,990			122,137		
	Microform Volume Equivalents	75,013			63,005			15,220		

Law Schools on the 1983 Approved List of the American Bar Association		Touro College School of Law 300 Nassau Road Huntington, New York 11743 516/421-2244 (Approved in 1983; Private) **			Union University Albany Law School 80 New Scotland Avenue Albany, New York 12208 518/445-2311 (Approved in 1930; Private)			Yeshiva University Benjamin N. Cardozo School of Law 55 Fifth Avenue New York, New York 10003 212/790-0463 (Approved in 1978; Private)		
		Total	Women	Minorities	Total	Women	Minorities	Total	Women	Minorities
1st Year Enrollment	Full-Time Part-Time	117 63	46 20	3 7	245 None	102	12	324 None	158	16
2nd Year Enrollment	Full-Time Part-Time	102 43	45 10	1 5	248 None	93	17	301 None	144	11
3rd Year Enrollment	Full-Time Part-Time	74 56	30 17	2 2	215 None	85	10	288 None	146	3
4th Year Enrollment	Full-Time Part-Time	86	13	2	None			None		
Graduate Enrollment	Full-Time Part-Time	None None			None None			None None		
Other Enrollment	Full-Time Part-Time	None None			None None			9 2	5 1	0 0
Fall, 1983, Enrollment	Full-Time Part-Time Total	293 248 541	121 60 181	6 16 22	708 708	280 280	39 39	922 2 924	453 1 454	30 0 30
Degrees Awarded through Summer, 1983	Full-Time	JD 91	25	1	JD 199	81	5	JD 277	143	0
	Part-Time									
Teachers	Full-Time Part-Time	17 10	3 0	0 1	24 3	6 0	2 0	30 17	5 1	1 0
Full-time Teaching Deans and Librarians		1	0	0	2	0	0	2	0	0
Tuition and Fees	Full-Time Part-Time	$5,600 $220/cr.hr.			$5,900			$7,425 $325/cr.hr.		
College Required—Degree or 3 years		D			D			3		
Weeks Required	Full-Time Part-Time	90 120			87			90		
Credits Required semester (s) or quarter (q)		84s			87s			84s		
Summer Programs	Accepts summer credit from other schools	Yes			Yes			No		
	Allows acceleration of graduation by attending summer sessions	Yes			No			No		
Joint Degrees		None			MBA 1	MPA 0		None		
Library	Total Hard Copy Volumes	64,560			114,634			123,675		
	Microform Volume Equivalents	20,309			44,728			86,002		

** Provisionally approved, status of graduates and students equal to that of fully approved law schools.

Law Schools on the 1983 Approved List of the American Bar Association

NORTH CAROLINA

Campbell University
School of Law
P.O. Box 158
Buies Creek, North Carolina 27506
919/893-4111
(Approved in 1979; Private)

Duke University
School of Law
Durham, North Carolina 27706
919/684-2834
(Approved in 1931; Private)

North Carolina Central University
School of Law
1801 Fayetteville Street
Durham, North Carolina 27707
919/683-6333
(Approved in 1950; Public)

		Campbell Total	Women	Minorities	Duke Total	Women	Minorities	NCCU Total	Women	Minorities
1st Year Enrollment	Full-Time	94	32	6	170	62	15	103	41	70
	Part-Time	None			None			43	23	9
2nd Year Enrollment	Full-Time	93	29	4	184	59	14	85	38	42
	Part-Time	None			None			10	7	1
3rd Year Enrollment	Full-Time	103	31	5	179	55	11	75	29	42
	Part-Time	None			None			4	3	1
4th Year Enrollment	Full-Time									
	Part-Time	None			None			10	2	0
Graduate Enrollment	Full-Time	None			8	1	5	None		
	Part-Time	None			None			None		
Other Enrollment	Full-Time	1	1	0	None			None		
	Part-Time	None			None			None		
Fall, 1983, Enrollment	Full-Time	291	93	15	541	177	45	263	108	154
	Part-Time							67	35	11
	Total	**291**	**93**	**15**	**541**	**177**	**45**	**330**	**143**	**165**
Degrees Awarded through Summer, 1983	Full-Time	JD 88	25	1	JD 186	63	11	JD 48	17	20
					LLM 7	2	4	LLB 1	1	0
					MCL 2	0	0			
	Part-Time									
Teachers	Full-Time	13	1	0	24	5	1	12	4	6
	Part-Time	4	0	0	8	0	2	7	4	4
Full-time Teaching Deans and Librarians		2	0	0	8	3	0	4	1	3
Tuition and Fees	Full-Time	$4,960			$8,320			$700 r $3,012 nr		
	Part-Time							$466/6-8 hrs. r $2,200/6-8 hrs. nr		
College Required—Degree or 3 years		3			D			3		
Weeks Required	Full-Time	96			96			93		
	Part-Time							144		
Credits Required semester (s) or quarter (q)		90s			86s			86s		
Summer Programs — Accepts summer credit from other schools		Yes			No			Yes		
Summer Programs — Allows acceleration of graduation by attending summer sessions		No			No			Yes		
Joint Degrees		None			MBA 5 MHA 0 MPP 2 MA/Hist. 0 MA/Phil. 0 MA/Pol.Sc. 0 MA/Econ. 0			None		
Library — Total Hard Copy Volumes		63,662			248,928			90,351		
Library — Microform Volume Equivalents		32,452			80,427			23,618		

Law Schools on the 1983 Approved List of the American Bar Association

University of North Carolina
School of Law
Chapel Hill, North Carolina 27514
919/962-5106
(Approved in 1923; Public)

Wake Forest University
School of Law
P.O. Box 7206
Winston-Salem, North Carolina 27109
919/761-5434
(Approved in 1935; Private)

NORTH DAKOTA

University of North Dakota
School of Law
Grand Forks, North Dakota 58202
701/777-2104
(Approved in 1923; Public)

		Total	Women	Minorities	Total	Women	Minorities	Total	Women	Minorities
1st Year Enrollment	Full-Time	229	103	18	173	63	9	103	30	4
	Part-Time	None			None			None		
2nd Year Enrollment	Full-Time	270	84	17	162	57	4	108	43	0
	Part-Time	None			None			None		
3rd Year Enrollment	Full-Time	221	94	10	164	48	8	88	25	2
	Part-Time	None			None			None		
4th Year Enrollment	Full-Time									
	Part-Time	None			None			None		
Graduate Enrollment	Full-Time	None			None			None		
	Part-Time	None			None			None		
Other Enrollment	Full-Time	None			None			None		
	Part-Time	None			None			None		
Fall, 1983, Enrollment	Full-Time	720	281	45	499	168	21	299	98	6
	Part-Time									
	Total	720	281	45	499	168	21	299	98	6
Degrees Awarded through Summer, 1983	Full-Time	JD 220	79	18	JD 160	40	6	JD 96	28	1
	Part-Time									
Teachers	Full-Time	29	6	2	15	1	0	11	2	0
	Part-Time	5	2	1	12	2	0	6	0	0
Full-time Teaching Deans and Librarians		3	1	0	3	0	0	3	1	0
Tuition and Fees	Full-Time	$793 r	$3,155 nr		$5,550			$1,168 r	$2,162 nr	
	Part-Time									
College Required—Degree or 3 years		D			D			D		
Weeks Required	Full-Time	96			90			90		
	Part-Time									
Credits Required semester (s) or quarter (q)		86s			89s			90s		
Summer Programs	Accepts summer credit from other schools	Yes			Yes			Yes		
	Allows acceleration of graduation by attending summer sessions	Yes			No			Yes		
Joint Degrees		MBA 5 PAA 2	MCRP 2	MPH 0	MBA 0			None		
Library	Total Hard Copy Volumes	221,511			93,335			129,921		
	Microform Volume Equivalents	33,392			81,243			92,139		

Law Schools on the 1983 Approved List of the American Bar Association

OHIO

		Capital University Law School 665 South High Street Columbus, Ohio 43215 614/445-8836 (Approved in 1923; Private)			Case Western Reserve University School of Law 11075 East Boulevard Cleveland, Ohio 44106 216/368-3280 (Approved in 1923; Private)			Cleveland State University Cleveland-Marshall College of Law Cleveland, Ohio 44115 216/687-2344 (Approved in 1957; Public)		
		Total	Women	Minorities	Total	Women	Minorities	Total	Women	Minorities
1st Year Enrollment	Full-Time	151	47	8	206	80	8	181	71	11
	Part-Time	81	22	4	None			120	46	4
2nd Year Enrollment	Full-Time	146	42	4	247	89	8	166	65	4
	Part-Time	80	23	3	None			109	32	8
3rd Year Enrollment	Full-Time	104	33	4	237	86	14	173	69	8
	Part-Time	60	16	2	None			102	34	7
4th Year Enrollment	Full-Time				None					
	Part-Time	63	19	3				97	24	9
Graduate Enrollment	Full-Time	None			None			None		
	Part-Time	None			None			3	0	0
Other Enrollment	Full-Time	3	2	0	None			16	7	2
	Part-Time	None			None			23	8	1
Fall, 1983, Enrollment	Full-Time	404	124	16	690	255	30	536	212	25
	Part-Time	284	80	12				454	144	29
	Total	**688**	**204**	**28**	**690**	**255**	**30**	**990**	**356**	**54**
Degrees Awarded through Summer, 1983	Full-Time	JD 109	26	4	JD 231	78	13	JD 184	72	11
	Part-Time	JD 98	32	1				JD 100 LLM 2	35 0	11 0
Teachers	Full-Time	22	3	1	26	3	1	39	3	2
	Part-Time	13	0	1	10	1	0	28	6	1
Full-time Teaching Deans and Librarians		2	0	0	2	1	1	5	2	0
Tuition and Fees	Full-Time	$5,380			$7,226			$2,400 r	$4,800 nr	
	Part-Time	$3,460						$92/cr.hr. r	$184/cr.hr. nr	
College Required—Degree or 3 years		D			D			D		
Weeks Required	Full-Time	96			96			90		
	Part-Time	156						120		
Credits Required semester (s) or quarter (q)		85s			88s			84s		
Summer Programs	Accepts summer credit from other schools	Yes			Yes			Yes		
	Allows acceleration of graduation by attending summer sessions	Yes			Yes			Yes		
Joint Degrees		None			MBA 2	MSW 3	MSLS 0	MBA 2		
Library	Total Hard Copy Volumes	150,257			196,055			128,897		
	Microform Volume Equivalents	18,101			24,277			89,254		

Law Schools on the 1983 Approved List of the American Bar Association		Ohio Northern University Claude W. Pettit College of Law Ada, Ohio 45810 419/772-2205 (Approved in 1948; Private)			Ohio State University College of Law 1659 North High Street Columbus, Ohio 43210 614/422-2631 (Approved in 1923; Public)			The University of Akron School of Law 302 East Buchtel Avenue Akron, Ohio 44325 216/375-7331 (Approved in 1961; Public)		
		Total	Women	Minorities	Total	Women	Minorities	Total	Women	Minorities
1st Year Enrollment	Full-Time Part-Time	204 None	57	13	217 None	88	22	91 93	35 37	2 3
2nd Year Enrollment	Full-Time Part-Time	144 None	40	9	209 None	86	19	99 80	45 26	5 10
3rd Year Enrollment	Full-Time Part-Time	150 None	40	9	209 None	77	26	92 107	30 29	5 0
4th Year Enrollment	Full-Time Part-Time	None			None			76	24	5
Graduate Enrollment	Full-Time Part-Time	None None			None None			None None		
Other Enrollment	Full-Time Part-Time	None None			None None			1 3	1 0	0 0
Fall, 1983, Enrollment	Full-Time Part-Time **Total**	498 **498**	137 **137**	31 **31**	635 **635**	251 **251**	67 **67**	283 359 **642**	111 116 **227**	12 18 **30**
Degrees Awarded through Summer, 1983	Full-Time	JD 177	39	9	209	69	7	JD 113	33	2
	Part-Time							JD 73	21	1
Teachers	Full-Time Part-Time	18 None	0	1	29 4	4 1	2 0	23 13	3 3	0 0
Full-time Teaching Deans and Librarians		2	1	0	3	1	0	3	0	0
Tuition and Fees	Full-Time Part-Time	$5,772			$2,316 r $5,337 nr			$2,060 r $3,470 nr $1,242 r $2,088 nr		
College Required—Degree or 3 years		D			D			D		
Weeks Required	Full-Time Part-Time	90			90			96 144		
Credits Required semester (s) or quarter (q)		129q			128q			84s		
Summer Programs	Accepts summer credit from other schools	Yes			Yes			Yes		
	Allows acceleration of graduation by attending summer sessions	Yes			Yes			Yes		
Joint Degrees		None			MAd 0 MBA 4 MCRP 0 MHA 1 MPA 3 MSW 0 MA/Journ. 1 MA/Comm. 1 MA/Nat.Res. 0			MBA 2 MA/Tax. 4		
Library	Total Hard Copy Volumes	138,931			390,512			144,067		
	Microform Volume Equivalents	13,931			64,821			15,396		

**Law Schools on the
1983 Approved List
of the American
Bar Association**

University of Cincinnati
College of Law
M. L. 40
Cincinnati, Ohio 45221
513/475-2536
(Approved in 1923; Public)

University of Dayton
School of Law
Dayton, Ohio 45469
513/229-3211
(Approved in 1975; Private)

University of Toledo
College of Law
2801 West Bancroft Street
Toledo, Ohio 43606
419/537-2882
(Approved in 1939; Public)

		Total	Women	Minorities	Total	Women	Minorities	Total	Women	Minorities
1st Year Enrollment	Full-Time	135	61	12	135	41	1	205	71	8
	Part-Time	None			None			76	18	7
2nd Year Enrollment	Full-Time	131	52	16	132	54	6	170	57	8
	Part-Time	None			None			56	21	5
3rd Year Enrollment	Full-Time	115	50	9	159	47	7	159	42	4
	Part-Time	None			None			49	13	2
4th Year Enrollment	Full-Time							60	23	0
	Part-Time	None			None					
Graduate Enrollment	Full-Time	None			None			None		
	Part-Time	None			None			None		
Other Enrollment	Full-Time	7	3	1	2	1	1	3	3	0
	Part-Time	None			None			2	1	1
Fall, 1983, Enrollment	Full-Time	388	166	38	428	143	15	537	173	20
	Part-Time							243	76	15
	Total	**388**	**166**	**38**	**428**	**143**	**15**	**780**	**249**	**35**
Degrees Awarded through Summer, 1983	Full-Time	JD 132	52	8	JD 142	43	4	JD 180	40	6
	Part-Time							JD 43	13	1
Teachers	Full-Time	20	5	1	17	0	0	26	5	0
	Part-Time	9	0	0	8	0	1	2	0	0
Full-time Teaching Deans and Librarians		2	0	1	2	0	0	5	1	0

		University of Cincinnati	University of Dayton	University of Toledo
Tuition and Fees	Full-Time	$2,878 r $5,607 nr	$5,266	$1,953 r $3,870 nr
	Part-Time		$208/cr.hr.	$1,302/8 hrs. r $2,580/8 hrs. nr
College Required—Degree or 3 years		D	D	D
Weeks Required	Full-Time	92	96	99
	Part-Time			132
Credits Required semester (s) or quarter (q)		88s	84s	126q
Summer Programs	Accepts summer credit from other schools	Yes	Yes	Yes
	Allows acceleration of graduation by attending summer sessions	Yes	Yes	Yes
Joint Degrees		MBA 0 MCP 0 MA/Phil. 0	MBA 1 MA/Phil. 0 MS/Ed.Adm. 0	MBA 4
Library	Total Hard Copy Volumes	126,464	96,609	140,936
	Microform Volume Equivalents	56,724	69,760	30,842

Law Schools on the 1983 Approved List of the American Bar Association

OKLAHOMA

		Oklahoma City University School of Law 2501 North Blackwelder Oklahoma City, Oklahoma 73106 405/521-5337 (Approved in 1960; Private)			Oral Roberts University O. W. Coburn School of Law 7777 South Lewis Avenue Tulsa, Oklahoma 74171 918/495-6039 (Approved in 1981; Private) **			University of Oklahoma College of Law 300 Timberdell Road Norman, Oklahoma 73019 405/329-8800 (Approved in 1923; Public)		
		Total	Women	Minorities	Total	Women	Minorities	Total	Women	Minorities
1st Year Enrollment	Full-Time Part-Time	125 83	36 31	3 4	89 None	23	10	227 None	81	18
2nd Year Enrollment	Full-Time Part-Time	103 46	31 15	1 2	47 None	7	3	200 None	82	14
3rd Year Enrollment	Full-Time Part-Time	101 98	34 31	8 10	20 None	3	1	223 None	86	15
4th Year Enrollment	Full-Time Part-Time	None			None			None		
Graduate Enrollment	Full-Time Part-Time	None None			None None			None None		
Other Enrollment	Full-Time Part-Time	None 6	0	0	None None			None None		
Fall, 1983, Enrollment	Full-Time Part-Time **Total**	329 233 **562**	101 77 **178**	12 16 **28**	156 **156**	33 **33**	14 **14**	650 **650**	249 **249**	47 **47**
Degrees Awarded through Summer, 1983	Full-Time	JD 93	28	5	JD 24	5	4	JD 218	90	20
	Part-Time	JD 39	6	2						
Teachers	Full-Time Part-Time	18 9	2 0	0 0	7 6	1 0	1 1	28 5	2 1	1 0
Full-time Teaching Deans and Librarians		3	1	0	3	0	0	3	1	0
Tuition and Fees	Full-Time Part-Time	$5,212 $172/cr.hr.			$4,080			$963 r	$2,667 nr	
College Required—Degree or 3 years		D			D			D		
Weeks Required	Full-Time Part-Time	90 120			90			96		
Credits Required semester (s) or quarter (q)		90s			90s			90s		
Summer Programs	Accepts summer credit from other schools	Yes			Yes			Yes		
	Allows acceleration of graduation by attending summer sessions	Yes			Yes			Yes		
Joint Degrees		MBA 0	M.Div. 0		MBA 0			MBA 3		
Library	Total Hard Copy Volumes	81,778			95,317			146,905		
	Microform Volume Equivalents	19,904			84,264			71,318		

** Provisionally approved, status of graduates and students equal to that of fully approved law schools.

**Law Schools on the
1983 Approved List
of the American
Bar Association**

OREGON

		University of Tulsa College of Law 3120 East 4th Place Tulsa, Oklahoma 74104 918/592-6000 (Approved in 1950; Private)			Lewis and Clark College Northwestern School of Law 10015 Southwest Terwilliger Boulevard Portland, Oregon 97219 503/244-1181 (Approved in 1970; Private)			University of Oregon School of Law 1101 Kincaid Street Eugene, Oregon 97403 503/686-3852 (Approved in 1923; Public)		
		Total	Women	Minorities	Total	Women	Minorities	Total	Women	Minorities
1st Year Enrollment	Full-Time Part-Time	150 78	50 27	3 8	161 86	56 33	7 8	166 None	56	14
2nd Year Enrollment	Full-Time Part-Time	130 38	42 16	10 2	139 87	65 32	10 2	162 None	51	11
3rd Year Enrollment	Full-Time Part-Time	134 42	46 11	3 3	138 69	55 26	6 5	156 None	48	15
4th Year Enrollment	Full-Time Part-Time	 37	 8	 1	 56	 20	 2	None		
Graduate Enrollment	Full-Time Part-Time	None None			None None			None None		
Other Enrollment	Full-Time Part-Time	2 5	0 2	0 0	None None			12 None	6	1
Fall, 1983, Enrollment	Full-Time Part-Time **Total**	416 200 **616**	138 64 **202**	16 14 **30**	438 298 **736**	176 111 **287**	23 17 **40**	496 **496**	161 **161**	41 **41**
Degrees Awarded through Summer, 1983	Full-Time	JD 115	43	5	JD 153	59	12	158	47	11
	Part-Time	JD 47	7	7	JD 65	24	1			
Teachers	Full-Time Part-Time	24 16	4 1	1 1	23 19	2 5	0 0	22 2	4 0	0 0
Full-time Teaching Deans and Librarians		2	1	0	3	2	0	1	0	1
Tuition and Fees	Full-Time Part-Time	$4,830 $3,550			$6,050 $4,285			$2,696 r $474/cr.hr. r	$3,944 nr $612/cr.hr. nr	
College Required—Degree or 3 years		D			D			D		
Weeks Required	Full-Time Part-Time	90 120			84 112			90		
Credits Required semester (s) or quarter (q)		88s			86s			85s		
Summer Programs	Accepts summer credit from other schools	Yes			Yes			Yes		
	Allows acceleration of graduation by attending summer sessions	Yes			Yes			Yes		
Joint Degrees		MBA 1 MA/Urb.Aff. 1 MA/Hist. 0 MS/Env.St. 0 MA/Mod. MA/Ed.Lead. 0 MS/Acct. 0 Letters 0 MS/Org.Bio. 0 MS/Genetics 0			None			None		
Library	Total Hard Copy Volumes	102,239			108,108			119,235		
	Microform Volume Equivalents	73,487			79,935			57,063		

Law Schools on the 1983 Approved List of the American Bar Association

PENNSYLVANIA

		Willamette University College of Law 250 Winter Street, S.E. Salem, Oregon 97301 503/370-6380 (Approved in 1938; Private)			Dickinson School of Law 150 South College Street Carlisle, Pennsylvania 17013 717/243-4611 (Approved in 1931; Private) *			Duquesne University School of Law 900 Locust Street Hanley Hall Pittsburgh, Pennsylvania 15282 412/434-6300 (Approved in 1960; Private)		
		Total	Women	Minorities	Total	Women	Minorities	Total	Women	Minorities
1st Year Enrollment	Full-Time Part-Time	148 None	46	10	173 None	66	5	100 105	41 36	7 4
2nd Year Enrollment	Full-Time Part-Time	136 None	55	5	164 None	60	7	103 90	41 39	5 8
3rd Year Enrollment	Full-Time Part-Time	121 None	34	9	169 None	67	3	101 92	32 33	2 4
4th Year Enrollment	Full-Time Part-Time	None			None			97	24	3
Graduate Enrollment	Full-Time Part-Time	None None			7 None	2	5	None None		
Other Enrollment	Full-Time Part-Time	None None	.		6 None	3	0	None 5	3	2
Fall, 1983, Enrollment	Full-Time Part-Time Total	405 405	135 135	24 24	519 519	198 198	20 20	304 389 693	114 135 249	14 21 35
Degrees Awarded through Summer, 1983	Full-Time	JD 131	44	6	JD 166 MCL 5	57 2	5 2	JD 98	42	6
	Part-Time							JD 92	28	5
Teachers	Full-Time Part-Time	16 4	2 0	0 0	19 20	2 2	0 0	17 17	2 1	1 1
Full-time Teaching Deans and Librarians		None			3	1	0	None		
Tuition and Fees	Full-Time Part-Time	$5,994			$4,410			$4,824 $3,528		
College Required—Degree or 3 years		D			D			3		
Weeks Required	Full-Time Part-Time	95			96			96 126		
Credits Required semester (s) or quarter (q)		88s			88s			89s		
Summer Programs	Accepts summer credit from other schools	Yes			Yes			Yes		
	Allows acceleration of graduation by attending summer sessions	Yes			No			No		
Joint Degrees		MA/Man. 10			None			None		
Library	Total Hard Copy Volumes	89,941			120,620			93,901		
	Microform Volume Equivalents	2,921			38,972			5,855		

* Independent law school, not affiliated with a university.

Law Schools on the 1983 Approved List of the American Bar Association

Temple University
School of Law
1719 North Broad Street
Philadelphia, Pennsylvania 19122
215/787-7861
(Approved in 1933; Public)

University of Pennsylvania
Law School
3400 Chestnut Street
Philadelphia, Pennsylvania 19104
215/898-7483
(Approved in 1923; Private)

University of Pittsburgh
School of Law
3900 Forbes Avenue
Pittsburgh, Pennsylvania 15260
412/624-6200
(Approved in 1923; Public)

		Total	Women	Minorities	Total	Women	Minorities	Total	Women	Minorities
1st Year Enrollment	Full-Time	295	145	44	214	91	36	213	88	18
	Part-Time	115	46	15	None			None		
2nd Year Enrollment	Full-Time	277	133	26	228	86	20	214	83	18
	Part-Time	115	49	11	None			None		
3rd Year Enrollment	Full-Time	262	108	36	218	73	33	198	85	13
	Part-Time	96	35	8	None			None		
4th Year Enrollment	Full-Time									
	Part-Time	111	42	7	None			None		
Graduate Enrollment	Full-Time	33	7	9	52	10	1	None		
	Part-Time	124	29	2	None			None		
Other Enrollment	Full-Time	None			4	0	4	None		
	Part-Time	None			None			None		
Fall, 1983, Enrollment	Full-Time	867	393	115	716	260	94	625	256	49
	Part-Time	561	201	43						
	Total	**1,428**	**594**	**158**	**716**	**260**	**94**	**625**	**256**	**49**
Degrees Awarded through Summer, 1983	Full-Time	JD 277 LLM 19	129 6	33 5	JD 223 LLM 35 SSD 1	78 8 0	22 0 0	JD 238	92	10
	Part-Time	JD 68 LLM 41	24 7	3 1						
Teachers	Full-Time	32	3	5	29	4	2	29	5	2
	Part-Time	61	10	5	14	3	0	9	1	0
Full-time Teaching Deans and Librarians		8	3	3	1	1	0	2	1	0
Tuition and Fees	Full-Time	$3,475 r	$6,569 nr			$9,435		$3,854 r	$7,284 nr	
	Part-Time	$134/cr.hr. r	$266/cr.hr. nr							
College Required—Degree or 3 years		D			D			D		
Weeks Required	Full-Time	96			96			96		
	Part-Time	128								
Credits Required semester (s) or quarter (q)		83s			90s			86s		
Summer Programs	Accepts summer credit from other schools	Yes			No			Yes		
	Allows acceleration of graduation by attending summer sessions	No			No			No		
Joint Degrees		None			MBA 5 MA/Pub.Pol. 3	MCRP 2 MA/Econ. 2	MA/M.E.St. 1 Ph.D./Econ. 0	MBA 0 RUP 0	MALIR 0 MPIA 2	MPA 0 MS/Pub.Man. 0
Library	Total Hard Copy Volumes	253,362			336,889			117,071		
	Microform Volume Equivalents	67,172			14,366			51,646		

Law Schools on the 1983 Approved List of the American Bar Association		Villanova University School of Law Villanova, Pennsylvania 19085 215/645-7000 (Approved in 1954; Private)			**PUERTO RICO** Catholic University of Puerto Rico School of Law Station 6 Ponce, Puerto Rico 00732 809/844-4150 (Approved in 1967; Private)			Inter-American University of Puerto Rico School of Law P.O. Box 8897 Fernandez Juncos Station Santurce, Puerto Rico 00910 809/727-1930 (Approved in 1969; Private)		
		Total	Women	Minorities	Total	Women	Minorities	Total	Women	Minorities
1st Year Enrollment	Full-Time Part-Time	224 None	111	10	56 73	23 24	0 0	177 158	83 43	0 0
2nd Year Enrollment	Full-Time Part-Time	210 None	89	15	41 38	13 8	0 0	150 102	68 38	0 0
3rd Year Enrollment	Full-Time Part-Time	216 None	96	6	42 20	18 4	0 0	133 74	60 20	0 0
4th Year Enrollment	Full-Time Part-Time	None			12	2	0	48	12	0
Graduate Enrollment	Full-Time Part-Time	None 257	62	2	None 41	10	0	None None		
Other Enrollment	Full-Time Part-Time	None None			None 2	1	0	24 29	10 14	0 0
Fall, 1983, Enrollment	Full-Time Part-Time Total	650 257 **907**	296 62 **358**	31 2 **33**	139 186 **325**	54 49 **103**	0 0 **0**	484 411 **895**	221 127 **348**	0 0 **0**
Degrees Awarded through Summer, 1983	Full-Time	JD 206	84	12	JD 37	10	0	JD 119	56	0
	Part-Time	LLM 19	3	0	JD 16	3	0	JD 66	19	0
Teachers	Full-Time Part-Time	26 11	4 2	1 0	11 14	2 1	9 14	24 32	10 6	23 31
Full-time Teaching Deans and Librarians		3	0	0	1	0	1	2	0	2
Tuition and Fees	Full-Time Part-Time	$5,905			$3,767 $2,875			$3,655 $2,755		
College Required—Degree or 3 years		D			D			D		
Weeks Required	Full-Time Part-Time	90			96 128			102 136		
Credits Required semester (s) or quarter (q)		86s			92s			90s		
Summer Programs	Accepts summer credit from other schools	No			Yes			No		
	Allows acceleration of graduation by attending summer sessions	No			Yes			No		
Joint Degrees		None			MBA 0			None		
Library	Total Hard Copy Volumes	215,366			91,042			93,337		
	Microform Volume Equivalents	36,984			18,459			23,753		

**Law Schools on the
1983 Approved List
of the American
Bar Association**

	SOUTH CAROLINA	SOUTH DAKOTA
University of Puerto Rico School of Law P.O. Box AZ U.P.R. Station Rio Piedras, Puerto Rico 00931 809/767-6208 (Approved in 1945; Public)	University of South Carolina School of Law Main and Greene Streets Columbia, South Carolina 29208 803/777-6617 (Approved in 1925; Public)	University of South Dakota School of Law Vermillion, South Dakota 57069 605/677-5443 (Approved in 1923; Public)

		Total	Women	Minorities	Total	Women	Minorities	Total	Women	Minorities
1st Year Enrollment	Full-Time Part-Time	129 28	64 9	0 3	258 None	90	27	68 None	15	1
2nd Year Enrollment	Full-Time Part-Time	87 49	46 19	3 0	241 None	74	15	64 None	13	0
3rd Year Enrollment	Full-Time Part-Time	91 46	41 22	4 0	245 None	71	19	86 None	20	1
4th Year Enrollment	Full-Time Part-Time	 67	 18	 4	None			None		
Graduate Enrollment	Full-Time Part-Time	None None			None None			None None		
Other Enrollment	Full-Time Part-Time	None 3	 0	 3	None None			None None		
Fall, 1983, Enrollment	Full-Time Part-Time **Total**	307 193 **500**	151 68 **219**	7 10 **17**	744 **744**	235 **235**	61 **61**	218 **218**	48 **48**	2 **2**
Degrees Awarded through Summer, 1983	Full-Time	JD 62	29	0	JD 233	69	12	JD 53	18	2
	Part-Time	JD 21	9	0						
Teachers	Full-Time Part-Time	28 13	2 2	26 12	37 9	3 1	0 0	12 1	1 0	0 0
Full-time Teaching Deans and Librarians		3	0	3	3	1	0	3	2	0
Tuition and Fees	Full-Time Part-Time	$1,425 r $1,120 r	$3,075 nr $3,040 nr		$1,640 r	$3,270 nr		$1,585 r	$2,712 nr	
College Required—Degree or 3 years		D			D			D		
Weeks Required	Full-Time Part-Time	108 144			95			102		
Credits Required semester (s) or quarter (q)		92s			88s			90s		
Summer Programs	Accepts summer credit from other schools	Yes			Yes			Yes		
	Allows acceleration of graduation by attending summer sessions	No			Yes			Yes		
Joint Degrees		None			MBA 2 MPA 1 MA/Crim.Jus. 0 MA/Bus. 0 MA/Acct. 0			MBA 4 MPA 0 MA/Pol.Sc. 0 MA/Acct. 0 MA/Econ. 0 MA/Ed.Adm. 0 MA/Eng. 0 MA/Hist. 0 MA/Ag.Econ. 0 MS/Psy. 0		
Library	Total Hard Copy Volumes	116,410			173,240			91,900		
	Microform Volume Equivalents	8,015			84,570			9,444		

AN OVERALL VIEW OF ABA-APPROVED LAW SCHOOLS

Law Schools on the 1983 Approved List of the American Bar Association

TENNESSEE

	Memphis State University Cecil C. Humphreys School of Law Memphis, Tennessee 38152 901/454-2421 (Approved in 1965; Public)			University of Tennessee College of Law 1505 West Cumberland Avenue Knoxville, Tennessee 37996-1800 615/974-4241 (Approved in 1925; Public)			Vanderbilt University School of Law Nashville, Tennessee 37240 615/322-2615 (Approved in 1925; Private)		
	Total	Women	Minorities	Total	Women	Minorities	Total	Women	Minorities
1st Year Enrollment Full-Time	149	55	16	179	68	15	183	78	7
Part-Time	51	20	5	None			None		
2nd Year Enrollment Full-Time	126	48	13	193	75	7	170	51	8
Part-Time	41	18	4	None			None		
3rd Year Enrollment Full-Time	132	45	11	203	72	8	172	44	8
Part-Time	22	5	1	None			None		
4th Year Enrollment Full-Time				None			None		
Part-Time	24	6	1						
Graduate Enrollment Full-Time	None			None			None		
Part-Time	None			None			None		
Other Enrollment Full-Time	None			None			None		
Part-Time	3	1	0	None			None		
Fall, 1983, Enrollment Full-Time	407	148	40	575	215	30	525	173	23
Part-Time	141	50	11						
Total	**548**	**198**	**51**	**575**	**215**	**30**	**525**	**173**	**23**
Degrees Awarded through Summer, 1983 Full-Time	JD 140	44	8	JD 190	65	2	JD 164	52	4
Part-Time	JD 24	5	1						
Teachers Full-Time	21	3	0	26	3	1	24	3	1
Part-Time	4	0	0	5	2	0	8	0	0
Full-time Teaching Deans and Librarians	3	1	0	2	0	0	5	1	1

Tuition and Fees	Full-Time	$1,034 r $2,792 nr	$1,068 r $2,966 nr	$7,823
	Part-Time	$48/cr.hr. r $124/cr.hr. nr	$68/cr.hr. r $154/cr.hr. nr	
College Required—Degree or 3 years		D	D	D
Weeks Required	Full-Time	96	90	96
	Part-Time	128		
Credits Required semester (s) or quarter (q)		90s	84s	88s
Summer Programs	Accepts summer credit from other schools	Yes	Yes	No
	Allows acceleration of graduation by attending summer sessions	Yes	Yes	No
Joint Degrees		MBA 2	MBA 6	MBA 6 M.Div. 1
Library	Total Hard Copy Volumes	125,587	140,992	130,982
	Microform Volume Equivalents	29,774	71,766	30,759

Law Schools on the 1983 Approved List of the American Bar Association

TEXAS

		Baylor University School of Law Waco, Texas 76798 817/755-1911 (Approved in 1931; Private)			St. Mary's University School of Law One Camino Santa Maria San Antonio, Texas 78284 512/436-3424 (Approved in 1948; Private)			Southern Methodist University School of Law Dallas, Texas 75275 214/692-2618 (Approved in 1927; Private)		
		Total	Women	Minorities	Total	Women	Minorities	Total	Women	Minorities
1st Year Enrollment	Full-Time Part-Time	189 None	54	2	213 None	78	26	228 1	97 1	28 0
2nd Year Enrollment	Full-Time Part-Time	151 None	49	0	213 None	94	25	235 None	98	17
3rd Year Enrollment	Full-Time Part-Time	93 None	28	2	177 None	64	25	240 None	100	16
4th Year Enrollment	Full-Time Part-Time	None			None			None		
Graduate Enrollment	Full-Time Part-Time	None None			None None			59 61	10 16	20 0
Other Enrollment	Full-Time Part-Time	None None			2 None	1	0	14 None	7	0
Fall, 1983, Enrollment	Full-Time Part-Time Total	433 433	131 131	4 4	605 605	237 237	76 76	776 62 838	312 17 329	81 0 81
Degrees Awarded through Summer, 1983	Full-Time	JD 140	29	3	JD 182	65	26	JD 231 LLM 29 MCL 26	89 6 4	11 0 21
	Part-Time									
Teachers	Full-Time Part-Time	14 2	0 1	0 0	22 22	1 3	1 2	32 9	2 0	0 0
Full-time Teaching Deans and Librarians		4	2	0	2	0	0	2	0	0
Tuition and Fees	Full-Time Part-Time	$2,939 $97/cr.hr.			$6,300			$7,766 $266/cr.hr.		
College Required—Degree or 3 years		3			D			D		
Weeks Required	Full-Time Part-Time	105			96			90 180		
Credits Required semester (s) or quarter (q)		120q			90s			90s		
Summer Programs	Accepts summer credit from other schools	Yes			Yes			Yes		
	Allows acceleration of graduation by attending summer sessions	Yes			Yes			Yes		
Joint Degrees		None			None			MBA 2	MPA 1	
Library	Total Hard Copy-Volumes	100,964			97,477			279,691		
	Microform Volume Equivalents	25,260			17,776			12,882		

Law Schools on the 1983 Approved List of the American Bar Association

		South Texas College of Law 1303 San Jacinto Street Houston, Texas 77002 713/659-8040 (Approved in 1959; Public) *			Texas Southern University Thurgood Marshall School of Law 3100 Cleburne Avenue Houston, Texas 77004 713/527-7112 (Approved in 1949; Public)			Texas Tech University School of Law Lubbock, Texas 79409 806/742-3791 (Approved in 1969; Public)		
		Total	Women	Minorities	Total	Women	Minorities	Total	Women	Minorities
1st Year Enrollment	Full-Time	182	51	6	225	99	185	181	61	19
	Part-Time	301	135	14	None			None		
2nd Year Enrollment	Full-Time	148	48	12	133	47	101	198	66	12
	Part-Time	195	78	9	None			None		
3rd Year Enrollment	Full-Time	203	84	22	88	33	75	218	60	7
	Part-Time	104	42	8	None			None		
4th Year Enrollment	Full-Time				None			None		
	Part-Time	52	13	2						
Graduate Enrollment	Full-Time	None			None			None		
	Part-Time	None			None			None		
Other Enrollment	Full-Time	None			None			None		
	Part-Time	None			None			None		
Fall, 1983, Enrollment	Full-Time	533	183	40	446	179	361	597	187	38
	Part-Time	652	268	33						
	Total	**1,185**	**451**	**73**	**446**	**179**	**361**	**597**	**187**	**38**
Degrees Awarded through Summer, 1983	Full-Time	JD 135	35	6	JD 108	36	92	JD 202	62	3
	Part-Time	JD 207	82	7						
Teachers	Full-Time	27	4	1	22	2	17	24	2	1
	Part-Time	15	1	1	1	0	1	4	0	0
Full-time Teaching Deans and Librarians		2	0	0	5	4	5	4	2	0
Tuition and Fees	Full-Time	$3,628			$576 r	$1,728 nr		$452 r	$1,532 nr	
	Part-Time	$2,628								
College Required—Degree or 3 years		D			D			D		
Weeks Required	Full-Time	90			96			90		
	Part-Time	120								
Credits Required semester (s) or quarter (q)		90s			90s			90s		
Summer Programs	Accepts summer credit from other schools	Yes			Yes			Yes		
	Allows acceleration of graduation by attending summer sessions	Yes			Yes			Yes		
Joint Degrees		None			MBA 0 MPA 0 PAA 1 MA/Hist. 0			MBA 6 MPA 0 MS/Ag.Econ. 0		
Library	Total Hard Copy Volumes	112,226			98,352			151,568		
	Microform Volume Equivalents	87,583			50,385			61,625		

* Independent law school, not affiliated with a university.

AN OVERALL VIEW OF ABA-APPROVED LAW SCHOOLS

Law Schools on the 1983 Approved List of the American Bar Association

University of Houston
Law Center
4800 Calhoun
Houston, Texas 77004
713/749-1422
(Approved in 1950; Public)

University of Texas
College of Law
727 East 26th Street
Austin, Texas 78705
512/471-5151
(Approved in 1923; Public)

UTAH

Brigham Young University
J.Reuben Clark Law School
Provo, Utah 84602
801/378-4274
(Approved in 1974; Private)

		Total	Women	Minorities	Total	Women	Minorities	Total	Women	Minorities
1st Year Enrollment	Full-Time	280	131	59	509	193	106	147	31	8
	Part-Time	82	32	14	None			None		
2nd Year Enrollment	Full-Time	276	111	38	681	267	132	146	30	8
	Part-Time	66	22	7	None			None		
3rd Year Enrollment	Full-Time	342	155	46	429	177	101	159	24	5
	Part-Time	75	34	12	None			None		
4th Year Enrollment	Full-Time				None			None		
	Part-Time	66	28	15						
Graduate Enrollment	Full-Time	None			9	1	3	None		
	Part-Time	None			None			None		
Other Enrollment	Full-Time	None			None			None		
	Part-Time	None			None			None		
Fall, 1983, Enrollment	Full-Time	898	397	143	1,628	638	342	452	85	21
	Part-Time	289	116	48						
	Total	**1,187**	**513**	**191**	**1,628**	**638**	**342**	**452**	**85**	**21**
Degrees Awarded through Summer, 1983	Full-Time	JD 239	121	17	JD 489 LLM 4 MCL 3	185 2 1	76 0 0	JD 143	16	8
	Part-Time	JD 50	20	6						
Teachers	Full-Time	39	6	4	48	4	2	19	3	0
	Part-Time	16	2	0	22	6	0	6	0	0
Full-time Teaching Deans and Librarians		5	0	0	7	2	0	4	0	0
Tuition and Fees	Full-Time	$440 r	$1,520 nr		$406 r	$1,266 nr		$2,460 [1]	$3,690 [2]	
	Part-Time	$420 r	$1,120 nr					$125/cr.hr. [1]	$188/cr.hr. [2]	
College Required—Degree or 3 years		D			D			D		
Weeks Required	Full-Time	90			96			90		
	Part-Time	120								
Credits Required semester (s) or quarter (q)		88s			85s			90s		
Summer Programs	Accepts summer credit from other schools	Yes			Yes			Yes		
	Allows acceleration of graduation by attending summer sessions	Yes			Yes			Yes		
Joint Degrees		MBA 8	RUP 1	MA/Hist. 1	MBA 2	PAA 6		MBA 7	MPA 1	MSJA 1
Library	Total Hard Copy Volumes	167,698			524,450			209,824		
	Microform Volume Equivalents	94,261			81,718			38,071		

[1] Member of the Church of Jesus Christ of Latter Day Saints.

[2] Not a member of the Church of Jesus Christ of Latter Day Saints.

AN OVERALL VIEW OF ABA-APPROVED LAW SCHOOLS

Law Schools on the 1983 Approved List of the American Bar Association		University of Utah College of Law Salt Lake City, Utah 84112 801/581-6833 (Approved in 1927; Public)			**VERMONT** Vermont Law School South Royalton, Vermont 05068 802/763-8303 (Approved in 1975; Private) *			**VIRGINIA** College of William and Mary Marshall Wythe School of Law Williamsburg, Virginia 23185 804/253-4304 (Approved in 1932; Public)		
		Total	Women	Minorities	Total	Women	Minorities	Total	Women	Minorities
1st Year Enrollment	Full-Time Part-Time	125 None	43	6	148 None	56	0	180 None	60	9
2nd Year Enrollment	Full-Time Part-Time	135 None	41	4	122 None	39	2	165 None	61	6
3rd Year Enrollment	Full-Time Part-Time	130 None	42	4	106 None	39	0	173 None	72	6
4th Year Enrollment	Full-Time Part-Time	None			None			None		
Graduate Enrollment	Full-Time Part-Time	4 3	3 0	1 0	None None			8 12	0 0	0 0
Other Enrollment	Full-Time Part-Time	None None			9 None	3	0	None None		
Fall, 1983, Enrollment	Full-Time Part-Time **Total**	394 3 **397**	129 0 **129**	15 0 **15**	385 **385**	137 **137**	2 **2**	526 12 **538**	193 0 **193**	21 0 **21**
Degrees Awarded through Summer, 1983	Full-Time	JD 128 LLM 1	36 0	5 0	JD 120 MSL 12	43 4	1 0	JD 172 LLM 15	56 3	6 0
	Part-Time							LLM 11	0	1
Teachers	Full-Time Part-Time	21 3	2 1	0 1	15 11	4 1	1 0	24 11	3 3	0 1
Full-time Teaching Deans and Librarians		3	1	0	1	0	0	3	0	0
Tuition and Fees	Full-Time Part-Time	$1,206 r	$3,474 nr			$6,300		$1,954 r $63/cr.hr. r	$4,868 nr $152/cr.hr. nr	
College Required—Degree or 3 years		3			D			D		
Weeks Required	Full-Time Part-Time	93			97			90		
Credits Required semester (s) or quarter (q)		88s			84s			90s		
Summer Programs	Accepts summer credit from other schools	Yes			Yes			Yes		
	Allows acceleration of graduation by attending summer sessions	Yes			No			Yes		
Joint Degrees		None			MSL 12			None		
Library	Total Hard Copy Volumes	229,648			62,174			127,168		
	Microform Volume Equivalents	49,560			31,156			51,335		

* Independent law school, not affiliated with a university.

Law Schools on the 1983 Approved List of the American Bar Association

George Mason University
School of Law
3401 North Fairfax Drive
Arlington, Virginia 22201
703/841-2600
(Approved in 1980; Public) **

University of Richmond
T. C. Williams School of Law
Richmond, Virginia 23173
804/285-6336
(Approved in 1928; Private)

University of Virginia
School of Law
Charlottesville, Virginia 22901
804/924-7343
(Approved in 1923; Public)

		Total	Women	Minorities	Total	Women	Minorities	Total	Women	Minorities
1st Year Enrollment	Full-Time	98	36	5	158	66	1	381	143	31
	Part-Time	85	40	8	None			None		
2nd Year Enrollment	Full-Time	60	33	3	137	56	3	370	138	30
	Part-Time	96	37	8	None			None		
3rd Year Enrollment	Full-Time	76	22	1	136	51	4	401	136	29
	Part-Time	63	31	3	None			None		
4th Year Enrollment	Full-Time				None			None		
	Part-Time	77	30	1						
Graduate Enrollment	Full-Time	None			None			19	2	2
	Part-Time	None			None			8	0	2
Other Enrollment	Full-Time	None			None			None		
	Part-Time	None			None			None		
Fall, 1983, Enrollment	Full-Time	234	91	9	431	173	8	1,171	419	92
	Part-Time	321	138	20				8	0	2
	Total	**555**	**229**	**29**	**431**	**173**	**8**	**1,179**	**419**	**94**
Degrees Awarded through Summer, 1983	Full-Time	JD 60	24	1	JD 142	58	2	JD 359 LLM 23	109 8	15 2
	Part-Time	JD 72	15	1				LLM 1 SJD 2	0 0	0 1
Teachers	Full-Time	21	4	4	17	2	0	39	2	0
	Part-Time	12	1	1	13	1	1	23	3	4
Full-time Teaching Deans and Librarians		4	1	0	3	1	0	4	0	0
Tuition and Fees	Full-Time	$1,974 r	$6,972 nr			$6,220		$2,448 r	$5,138 nr	
	Part-Time	$47/cr.hr. r	$166/cr.hr. nr							
College Required—Degree or 3 years			D			D			D	
Weeks Required	Full-Time		99			96			95	
	Part-Time		132							
Credits Required semester (s) or quarter (q)			126q			90s			86s	
Summer Programs — Accepts summer credit from other schools			Yes			Yes			Yes	
Summer Programs — Allows acceleration of graduation by attending summer sessions			Yes			Yes			No	
Joint Degrees			None		MBA 0	MSW 3	RUP 0	MBA 8 MA/Hist. 2 MA/Soc. 0 Ph.D./Gov.&For.Aff.0	MPP 0 MA/Econ. 0 MA/Mar.Aff. 0	MA/Gov.& For.Aff. 0 MA/Phil. 0 MS/Acct. 0
Library — Total Hard Copy Volumes			134,184			73,071			369,264	
Library — Microform Volume Equivalents			45,640			42,049			128,290	

** Provisionally approved, status of graduates and students equal to that of fully approved law schools.

Law Schools on the 1983 Approved List of the American Bar Association

WASHINGTON

		Washington and Lee University School of Law Lewis Hall Lexington, Virginia 24450 703/463-9111 (Approved in 1923; Private)			Gonzaga University School of Law P. O. Box 3528 Spokane, Washington 99220-3528 509/328-4220 (Approved in 1951; Private)			University of Puget Sound School of Law 950 Broadway Plaza Tacoma, Washington 98402 206/756-3500 (Approved in 1973; Private)		
		Total	Women	Minorities	Total	Women	Minorities	Total	Women	Minorities
1st Year Enrollment	Full-Time	119	34	5	161	35	15	259	102	19
	Part-Time	None			5	1	0	88	33	10
2nd Year Enrollment	Full-Time	128	44	4	177	58	8	253	110	10
	Part-Time	None			3	2	0	51	26	8
3rd Year Enrollment	Full-Time	106	29	2	174	55	8	263	117	19
	Part-Time	None			7	5	0	24	7	3
4th Year Enrollment	Full-Time									
	Part-Time	None			25	6	2	26	8	0
Graduate Enrollment	Full-Time	None			None			None		
	Part-Time	None			None			None		
Other Enrollment	Full-Time	None			None			10	6	0
	Part-Time	None			None			None		
Fall, 1983, Enrollment	Full-Time	353	107	11	512	148	31	785	335	48
	Part-Time				40	14	2	189	74	21
	Total	353	107	11	552	162	33	974	409	69
Degrees Awarded through Summer, 1983	Full-Time	JD 123	36	6	JD 154	41	5	JD 275	77	11
	Part-Time				JD 15	4	2	JD 49	16	1
Teachers	Full-Time	17	3	1	19	2	0	31	6	0
	Part-Time	5	0	0	8	0	0	6	1	0
Full-time Teaching Deans and Librarians		3	0	0	1	0	0	3	0	0
Tuition and Fees	Full-Time	$5,900			$5,790			$6,000		
	Part-Time				$3,474			$4,000		
College Required—Degree or 3 years		D			D			D		
Weeks Required	Full-Time	90			90			90		
	Part-Time				120			135		
Credits Required semester (s) or quarter (q)		85s			90s			90s		
Summer Programs	Accepts summer credit from other schools	Yes			Yes			Yes		
	Allows acceleration of graduation by attending summer sessions	Yes			Yes			Yes		
Joint Degrees		None			MBA 2	MS/Tax. 2		None		
Library	Total Hard Copy Volumes	123,176			118,869			99,241		
	Microform Volume Equivalents	98,533			67,957			91,869		

Law Schools on the 1983 Approved List of the American Bar Association		University of Washington School of Law Condon Hall JB-20 1100 N. E. Campus Parkway Seattle, Washington 98105 206/543-4550 (Approved in 1924; Public)			**WEST VIRGINIA** West Virginia University College of Law P.O. Box 6130 Morgantown, West Virginia 26506 304/293-5301 (Approved in 1924; Public)			**WISCONSIN** Marquette University Law School 1103 West Wisconsin Avenue Milwaukee, Wisconsin 53233 414/224-7090 (Approved in 1925; Private)		
		Total	Women	Minorities	Total	Women	Minorities	Total	Women	Minorities
1st Year Enrollment	Full-Time Part-Time	137 None	58	17	113 None	39	1	165 None	57	18
2nd Year Enrollment	Full-Time Part-Time	143 None	65	12	127 None	57	4	146 None	51	3
3rd Year Enrollment	Full-Time Part-Time	148 None	61	25	121 None	45	3	156 None	49	5
4th Year Enrollment	Full-Time Part-Time	None			None			None		
Graduate Enrollment	Full-Time Part-Time	32 None	3	20	None None			None None		
Other Enrollment	Full-Time Part-Time	None None			None None			3 None	1	0
Fall, 1983, Enrollment	Full-Time Part-Time **Total**	460 **460**	187 **187**	74 **74**	361 **361**	141 **141**	8 **8**	470 **470**	158 **158**	26 **26**
Degrees Awarded through Summer, 1983	Full-Time Part-Time	JD 141 LLM 19	47 3	15 8	JD 154	63	1	JD 157	61	5
Teachers	Full-Time Part-Time	27 None	1	1	21 3	1 0	1 0	20 9	4 1	0 0
Full-time Teaching Deans and Librarians		3	1	0	3	0	0	3	1	0
Tuition and Fees	Full-Time Part-Time	$1,884 r $178-$538/ qtr.hr. r	$4,686 nr $447-$1,339/ qtr.hr. nr		$1,150 r	$3,140 nr		$5,660		
College Required—Degree or 3 years		D			D			D		
Weeks Required	Full-Time Part-Time	108			90			90		
Credits Required semester (s) or quarter (q)		135q			90s			90s		
Summer Programs	Accepts summer credit from other schools	Yes			Yes			Yes		
	Allows acceleration of graduation by attending summer sessions	Yes			Yes			No		
Joint Degrees		MBA 6 PAA 2 MA/Phil. 1	MHA 0 MA/Comm. 0 MA/Hist. 0	MLS 4 MA/Econ. 1 MA/E. Asian St. 1	MBA 0	MPA 1 Ph.D./Pol.Sc. 0		MBA 0		
Library	Total Hard Copy Volumes	343,119			130,687			105,745		
	Microform Volume Equivalents	49,921			10,381			8,896		

Law Schools on the 1983 Approved List of the American Bar Association		University of Wisconsin Law School Madison, Wisconsin 53706 608/262-2240 (Approved in 1923; Public)			WYOMING University of Wyoming College of Law P.O. Box 3035 University Station Laramie, Wyoming 82071-3035 307/766-6416 (Approved in 1923; Public)		
		Total	Women	Minorities	Total	Women	Minorities
1st Year Enrollment	Full-Time Part-Time	264 44	111 23	24 2	80 None	29	0
2nd Year Enrollment	Full-Time Part-Time	298 22	128 11	20 0	64 None	19	3
3rd Year Enrollment	Full-Time Part-Time	275 4	105 3	23 0	59 None	11	2
4th Year Enrollment	Full-Time Part-Time	None			None		
Graduate Enrollment	Full-Time Part-Time	5 None	3	2	None None		
Other Enrollment	Full-Time Part-Time	11 None	4	0	None None		
Fall, 1983, Enrollment	Full-Time Part-Time Total	853 70 923	351 37 388	69 2 71	203	59 59	5 5
Degrees Awarded through Summer, 1983	Full-Time	JD 277 LLM 1 SJD 1	124 0 0	16 1 1	JD 67	20	2
	Part-Time						
Teachers	Full-Time Part-Time	39 10	5 3	1 0	12 None	1	0
Full-time Teaching Deans and Librarians		3	1	0	6	4	0
Tuition and Fees	Full-Time Part-Time	$1,676 r $70/cr.hr. r	$5,073 nr $212/cr.hr. nr		$616 r	$2,076 nr	
College Required—Degree or 3 years		D			D		
Weeks Required	Full-Time Part-Time	90 120			90		
Credits Required semester (s) or quarter (q)		90s			86s		
Summer Programs	Accepts summer credit from other schools	Yes			Yes		
	Allows acceleration of graduation by attending summer sessions	Yes			Yes		
Joint Degrees		ML&T 3			MBA 0		
Library	Total Hard Copy Volumes	253,803			85,222		
	Microform Volume Equivalents	40,328			42,432		

Special Program Approved by the American Bar Association, 1983

VIRGINIA

The Judge Advocate General's School
(Officer Residence Graduate Course,
Specialized Program beyond first degree
in law) U. S. Army
Charlottesville, Virginia 22901
804/977-4930
(Approved in 1965; Public)[*]

		Total	Women	Minorities
1st Year Enrollment	Full-Time	None		
	Part-Time	None		
2nd Year Enrollment	Full-Time	None		
	Part-Time	None		
3rd Year Enrollment	Full-Time	None		
	Part-Time	None		
4th Year Enrollment	Full-Time	None		
	Part-Time			
Graduate Enrollment	Full-Time	77	6	6
	Part-Time	None		
Other Enrollment	Full-Time	None		
	Part-Time	None		
Fall, 1983, Enrollment	Full-Time	77	6	6
	Part-Time			
	Total	**77**	**6**	**6**
Degrees Awarded through Summer, 1983	Full-Time	87[*]	5	6
	Part-Time			
Teachers	Full-Time	31	0	1
	Part-Time	7	0	0
Full-time Teaching Deans and Librarians		3	0	0
Tuition and Fees	Full-Time	None		
	Part-Time			
College Required—Degree or 3 years		D		
Weeks Required	Full-Time	42		
	Part-Time			
Credits Required semester (s) or quarter (q)		q		
Summer Programs	Accepts summer credit from other schools	No		
	Allows acceleration of graduation by attending summer sessions	No		
Joint Degrees		None		
Library	Total Hard Copy Volumes	27,652		
	Microform Volume Equivalents	853		

[*] The Judge Advocate General's School is fully approved by the ABA as a graduate course; however, no degree ABA awarded. Students are provided a certificate of completion of the course.